Triumph TR 2, 3, 3A, 4, 4A Owners Workshop Manual

by J H Haynes
Member of the Guild of Motoring Writers

B L Chalmers - Hunt R Tech Eng, AMIMI, AMIRTE, AMVBRA
and J L S Maclay

Models covered
TR2, TR3 and TR3A, 1991 cc
TR4 and TR4A, 2138 cc

ISBN 978 0 85733 701 6

© Haynes Group Limited 1971, 1980, 1984, 1986

ABCDE
2

All rights reserved. No part of this book may be reproduced or transmitted in any form or by any means, electronic or mechanical, including photocopying, recording or by any information storage or retrieval system, without permission in writing from the copyright holder.

Printed in India   (028-11M3)

Haynes Group Limited
Sparkford, Yeovil,
Somerset BA22 7JJ, England

Haynes North America, Inc
2801 Townsgate Road,
Suite 340, Thousand Oaks,
CA 91361, USA

Disclaimer
There are risks associated with automotive repairs. The ability to make repairs depends on the individual's skill, experience and proper tools. Individuals should act with due care and acknowledge and assume the risk of performing automotive repairs.

The purpose of this manual is to provide comprehensive, useful and accessible automotive repair information, to help you get the best value from your vehicle. However, this manual is not a substitute for a professional certified technician or mechanic.

This repair manual is produced by a third party and is not associated with an individual vehicle manufacturer. If there is any doubt or discrepancy between this manual and the owner's manual or the factory service manual, please refer to the factory service manual or seek assistance from a professional certified technician or mechanic.

Even though we have prepared this manual with extreme care and every attempt is made to ensure that the information in this manual is correct, neither the publisher nor the author can accept responsibility for loss, damage or injury caused by any errors in, or omissions from, the information given.

Acknowledgements

Thanks are due to the British Leyland Motor Corporation for their assistance with regard to the use of technical material and illustrations and to the 'Autocar' for permission to use the cutaway illustration on the cover.

The Champion Sparking Plug Company supplied the illustrations showing the various spark plug conditions.

The bodywork repair photographs used in this manual were provided by Holt Lloyd Ltd. who supply 'Turtle Wax', 'Dupli-color Holts' and other Holts range products.

Castrol Limited supplied the lubrication data.

Thanks are especially due to R.T.Grainger, D.Stead, J.R.S.Hall for their assistance when working on the car and to Brig.K.F.Kinchin for advice on the text.

Whilst every care is taken to ensure that the information in this manual is correct bearing in mind the changes in design and specification which are a continuous process, even within a model range, no liability can be accepted by the authors and publishers for any loss, damage or injury caused by any errors or omissions in the information given.

Photographic Captions & Cross References

The book is divided into twelve chapters. Each chapter is divided into numbered sections which are headed in bold type between horizontal lines. Each section consists of serially numbered paragraphs.

There are two types of illustration. (1) Figures which are numbered according to Chapter and sequence of occurrence in that chapter and having an individual caption to each figure. (2) Photographs which have a reference number in the bottom left-hand corner. All photographs apply to the chapter in which they occur so that the reference figures pinpoint the pertinent section and paragraph numbers.

Procedures, once described in the text, are not normally repeated. If it is necessary to refer to another chapter the reference will be given in chapter number and section number thus:— Chapter 1/6.

If it is considered necessary to refer to a particular paragraph in another chapter the reference is 'Chapter 1/6:5'. Cross references given without use of the word 'Chapter' apply to sections and/or paragraphs in the same chapter, e.g., 'see section 8' means also 'in this chapter'.

When the left or right-hand side of a car is mentioned it is as if one was looking in the forward direction of travel.

TRIUMPH TR3

TRIUMPH TR2

TWO VIEWS OF THE TRIUMPH TR3A

TWO VIEWS OF THE TRIUMPH TR4

THREE-QUARTERS & SIDE VIEW OF THE TRIUMPH TR4A

Contents

The main Chapter headings are shown below. Because the Manual covers TR2, 3, 3A, 4 and 4A to avoid complication, detailed headings are found at the commencement of each Chapter.

		Page
	Introduction	6
	Ordering Spare Parts	6
	Routine Maintenance	7
	Recommended Lubricants TR2, 3, 3A	10
	Recommended Lubricants TR4, 4A	12

Chapter		Page
1	Engine	14
2	Cooling System	60
3	Fuel System & Carburation	74
4	Ignition System	94
5	Clutch & Actuating Mechanism	106
6	Gearbox	122
7	Propeller Shaft & Universal Joints	154
8	Rear Axle	158
9	Braking System	176
10	Electrical System	206
11	Suspension - Dampers - Steering	232
12	Bodywork & Underframe	268
	Use of English	298
	Conversion factors	299
	Safety first!	300
	Index	301

Introduction

This is a manual for do-it-yourself TR2, TR3, TR3A, TR4 and TR4A owners. It shows how to maintain these cars in first class condition and how to carry out repairs when components become worn or break. Regular and careful maintenance is essential if maximum reliability and minimum wear are to be achieved.

The step-by-step photographs show how to deal with the major components and in conjunction with the text and exploded illustrations should make all the work quite clear - even to the novice who has never previously attempted the more complex jobs.

Although TR's are hardwearing and robust, it is inevitable that their reliability and performance will decrease as they become older. Repairs and general reconditioning will become necessary if the car is to remain roadworthy. Early models requiring attention are frequently bought by the more impecunious motorist who can least afford the repair prices charged in garages, even though these prices are usually quite fair, bearing in mind overheads and the high cost of capital equipment and skilled labour.

It is in these circumstances that this manual will prove to be of maximum assistance, as it is the ONLY workshop manual written from practical experience specially to help TR2, TR3, TR3A, TR4 and TR4A owners.

Manufacturer's official manuals are usually splendid publications which contain a wealth of technical information. Because they are issued primarily to help the manufacturers authorised dealers and distributors they tend to be written in very technical language, and tend to skip details of certain jobs which are common knowledge to garage mechanics. Owner's workshop manuals are different as they are intended primarily to help the owner. They therefore go into many of the jobs in great detail with extensive photographic support to ensure everything is properly understood so that the repair is done correctly.

Owners who intend to do their own maintenance and repairs should have a reasonably comprehensive tool kit. Some jobs require special service tools, but in many instances it is possible to get round their use with a little care and ingenuity. For example a 3½ inch diameter jubilee clip makes a most efficient and cheap piston ring compressor.

Throughout this manual ingenious ways of avoiding the use of special equipment and tools are shown. In some cases the proper tool must be used. Where this is the case a description of the tool and its correct use is included.

When a component malfunctions repairs are becoming more and more a case of replacing the defective item with an exchange rebuilt unit. This is excellent practice when a component is thoroughly worn out, but is a waste of good money when overall the component is only half worn, and requires the replacement of but a single small item to effect a complete repair. As an example, a non-functioning dynamo can frequently be repaired quite satisfactorily just by fitting new brushes.

A further function of this manual is to show the owner how to examine malfunctioning parts; determine what is wrong, and then how to make the repair.

Given the time, mechanical do-it-yourself aptitude, and a reasonable collection of tools, this manual will show the ordinary private owner how to maintain and repair his car really economically.

Ordering Spare Parts

Always order genuine British Leyland spare parts from your nearest Triumph dealer or local garage. Authorised dealers carry a comprehensive stock of GENUINE PARTS and can supply most items over the counter.

When ordering new parts it is essential to give full details of your car to the storeman. He will want to know models and chassis or commission numbers, and in the case of engine spares the engine number. Year of manufacture is helpful too. If possible take along the part to be replaced.

If you want to re-touch the paintwork you can obtain an exact match (providing the original paint has not faded) by quoting the paint code number in conjunction with the model number.

The chassis or commission number as it is called at the factory is stamped on a model identification plate located on a plate attached to the right hand side of the bulkhead under the bonnet (TR2, TR3 and TR3A models) or on the left hand side of the bulkhead by the windscreen wiper motor (TR4 and TR4A models).

The engine number is stamped on a flat surface on the left hand side of the engine immediately under number 4 spark plug.

When obtaining new parts remember that many assemblies can be exchanged. This is very much cheaper than buying them outright and throwing away the old part.

Routine Maintenance

The maintenance instructions listed below are basically those recommended by the manufacturer. They are supplemented by additional maintenance tasks which, through practical experience, the author recommends should be carried out at the intervals suggested.

It should be pointed out that until late 1963 the recommended service scheme suggested intervals of 1,000, 3,000, 6,000 and 12,000 but the general tendency is for car manufacturers to recommend lengthier service intervals due to better materials and lubricants now being available. The service procedure outlined below can be safely used on all models of cars covered by this manual, but care must be taken with the older models as there will be a certain amount of wear which could allow oil and grease to seep out more quickly than when the car was new. Therefore, some parts, such as ball joints and swivel pins, could require more frequent attention.

On earlier service schemes it was recommended that the gearbox and rear axle were drained regularly but now it is only necessary to regularly check the level and top up with cars produced since July 1963.

The additional tasks are indicated by an asterisk and are primarily of a preventive nature in that they will assist in eliminating the unexpected failure of a component due to fair wear and tear.

The levels of engine oil, radiator cooling water, windscreen washer water and battery electrolyte, also the tyre pressures, should be checked weekly or more frequently if experience dictates this to be necessary. Similarly, it is wise to check the level of fluids in the clutch and brake master cylinder reservoirs at monthly intervals. If not checked at home it is advantageous to use regularly the same garage for this work as they will get to know your preferences for particular oils and the pressures at which you like to run your tyres.

6,000 miles

EVERY 6,000 miles (or six months if 6,000 miles are not exceeded).

1. Run the engine until it is hot and place a container of at least 10 pints capacity under the drain plug on the left hand side of the sump and allow the oil to drain for at least 10 minutes. Clean the plug and the area around the plug hole in the sump and replace the plug, tightening it firmly. Clean the oil filler with petrol, refill the sump with 10 pints of a recommended grade of oil (see page 11) and clean off any oil which may have been spilt over the engine or its components. The interval between oil changes should be reduced in very hot or dusty conditions or during cold weather with much slow stop/start driving.
2. Check the valve clearances and adjust, if necessary, as described on Page 48.
3. Check and adjust, if necessary, the engine slow-running as described on Pages 86 or 88.
4. Check and adjust the brakes, if necessary. The procedure is described on Pages 180 and 182.
5. Examine and remedy any defects in the braking system and ensure that there is adequate clearance between the brake pipes and any chassis or other components to eliminate chafing.
6. Examine the tyres and, should wear be apparent, take the appropriate action to correct the cause, e.g., misalignment, poor balancing, over or under inflation. If in any doubt a Triumph repair garage should be consulted especially where alignment is suspect because complicated and expensive equipment is required to carry out the necessary check. Remove any flints or other road matter from the treads. Check wheel nuts for tightness.
7. Apply grease (see Page 11) to the handbrake cable guide and the compensator sector.
8. Lubricate with a recommended grade of oil (Page 11) all hinges, catches and controls to allow them to work freely and prevent unnecessary wear.
9. Remove the plug for the upper and lower steering swivels and fit screwed grease nipples (if not already fitted). Jack up the front road wheels and apply a grease gun filled with a recommended HYPOID oil (see Page 11) and pump until oil exudes from the swivels.
10. Remove the sparking plugs for cleaning and reset the gaps to 0.025 inch (.64 mm). Clean the ceramic insulators and examine them for cracks or other damage likely to cause 'tracking'. Test the plugs before refitting and renew any which are suspect.
11. Release the spring clips and remove the distributor cap and rotor arm. Apply a few drops of thin oil (see Page 11) over the screw in the centre of the cam spindle and on the moving contact breaker pivot. Grease the cam surface very lightly. Remove any excess oil or grease with a clean rag. Apply a few drops of oil through the hole in the contact breaker base plate to lubricate the automatic timing control.

Routine Maintenance

12 Clean and adjust the contact breaker points as described on Page 96.

13 The various types of air cleaner are described on Page 76 and these should be cleaned or the paper elements renewed as appropriate. In very dusty conditions the intervals for carrying out this task may well have to be reduced considerably.

14 The fan belt must be tight enough to drive the generator without over-loading the generator and water pump bearings. The method of adjusting the fan belt is described on Page 68 and is correct when it can be pressed inwards ¾ inch (19 mm) on the longest run - from the generator pulley to the crankshaft pulley.

15 Check the operation of all electrical equipment particularly stop/tail lamps, plate illumination and side lamps. Adjust, if necessary, the headlamp settings.

16 Remove the hexagon caps from the carburettor dashpots and top them up to within ½ inch of the top with SAE 20 oil (see Page 80). Remove the float chambers, empty away any sediment, check the condition of the needle valve, clean and reassemble. Remove the filter in the carburettors if fitted.

17 With the car standing on level ground check the level of oil in the gearbox by removing the oil filler level plug on the left hand side of the gearbox. Top up, if necessary, with SAE 90 EP oil until the oil starts to run out of the filler hole.

18 Lubricate the clutch and brake pedal pivot bushes.

19 Lubricate the propeller shaft grease nipple, if fitted, using a grease gun filled with a recommended HYPOID oil (see Page 11).

20 Remove the front wheel trim and apply a recommended grease to the front hub bearing grease nipple (early TR2 and TR3 models).

21 Check the level of oil in the steering box and top up if necessary with the recommended grade oil (see Page 11).

22 Check the level of oil in the rear axle and top up if necessary with the recommended grade oil (see Page 11). Remove the rear wheel trims and apply five strokes of the grease gun to the exposed nipples.

*23 Give the bodywork and chromium trim a thoroughly good wax polish. If a chromium cleaner is used to remove rust, on any part of the car's plated parts, remember that the cleaner also removes part of the chromium, so use carefully.

*24 Remove the carpets or mats and thoroughly clean the interior of the car. Beat out or vacuum clean the carpets. If the upholstery is soiled apply an upholstery cleaner with a damp sponge and wipe off with a clean dry cloth.

*25 Hoods and tonneau covers should be cleaned with a plain soap and water solution. Detergents, caustic soaps or spirit cleaners should never be used.

12,000 miles

EVERY 12,000 miles (or every 12 months if 12,000 miles are not exceeded).

1. On post July 1963 models, with the car standing on level ground, remove the oil level plug on the left hand side of the gearbox. Top up, if necessary, with SAE 90 EP oil until the oil starts to run out of the filler hole. On pre July 1963 models the gearbox must be drained and refilled with the recommended grade oil. The capacity is 1½ pints, with overdrive 2¾ pints.

2. Unscrew the oil filter bowl from the left hand side of the engine and discard the old element. Wash out the bowl, fit a new element and sealing ring and refit. Top up the oil level once the engine has run.

3. Disconnect the fuel pipe from the suction side of the

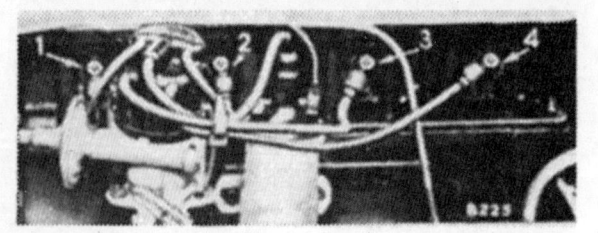

Correct fitting of H.T. Ignition leads from distributor to sparking plugs.

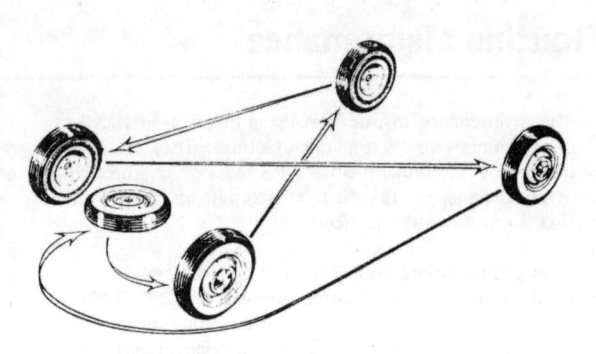

Manufacturers recommended tyre rotation pattern

CLUTCH LINKAGE
1 Bleed nipple
2 Adjusting rod
3 Locknut
4 Clevis
5 Cross shaft greaser

REAR HUB & BACKING PLATE
1 Brake adjuster
2 Hub greaser
3 Bleed nipple

Routine Maintenance

fuel pump and plug the end of the pipe with a pencil or piece of tapered wood to prevent loss of petrol. Unscrew the stirrup nut under the glass bowl, swing the stirrup to one side and remove the bowl. Swill out the sediment bowl and wipe it clean. Take care not to damage the bowl by overtightening the stirrup nut, only tighten sufficiently to ensure a fuel tight joint. Reconnect the fuel pipe and prime the carburettors.

4. Jack up the car and remove the road wheels and brake drums. Remove the dust from the drums and clean the backplates. Examine the brake shoes and renew worn or contaminated shoes. Reassemble and adjust. Examine the front disc pads for wear and deterioration (see Page 196).

5. Examine and, if necessary, tighten the front and rear suspension attachments, steering connections, water pump, starter motor, generator, and generator pulley and all universal joints and their nuts and bolts.

6. Inject a few drops of engine oil (see Page 11) through the hole in the rear of the generator.

7. It is recommended that new spark plugs be fitted every 12,000 miles.

8. Check the level of oil in the steering box and top up if necessary (TR2, TR3 and TR3A models). On other models remove the plug from the top of the steering unit and fit a screwed grease nipple. Apply a grease gun filled with a recommended grease (see Page 11) and give it five strokes only. Remove the nipple and refit the plug. Over greasing can cause damage to the rubber bellows.

9. The front hubs must be repacked with grease (see Page 11). Full details are given in Page 238 (all models except early TR2 and TR3 models).

10 Unscrew the plug from the top of the water pump and fit a screwed grease nipple. Apply the grease gun filled with a recommended grease giving it five strokes only. Remove the nipple and refit the plug.

11 Dismantle, clean and reassemble the crankshaft breather valve. Ensure the breather hole in the oil filler cap is free from obstruction.

*12 It is a sound scheme to visit your local main agent and have the underside of the body steam cleaned. This will take about 1½ hours and cost about £4. All traces of dirt and oil will be removed and the underside can then be inspected carefully for rust, damaged hydraulic pipes, frayed electrical wiring and similar maladies. The car should be greased on completion of this job.

*13 At the same time the engine compartment should be cleaned in the same manner. If steam cleaning facilities are not available then brush 'Gunk' or a similar cleaner over the whole engine and engine compartment with a stiff paint brush working it well in where there is an accumulation of oil and dirt. Do not paint the ignition system but protect it with oily rags when the Gunk is washed off, as the Gunk is washed away it will take with it all traces of oil and dirt, leaving the engine looking clean and bright.

36,000 miles

EVERY 36,000 miles (or every 2 years).

1. Carry out the maintenance tasks listed for the 6,000 and 12,000 miles services.

2. All seals, flexible hoses, etc., throughout the braking system should be removed and renewed, brake cylinders and pistons should be examined and replaced, if wear is found, and the brake pipes replaced if any damage is present.

*3. Drain and refill the gearbox and rear axle with the appropriate grades of oil (see Page 11). This is recommended so that any minute particles of metal are carried away in the old oil so helping to prevent further wear.

Filling Carburettor Dash Pots (S.U.)

Front Suspension and Steering Grease Points TR3, 3A, 4, 4A

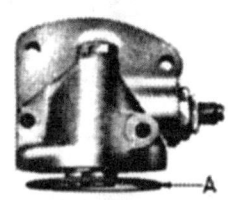

OIL FILTER
A. Washer
B. Element
C. Securing bolt

LUBRICATION CHART TR2, 3, 3A

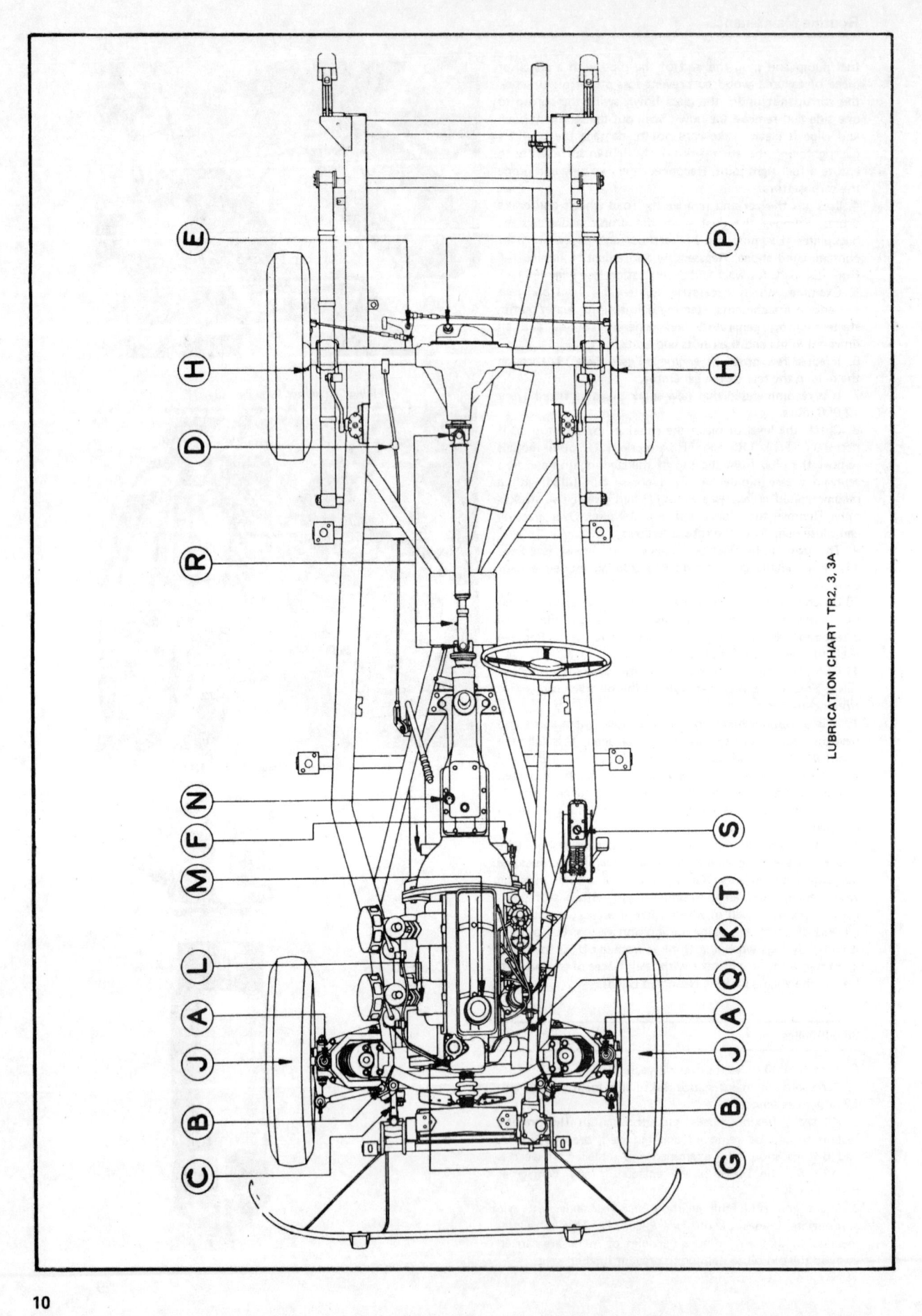

Ref.	ITEMS	DETAILS	Mileage Interval (Thousands of Miles)	RECOMMENDED LUBRICANTS
A	Steering Swivels... ... ... (4 nipples)	THREE OR FOUR STROKES	1	Castrol LM Grease
B	Outer Tie Rod Ball Joints.. ... ... (4 nipples)		1	Castrol LM Grease
C	Steering Slave Drop Arm Pivot... ... ... (1 nipple)		1	Castrol LM Grease
	Lower Wishbone Outer Bushes ... ... (4 nipples)		1	Castrol LM Grease
D	Cable... ... ... (1 nipple)	FIVE STROKES	5	Castrol LM Grease
	Handbrake			
E	Compensator ... ... (2 nipples)		5	Castrol LM Grease
F	Clutch Shaft Bearings ... ... (2 nipples)		5	Castrol LM Grease
G	Engine Water Pump ... ... (1 nipple)		5	Castrol LM Grease
H	Rear ... ... (2 nipples)		5	Castrol LM Grease
	Hubs			
J	Front ... ... (2 nipples) Fitted up to Commission No.TS.5348 only		5	Castrol LM Grease
K	Ignition Distributor	OIL AS RECOMMENDED	5	Castrol GTX
	Handbrake Lever		5	Castrol GTX
	Carburetter Dashpots and Control Linkages		5	Castrol GTX
	Door Locks, Hinges, Bonnet Safety Catch, Boot and Spare Wheel Locks		5	Castrol GTX
	Dynamo — 250 miles		10	
L		Top up oil level		Castrol GTX
M	Engine Sump	Drain and refill with new oil	2½	Castrol GTX
	Oil Filler Cap	Wash	5	
N	Gearbox	Top up oil level	5	Castrol GTX
		Drain and refill with new oil	10	
P	Rear Axle	Top up oil level	5	Castrol Hypoy
Q	Steering Gearbox (1 nipple)		5	Castrol Hypoy
R	Propeller Shaft Splines	Three or four strokes with gun	5	Castrol LM Grease
	Universal Joints (2 nipples)			
	Road Springs	Clean and oil	5	Old Engine Oil
	Air Cleaners	Oil as recommended	5	Castrol GTX
S	Hydraulic Brake and Clutch Reservoir	Top up fluid level	5	Lockheed Brake Fluid
T	Oil Cleaner	Renew cartridge	10	

(Grease Gun: A–K; Oil Can: L–T)

11

LUBRICATION CHART TR4, 4A

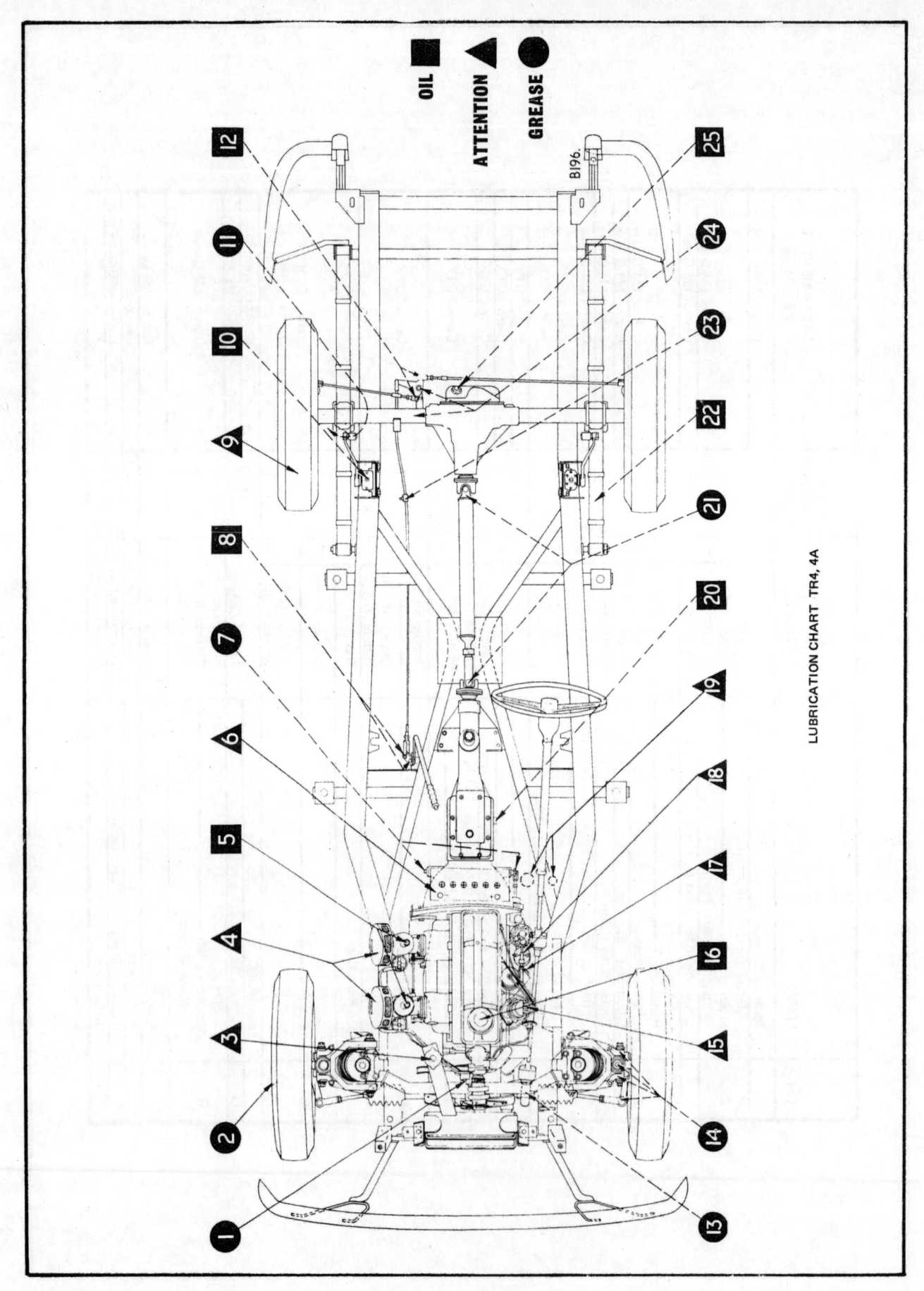

Ref.	Items	Details	Mileage Intervals
9	Tyre pressures		Weekly
3	Radiator water level	Top up	Weekly
6	Battery	Top up	Monthly
	Steering Swivels (4 nipples)		3,000
14	Outer tie rod ball joints (4 nipples)	Grease gun	3,000
	Steering Slave drop arm pivot		3,000
14	Lower wishbone outer bushes (4 nipples)		3,000
21	Propeller shaft Splines (1 nipple) Universal joints (2 nipples)	Gun Three of four strokes	3,000
19	Hydraulic brake and clutch reservoirs	Top up fluid level	3,000
5	Carburetter dashpots and control linkages	Oil as recommended	3,000
16	Engine 250 miles	Oil can Top up oil level	3,000
		Drain & refill with new oil	6,000
20	Gearbox	Top up oil level	6,000
23	Handbrake Cable (1 nipple)	Grease gun	3,000
24	Compensator (2 nipples)		3,000
7	Clutch cross shaft bearings (2 nipples)	Grease gun	3,000
1	Engine water pump (1 nipple)		6,000
11	Hubs — Rear (2 nipples)		12,000
15	Ignition distributor	Oil can	6,000
8	Handbrake lever		6,000
	Door locks, hinges, bonnet safety-catch, boot and wheel locks.		6,000
	Generator		12,000
	Oil filler cap	Wash	6,000
25	Rear axle	Drain & refill with new oil	6,000
13	Steering unit	Grease five strokes	6,000
4	Air cleaners	Oil as recommended	6,000
17	Oil filter	Renew cartridge	6,000
18	Fuel pump	Clean out filter bowl	6,000
2	Hubs - Front	Remove and re-pack	12,000 or 24,000
22	Rear road springs	Clean and oil	12,000

Recommended Lubricants British Isles		(Castrol) (All Seasons)
Component		Lubricant
Engine sump		Castrol GTX
Carburetter Dashpots		Castrol GTX
Gearbox, Overdrive, Rear Axle.		Castrol Hypoy
Steering Unit Grease Gun Front Wheel Hubs.		Castrol LM Grease
Oil Can		Everyman Oil
Rear Road Springs		Old Engine Oil
Brake Cables		Castrol LM Grease
Clutch and Brake Reservoir	Girling	Castrol Girling Brake Fluid
	Lockheed	Lockheed super heavy duty brake fluid
Anti-freeze.		Castrol Anti-freeze

Chapter 1/Engine

Contents

General Description ... 1	Timing Chain Tensioner - Examination & Renovation ... 36
Routine Maintenance ... 2	Rockers & Rocker Shaft - Examination & Renovation ... 37
Major Operations with Engine in Place ... 3	Tappets - Examination & Renovation ... 38
Major Operations with Engine Removed ... 4	Flywheel Starter Ring - Examination & Renovation ... 39
Methods of Engine Removal ... 5	Flywheel Starter Ring - Examination & Renovation (TR4, 4A) ... 40
Engine Removal without Gearbox ... 6	Oil Pump - Examination & Renovation ... 41
Engine Removal with Gearbox ... 7	Cylinder Head - Decarbonisation ... 42
Dismantling the Engine - General ... 8	Valve Guides - Examination & Renovation ... 43
Removing Ancillary Engine Components ... 9	Sump - Examination & Renovation ... 44
Cylinder Head Removal - Engine on Bench ... 10	Engine Reassembly - General ... 45
Cylinder Head Removal - Engine in Car ... 11	Crankshaft - Replacement ... 46
Valve Removal ... 12	Piston & Connecting Rod - Reassembly ... 47
Valve Guide - Removal ... 13	Piston Ring - Replacement ... 48
Dismantling the Rocker Assembly ... 14	Piston - Replacement ... 49
Timing Cover, Gears and Chain - Removal ... 15	Connecting Rod to Crankshaft - Reassembly ... 50
Camshaft - Removal ... 16	Front & Rear Crankshaft Bearing Sealing Block & Seals ... 51
Distributor Drive - Removal ... 17	Front End Plate - Reassembly ... 52
Sump, Piston, Connecting Rod, Big End Bearing & Liner - Removal ... 18	Camshaft - Replacement ... 53
Gudgeon Pin - Removal ... 19	Timing Gears, Chain Tensioner, Cover - Replacement (Marked Sprockets) ... 54
Piston Ring - Removal ... 20	Oil Pump - Replacement ... 55
Flywheel & Engine End Plate - Removal ... 21	Sump - Replacement ... 56
Crankshaft & Main Bearing - Removal ... 22	Valve & Valve Spring - Reassembly ... 57
Lubrication & Crankcase Ventilation System - Description ... 23	Rocker Shaft & Tappet - Reassembly ... 58
Oil Filter - Removal & Replacement ... 24	Cylinder Head - Replacement ... 59
Oil Pressure Relief Valve - Removal & Replacement ... 25	Rocker Arm/Valve - Adjustment ... 60
Oil Pump - Removal & Dismantling ... 26	Timing Gears, Chain Tensioner, Cover - Replacement (Unmarked Sprockets) ... 61
Timing Chain Tensioner - Removal & Replacement ... 27	Thermostat Housing & Water Pump - Refitting ... 62
Examination & Renovation - General ... 28	Oil Filter Head - Refitting ... 63
Crankshaft - Examination & Renovation ... 29	Fuel Pump - Refitting ... 64
Big End & Main Bearings - Examination & Renovation ... 30	Distributor Drive Shaft, Pedestal & Distributor - Refitting ... 65
Cylinder Liner Bores - Examination & Renovation ... 31	Crankshaft Rear Oil Seal, Spigot, Flywheel & Clutch - Refitting ... 66
Pistons & Piston Rings - Examination & Renovation ... 32	Final Assembly ... 67
Camshaft & Camshaft Bearing - Examination & Renovation ... 33	Engine - Replacement ... 68
Valves & Valve Seals - Examination & Renovation ... 34	
Timing Gears & Chain - Examination & Renovation ... 35	

Specifications

	TR4, 4A	TR2, 3, 3A
Type	O.H.V. water cooled using wet liners	
Number of cylinders	4	
Compression ratio	9.0:1	8.5:1
Cubic capacity	2.138 cc (130.5 in^2)	TR2,3 1991 cc (121.5 in^2)
		TR3A 2138 cc (130.5 in^2)
Bore	3.386 inch	3.268 inch
Stroke	3.622 inch	

Chapter 1/Engine

	TR4, 4A	TR2, 3, 3A
Firing order	1 - 3 - 4 - 2	
Ignition timing	4° B.T.D.C.	

Crankshaft
Material	Molybdenum - manganese steel	
Type	Counter-balanced	
Thrust taken at	Centre bearing	
Number of journals	3	
Main bearing journal diameter	2.4790 to 2.4795 inch	
1st undersize	0.010 inch	
2nd undersize	0.020 inch	
3rd undersize	0.030 inch	
End float	0.004 to 0.006 inch	
Crankpin bearing journal diameter	2.0861 to 2.086 inch	
1st undersize	0.010 inch	
2nd undersize	0.020 inch	
3rd undersize	0.030 inch	
Main bearing clearance:		
New	0.0015 to 0.0025 inch	
Wear limit	0.0031 inch	

Connecting Rods
Type	Steel forging	
Removal method	Upwards through liner bore	
Length (centre to centre)	6.248 to 6.252 inch	
Big end:		
Bore	2.2327 to 2.2335 inch	
Width	1.1775 to 1.1795 inch	
Big end bearing clearance:		
New	0.0028 to 0.0040 inch	
Wear limit	0.005 inch	
Big end bearing width	0.965 to 0.975 inch	
Small end bearing bore:		
Reamed	0.8742 to 0.8758 inch	
Width	1.070 to 1.090 inch	
Connecting rod end float on crankpin	0.007 to 0.014 inch	
Undersize big end bearings:		
1st undersize	0.010 inch	
2nd undersize	0.020 inch	
3rd undersize	0.030 inch	
Maximum connecting rod bend and twist	0.002 inch	

Piston
Type	'Aeroflex' light alloy	
Grades	3 — F.G.H.	
Number of rings	3	
Type of rings	2 compression, 1 oil scraper	
Piston ring gaps	0.010 to 0.015 inch	0.003 to 0.010 inch
Piston rings:		
Width - top	0.0615 to 0.0625 inch	0.061 to 0.062 inch
- centre	0.0615 to 0.0625 inch	0.061 to 0.062 inch
- scraper	0.1552 to 0.1562 inch	0.155 to 0.156 inch
- new clearance	0.0010 to 0.0030 inch	
- wear limit	0.0038 inch	
Grading dimensions for standard bore:		
Cylinder liner bore - F	3.3854 to 3.3857 inch	
- G	3.3858 to 3.3861 inch	
- H	3.3862 to 3.3865 inch	
Piston top diameter - F	3.3803 to 3.3807 inch	
- G	3.3807 to 3.3811 inch	
- H	3.3811 to 3.3815 inch	
Piston bottom diameter - F	3.3818 to 3.3822 inch	
- G	3.3822 to 3.3826 inch	
- H	3.3826 to 3.3830 inch	

Gudgeon pin
Length	2.916 to 2.920 inch	
Diameter	0.87485 to 0.8751 inch	
Clearance	0.00005 to 0.00045 inch	

Chapter 1/Engine

	TR4, 4A	TR2, 3, 3A
Cylinder Liners		
Type	Wet	
Material	Nickel - chrome - iron	
Position when fitted (relative to top of block)	0.003 to 0.005 inch proud	
Method of retention	Cylinder head	
Bore diameter grades:		
Grade F	3.3854 to 3.3857 inch	3.2673 to 3.2676 inch
G	3.3858 to 3.3861 inch	3.2677 to 3.2680 inch
H	3.3862 to 3.3865 inch	3.2681 to 3.2684 inch
Maximum clearance to piston:		
Top	.007 inch	
Bottom	.005 inch	
Camshaft		
Number of bearings	4	
Front journal diameter	1.871 to 1.872 inch	
Centre, intermediate & rear journal diameter	1.7153 to 1.7158 inch	
Front bearing length	1.870 to 1.872 inch	
Intermediate bearing length	0.740 to 0.760 inch	
Centre & rear bearing length	1.190 to 1.210 inch	
Journal length:		
Front	1.8760 to 1.8775 inch	
Centre	1.115 to 1.135 inch	
Intermediate	0.740 to 0.760 inch	
Rear	1.3025 to 1.3225 inch	
Front bearing internal diameter	1.8748 to 1.8757 inch	
Centre, intermediate & rear journal internal diameter	1.71725 to 1.71825 inch	
Clearance between front bearing & journal:		
New	0.0028 to 0.0047 inch	
Wear limit	0.0059 inch	
Cam lift (maximum)	0.260 inch	
Camshaft end float	0.004 to 0.0075 inch	
Tappets		
Length	1.969 to 1.971 inch	
Block bore for tappet	0.9373 to 0.9380 inch	
Stem diameter	0.9367 to 0.9371 inch	
Clearance in block:		
New	0.0002 to 0.0013 inch	
Wear limit	0.0016 inch	
Valves		
Head diameter:		
Inlet	1.558 to 1.526 inch	
Exhaust	1.299 to 1.303 inch	
Angle of seat:		
Valves	45°	
Cylinder head	44½°	
Valve stem diameter:		
Inlet	0.310 to 0.311 inch	
Exhaust	0.3705 to 0.3715 inch	
Valve guide bore:		
Inlet	0.312 to 0.313 inch	
Exhaust	0.3745 to 0.3755 inch	
Stem to guide clearance:		
Inlet:		
New	0.001 to 0.003 inch	
Wear limit	0.0038 inch	
Exhaust:		
New	0.003 to 0.005 inch	
Wear limit	0.0063 inch	
Valve springs		
Number of springs per valve:		
Inlet	2	2
Exhaust	3	2
Free length:		
Inner	1.88 to 1.90 inch	2.080 inch
Outer	1.94 to 1.96 inch	1.980 inch
Auxiliary inner (exhaust only)	1.55 to 1.57 inch	1.540 inch

Chapter 1/Engine

	TR4, 4A	TR2, 3, 3A
Valve clearance (cold)		
Inlet	0.010 inch	
Exhaust	0.010 inch	
Timing only	0.040 inch	
Valve timing		
Inlet valve opens	17º B.T.D.C.	15º B.T.D.C.
Inlet valve closes	57º A.B.D.C.	55º A.B.D.C.
Exhaust valve opens	57º B.B.D.C.	55º B.B.D.C.
Exhaust valve closes	17º A.T.D.C.	15º A.T.D.C.
Valve guides		
Material	Cast iron	
Inside diameter:		
Inlet	.3120 to .3130 inch	
Exhaust	.3745 to .3755 inch	
Fitted height above spring seat	.780 inch	
Camshaft drive		
Type	Duflex chain	
Fit of gear on camshaft	Slide	
How secured	Setscrews	
Fit of gear on crankshaft	Slide	
How secured	Woodruff key and dog nut	
Lubrication system		
Type	Pressure	
Type of pump	Double eccentric rotor	
Type of pump drive	Skew gear	
Normal pressure	70 PSI at 2,000 r.p.m.	
Relief valve opens at	70 PSI	
Filter:		
Type	By-pass fitted to engine number TS 12650E	
	Full flow after engine number TS 12650E	
Location	External	
Capacity	1 pint	
Oil pump		
Outer rotor:		
External diameter	1.5965 to 1.5975 inch	
Housing internal diameter	1.603 to 1.604 inch	
Depth of rotor	1.4985 to 1.4995 inch	
Housing depth	1.500 to 1.501 inch	
Inner rotor:		
Major diameter	1.171 to 1.172 inch	
Minor diameter	0.729 to 0.731 inch	
Rotor depth	1.4985 to 1.4995 inch	
Spindle diameter	0.4980 to 0.4985 inch	
Bore in housing for spindle	0.4995 to 0.5010 inch	
Spindle clearance in housing	0.001 to 0.003 inch	
Torque Wrench Settings		
Cylinder head	100 to 105 lb.ft.	
Connecting rod caps	55 to 60 lb.ft.	
Main bearing caps	85 to 90 lb.ft.	
Flywheel attachment to crankshaft	42 to 46 lb.ft.	
Timing Chain wheel to camshaft	24 to 26 lb.ft.	
Manifold attachment	22 to 24 lb.ft.	
Oil pump attachments	12 to 14 lb.ft.	
Rear oil seal attachment	8 to 10 lb.ft.	
Clutch attachment	20 lb.ft.	
Attachment of end plates	14 to 16 lb.ft.	
Attachment of oil filters	18 to 20 lb.ft.	
Timing cover	14 to 16 lb.ft.	
Sump attachment	16 to 18 lb.ft.	
Pulley to water pump spindle	16 to 18 lb.ft.	
Dynamo bracket to block	16 to 18 lb.ft.	
Dynamo to bracket and pedestal	16 to 18 lb.ft.	
Rocker pedestal	24 to 26 lb.ft.	

Chapter 1/Engine

Oil gallery plugs	24 to 26 lb.ft.
Attachment of starter motor	26 to 28 lb.ft.
Petrol pump attachment	12 to 14 lb.ft.
Thermostat assembly to cylinder head	12 to 14 lb.ft.
Inlet to exhaust manifold	12 to 14 lb.ft.
Dynamo to pedestal front	16 to 18 lb.ft.

1. General Description

The engine and gearbox are bolted together in the conventional manner and supported by rubber mountings at three points in the interests of silence and lack of vibration.

There have been several modifications to the engine and these will be covered in their respective sections. Full technical details are given in the specification section at the beginning of this Chapter.

The engine is a four cylinder overhead valve type operating on the 'Otto' four stroke cycle. Two valves per cylinder are mounted vertically in the cast iron cylinder head and run in pressed in valve guides. They are operated by rocker arms, pushrods and tappets from the camshaft which is located at the base of the cylinder bores in the left hand side of the engine. The correct valve stem to rocker pad clearance can be obtained by the adjusting screws in the ends of the rocker arms.

The cylinder block and upper half of the crankcase are cast together. The bottom half of the crankcase consists of a pressed steel sump.

The pistons are made from anodised aluminium. Two compression rings and a slotted oil ring are fitted.
The gudgeon pin is retained in the little end of the connecting rod by circlips.

Renewable steel backed shell type bearings are fitted.

At the front of the engine a twin track chain drives the camshaft via the camshaft and crankshaft chain wheels which are enclosed in a pressed steel cover.

The chain is tensioned automatically by a spring blade which presses against the non driving side of the chain, so avoiding any lash or rattle.

On earlier engines the camshaft runs directly in the block but in later models three steel backed alloy bearings are used. End float of the camshaft is controlled by the length of the front camshaft bearing.

The statically and dynamically balanced forged steel crankshaft is supported by three renewable thinwall shell main bearings which are in turn supported by substantial webs which form part of the crankcase. Crankshaft end float is controlled by semi-circular thrust washers located on each side of the centre main bearing.

The engine uses wet cylinder liners which are fitted and sealed with special liner gaskets into the bores in the crankcase. The liners are held in position by the cylinder head.

The centrifugal water pump and dynamo are driven from the crankshaft pulley wheel by a rubber/fabric belt whilst the radiator cooling fan is mounted on an extension from the crankshaft.

The distributor is mounted in the middle of the left hand side of the cylinder block and advances and retards the ignition timing by mechanical and vacuum means. The distributor is driven at half crankshaft speed by a short skew gear from a skew gear on the camshaft located between the second and third journals.

The oil pump is located in the crankcase and is driven by a short shaft from the skew gear on the camshaft. The tachometer drive is taken on second skew gear on the distributor drive shaft.

Lubricating oil is drawn from the supply in the sump through a wire mesh filter and passes to an oil gallery which runs the length of the left hand side of the engine.

On earlier engines covered by this manual the oil is passed to a by pass oil filter into which is built a pressure relief valve designed to open at a pressure of approximately 70 PSI allowing some of the oil to pass through the filter and then return to the sump. Later engines however have a full flow filter whereby all the oil passes through the filter on its way to the main oil gallery. A pressure relief valve allows excess oil to return to the sump and again operates at a pressure of approximately 70 PSI. Oil is then distributed to the various parts of the engine via drillings and full details of the circulation are given in Section 23 of this Chapter.

Attached to the end of the crankshaft by four bolts and dowels is the flywheel to which is bolted to the Borg and Beck clutch. Attached to the engine end plate is the gearbox bell housing.

Due to the simplicity in design of the engine most jobs can be done without having to remove it from the car.

2. Routine Maintenance

1. Once a week, or more frequently if necessary, remove the dipstick and check the engine oil level which should be at the 'MAX' mark. Top up the oil in the sump with the recommended grade (see Page 11 for details). On no account allow the oil to fall below the 'MIN' mark on the dipstick.
2. Every 6,000 miles run the engine till it is hot, place a container with a capacity of at least 11 pints under the drain plug in the sump, undo and remove the drain plug and allow the oil to drain for at least ten minutes. While the oil is draining wash the oil filler cap gauze in petrol, shake dry and re-oil.
3. Clean the drain plug, ensure the washer is in place and return the plug to the sump, tightening the plug firmly. Refill the sump with 11 pints Castrol GTX. Every 12,000 miles the oil filter element should be renewed as described in Section 24.
4. In very hot or dusty conditions, in cold weather with much slow stop/start driving, with much use of the choke, or when the engine has covered a very high mileage, it is beneficial to change the engine oil every 3,000 miles and the filter every 6,000 miles.

3. Major Operations with Engine in Place

The following major operations can be carried out to the engine with it in place in the body frame:-

a) Removal and replacement of the cylinder head assembly.
b) Removal and replacement of the sump.
c) Removal and replacement of the big end bearings.
d) Removal and replacement of the pistons and connecting rods.
e) Removal and replacement of the timing chain and gears and the timing cover oil seal.

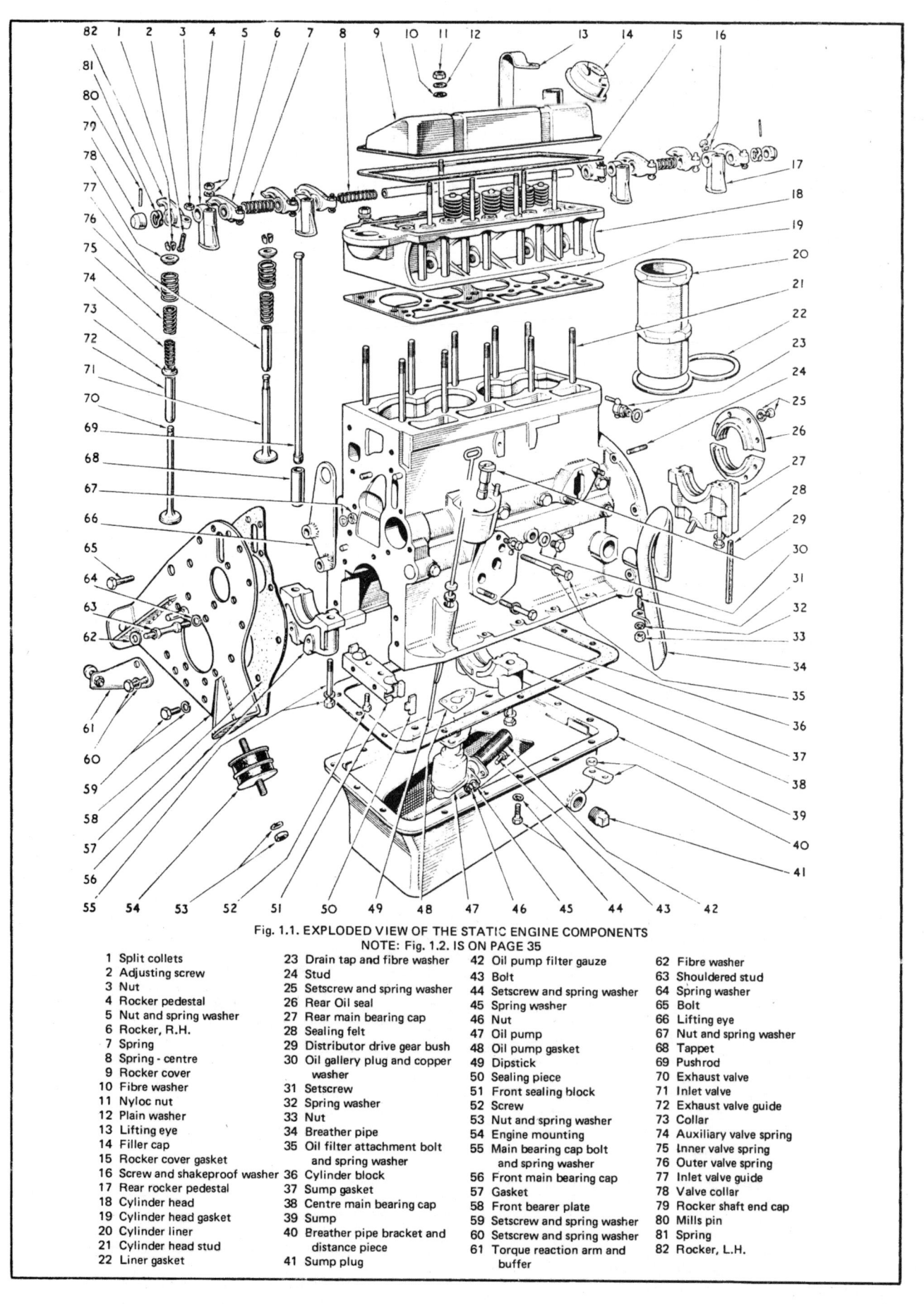

Fig. 1.1. EXPLODED VIEW OF THE STATIC ENGINE COMPONENTS
NOTE: Fig. 1.2. IS ON PAGE 35

1 Split collets
2 Adjusting screw
3 Nut
4 Rocker pedestal
5 Nut and spring washer
6 Rocker, R.H.
7 Spring
8 Spring - centre
9 Rocker cover
10 Fibre washer
11 Nyloc nut
12 Plain washer
13 Lifting eye
14 Filler cap
15 Rocker cover gasket
16 Screw and shakeproof washer
17 Rear rocker pedestal
18 Cylinder head
19 Cylinder head gasket
20 Cylinder liner
21 Cylinder head stud
22 Liner gasket
23 Drain tap and fibre washer
24 Stud
25 Setscrew and spring washer
26 Rear Oil seal
27 Rear main bearing cap
28 Sealing felt
29 Distributor drive gear bush
30 Oil gallery plug and copper washer
31 Setscrew
32 Spring washer
33 Nut
34 Breather pipe
35 Oil filter attachment bolt and spring washer
36 Cylinder block
37 Sump gasket
38 Centre main bearing cap
39 Sump
40 Breather pipe bracket and distance piece
41 Sump plug
42 Oil pump filter gauze
43 Bolt
44 Setscrew and spring washer
45 Spring washer
46 Nut
47 Oil pump
48 Oil pump gasket
49 Dipstick
50 Sealing piece
51 Front sealing block
52 Screw
53 Nut and spring washer
54 Engine mounting
55 Main bearing cap bolt and spring washer
56 Front main bearing cap
57 Gasket
58 Front bearer plate
59 Setscrew and spring washer
60 Setscrew and spring washer
61 Torque reaction arm and buffer
62 Fibre washer
63 Shouldered stud
64 Spring washer
65 Bolt
66 Lifting eye
67 Nut and spring washer
68 Tappet
69 Pushrod
70 Exhaust valve
71 Inlet valve
72 Exhaust valve guide
73 Collar
74 Auxiliary valve spring
75 Inner valve spring
76 Outer valve spring
77 Inlet valve guide
78 Valve collar
79 Rocker shaft end cap
80 Mills pin
81 Spring
82 Rocker, L.H.

19

Chapter 1/Engine

f) Removal and replacement of the camshaft.
g) Removal and replacement of the oil pump.

4. Major Operations with Engine Removed

The following major operations can be carried out with the engine out of the body and on the bench or floor:-

a) Removal and replacement of the main bearings.
b) Removal and replacement of the crankshaft.
c) Removal and replacement of the flywheel.

5. Methods of Engine Removal

There are two methods of engine removal. The engine can either be removed complete with gearbox, or the engine can be removed without the gearbox by separating it at the gearbox bell housing. Both methods are described. Irrespective of whether the Triumph engine is removed with or without the gearbox, it will be found to be one of the easiest units to take out and replace, apart from its size and weight. No pit or ramps are necessary as the jobs usually done underneath, such as propshaft/gearbox separation are all done from inside the car. As a further bonus engine accessibility is excellent.

6. Engine Removal without Gearbox

1. Practical experience has proved that the engine can be easily removed in about three hours (less with experience) by adhering to the following sequence of operations.
2. It must be pointed out that the basic procedures for removing the engine on all models covered by this manual is identical but there may be slight differences which will be apparent as work progresses.
3. Open the bonnet and prop it up to expose the engine and ancillary components. Turn on the water drain taps to be found at the bottom of the radiator and on the side of the cylinder block. NOTE: Do not drain the water in your garage or the place where you will remove the engine if receptacles are not at hand to catch the water.
4. Place a container with a capacity of at least 11 pints under the drain plug in the sump, undo and remove the drain plug, and allow the oil to drain for at least ten minutes. Replace the drain plug.
5. A second person's assistance will be necessary to remove the bonnet. Using a pencil, mark the outline of the hinge on the bonnet lid to assist refitting.
6. TR2, 3 and 3A models — Undo the two nuts which secure the bonnet hinge to the underside of the dash panel from inside the car and with the assistance of the second person lift away the bonnet.
7. TR4 and 4A models — Undo the three bolts on each hinge securing the hinge to the bonnet. Remove the bolts, spring and plain washers (photo).
8. TR4 and 4A models — It should be observed that there is a further bolt on the side of each hinge which must be removed. Lift away the bolt, spring and plain washers. Note that this bolt is longer than the other three bolts (photo).
9. TR4 and 4A models — Undo the nyloc nut securing the bonnet stay to the underside of the bonnet and remove the nut and plain washer (photo).
10. With the assistance of the second person lift away the bonnet (photo).
11. Put the bonnet in one corner out of the way where it will not be scratched or damaged. It will assist working on the engine if any wing mirrors are removed.
12. Place some old blankets over the wings and the front of the car so that the paintwork is not damaged.
13. Remove the dynamo securing bolts and lift away the unit from the side of the engine.
14. Disconnect the battery earth terminal from the battery terminal post and the negative lead from the starter solenoid switch. Undo the battery retaining wing nut and clamp bracket and lift away the battery (photo).
15. TR2, 3 and 3A models — Remove the radiator as detailed in Chapter 2, Section 6, paragraphs 3 to 11 inclusive.
16. TR4 and 4A models — Remove the radiator as detailed in Chapter 2, Section 7, paragraphs 3 to 7 inclusive.
17. As the fan assembly is accurately balanced care must be taken to note the exact location of each part. During manufacture once the unit has been balanced, the balancing plate is drilled right through and the hub extension just touched with the drill to give a datum. If the assembly is just to be dismantled re-balancing will not be necessary but if new parts are to be fitted a special jig will be necessary and this is best left to the local Triumph agent.
18. Using a scriber mark the balancing plate and fan assembly so that the front of each part will be easily recognised.
19. Using a screwdriver ease back the lock plate tabs locking the hub extension nuts on the pulley flange and undo the six nuts. On later engines nyloc nuts and plain washers were fitted instead of locking plates (photo).
20. With a screwdriver ease back the locking plate tab and undo the four bolts holding the fan blades to the fan pulley hub extension (photo).
21. Lift away the bolts, lock plate, plain washers and a balance plate if one has been previously fitted (photo). Also remove the fan blades, split rubber bushes, metal sleeves and plain washers.
22. Undo the starter dog or extension bolt (photo).
23. Withdraw the starter dog or bolt through the fan pulley hub extension noting any shims that may be under the head of the starter dog or bolt (photo).
24. Carefully tap the crankshaft pulley from the end of the crankshaft using a soft faced hammer and lift away the pulley (photo).
25. Disconnect the carburettor choke control cable from the choke linkage (photo).
26. Extract the split pin from the carburettor control linkage ball joint end and undo the socket screw sufficiently to release the ball joint from its seating (photo). Screw in the socket screw so that it does not fall out.
27. Undo the tachometer drive cable knurled retainer from the side of the distributor pedestal and separate the drive cable (photo).
28. Coil the tachometer cable and tie back out of the way.
29. Close the fuel line tap (where fitted) on the end of the main fuel line to the pump inlet flexible hose connection and disconnect the fuel line to the fuel pump (photo).
30. Undo the fuel line connection from the pump to the carburettors at the front carburettor.
31. Undo the four nuts securing the inlet manifold to the side of the cylinder head. Lift away the nuts, plain washers and metal clamping pieces (photo).
32. Undo the two nuts securing the studs on the underside of the inlet manifold to the exhaust manifold and lift away the nuts and plain washers (photo).
33. Disconnect the distributor vacuum line from the front carburettor body.
34. Disconnect the two throttle linkage return springs from the underside of the linkage.
35. Undo the nuts holding the carburettors to the inlet manifold and remove the nuts and plain and spring washers.
36. Carefully remove the carburettors from the inlet mani-

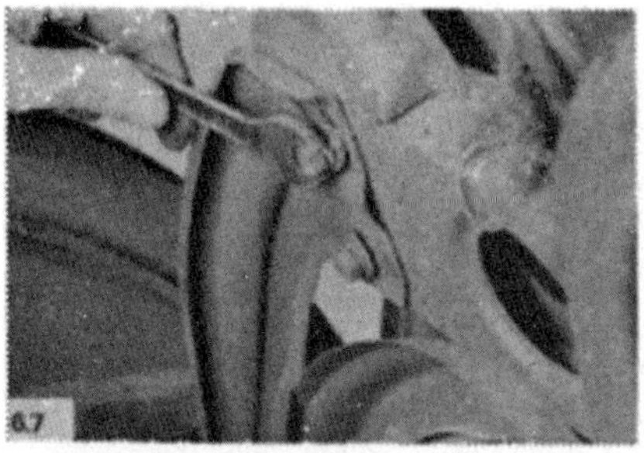
6.7

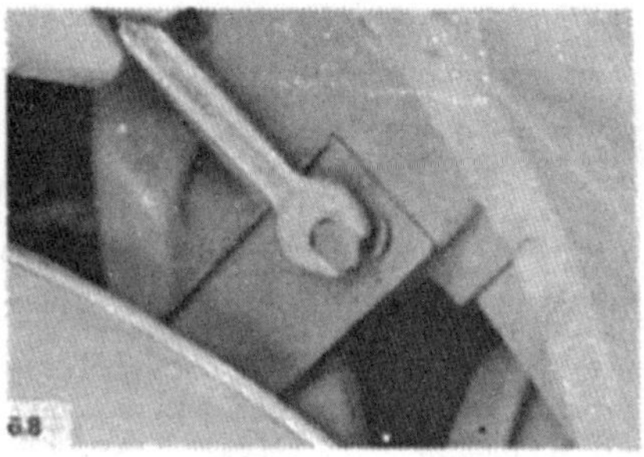
6.8

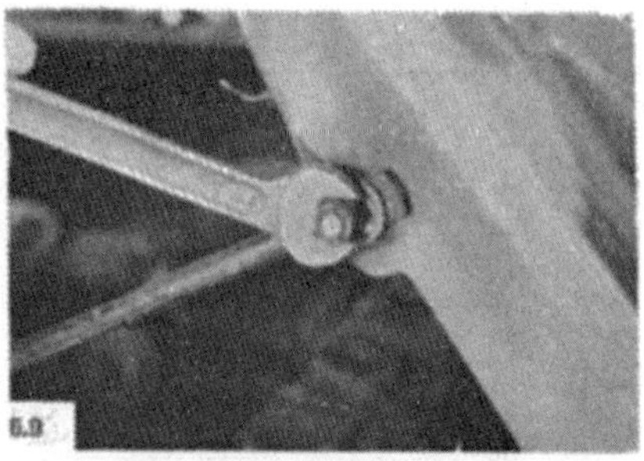
6.9

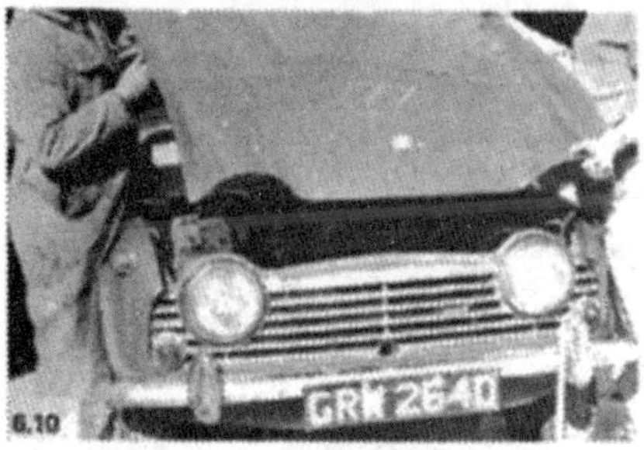

6.10

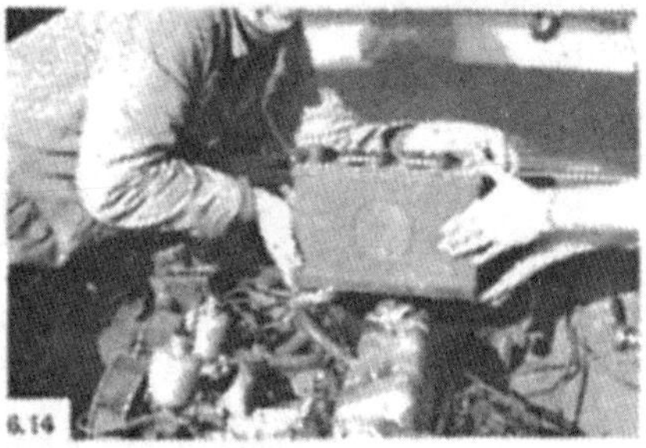
6.14

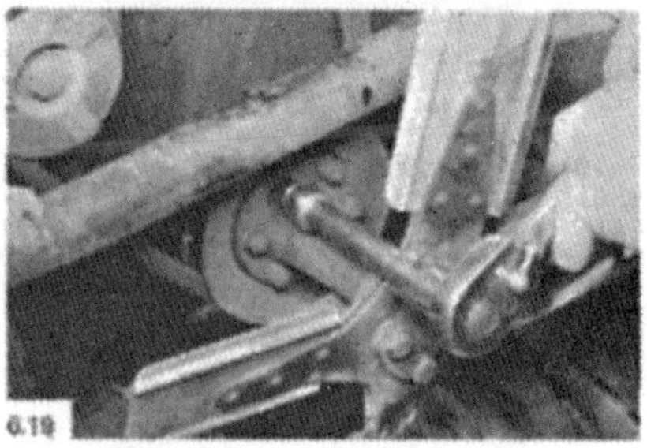
6.19

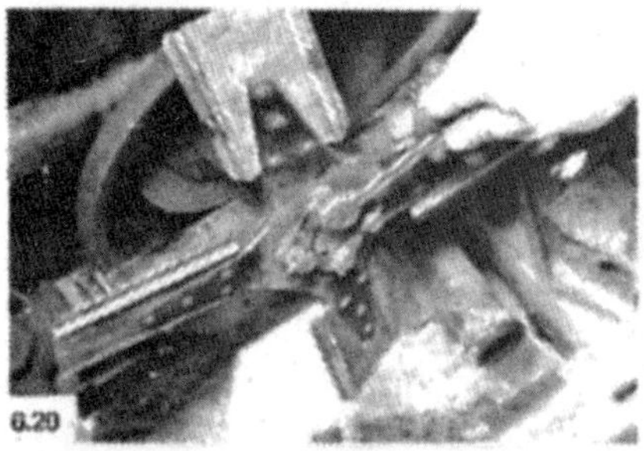
6.20

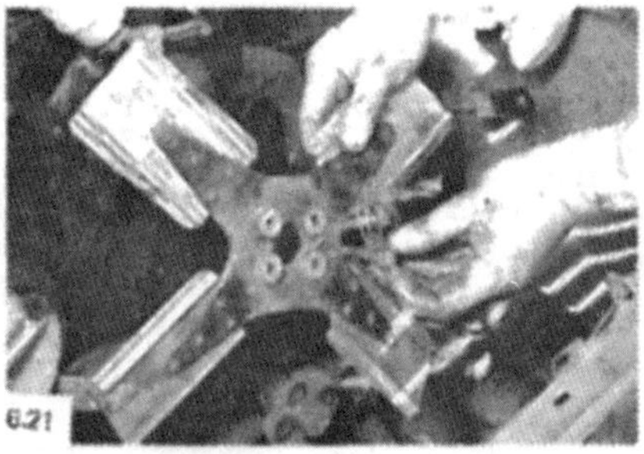
6.21

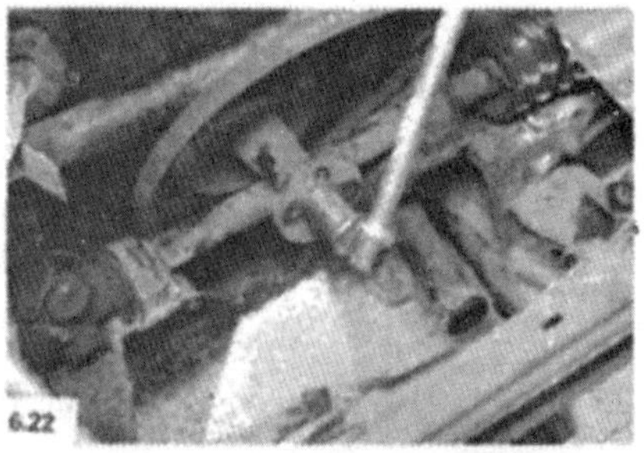
6.22

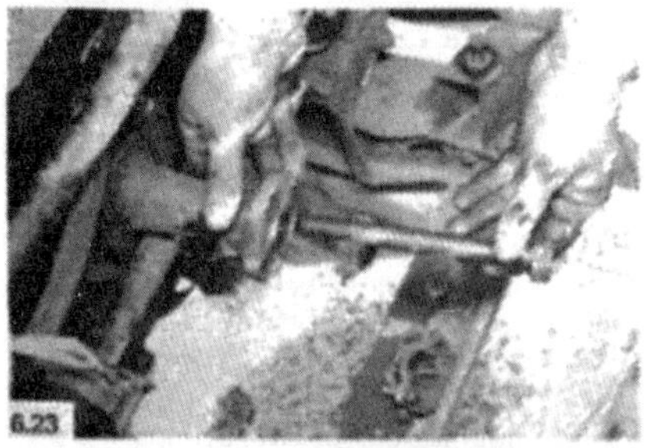
6.23

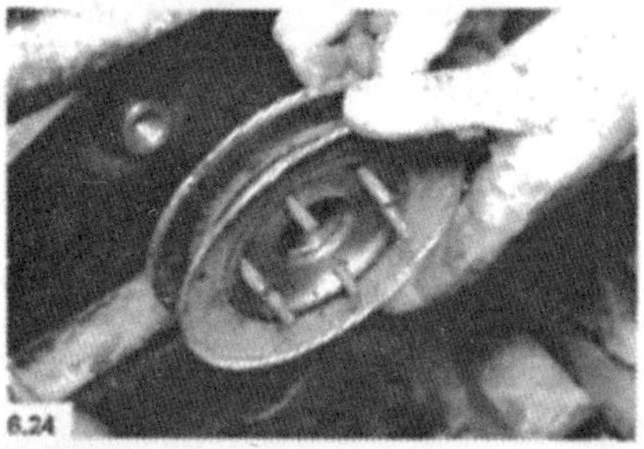
6.24

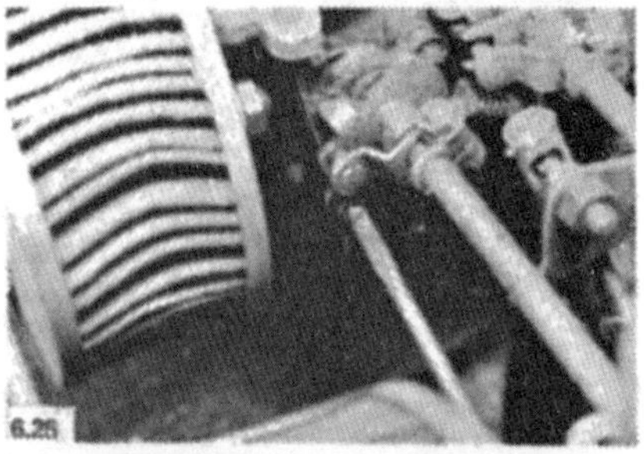
6.25

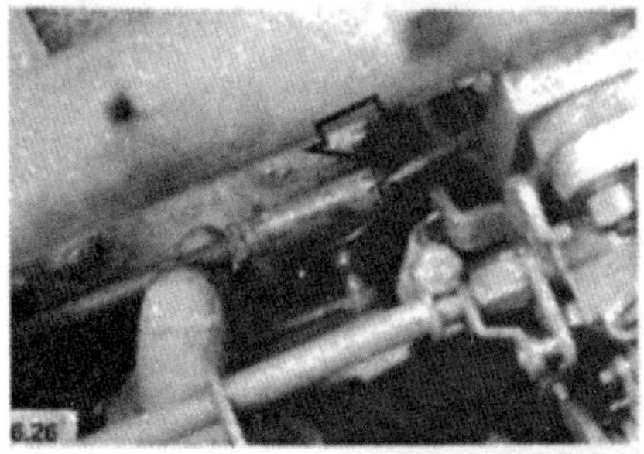
6.26

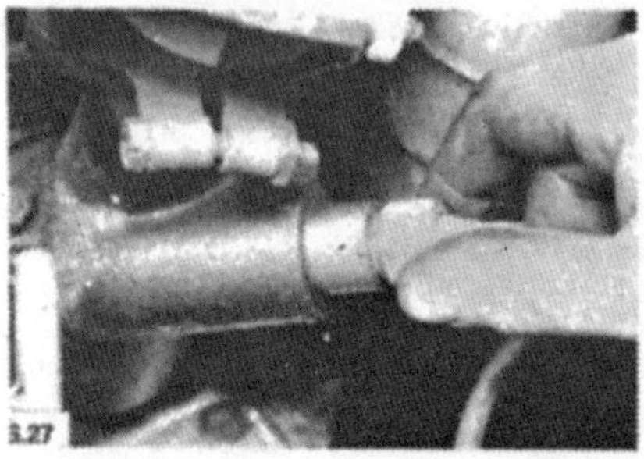
6.27

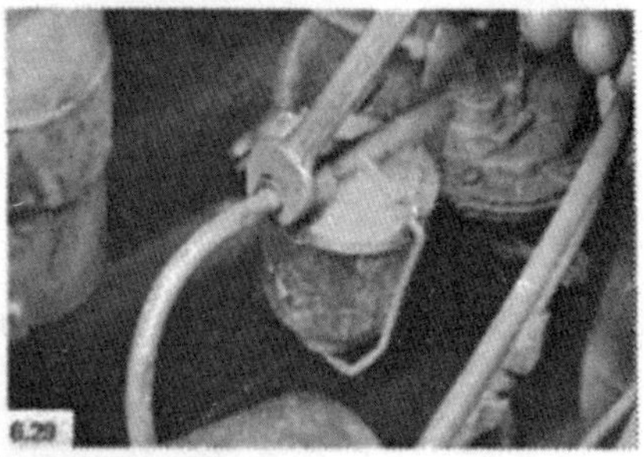
6.29

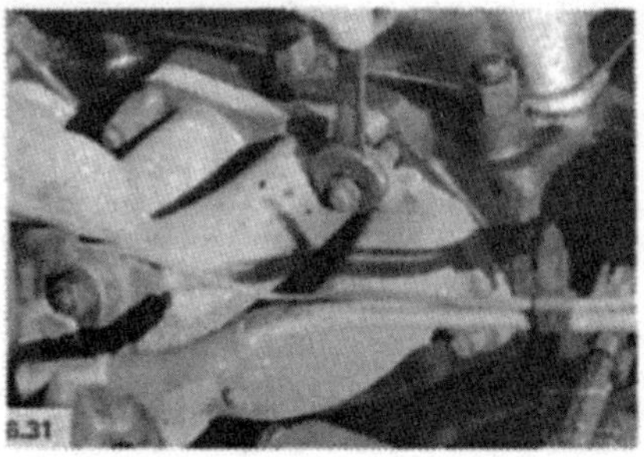
6.31

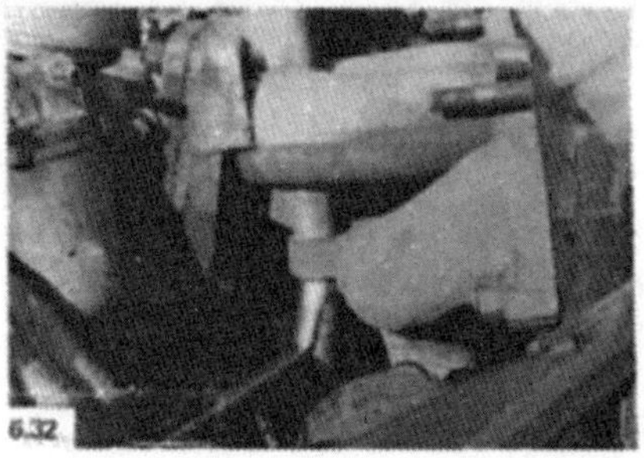
6.32

Chapter 1/Engine

fold followed by the gaskets and insulation pieces (photo).
37 Undo the two nuts securing the lower part of the manifold, mounting flanges to the cylinder head and lift away the nuts and spring washers (photo).
38 Undo the heater return hose pipe connection clip and disconnect the hose from the metal pipe at the rear of the engine (photo).
39 Undo the heater feed pipe connection clip and disconnect the hose from the heater water valve connection (photo).
40 Undo the heater water valve control outer cable connection from the bracket on the side of the water valve body (photo).
41 Using a pair of pliers and an open ended spanner disconnect the heater water valve inner control cable from the lever (photo).
42 Separate the inner control cable from the lever.
43 Undo the heater return pipe connection to be found at the rear of the water pump (photo).
44 Undo the nut securing the heater return pipe bracket to the rear right hand side of the engine by the inlet manifold and lift away the pipe (photo).
45 Disconnect the crankcase emission control valve pipe connection from the side of the valve rocker cover and withdraw the inlet manifold from the side of the cylinder head (photo).
46 Undo the four nuts securing the exhaust downpipe flange to the exhaust manifold (photo). Remove the nuts and separate the joint noting the gasket positioned between the two faces.
47 The exhaust manifold may now be removed from the side of the cylinder head (photo).
48 Remove the heavy duty lead from the rear of the starter motor.
49 Undo the two starter motor retaining nuts and bolts and lift away the starter motor (photo).
50 Slacken the hose clip on the side of the water pump and disconnect the hose from the union (photo).
51 The rubber hose and metal pipe which connects the radiator bottom tank to the water pump may now be lifted away (photo).
52 Disconnect the terminal from the water temperature gauge sender unit situated at the rear of the thermostat housing (photo).
53 Disconnect the positive (+) cable from the ignition coil (photo).
54 Undo and remove the nut and bolt securing the engine earth cable to the rear of the engine timing chain cover (photo).
55 From inside the car lift away both seat cushions and also the carpeting from the front boot wells.
56 Undo and remove the eight nuts securing the seats to their runners. Lift away the front seats to give better access to the floor centre section.
57 Make a note of the electrical cable connections at the rear of the switch and disconnect the electrical terminals. If a radio set is fitted this should be removed from its mounting (photo, Chapter 6, 3.6).
58 Slacken the gear change lever knob locknut and unscrew the knob. Also unscrew the locknut (photo, Chapter 6, 3.7).
59 Withdraw the gear change lever rubber boot from the gear change lever (photo, Chapter 6, 3.8).
60 Disconnect the two dip switch cables from their snap connectors and remove the dip switch.
61 Undo the two bolts holding the panel to the underside of the instrument panel switch console (photo, Chapter 6, 3.10).
62 Undo the four bolts holding the fascia support to the floor panels (photo, Chapter 6, 3.11).
63 Disconnect the two heater control cables, one of which is shown in photo 3.12, Chapter 6.
64 Withdraw the centre console from under the switch panel and lift away from the car (photo, Chapter 6, 3.13).
65 Undo the sixteen bolts with plain washers holding the floor centre section to the floor panels and lift away the complete centre section.
66 Place a rope sling around the front and rear of the engine or chains and hooks to the front and rear of the cylinder head and take the weight of the engine from the mountings.
67 Using a garage hydraulic jack or other suitable means support the weight of the gearbox and overdrive unit if fitted.
68 Undo the two nuts (8) which secure the engine front end plate mounting to the rubber mountings (Fig. 1.5 and photo).
69 Undo the nuts and bolts which secure the clutch bell housing to the engine backplate. The top nuts and bolts are only accessible from inside the car.
70 Check that all electrical connections and pipes have been disconnected from the engine and that all vulnerable parts are protected or moved to one side parallel in movement until the gearbox first motion shaft (input) is free of the clutch.
71 Raise the engine and tilt the front end upwards (photo).
72 Continue raising the engine making sure the front engine plate mounting feet clear the inside wing panels (photo).
73 Finally lift the engine to clear the front panels and pull the engine away from the front of the car (photo).
74 Carefully lower the engine to the ground.
75 To complete the job clear out any loose nuts and bolts and tools from the engine compartment and place them where they will not be misplaced.

7. Engine - Removal with Gearbox

1. Practical experience has proved that the engine and gearbox can be removed in about four and a quarter hours (less with experience) by adhering to the following sequence of operations.
2. It must be pointed out that the basic procedures for removing the engine on all models covered by this manual is identical but there may be slight differences which will be apparent as work progresses. Follow the instructions in Section 6, paragraphs 3 to 68 inclusive.
3. Undo the two bolts which hold the clutch slave cylinder mounting bracket to the gearbox and tie back the slave cylinder out of the way. By this means unless the clutch pedal is accidentally depressed the clutch hydraulic system need not be bled.
4. Disconnect the propeller shaft universal joint flange from the gearbox extension housing or overdrift unit flange by undoing the four nuts and bolts. Carefully lower the propeller shaft to the floor.
5. Using a pair of pliers undo the speedometer drive cable knurled collar from the gearbox extension housing (standard gearbox) or rear of the overdrive unit (photo, Chapter 6, 3.16).
6. Undo and remove the right hand overdrive or gearbox silent block mounting bolt followed by the nut and spring washer. Then undo the bracket to chassis mounting nut and bolt (photo, Chapter 6, 3.18).
7. Lift away the bracket noting that the nut is welded to the underside to assist refitting (photo, Chapter 6, 3.19).
8. Remove the bolt and washer securing the gearbox remote control support stay to the silentbloc mounting (standard gearbox) or silentbloc mounting flange on the side of the overdrive unit (photo, Chapter 6, 3.20).
9. Lift away the little spacer from between the stay and overdrive unit mounting flange (photo, Chapter 6, 3.21).
10 Disconnect the two wires from their terminals on the

6.36

6.37

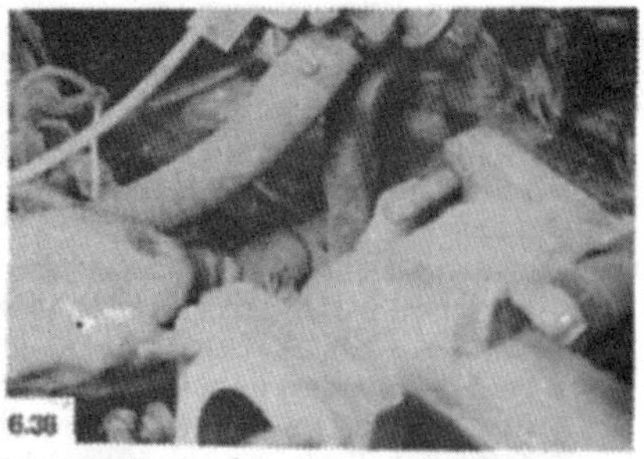
6.38

6.39

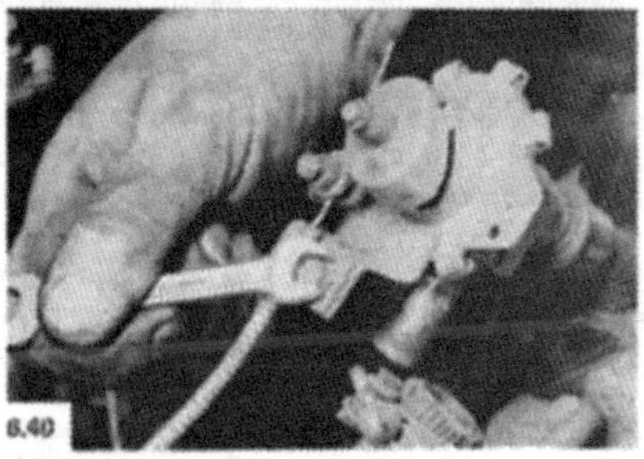
6.40

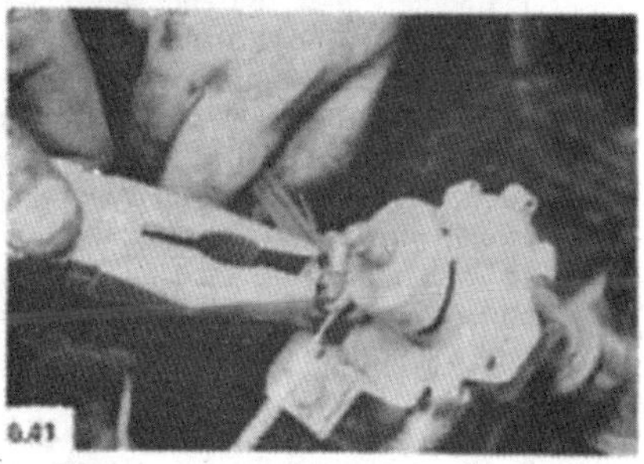
6.41

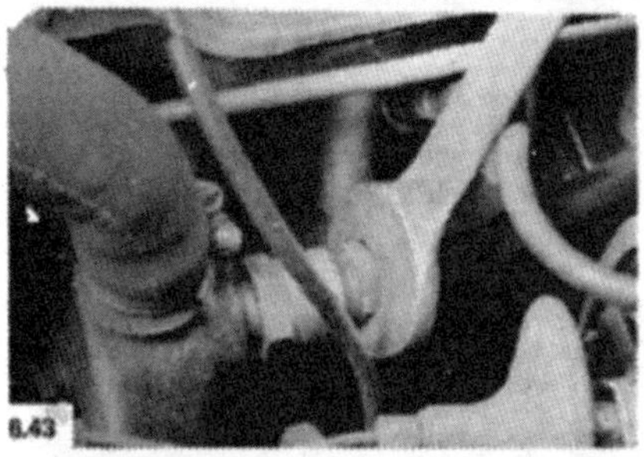
6.43

6.44

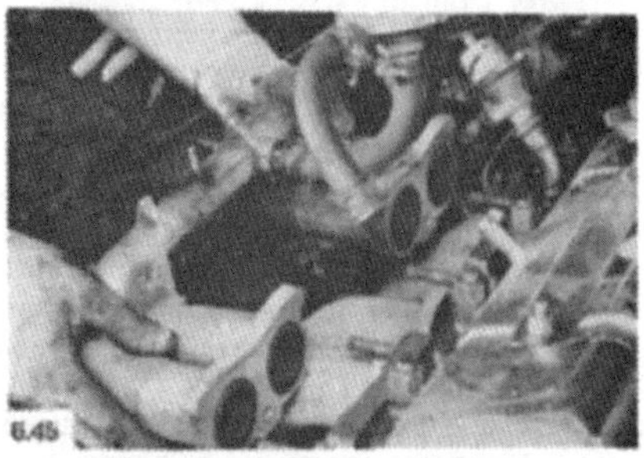
6.45

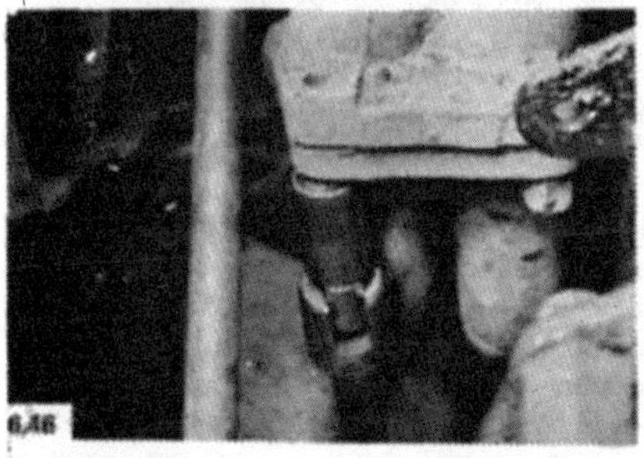
6.46

6.47

6.48

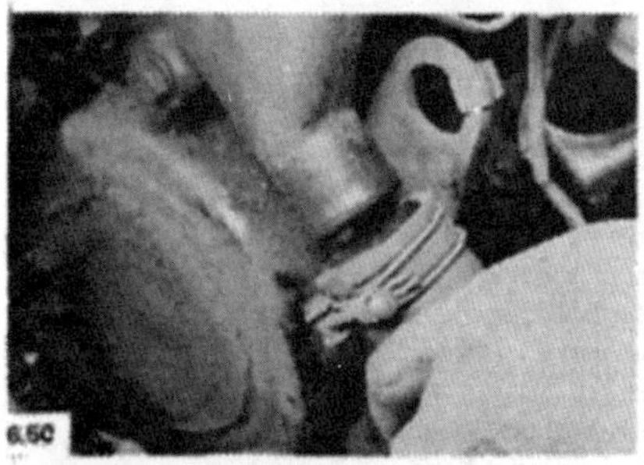
6.50

6.51

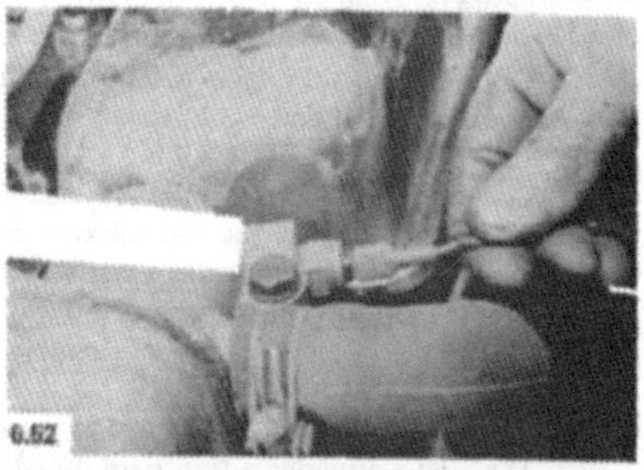
6.52

6.53

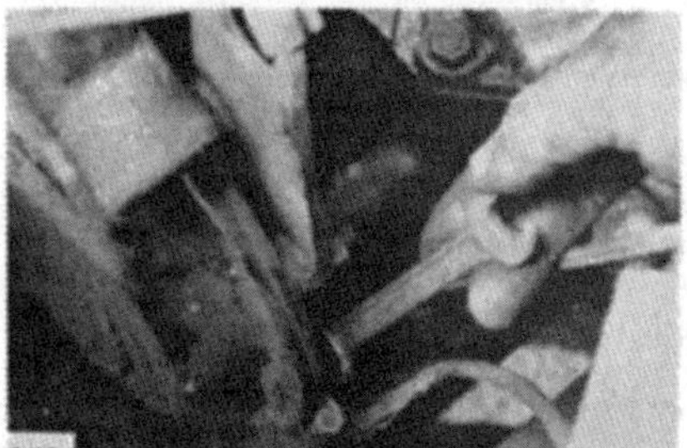
6.54

6.68

Chapter 1/Engine

reverse light switch and also the two wires from the solenoid if the overdrive unit is fitted.
11 Turn the gearbox rear mounting through 90° and lift away from the underside of the unit (photo, Chapter 6, 3.31).
12 Remove the gearbox support and allow the weight of the engine and gearbox unit to be taken by the sling.
13 Check that all electrical connections and pipe have been disconnected from the engine and gearbox and that all vulnerable parts are protected or moved to one side.
14 Carefully ease the complete power unit forwards and then raise the front of the engine so that the front engine plate feet clear the inside wing panels.
15 Continue to raise the front of the power unit as well as pulling forwards until it is over the engine compartment. Pull the unit over the front of the engine compartment and carefully lower to the ground.
16 To complete the job clear out any loose nuts, bolts or tools from the engine compartment and place them where they will not be misplaced.

8. Dismantling the Engine - General

1. It is best to mount the engine on a dismantling stand, but if one is not available, then stand the engine on a strong bench so as to be at a comfortable working height. Failing this, the engine can be stripped down on the floor.
2. During the dismantling process the greatest care should be taken to keep the exposed parts free from dirt. As an aid to achieving this, it is a sound scheme to thoroughly clean down the outside of the engine, removing all traces of oil and congealed muck.
3. Use paraffin or a good grease solvent such as 'Gunk'. The latter compound will make the job much easier, as, after the solvent has been applied and allowed to stand for a time, a vigorous jet of water will wash off the solvent and all the grease and filth. If the dirt is thick and deeply embedded, work the solvent into it with a stiff paintbrush.
4. Finally wipe down the exterior of the engine with rags and only then, when it is quite clean, should the dismantling process begin. As the engine is stripped, clean each part in a bath of paraffin or petrol.
5. Never immerse parts with oilways in paraffin, i.e., the crankshaft, but to clean wipe down carefully with a petrol dampened rag. Oilways can be cleaned out with pipe cleaners. If an air line is present all parts can be blown dry and the oilways blown through as an added precaution.
6. Re-use of old engine gaskets is a false economy and can give rise to oil and water leaks, if nothing worse. To avoid the possibility of trouble after the engine has been reassembled always use new gaskets throughout.
7. Do not throw the old gaskets away as it sometimes happens that an immediate replacement cannot be found and the old gasket is then very useful as a template. Hang up the old gaskets as they are removed on a suitable hook or nail.
8. To strip the engine it is best to work from the top down. The sump provides a firm base on which the engine can be supported in an upright position. When the stage where the sump must be removed is reached, the engine can be turned on its side and all other work carried out with it in this position.
9. Wherever possible, replace nuts, bolts and washers finger tight from wherever they were removed. This helps avoid later loss and muddle. If they cannot be replaced then lay them out in such a fashion that it is clear from where they came.
10 If the engine was removed with the gearbox separate them by undoing the nuts and bolts which hold the bellhousing to the engine endplate.
11 Also undo the two bolts holding the starter motor in place and lift off the motor. Note and retain the distance piece and any shims which may be fitted.
12 Carefully pull the gearbox complete with bellhousing off the engine.

9. Removing Ancillary Engine Components

1. Before basic engine dismantling begins the engine should be stripped of all its ancillary components. These items must also be removed if a factory exchange unit is being purchased. It will be observed that if the engine removal sequences were followed in the previous sections some of the items now fitted will have already been removed.

   Dynamo and dynamo brackets.
   Water pump and thermostat housing.
   Starter motor.
   Distributor and spark plugs.
   Inlet and exhaust manifold and carburettors.
   Fuel pump and fuel pipe.
   Oil filter and dipstick.
   Oil filler cap.
   Clutch assembly.
   Breather pipe and oil pressure switch.
   Auxiliary header tank (where fitted).

2. Without exception all these items can be removed with the engine in the car if it is merely an individual item which requires attention. (It is necessary to remove the gearbox if the clutch is to be renewed with the engine 'in situ'.)
3. Starting work on the right hand side of the engine, slacken off the dynamo retaining bolts, and remove the unit and then the support brackets.
4. Take off the distributor and housing after undoing the two nuts and washers which hold the bottom flange of the distributor housing to the cylinder block. Retain and note the shims between the housing and block. Do not loosen the square nut on the clamp at the base of the distributor body or the timing will be lost. Undo the spark plugs.
5. Note that the fuel pump is held in place by two nuts and washers. One of these nuts holds the bracket for the oil pressure pipe. Lift away the pump together with the gasket and packing pieces.
6. Undo and remove the low oil pressure warning sender unit (if fitted) or the oil pressure gauge pipe at the main oil gallery.
7. Undo the oil filter centre bolt and lift away the bowl and element.
8. Moving to the front of the engine undo the two bolts that hold the thermostat housing onto the top of the water pump and lift away the bolts, spring washers, and thermostat housing. Note the gasket placed between the housing and pump mating faces.
9. Undo the nuts and washers which hold the inlet and exhaust manifolds to the cylinder head.
10 Lift off the inlet and exhaust manifolds together with the carburettors. If stiff tap the manifolds gently with a piece of wood.
11 Undo the bolts which hold the water pump in place on the front of the block. Note the bolts are of different lengths so they must be replaced in their original positions.
12 Undo the breather pipe support bracket and remove by twisting and pulling as it is a press fit into the side of the crankcase.
13 Undo a quarter of a turn at a time the six bolts which hold the clutch pressure plate onto the flywheel.

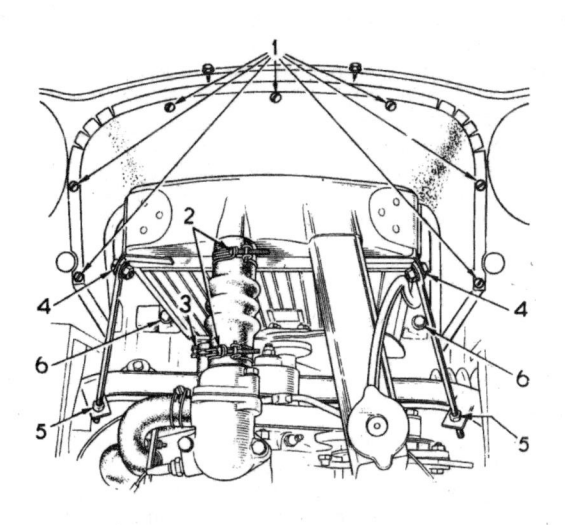

Fig. 1.3. ENGINE COMPARTMENT AIR DEFLECTOR
AND RADIATOR MOUNTING POINTS
(TR4, 4A)

1 Air deflector attachment screws
2 Top hose clips
3 Bottom hose clips
4 Radiator stay attachments
5 Adjusting nuts
6 Radiator attachments

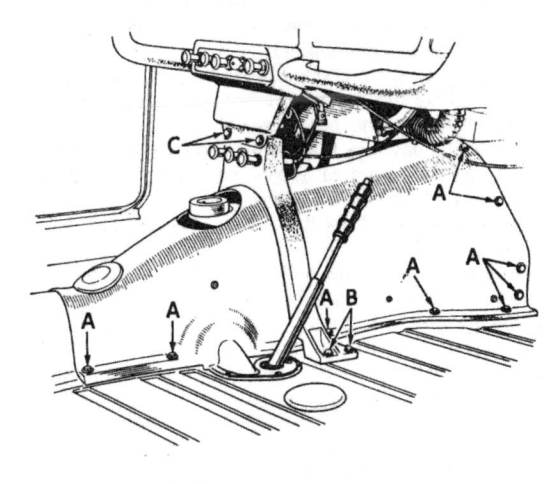

Fig. 1.4. Gearbox cover mounting points

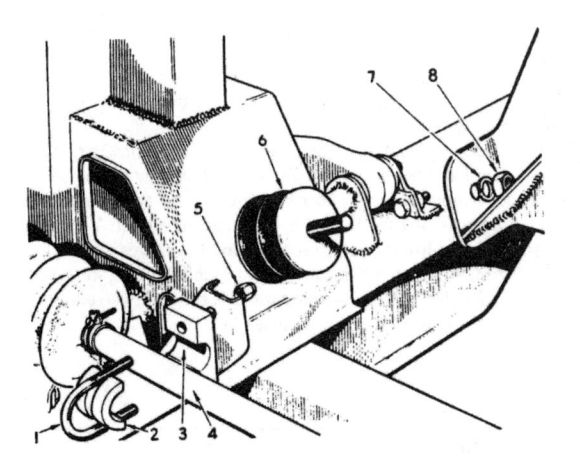

Fig. 1.5. ENGINE MOUNTING TO CHASSIS

1 'U' bolt
2 Clamp (outer)
3 Clamp (inner)
4 Steering unit
5 Nyloc nut
6 Engine mounting
7 Lockwasher
8 Nut

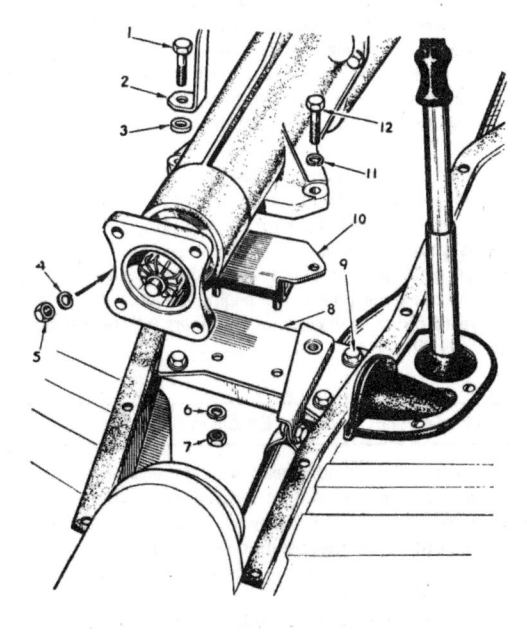

Fig. 1.6. GEARBOX MOUNTING COMPONENTS

1 Bolt
2 Stay
3 Washer
4 Washer
5 Nyloc nut
6 Washer
7 Nut
8 Crossmember
9 Bolt
10 Rear mounting
11 Washer
12 Bolt

25

Chapter 1/Engine

14 Lift off the pressure plate together with the loose friction plate. Check that all the items listed in paragraph 1 of this Section have been removed. The engine is now stripped of ancillary equipment and ready for major dismantling.

10. Cylinder Head Removal - Engine on Bench

1. With the engine out of the car and standing on its sump on the bench or on the floor remove the cylinder head as follows:-
2. Unscrew the two rocker cover retaining nyloc nuts and lift away the nuts, plain washer and fibre washer followed by the rocker cover and its gasket.
3. Unscrew the four rocker pedestal nuts half a turn at a time until all are free and then remove the nuts and spring washers followed by the rocker assembly.
4. Lift out the pushrods keeping them in the relative order in which they were removed. The easiest way to do this is to push them through a sheet of thick paper or thin card in the correct sequence. Mark the card to indicate which end the front pushrod is at.
5. Slacken the ten cylinder head nuts half a turn at a time in the order shown in Fig. 1.7 and when all free remove the nuts and plain washers.
6. The cylinder head may now be removed by lifting upwards. If the head is jammed try to rock it to break the seal. Under no circumstances try to prise it apart from the block with a screwdriver or cold chisel as damage may be done to the faces of the head or block. If the head will not readily free do not under any circumstances try to free the head by replacing the spark plugs and rotating the engine flywheel as the liners are held in place by the cylinder head and using this method may loosen them. Strike the head sharply with a plastic headed hammer, or with a hammer with an interposed piece of wood to cushion the blows but under no circumstances hit the head directly with a metal hammer as this may cause the iron casting to fracture. Several sharp taps with the hammer at the same time pulling upwards should free the head. Lift the head off and place on one side.
7. As soon as the cylinder head has been removed it is advisable to hold the liners in position by using thick washers and a distance tube on the adjoining cylinder head studs as shown in Fig. 1.8. If the liners are moved the 'figure of eight' joints will leak and allow water to enter the sump. At the same time if the engine is more than two or three years old it is likely that the liners will be rusted in place fairly firmly.

11. Cylinder Head Removal - Engine in Car

To remove the cylinder head with the engine still in the car the following additional procedure to that in the previous section must be followed. This procedure should be carried out before that listed in Section 10.
1. Disconnect the battery by removing the lead from the positive terminal.
2. Drain the water from the cooling system by turning on the taps at the base of the radiator and at the bottom left hand corner of the cylinder block.
3. Slacken the top radiator hose clips and remove the hose.
4. Slacken the by pass hose clips from the thermostat housing and water pump and remove the by pass hose.
5. Disconnect the heater hose from the tap located on the right hand rear side of the cylinder head.
6. Mark the four spark plug high tension leads to ensure correct refitting and remove the leads.

7. Remove the carburettors from the inlet manifold as described in Chapter 3.
8. Undo the four nuts securing the inlet manifold to the side of the cylinder head. Lift away the nuts, plain washer and metal clamping pieces.
9. Undo the two nuts securing the studs to the underside of the inlet manifold to the exhaust manifold and lift away the nuts and plain washers.
11 Undo the two nuts securing the lower part of the manifold mounting flanges to the cylinder head and lift away the nuts and spring washers.
11 Disconnect the crankcase emission control valve pipe connection for the side of the valve rocker cover and withdraw the inlet manifold from the side of the cylinder head.
12 Undo the four nuts securing the exhaust downpipe flange to the exhaust manifold. Remove the nuts and separate the joint noting the gasket positioned between the two faces.
13 The exhaust manifold may now be removed from the side of the cylinder head followed by the gasket.
14 The procedure is now the same as for removing the cylinder head when on the bench.

12. Valve Removal

1. The component parts of the valve assembly are shown in Fig. 1.9.
2. Before the valves are removed it is recommended that the cylinder head be decarbonised by using a soft metal scraper or a wire brush in an electric drill (photo).
3. The valves can be removed from the cylinder head by the following method. Compress each spring in turn with a valve spring compressor until the two halves of the collets can be removed. Release the compressor and remove the valve collar, valve spring and collar. The valve may then be withdrawn from the combustion chamber side of the cylinder head.
4. If, when the valve spring compressor is screwed down, the valve spring retaining collar refuses to free and expose the split collet, do not continue to screw down on the compressor as there is a likelihood of damaging it.
5. Gently tap the top of the tool directly over the collets with a light hammer. This will free the collets. To avoid the compressor jumping off the valve spring retaining collar when it is tapped, hold the compressor firmly in position with one hand.
6. It is essential that the valves are kept in their correct sequence unless they are so badly worn that they are to be renewed. If they are going to be kept and used again, place them in a sheet of card having eight holes numbered 1 to 8 corresponding with the relative positions the valves were in when fitted. Also keep the valve springs, collets, etc., in the correct order. Note that on some models the inlet valve has three springs whilst the exhaust valve has two.

13. Valve Guide - Removal

If it is wished to remove the valve guides they can be removed from the cylinder head in the following manner. Measure the distance between the top of the valve guide and the spring seat to ensure correct fitting of the new guide. Place the cylinder head with the gasket face on the bench and with a suitable hard steel punch drift the guides out of the cylinder head.

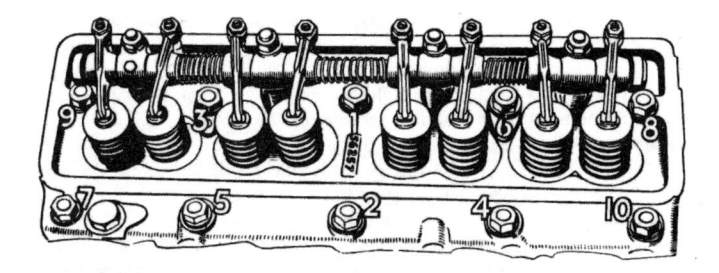

Fig. 1.7. Correct sequence for slackening or tightening cylinder head nuts

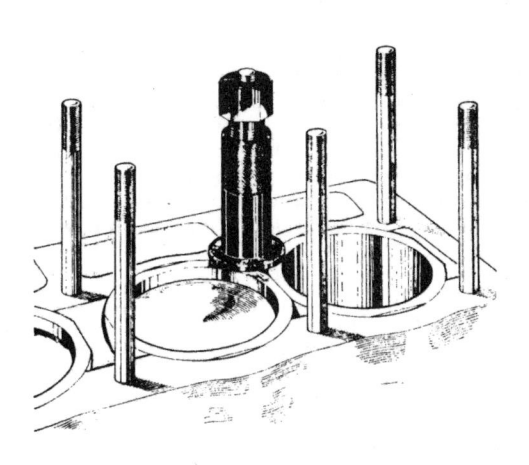

Fig. 1.8. Method of retaining cylinder liners using washers, a piece tube and a nut

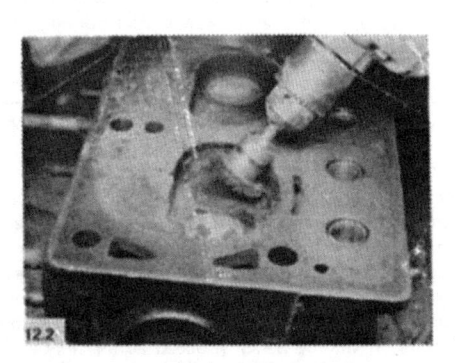

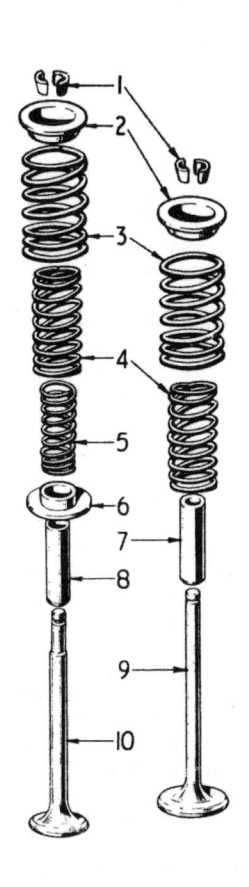

Fig. 1.9. VALVES AND VALVE SPRINGS
1 Split collets
2 Upper collars
3 Outer valve springs
4 Inner valve springs
5 Auxiliary valve spring
6 Lower collars
7 Inlet valve guide
8 Exhaust valve guide
9 Inlet valve
10 Exhaust valve

NOTE: On TR2, 3, 3A models only two springs are fitted to the exhaust valve. The auxiliary valve spring (5) is ommitted.

27

Chapter 1/Engine

14. Dismantling the Rocker Assembly

1. To dismantle the rocker assembly as shown in Fig. 1.10, release the rocker shaft locating screw, remove the pins and caps, and spring washers from each end of the shaft and slide from the shaft the pedestals, rocker arms, and rocker spacing springs.
2. From the end of the shaft undo the plug which gives access to the inside of the rocker shaft which can now be cleaned of sludge, etc. Ensure that the rocker arm lubricating holes are clear.

15. Timing Cover, Gears and Chain - Removal

The timing cover, gears and chain can be removed with the engine in the car, provided that the radiator and front grille are first removed. The fan assembly will also have to be removed from the end of the crankshaft. Full details of these operations are given in Chapter 2. Then proceed as follows.

1. The crankshaft pulley wheel may pull off quite easily. If not place two large screwdrivers behind the crankshaft pulley wheel at 180° to each other, and carefully lever off the wheel. It is preferable to use a proper pulley wheel extractor if this is available, but large screwdrivers or tyre levers are quite suitable, providing care is taken not to damage the pulley flange.
2. Remove the Woodruff key from the crankshaft nose with a pair of pliers and note how the channel in the pulley is designed to fit over it. Place the Woodruff key in a glass jam jar as it is a very small part and can easily become lost.
3. Unscrew the bolts holding the timing cover to the front engine plate and block.
4. Pull off the timing chain cover and gasket followed by the oil thrower. Note which way round the thrower fits (the concave side faces the sprocket).
5. Check the wear on the timing chain by putting a straight edge across the sprockets and if the maximum gap between the straight edge and the chain exceeds 0.4 inch when the chain is pulled away from the straight edge the chain must be renewed. If the chain is worn the sprockets are also probably worn as well so always fit a new set of sprockets and chain.
6. Using a screwdriver unlock the camshaft sprocket tab washer and undo the two retaining bolts.
7. With two screwdrivers or tyre levers carefully ease the two sprockets forwards if the timing chain is still fitted, until the sprockets are clear of their mountings.
8. If the gear wheels are locked solid then it will be necessary to use a proper gear wheel and pulley extractor, and if one is available this should be used anyway in preference to screwdrivers or tyre levers.
9. Should the timing chain have been noisy inspect the timing chain tensioner for signs of wear. It may be removed by extracting the split pin and lifting away the washer. The tensioner may then be removed.

16. Camshaft - Removal

The camshaft can be removed with the engine in place in the car, or with the engine on the bench. If the camshaft is to be removed with the engine in the car, the radiator and fan belt must be removed after the cooling system has been drained. The inlet and exhaust manifolds, rocker gear, pushrods, cylinder head, and tappets must be removed. The fan assembly, timing cover, sprockets and chain must be removed as described in Section 15. It is also necessary to remove the distributor drive gear as described in Section 17. With the drive gear out of the way work may proceed as follows.

1. It should be noted that on the engines fitted to the earlier models of cars covered by this manual, the camshaft runs directly in the cylinder block whilst on the later engines bi-metal bearings are used. There are three screws which hold the bearings in place situated on the left hand side of the cylinder block. Again on the later engines the rear bearing is covered by a seal plug and it is only accessible when the gearbox and flywheel have been removed.
2. If the fuel pump is still in position, close the main fuel line tap, where fitted, and disconnect the fuel pump inlet and outlet connections.
3. Undo the two nuts securing the fuel pump in position, remove the nuts and spring washers and lift away the pump followed by the gasket and packing pieces.
4. Disconnect the tachometer drive cable from the side of the distributor pedestal.
5. Undo the two nuts that secure the distributor pedestal to the side of the cylinder block. The distributor clamp bolts should not be disturbed otherwise the timing setting will be lost. Lift away the nuts and spring washers followed by the distributor and pedestal and its gasket from the cylinder block.
6. It will be observed that the distributor drive gear will also be withdrawn with the distributor and pedestal.
7. Using a dial indicator gauge or feeler gauges measure the end float of the camshaft. It should be between 0.003 and 0.0075 inch (Fig. 1.11). If these limits are exceeded the front bearing will have to be either renewed if the end float is excessive or refaced if the end float is not sufficient.
8. Undo the two bolts which secure the camshaft bearing to the cylinder block, remove the bolts and spring washers followed by the bearing itself. The camshaft may then be withdrawn. Take great care to ensure that the cam lobes do not damage the soft metal bearings (if fitted) as it is being withdrawn.

17. Distributor Drive - Removal

1. To remove the distributor drive with the sump still in position first remove the tachometer drive cable from the side of the distributor pedestal.
2. Undo the two nuts that secure the distributor pedestal to the side of the cylinder block. The distributor clamp bolts should not be disturbed, otherwise the timing setting will be lost. Lift away the nuts and spring washers followed by the distributor and pedestal and its gasket from the cylinder block.
3. Using a pair of long nosed pliers lift out the drive shaft. As the shaft is being withdrawn it will be necessary to turn it slightly to allow the shaft skew gears to disengage with the camshaft skew gear.

18. Sump, Piston, Connecting Rod, Big End Bearing and Liner - Removal

1. The sump, pistons, connecting rods and liners can be removed with the engine still in the car or with the engine on the bench. If in the car it is recommended that the car is placed over a pit or on a ramp due to the low ground clearance and lack of space. Then proceed as for removing the cylinder head with the engine in the car as described in Section 11. If on the bench proceed as for removing the cylinder with the engine in this position, as described in Section 10. The pistons and connecting rods are drawn up out of the top of the cylinder bores.

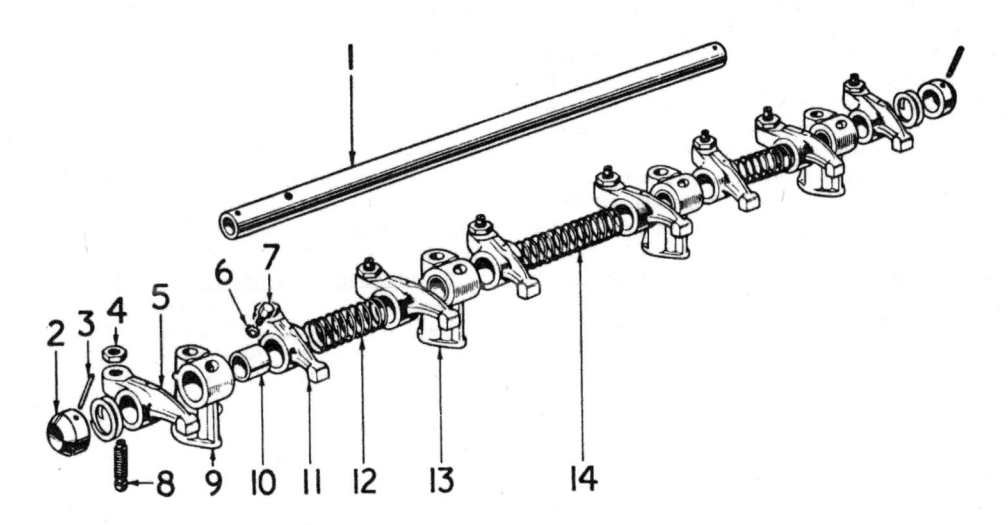

Fig. 1.10. VALVE ROCKER ASSEMBLY COMPONENTS

1 Rocker shaft
2 End cap
3 Mills pin
4 Locknut
5 Rocker, R.H.
6 Shakeproof washer
7 Screw
8 Adjuster
9 Rocker pedestal (rear)
10 Rocker bush
11 Rocker, L.H.
12 Spring
13 Rocker pedestal
14 Spring

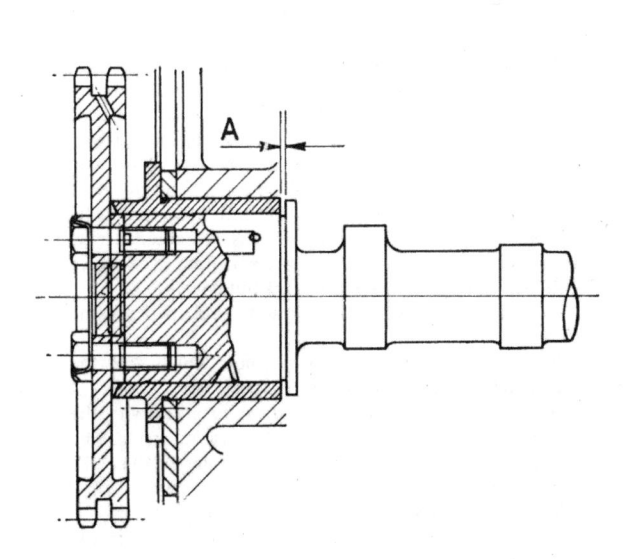

Fig. 1.11. CAMSHAFT END FLOAT
A—0.003" to 0.0075" (0.08 mm to 0.19 mm)

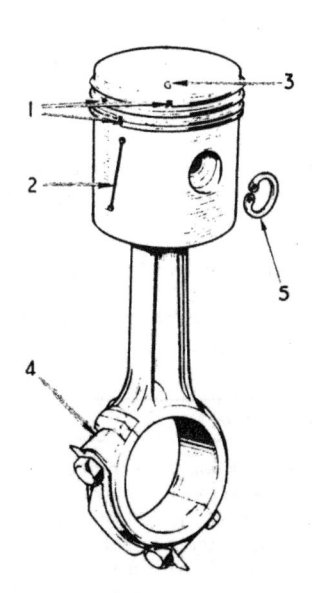

Fig. 1.12. PISTON AND CONNECTING ROD ASSEMBLY. NOTE LETTER 'G' STAMPED ON PISTON CROWN AND POSITIONING OF RING GAPS

1 Piston rings
2 Slot in piston
3 Identification symbol
4 Cap
5 Circlip

29

Chapter 1/Engine

2. Remove the bolts, and washers holding the sump in position. Remove the sump and the sump gasket.
3. If locking tabs are fitted to the connecting rod big end bolts these should be knocked back using a chisel and hammer. Alternatively spring washers may be fitted.
4. Remove the bolts and locking tabs keeping the bolts in sets to ensure correct refitting to the connecting rods.
5. Remove the end caps one at a time, taking care to keep them in the right order and the correct way round. Also ensure that the shell bearings are kept with their correct connecting rods and caps unless they are to be removed. Normally the numbers 1 to 4 are stamped on adjacent sides of the big end caps and connecting rods, indicating which cap fits on which rod and which way round the cap fits. If no numbers or lines can be found then with a sharp screwdriver or file scratch mating marks across the joint from the rod to the cap. One line for connecting rod No. 1, two for connecting rod No. 2 and so on. This will ensure there is no confusion later as it is most important that the cap go back in the correct position on the connecting rods from which they were removed.
6. If the big end caps are difficult to remove they may be gently tapped with a soft faced hammer.
7. To remove the shell bearings, press the bearing opposite the groove in both the connecting rod and the connecting rod caps and the bearings will slide out easily.
8. Withdraw the pistons and connecting rods upwards and ensure that they are kept in the correct order for replacement in the same bore. Refit the connecting rod caps and bearing to the rods if the bearings do not require renewal to minimise the risk of getting the caps and rods muddled.
9. It is important to note that when the cylinder head has been removed the liners must be held down in position using washers and a spacer tube on the adjacent cylinder block studs otherwise the figure of eight washers may move causing water to find its way into the sump.
10 To remove the liners using a block of wood slightly larger in diameter than the bore push the liners upwards and remove the top of the block. If the liners are to be refitted mark them so that they may be refitted in their original positions.

19. Gudgeon Pin - Removal

1. To remove the gudgeon pin to free the piston from the connecting rod, remove one of the circlips at either end of the pin with a pair of circlip pliers.
2. Place the piston in a pan of hot water so as to expand the gudgeon pin boss and press out the pin from the rod and piston with the fingers.
3. Make sure that the gudgeon pins are kept with the same piston for ease of refitting.

20. Piston Ring - Removal

1. To remove the piston rings, slide them carefully over the top of the piston, taking care not to scratch the aluminium alloy. Never slide them off the bottom of the piston skirt. It is very easy to break the iron piston rings if they are pulled off roughly so this operation should be done with extreme caution. It is helpful to make use of an old hacksaw blade, or better still, an old .020 inch feeler gauge.
2. Lift one end of the piston ring to be removed out of its groove and insert the end of the feeler gauge under it.
3. Turn the feeler gauge slowly round the piston and as the ring comes out of its groove apply slight upward pressure so that it rests on the land above. It can be eased off the piston with the feeler gauge stopping it from slipping into any empty groove if it is any but the top piston ring that is being removed.

21. Flywheel and Engine End Plate - Removal

It is possible for the flywheel to be removed from the engine whilst the engine is in position in the car and to do this remove the gearbox as described in Chapter 6, Section 3. Then proceed as follows.
1. If the clutch unit is still in position on the rear face of the flywheel slacken the six securing bolts in a diagonal manner half a turn at a time ensuring that the cover is not held by the dowels. Remove the bolts and spring washers and lift away the clutch cover and driven plate.
2. Bend back the locking plates securing the flywheel retaining bolts and undo the bolts. Lift away the flywheel from the rear of the crankshaft. NOTE: Some difficulty may be experienced in removing the bolts by the rotation of the crankshaft every time pressure is put on the spanner. To lock the crankshaft in position while the bolts are removed, use a screwdriver as a wedge between a backplate stud and the ring gear. Alternatively a wooden wedge can be inserted between the crankshaft and side of the block inside the crankcase.
3. The engine end plate is held in position by a number of bolts and spring washers of varying size. Release the bolts noting where different sizes fit and place them together to ensure none of them become lost. Lift away the end plate from the block complete with the paper gasket.
4. The front engine end plate is removed in the same way as the rear end plate but if it is being removed with the engine 'in situ' the front engine mounting will have to be disconnected and the weight of the unit supported on a jack or other suitable means. The radiator, timing cover, timing chain wheels and chain will have to be removed first.

22. Crankshaft and Main Bearing - Removal

With the engine out of the car, remove the timing chain wheel, sump, oil pump and the big end bearings, pistons, flywheel and engine end plates as has already been described in Sections 15, 18 and 21. Removal of the crankshaft can only be attempted with the engine on the bench or floor.
1. Check the crankshaft end float using feeler gauges placed between the crankshaft main bearing journal well and the thrust washers, as shown in Fig. 1.14. Move the crankshaft forwards as far as it will go using two tyre levers to obtain a maximum reading. The end float should be between 0.004 and 0.006 inch. If this is exceeded new thrust washers must be fitted. If the end float is excessive 0.005 inch oversize thrust washers are obtainable.
2. Remove the front sealing block and the shaped packing pieces.
3. Undo by one turn at a time the nuts which hold the three main bearing caps in place.
4. Unscrew the nuts and remove them together with the washers. It may be found that the rear bearing cap may be very hard to remove which, if the case, refer to Fig. 1.15 and make up the extractor shown.
5. Take care to keep the bearing shells in the right caps.
6. When removing the centre main bearing cap, note the bottom semi-circular halves of the thrust washers, one half lying on either sides of the main bearing. Lay them with the centre bearing along the correct side. Free the two halves of the rear oil seal from the main bearing and cap and rear end of the crankcase.
7. Slightly rotate the crankshaft to free the upper halves of the bearing shells and thrust washers which should now be

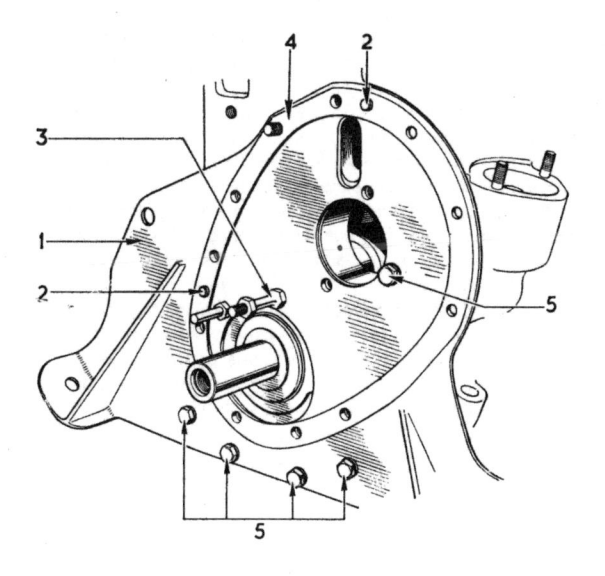

Fig. 1.13. ENGINE FRONT PLATE
1 Engine bearer plate
2 Dowels
3 Stud
4 Timing cover gasket
5 Bolts

Fig. 1.14. Crankshaft and float measurement using feeler gauges

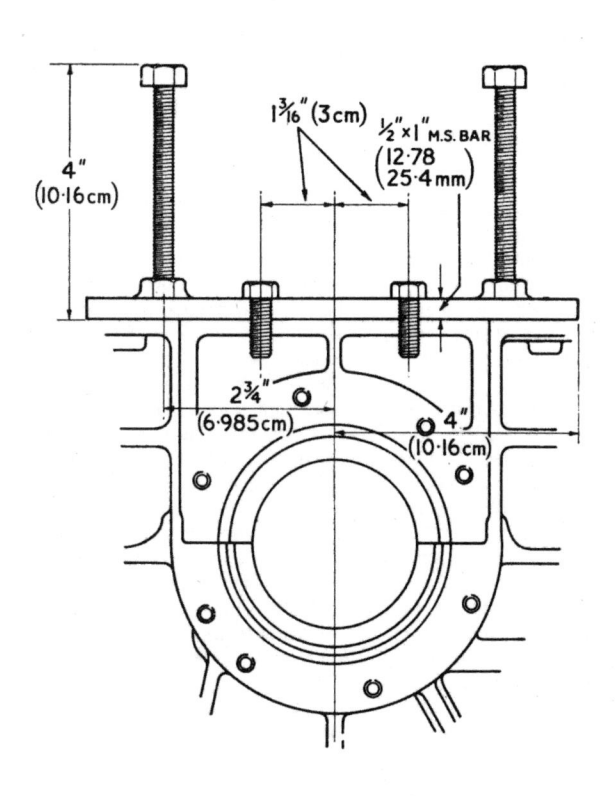

Fig. 1.15 Use of home made tool to remove rear main bearing cap

Chapter 1/Engine

extracted and placed over the correct bearing cap.
8. Remove the crankshaft by lifting it away from the crankcase.

23. Lubrication and Crankcase Ventilation System - Description

1. A forced feed system of lubrication is fitted with oil circulated round the engine from the sump below the block. The level of engine oil in the sump is indicated on the dipstick which is fitted on the right hand side of the engine. It is marked to indicate the optimum level which is the maximum mark.
2. The level of the oil in the sump, ideally, should not be above or below this line. Oil is replenished via the filler cap on the rocker cover.
3. The eccentric rotor type oil pump is bolted in the left hand side of the crankcase and is driven by a short shaft from the skew gear on the camshaft which also drives the distributor shaft.
4. The pump is the non-draining variety to allow rapid pressure build up when starting from cold.
5. Oil is drawn into the pump from the sump via the pick up pipe. From the oil pump the lubricant passes through a non adjustable relief valve to the by pass (early models only) or full flow filter. Filtered oil enters the main gallery which runs the length of the engine on the left hand side. Drillings from the main gallery carry the oil to the crankshaft and camshaft journals.
6. The crankshaft is drilled so that oil under pressure reaches the crankpins from the crankshaft journals. The cylinder bores, pistons and gudgeon pins are all lubricated by splash and oil mist.
7. Oil is fed to the valve gear via the hollow rocker shaft at a reduced pressure by means of a scroll and two flats on the camshaft journal.
8. Drillings and grooves in the camshaft front journal lubricate the camshaft thrust plate, and the timing chain and gearwheels. Oil returns to the sump by gravity, the pushrods and cam followers being lubricated by oil returning via the pushrod drillings in the block.
9. Any one of three types of crankcase ventilation system may be fitted depending on the model and its year of manufacture. The three systems are known as 'open ventilation', 'closed ventilation' and emission control.
10 'Open ventilation' is very straightforward and is only fitted to early models. It comprises an angled tube fitted on the right hand side of the engine which relieves crankcase pressure directly into the air.
11 'Closed ventilation' is a slightly more sophisticated system with crankcase pressure being relieved by means of a rubber pipe from the rocker cover to the air cleaner. The hole for the open road tube is blocked over and the possibility of crankcase fumes entering the car is considerably reduced.
12 'Emission control' is similar to 'closed ventilation' but more efficient and complicated. An emission control valve is positioned on top of the inlet manifold to which it is connected. It is also connected to a tube from the rocker cover. The control valve works by manifold depression so that when the depression is greatest (i.e. on the over-run) crankcase gas flow is restricted. A special oil filler cap is also used and this contains a non-return valve which ensures that crankcase and atmospheric pressures are kept in balance.

24. Oil Filter - Removal and Replacement

1. It is very easy to change the oil filters on all models.

2. Undo the long filter centre bolt which holds the bowl in place (photo).
3. With the bolt released carefully lift away the filter bowl which contains the filter and will also be full of oil (photo). It is helpful to have a large basin under the filter body to catch the amount which is bound to spill (photo).
4. Throw the old filter away and thoroughly clean down the filter bowl, the bolt and associated parts positioned as shown on Page 8 . When clean wipe dry using a clean non fluffy rag.
5. A rubber sealing ring is located in a groove round the head of the oil filter and forms an effective leak proof joint between the filter head and the filter bowl. A new rubber sealing ring is supplied with each new filter element.
6. Carefully prise out the oil sealing ring from the locating groove (photo). If the ring has become hard and is difficult to move take care not to damage the sides of the sealing ring groove.
7. With the old ring removed, fit the new ring in the groove at four equidistant points and press it home a segment at a time. Do not insert the ring at just one point and work round the groove pressing it home as, using this method, it is easy to stretch the ring and be left with a small loop of rubber which will not fit into the locating groove.
8. If the bolt has been removed from the filter bowl first place the seal under the head of the bolt and insert into the bowl. Slide on the spring, washer, bolt, seal and element seal with the concave side facing the bottom of the bowl. Using a piece of rube or a small diameter box spanner slide the circlip down the centre bolt.
9. Slide the new element into the oil filter bowl (photo).
10 With the bolt pressed hard up against the filter bowl body (to avoid leakage) three quarter fill the bowl with engine oil.
11 Offer up the bowl to the rubber sealing ring and before finally tightening down the centre bolt, check that the lip of the filter bowl is resting squarely on the rubber sealing ring and is not offset and off the ring. If the bowl is not seating properly, rotate it until it is located correctly. Run the engine and check the bowl for leaks.

25. Oil Pressure Relief Valve - Removal and Replacement

1. To prevent excessive oil pressure, for example when the engine is cold, an oil pressure relief valve is built into the head of the external oil filter and this is set at the factory to limit the oil pressure to 70 lb. sq. in. The normal oil pressure at an engine speed of 2,000 r.p.m. should be 70 lb. sq. in. The pressure will be lower when the engine is warm and at idling speed.
2. If the oil pressure is continually low then the cause of the trouble could be worn bearings, low oil level in the sump, oil too thick due either to wrong grade of oil or dirty oil, a clogged filter or dirt trapped in the pressure relief valve.
3. To remove the oil pressure relief valve unscrew the complete assembly from the filter head assembly without disturbing the adjustment and clean the ball and its seat.
4. If the oil pressure relief valve appears to be satisfactory the pressure gauge could be at fault and may be checked by substitution or at the local agents.

26. Oil Pump - Removal and Dismantling

1. The oil pump does not usually wear by any appreciable amount as it is continually lubricated. However, if oil changes have been infrequent then oil contamination will result and this can be a main factor in determining the life of the pump. It is usually necessary to fit a new or recon-

32

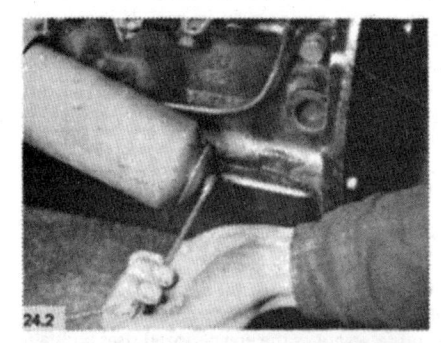

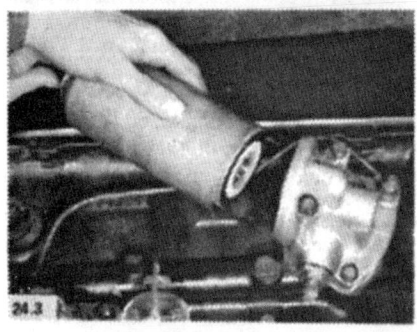

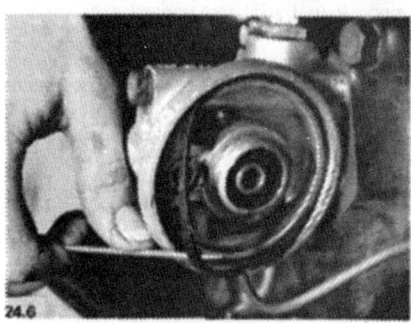

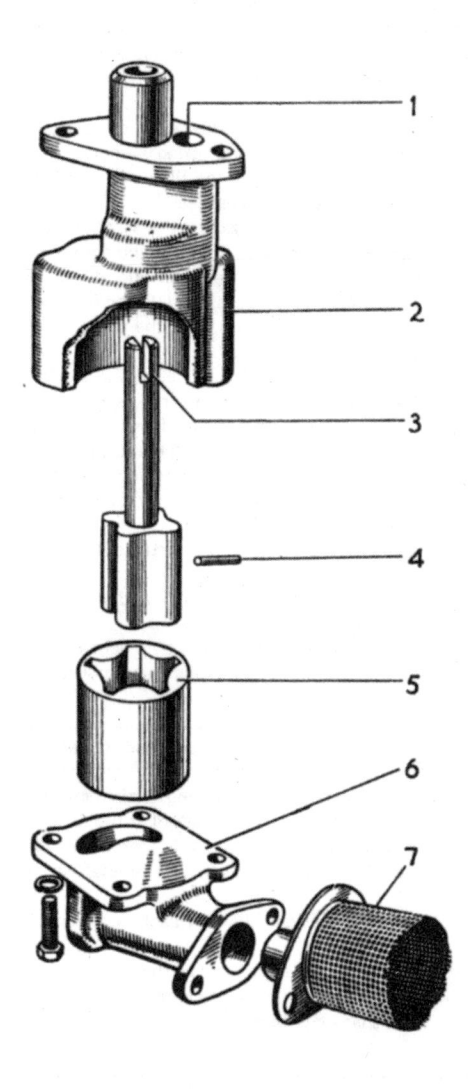

Fig. 1.16. OIL PUMP COMPONENT PARTS
1 Oil pump outlet
2 Oil pump body
3 Shaft and inner rotor
4 Securing pin
5 Outer rotor
6 End plate
7 Filter

ditioned pump when the engine is undergoing major reconditioning.

2. The oil pump may be removed with the engine in position in the car. First remove the sump after draining all the oil into a container having a capacity of at least 11 pints. Refit the drain plug.

3. Undo the fifteen bolts that secure the sump to the underside of the crankcase and lift away the bolts and spring washers.

4. Carefully lower the front end of the sump first and manipulate the sump baffle over the oil pump and gauze filter. Also remove the sump gasket. It is recommended that a new sump gasket be fitted upon reassembling the sump to the crankcase.

5. Undo the three bolts that secure the oil pump to the block and lift away the bolts and spring washers.

6. Withdraw the oil pump with the filter still attached from the crankcase followed by the gasket.

7. Undo the two bolts that secure the filter gauze to the side of the pump and lift away the bolts and spring washers.

8. Note which way round the filter mounting plate is fitted to the pump body as it is possible for it to be fitted back the wrong way in which case the sump cannot be refitted. Remove the filter gauze.

9. The gauze may be cleaned with petrol and a stiff brush like an old toothbrush. Do not use rag as the fibres will catch on the gauze and those can be difficult to remove.

10 Unscrew the four bolts holding the end plate onto the pump body. Lift away the bolts and spring washers. Scribe a mark on the end plate and pump body to ensure correct refitting and remove the end plate.

11 The rotors and shaft may now be lifted out of the pump body.

12 Thoroughly wash all parts in petrol and wipe dry using a non fluffy rag.

13 Lubricate the rotors and shaft with a light machine oil and reassemble ready for examination and measurement.

27. Timing Chain Tensioner - Removal and Replacement

1. With time the spring blade timing chain tensioner will become worn and it should be renewed at the same time as the timing chain. Wear can be clearly seen as two grooves on the face of the tensioner where it presses against the chain.

2. To remove the tensioner bend it back and then pull out from its securing pins.

3. On replacement fit the open end of the tensioner over the pin and press the blade into place with the aid of a screwdriver until it snaps into place.

28. Examination and Renovation - General

With the engine stripped down and all parts thoroughly cleaned, it is now time to examine everything for wear. The following items should be checked and where necessary renewed or renovated as described in the following sections.

29. Crankshaft - Examination and Renovation

Examine the crankpin and main journal surfaces for signs of scoring or scratches. Check the ovality of the crankpins at different positions with a micrometer. If more than 0.001 inch out of round, the crankpins will have to be reground. It will also have to be reground if there are any scores or scratches present. Also check the journals in the same fashion. On highly tuned engines the centre main bearing has been known to break up. This is not always immediately apparent, but slight vibration in an otherwise normally smooth engine and a very slight drop in oil pressure under normal conditions are immediate clues. If the centre main bearing is suspected of failure it should be immediately investigated by dropping the sump and removing the centre main bearing cap. Failure to do this will result in a badly scored centre main journal. If it is necessary to regrind the crankshaft and fit new bearings your local Triumph garage or engineering works will be able to decide how much metal to grind off and the correct undersize shells to fit.

30. Big End and Main Bearings - Examination and Renovation

Big end bearing failure is accompanied by a noisy knocking from the crankcase and a slight drop in oil pressure. Main bearing failure is accompanied by vibration which can be quite severe as the engine speed rises and falls and a drop in oil pressure.

Bearings which have not broken up, but are badly worn, will give rise to low oil pressure and some vibration. Inspect the big ends, main bearings, and thrust washers for signs of general wear, scoring, pitting and scratches. The bearings should be matt grey in colour. With lead indium bearings should a trace of copper colour be noticed the bearings are badly worn as the lead bearing material has worn away to expose the indium underlay. Renew the bearings if they are in this condition or if there is any sign of scoring or pitting.

The undersizes available are designed to correspond with the regrind sizes, i.e., .010 inch bearings are correct for a crankshaft reground .010 undersize. The bearings are in fact slightly more than the stated undersize as running clearances have been allowed for during their manufacture.

Very long engine life can be achieved by changing big end bearings at intervals of 30,000 miles, irrespective of bearing wear. Normally crankshaft wear is infinitesimal and a change of bearings will ensure mileages of between 100,000 to 120,000 miles before crankshaft regrinding becomes necessary. Crankshafts normally have to be reground because of scoring due to bearing failure.

31. Cylinder Liner Bores - Examination and Renovation

1. The cylinder bores must be examined for taper, ovality, scoring and scratches. Start by carefully examining the top of the cylinder bores. If they are at all worn a very slight ridge will be found on the thrust side. This marks the top of the piston ring travel. The owner will have a good indication of the bore wear prior to dismantling the engine, or removing the cylinder head. Excessive oil consumption accompanied by blue smoke from the exhaust is a sure sign of worn cylinder bores and piston rings.

2. Measure the bore diameter just under the ridge with a micrometer and compare it with the diameter at the bottom of the bore, which is not subject to wear. If the differences between the two measurements are more than .006 then it will be necessary to fit special pistons and rings or to have the cylinders rebored and fit oversize pistons. If no micrometer is available remove the ring from a piston and place the piston in each bore in turn about ¾ inch below the top of the bore. If an 0.010 inch feeler gauge can be slid between the piston and the cylinder wall on the thrust side of the bore then remedial action must be taken. Three sizes of pistons are available and details of these sizes are given in the specifications at the beginning of this Chapter.

3. These are accurately machined in just below these

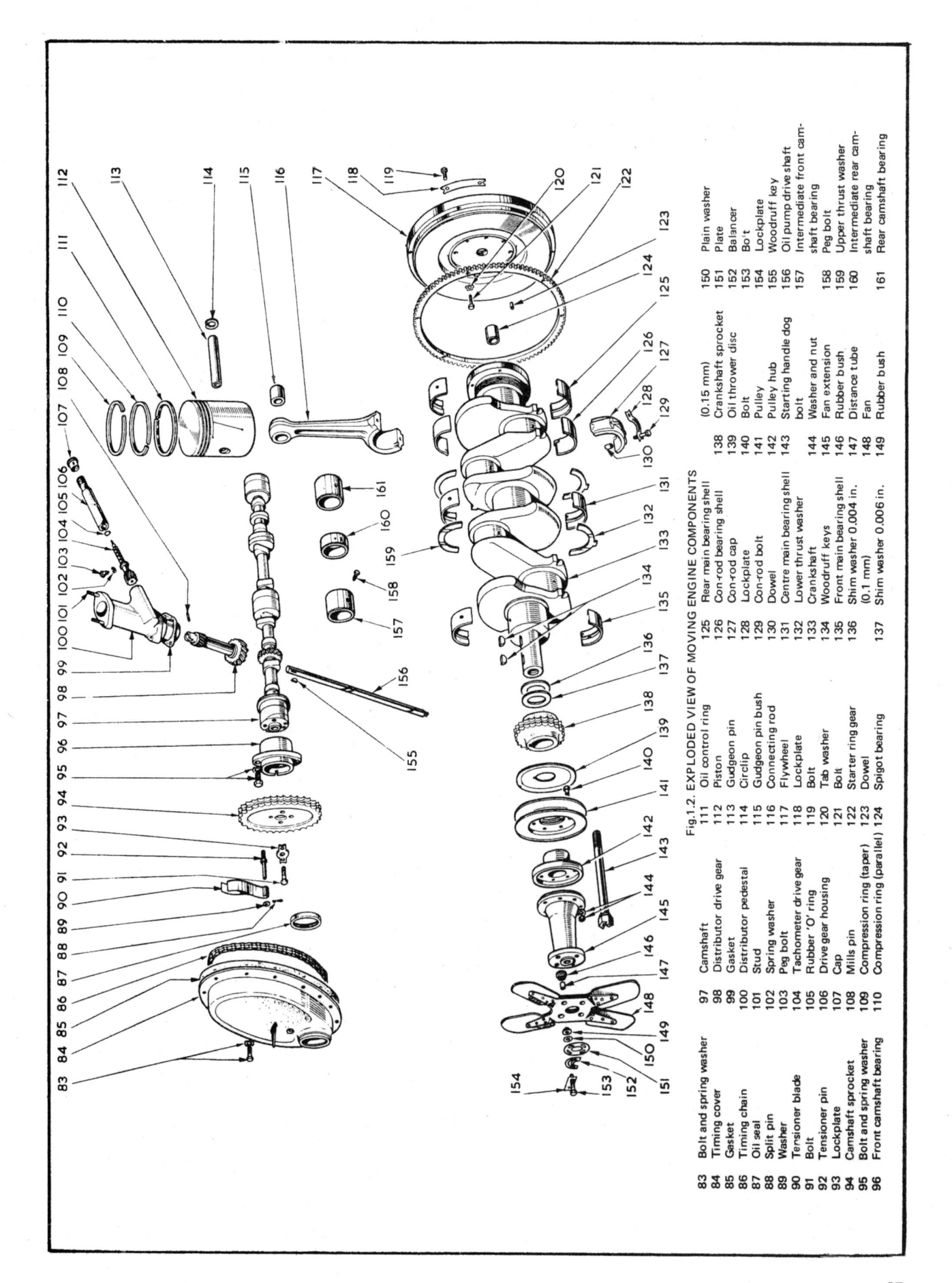

Fig.1.2. EXPLODED VIEW OF MOVING ENGINE COMPONENTS

83	Bolt and spring washer	97	Camshaft	111	Oil control ring	
84	Timing cover	98	Distributor drive gear	112	Piston	
85	Gasket	99	Gasket	113	Gudgeon pin	
86	Timing chain	100	Distributor pedestal	114	Circlip	
87	Oil seal	101	Stud	115	Gudgeon pin bush	
88	Split pin	102	Spring washer	116	Connecting rod	
89	Washer	103	Washer	117	Flywheel	
90	Tensioner blade	104	Tachometer drive gear	118	Lockplate	
91	Bolt	105	Rubber 'O' ring	119	Bolt	
92	Tensioner pin	106	Drive gear housing	120	Tab washer	
93	Lockplate	107	Cap	121	Bolt	
94	Camshaft sprocket	108	Mills pin	122	Starter ring gear	
95	Bolt and spring washer	109	Compression ring (taper)	123	Dowel	
96	Front camshaft bearing	110	Compression ring (parallel)	124	Spigot bearing	

125	Rear main bearing shell	138	(0.15 mm)	
126	Con-rod bearing shell	139	Crankshaft sprocket	
127	Con-rod cap	140	Oil thrower disc	
128	Lockplate	141	Bolt	
129	Con-rod bolt	142	Pulley	
130	Dowel	143	Pulley hub	
131	Centre main bearing shell	144	Starting handle dog bolt	
132	Lower thrust washer	145	Washer and nut	
133	Crankshaft	146	Fan extension	
134	Woodruff keys	147	Rubber bush	
135	Front main bearing shell	148	Distance tube	
136	Shim washer 0.004 in. (0.1 mm)	149	Fan	
137	Shim washer 0.006 in.		Rubber bush	

150	Plain washer
151	Plate
152	Balancer
153	Bolt
154	Lockplate
155	Woodruff key
156	Oil pump drive shaft
157	Intermediate front camshaft bearing
158	Peg bolt
159	Upper thrust washer
160	Intermediate rear camshaft bearing
161	Rear camshaft bearing

Chapter 1/Engine

measurements so as to provide correct running clearances in bores bored out to the exact oversize dimensions.

4. If the bores are slightly worn but not so badly worn as to justify reboring them, then special oil control rings and pistons can be fitted which will restore compression and stop the engine burning oil. Several different instructions concerning their fitting must be followed closely.

5. If the liner bores are badly worn then they may be either sent away for reboring or alternatively new liners may be obtained and fitted.

6. Should the liners have been disturbed they must be completely removed from the cylinder block and new seals fitted otherwise once the seals have been disturbed the chances are that water will leak into the sump.

7. It is possible that if the liners are only very slightly worn for the liners to be removed and refitted 90° from their original position so minimising piston slap. It will of course be necessary to fit new seals.

8. To refit the liners first clean the bottom of the liner with a wire brush to remove all signs of corrosion. Wipe clean with a non fluffy rag.

9. Smear the liner and seal areas with a sealing compound and fit the liners in position taking extreme care not to damage the plastic seal.

10 Retain the liners in position with washers and a spacer tube fitted to the adjoining cylinder studs.

11 Using a feeler gauge and straight edge check that the liner protrudes above the face of the cylinder block by between 0.003 and 0.005 inch to give the required nip by the cylinder head.

12 Three sizes of liners are available and are identified by letters stamped on the top face of the liner.

13 If new pistons are being fitted and the liners have not been reground, it is essential to slightly roughen the hard glaze on the side of the bores with fine glass paper so that new pistons will have a chance to bed in properly.

32. Pistons and Piston Rings - Examination and Renovation

If the old pistons are to be refitted carefully remove the piston rings and then thoroughly clean them. Take particular care to clean out the piston ring grooves. At the same time do not scratch the aluminium in any way. If new rings are to be fitted to the old pistons then the top ring should be stepped so as to clear the ridge left above the previous top ring. If a normal but oversize new ring is fitted it will hit the ridge and break because the new ring will not have worn in the same way as the old, which will have worn in union with the ridge.

Before fitting the rings on the pistons each should be inserted approximately 3 inches down the cylinder bore and the gap measured with a feeler gauge as shown in Fig. 1.17. This should be between .015 inch and .038 inch. It is essential that the gap should be measured at the bottom of the ring travel, as if it is measured at the top of a worn bore and gives a perfect fit, it could easily seize at the bottom. If the ring gap is too small rub down the ends of the ring with a very fine file until the gap, when fitted, is correct. To keep the rings square in the bore for measurement line each up in turn by inserting an old piston in the bore upside down, and use the piston to push the ring down about 3 inches. Remove the piston and measure the piston ring gap.

When refitting new pistons and rings to a rebored engine the piston ring gap can be measured at the top of the bore as the bore will not now taper. It is not necessary to measure the side clearance in the piston ring grooves with the rings fitted as the groove dimensions are accurately machined during manufacture. When fitting new oil control rings to old pistons it may be necessary to have the groove in this instance widened by machining to accept the new wider rings. In this instance the manufacturers representative will make this quite clear and will supply the address to which the pistons must be sent for machining.

33. Camshaft and Camshaft Bearings - Examination and Renovation

On earlier engines the camshaft runs direct in the block and wear of the journal and bearings is negligable. On the later engines pre-formed camshaft bearings are fitted and these can be replaced. This is an operation for your Triumph dealer or the local engineering works as it demands the use of specialised equipment. The bearings are removed with a special drift after which new bearings are pressed in, care being taken to ensure the oil holes in the bearings lineup with those in the block. On no account can the bearings be reamed in position.

The camshaft itself should show no signs of wear, but, if very slight scoring on the cams is noticed, the score marks can be removed by very gently rubbing down with a very fine emery cloth. The greatest care should be taken to keep the cam profiles smooth and not to break through the case hardening.

34. Valves and Valve Seats - Examination and Renovation

1. Examine the heads of the valves for pitting and burning, especially the heads of the exhaust valves. The valve seatings should be examined at the same time. If the pitting on valve and seat is very slight the marks can be removed by grinding the seats and valves together with coarse, and then fine, valve grinding paste. Where bad pitting has occurred to the valve seats it will be necessary to recut them and fit new valves. If the valve seats are so worn that they cannot be recut, then it will be necessary to fit new valve seat inserts. These latter two jobs should be entrusted to the local Triumph agent or engineering works. In practice it is very seldom that the seats are so badly worn that they require renewal. Normally, it is the exhaust valve that is too badly worn for replacement, and the owner can easily purchase a new set of valves and match them to the seats by valve grinding.

2. Valve grinding is carried out as follows. Smear a trace of coarse carborundum paste on the seat face and apply a suction grinder tool to the valve head. With a semi-rotary motion, grind the valve head to its seat, lifting the valve occasionally to redistribute the grinding paste (photo). When a dull matt even surface finish is produced on both the valve seat and the valve, wipe off the paste and repeat the process with fine carborundum paste, lifting and turning the valve to redistribute the paste as before. A light spring placed under the valve head will greatly ease this operation. When a smooth unbroken ring of light grey matt finish is produced on both valve and valve seat faces, the grinding operation is completed.

3. Scrape away all carbon from the valve head and the valve stem. Carefully clean away every trace of grinding compound, taking great care to leave none in the ports or in the valve guides. Clean the valves and valve seats with a paraffin soaked rag then with a clean rag, and finally, if an air line is available, blow the valves, valve guides and valve ports clean.

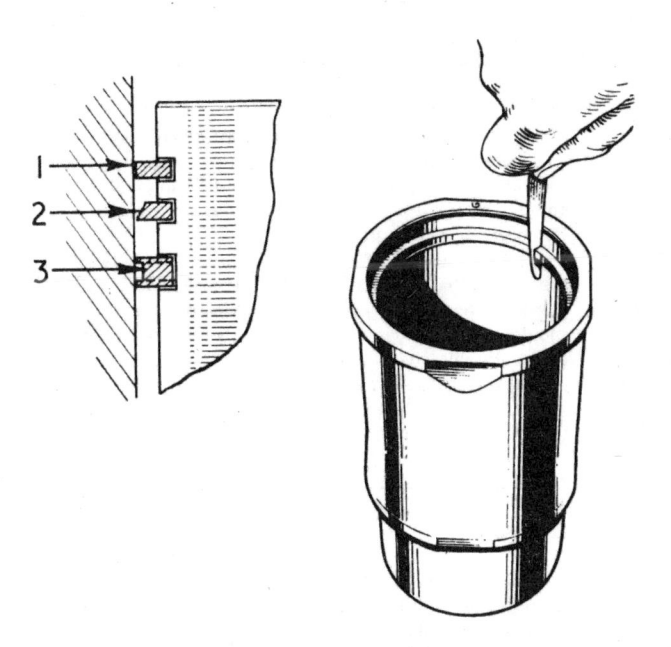

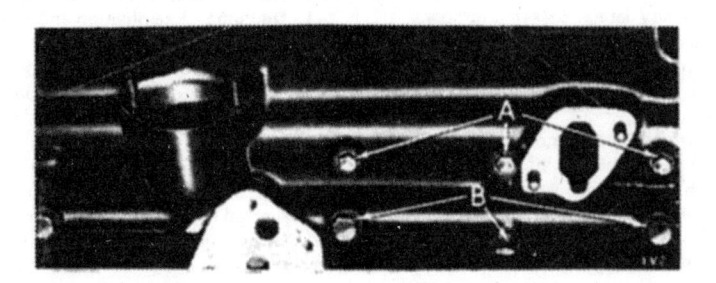

Fig. 1.17. PISTON RING GAP
MEASUREMENT
1 Plain compression ring 3 Oil control ring
2 Taper faced compression ring

Fig. 1.18. Camshaft bearing locating screws A. Oil gallery sealing plugs B.

Chapter 1/Engine

35. Timing Gears and Chain - Examination and Renovation

Examine the teeth on both the crankshaft gearwheel and the camshaft gearwheel for wear. Each tooth forms an inverted 'V' with the gearwheel periphery, and if worn, the side of each tooth under tension will be slightly concave in shape when compared with the other side of the tooth, i.e., one side of the inverted 'V' will be concave when compared with the other. If any sign of wear is present the gearwheels must be renewed.

Examine the links of the chain for side slackness and renew the chain if any slackness is noticeable when compared with a new chain. It is a sensible precaution to renew the chain at about 30,000 miles and at a lesser mileage if the engine is stripped down for a major overhaul. The actual rollers on a very badly worn chain may be slightly grooved.

36. Timing Chain Tensioner - Examination and Renovation

1. If the timing chain is badly worn it is more than likely that the tensioner will be too.
2. Examine the side of the tensioner which bears against the chain and renew it if it is grooved or ridged. See Section 27 for details.

37. Rockers and Rocker Shaft - Examination and Renovation

Remove the threaded plug with a screwdriver from the end of the rocker shaft and thoroughly clean out the shaft. As it acts as the oil passage for the valve gear also ensure the oil holes in it are quite clear after having cleaned them out. Check the shaft for straightness by rolling it on the bench. It is most unlikely that it will deviate from normal, but, if it does, then a judicious attempt must be made to straighten it. If this is not successful purchase a new shaft. The surface of the shaft should be free from any worn ridges caused by the rocker arms. If any wear is present, renew the shaft. Wear is only likely to have occurred if the rocker shaft oil holes have become blocked.

Check the rocker arms for wear of the rocker bushes, for wear at the rocker arm face which bears on the valve stem, and for wear of the adjusting ball ended screws. Wear in the rocker arm bush can be checked by gripping the rocker arm tip and holding the rocker arm in place on the shaft, noting if there is any lateral rocker arm shake. If shake is present, and the arm is very loose on the shaft, a new bush or rocker arm must be fitted.

Check the tip of the rocker arm where it bears on the valve head for cracking or serious wear on the case hardening. If none is present reuse the rocker arm. Check the lower half of the ball on the end of the rocker arm adjusting screw. On high performance engines wear on the ball and top of the pushrod is easily noted by the unworn 'pip' which fits in the small central oil hole on the ball. The larger this 'pip' the more wear has taken place to both the ball and the pushrod. Check the pushrods for straightness by rolling them on the bench. Renew any that are bent.

38. Tappets - Examination and Renovation

Examine the bearing surface of the tappets which lie on the camshaft. Any indentation in this surface or any cracks indicate serious wear and the tappets should be renewed. Thoroughly clean them out, removing all traces of sludge. It is most unlikely that the sides of the tappets will prove worn, but, if they are a very loose fit in their bores and can readily be rocked, they should be exchanged for new units. It is very unusual to find any wear in the tappets, and any wear present is likely to occur only at very high mileages.

39. Flywheel Starter Ring - Examination and Renovation (TR2, 3, 3A)

If the teeth on the flywheel starter ring are badly worn, or if some are missing, then it will be necessary to remove the ring. This is achieved by splitting the ring with a cold chisel. The greatest care should be taken not to damage the flywheel during this process.

To fit a new ring heat it gently in boiling water. With the ring at this temperature, fit it to the flywheel with the front of the teeth facing the flywheel register. The ring should be tapped gently down onto its register and left to cool naturally when the shrinkage of the metal on cooling will ensure that it is a secure and permanent fit. Great care must be taken not to overheat the ring, as if this happens, the temper of the ring will be lost.

40. Flywheel Starter Ring - Examination and Renovation (TR4, 4A)

If the teeth on the flywheel starter ring are found to be worn in two positions caused by the engine stopping on the compression stroke with the ignition switch off it is possible to remove the ring gear and replace it 60° further round on the flywheel. This is of course presuming that the teeth are not too badly worn to cause non engagement or jamming.

Mark the T.D.C. position on the flywheel, knock back the tabs and undo the six bolts securing the ring gear to the flywheel. Obtain some short pieces of ¼ inch diameter rod and insert these into the tapped holes as shown in the insert in Fig. 1.19. Replace the bolts and gently screw in, so causing the rods to push the ring gear off.

Move the position of the ring gear through 60° and replace on the flywheel. Replace the bolts and tighten the bolts in a diagonal manner until the ring gear is in position. Lock by bending over the lockwasher tabs.

Measure the position of the new T.D.C. position from the previous made mark on the flywheel and mark the face of the ring gear with a file.

41. Oil Pump - Examination and Renovation

Thoroughly clean all the component parts in petrol and then check the rotor end float and lobe clearances in the following manner.

Position the rotors in the pump and place the straight edge of a steel ruler across the joint face of the pump. Measure the gap between the bottom of the straight edge and the top of the rotors with a feeler gauge as in Fig. 1.20. If the measurement exceeds .005 inch (.127 mm) then check the lobe clearances as described in the following paragraphs. If the lobe clearances are correct, then lap the joint face on a sheet of plate glass.

Measure with a feeler gauge the gap between the inner and outer rotors. It should not be more than 0.010 inch as shown in Fig. 1.21.

Then measure the gap between the outer rotor and the side of the pump body (Fig. 1.22) which should not exceed 0.008 inch. It is essential to renew the pump if the measurements are outside these figures. It can be safely assumed that at any major reconditioning the pump will need renewal.

As will be seen from Fig. 1.16 the oil pump is driven by

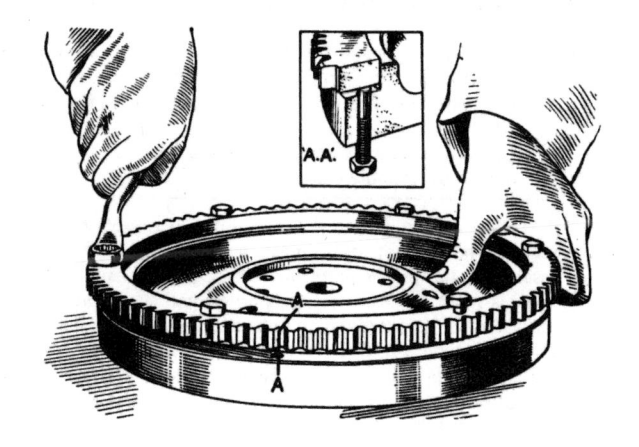

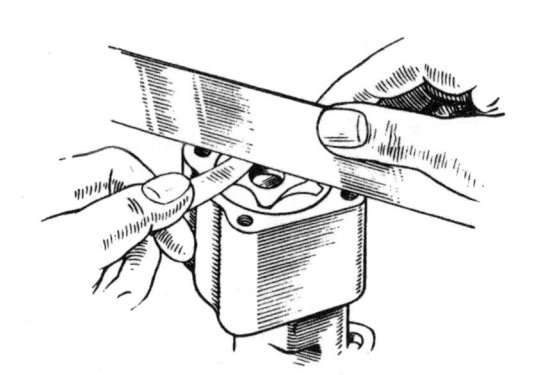

Fig. 1.19. Method of removal and refitting starter ring gear TR4, 4A

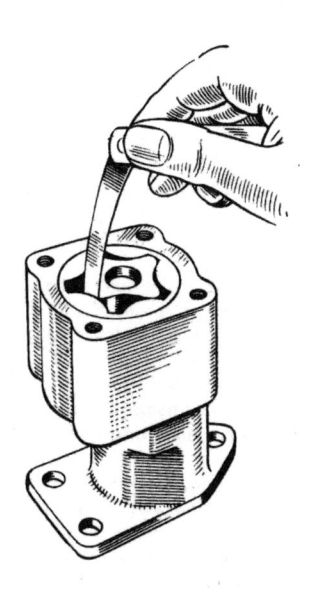

Fig. 1.20. Use of steel rule and feeler gauges to determine oil pump rotor to casing gap

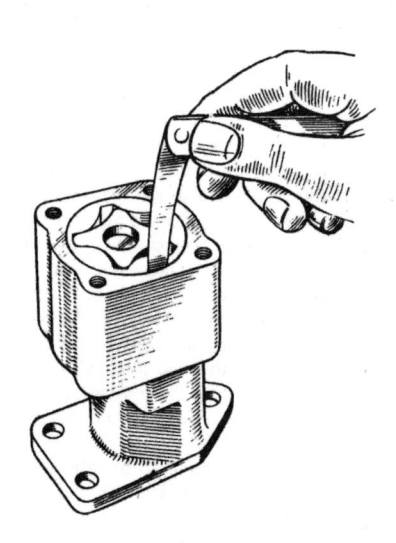

Fig. 1.21. Use of feeler gauge to measure inner rotor to outer rotor clearance

Fig. 1.22. Use of feeler gauge to measure clearance between outer rotor and body

39

Chapter 1/Engine

the shaft and key from the gear on the camshaft.

If a case of total loss of oil pressure is being investigated this can usually be attributed to a failure of the shaft on its key. Whilst the pump is away from the engine check the shaft and key.

42. Cylinder Head - Decarbonisation

This can be carried out with the engine either in or out of the car. With the cylinder head off carefully remove with a wire brush and blunt scraper all traces of carbon deposits from the combustion spaces and the ports. The valve head stems and valve guides should also be freed from any carbon deposits. Wash the combustion spaces and ports down with petrol and scrape the cylinder head surface free of any foreign matter with the side of a steel rule, or a similar article.

Clean the pistons and top of the cylinder bores. If the pistons are still in the block then it is essential that great care is taken to ensure that no carbon gets into the cylinder bores as this could scratch the cylinder walls or cause damage to the piston and rings. To ensure this does not happen, first turn the crankshaft so that two of the pistons are at the top of their bores. Stuff rag into the other two bores or seal them off with paper and masking tape. The waterways should also be covered with small pieces of masking tape to prevent particles of carbon entering the cooling system and damaging the water pump.

There are two schools of thought as to how much carbon should be removed from the piston crown. One school recommends that a ring of carbon should be left round the edge of the piston and on the cylinder bore wall as an aid to low oil consumption. Although this is probably true for early engines with worn bores, on later engines the thought of the second school can be applied, which is that for effective decarbonisation all traces of carbon should be removed.

If all traces of carbon are to be removed, press a little grease into the gap between the cylinder walls and the two pistons which are to be worked on. With a blunt scraper carefully scrape away the carbon from the piston crown, taking great care not to scratch the aluminium. Also scrape away the carbon from the surrounding lip of the cylinder wall. When all carbon has been removed, scrape away the grease which will now be contaminated with carbon particles, taking care not to press any into the bores. To assist prevention of carbon build-up the piston crown can be polished with a metal polish such as Brasso. Remove the rags or masking tape from the other two cylinders and turn the crankshaft so that the two pistons which were at the bottom are now at the top. Place a rag or masking tape in the cylinders which have been decarbonised and proceed as just described.

If a ring of carbon is going to be left round the piston then this can be helped by inserting an old piston ring into the top of the bore to rest on the piston and ensure that carbon is not accidentally removed. Check that there are no particles of carbon in the cylinder bores. Decarbonising is now complete.

43. Valve Guides - Examination and Renovation

Examine the valve guides internally for wear. If the valves are a very loose fit in the guides and there is the slightest suspicion of lateral rocking using a new valve, then new guides will have to be fitted. If the valve guides have been removed compare them internally by visual inspection with a new guide as well as testing them for rocking with a new valve.

44. Sump - Examination and Renovation

1. Before examination thoroughly wash out the sump with petrol.
2. Check the underside for dents and fractures which, if evident, mean that the sump pressing should be renewed.
3. Scrape all traces of the old sump gasket from the flange.

45. Engine Reassembly - General

1. To ensure maximum life with minimum trouble from a rebuilt engine, not only must everything be correctly assembled, but all the parts must be spotlessly clean, all the oilways must be clear, locking washers and spring washers must always be fitted where indicated and all bearing and other working surfaces must be thoroughly lubricated during assembly. Before assembly begins renew any bolts or studs, the threads of which are to any way damaged, and whenever possible use new spring washers.
2. Check the core plugs for signs of weeping and renew any that are suspect.
3. To do this drive a punch through the centre of the core plug.
4. Using the punch as a lever lift out the old core plug.
5. Thoroughly clean the core plug orifice and using a thin headed hammer as an expander firmly tap a new core plug in place, convex side facing out.
6. Apart from your normal tools, a supply of clean rag, an oil can filled with engine oil (an empty plastic detergent bottle thoroughly cleaned and washed out will invariably do just as well), a new supply of assorted spring washers, a set of new gaskets and a torque spanner should be collected together.

46. Crankshaft - Replacement

Ensure that the crankcase is thoroughly clean and that all oilways are clear. A thin twist drill or a pipe cleaner is useful for cleaning them out. If possible blow them out with compressed air.

Treat the crankshaft in the same fashion and then inject engine oil into the crankshaft oilways.

1. Commence work on rebuilding the engine by first refitting the crankcase half of the scroll type rear oil seal. Replace the four bolts with spring washers and lightly tighten. Using a soft faced hammer position the seal edge so that it is flush with the main bearing cap face. Tighten the four bolts fully.
2. If the old main bearing shells are to be replaced (a false economy unless they are virtually as new) fit the three upper halves of the main bearing shells to their location in the crankcase, after wiping the locations clean (photo).
3. Note that at the back of each bearing shell is a tab which engages in locating grooves in either the crankcase or the main bearing cap housings.
4. If new bearings are being fitted, carefully clean away all traces of the protective grease with which they are coated.
5. With the three upper bearing shells securely in place, wipe the lower bearing cap housings and fit the three lower shell bearings to their caps ensuring that the right shell goes into the right cap if the old bearings are being refitted.
6. Wipe the recesses either side of the centre main bearing which locate the thrust washers.
7. Generously lubricate the crankshaft journals and the upper and lower main bearing shells and carefully lower the

Fig. 1.23. Method of fitting the sealing block to the front crankshaft bearing

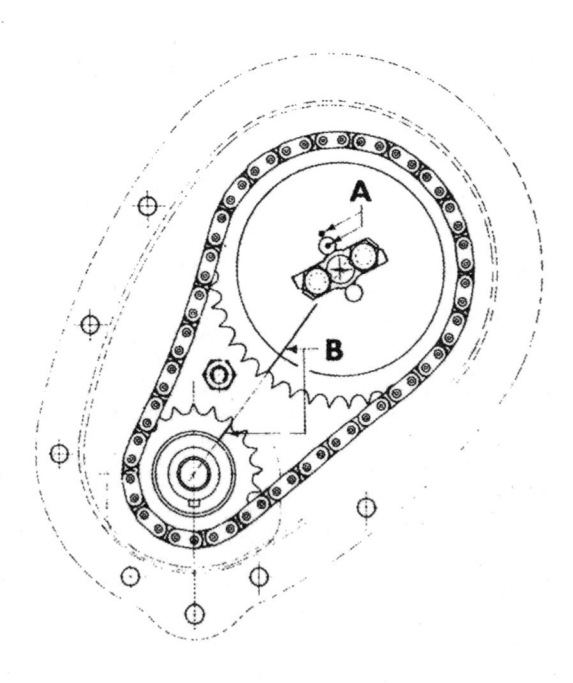

Fig. 1.24. Correct position of timing marks when No. 1 piston is at T.D.C. on the compression stroke

41

Chapter 1/Engine

crankshaft into place (photo).

8. Fit the upper halves of the thrust washer into their grooves either side of the centre main bearing (photo) so their oil grooves face outwards away from the bearing.

9. Fit the main bearing caps in position ensuring they locate properly (photo). The mating surfaces must be spotlessly clean or the caps will not seat correctly. As the bearing caps were assembled to the cylinder block and then line bored during manufacture, it is essential that they are returned to the same positions from which they were removed.

10 The two thrust washers for the centre main bearing cap are tabbed and should be held in place before the cap is refitted using grease (photo). Again ensure the oil grooves face outwards.

11 Refit the main bearing cap bolts, spring washers or locking tabs whichever were fitted and tighten using a torque wrench set to 85 to 90 lb. (photo).

12 Test the crankshaft for freedom of rotation. Should it be very stiff to turn or possess high spots a most careful inspection must be made, preferably by a qualified mechanic with a micrometer to find the cause of the trouble. It is very seldom that any trouble of this nature will be experienced when fitting the crankshaft.

13 Check the crankshaft end float with a feeler gauge measuring the longitudinal movement between the crankshaft and the bearing cap. End float should be between 0.004 and 0.006 inch. If end float is excessive oversize thrust washers can be fitted.

47. Piston and Connecting Rod - Assembly

1. If the same pistons are being used then they must be mated to the same connecting rod with the same gudgeon pin. If new pistons are being fitted it does not matter which connecting rod they are used with, and as they come with new gudgeon pins, these should be fitted to the connecting rods on the basis of selective assembly.

2. Because aluminium alloy, when hot, expands more than steel, the gudgeon pin may be a very tight fit in the piston when cold. To avoid any damage to the piston it is best to heat it in near boiling water when the pin will slide in and out easily (photo).

3. Remove the circlip from either side of a new piston and using the thumb push the gudgeon pin out of the piston (photo). Hold the piston with rag if very hot.

4. Lay the correct piston adjacent to each connecting rod and remember that the same rod and piston must go back into the same bore. If new pistons are being used it is only necessary to ensure that the right connecting rod is placed in each bore.

5. Fit a gudgeon pin circlip in position at one end of the gudgeon pin hole in the piston.

6. Note the mark indicating the front of the piston and mount the piston between two soft wood pieces in a vice as shown in the photo. Insert the connecting rod little end into the gudgeon pin boss so that the connecting rod cap will be towards the camshaft side of the engine.

7. Slide the gudgeon pin into position through the hole in the piston and through the connecting rod little end until it rests against the previously fitted circlip. Note the pins should be a push fit when the piston and pin are worn.

8. Fit the second circlip in position (photo). Repeat this procedure for all four pistons and connecting rods.

9. Where special oil control pistons are being fitted should the position of the top ring be the same as the position of the top ring of the old piston ensure that a groove has been machined on the top of the new ring so no fouling occurs between the unworn portion at the top of the bore and the piston ring when the latter is at the top of its stroke.

48. Piston Ring - Replacement

1. Check that the piston ring grooves and oilways are thoroughly clean and unblocked. Piston rings must always be fitted over the head of the piston and never from the bottom.

2. The easiest method to use when refitting rings is to wrap a .020 inch feeler gauge round the top of the piston and place the rings one at a time, starting with the bottom oil control ring, over the feeler gauge.

3. The feeler gauge, complete with ring, can then be slid down the piston over the other piston ring grooves until the correct groove is reached. The piston ring is then slid gently off the feeler gauge into the groove.

4. An alternative method is to fit the rings by holding them slightly open with the thumbs. This method requires a steady hand and great care as it is easy to open the ring too much and break it.

49. Piston - Replacement

The pistons, complete with connecting rods, can be fitted to the cylinder liner bores in the following sequence.

1. With a wad of clean rag wipe the cylinder bores clean.

2. The pistons, complete with connecting rods, are fitted into their bores from the top of the block.

3. Wipe the connecting rod half big end bearing seat clean and insert the bearing shell ensuring that the tag of the bearing lines up in the cut out portion of the connecting rod. Check that the oil hole in the bearing lines up with the drilling in the connecting rod (photo). Well lubricate the piston and bore with clean engine oil.

4. As each piston is inserted into its bore ensure that it is the correct piston/connecting rod assembly for that particular bore and that the connecting rod is the right way round, and that the front of the piston is towards the front of the bore, i.e., towards the front of the engine (photo).

5. The piston will only slide into the bore as far as the oil control ring (photo).

6. It is then necessary to compress the piston rings in a clamp and to gently tap the piston into the cylinder bore with a wooden or plastic hammer (photo). If a proper piston ring clamp is not available then a 3½ inch jubilee clip does the job very well.

50. Connecting Rod to Crankshaft - Reassembly

1. If the old bearings are nearly new and are being refitted ensure they are replaced in their correct locations on the correct rods.

2. Generously lubricate the crankpin journals with engine oil and turn the crankshaft so that the crankpin is in the most advantageous position for the connecting rod to be drawn into it.

3. Wipe the connecting rod bearing cap and back of the shell bearing clean and fit the shell bearing in position, ensuring that the locating tongue at the back of the bearing engages with the locating groove in the connecting rod cap.

4. Generously lubricate the shell bearing and offer up the connecting rod bearing cap to the connecting rod (photo).

5. Fit the connecting rod bolts with the one piece locking tab under them where fitted and tighten the bolts using a torque wrench (photo) set to 55 to 60 lb.ft.

6. With a hammer or a pair of pliers knock up the locking tabs where fitted against the bolt head.

46.2

46.7

46.8

46.9

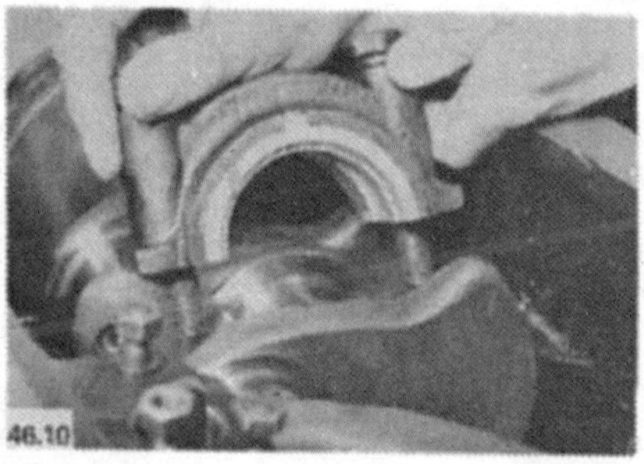
46.10

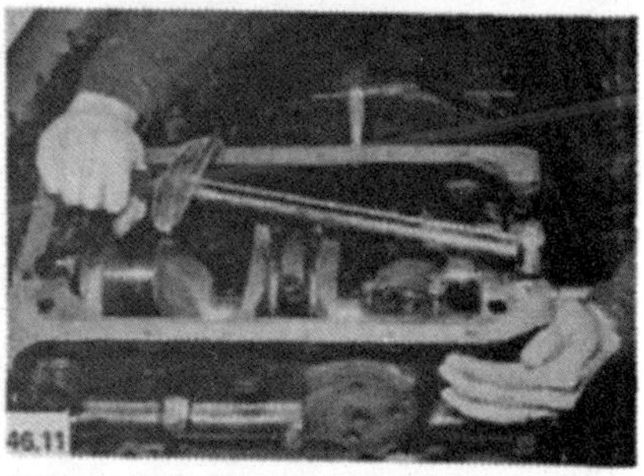
46.11

47.2

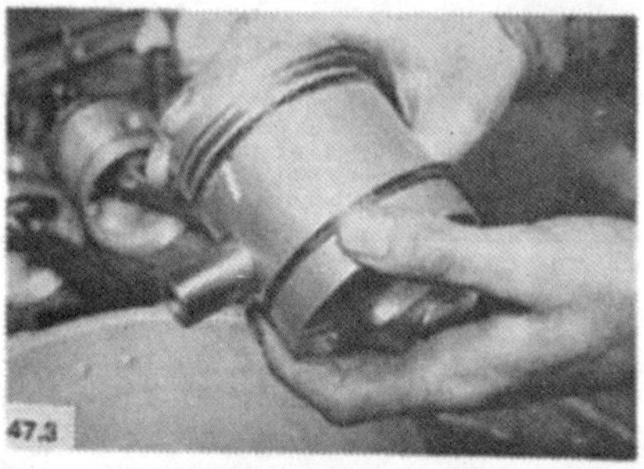
47.3

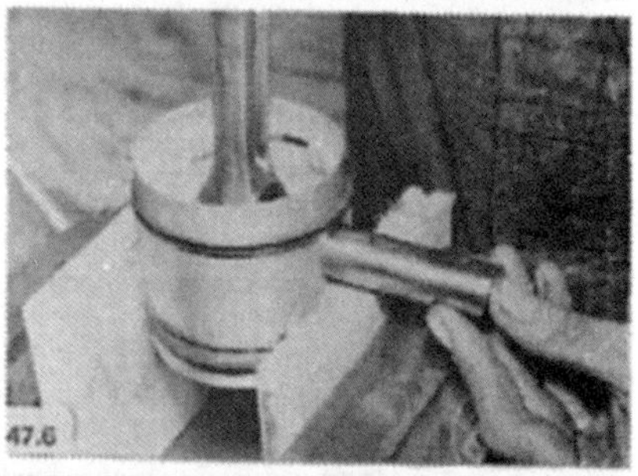
47.6

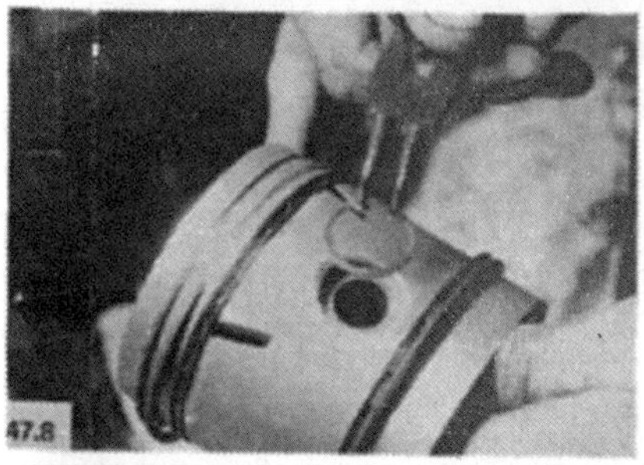
47.8

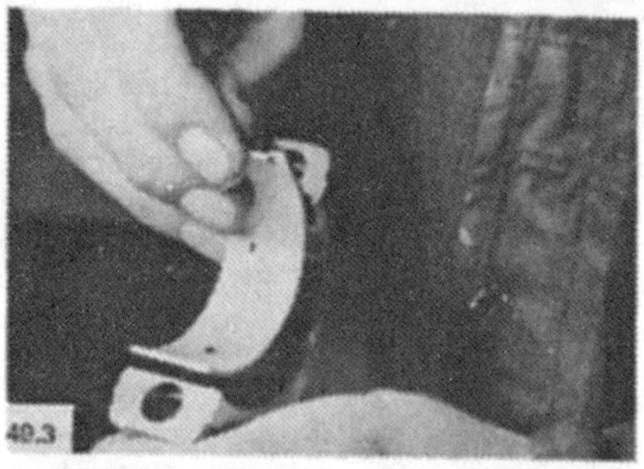
49.3

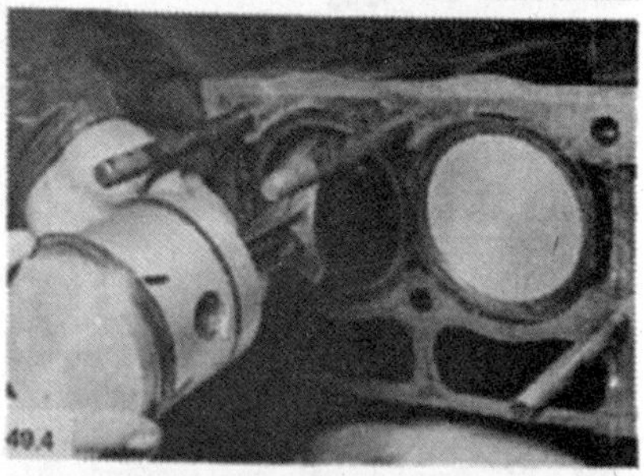
49.4

49.5

49.6

50.4

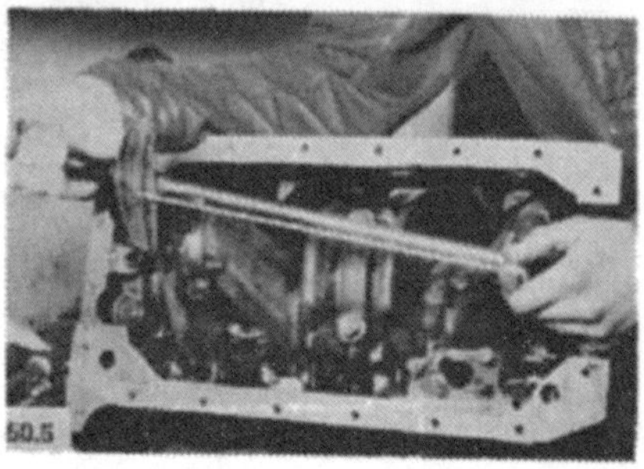
50.5

Chapter 1/Engine

7. When all the connecting rods have been fitted rotate the crankshaft to check that everything is free, and that there are no high spots causing binding. Ensure that the cylinder liner retainers are in place before doing this.

51. Front and Rear Crankshaft Bearing Sealing Block and Seals

1. Smear the ends of the front crankshaft bearing sealing block with a jointing compound and fit new 'T' shaped sealing pieces to the block (photo).
2. Carefully fit the block into position taking care that the sealing blocks do not drop out (photo).
3. Fit the two securing bolts into position but do not tighten fully. Using a straight edge align the front of the sealing block with the front of the crankcase and when correct tighten the two bolts (photo and Fig. 1.23).
4. Using a sharp knife trim off the end of the sealing pieces (photo).
5. Soak the crankshaft rear main bearing cap sealing felt in liquid jointing compound and carefully slide the felt down the channel as shown in the photo. When it is in the fully down position trim the end with a sharp knife.

52. Front End Plate - Reassembly

1. Fit a new gasket in place over the front of the cylinder block (photo).
2. Lower the front end plate into place noting the dowel and dowel hole.
3. Refit the shouldered stud into its position just below the crankshaft (photo) and tighten using an open ended spanner.
4. Replace the other front end plate retaining bolts fitted with spring washers and tighten in a diagonal manner (photo).

53. Camshaft - Replacement

1. Wipe the camshaft journals clean and lubricate them generously with clean engine oil.
2. Insert the camshaft into the crankcase gently (photo) taking care not to damage the camshaft bearings with the sharp edged cams.
3. Carefully fit the camshaft front bearing into place, noting that the one side has a flat which must be positioned next to the bolt hole (photo).
4. Replace the two camshaft bearing retaining bolts with spring washers and tighten (photo).
5. Using a dial indicator gauge measure the end float of the camshaft and this should be between 0.003 and 0.0075 inch. As the front bearing controls the end float to increase the end float lightly rub the end of the bearing with a file or emery cloth. To decrease the end float a new bearing must be fitted.

54. Timing Gears, Chain Tensioner, Cover - Replacement (Marked Sprockets)

1. Replace the crankshaft woodruff key and rotate the crankshaft until the key is vertical to the sump face and next to it (see Fig. 1.24).
2. If the original sprockets are to be fitted they will have been already marked. If they show no signs of centre punch or scribe line marks the sprockets should be fitted as described later in Section 61.
3. Identify the centre punch marks on the face of the camshaft and the camshaft sprocket (photo) and assemble the sprocket to the crankshaft with the centre punch marks over each other.
4. Refit the camshaft sprocket retaining bolts and tab washer. Tighten the bolts and bend over the corners of the tab washer using a screwdriver or chisel and hammer (photo).
5. Replace any shims that were removed from between the front of the crankshaft and the sprocket and slide the crankshaft sprocket onto the end of the crankshaft so that the key way in the sprocket hub aligns with the crankshaft key. Push it on as far as it will go.
6. With the two sprockets in position place a straight edge across the sides of the sprockets (photo) and measure the gap (if any) between the straight edge and the sprocket. If a gap exists a suitable number of packing washers must be placed on the crankshaft to bring the sprocket onto the same plane as the camshaft sprocket.
7. Turn the crankshaft and camshaft sprockets until the two scribed lines are exactly opposite to each other as shown in the photo.
8. Refit the timing chain and insert the joint link from the front. It cannot be fitted from the rear forwards as there is insufficient room (photo). Fit the centre bridge piece.
9. Holding the joining link side piece with a pair of pointed nosed pliers carefully fit it to the rear of the chain joint link (photo).
10 Again using the pliers refit the locking spring link with the open end upwards so that it is not facing the direction of rotation (photo).
11 Replace the oil thrower on to the end of the crankshaft so that the concave face is towards the sprocket (photo).
12 The oil seal in the front of the timing cover should be renewed. To remove it carefully drive it out with a screwdriver taking care not to damage the timing cover in the process (photo).
13 Insert a new seal, making sure it is fitted the correct way round as shown in the photo.
14 Using a drift and hammer tapping in a diagonal manner gradually fit the seal into its housing. Ensure that it is kept square and is fitted in as far as it will go.
15 Refit the timing chain tensioner fulcrum bolt to the front of the crankcase adjacent to the crankshaft sprocket wheel.
16 Slide the end of the tensioner over the fulcrum bolt (photo) followed by the plain washer.
17 Insert the split pin locking the tensioner and washer in place on the fulcrum bolt (photo). Fit a new fibre washer to the extended stud.
18 Lubricate the front cover oil seal, fit a new gasket on the end plate holding it in position with a few dabs of grease and fit the cover at an angle so as to catch the tensioner spring against the side of the chain (photo). Swing the cover into position and secure by tightening several bolts finger tight.
19 Refit the remaining timing cover retaining bolts but do not tighten fully at this stage.
20 Replace the crankshaft pulley onto the end of the crankshaft so that it will centralise the timing cover and tighten the cover retaining bolts fully.

55. Oil Pump - Replacement

1. Fit the gauze filter to the oil pump noting that it must be fitted so that the top of the gauze is in the same plane as the edge of the casing as shown in photo 56.1.
2. Place a new gasket on the crankcase mounting for the oil pump and refit the oil pump. Refit the spring washers and nuts (photo).

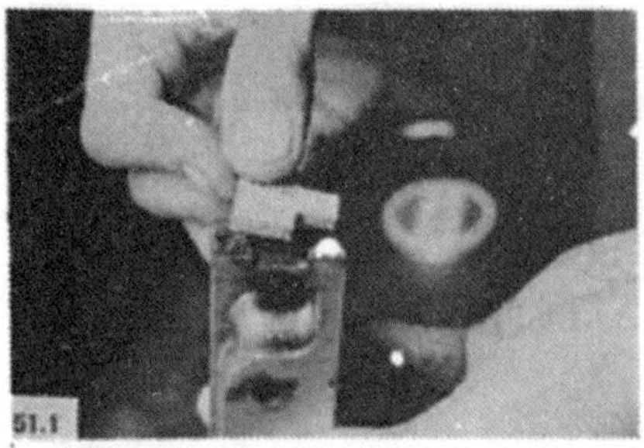

51.1

51.2

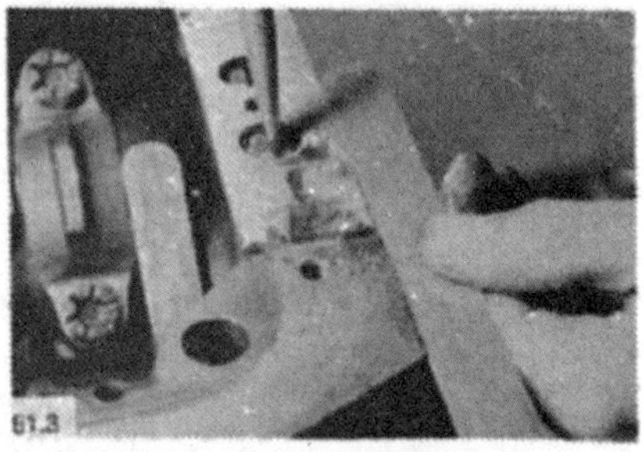

51.3

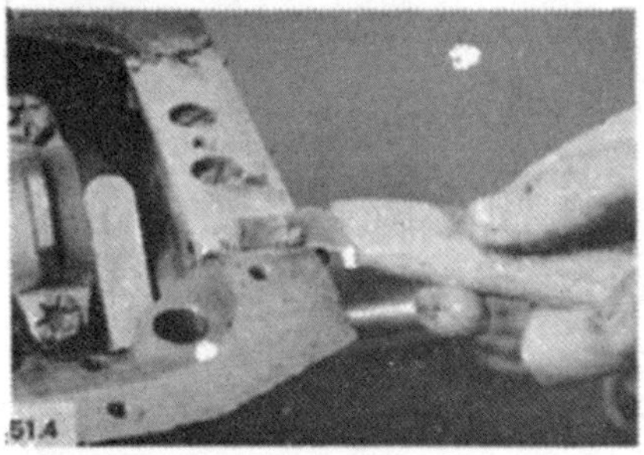

51.4

51.5

52.1

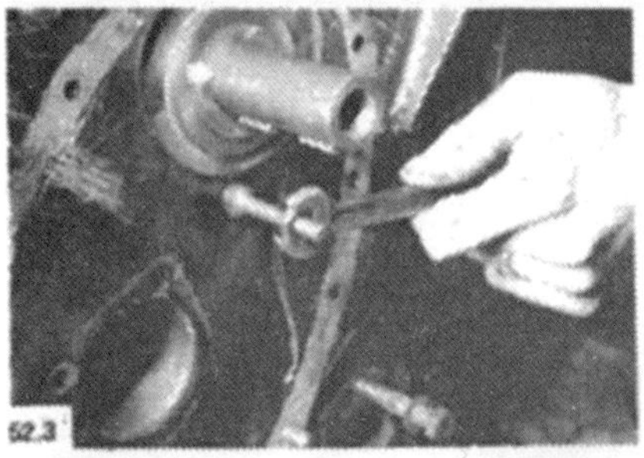

52.3

53.4

53.2

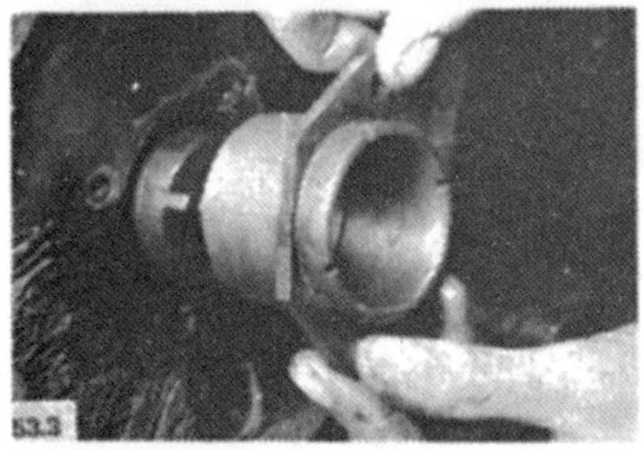

53.3

52.4

54.3

54.4

54.5

54.6

54.7

54.8

54.9

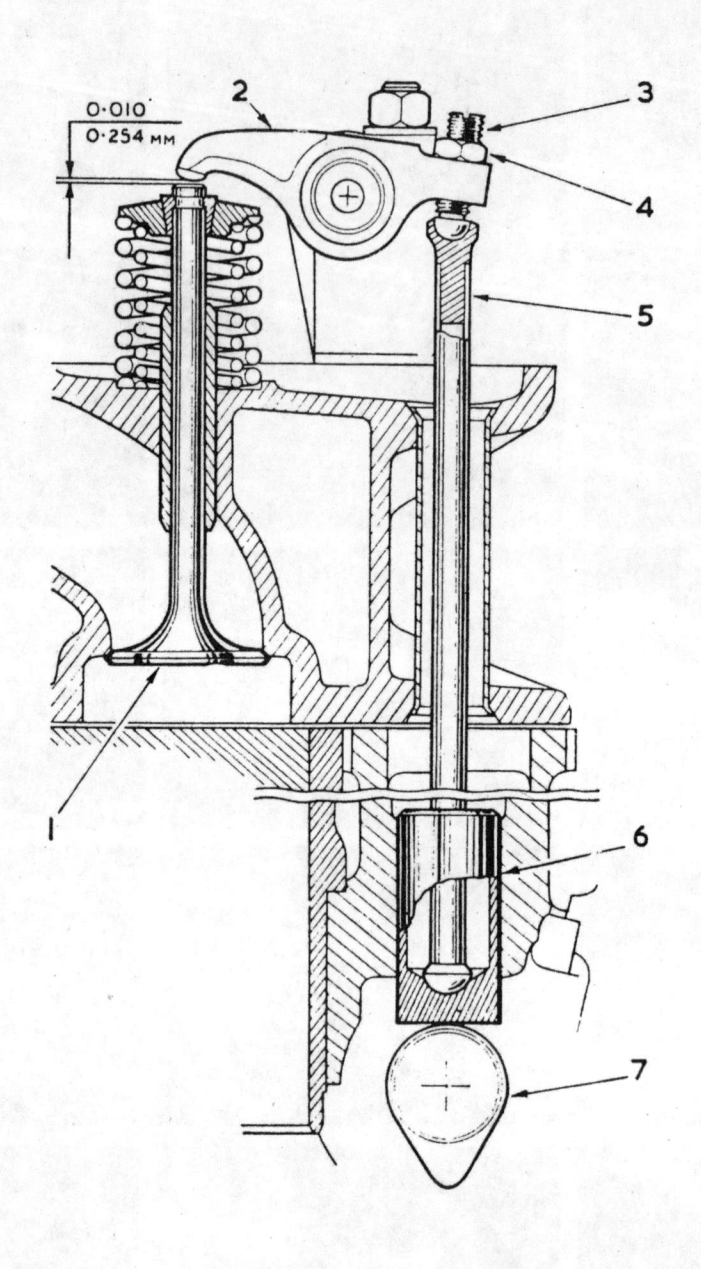

Fig. 1.25. CORRECT VALVE ROCKER
CLEARANCE (ARROWED)

1 Valve
2 Rocker
3 Adjuster
4 Locknut
5 Pushrod
6 Tappet
7 Camshaft

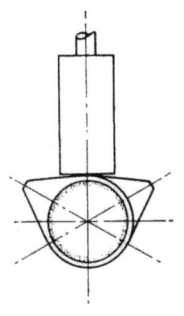

Fig. 1.26. The cams positioned at the point of balance

Chapter 1/Engine

56. Sump - Replacement

1. After the sump has been thoroughly cleaned, scrape all traces of the old sump gasket from the sump and crankcase flanges, fit a new gasket in place holding it in position with a little grease and then refit the sump (photo).
2. Replace all fifteen sump retaining bolts and spring washers noting that the bolt shown in the photo is longer than the rest as it also has to retain the crankcase breather downpipe bracket (photo).
3. Tighten all the bolts in a diagonal manner until all are tight (photo). The bolt shown in photo 56:2 may either be left slack or the bracket refitted at this time.

57. Valve and Valve Spring - Reassembly

To refit the valves and valve springs to the cylinder head proceed as follows.
1. Rest the cylinder head on its side.
2. Fit each valve and valve spring in turn, wiping down and lubricating each valve stem as it is inserted into the same valve guide from which it was removed.
3. Build up each valve assembly by first fitting the lower collar (exhaust valve only).
4. Then fit the valve springs as illustrated in Fig. 1.9, noting that the exhaust valve has three springs and the inlet valve two springs.
5. Refit the upper collar (photo).
6. Move the cylinder head towards the edge of the bench and fit the valve spring compressor ensuring that the base of the valve spring compressor is on the valve head. Compress the spring (photo) until there is sufficient room to insert the cotters.
7. Carefully fit the two cotters into the upper collar (photo) and when in position release the valve spring compressor.
8. Repeat this procedure until all eight valve and valve springs are fitted.

58. Rocker Shaft and Tappet - Reassembly

1. Fit an end cap and pin to one end of the shaft and then slide on the spring, rockers, distance springs, and rocker pedestals in their correct order as shown in Fig. 1.10.
2. Make sure that the Phillips screw on the rear rocker pedestal engages properly with the rocker shaft.
3. When all is correctly assembled fit the remaining end cap and oil the components thoroughly.
4. With the tappets in their storage rack (photo A) (part of an old egg box) first lubricate the tappets and with the engine in its normal upright position carefully insert each tappet into its respective bore using a pair of pointed pliers (photo B).

59. Cylinder Head - Replacement

1. Thoroughly clean the cylinder block top face and then refit the cylinder head studs using the double nut method (photo).
2. Note that the two longer studs must be fitted to the last two holes towards the rear of the block on the right hand side.
3. Fit a new gasket in place. If one side of the gasket is marked 'TOP' it must naturally be fitted with this side facing upwards.
4. Generously lubricate each cylinder with engine oil.
5. Ensure that the cylinder head face is perfectly clean and then lower the cylinder head into place (photo) keeping it parallel to the block to avoid binding of any of the studs.
6. With the head in place fit the lifting eye over the two rear right hand studs and the accelerator cable attachment bracket to the next stud along.
7. Fit the cylinder head nuts and washers and tighten down the nuts half a turn at a time in the order shown in Fig. 1.7 to a torque of 100 to 105 lb.ft. (photo A). Because of the close proximity of the rear rocker cover stud to the cylinder head nut (arrowed photo B) remove the stud so the socket can fit over the nut.
8. Insert the pushrods into the block so the ball end rests in the tappet. Ensure the pushrods are replaced in the same order in which they were removed (photo).
9. Then refit the rocker shaft ensuring that the rocker arm ball joints seat in the pushrod cups.
10 Replace the four rocker pedestal nuts and washers and tighten them down evenly to a torque setting of 25 lb.ft. (photo).

60. Rocker Arm/Valve - Adjustment

1. The valve adjustments should be made with the engine cold. The importance of correct rocker arm/valve stem clearances cannot be overstressed as they vitally affect the performance of the engine.
2. If the clearances are set too open, the efficiency of the engine is reduced as the valves open late and close earlier than was intended. If, on the other hand, the clearances are set too close there is a danger that the stems will expand upon heating and not allow the valves to close properly which will cause burning of the valve head and seat and possible warping.
3. If the engine is in the car to get at the rockers it is merely necessary to remove the two holding down nuts from the rocker cover and then to lift the rocker cover and gasket away.
4. It is important that the clearance is set when the tappet of the valve being adjusted is on the heel of the cam (i.e., opposite the peak). This can be done by carrying out the adjustments in the following order, which also avoids turning the crankshaft more than necessary.

Valve fully open	Check and adjust
Valve No. 8	Valve No. 1
Valve No. 6	Valve No. 3
Valve No. 4	Valve No. 5
Valve No. 7	Valve No. 8
Valve No. 1	Valve No. 8
Valve No. 3	Valve No. 6
Valve No. 5	Valve No. 4
Valve No. 2	Valve No. 7

5. The correct valve clearance of .010 inch is obtained by slackening the hexagon locknut with a spanner while holding the ball against rotation with the screwdriver. Then, still pressing down with the screwdriver, insert a feeler gauge in the gap between the valve stem head and the rocker arm and adjust the ball pin until the feeler gauge will just move in and out without nipping, and, still holding the ball pin in the correct position, tighten the locknut (photo).
6. An alternative method is to set the gaps with the engine running at idling speed and although this looks impressive and may be faster it is no more reliable.
7. Whenever the rocker cover is disturbed it is recommended that a new gasket is fitted. Clean all traces of the old gasket from the flange on the rocker cover and cylinder head surface. Fit a new gasket and carefully replace the rocker cover (photo).

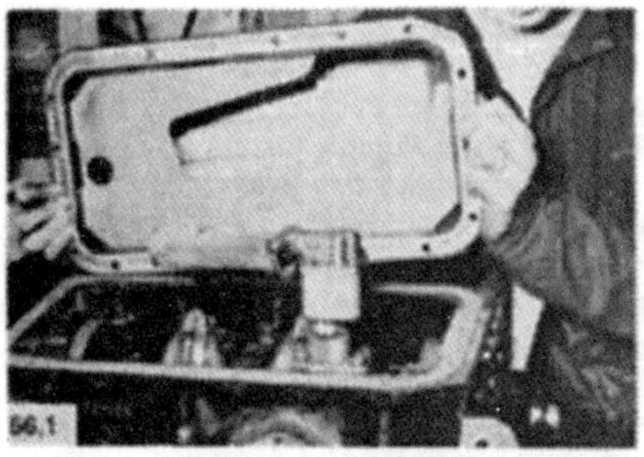

56.1

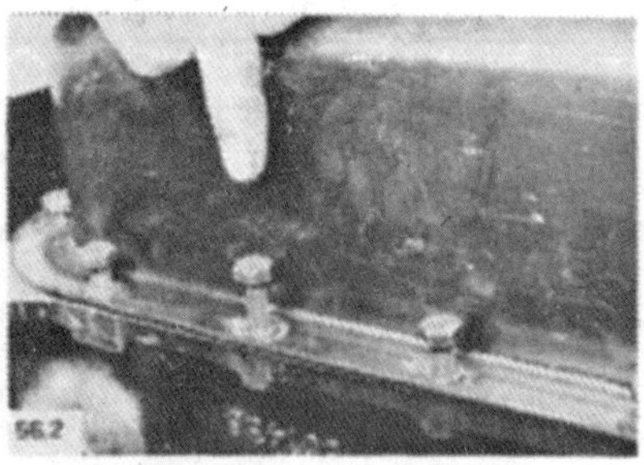

56.2

56.3

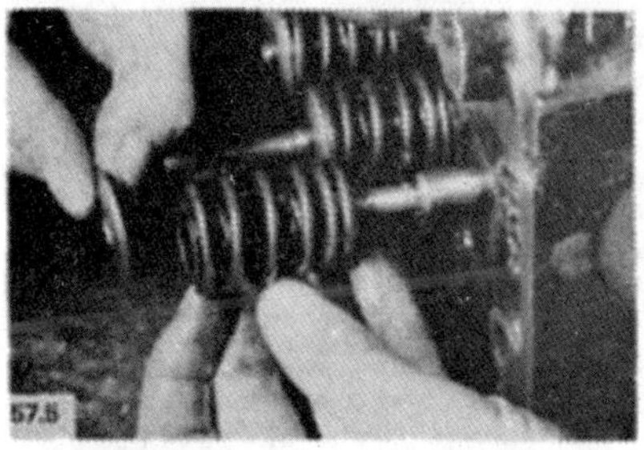

57.5

57.6

57.7

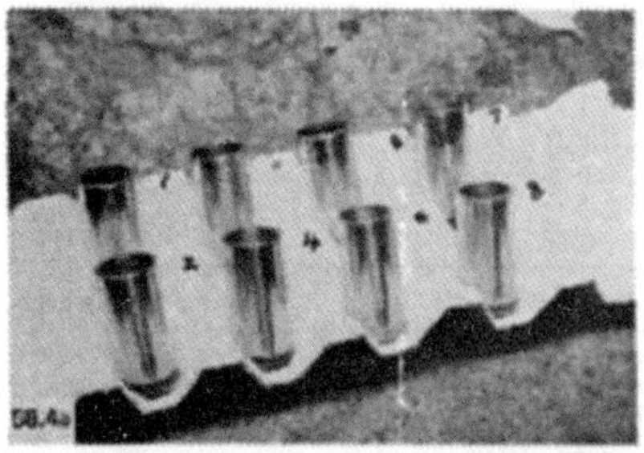

58.4a

58.4b

59.1

59.5

59.7a

59.7b

59.8

59.10

60.5

60.7

Chapter 1/Engine

8. Refit the plain washer and nyloc nuts to each rocker cover retaining stud and just tighten the nuts so as to give a good gasket seal. Check that the gasket is still in its correct position whilst the nuts are being tightened (photo).
9. Overtightening the nuts will strain the rocker cover, causing it to splay out at its centre.

61. Timing Gears, Chain Tensioner, Cover - Replacement (Unmarked Sprockets)

1. Refitting the camshaft drive sprockets that do not have any markings on them requires a special procedure which can only be completed with the valve components and cylinder head fully assembled and correctly adjusted as necessary.
2. Temporarily refit the camshaft sprocket and hold in position with the two retaining bolts. Just tighten sufficiently to hold the sprocket in position.
3. Rotate the camshaft until the first pushrod from the front of the engine is at its highest position. Adjust the last rocker No. 8 clearance to 0.040 inch.
4. Repeat the procedure using the position of number 2 pushrod to set the rocker clearance on number 7.
5. Rotate the camshaft until both No. 7 and 8 valves are closed and with a slight rotation in either direction starts to open one or other valves. The cams will now be at the point of balance as shown in Fig. 1.26.
6. Without moving the camshaft at all remove the sprocket retaining bolts and lift away the sprocket.
7. Rotate the crankshaft so that the Woodruff key is positioned vertically downwards and Nos. 1 and 4 pistons are at their T.D.C. positions.
8. Put the chain around both sprockets and carefully push the sprockets into place.
9. Manipulate the camshaft sprocket by slipping a link at a time or reversing the sprocket until a pair of holes coincide EXACTLY with those of the camshaft. Half tooth adjustments are given by using the second pair of holes in the camshaft sprocket.
10 For quarter tooth adjustments reverse the camshaft sprocket. A three quarter tooth adjustment is a combination of reversing the sprocket and using the second pair of holes in the sprocket.
11 Secure the camshaft sprocket using the tab washer and two bolts and test the rocker clearances on No. 7 and 8 rockers to ensure they are still equal indicating the camshaft has not moved.
12 If all is well reset the rocker clearance to 0.010 inch.
13 Using a centre punch mark the two sprockets as shown in Fig. 1.24 so that upon dismantling timing identification will not be lost.
14 It will now be necessary to check the sprocket alignment. Remove the camshaft and crankshaft sprockets and the timing chain.
15 Replace any shims that were removed from between the front of the crankshaft and the sprocket and slide the crankshaft sprocket onto the end of the crankshaft so that the key way in the sprocket hub aligns with the crankshaft key. Push it on as far as it will go.
16 With the two sprockets in position place a straight edge across the sides of the sprockets and measure the gap (if any) between the straight edge and the sprocket. If a gap exists a suitable number of packing washers must be placed on the crankshaft to bring the sprocket onto the same place as the camshaft.
17 Turn the crankshaft and camshaft sprockets until the previously made identification marks are exactly opposite to each other. Now follow the instructions in Section 54, paragraphs 8 to 20.

62. Thermostat Housing and Water Pump - Refitting

1. If the thermostat housing has been dismantled first check and file flat if necessary to two half mating faces.
2. Insert the thermostat and fit a new gasket.
3. Refit the top half of the housing ensuring the hose union is towards the lower part of the housing (see photo 62.6).
4. Replace the two retaining bolts with spring washers and tighten securely.
5. Clean the face of the cylinder head and also the mating face of the thermostat housing and fit a new gasket.
6. Place the thermostat housing on the cylinder head (photo).
7. Refit the two thermostat housing bolts and spring washers and tighten securely (photo).
8. Clean the mounting face for the water pump on the front of the crankcase and fit a new gasket (photo). This may be held in place with grease.
9. Ensure the mating face of the water pump is clean and free from any jointing compound or parts of the old gasket and offer up to the cylinder block (photo).
10 Refit the water pump retaining bolts ensuring that the bolts are fitted in their original positions as were noted during engine dismantling. Tighten the bolts securely (photo).

63. Oil Filter Head - Refitting

1. Ensure that the mating faces of the oil filter head to the cylinder block are free of signs of old jointing compound or gasket.
2. Fit a new filter head gasket having first inserted the four retaining bolts. Note that they are of different lengths, the longer one being fitted to the top right and bottom right hand sides (photo).
3. The bolt on the bottom left is hollow and also secures the oil pressure gauge pressure pipe union. Assemble the union to the bolt with fibre washers on either side of the union and fit to the filter head (photo).
4. With the four bolts with spring washers in position tighten the bolts in a diagonal manner (photo).
5. On some engines a special stud was fitted instead of the bolt, in which case the pressure pipe was connected to the filter head instead.

64. Fuel Pump - Refitting

1. With the mating faces of the fuel pump and crankcase clean, fit a new gasket taking care not to tear it as it is passed over the threaded section of the two studs. If any packing pieces were found during removal these must be refitted.
2. Offer the pump up to the crankcase and manipulate it so that the rocker arm is to the front of the camshaft (photo).
3. Refit the left hand nut and spring washer and to the right stud attach the oil pressure pipe clip. Refit the right hand nut and spring washer and tighten the two nuts (photo).

65. Distributor Drive Shaft, Pedestal and Distributor - Refitting

1. Set the crankshaft so that numbers 1 and 4 pistons are exactly at their T.D.C. positions indicated by the pointer on the timing cover being lined up with the small hole in the rear of the crankshaft pulley. Also ensure that No. 1

Fig. 1.27. DISTRIBUTOR DRIVE SHAFT & PEDESTAL PARTS

1 Distributor pedestal
2 Distributor drive gear
3 0.5" I.D. washer
4 Oil pump drive shaft bush
5 Oil pump drive shaft
6 Oil pump rotor shaft

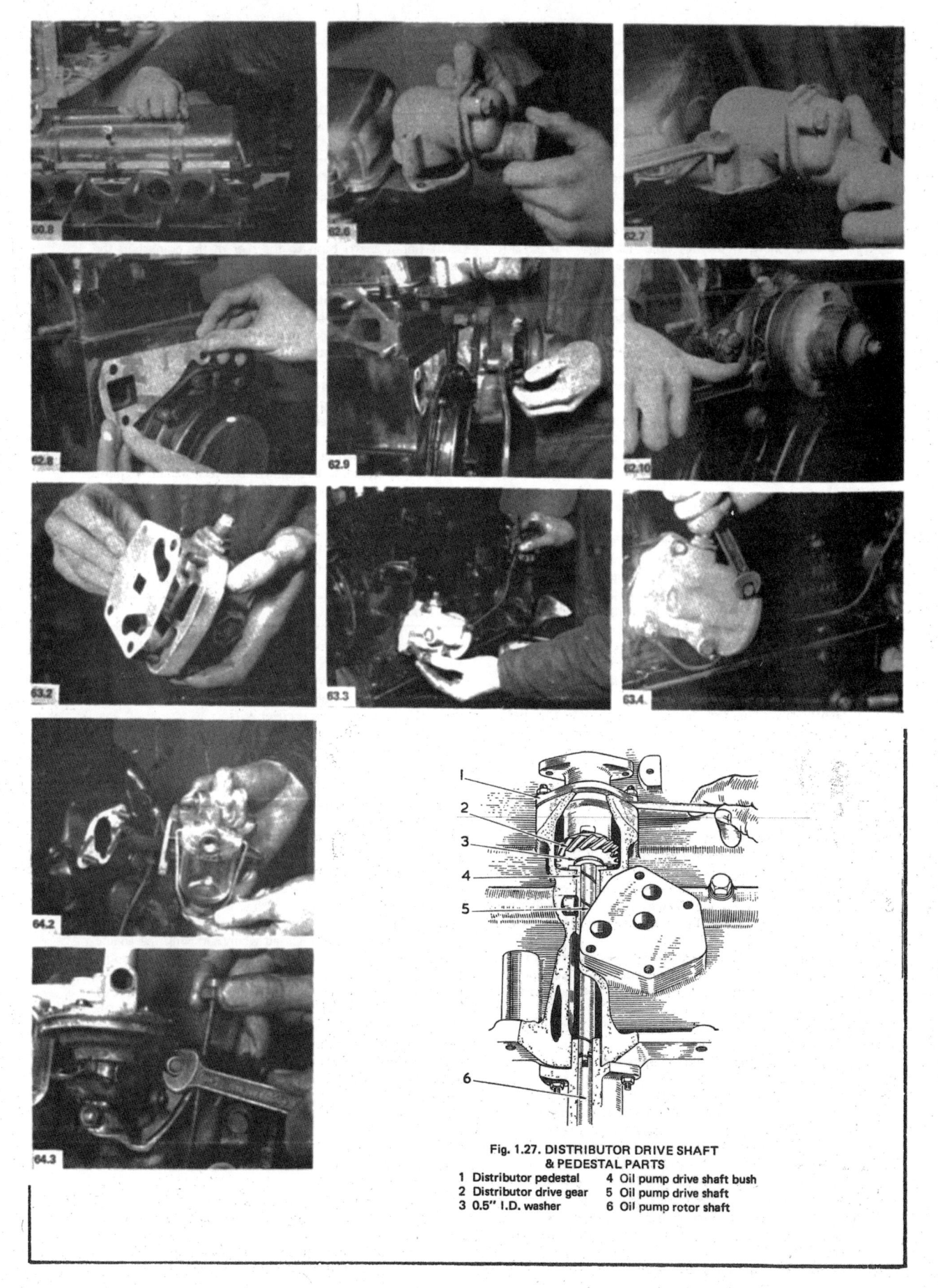

51

Chapter 1/Engine

piston is on its compression stroke. To do this either remove a plug, and with your thumb cover the plug hole feel the compression developing, or if the rocker cover is off note that on the compression stroke both valves should be closed. This check is vital as otherwise it is easy to set the distributor so the timing is 180° out.

2. When fitting the distributor drive not only must it be correctly positioned for timing purposes as shown in Fig. 1.28, but the key on the end of the drive shaft to the oil pump must engage with the slot in the top of the oil pump rotor shaft. If the key does not engage in the slot then turn the oil pump rotor shaft an eighth of a turn at a time with a long screwdriver (photo) until engagement is made.

3. Generously lubricate the oil pump drive shaft bush, and the drive shaft.

4. It is important that there is an end float of between 0.003 and 0.007 inch for the distributor drive gear. To obtain this first obtain a 0.5 inch internal diameter washer and measure its thickness accurately.

5. Assemble the washer with the distributor drive gear onto the oil pump drive shaft so that the washer is between the gear and the top of the oil pump drive shaft bushing (Fig. 1.27). Check that the shaft is still engaged with the oil pump.

6. Fit the distributor pedestal onto the cylinder block.

7. Using feeler gauges determine the distance between the distributor pedestal and its mating face of the cylinder block.

8. Compare this measurement with the thickness of the washer that was assembled to the drive gear, the difference represents the amount of end float. Once the amount has been determined measure the thickness of a new gasket and calculate the thickness of shim required to give the end float of between 0.003 and 0.007 inch.

9. Remove the drive gear and extract the washer using a bent piece of wire.

10 Gently lower the distributor drive gear onto the shaft. Allow it to rotate as the gear teeth mesh with the camshaft gear (photo). Ensure the key on the end of the shaft engages with the slot in the oil pump rotor shaft.

11 The correct position for the distributor drive slot must be as shown in the photograph and also in Fig. 1.28 when the number 1 cylinder is on the compression stroke.

12 Refer to Fig. 1.28 and note that the arrow indicates a small notch cut out of the inside periphery larger offset. This must be positioned as shown so that when the distributor is refitted the rotor arm segment must point to No. 1 valve pushrod tube in the cylinder head. (Check this by actually placing the distributor on the end of the drive shaft.)

13 Fit any necessary shims and the new gasket onto the distributor pedestal mounting on the cylinder block, taking care not to tear it when passing it over the threaded portion of the studs.

14 Refit the pedestal with the tachometer drive facing towards the rear (photo).

15 Replace the spring washers and nuts and tighten securely (photo).

16 Lower the distributor into position on the pedestal. Point the rotor arm segment beak towards Number 1 pushrod tube and by twisting very slightly in one or other direction the drive should slot into the distributor drive gear (photo). If it does not slot in easily the meshing of the distributor drive shaft to the camshaft is probably incorrect.

17 Provided that the distributor clamp has not been disturbed the ignition timing should be correct. Replace the clamp retaining spring washers and nuts and tighten securely (photo).

18 Replace the distributor cap and secure with the two clips (photo).

66. Crankshaft Rear Oil Seal, Spigot, Flywheel and Clutch - Refitting

1. Refit the lower half of the crankshaft oil seal to the main bearing cap and secure with the four bolts and spring washers (Fig. 1.29).

2. Should it be found necessary to fit a new first motion shaft (input shaft) bush to the rear of the crankshaft the old bush may be removed by screwing in a tap of suitable size and pulling out the tap with the bush attached.

3. The new one should be soaked in oil for twenty-four hours or for one hour in hot oil.

4. Insert the new spigot bush into the end of the crankshaft and tap home gently with a soft faced hammer (photo).

5. Wipe the flange on the rear of the crankshaft and the mating face of the flywheel and fit the flywheel to the crankshaft carefully aligning the dowel in the flange with the hole in the flywheel (photo).

6. Refit the four flywheel and retaining bolts and tighten in a diagonal manner. Use a torque wrench to finally tighten the bolts set to a reading of between 42 and 46 lb.ft. (photo). To prevent the flywheel turning while it is being tightened place a screwdriver between a stud and the flywheel teeth as shown in the photo.

7. Refit the clutch unit to the flywheel as described in Chapter 5, Section 6.

67. Final Assembly

1. Fit a new gasket to the rocker cover and carefully fit the cover in place.

2. Replace washers over the rocker cover holding down studs ensuring the sealing washer lies under the flat steel washer. Replace the rocker cover nuts.

3. Fit new sparking plugs. Reconnect the ancillary component to the engine in the reverse order to which they were removed.

68. Engine - Replacement

Although the engine can be replaced with one man and a suitable winch, it is easier if two are present, one to lower the engine into the engine compartment and the other to guide the engine into position and to ensure that it does not foul anything. Generally speaking, engine replacement is a reversal of the procedures used when removing the engine (see Sections 6 or 7) but one or two added tips may come in useful.

1. Ensure all the loose leads, cables, etc., are tucked out of the way. If not it is easy to trap one and so cause much additional work after the engine is replaced.

2. Fit the starter motor and oil filter before lowering the engine and gearbox into place.

3. After the dynamo has been replaced it is advisable to fit a new fan belt.

4. Carefully lower the engine into position and then refit the following:-

a) Gearbox mounting nuts and washers.
b) Front mountings.
c) Propeller shaft to gearbox.
d) Reconnect the clutch pipe to the master cylinder.
e) Speedometer cable.
f) Gearchange remote control and lever (solenoid wires if fitted).

Fig. 1.28. Correct position of distributor drive shaft for distributor refitting

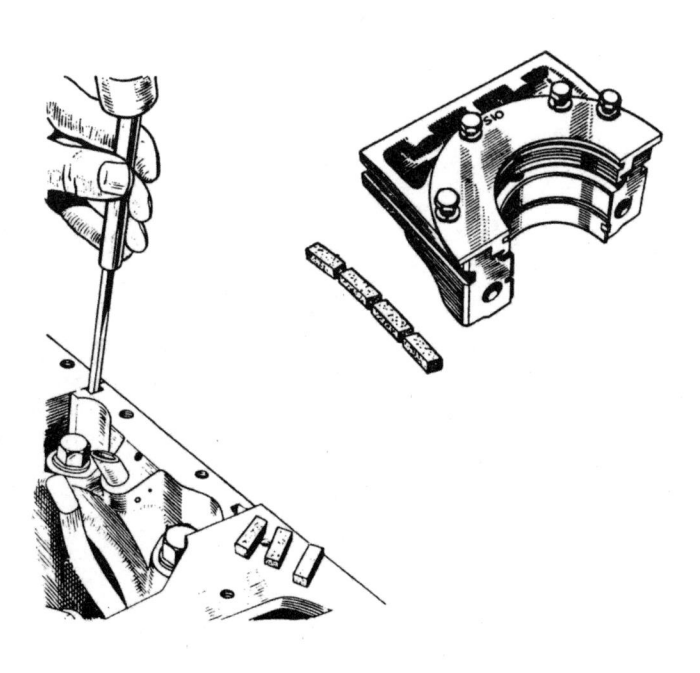

Fig. 1.29. Crankshaft rear oil seal refitting method

Chapter 1/Engine

g) Gearbox cover and carpets etc. (refill gearbox first).
h) Oil pressure gauge pressure pipe.
i) Rev. counter drive (if fitted).
j) Wires to coil, distributor and dynamo.
k) Carburettor controls.
l) Fuel pipe to pump and carburettors.
m) Air cleaner/s.
n) Exhaust manifold to pipe and bracket.
o) Earth and starter motor cables.
p) Radiator and hoses and any items hung on radiator attachment bolts.
q) Heater hoses.
r) Water temperature cable.
s) Vacuum advance and retard pipe.
t) Battery.

5. Finally, check that the drain taps are closed and refill the cooling system with water and the engine with the correct grade of oil. Prime the carburettors by working the fuel pump manually, pull out the choke, and start the engine (if you are lucky it will fire first time). Carefully check for oil or water leaks. There should be no leaks if the engine has been reassembled carefully, all nuts and bolts tightened down correctly, and new gaskets and joints used throughout.

6. After 500 miles check the tightness of the cylinder head nuts with a torque wrench, change the oil and the filter, and recheck the rocker arm to valve stem clearances.

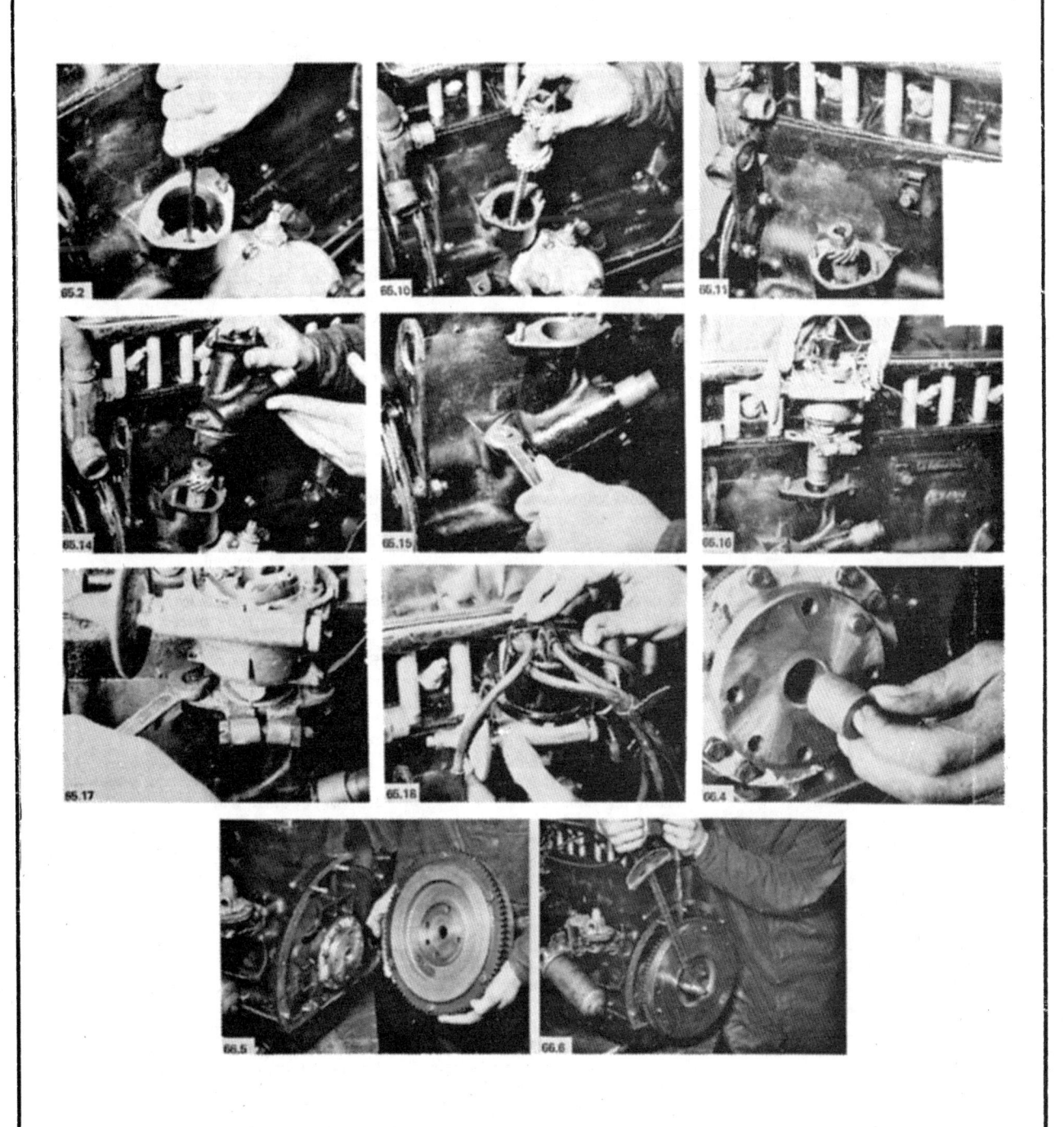

55

Fault Finding Chart - Engine

Cause	Trouble	Remedy
SYMPTOM: ENGINE FAILS TO TURN OVER WHEN STARTER BUTTON PULLED		
No current at starter motor	Flat or defective battery.	Charge or replace battery. Push-start car.
	Loose battery leads.	Tighten both terminals and earth ends of earth lead.
	Defective starter solenoid or switch or broken wiring.	Run a wire direct from the battery to the starter motor or by-pass the solenoid.
	Engine earth strap disconnected.	Check and retighten strap.
Current at starter motor	Jammed starter motor drive pinion.	Place car in gear and rock from side to side. Alternatively free exposed square end of shaft with spanner.
	Defective starter motor.	Remove and recondition.
SYMPTOM: ENGINE TURNS OVER BUT WILL NOT START		
No spark at sparking plug	Ignition damp or wet	Wipe dry the distributor cap and ignition leads.
	Ignition leads to spark plugs loose.	Check and tighten at both spark plug and distributor cap ends.
	Shorted or disconnected low tension leads.	Check the wiring on the CB and SW terminals of the coil and to the distributor.
	Dirty, incorrectly set, or pitted contact breaker points.	Clean, file smooth and adjust.
	Faulty condenser.	Check contact breaker points for arcing, remove and fit new.
	Defective ignition switch.	By-pass switch with wire.
	Ignition leads connected wrong way round.	Remove and replace leads to spark plugs in correct order.
	Faulty coil.	Remove and fit new coil.
	Contact breaker point spring earthed or broken.	Check spring is not touching metal part of distributor. Check insulator washers are correctly placed. Renew points if the spring is broken.
No fuel at carburettor float chamber or at jets.	No petrol in petrol tank.	Refill tank!
	Vapour lock in fuel line. (In hot conditions or at high altitude.)	Blow into petrol tank, allow engine to cool, or apply a cold wet rag to the fuel line.
	Blocked float chamber needle valve.	Remove, clean and replace.
	Fuel pump filter blocked.	Remove, clean and replace.
	Choked or blocked carburettor jets.	Dismantle and clean.
	Faulty fuel pump.	Remove, overhaul and replace. Check CB points on S.U. pumps.
Excess of petrol in cylinder or carburettor flooding.	Too much choke allowing too rich a mixture to wet plugs.	Remove and dry sparking plugs or with wide open throttle, push-start the car.
	Float damaged or leaking or needle not seating.	Remove, examine, clean and replace float and needle valve as necessary.
	Float lever incorrectly adjusted.	Remove and adjust correctly.
SYMPTOM: ENGINE STALLS AND WILL NOT START		
No spark at sparking plug	Ignition failure - Sudden.	Check over low and high tension circuits for breaks in wiring.
	Ignition failure - Misfiring precludes total stoppage.	Check contact breaker points, clean and adjust. Renew condenser if faulty.
	Ignition failure - In severe rain or after traversing water splash.	Dry out ignition leads and distributor cap.
No fuel at jets.	No petrol in petrol tank.	Refill tank!
	Petrol tank breather choked.	Remove petrol cap and clean out breather hole or pipe.
	Sudden obstruction in carburettor(s).	Check jets, filter and needle valve in float chamber for blockage.
	Water in fuel system.	Drain tank and blow out fuel lines.
SYMPTOM: ENGINE MISFIRES OR IDLES UNEVENLY		
Intermittent sparking at sparking plug	Ignition leads loose.	Check and tighten as necessary at spark plug and distributor cap ends.

Fault Finding Chart - Engine

Cause	Trouble	Remedy
	Battery leads loose on terminals.	Check and tighten terminal leads.
	Battery earth strap loose on body attachment point.	Check and tighten earth lead to body attachment point.
	Engine earth lead loose.	Tighten lead.
	Low tension leads to SW and CB terminals on coil loose.	Check and tighten leads if found loose.
	Low tension lead from CB terminal side to distributor loose.	Check and tighten if found loose.
	Dirty, or incorrectly gapped plugs.	Remove, clean and regap.
	Dirty, incorrectly set, or pitted contact breaker points.	Clean, file smooth and adjust.
	Tracking across inside of distributor cover.	Remove and fit new cover.
	Ignition too retarded.	Check and adjust ignition timing.
	Faulty coil.	Remove and fit new coil.
Fuel shortage at engine	Mixture too weak.	Check jets, float chamber needle valve and filters for obstruction. Clean as necessary.
	Air leak in carburettor(s).	Remove and overhaul carburettor.
	Air leak at inlet manifold to cylinder head or inlet manifold to carburettor.	Test by pouring oil along joints. Bubbles indicate leak. Renew manifold gasket as appropriate.
Mechanical wear	Incorrect valve clearances.	Adjust rocker arms to take up wear.
	Burnt out exhaust valves.	Remove cylinder head and renew defective valves.
	Sticking or leaking valves.	Remove cylinder head, clean, check and renew valves as necessary.
	Weak or broken valve springs.	Check and renew as necessary.
	Worn valve guides or stems.	Renew valve guides and valves.
	Worn pistons and piston rings.	Dismantle engine, renew pistons and rings.

SYMPTOM: LACK OF POWER AND POOR COMPRESSION

Cause	Trouble	Remedy
Fuel/air mixture leaking from carburettor	Burnt out exhaust valves.	Remove cylinder head, renew defective valves.
	Sticking or leaking valves.	Remove cylinder head, clean, check and renew valves as necessary.
	Worn valve guides and stems.	Remove cylinder head and renew valves and valve guides.
	Weak or broken valve springs.	Remove cylinder head, renew defective springs.
	Blown cylinder head gasket (Accompanied by increase in noise).	Remove cylinder head and fit new gasket.
	Worn pistons and piston rings.	Dismantle engine, renew pistons and rings.
	Worn or scored cylinder bores.	Dismantle engine, rebore, renew pistons and rings.
Incorrect adjustments	Ignition timing wrongly set. Too advanced or retarded.	Check and reset ignition timing.
	Contact breaker points incorrectly gapped.	Check and reset contact breaker points
	Incorrect valve clearances.	Check and reset rocker arm to valve stem gap.
	Incorrectly set sparking plugs.	Remove, clean and regap.
	Carburation too rich or too weak.	Tune carburettor(s) for optimum performance.
Carburation and ignition faults	Dirty contact breaker points.	Remove, clean and replace.
	Fuel filters blocked causing top end fuel starvation.	Dismantle, inspect, clean and replace all fuel filters.
	Distributor automatic balance weights or vacuum advance and retard mechanisms not functioning correctly.	Overhaul distributor.
	Faulty fuel pump giving top end fuel starvation.	Remove, overhaul or fit exchange reconditioned fuel pump.

Fault Finding Chart - Engine

Cause	Trouble	Remedy
SYMPTOM: EXCESSIVE OIL CONSUMPTION		
Oil being burnt by engine	Badly worn, perished or missing valve stem oil seals.	Remove, fit new oil seals to valve stems.
	Excessively worn valve stems and valve guides.	Remove cylinder head and fit new valves and valve guides.
	Worn piston rings.	Fit oil control rings to existing pistons or purchase new pistons.
	Worn pistons and cylinder bores.	Fit new pistons and rings, rebore cylinders.
	Excessive piston ring gap allowing blow-by.	Fit new piston rings and set gap correctly.
	Piston oil return holes choked.	Decarbonise engine and pistons.
Oil being lost due to leaks	Leaking oil filter gasket.	Inspect and fit new gasket as necessary.
	Leaking rocker cover gasket.	" " " " " "
	Leaking tappet chest gasket.	" " " " " "
	Leaking timing case gasket.	" " " " " "
	Leaking sump gasket.	" " " " " "
	Loose sump plug.	Tighten, fit new gasket if necessary.
SYMPTOM: UNUSUAL NOISES FROM ENGINE		
Excessive clearances due to mechanical wear	Worn valve gear. (Noisy tapping from rocker box).	Inspect and renew rocker shaft, rocker arms, and ball pins as necessary.
	Worn big end bearing. (Regular heavy knocking).	Drop sump, if bearing broken up clean oil pump and oilways, fit new bearings. If bearings not broken but worn fit bearing shells.
	Worn timing chain and gears. (Rattling from front of engine).	Remove timing cover, fit new timing wheels and timing chain.
	Worn main bearings. (Rumbling and vibration).	Drop sump, remove crankshaft, if bearings worn but not broken up, renew. If broken up strip oil pump and clean out oilways.
	Worn crankshaft. (Knocking, rumbling and vibration).	Regrind crankshaft, fit new main and big end bearings.

Castrol GRADES

Castrol Engine Oils

Castrol GTX

An ultra high performance SAE 20W/50 motor oil which exceeds the latest API MS requirements and manufacturers' specifications. Castrol GTX with liquid tungsten† generously protects engines at the extreme limits of performance, and combines both good cold starting with oil consumption control. Approved by leading car makers.

Castrol XL 20/50

Contains liquid tungsten†; well suited to the majority of conditions giving good oil consumption control in both new and old cars.

Castrolite (Multi-grade)

This is the lightest multi-grade oil of the Castrol motor oil family containing liquid tungsten†. It is best suited to ensure easy winter starting and for those car models whose manufacturers specify lighter weight oils.

Castrol Grand Prix

An SAE 50 engine oil for use where a heavy, full-bodied lubricant is required.

Castrol Two-Stroke-Four

A premium SAE 30 motor oil possessing good detergency characteristics and corrosion inhibitors, coupled with low ash forming tendency and excellent anti-scuff properties. It is suitable for all two-stroke motor-cycles, and for two-stroke and small four-stroke horticultural machines.

Castrol CR (Multi-grade)

A high quality engine oil of the SAE-20W/30 multi-grade type, suited to mixed fleet operations.

Castrol CRI 10, 20, 30

Primarily for diesel engines, a range of heavily fortified, fully detergent oils, covering the requirements of DEF 2101-D and Supplement 1 specifications.

Castrol CRB 20, 30

Primarily for diesel engines, heavily fortified, fully detergent oils, covering the requirements of MIL-L-2104B.

Castrol R 40

Primarily designed and developed for highly stressed racing engines. Castrol 'R' should not be mixed with any other oil nor with any grade of Castrol.

†*Liquid Tungsten is an oil soluble long chain tertiary alkyl primary amine tungstate covered by British Patent No. 882,295.*

Castrol Gear Oils

Castrol Hypoy (90 EP)

A light-bodied powerful extreme pressure gear oil for use in hypoid rear axles and in some gearboxes.

Castrol Gear Oils (continued)

Castrol Hypoy Light (80 EP)

A very light-bodied powerful extreme pressure gear oil for use in hypoid rear axles in cold climates and in some gearboxes.

Castrol Hypoy B (90 EP)

A light-bodied powerful extreme pressure gear oil that complies with the requirements of the MIL-L-2105B specification, for use in certain gearboxes and rear axles.

Castrol Hi-Press (140 EP)

A heavy-bodied extreme pressure gear oil for use in spiral bevel rear axles and some gearboxes.

Castrol ST (90)

A light-bodied gear oil with fortifying additives

Castrol D (140)

A heavy full-bodied gear oil with fortifying additives.

Castrol Thio-Hypoy FD (90 EP)

A light-bodied powerful extreme pressure gear oil. This is a special oil for running-in certain hypoid gears.

Automatic Transmission Fluids

Castrol TQF

(Automatic Transmission Fluid)

Approved for use in all Borg-Warner Automatic Transmission Units. Castrol TQF also meets Ford specification M2C 33F.

Castrol TQ Dexron®

(Automatic Transmission Fluid)

Complies with the requirements of Dexron® Automatic Transmission Fluids as laid down by General Motors Corporation.

Castrol Greases

Castrol LM

A multi-purpose high melting point lithium based grease approved for most automotive applications including chassis and wheel bearing lubrication.

Castrol MS3

A high melting point lithium based grease containing molybdenum disulphide.

Castrol BNS

A high melting point grease for use where recommended by certain manufacturers in front wheel bearings when disc brakes are fitted.

Castrol Greases (continued)

Castrol CL

A semi-fluid calcium based grease, which is both waterproof and adhesive, intended for chassis lubrication.

Castrol Medium

A medium consistency calcium based grease.

Castrol Heavy

A heavy consistency calcium based grease.

Castrol PH

A white grease for plunger housings and other moving parts on brake mechanisms. *It must NOT be allowed to come into contact with brake fluid when applied to the moving parts of hydraulic brakes.*

Castrol Graphited Grease

A graphited grease for the lubrication of transmission chains.

Castrol Under-Water Grease

A grease for the under-water gears of outboard motors.

Anti-Freeze

Castrol Anti-Freeze

Contains anti-corrosion additives with ethylene glycol. Recommended for the cooling systems of all petrol and diesel engines.

Speciality Products

Castrol Girling Damper Oil Thin

The oil for Girling piston type hydraulic dampers.

Castrol Shockol

A light viscosity oil for use in some piston type shock absorbers and in some hydraulic systems employing synthetic rubber seals. It must not be used in braking systems.

Castrol Penetrating Oil

A leaf spring lubricant possessing a high degree of penetration and providing protection against rust.

Castrol Solvent Flushing Oil

A light-bodied solvent oil, designed for flushing engines, rear axles, gearboxes and gearcasings.

Castrollo

An upper cylinder lubricant for use in the proportion of 1 fluid ounce to two gallons of fuel.

Everyman Oil

A light-bodied machine oil containing anti-corrosion additives for both general use and cycle lubrication.

Chapter 2/Cooling System

Contents

General Description	1	Water Pump - Removal & Replacement	9
Routine Maintenance	2	Water Pump - Dismantling & Reassembly	10
Cooling System - Draining	3	Anti-Freeze Mixture	11
Cooling System - Flushing	4	Temperature Gauge - Fault Finding	12
Cooling System - Filling	5	Temperature Gauge & Sender Unit - Removal & Replacement	13
Radiator - Removal, Inspection, Cleaning & Replacement (TR2, 3 & 3A)	6	Fan Belt - Adjustment	14
Radiator - Removal, Inspection, Cleaning & Replacement (TR4 & 4A)	7	Fan Belt - Removal & Replacement	15
		Fan Assembly	16
Thermostat - Removal, Testing & Replacement	8	Modified Radiator (TR4A models)	17

Specifications

Type of system	Pressurised, pump impeller and fan assisted
Normal temperature	Should not exceed 85ºC (185ºF)
Thermostat:	
Starts opening	70ºC (158ºF)
Fully open	92ºC (197ºF)
Maximum lift	.281 to .407 inch (7.137 to 10.337 mm)
Pressure cap release pressure	3¼ to 4¼ lb/sq.inch
Fan blades:	
Diameter	12½ inch
Number of blades	4
Tension of fan belt	¾ inch movement midway between the dynamo and crank-shaft pulley wheels
Type of water pump	Centrifugal
Water pump drive	Belt from crankshaft pulley

Capacities

TR2, 3 & 3A	
Standard	13 pints (15.612 U.S. pints, 7.4 litres)
With heater	14 pints (16.823 U.S. pints, 8.0 litres)
TR4, 4A	
TR4 (old type radiator)	13 pints (15.612 U.S. pints, 7.4 litres)
TR4 and TR4A new type radiator	10 pints (12.009 U.S. pints, 5.7 litres)
Heater	1 pint (1.201 U.S. pints, 0.568 litres)

Torque Wrench Settings

Water pump attachment	26 to 28 lb.ft. (3.595 to 3.871 Kg.m)
Thermostat assembly to cylinder head	16 to 18 lb.ft. (2.212 to 2.489 Kg.m)
Water pump body	26 to 28 lb.ft. (3.595 to 3.871 Kg.m)

1. General Description

The engine cooling water is circulated by a thermo-siphon, water pump assisted, system and the coolant is pressurised. This to prevent both the loss of water down the overflow pipe with the radiator cap in position and to prevent premature boiling in adverse conditions.

The radiator cap is pressurised and increases the boiling point to 225ºF. If the water temperature exceeds this figure and the water boils, the pressure in the system forces the internal part of the cap off its seat, thus exposing the overflow pipe down which the steam from the boiling water escapes, thus relieving the pressure.

It is, therefore, important to check that the radiator cap is in good condition and that the spring behind the sealing washer has not weakened. Most garages have a special machine in which radiator caps can be tested.

The cooling system comprises the radiator, top and bottom water hoses, heater hose (if heater/demister fitted),

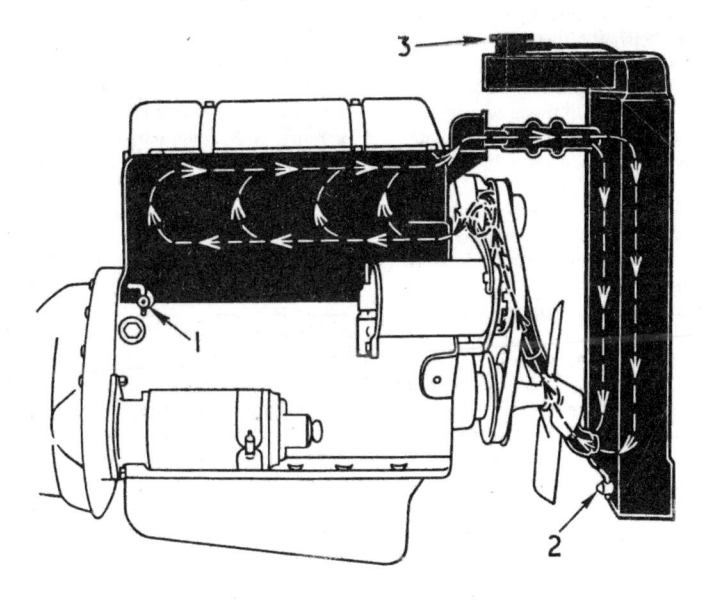

Fig. 2.1. CIRCULATION OF WATER
THROUGH COOLING
SYSTEM
1 Cylinder block drain tap 3 Radiator filler cap
2 Radiator drain tap

Fig. 2.1.A. Water pump grease nipple (arrowed)

Chapter 2/Cooling System

the impellor water pump (mounted on the front of the engine and driven by the fan belt), the thermostat and the two drain taps as shown in Fig. 2.1.

The system functions in the following fashion. Cold water in the bottom of the radiator circulates up the lower radiator hose to the water pump where it is pushed round the water passages in the cylinder block, helping to keep the cylinder bores and pistons cool.

The water then travels up into the cylinder head and circulates round the combustion spaces and valve seats absorbing more heat, and then, when the engine is at its proper operating temperature, travels out of the cylinder head, past the open thermostat into the upper radiator hose and so into the radiator header tank.

The water travels down the radiator where it is rapidly cooled by the in-rush of cold air through the radiator core, which is created by both the fan and the motion of the car. The water, now cold, reaches the bottom of the radiator, when the cycle is repeated.

When the engine is cold the thermostat (which is a valve which opens and closes according to the temperature of the water) maintains the circulation of the same water in the engine.

Only when the correct minimum operating temperature has been reached, as shown in the specification, does the thermostat begin to open, allowing water to return to the radiator.

The header tank on the earlier models of the TR4 was separate from the radiator but on later models and the TR4A the header tank was incorporated in the top of the radiator as is usual practice with most cars.

The coolant overflow from the neck of the radiator filler cap on all models except the TR4A passes down an overflow pipe and discharges onto the road. TR4A models have the overflow pipe connected to an expansion bottle so that as the coolant temperature drops a partial vacuum exists in the radiator and the overflow is drawn back from the expansion bottle, through a little vacuum relief valve in the filler cap back into the radiator top tank. The modified radiator is shown in Fig. 2.10.

2. Routine Maintenance

1. Check the level of water in the radiator once a week or more frequently if necessary, and top up with a soft water (rain water is excellent) as required.
2. Once every 6,000 miles check the fan belt for wear and correct tension and renew or adjust the belt as necessary (see Section 14 for details).
3. Once every 12,000 miles unscrew the plug from the top of the water pump, fit a grease nipple and give five strokes with the grease gun supplied. On later models a grease nipple is fitted as standard. Do not overgrease or the seal may be rendered inoperative. Replace the plug and screw down.

3. Cooling System - Draining

1. With the car on level ground drain the system as follows.
2. If the engine is cold remove the filler cap from the radiator by turning the cap anti-clockwise. If the engine is hot, having just been run, then turn the filler cap very slightly until the pressure in the system has had time to disperse. Use a rag over the cap to protect your hand from escaping steam. If, with the engine very hot, the cap is released suddenly, the drop in pressure can result in the water boiling. With the pressure released the cap can be removed.

3. If anti-freeze is in the radiator drain it into a clean bucket or bowl for re-use.
4. Open the two drain taps (Fig. 2.1.) and ensure the heater control is in the hot position. On later models drain plugs may be fitted instead of taps. Remove the plugs with a spanner. The drain taps are located at the bottom of the radiator and at the rear on the right hand side of the block.
5. When the water has finished running, probe the drain tap orifices with a short piece of wire to dislodge any particles or rust or sediment which may be blocking the taps and preventing all the water draining out.

4. Cooling System - Flushing

1. With time, the cooling system will gradually lose its efficiency as the radiator becomes choked with rust, scales, deposits from the water and other sediment. To clear the system out, remove the radiator cap and the drain taps and leave a hose running in the radiator cap orifice for ten to fifteen minutes.
2. Then close the drain taps and refill with water and a proprietary cleaning compound. Run the engine for 10 to 15 minutes and then drain it and flush out thoroughly for a further ten minutes. All sediment and sludge should now have been removed.
3. In very bad cases the radiator should be reverse flushed. This can be done with the radiator in position. The cylinder block tap is closed and a hose placed over the open radiator drain tap. Water, under pressure, is then forced up through the radiator and out of the header tank filler orifice.
4. The hose is then removed and placed in the filler orifice and the radiator washed out in the usual fashion.

5. Cooling System - Filling

1. Close the two drain taps (Fig. 2.1).
2. Fill the system ensuring that no air locks develop. If a heater is fitted, check that the valve to the heater unit is open, otherwise an air lock may form in the heater. The best type of water to use in the cooling system is rain water, so use this whenever possible.
3. Do not fill the system higher than within ½ inch of the filler orifice. Overfilling will merely result in wastage, which is especially to be avoided when anti-freeze is in use.
4. Only use anti-freeze mixture with a glycerine or ethylene base.
5. Replace the filler cap and turn it firmly clockwise to lock it in position.

6. Radiator - Removal, Inspection, Cleaning and Replacement (TR2, 3 and 3A)

1. To remove the radiator first drain the cooling system as described in Section 3.
2. With the bonnet supported in the fully open position disconnect the earth terminal from the battery.
3. Undo and remove the two nuts and bolts that secure the two 'U' bolts on the top of the wings to the reinforcement bar of the cowling.
4. Make a note of the electrical cable connections and disconnect the electrical cables from their connectors located beside the radiator on the cowling.
5. If the bonnet lock is cable operated as on early models disconnect the cable from its clip on the centre of the front of the cowling reinforcement bar.
6. Undo and remove the six bolts situated on each side securing the outer edges of the radiator cowling to the

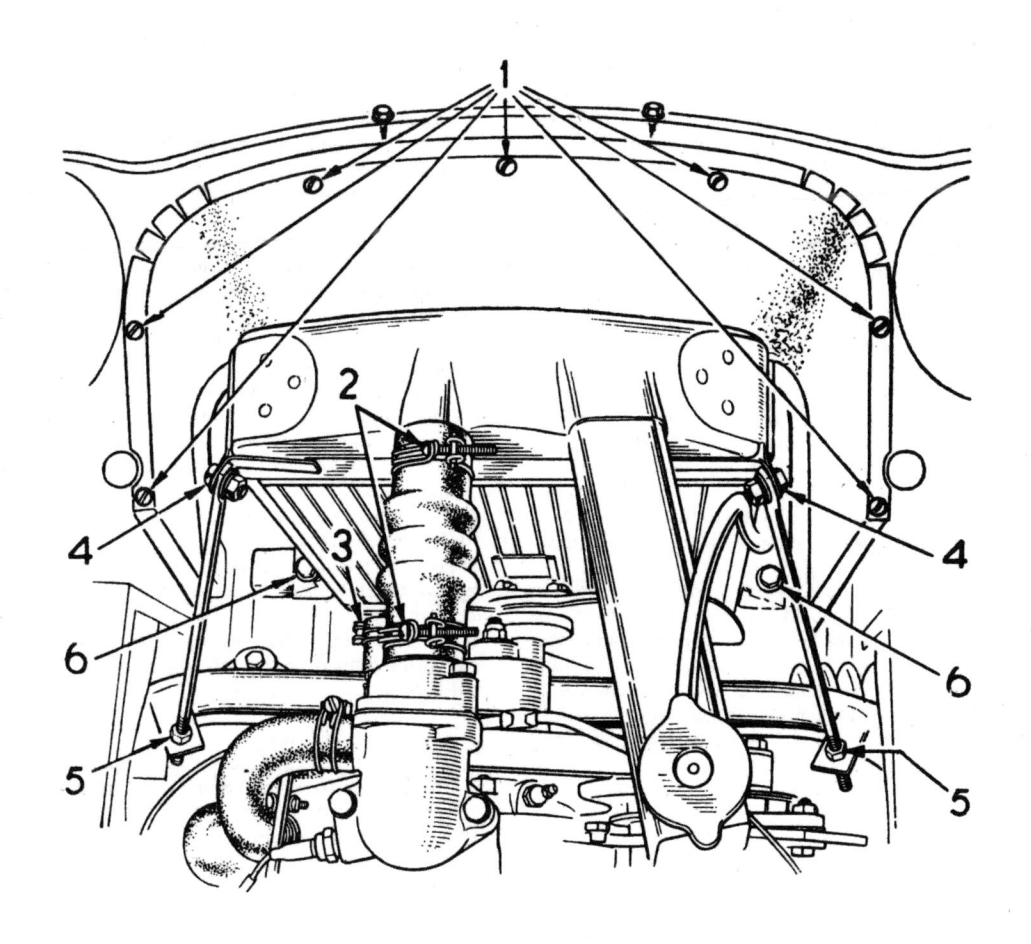

Fig. 2.2. RADIATOR AND AIR DEFLECTOR
WITHIN ENGINE COMPARTMENT
1 Air deflector retaining screws 4 Radiator stay attachment
2 Top hose clips   5 Adjustment nuts
3 Bottom hose clips   6 Radiator mountings

Chapter 2/Cooling System

front wings. It should be specially noted that these bolts are fitted horizontally from the inside of the wheel arches and should not be confused with the row of bolts positioned vertically on the wheel arch.

7. Disconnect the cowling stay to the chassis by undoing the nut, bolt and lockwasher. Next undo the bolt securing the starting handle in place and finally lift the lower section of the cowling upwards and forwards so as to release the water seal and then lift the cowling away from the brackets on the top of the wing panels.

8. Undo the jubilee clip which holds the radiator top hose to the radiator followed by the jubilee clip which holds the bottom radiator hose to the radiator. Disconnect the overflow pipe from the neck of the radiator filler cap.

9. Undo the nuts and bolts that secure the two reinforcement stays to the top covers of the radiator.

10 Unscrew the two bolts and lockwashers that secure the brackets on the sides of the radiator. Remove the radiator from the engine compartment taking great care not to damage the radiator matrix on the fan blades.

11 Lift away the radiator packing pieces fitted between the brackets and chassis members.

12 With the radiator away from the car any leaks can be soldered up or repaired with a substance such as 'Cataloy'. Clean out the inside of the radiator by flushing as detailed in Section 4. When the radiator is away from the car it is advantageous to invert if for reverse flushing. Clean the exterior of the radiator by hosing down the radiator matrix with a strong jet of water to clear away any road dirt, dead flies, etc.

13 Inspect the radiator hoses for cracks, internal or external perishing, and damage caused by overtightening of the securing clips. Replace the hoses as necessary. Examine the radiator hose securing clips and renew them if they are rusted or distorted. The drain taps should be renewed if leaking, but ensure that the leak is not a faulty washer behind the tap. If the tap is suspected try a new washer to see if this clears the trouble first.

14 Refitting the radiator is the reverse sequence to removal, but there are several points to note to ensure that no trouble is experienced during or after refitting.

15 Position the radiator packing pieces before the radiator is replaced in the engine compartment.

16 Carefully fit the water sealing beading to the cowling ensuring that the hole in the beading is over the top hole of the cowling. The remaining elongated holes in the beading should then line up with the lower holes in the cowling.

17 On early models fitted with a cable release bonnet lock, reconnect the cable and adjust as necessary taking care not to force the bonnet closed if the lock is not correctly adjusted otherwise damage could result.

18 Reconnect the electrical cables to their connectors on the cowling in the correct order and then refit the battery earth terminals.

19 Fill the cooling system as detailed in Section 5 and run the engine until it reaches normal operating temperature. Check for leaks.

7. Radiator - Removal, Inspection, Cleaning and Replacement (TR4 and 4A)

1. To remove the radiator first drain the cooling system as described in Section 3.
2. Undo and remove the seven screws (1) (Fig. 2.2.) which secure the air deflector to the front panel and lift away the air deflector.
3. Undo the jubilee clips (2) which hold the radiator top hose to the radiator followed by the jubilee clip (3) which holds the bottom radiator hose to the radiator. Disconnect the overflow pipe from the neck of the radiator filler cap.
4. Undo the nuts and bolts (4) that secure the two reinforcement stays to the top corners of the radiator.
5. Slacken and remove the radiator stay retaining nuts from the front crossmember bracket and lift the two stays away
6. Undo and remove the two radiator mounting nuts and bolts and lift the radiator from the engine compartment taking great care not to damage the radiator matrix on the fan blades.
7. Lift away the radiator packing pieces fitted between the lower radiator mounting and chassis brackets.
8. With the radiator away from the car any leaks can be soldered up or repaired with a substance such as 'Cataloy'. Clean out the inside of the radiator by flushing as detailed in Section 4. When the radiator is away from the car it is advantageous to invert it for reverse flushing. Clean the exterior of the radiator by hosing down the radiator matrix with a strong jet of water to clear away any road dirt, dead flies, etc.
9. Inspect the radiator hoses for cracks, internal or external perishing, and damage caused by overtightening of the securing clips. Replace the hoses as necessary. Examine the radiator hose securing clips and renew them if they are rusted or distorted. The drain taps should be renewed if leaking, but ensure that the leak is not a faulty washer behind the tap. If the tap is suspected try a new washer to see if this clears the trouble first.
10 Refitting the radiator is the reverse sequence to removal.
11 Position the packing pieces fitted between the lower radiator mounting and chassis brackets before replacing the radiator.
12 Fill the cooling system as detailed in Section 5 and run the engine until it reaches normal operating temperature. Check for leaks.

8. Thermostat - Removal, Testing and Replacement

1. To remove the thermostat partially drain the cooling system (4 pints is enough), loosen the upper radiator hose jubilee clips
2. Undo the three nuts from the thermostat housing front cover and lift away the nuts and spring washers.
3. On later models the thermostat housing front cover is retained by two long bolts and spring washers and these should be removed.
4. Release the petrol pipe retaining clip from the lower right hand stud (early models).
5. Carefully separate the two halves of the thermostat housing and lift away the gasket. Take care not to damage it if a new one is not available.
6. Lift the thermostat from the thermostat housing body.
7. Test the thermostat for correct functioning by dangling it by a length of wire or string in a saucepan of cold water together with a thermometer.
8. Heat the water and note when the thermostat begins to open. This temperature is stamped on the flange of the thermostat and is also given in the specifications on page 60.
9. Discard the thermostat if it opens too early. Continue heating the water until the thermostat is fully open. Then let it cool down naturally. If the thermostat will not open fully in boiling water, or does not close down as the water cools then a new one must be fitted.
10 If the thermostat is stuck open when cold this will have been apparent when removing it from the housing.
11 Replacing the thermostat is a reversal of the removal procedure. If at all possible always use a new paper gasket

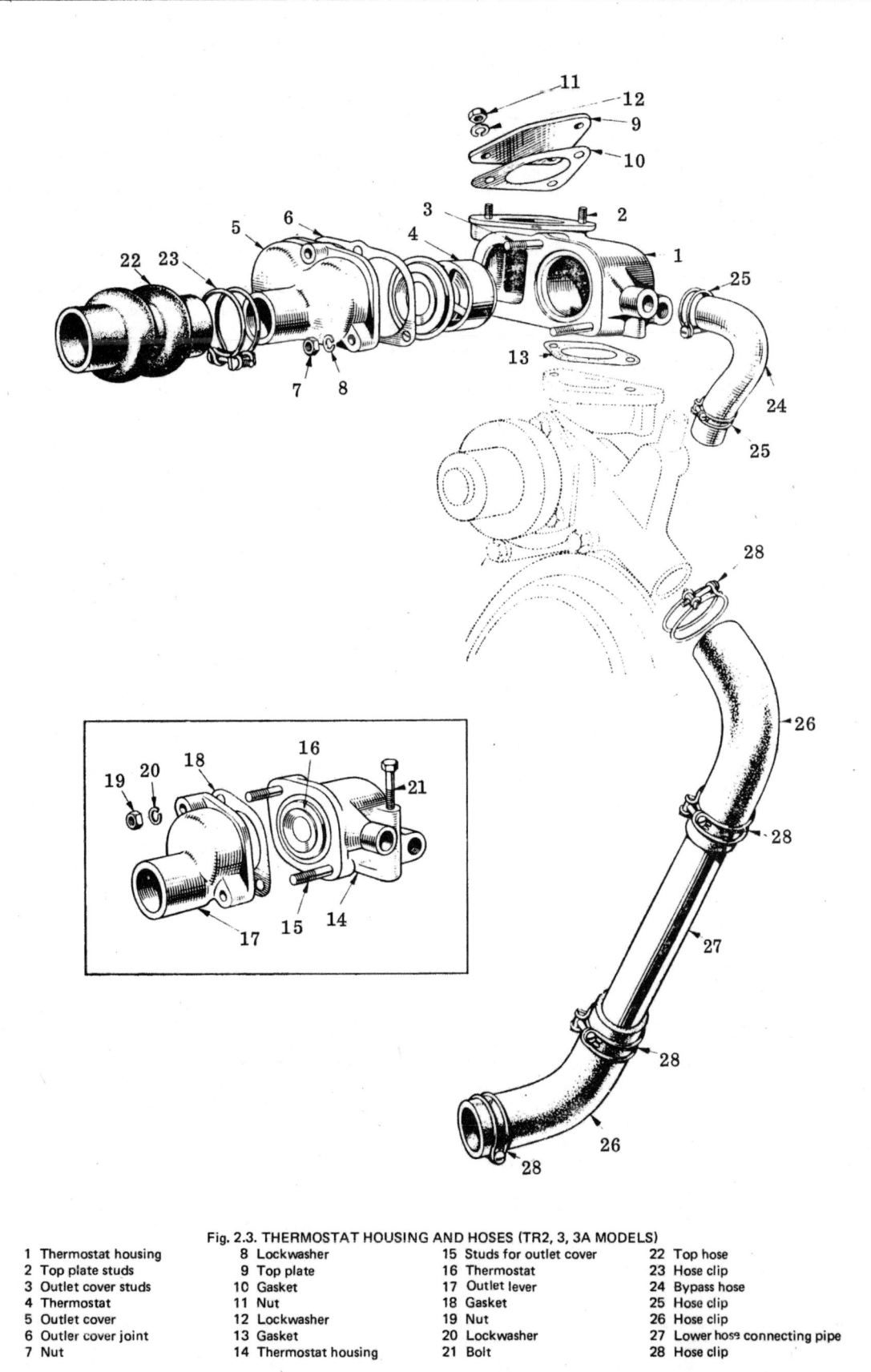

Fig. 2.3. THERMOSTAT HOUSING AND HOSES (TR2, 3, 3A MODELS)

1 Thermostat housing	8 Lockwasher	15 Studs for outlet cover	22 Top hose
2 Top plate studs	9 Top plate	16 Thermostat	23 Hose clip
3 Outlet cover studs	10 Gasket	17 Outlet lever	24 Bypass hose
4 Thermostat	11 Nut	18 Gasket	25 Hose clip
5 Outlet cover	12 Lockwasher	19 Nut	26 Hose clip
6 Outler cover joint	13 Gasket	20 Lockwasher	27 Lower hose connecting pipe
7 Nut	14 Thermostat housing	21 Bolt	28 Hose clip

65

Chapter 2/Cooling System

between the thermostat housing front cover and the body. Renew the complete housing if it is badly corroded.

9. Water Pump - Removal and Replacement

1. If the water pump is badly worn normal practice is to fit an exchange reconditioned unit. Drain the complete cooling system as described in Section 3.
2. Slacken the generator adjustment bolts (5) (Fig. 2.5.) and the two pivot bolts (3 and 4) and push the generator towards the engine. Lift off the fan belt from the water pump pulley.
3. Undo the heater pipe union from the rear of the water pump body (1) (Fig. 2.6.) if a heater is fitted.
4. Undo the jubilee clips holding the bypass hose, and bottom hose from the water pump body.
5. Unscrew the generator adjustment link bolt from the front of the generator.
6. Undo the three bolts with spring washers (25) securing the water pump to the front of the cylinder block. It should be observed that the longer right hand bolt not only holds the pump body to the cylinder block but also holds the bearing housing (22) to the body of the pump. It cannot be completely removed until the pulley has been removed from the water pump shaft.
7. Lift the water pump away from the engine followed by the gasket.
8. Refitting is a straight forward reversal of the removal sequence. Note that the fan belt tension must be correct when all is reassembled. If the fan belt is too tight undue strain will be placed on the water pump and dynamo bearings, and if the belt is too loose it will slip and wear rapidly as well as giving rise to low electrical output from the dynamo.

10. Water Pump - Dismantling and Reassembly

1. If it is wished to repair the pump first ascertain that spare parts are available as less and less firms stock spare parts as opposed to rebuilt pump units.
2. Undo the nut (7) (Fig. 2.6.) and lift away together with spring washer (6). Also undo the two bolts (20) and remove together with spring washer (21). Separate the bearing housing assembly (22) from the body (1).
3. Undo the nyloc nut (15) from the end of the spindle (17) and lift away the nut and plain washer (14).
4. With the aid of a three leg puller withdraw the pulley (13) from the shaft (17). Lift away the woodruff key (19) from the shaft.
5. Using a small three leg puller withdraw the impellor (24) from the shaft (17). The seal (23) may now be removed.
6. Using a small screwdriver release the circlip (12) from its seating in the bearing housing (22) and using a soft faced hammer gently tap out the shaft (17) together with the bearings (10), distance tube (11), spinner (8), and distance washer (9) from the bearing housing (22).
7. Remove the spinner (8) and abutment washer (9) from the shaft (17).
8. The bearings and distance piece may be removed by placing vertically on the top of vice jaws that are opened sufficiently to accept the shaft (17) and tapping the shaft with a soft faced hammer.
9. If the pump is badly worn the bearing will require renewal and the gland face on the housing recut (this is a job for a Triumph garage or your local engineering works). A new seal and bellows assembly (23) and spinner (8) together with new gaskets (3, 26) must also be obtained.
10 Reassembly of the water pump is a reversal of the above sequence. The following additional points should be noted.
11 Position the bearings with their built in seals facing outwards away from each other. Pack the bearings and area around the distance piece with a water proof grease.
12 The shaft and bearings are fitted to the housing with the aid of a drift made from a piece of tubing.
13 Press the impellor onto the spindle until a 0.085 inch clearance exists between the flat face of the impellor and housing (Fig. 2.7.). The impellor should then be soldered to the shaft to prevent water seepage down the spindle.
14 If the impellor is not a tight fit onto the shaft new parts must be fitted.
15 Before refitting the pulley (13) insert the bolt (20) and spring washer through its hole in the bearing housing.
16 Refit the bearing housing (22) to the body (1) using a new gasket (3) and if wished use a non-hardening sealer between the faces to be joined.

11. Anti-Freeze Mixture

1. In circumstances where it is likely that the temperature will drop to below freezing it is essential that some of the water is drained and an adequate amount of ethylene glycol anti-freeze such as Bluecol is added to the cooling system.
2. If Bluecol is not available any anti-freeze which conforms with specification B.S. 3151 or B.S. 3152 can be used. Never use an anti-freeze with an alcohol base as evaporation is too high.
3. Bluecol anti-freeze with an anti-corrosion additive can be left in the cooling system for up to two years, but after six months it is advisable to have the specific gravity of the coolant checked at your local garage, and thereafter once every three months.
4. Listed below are the amounts of Bluecol which should be added to ensure adequate protection down to the temperature given:-

Amount of A.F.	Protection to
1.7 pints (1 litre)	−17.8ºC (0ºF)
2.0 pints (1.3 litres)	−28.9ºC (−20ºF)
2.3 pints (1.43 litres)	−34.5ºC (−30ºF)
3.0 pints (1.7 litres)	−40ºC (−40ºF)

12. Temperature Gauge - Fault Finding

1. If the temperature gauge fails to work either the gauge, the sender unit, the wiring or the connections are at fault.
2. It is not possible to repair the gauge or the sender unit and they must be replaced by new units if at fault.
3. First check the wiring connections and if sound check the wiring for breaks using an ohmmeter. The sender unit and gauge should be tested by substitution.

13. Temperature Gauge and Sender Unit - Removal and Replacement

1. For details of how to remove and replace the temperature gauge see Chapter 10, Section 38.
2. To remove the sender unit disconnect the battery, pull off the wire at the snap connector on the unit located on the side of the thermostat housing. Undo the unit with a spanner.
3. On replacement renew the fibre washer to prevent the possibility of leaks developing.

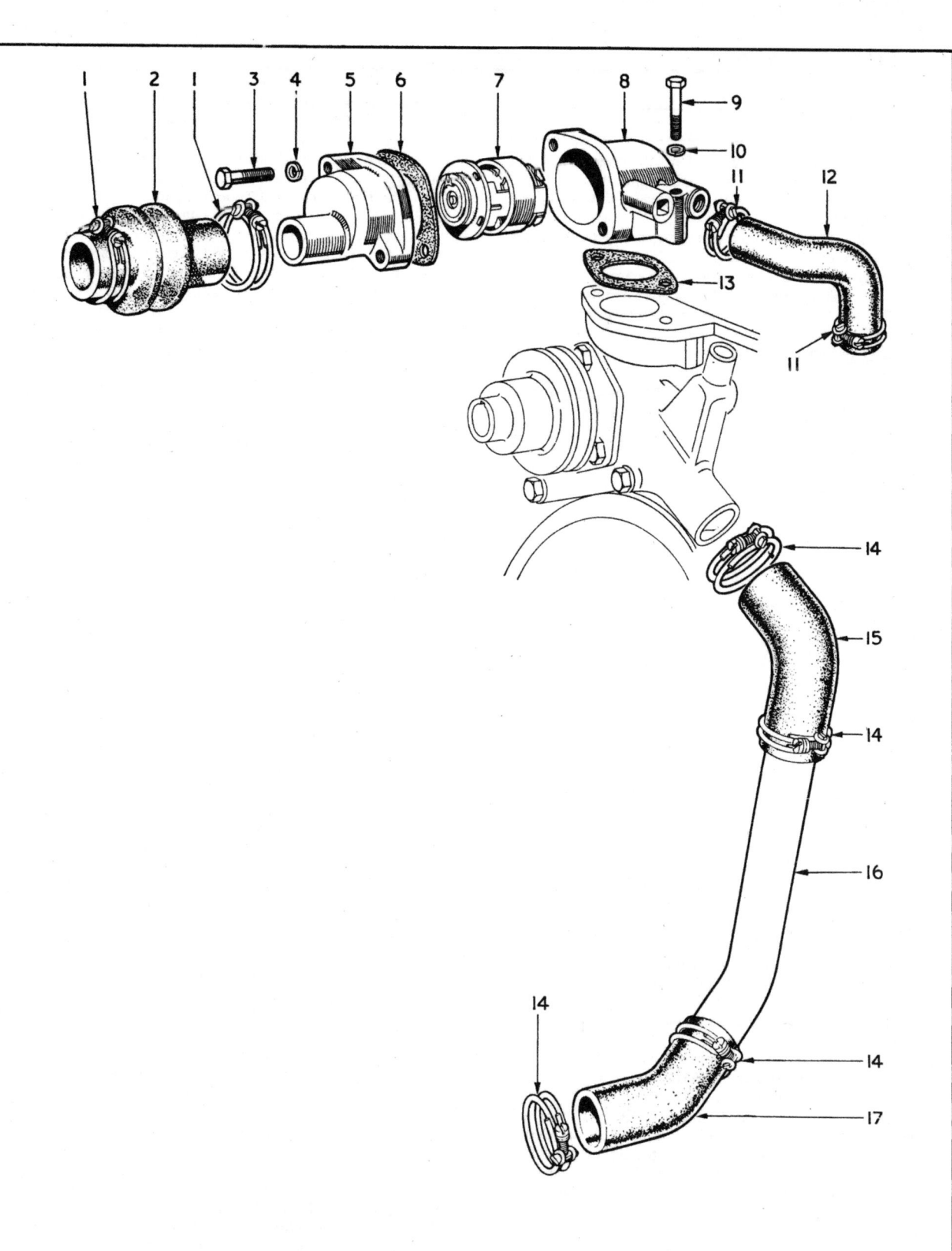

Fig. 2.4. THERMOSTAT HOUSING AND COOLING SYSTEM HOSES (TR4 & 4A MODELS)

1 Clips
2 Top water hose
3 Bolt
4 Spring washer
5 Top elbow
6 Gasket
7 Thermostat
8 Thermostat housing
9 Bolt
10 Spring washer
11 Clips
12 Bypass hose
13 Gasket
14 Clips
15 Bottom water hose (upper)
16 Bottom water pipe
17 Bottom water hose (lower)

Chapter 2/Cooling System

14. Fan Belt - Adjustment

1. It is important to keep the fan belt correctly adjusted and although not listed by the manufacturer, it is considered that this should be a regular maintenance task performed every 6,000 miles.
2. If the belt is too loose it will slip, wear rapidly and cause the dynamo and water pump to malfunction. If the belt is too tight the dynamo and water pump bearings will wear rapidly causing premature failure of these components.
3. The fan belt tension is correct when there is ¾ inch of lateral movement at the midpoint position of the belt between the dynamo pulley wheel and the crankshaft pulley wheel.
4. To adjust the fan belt, slacken the dynamo securing bolts (1, 2, 3, 4) (Fig. 2.5) and move the dynamo either in or out until the correct tension is obtained. It is easier if the dynamo bolts are only slackened a little so it requires some force to move the dynamo. In this way the tension of the belt can be arrived at more quickly than by making frequent adjustments.
5. With the dynamo bolts only slightly loosened, difficulty may be experienced in moving the dynamo away from the engine. A long spanner placed behind the dynamo and resting against the block serves as a very good lever and can be held in this position while the dynamo bolts are tightened. On no account overtighten the fan belt. It is better for the belt to be too loose than too tight.

15. Fan Belt - Removal and Replacement

1. If the fan belt is worn or has stretched unduly it should be replaced. The most usual reason for replacement is that the belt has broken in service. It is therefore recommended that a spare belt is always carried as a spare and is fitted as detailed below.
2. Loosen the two dynamo pivot bolts and the nut on the adjusting link and push the dynamo towards the engine.
3. Undo and remove the three bolts each side of the cross tube positioned directly by the crankshaft pulley. Move the cross tube to one side. The reason for moving the cross tube is that it is very near to the pulley and it is not possible to fit a new fan belt to the pulley with the cross tube in position.
4. Slip the belt over the crankshaft, dynamo and water pump pulleys.
5. Adjust the belt as described in Section 14 and tighten the dynamo mounting nuts. NOTE: After fitting a new belt it will require adjustment 250 miles later.
6. Before refitting the cross member obtain a spare fan belt and bind it tightly to the cross member in such a position that it may be slipped onto the crankshaft pulley at some future date. It will save the trouble of removing the cross member if the belt breaks some time in the future.

16. Fan Assembly

1. The fan assembly parts are shown in Fig. 1.2. and to remove it from the front of the engine the radiator must be removed as described in either Section 6 or 7 of this Chapter.
2. As the fan assembly is accurately balanced care must be taken to note the exact location of each part. During manufacture, once the unit has been balanced, the balancing plate is drilled right through and the hub extension just touched with the drill to give a datum. If the assembly is just to be dismantled re-balancing will not be necessary but if new parts are to be fitted a special jig will be necessary and this is best left to the local Triumph agents.
3. Using a scriber, mark the balancing plate and fan assembly so that the front of each part will be easily recognised.
4. With a screwdriver ease back the locking plate tab and undo the four bolts holding the fan blades to the fan pulley hub extension. Lift away the fan bolts, lock plates, plain washers and a balance plate if one has been previously fitted. Also lift away the extension bolt locking plate.
5. Carefully remove the fan blades, split rubber bushes, metal sleeves and plain washers.
6. Undo the starter dog or extension bolt and withdraw through the fan pulley hub extension noting any shims that may be under the head of the starter dog bolt.
7. Carefully tap on the front flange of the hub extension to separate it from the end of the crankshaft. Lift away the hub extension, hub fan belt pulley and woodruff key from the end of the crankshaft.
8. To separate the hub extension from the hub and pulley ease back the lock plate tabs from the six nuts and bolts. On later engines nyloc nuts and plain washers were fitted instead of locking plates.
9. Undo the nuts and bolts and separate the parts.
10 To refit the fan assembly first ensure that the fan blades are securely riveted to the fan assembly.
11 Put the two pulley pressings together so that on the flatter one the drilled hole is uppermost and the second pressing is on top.
12 Position the hub (142) (Fig. 1.2) through the pulley pressing so that the keyway is facing downwards 180º away from the hole in the rear pulley pressing. This is very important otherwise the T.D.C. notch on the pulley will be incorrectly positioned.
13 Replace the nuts (144), bolts (140) and washers. On the earlier models of engine lockplates were used and may be discarded provided the nyloc nuts and plain washers are used.
14 Refit the rubber sleeves (146) onto the fan assembly (148) and position the metal sleeves (147) through the centre of the rubber sleeves.
15 Put one lock plate (154) onto each pair of fan securing bolts (153) whilst onto the second pair of bolts fit the balance piece (152) followed by a plain washer (150) to every bolt (153).
16 Refit the previously noted shims under the head of the long starter dog bolt or plain bolt to secure the hub extension and pulley onto the end of the crankshaft.
17 Tighten the bolt until the jaws of the starter dog lie at the 'ten to four' position which is the ideal position to ensure easy engine starting when using a starting handle. If difficult to obtain undo the bolt and either remove or fit more shims as necessary until the desired position is obtained.
18 Refit the fan assembly to the extension hub carefully ensuring that the 5/32 inch hole in the web is over the dimple on the hub extension. Refit the starter dog bolt locking washer (151) so that the larger diameter plain washers are between it and the rubber sleeves on the fan assembly.
19 Replace the fan retaining bolts (153) together with their lock plates and washers and tighten fully. The balance piece (152) should be fitted so that the 5/32 inch hole in it lines up with the hole in the fan assembly.
20 Bend over the lock tabs to secure the bolts in position.
21 Replace the radiator and front cowl as detailed in Section 6 or 7 of this Chapter.

Fig.2.6. WATER PUMP COMPONENT PARTS

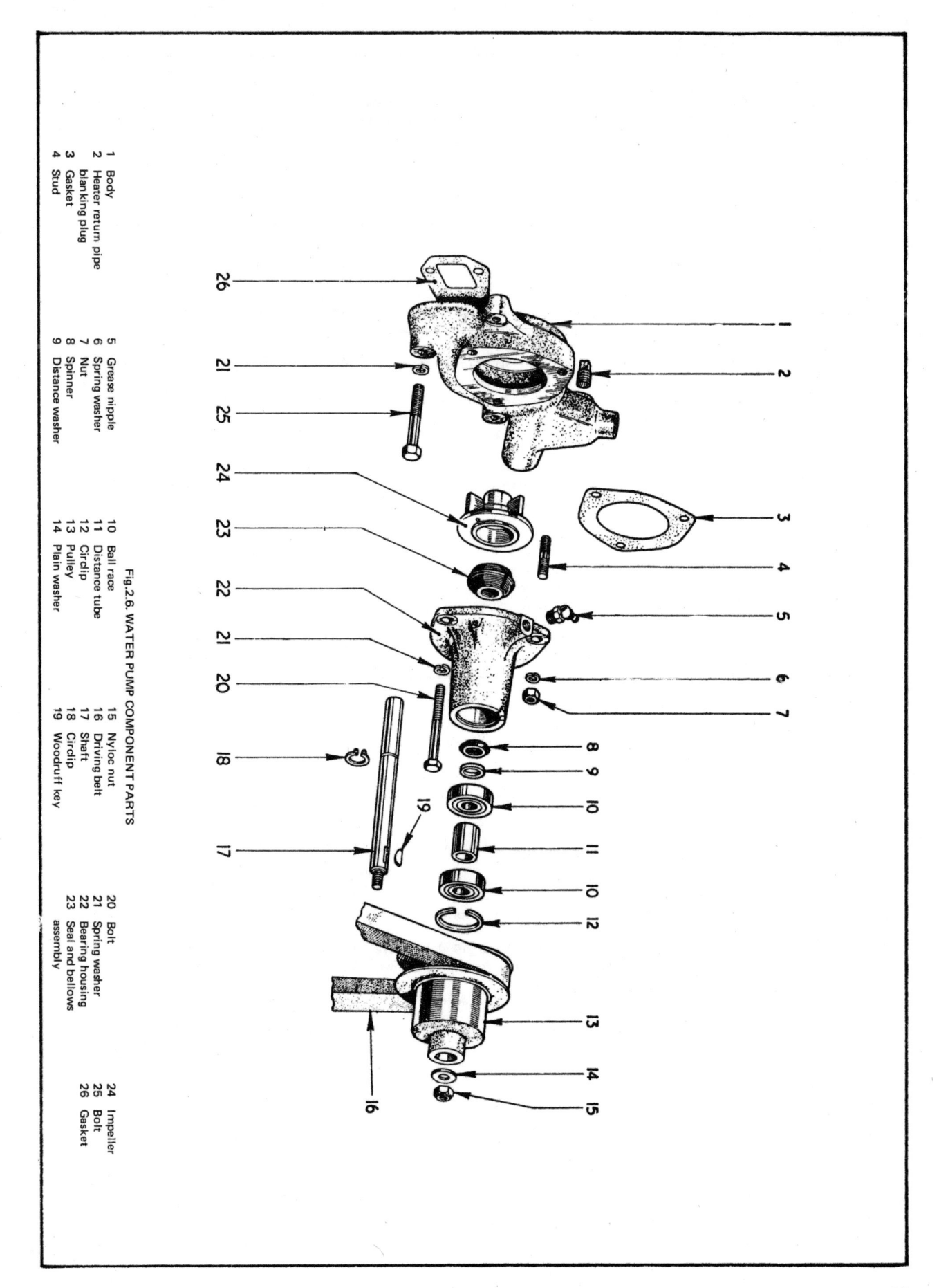

1 Body
2 Heater return pipe
3 Gasket
4 Stud
5 Grease nipple
6 Spring washer
7 Nut
8 Spinner
9 Distance washer
10 Ball race
11 Distance tube
12 Circlip
13 Pulley
14 Plain washer
15 Nyloc nut
16 Driving belt
17 Shaft
18 Circlip
19 Woodruff key
20 Bolt
21 Spring washer
22 Bearing housing
23 Seal and bellows assembly
24 Impeller
25 Bolt
26 Gasket

blanking plug

Chapter 2/Cooling System

17. Modified Radiator (TR4A models)

The radiator was modified upon the introduction of the TR4A whereby a coolant overflow bottle was fitted and the design of the top radiator tank reduced in size. Fig. 2.10 shows the new design.

Fault Finding Chart - Cooling System

Cause	Trouble	Remedy
SYMPTOM: OVERHEATING		
Heat generated in cylinder not being successfully disposed of by radiator	Insufficient water in cooling system	Top up radiator.
	Fan belt slipping (accompanied by a shrieking noise on rapid engine acceleration	Tighten fan belt to recommended tension or replace if worn.
	Radiator core blocked or radiator grille restricted	Reverse flush radiator, remove obstructions.
	Bottom water hose collapsed, impeding flow	Remove and fit new hose.
	Thermostat not opening properly	Remove and fit new thermostat.
	Ignition advance and retard incorrectly set (accompanied by loss of power, and perhaps, misfiring)	Check and reset ignition timing.
	Carburettor(s) incorrectly adjusted (mixture too weak)	Tune carburettor(s).
	Exhaust system partially blocked	Check exhaust pipe for constrictive dents and blockages.
	Oil level in sump too low	Top up sump to full mark on dipstick.
	Blown cylinder head gasket (Water/steam being forced down the radiator overflow pipe under pressure)	Remove cylinder head, fit new gasket.
	Engine not yet run-in	Run-in slowly and carefully.
	Brakes binding	Check and adjust brakes if necessary.
SYMPTOM: UNDERHEATING		
Too much heat being dispersed by radiator	Thermostat jammed open	Remove and renew thermostat.
	Incorrect grade of thermostat fitted allowing premature opening of valve	Remove and replace with new thermostat which opens at a higher temperature.
	Thermostat missing	Check and fit correct thermostat.
SYMPTOM: LOSS OF COOLING WATER		
Leaks in system	Loose clips on water hoses	Check and tighten clips if necessary.
	Top, bottom, or by-pass water hoses perished and leaking.	Check and replace any faulty hoses.
	Radiator core leaking	Remove radiator and repair.
	Thermostat gasket leaking	Inspect and renew gasket.
	Radiator pressure cap spring worn or seal ineffective	Renew radiator pressure cap.
	Blown cylinder head gasket (pressure in system forcing water/steam down overflow pipe	Remove cylinder head and fit new gasket.
	Cylinder wall or head cracked	Dismantle engine, dispatch to engineering works for repair.

Fig. 2.5. Generator mounting and adjustment bolts

Fig. 2.7. Use of a feeler gauge to set clearances of 0.085 inch between water impeller and bearing housing.

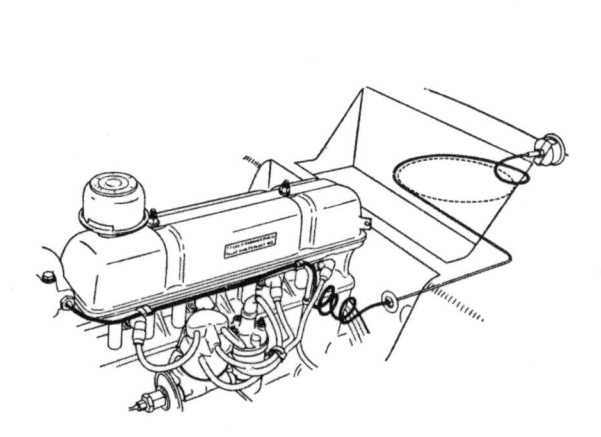

Fig. 2.8. Correct positioning of water temperature gauge capilliary tube. Note: The dotted circle shows the position of the heater if one is fitted.

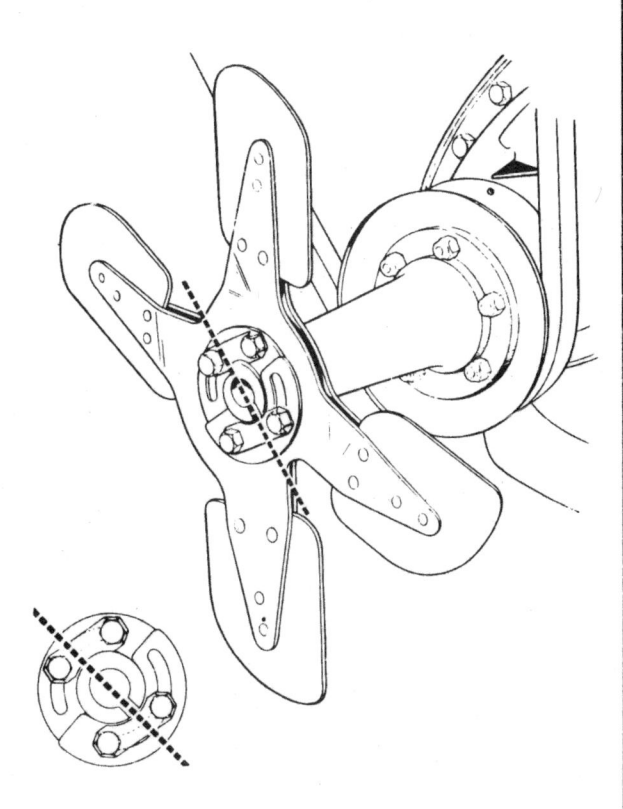

Fig. 2.9. Correct positioning of the fan and starter dog assembly for easy use of the starter handle

71

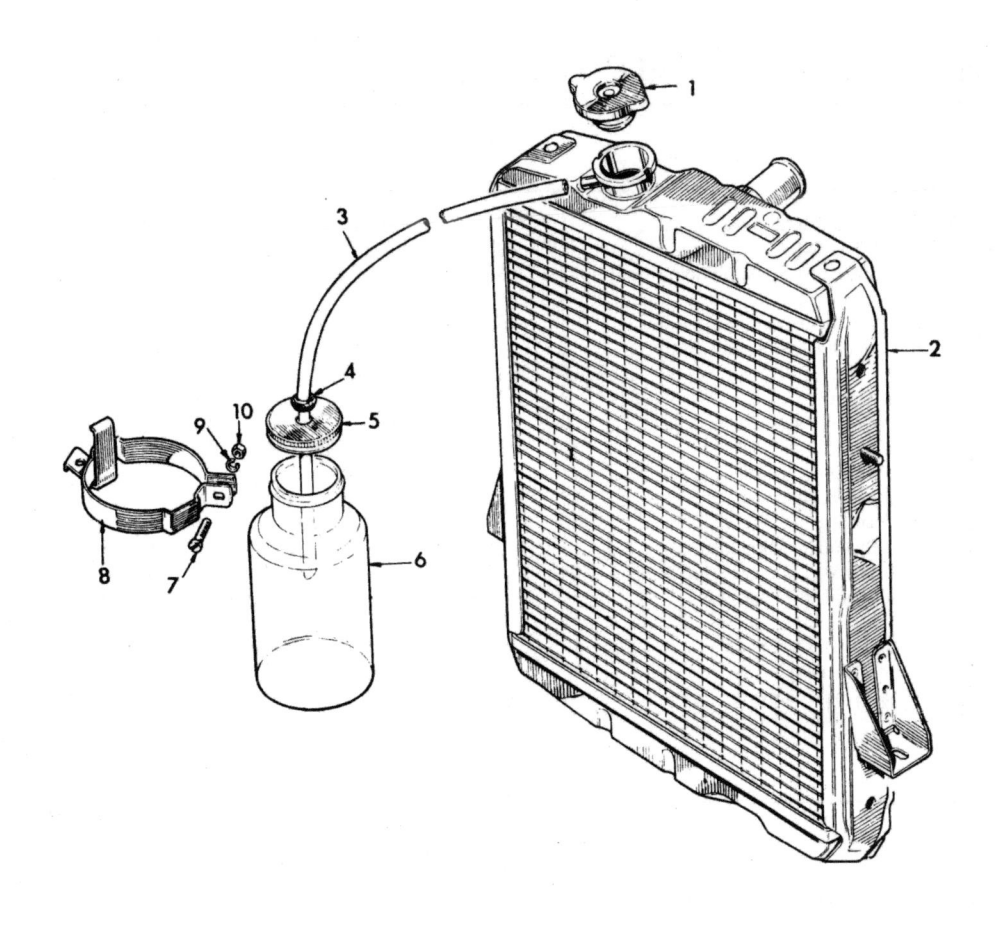

Fig. 2.10. MODIFIED RADIATOR FITTED TO
TR4A MODELS

1 Radiator filler cap   6 Overflow bottle
2 Radiator block   7 Bolt
3 Hose   8 Bracket
4 Grommet   9 Spring washer
5 Cap   10 Nut

Chapter 3/Fuel System and Carburation

Contents

General Description (TR2, 3 & 3A) ...	1
General Description (TR4 & 4A) ...	2
Air Cleaner - Removal, Replacement & Servicing ...	3
A.C. Fuel Pump - Description ...	4
A.C. Fuel Pump - Routine Maintenance ...	5
A.C. Fuel Pump - Removal & Replacement ...	6
A.C. Fuel Pump - Testing ...	7
A.C. Fuel Pump - Dismantling ...	8
A.C. Fuel Pump - Examination & Reassembly ...	9
S.U. Carburettor - Routine Maintenance ...	10
S.U. Carburettor - Description ...	11
S.U. Carburettor - Removal & Refitting ...	12
S.U. Carburettor - Dismantling ...	13
S.U. Carburettor Float Chamber - Dismantling, Examination & Reassembly ...	14
S.U. Carburettor Float Chamber - Fuel Level Adjustment ...	15
S.U. Carburettor - Examination & Repair ...	16
S.U. Carburettor - Piston Sticking ...	17
S.U. Carburettor - Float Needle Sticking ...	18
S.U. Carburettor - Float Chamber Flooding ...	19
S.U. Carburettor - Water & Dirt in Carburettor ...	20
S.U. Carburettor - Jet Centering ...	21
S.U. Carburettors - Adjustment & Tuning ...	22
S.U. Carburettors - Jet & Throttle Interconnection Adjustment ...	23
Synchronisation of Twin S.U. Carburettors ...	24
Stromberg 175 CD Carburettor - Description ...	25
Stromberg 175 CD Carburettor - Adjustment ...	26
Stromberg 175 CD Carburettor - Float Chamber Fuel Level Adjustment ...	27
Stromberg 175 CD Carburettor - Removal & Refitting ...	28
Stromberg 175 CD Carburettor - Dismantling & Reassembly ...	29
Synchronization of Twin Stromberg Carburettors ...	30
Fuel Line Tap ...	31
Fuel Tank - Removal & Replacement ...	32
Crankcase Breather Valve (TR4A) ...	33

Specifications

Fuel Pump
Type ... A.C. mechanical UE
Drive ... From camshaft
Operating pressure ... 1¼ to 2½ lb/sq.in.

Carburettors
TR2
  Type ... Twin S.U. H4
  Needle size:
    Standard ... FV
    High speed ... GC
TR3, TR3A, TR4
  Type ... Twin S.U. H6
  Needle size:
    Early before engine number TS 10037E ... TD
    Later after engine number TS 10037E ... TESM
    (To be fitted as a replacement for earlier size)
TR4A
  Type ... Twin Stromberg 175 CD Horizontal
  Needle size:
    Early up to engine number CTC 54939 ... 2E
    Later after engine number CTC 54939 ... 2H

Air cleaners
TR2
  Make ... A.C. Sphinx
  Type ... 7222 575 oil damped elements or paper element type
TR3, TR4, TR4A
  Similar to TR2 but offset

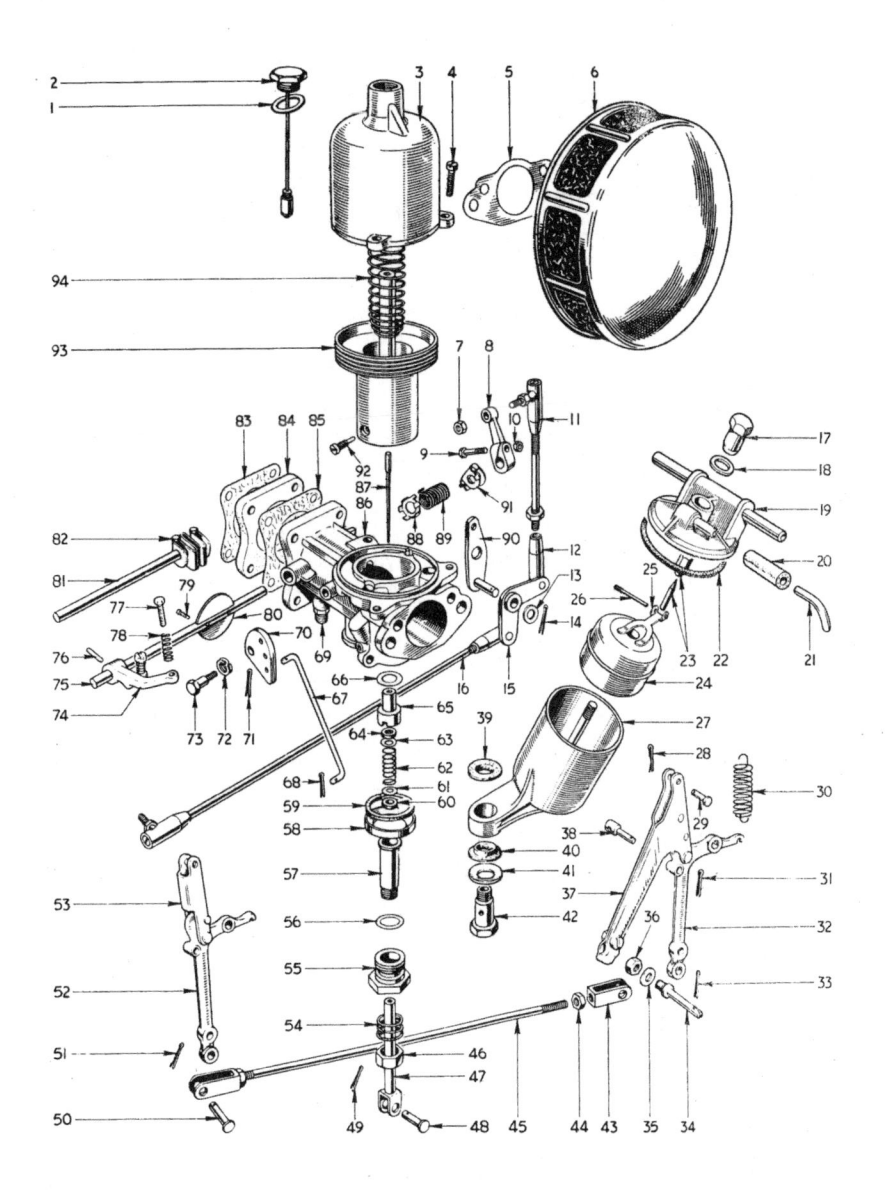

Fig. 3.5. S.U. CARBURETTOR COMPONENT PARTS (TYPE H.5)

1 Fibre washer	26 Hinge pin	49 Split pin	72 Double spring washer
2 Damper assembly	27 Float chamber	50 Clevis pin	73 Shouldered bolt
3 Suction chamber	28 Split pin	51 Split pin	74 Throttle stop
4 Screw	29 Clevis pin	52 Jet lever	75 Throttle spindle
5 Gasket	30 Jet lever return spring	53 Jet lever link	76 Pin
6 Air cleaner	31 Split pin	54 Loading spring	77 Stop adjusting screw
7 Nut	32 Jet lever	55 Jet locking nut	78 Spring
8 throttle lever	33 Split pin	56 Washer	79 Throttle butterfly screw
9 Pinch bolt	34 Choke cable connector	57 Bottom half jet bearing	80 Butterfly
10 Nut	35 Washer	58 Sealing ring	81 Throttle connecting rod
11 Link rod coupling	36 Nut	59 Cork washer	82 Coupling
12 Link rod coupling	37 Jet link and choke cable support	60 Cork gland washer	83 Gasket
13 Plain washer	38 Clevis pin	61 Copper gland washer	84 Insulator
14 Split pin	39 Washer	62 Spring between gland washer	85 Gasket
15 Relay lever	40 Shouldered washer	63 Copper gland washer	86 Carburettor body
16 Link rod assembly	41 Washer	64 Cork gland washer	87 Needle
17 Cap nut	42 Float chamber attachment bolt	65 Top half jet bearing	88 Anchor plate
18 Washer	43 Fork end	66 Washer	89 Return spring
19 Front chamber cover	44 Nut	67 Choke/throttle interconnecting link	90 Pivot lever
20 Fuel pipe coupling	45 Jet control connecting link	68 Split pin	91 End clip
21 Fuel pipe	46 Jet adjusting nut	69 Vacuum union	92 Needle locking screw
22 Joint washer	47 Jet head	70 Lever cam	93 Piston
23 Needle valve	48 Clevis pin	71 Split pin	94 Piston spring
24 Float			
25 Fork			

75

Chapter 3/Fuel System & Carburation

Fuel Tank Capacities
TR2, TR3, TR3A ... ... 12 gallons
TR4, TR4A ... ... 11¾ gallons

1. General Description (TR2, 3 and 3A)

The fuel system on these models comprises a 12½ gallon (12 gallon TR3 and 3A) fuel tank located in the front section of the rear luggage compartment over the rear axle. The fuel line from the tank to the pump passes along the left hand side of the car and as the fuel tank is above the level of the pump a special tap is fitted into the line as it emerges into the engine compartment to prevent syphoning of fuel when the line is disconnected from the pump. The fuel tank has a built in venting pipe (8) (Fig. 3.1) which means that ventilation is not through the filler cap. To enable complete draining of the tank a drain plug is fitted to the lowest part of the tank.

Fuel is drawn from the tank to the carburettor installation by an AC mechanical fuel pump positioned on the left hand side of the crankcase and is driven by an eccentric on the camshaft. The pump has a glass sediment bowl and a wire gauze filter to remove any particles of dirt or water from the fuel. Due to normal engine movement on its rubber mountings a flexible hose (19) connects the fuel tap on the main line to the pump.

Twin S.U. carburettors are fitted as standard onto a manifold on the right hand side of the engine and are fed with fuel by a metal pipe connecting the carburettor float chambers to the fuel feed pump, this pipe passing around the front of the engine. At certain times a thimble type gauze filter was fitted to the fuel inlet connection to the carburettors. Individual oil dampened AC Sphinx canister type air filters are fitted to each carburettor to ensure that the air is adequately freed of dust before entering the carburettors.

During the long production run of the TR2, 3 and 3A models slight modifications have been incorporated into the fuel system. S.U. carburettors type H4 were fitted to the TR2 models which were then changed to H6 type upon the introduction of the TR3 model. As the latter carburettor has a four point fixing to the manifold instead of two point fixing the manifold was modified accordingly as well as increasing the bore diameter to accommodate the larger ports of the high port cylinder head.

The TR3 fuel tank was redesigned to accommodate the rear seats and this necessitated the reduction in capacity to 12 gallons.

2. General Description (TR4 and 4A)

The fuel system on these models comprise a 11¾ gallon fuel tank located in the front of the rear luggage compartment over the rear axle. The fuel line from the tank to the pump passes along the left hand side of the car and as the fuel tank is above the level of the pump a special tap is fitted into the line as it emerges into the engine compartment to prevent syphoning of fuel when the line is disconnected from the pump. The fuel tank has a built in venting pipe (8) (Fig. 3.1) which means that ventilation is not through the filler cap. To enable complete draining of the tank a drain plug is fitted to the lowest part of the tank.

Fuel is drawn from the tank to the carburettor installation by an AC mechanical fuel pump positioned on the left hand side of the crankcase and is driven by an eccentric on the camshaft. The pump has a glass sediment bowl and a wire gauze filter to remove any particles of dirt or water from the fuel. Due to normal engine movement on its rubber mountings a flexible hose (19) connects the fuel tap on the main line to the pump.

Like the previous models twin carburettors are fitted as standard. The TR4 is fitted with twin S.U. type H6 carburettors whilst the TR4A is fitted with twin Stromberg CD carburettors.

Two types of air cleaners were fitted to these models. The differences being that one type was of a wire gauze element individually fitted to the carburettor air intakes whilst the second type was of the paper element design, in this latter instance both elements being housed in a single cover as shown in Fig. 3.2. The second type are not serviceable and the elements must be renewed. The earlier types may be washed in petrol and resoaked in oil. Full details are given in Section 3 of this Chapter.

3. Air Cleaners - Removal, Replacement and Servicing

TR2, 3 and 3A
1. Every 3,000 miles the wire gauze air cleaner elements should be removed by undoing the two bolts which hold each cleaner to the carburettor, thoroughly wash the elements in petrol and when dry soak in engine grade oil. Do not refit until the surface oil has drained away.
2. Upon replacement renew the air cleaner/carburettor gaskets if necessary and make sure that the holes in the gaskets are correctly aligned and the filter elements correctly positioned.

TR4 and 4A
3. Wire gauge element - For servicing details see earlier in this Section.
4. Paper Element - Every 3,000 miles the cleaner elements should be removed by undoing the bolts which hold the air cleaner cover to the carburettor flanges. The paper element cleaner should have all foreign matter blown or gently brushed from them at 3,000 mile intervals and every 12,000 miles new paper element cleaners should be fitted.
5. Upon replacement renew the air cleaner/carburettor gaskets if necessary and also the cover joint washer. Make sure that the holes in the carburettor flange gaskets are correctly aligned and the filter elements correctly positioned in their cover to allow the bolts to pass through them.

4. A.C. Fuel Pump - Description

The mechanically operated A.C. fuel pump is actuated through a spring loaded rocker arm (23) (Fig. 3.3) by an eccentric on the engine camshaft. The diaphragm assembly (12) is connected to the rocker arm (23) by the link arm (24).

As the engine camshaft rotates, the eccentric moves the pivoted rocker arm outwards which in turn pulls the diaphragm pull rod down against the pressure of the diaphragm spring (13).

This creates sufficient vacuum in the pump chamber to draw in fuel from the tank through the fuel filter gauze (4) located in the top of the sediment bowl (2) and the inlet valve (10).

The rocker arm is held in constant contact with the

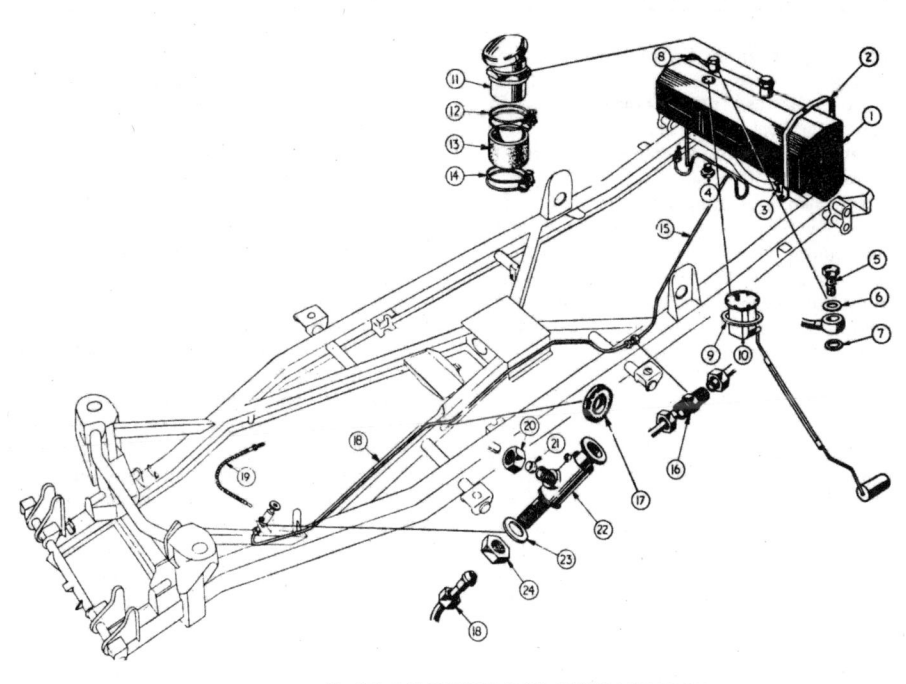

Fig. 3.1. LAYOUT OF FUEL LINES AND TANK

1 Petrol tank
2 Petrol tank strap
3 Fixing bolt for 2
4 Drain plug
5 Banjo bolt
6 Fibre washer
7 Fibre washer
8 Vent pipe
9 Cork washer
10 Gauge unit
11 Filler assembly
12 Hose clip
13 Hose
14 Hose clip
15 Pipe
16 Connector
17 Rubber grommet
18 Pipe
19 Hose
20 Union nut
21 Brass olive
22 Tap
23 Washer
24 Locknut

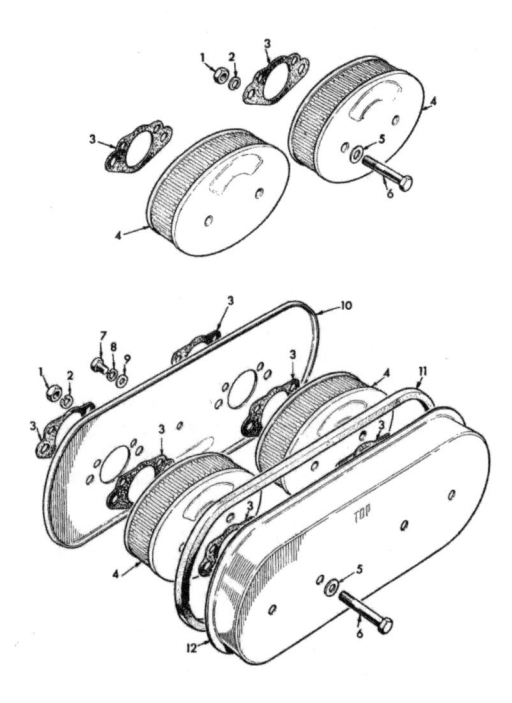

Fig. 3.2. PAPER ELEMENT AIR CLEANERS

1 Nut
2 Spring washer
3 Joint washer
4 Air cleaner
5 Washer
6 Bolt
7 Bolt
8 Spring washer
9 Washer
10 Backplate
11 Joint washer
12 Cover pressing

77

Chapter 3/Fuel System & Carburation

eccentric by an anti-rattle spring (25) and as the engine camshaft continues to rotate the eccentric allows the rocker arm to move inwards. The diaphragm spring (13) is thus free to push the diaphragm (12) upwards so forcing the fuel in the pump chamber out to the carburettor through the non-return outlet valve (10).

When the float chamber in the carburettor is full the float chamber needle valve will close so preventing further flow from the fuel pump.

The pressure in the delivery line will hold the diaphragm downwards against the pressure of the diaphragm spring, and it will remain in this position until the needle valve in the float chamber opens to admit more petrol.

5. A.C. Fuel Pump - Routine Maintenance

1. Every 6,000 miles (3,000 miles in very dusty conditions) slacken the wire stirrup thumb screw and move the stirrup to one side.
2. Lift off the glass bowl (2) (Fig. 3.3) followed by the cork seal (3) and gauze filter. Clean out any sediment in the bowl.
3. Inspect the filter gauze for sediment and clean it with petrol and a soft brush if dirty.
4. Check the condition of the cork gasket and renew if it has hardened or broken. Replacement is a straightforward reversal of the removal sequence. Do not overtighten the stirrup clamp nut otherwise the glass bowl will crack.

6. A.C. Fuel Pump - Removal and Replacement

1. Close the fuel line tap located on the end of the main fuel line within the engine compartment to stop full syphoning out when the inlet connection on the pump is disconnected. The tap is shown in Fig. 3.1.
2. Remove the fuel inlet and outlet pipes by unscrewing the union nuts.
3. Undo the two nuts and spring washers which hold the pump to the crankcase. Note the special nut at the rear of the pump with a slotted head. Ensure that it is replaced on the correct stud, i.e., the stud nearest to the rear of the engine.
4. Lift the pump together with the gasket and packing pieces away from the crankcase. Note that the oil pressure pipe is clipped to the rear stud.
5. Replacement of the pump is a reversal of the above procedure. Remember to use a new gasket between the crankcase and fuel pump to ensure no oil leaks. Ensure that both faces of the flange are perfectly clean and check that the rocker arm lies on top of the camshaft eccentric and not underneath it.

7. A.C. Fuel Pump - Testing

Presuming that the fuel lines and unions are in good condition and that there are no leaks anywhere, check the performance of the fuel pump in the following manner. Disconnect the fuel pipe at the carburettor inlet union, and the high tension lead to the coil, and with a suitable container or a large rag in position to catch the ejected fuel, turn the engine over on the starter motor solenoid. A good spurt of petrol should emerge from the end of the pipe every second revolution.

8. A.C. Fuel Pump - Dismantling

1. Clean the outside of the pump and wipe dry using a dry non fluffy rag.
2. Using a file make a mark on the flanges of the upper (7) (Fig. 3.3) and lower body (26) to ensure that they are correctly reassembled.
3. Unscrew the stirrup thumb screw (1) and swing the stirrup out of the way. Hold the glass bowl to ensure that it does not drop. Lift away the sediment bowl followed by the cork seal (3) and gauze filter (4). Inspect the cork gasket (3) for signs of damage or flattening and obtain a new one ready for reassembling.
4. Undo and remove the six body securing screws (5) and spring washers (6) and separate the two halves.
5. Invert the upper body (7) and undo the two valve retaining plate screws (8) and lift away the screws (8), retaining plate (9), the two valve assemblies (10) and the valve gasket (11) from the upper body.
6. Note the position of the lip on the diaphragm (12) relative to the lower body (26) to ensure correct reassembly and remove the diaphragm (12) by rotating through 90° in an anti-clockwise direction and lifting it away from the lower body and the link (24).
7. It is recommended that the lower body parts are not dismantled unless either the seal (15), hand priming lever (16) or the link assembly require attention.

9. A.C. Fuel Pump - Examination and Reassembly

1. Check the condition of the cork sediment bowl sealing washer and if it has hardened or broken it must be replaced. The diaphragm should be checked similarly and replaced if faulty. Clean the pump thoroughly and agitate the valves in paraffin or petrol to clean them out. This will also improve the contact between the valve seat and the valve. It is unlikely that the pump body will be damaged but check for fractures and cracks.
2. To reassemble the pump proceed as follows. If the lower body (26) (Fig. 3.3) has been dismantled replace the rocker arm assembly comprising the operating link (24), rocker arm (23), anti-rattle spring (25) and washers (22) in their relative positions in the lower body. Align the holes in the body and insert the pivot pin (21).
3. Refit the circlips to the grooves in each end of the pivot pin.
4. Invert the upper body (7) and replace the gasket (11), valves (10), valve retaining plate (9) and tighten the two plate retaining screws (8). The two valves are interchangable so care must be taken to ensure they are fitted the correct way round. The inlet valve should be fitted into the offset and shallower part with its spring facing the diaphragm, whilst the outlet valve is fitted to the centre part with its spring facing away from the diaphragm.
5. Place the seal (15) and retainer (14) in the lower body (26) and place the diaphragm spring (13) over them.
6. Replace the diaphragm and pull rod assembly with the pull rod downwards and the small tab on the diaphragm line up to the previously noted position which should have been adjacent to the centre of the flange and rocker arm.
7. With the body of the pump held so that the rocker arm is facing away from one, press down the diaphragm, turning it a quarter of a turn to the left at the same time. This engages the slot on the pull rod with the operating lever. The small tab on the diaphragm should now be at an angle of 90° to the rocker arm and the diaphragm should be firmly located.
8. Move the rocker arm until the diaphragm is level with

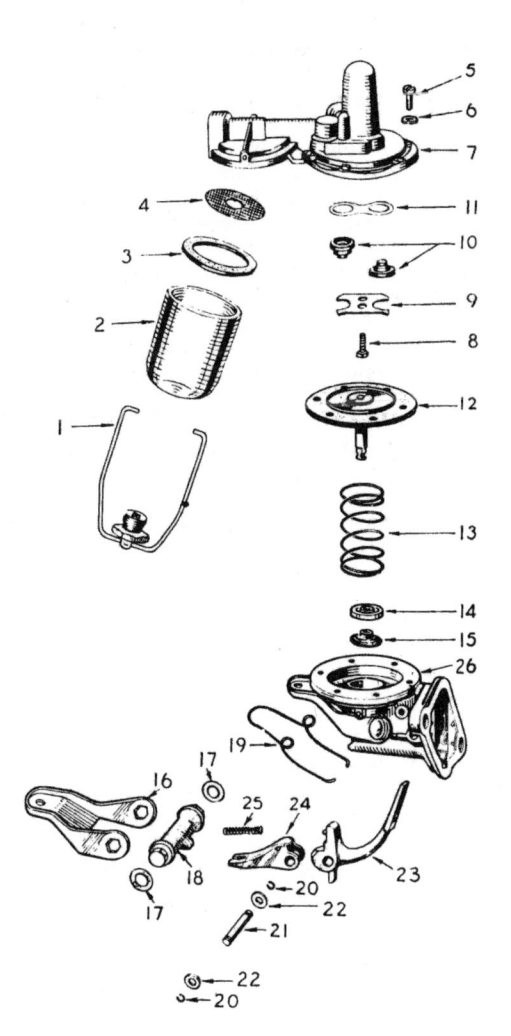

Fig.3.3. A.C. FUEL PUMP

1. Stirrup
2. Glass sediment bowl
3. Cork seal
4. Gauze filter
5. Securing screw
6. Lock washer
7. Upper body
8. Screw for retaining plate
9. Valve retaining plate
10.* Inlet and outlet valve assemblies
11. Valve gasket
12. Diaphragm assembly
13. Diaphragm spring
14. Oil seal retainer
15. Oil seal
16. Primer lever
17. Cork washer
18. Primer lever shaft
19. Hand primer spring
20. Circlip
21. Rocker arm pin
22. Washer
23. Rocker arm
24. Link lever
25. Rocker arm spring
26. Lower body

*These valves are identical, but on fitting them to the upper body the spring of the inlet valve is pointing towards the diaphragm and the spring of the outlet valve away from the diaphragm, as shown in the illustration.

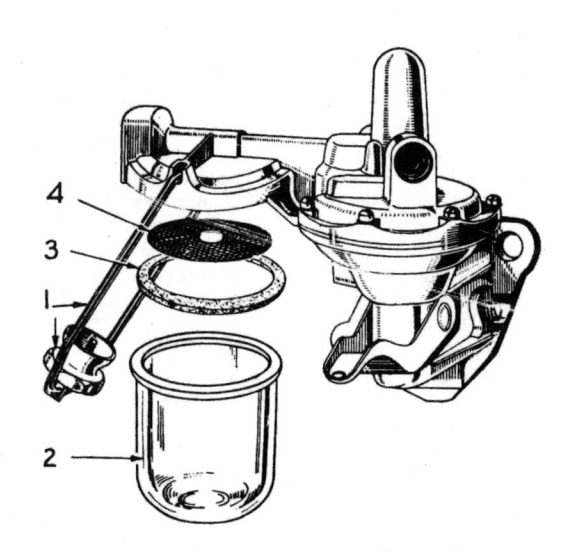

Fig. 3.3A. MAIN PARTS OF THE A.C. FUEL PUMP
1 Retaining stirrup
2 Cork seal
3 Glass sediment bowl
4 Gauze filter

79

Chapter 3/Fuel System & Carburation

the body flanges and hold the arm in this position. Re-assemble the two halves of the pump ensuring that the previously made marks on the flanges are adjacent to each other.

9. Insert the six screws and lockwashers and tighten them down finger tight.

10 Move the rocker arm up and down several times to centralise the diaphragm, and then with the arm held down, tighten the screws securely in a diagonal sequence.

11 Replace the gauze filter, cork washer and sediment bowl and refit the stirrup thumbscrew to the base of the sediment bowl. Tighten lightly only to ensure a fuel tight joint as overtightening will crack the bowl.

10. S.U. Carburettor - Routine Maintenance

1. Once every 3,000 miles undo the hexagon caps on the dashpot/s and top them up within ½ inch of the top with Castrolite or a similar S.A.E. 20 oil as shown under 'Recommended Lubricants', page 11.

2. Once every 6,000 miles adjust the carburettor slow running and tune the carburettors if necessary. See Sections 22 and 23 for further details. Check the fuel lines and the union joints for leaks or weeping and replace defective washers if required.

3. Also every 6,000 miles remove the float chambers from the carburettors, empty away any sediment, check the condition of the needle valve and clean and reassemble. Remove and clean the filters in the carburettors and fuel pump where these are fitted.

11. S.U. Carburettor - Description

The variable choke S.U. carburettor is a relatively simple instrument and is basically the same irrespective of its size and type. It differs from most other carburettors in that instead of having a number of various sized fixed jets for different conditions, only one variable jet is fitted to deal with all possible conditions.

Air passing rapidly through the carburettor choke draws petrol from the jet so forming the petrol/air mixture. The amount of petrol drawn from the jet depends on the position of the tapered carburettor needle, which moves up and down the jet orifice according to engine load and throttle opening, thus effectively altering the size of the jet so that exactly the right amount of fuel is metered for the prevailing road conditions.

The position of the tapered needle in the jet is determined by engine vacuum. The shank of the needle is held at its top end in a piston which slides up and down the dashpot in response to the degree of manifold vacuum. This is directly controlled by the position of the throttle.

With the throttle fully open, the full effect of the inlet manifold vacuum is felt by the piston which has an air bleed into the choke tube on the outside of the throttle. This causes the piston to rise fully, bringing the needle with it. With the accelerator partially closed only slight inlet manifold vacuum is felt by the piston (although, of course, on the engine side of the throttle the vacuum is now greater) and the piston only rises a little, blocking most of the jet orifice with the metering needle.

To prevent the piston fluttering and to give a richer mixture when the accelerator is suddenly depressed, an oil damper and light spring are fitted inside the dashpot.

The only portion of the piston assembly to come into contact with the piston chamber or dashpot is the actual central piston rod. All the other parts of the piston assembly, including the lower choke portion, have sufficient clearances to prevent any direct metal to metal contact which is essential if the carburettor is to work properly.

The correct level of the petrol in the carburettor is determined by the level of the float in the float chamber. When the level is correct the float rises and by means of a lever resting on top of it closes the needle valve in the cover of the float chamber. This closes off the supply of fuel from the pump. When the level in the float chamber drops as fuel is used in the carburettor the float sinks. As it does, the float needle comes away from its seat so allowing more fuel to enter the float chamber and restore the correct level.

12. S.U. Carburettor - Removal and Refitting

1. Undo the air filter to carburettor retaining bolts and lift away the air filter and paper gaskets.

2. If a closed circuit breathing system is fitted disconnect the breather pipe to the rocker cover.

3. Close the main fuel line petrol tap situated on the end of the main fuel line as it emerges into the engine compartment to stop the possibility of syphoning.

4. Disconnect the fuel lines from the carburettor float chamber covers and also the distributor automatic advance/retard pipe from the carburettor body.

5. Refer to Fig. 3.4 and disconnect the accelerator rod (77) followed by the mixture control cable from the linkage (25).

6. Slacken the throttle spindle clamp (76) and remove the jet control connection link (66) by first extracting the split pin (70). Withdraw the clevis pin (69). Undo the nut (72) and lift away the swivel pin (71) and plain washer (73).

7. On earlier models undo the two nuts holding each carburettor to the inlet manifold and withdraw the carburettors from the manifold followed by the gaskets (83, 85) (Fig. 3.5) and the insulator (84).

8. On later models undo the four nuts holding each carburettor to the inlet manifold and withdraw the carburettors from the manifold followed by the gaskets (83, 85) and the insulator (84).

9. Refitting the carburettors is the reverse sequence to removal. Check that the holes in the air filter line up with the matching holes in the carburettor flanges. Also ensure that the gaskets are fitted the correct way round. Finally top up the dampers with correct grade oil.

13. S.U. Carburettors - Dismantling

1. The S.U. carburettor is a straightforward instrument to service, but at the same time it is a delicate unit and clumsy handling can cause much damage. In particular, it is easy to knock the finely tapering needle out of true, and the greatest care should be taken to keep all parts associated with the dashpot scrupulously clean.

2. Remove the oil dashpot damper (3) (Fig. 3.4) by unscrewing it and lifting it away together with the fibre washer (4).

3. Turn the carburettor upside down and allow the oil in the damper well to drain out.

4. Scribe a mark on the suction chamber (2) and body (1) so that they may be correctly reassembled and undo the three screws (8).

5. Carefully lift off the suction chamber (2) followed by the spring (7). The piston may next be removed by lifting upwards until the needle is clear of the bridge of the body. It is recommended that the piston is stood upright on the top of a small glass jar so that the needle is inside the jar for protection against possible damage.

6. If necessary the needle (5) may be removed from the

Fig. 3.4. S.U. CARBURETTOR TYPE H.4

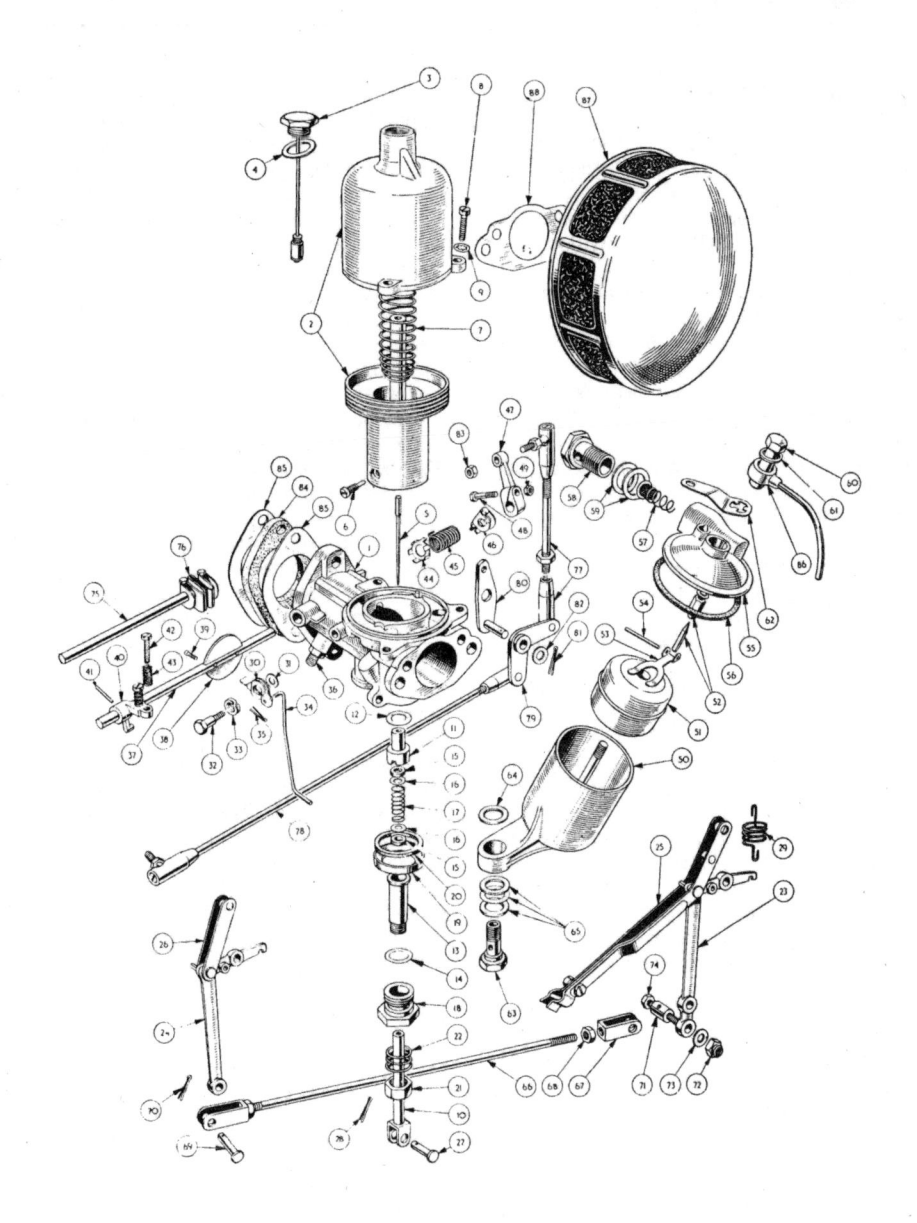

1 Body assembly
2 Suction chamber assembly
3 Damper assembly
4 Washer
5 Jet needle
6 Needle locking screw
7 Piston spring
8 Securing screw
9 Shakeproof washer
10 Jet head
11 Top half jet bearing
12 Washer
13 Bottom half jet bearing
14 Washer
15 Cork gland washer
16 Copper gland washer
17 Spring
18 Jet locking nut
19 Sealing ring
20 Cork washer
21 Jet adjusting nut
22 Loading spring
23 Jet lever

24 Jet lever
25 Jet lever link
26 Jet lever link
27 Clevis pin
28 Split pin
29 Jet lever return spring
30 Rocker lever
31 Washer for 30
32 Rocker lever bolt
33 Spring washer
34 Connecting rod
35 Split pin
36 Ignition connection union
37 Throttle spindle
38 Throttle disc
39 Throttle disc attachment screws
40 Throttle stop
41 Taper pin
42 Stop adjusting screw
43 Locking screw spring
44 Anchor plate
45 Return spring

46 End clip
47 Throttle lever
48 Pinch bolt
49 Nut for 48
50 Float chamber
51 Float
52 Needle and seat assembly
53 Hinged lever
54 Pin for hinged lever
55 Float chamber cover
56 Joint washer
57 Petrol inlet filter
58 Banjo bolt
59 Fibre washer
60 Cap nut
61 Aluminium washer
62 Float chamber support arm
63 Float chamber attachment bolt
64 Fibre washer
65 Washer
66 Jet control connecting rod

67 Fork end
68 Nut on fork end
69 Clevis pin
70 Split pin
71 Choke cable swivel pin
72 Nyloc nut
73 Plain washer
74 Screw
75 Throttle spindle connecting rod
76 Folding coupling
77 Short link rod assembly
78 Long link rod assembly
79 Bell crank lever
80 Pivot lever
81 Split pin
82 Plain washer
83 Nut
84 Insulating packing
85 Joint washer
86 Carburettor overflow pipe
87 Air cleaner
88 Air cleaner gasket

81

piston by undoing the screw (6) and withdrawing the needle. Note the position of the shoulder for correct refitting (See Fig. 3.4.A).

7. Undo the float chamber (50) to body (1) retaining bolt (63) and separate the two parts. Note the position of the washers (64, 65) to ensure correct reassembly.

8. Undo the bolt (60) on the top of the float chamber (50) and lift away the spill pipe (86) followed by the float chamber cover (55).

9. Invert the float chamber (50) and remove the float (51) making a note which way round it fits.

10 To remove the needle valve assembly (52) from the float chamber cover first carefully extract the pin (54) which will then free the fork (53). Using a small box spanner unscrew the needle valve assembly (52) from the float chamber cover (56).

11 Extract the split pin (28) from the clevis pin (27) in the jet head assembly (10) and remove the clevis pin (27). Carefully withdraw the jet head (10) downwards from the jet assembly.

12 Using an open ended spanner undo the jet assembly locking nut (18) which will allow all the components to be removed from the body. Take extreme caution with removing the various parts and note the exact position of items for correct reassembly.

13 Undo the jet adjustment nut (21) from the lower half of the jet bearing (13) and the parts of the jet assembly may be completely separated.

14 Normally it is not necessary to dismantle the carburettor any further but if, because of wear or for some other reason it is necessary to remove the throttle and spindle, undo the two throttle disc to spindle screws noting that the circumference is tapered and must be refitted the correct way round. Slide out the throttle spindle (37) from the body.

15 Reassembly is a straightforward reversal of the dismantling procedure. It will, however, be necessary to centre the jet and the procedure for this is given in Section 21 of this Chapter.

16 Whenever the carburettor is dismantled it is recommended that new washers and gaskets are always used, especially in the jet assembly. This is because the washers settle to a certain working position and when disturbed do not return to their original position. Check that the carburettor mounting flange is not distorted and always fit a new gasket and insulator if signs of distortion are evident.

14. S.U. Carburettor Float Chamber - Dismantling, Examination and Reassembly

1. To dismantle the float chamber, first disconnect the inlet pipe from the fuel pump at the top of the float chamber if this has not already been done.

2. Lift away the float chamber cover and spill pipe noting the position of any washers.

3. If it is not wished to remove the float chamber completely and the carburettor is still attached to the engine, carefully insert a thin piece of bent wire under the float and lift the float out.

4. To remove the float chamber from the carburettor body undo the bolt located on the extension of the float chamber.

5. Make a note carefully of the seals and washers and on reassembly ensure they are replaced in the correct order. If the float chamber is removed completely it is a simple matter to turn it upside down to drop the float out. Check that the float is not cracked or leaking by immersion in warm water. If it is, it must be repaired or renewed.

6. The float chamber cover contains the needle valve assembly which regulates the amount of fuel which is fed into the float chamber.

7. One end of the float lever rests on top of the float rising and falling with it, while the other end pivots on a hinge pin which is held by two lugs. On the float cover side of the float lever is a needle which rises and falls in its brass seating according to the movement of the lever.

8. With the cover in place the hinge pin is held in position by the walls of the float chamber. With the cover removed the pin is easily pushed out so freeing the float lever and the needle.

9. Examine the tip of the needle and the needle seating for wear. Wear is present when there is a discernable ridge in the chamfer of the needle. If this is evident then the needle and seating must be renewed. This is a simple operation and the hexagon head of the needle housing is easily screwed out using a small box spanner.

10 Never renew either the needle or the seating without renewing the other part as otherwise it will not be possible to obtain a fuel tight joint.

11 Clean the fuel chamber out thoroughly. Reassembly is a reversal of the dismantling procedure detailed above. Before replacing the float chamber cover check that the fuel level setting is correct as detailed in Section 15.

15. S.U. Carburettor Float Chamber - Fuel Level Adjustment

1. It is essential that the fuel level in the float chamber is always correct otherwise excessive fuel consumption may occur. Carry out fuel level adjustment of the float chamber cover in the following manner.

2. Refer to Fig. 3.6. and hold the float chamber cover upside down. Place a 7/16 inch diameter bar, or shank of a drill across the centre of the cover. Check if the forked lever does not contact both the needle valve and the bar or drill and adjust as necessary by bending the lever at the commencement of the forked section. It is important that both prongs of the fork are level with each other.

16. S.U. Carburettor - Examination and Repair

The S.U. carburettor generally speaking is most reliable, but even so it may develop one of several faults which may not be readily apparent unless a careful inspection is carried out. The common faults the carburettor is prone to are:-

1) Piston sticking.
2) Float needle sticking.
3) Float chamber flooding.
4) Water and dirt in the carburettor.

In addition the following parts are susceptible to wear after long mileages; as they vitally affect the economy of the engine they should be checked and renewed, where necessary, every 24,000 miles.

a) The carburettor needle. If this has been incorrectly assembled at some time so that it is not centrally located in the jet orifice, then the metering needle will have a tiny ridge worn on it. If a ridge can be seen then the needle must be renewed. S.U. carburettor needles are made to very fine tolerances and should a ridge be apparent no attempt should be made to rub the needle down with fine emery paper. If it is wished to clean the needle it can be polished lightly with metal polish.

b) The carburettor jet. If the needle is worn it is likely that the rim of the jet will be damaged where the needle has been striking it. It should be renewed as otherwise

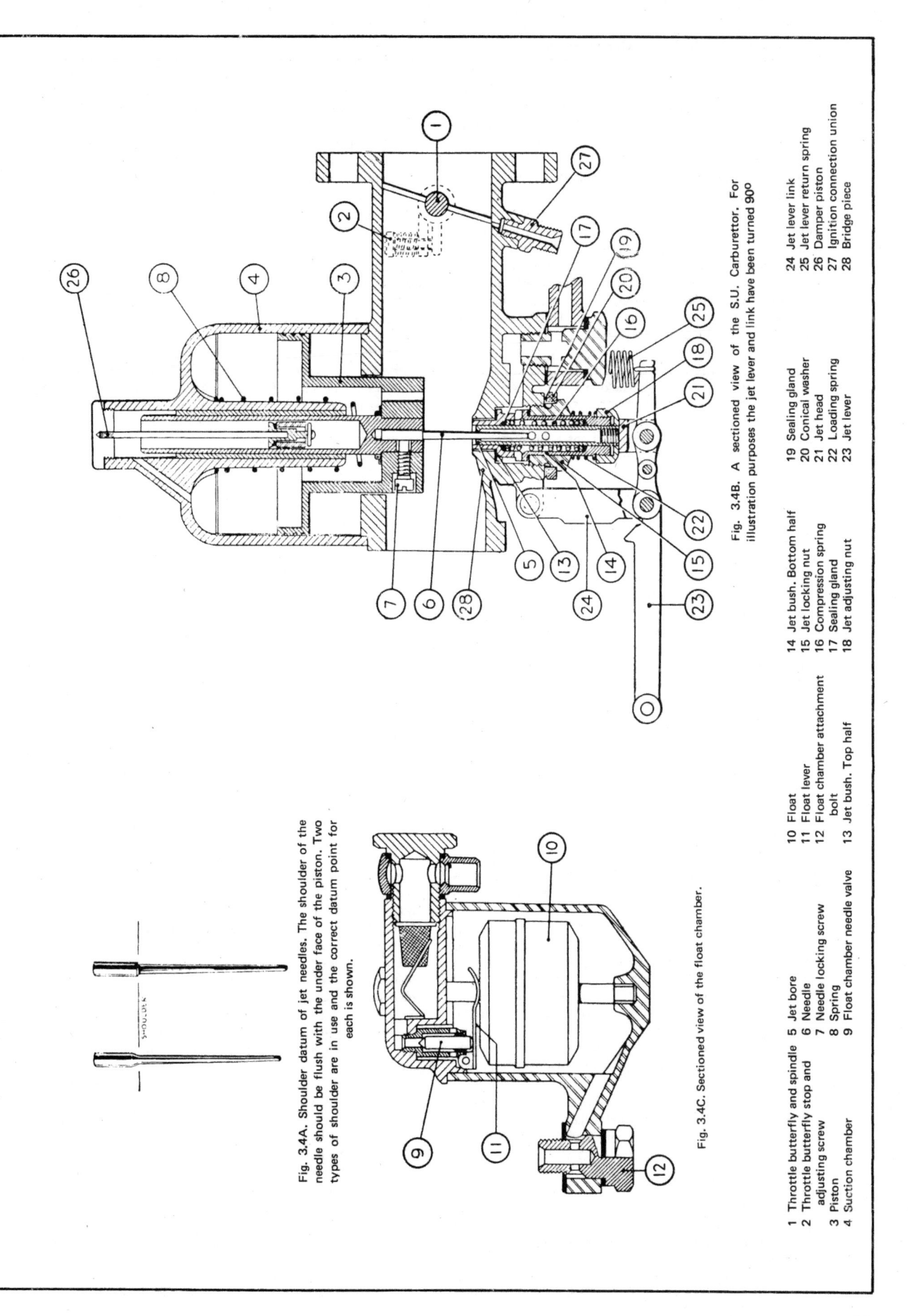

Fig. 3.4A. Shoulder datum of jet needles. The shoulder of the needle should be flush with the under face of the piston. Two types of shoulder are in use and the correct datum point for each is shown.

Fig. 3.4B. A sectioned view of the S.U. Carburettor. For illustration purposes the jet lever and link have been turned 90°.

Fig. 3.4C. Sectioned view of the float chamber.

1 Throttle butterfly and spindle
2 Throttle butterfly stop and adjusting screw
3 Piston
4 Suction chamber
5 Jet bore
6 Needle
7 Needle locking screw
8 Spring
9 Float chamber needle valve
10 Float
11 Float lever
12 Float chamber attachment bolt
13 Jet bush. Top half
14 Jet bush. Bottom half
15 Jet locking nut
16 Compression spring
17 Sealing gland
18 Jet adjusting nut
19 Sealing gland
20 Conical washer
21 Jet head
22 Loading spring
23 Jet lever
24 Jet lever link
25 Jet lever return spring
26 Damper piston
27 Ignition connection union
28 Bridge piece

83

Chapter 3/Fuel System & Carburation

fuel consumption will suffer. The jet can also be badly worn or ridged on the outside from where it has been sliding up and down between the jet bearings every time the choke has been pulled out. Removal and renewal is the only answer here as well.

c) Check the edges of the throttle and the choke tube for wear. Renew if worn.

d) The washers fitted to the base of the jet, to the float chamber, and to the petrol inlet union may all leak after a time and can cause much fuel wastage. It is wisest to renew them automatically when the carburettor is stripped down.

e) After high mileages the float chamber needle and seat are bound to be ridged. They are not an expensive item to replace and should be renewed as a set. They should never be renewed separately.

17. S.U. Carburettor - Piston Sticking

1. The hardened piston rod which slides in the centre guide tube in the middle of the dashpot is the only part of the piston assembly (which comprises the jet needle, suction disc, and piston choke) that should make contact with the dashpot.

2. The piston rim and the choke periphery are machined to very fine tolerances so that they will not touch the dashpot or the choke tube walls.

3. After high mileages wear in the centre guide tube (especially on semi-downdraught S.U's.) may allow the piston to touch the dashpot wall. This condition is known as sticking.

4. If piston sticking is suspected or it is wished to test for this condition, rotate the piston about the centre guide tube at the same time sliding it up and down inside the dashpot.

5. If any portion of the piston makes contact with the dashpot wall then that portion of the wall must be polished with metal polish until clearance exists. In extreme cases, fine emery cloth can be used.

6. The greatest care should be taken to remove only the minimum amount of metal to provide the clearance, as too large a gap will cause air leakage and will upset the functioning of the carburettor.

7. Clean down the walls of the dashpot and the piston rim and ensure that there is no oil on them. A trace of oil may be judiciously applied to the piston rod.

8. If the piston is sticking under no circumstances try to clear it by trying to alter the tension of the light return spring.

18. S.U. Carburettor - Float Needle Sticking

1. If the float needle sticks the carburettor will soon run dry and the engine will stop despite there being fuel in the tank.

2. The easiest way to check a suspected sticking float needle is to remove the inlet pipe at the carburettor and spin the engine.

3. If fuel spurts from the end of the pipe (direct it towards the ground or into a wad of cloth or jar), then the fault is almost certain to be a sticking float needle.

4. Remove the float chamber and dismantle the valve as detailed on page 82 and clean the housing and float chamber out thoroughly.

19. S.U. Carburettor - Float Chamber Flooding

If fuel emerges from the small breather hole or spill pipe in the cover of the float chamber this condition is known as flooding. It is caused by the float chamber needle not seating properly in its housing, normally because a piece of dirt or foreign matter has become jammed between the needle and the needle housing. Alternatively, the float may have developed a leak or be maladjusted so that it is holding open the float chamber needle valve even though the chamber is full of petrol. Remove the float chamber cover, clean the needle assembly, check the setting of the float, and shake the float to verify if any petrol has leaked into it.

20. S.U. Carburettor - Water and Dirt in Carburettor

1. Because of the size of the jet orifice, water or dirt in the carburettor is normally easily cleared.

2. If dirt in the carburettor is suspected lift the piston assembly and flood the float chamber. The normal level of fuel should be about $1/16$ inch below the top of the jet and on flooding the carburettor the fuel should well up out of the jet hole.

3. If very little or no petrol appears, start the engine (the jet is never completely blocked) and with the throttle fully open, blank off the air intake. This will create a partial vacuum in the choke tube and help to suck out any foreign matter from the jet tube. Release the throttle as soon as the engine starts to race. Repeat this procedure several times, stop the engine, and then check the carburettor as detailed in the first paragraph.

4. If this has failed to do the trick then there is no alternative but to remove and blow out the jet.

21. S.U. Carburettor - Jet Centering

1. This sequence of operations will be necessary whenever the carburettor has been completely stripped down or when a new jet needle (5) (Fig. 3.4) is fitted or the jet locking nut (18) distorted.

2. If the carburettor has not been dismantled unscrew and remove the damper assembly from the top of the carburettor.

3. Extract the split pin (28) and remove the clevis pin (27) from the jet head (10). Disconnect the linkage from the jet head (10).

4. Carefully withdraw the jet head downwards and unscrew the jet adjusting nut (21). Lift away the spring (22) and replace the adjusting nut and screw it up as far as it will go taking extreme care not to overtighten.

5. Slacken the locknut (18) by about half a turn.

6. Using a small knife or electricians screwdriver through the air intake end of the carburettor raise the piston to its highest point of travel and then allow it to drop under its own weight.

7. Insert a pencil or the electricians screwdriver through the damper hole in the top of the carburettor and gently push the piston down to the bottom of its travel if it is not already there.

8. If the piston does not move freely repeat the lifting and pressing down operation and after a further three times it should be free. If not, remove the suction chamber and piston (2) and clean them.

9. Gently press the piston down and at the same time tighten the locknut (18). Then lift up the piston and allow it to drop under its own weight. A metallic noise should be heard as it contacts the bridge.

10 Pull the jet head (10) down as far as it will go and repeat the piston drop test and compare the metallic noise previously obtained. If it is harder for the second test the jet must be centred again.

11 If after several attempts satisfactory results are not

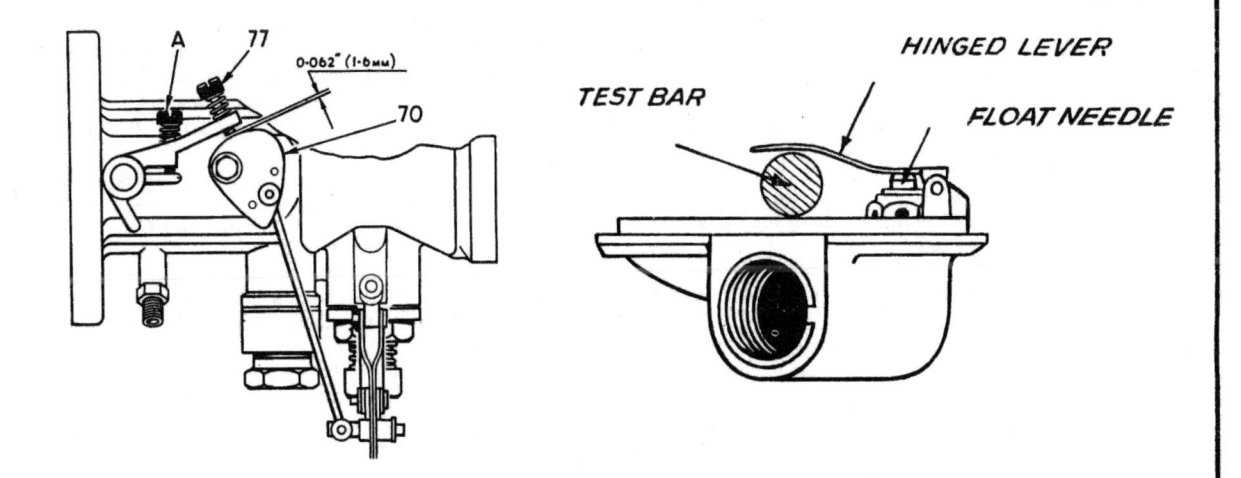

Fig. 3.5A.(1) Jet and throttle interconnection adjustment

Fig. 3.6. S.U. Carburettor float chamber hinged lever setting.

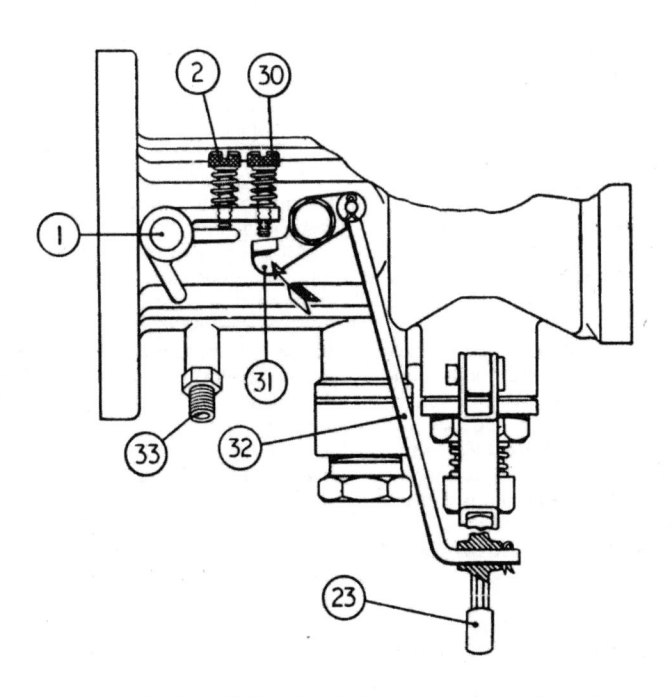

Fig. 3.5A. (2) Throttle and mixture control interconnection.
Early TR Models.

Chapter 3/Fuel System & Carburation

obtained the cause is probably a bent needle.

12 When satisfactory results have been obtained, carefully withdraw the jet head (10) and refit the spring (22) under the adjusting nut (21) and replace the jet head. Screw the adjusting nut (21) up as far as it will go taking care not to strain it and then undo it two and a half turns which is a rough setting for the correct mixture strength.

22. S.U. Carburettor - Adjustment and Tuning

1. To adjust and tune the S.U. carburettor proceed in the following manner. Check the colour of the exhaust idling speed with the choke fully in.
2. If the exhaust tends to be black, and the tailpipe interior is also black it is a fair indication that the mixture is too rich.
3. If the exhaust is colourless and the deposit in the exhuast pipe is a very light grey it is likely that the mixture is too weak.
4. This condition may also be accompanied by intermittent misfiring, while too rich a mixture will be associate with 'hunting'. Ideally the exhaust should be colourless with a medium grey pipe deposit.
5. Once the engine has reached its normal operating temperature, disconnect the carburettors so each can be worked independently by slackening the bolts on the interconnecting shaft.
6. Only two adjustments are provided on the S.U. carburettor. Idling speed is governed by the throttle adjusting screw, and the mixture strength by the jet adjusting screw. The S.U. carburettor is correctly adjusted for the whole of its engine revolution range when the idling mixture strength is correct.
7. Idling speed adjustment is effected by the idling adjusting screw. To adjust the mixture set the engine to run at about 1,000 r.p.m. by screwing in the idling screw. Repeat this procedure for each instrument in turn.
8. Check the mixture strength by lifting the piston of the carburettor approximately 1/32 inch (8 mm) with a thin wire spoke or small screwdriver so as to disturb the airflow as little as possible, when, if,

a) the speed of the engine increases appreciably the mixture is too rich.
b) the engine speed immediately decreases the mixture is too weak.
c) the engine speed increases very slightly the mixture is correct.

9. To enrich the mixture rotate the adjusting screw which is the screw at the bottom of the carburettor, in an anticlockwise direction, i.e., downward. To weaken the mixture rotate the jet adjusting screw in a clockwise direction, i.e. upwards. Only turn the adjusting screw a flat at a time and check the mixture strength between each turn. It is likely that there will be a slight increase or decrease in r.p.m. after the mixture adjustment has been made so the throttle idling adjusting screw should now be turned so that the engine idles at between 600 and 700 r.p.m.

23. S.U. Carburettor - Jet and Throttle Interconnection Adjustment

1. When the choke is pulled right out, the jet is lowered to enrich the mixture. At the same time the interconnecting rod operates a cam which opens the throttle slightly and then opens it further as the choke is pushed in, so as to give a fast idling speed. When fully pushed in the choke closes the throttle.
2. To ensure the position of the throttle is correct in relationship to the position of the jet establish that a clearance of 1/16 inch (1.5 mm) exists between the end of the adjustment screw (77) in Fig.3.5a and the rocker lever cam (70). Take this measurement with the choke fully in, and the engine warm and idling normally. Adjust the screw (77) as required to give the correct gap. This adjustment must always be made after the throttle stop screw 'A' has been turned.

24. Synchronisation of Twin S.U. Carburettors

1. First ensure that the mixture is correct in each instrument. With twin S.U. carburettors, in addition to the mixture strength being correct for each instrument, the idling suction must be equal on both. It is best to use a vacuum synchronising device such as the Motor Meter synchro-tester. If this is not available, it is possible to obtain fairly accurate synchronization by listening to the hiss made by the air flow into the intake throats of each carburettor.
2. The aim is to adjust the throttle butterfly disc so that an equal amount of air enters each carburettor. Loosen the clamping bolts on the throttle spindle connections. Listen to the hiss from each carburettor and if a difference in intensity is noticed between them, then unscrew the throttle adjusting screw on the other carburettor until the hiss from both the carburettors are the same.
3. With a vacuum synchronization device all that it is necessary to do is to place the instrument over the mouth of each carburettor in turn and adjust the adjusting screws until the reading on the gauge is identical for both carburettors.
4. Tighten the clamping bolts on the throttle spindle connections which connect the throttle disc of the two carburettors together, at the same time holding down the throttle adjusting screws against their idling stops. Synchronization of the two carburettors is now complete.

25. Stromberg 175 CD Carburettor - Description

TR4A models covered by this manual were fitted with Stromberg 175 CD carburettors instead of the twin S.U. carburettors fitted to the earlier models.

Although the principle of operation is similar to that of the S.U. carburettor there are certain constructional differences which are described below.

When starting from cold pulling the choke out rotates the lever (6) and bar (20) (All references are to Fig. 3.7.) which lifts the piston type air valve and needle (18, 29). On no account should the accelerator be pressed before the engine fires. The metering needle tapers slightly and fits into the jet orifice (19). The higher the needle is raised the richer the mixture becomes, because of the increased discharge area available at the mouth of the jet.

At the same time as the choke is pulled out a cam on the lever (6) opens the throttle beyond its normal idling position, the extent to which the throttle is opened, depending on the setting of the fast idle screw (4).

As soon as the engine starts, increased vacuum in the inlet manifold lifts the piston (18), so weakening the mixture to prevent the engine stalling because of over richness. As the engine warms up the choke is pushed in gradually until the lever (6) is back in its normal position.

When the throttle is opened the decrease in pressure in the induction manifold is also felt in the suction chamber (24), above the piston (18) because of the drilling (25) in the piston base. Because the suction chamber is sealed from

Fig. 3.7. SECTIONAL VIEW OF STROMBERG 175 CD CARBURETTOR

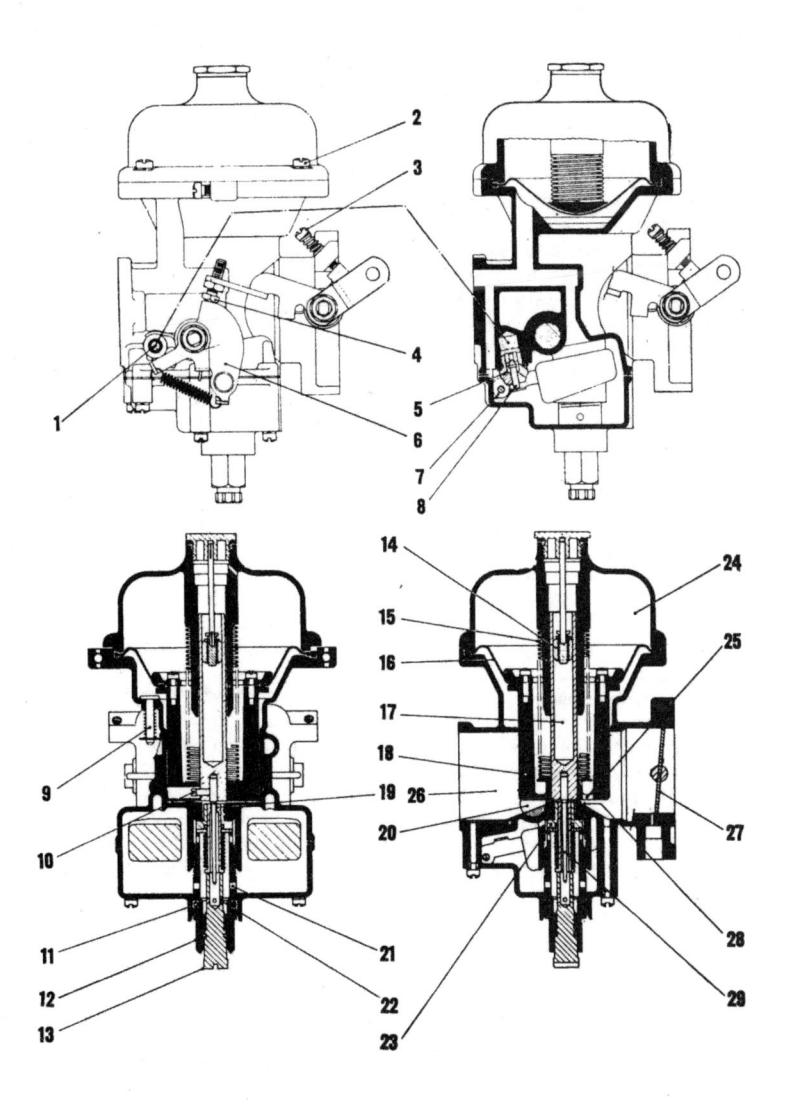

1 Petrol inlet	9 Spring-loaded pin	17 Guide rod	25 Air valve drilling
2 Screws	10 Locking screw	18 Air valve piston	26 Bore
3 Throttle stop screw	11 'O' ring	19 Jet orifice	27 Throttle
4 Screw	12 Jet assembly	20 Starter bar	28 Bridge
5 Needle seating	13 Jet adjusting screw	21 Inlet hole	29 Metering needle
6 Lever	14 Damper	22 Inlet hole	
7 Float arm	15 Coil spring	23 Orifice bush	
8 Needle	16 Diaphragm	24 Chamber	

87

Chapter 3/Fuel System & Carburation

the main body (25) by means of a diaphragm (16) pressure above the piston is decreased and the piston lifts. As this happens, the choke area is increased and the depression above the piston is reduced. In this way the pressure drop across the jet orifice and air velocity remains virtually constant at all speeds irrespective of throttle opening. Thus the piston rises and falls, and the choke area varies as the engine's demands alter. The tapered needle protruding from the base of the piston moves up and down in the jet, and the space between the needle and the jet increases and decreases as the piston rises and falls.

This of course, varies the mixture strength, and accounts for the influence of needle shape on engine performance.

Snap acceleration requires a richer mixture. The Stromberg is now faced with an additional difficulty; sudden throttle opening could increase suction over the piston to such an extent that the piston would rise very rapidly to the top of the chamber. This would lower the depression in the jet and cause a weakening of the mixture just when it should be enriched. In fact, this difficulty is avoided by the inclusion of a piston damper in the design. The oil well in the middle of the piston rod has a spindle in it which is attached to the screw cap. On the end of the spindle is a sleeve which provides opposition to the oil flow as the piston rises, but not when it falls. This obstruction decreases the speed of the piston's rise and thus increases mixture strength when the throttle is opened suddenly. The level of this S.A.E. 20 oil should be up to ¼ inch of the end of the well.

26. Stromberg 175 CD Carburettor - Adjustment

1. As there is no separate idling jet, the mixture for all conditions is supplied by the main jet and variable choke. Thus the strength of the mixture throughout the range depends on the height of the jet in the carburettor body and when the idling mixture is correct, the mixture will be correct throughout the range. A slotted nut (13) at the base of the carburettor increases or decreases the strength of the mixture. Turning the nut clockwise raises the jet and weakens the mixture. Turning the jet anti-clockwise enriches the mixture. The idling speed is controlled by the throttle stop screw (3).
2. To adjust a Stromberg 175 CD carburettor from scratch, run the engine until it is at its normal working temperature and then remove the air cleaner and damper and cap assembly. Press and hold the piston down with a length of wire held in the oil well so the underside of the piston rests on the bridge of the choke (27). With a coin, screw up clockwise the slotted jet adjustment nut (13) until the head of the jet can be felt to just touch the underside of the piston.
3. Then, from the position referred to in the previous paragraph, turn the jet screw anti-clockwise three full turns. This will give an appropriate setting. Start the engine and adjust the idle screw (3) so the engine runs fairly slowly and smoothly (about 600/800 r.p.m.) without rocking on its mountings. To get the engine to run smoothly at this speed it may be necessary to turn the jet adjustment nut a small amount in either direction.
4. To test if the correct setting has been found lift the piston 1/32 inch through the air intake with an electrical spanner or wire spoke. This is a very small amount and care should be taken to lift the piston only fractionally. If the engine speed rises the mixture is too rich and if it hesitates or stalls it is too weak. Re-adjust the jet adjusting nut and recheck. All is correct when the engine speed does not increase when the piston is lifted the requisite amount.

27. Stromberg 175 CD Carburettor - Float Chamber Fuel Level Adjustment

1. Take off the air cleaners as described in Section 3 of this chapter, and then remove the carburettor from the engine.
2. Undo the five small screws which hold the float chamber to the base of the carburettor body.
3. Turn the carburettor body upside down and accurately measure the highest point of the floats which should be 0.73 in. (18.5 mm) above the flange normally adjacent to the float chamber (See Fig. 3.8). During this operation ensure that the needle is against its seating. To reset the level carefully bend the tag which bears against the end of the needle.

28. Stromberg 175 CD Carburettor - Removal and Refitting

1. Undo the air filter to carburettor retaining bolts and lift away the air filters and paper gaskets.
2. Refer to Fig. 3.9. which shows the linkage and disconnect the accelerator rod, choke cable and fuel lines at the carburettors.
3. Undo the two clamps that secure the throttle spindles and the mixture control rods between the two carburettors.
4. Undo the four bolts that secure each carburettor to the induction manifold and lift away the carburettors.
5. Refitting is the reverse sequence to removal.

29. Stromberg 175 CD Carburettor - Dismantling and Reassembly

1. With the carburettors on the bench undo and remove the damper cap and plunger (1) (Fig. 3.11). Then undo the four screws (2) which hold the suction chamber cover (3) in place and lift off the cover.
2. The piston (7) complete with the needle (51) and diaphragm (6) is then lifted out. Handle the assembly with the greatest of care as it is very easy to knock the needle out of true.
3. The bottom of the float chamber (36) is removed by undoing the five screws (39, 40) and the spring washers which hold it in place. Take out the pin and remove the float assembly (35).
4. If wished the needle (51) may be removed from the piston (7) by undoing the grub screw (8).
5. To remove the diaphragm (6) from the piston simply undo the four screws and washers (56) which hold the diaphragm retaining ring (55) in place.
6. The jet (43) and associated parts are removed after the jet locking nut has been undone.
7. On reassembly there are several points which should be noted particularly. The first is that if fitting a new needle to the piston ensure it has the same markings as the old stamped on it, and fit it so that the needle shoulder is perfectly flush with the base of the piston.
8. Thoroughly clean the piston and its cylinder in paraffin and when replacing the jet centralise it as described in paragraphs 12 and 14.
9. Refit the jet and associated parts, lift the piston and tighten the jet assembly.
10 Turn the mixture adjusting nut clockwise until the tip of the jet is just above the choke bridge. Now loosen the jet assembly about one turn so as to free the orifice bush (47).
11 Allow the piston to fall. As it descends the needle will enter the orifice and automatically centralise it. With the needle still in the orifice tighten the jet assembly slowly, frequently raising and dropping the piston ¼ inch to ensure

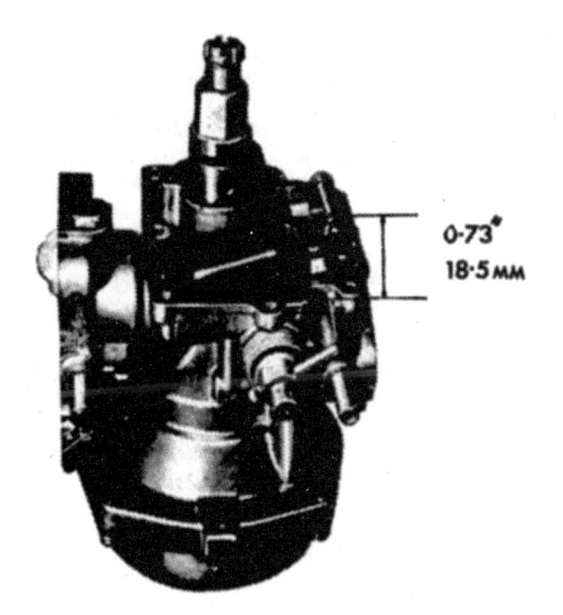

Fig. 3.8. The float level is correct when the distance between the bottom of the float and the flange is 0.73″ (18.5 mm).

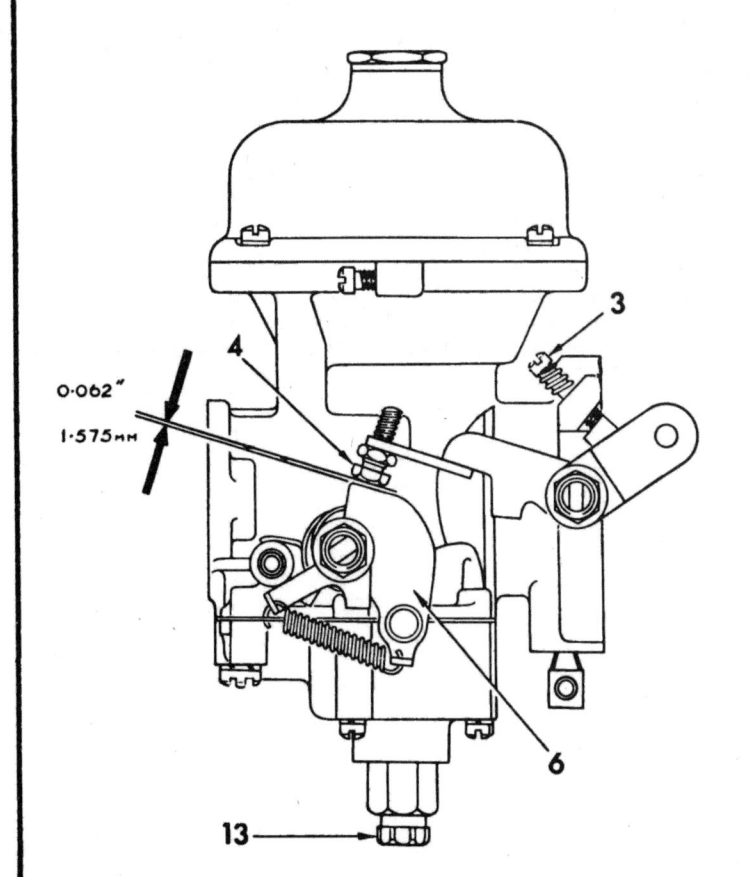

Fig. 3.9. Linkage between the two carburettors.

3 Throttle stop screw
4 Throttle interconnection adjustment screw
13 Jet adjusting screws
18 Air valve
30 Throttle interconnection clamping bolts

Fig. 3.10. THE GAP BETWEEN THE TWO ARROWS AND EXTENDED LINES SHOULD BE 0.062″ (1.575 mm)

3 Throttle stop screw
4 Screw
6 Lever
13 Jet adjusting screw

89

Chapter 3/Fuel System & Carburation

the orifice bush has not moved. Finally check that the piston drops freely without hesitation and hits the bridge with a soft metallic sound.

12 Make sure that the holes in the diaphragm line up with the screw holes in the piston and retaining ring, and that the diaphragm is correctly positioned. Reassembly is otherwise a straightforward reversal of the dismantling sequence.

30. Synchronization of Twin Stromberg Carburettors

1. Slacken off the clamping bolts (30) (Fig. 3.9) on the throttle spindle couplings between the two carburettors.
2. Unscrew both throttle stop screws (3) to allow the throttles in each carburettor to close completely. Now retighten the clamping bolts.
3. Ensure that the screw (4) is adjusted to give a gap of 1/16 inch (1.575 mm) as shown in Fig. 3.10.
4. Screw in the throttle stop screws (3) until they just make contact with the carburettor body. Then rotate each screw one complete turn thus opening both throttles an equal amount.
5. The two carburettors are now synchronized and tuning adjustments as detailed in Section 26 must now be carried out.

31. Fuel Line Tap

The tap is situated on a bracket on the side of the left hand chassis member and is of the Ewarts push and pull type. It is locked in the open position by rotating the plunger head in an anti-clockwise direction about 1/8 of a turn.

Should the tap show signs of leaking remove the small round head screw on the side of the tap body and extract the plunger assembly. Inspect the cork seal and if it shows signs of damage it should be renewed and to do this unlock the lock nut situated at the top of the plunger and unscrew the centre rod.

If the cork is not damaged it may be made to fit better into the tap by screwing in the centre rod. This will cause the cork to expand, therefore making it a tighter fit in the tap, thereafter making the tap harder to open and close.

32. Fuel Tank - Removal and Replacement

1. If it is known beforehand that the fuel tank is to be removed, it is advisable to allow the level of fuel to drop so that the minimum has to be drained from the tank.
2. For safety reasons disconnect the battery earth terminal and remove the filler cap.
3. Place a container under the fuel tank of a suitable capacity to collect fuel from the tank and remove the drain plug situated in the centre of the tank.
4. Undo and remove the centre capping of the rear elbow rail retaining screws and slide the capping to one side until its other end is clear of the side capping. Withdraw the centre section.
5. Empty the luggage compartment of tools, etc., and undo the carpet fixing screws and lift away the carpet. Undo and remove the fuel tank cover board fixing screws. Ease the board from the side capping and upper retaining clips and lift away the cover board.
6. Slacken the filler hose clips on the filler pipe assembly. Gently ease the short hose from the tank filler neck.
7. Undo and remove the banjo bolt securing the vent pipe to the tank.
8. Disconnect the electric cable from the fuel gauge tank sender unit.
9. Undo the petrol feed pipe from the underside of the tank taking care not to kink the metal pipe.
10 Undo and remove the four tank securing bolts and lock washers and lift away the tank retaining straps and felt packing.
11 The fuel tank may now be lifted away from the car.
12 Refitting is the reverse sequence to removal.

33. Crankcase Breather Valve (TR4A)

1. On TR4A models covered by this manual closed circuit breathing was fitted to cars destined for certain markets. If fitted the system should be serviced as follows.
2. Every 20,000 miles the crankcase emission control mounted on the inlet manifold must be serviced. This enables the fumes created in the crankcase to be fed into the inlet manifold where they are carried in with the petrol/air mixture and burnt in the cylinders.
3. Referring to Fig. 3.12 remove the interconnecting pipes (8, 11), remove the spring clip (1) and cover plate (2) and lift out the rubber diaphragm (3) noting the correct fitting position of its top face.
4. Remove the spring (4) and clean all the components, pipes and the body in clean petrol or methylated spirits.
5. Renew the diaphragm if this appears to be damaged in any way and reassemble in the reverse order to the above procedure.

Fig. 3.11. STROMBERG 175 CD CARBURETTOR COMPONENT PARTS

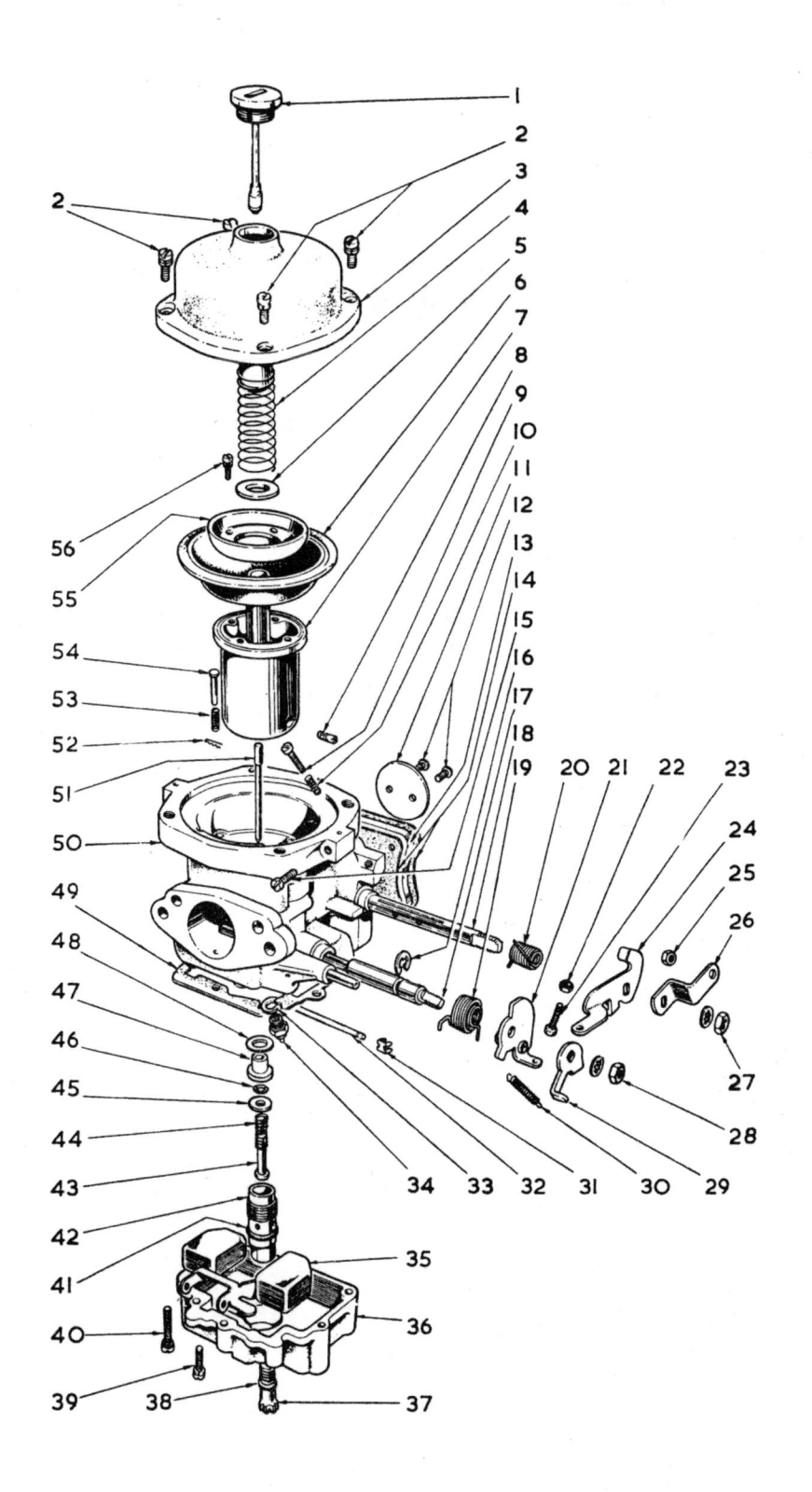

1 Damper
2 Screw
3 Cover
4 Return spring
5 Washer
6 Diaphragm air valve
7 Air valve
8 Locking screw
9 Clamping screw
10 Spring
11 Butterfly
12 Screw
13 Insulating washer
14 Joint
15 Screw
16 Retaining ring
17 Starter bar
18 Spindle
19 Spring
20 Spring
21 Lever
22 Nut
23 Screw
24 Lever
25 Nut
26 Lever
27 Nut
28 Nut
29 Lever
30 Spring
31 Clip
32 Fulcrum pin
33 Washer seating
34 Needle valve
35 Float assembly
36 Float chamber
37 Adjusting screw
38 'O' ring
39 Screw (short)
40 Screw (long)
41 'O' ring
42 Bushing screw
43 Jet
44 Spring
45 Washer
46 'O' ring
47 Jet bush
48 Washer
49 Gasket
50 Body
51 Needle
52 Clip
53 Spring
54 Pin
55 Retaining ring
56 Screw

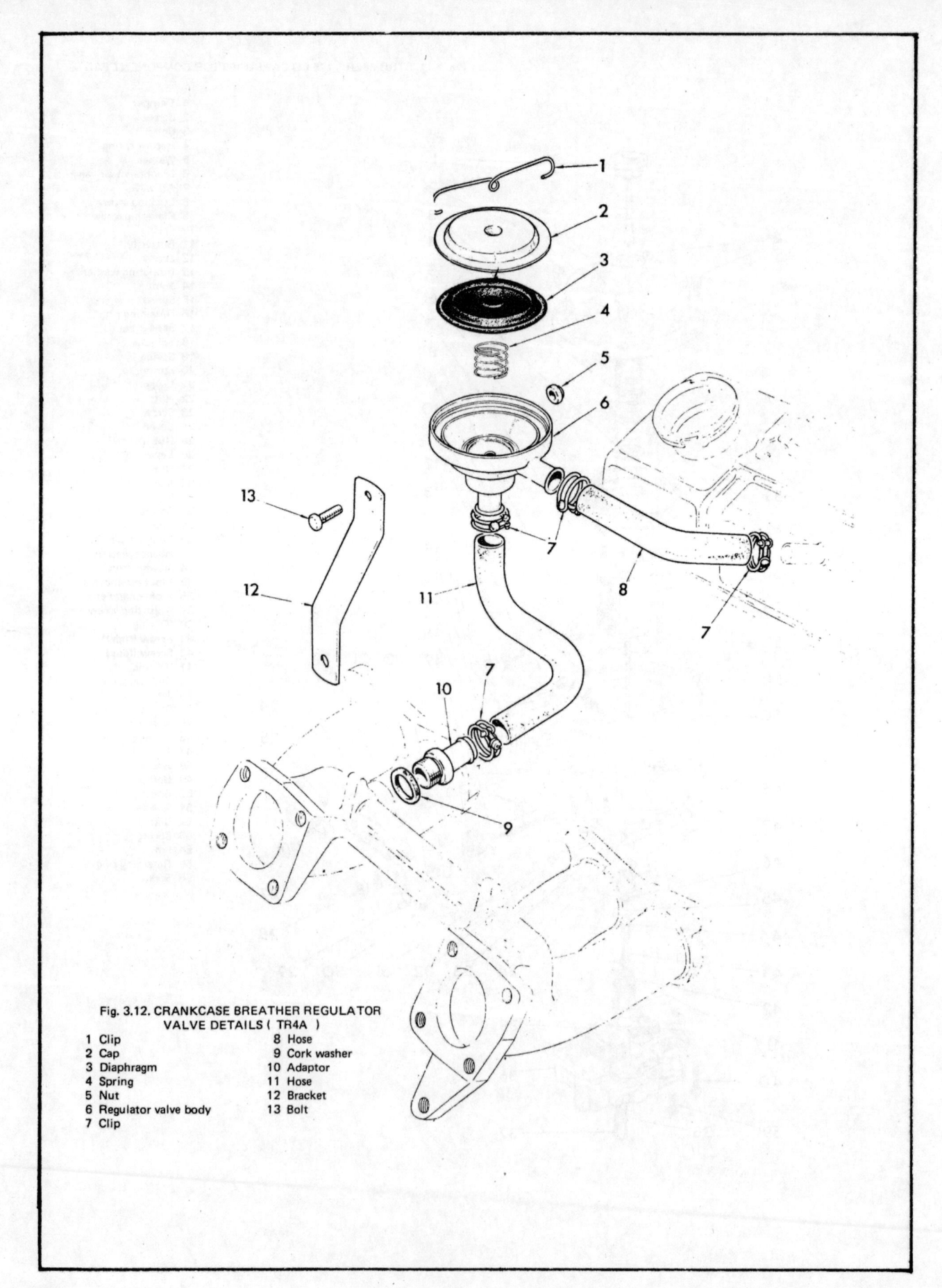

Fig. 3.12. CRANKCASE BREATHER REGULATOR
VALVE DETAILS (TR4A)

1 Clip
2 Cap
3 Diaphragm
4 Spring
5 Nut
6 Regulator valve body
7 Clip
8 Hose
9 Cork washer
10 Adaptor
11 Hose
12 Bracket
13 Bolt

Fault Finding Chart - Fuel System & Carburation

Cause	Trouble	Remedy
SYMPTOM: FUEL CONSUMPTION EXCESSIVE		
Carburation and ignition faults	Air cleaner choked and dirty giving rich mixture.	Remove, clean and replace air cleaner.
	Fuel leaking from carburettor(s), fuel pumps, or fuel lines.	Check for and eliminate all fuel leaks. Tighten fuel line union nuts.
	Float chamber flooding.	Check and adjust float level.
	Generally worn carburettor(s).	Remove, overhaul and replace.
	Distributor condenser faulty.	Remove, and fit new unit.
	Balance weights or vacuum advance mechanism in distributor faulty.	Remove, and overhaul distributor.
Incorrect adjustment	Carburettor(s) incorrectly adjusted mixture too rich.	Tune and adjust carburettor(s).
	Idling speed too high.	Adjust idling speed.
	Contact breaker gap incorrect.	Check and reset gap.
	Valve clearances incorrect.	Check rocker arm to valve stem clearances and adjust as necessary.
	Incorrect set sparking plugs.	Remove, clean, and regap.
	Tyres under-inflated.	Check tyre pressures and inflate if necessary.
	Wrong sparking plugs fitted.	Remove and replace with correct units.
	Brakes dragging.	Check and adjust brakes.
SYMPTOM: INSUFFICIENT FUEL DELIVERY OR WEAK MIXTURE DUE TO AIR LEAKS		
Dirt in system	Petrol tank air vent restricted.	Remove petrol cap and clean out air vent.
	Partially clogged filters in pump and carburettor(s).	Remove and clean filters.
	Dirt lodged in float chamber needle housing.	Remove and clean out float chamber and needle valve assembly.
	Incorrectly seating valves in fuel pump.	Remove, dismantle, and clean out fuel pump.
Fuel pump faults	Fuel pump diaphragm leaking or damaged.	Remove, and overhaul fuel pump.
	Gasket in fuel pump damaged.	Remove, and overhaul fuel pump.
	Fuel pump valves sticking due to petrol gumming.	Remove and thoroughly clean fuel pump.
Air leaks	Too little fuel in fuel tank. (Prevalent when climbing steep hills.)	Refill fuel tank.
	Union joints on pipe connections loose.	Tighten joints and check for air leaks.
	Split in fuel pipe on suction side of fuel pump.	Examine, locate, and repair.
	Inlet manifold to block or inlet manifold to carburettor(s) gasket leaking.	Test by pouring oil along joints - bubbles indicate leak. Renew gasket as appropriate.

Chapter 4/Ignition System

Contents

General Description ... 1	Distributor - Reassembly ... 9
Contact Breaker - Adjustment ... 2	Ignition Timing ... 10
Removing & Replacing Contact Breaker Points ... 3	Sparking Plug Leads ... 11
Condenser - Removal, Testing & Replacement ... 4	Ignition System - Fault Finding ... 12
Distributor Lubrication ... 5	Ignition System - Fault Symptoms ... 13
Distributor - Removal ... 6	Fault Diagnosis - Engine Fails to Start ... 14
Distributor - Dismantling ... 7	Fault Diagnosis - Engine Misfires ... 15
Distributor - Inspection & Repair ... 8	

Specifications

	TR2, 3, 3A	TR4, 4A
Firing Order	1, 3, 4, 2	1, 3, 4, 2
Ignition Timing	4° B.T.D.C.	4° B.T.D.C.
Sparking Plugs:		
Reach	½ inch	½ inch
Gap	0.032 inch	0.025 inch
Type - normal road use	Champion L.10.S	Lodge CNY
- high speed touring	Champion L.11.S	Lodge HN
- competition work	Champion L.11.S	Lodge 2HN
- low octane use	Champion L.10	Lodge CN
Distributor:		
Type	Lucas DM2 type V.167	Lucas 25.D4
Rotation	Anti-clockwise	Anti-clockwise
Contact breaker point gap	0.015 inch	0.015 inch
Automatic advance	Centrifugal and vacuum	Centrifugal and vacuum
Contact breaker spring - tension	20 to 24 ounces measured at points	20 to 24 ounces
Max. advance (crankshaft degrees)	15 degrees	11 degrees
Vacuum advance (crankshaft degrees)	8 degrees	5.5 degrees
Automatic advance commences	200 r.p.m.	350 r.p.m. (H.C.)
		400 r.p.m. (L.C.)
Condenser capacity	.2 microfarad	.2 microfarad
Coil:		
Type	Lucas HA12	Lucas HA12
Resistance 20°C (68°F) in primary winding	3.1 to 3.5 ohms	3.1 to 3.5 ohms
Consumption - ignition switched on at 1,000 r.p.m.	3.9 amps	3.9 amps

1. General Description

In order that the engine can run correctly it is necessary for an electrical spark to ignite the fuel/air mixture in the combustion chamber at exactly the right moment in relation to engine speed and load. The ignition system is based on feeding low tension voltage from the battery to the coil where it is converted to high tension voltage. The high tension voltage is powerful enough to jump the sparking plug gap in the cylinders many times a second under high compression pressures, providing that the system is in good condition and that all adjustments are correct.

The ignition system is divided into two circuits; the low tension circuit and the high tension circuit.

The low tension circuit (sometimes known as the primary circuit) consists of the battery, lead to the control box, lead to the ignition switch, lead from the ignition switch to the low tension or primary coil windings (terminal SW), and the lead from the low tension coil windings (coil terminal CB) to the contact breaker points and condenser in the distributor.

Fig. 4.1. DISTRIBUTOR COMPONENT PARTS TR4, 4A

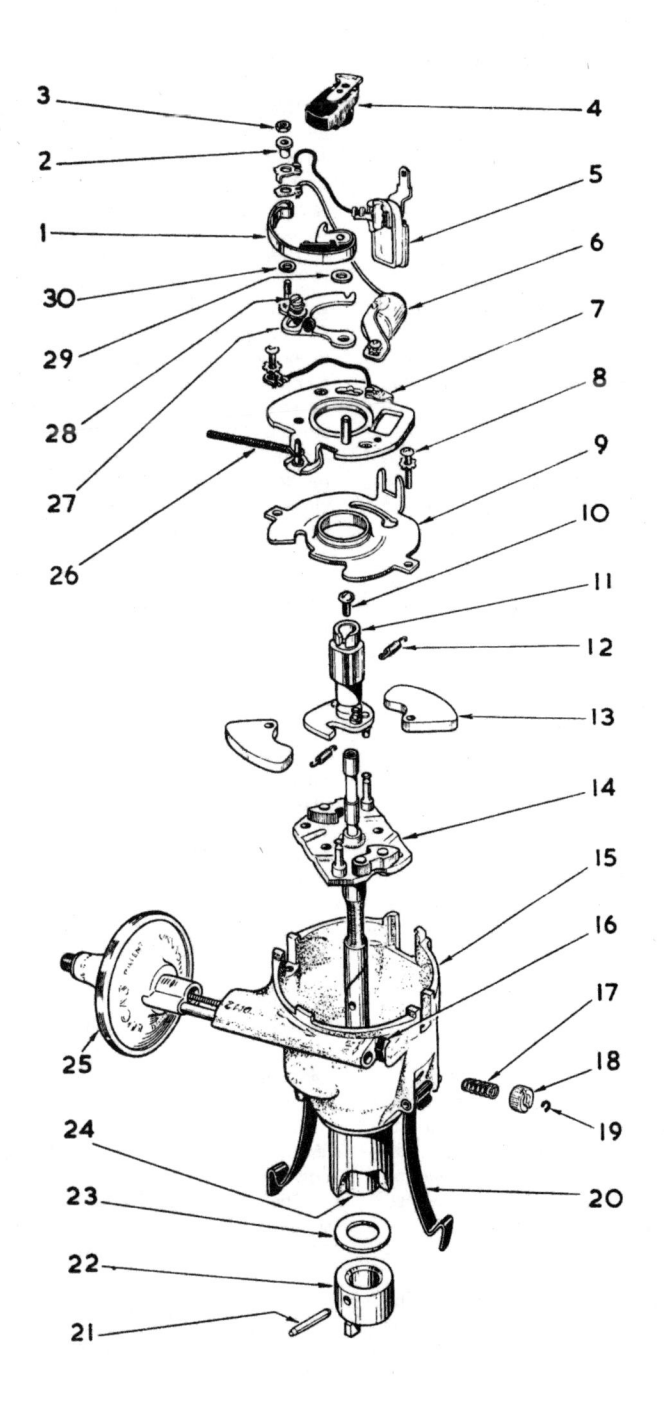

1 Spring contact
2 Insulating sleeve
3 Nut
4 Rotor arm
5 L.T. terminal
6 Capacitor
7 Contact plate
8 Screw
9 Base plate
10 Screw
11 Cam
12 Centrifugal spring
13 Centrifugal weights
14 Action plate and shaft assembly
15 Distributor body
16 Ratchet spring
17 Coiled spring
18 Adjusting nut
19 Circlip
20 Cap retainer
21 Pin
22 Driving dog
23 Washer
24 Bearing sleeve
25 Vacuum unit
26 Vacuum connecting spring
27 Fixed contact
28 Screw
29 Insulating washer
30 Insulating washer

Chapter 4/Ignition System

The high tension circuit consists of the high tension or secondary coil windings, the heavy ignition lead from the centre of the coil to the centre of the distributor cap, the rotor arm, and the sparking plug leads and sparking plugs. The system functions in the following manner:-

Low tension voltage is changed in the coil into high tension voltage by the opening and closing of the contact breaker points in the low tension circuit. High tension voltage is then fed via the carbon brush in the centre of the distributor cap to the rotor arm of the distributor. The rotor arm revolves inside the distributor cap and each time it comes in line with one of the four metal segments in the cap, which are connected to the sparking plug leads, the opening and closing of the contact breaker points causes the high tension voltage to build up, jump the gap from the rotor arm to the appropriate metal segment and so via the sparking plug lead to the sparking plug where it finally jumps the spark plug gap before going to earth.

The ignition is advanced and retarded automatically, to ensure the spark occurs at just the right instant for the particular load at the prevailing engine speed.

The ignition advance is controlled both mechanically and by a vacuum operated system. The mechanical governor mechanism comprises two lead weights which move out from the distributor shaft as the engine speed rises due to centrifugal force. As they move outwards they rotate the cam relative to the distributor shaft, and so advance the spark. The weights are held in position by two light springs and it is the tension of the springs which is largely responsible for correct spark advancement.

The vacuum control consists of a diaphragm, one side of which is connected via a small bore tube to the carburettor, and the other side to the contact breaker plate. Depression in the inlet manifold and carburettor, which varies with engine speed and throttle opening, causes the diaphragm to move, so moving the contact breaker plate, and advancing or retarding the spark. A fine degree of control is achieved by a spring in the vacuum assembly.

2. Contact Breaker - Adjustment

1. To adjust the contact breaker points to the correct gap, first pull off the two clips securing the distributor cap to the distributor body, and lift away the cap. Clean the cap inside and out with a dry cloth. It is unlikely that the four segments will be badly burned or scored, but if they are the cap will have to be renewed.
2. Push in the carbon brush located in the top of the cap once or twice to make sure that it moves freely.
3. Gently prise the contact breaker points open to examine the condition of their faces. If they are rough, pitted or dirty, it will be necessary to remove them for resurfacing, or for replacement points to be fitted.
4. Presuming the points are satisfactory, or that they have been cleaned and replaced, measure the gap between the points by turning the engine over until the contact breaker arm is on the peak of one of the four cam lobes.
5. A 0.015 inch feeler gauge should now just fit between the points.
6. If the gap varies slacken the contact plate securing screw (arrowed).
7. Adjust the contact gap by inserting a screwdriver in the notched hole (arrowed) at the end of the plate. Turning clockwise to decrease and anti-clockwise to increase the gap. Tighten the securing screw and check the gap again (small arrow).
8. Replace the rotor arm and distributor cap and clip the spring blade retainers into position.

3. Removing and Replacing Contact Breaker Points

1. If the contact breaker points are burned, pitted or badly worn, they must be removed and either replaced, or their faces must be filed smooth.
2. To remove the points unscrew the terminal nut and remove it together with the steel washer under its head. Remove the flanged nylon bush and then the condenser lead and the low tension lead from the terminal pin. Lift off the contact breaker arm and then remove the large fibre washer from the terminal pin.
3. The adjustable contact breaker plate is removed by unscrewing the one holding down screw and removing it, complete with spring and flat washer.
4. To reface the points rub their faces on a fine carborundum stone or on fine emery paper. It is important that the faces are rubbed flat and parallel to each other so that there will be complete face to face contact when the points are closed. One of the points will be pitted and the other will have deposits on it.
5. It is necessary to completely remove the built up deposits but not necessary to rub the pitted point right down to the stage where all the pitting has disappeared, though obviously if this is done it will prolong the time before the operation of refacing the points has to be repeated.
6. To replace the points first position the adjustable contact breaker plate over the terminal pin (arrowed, see photo).
7. Secure the contact plate by screwing in the screw (arrowed) which should have a spring and a flat washer under its head.
8. Then fit the fibre washer (arrowed) over the terminal pin.
9. Next fit the contact breaker arm complete with spring over the terminal pin.
10 Drop the fibre washer over the terminal bolt (arrowed).
11 Then bend back the spring of the contact breaker arm and fit it over the terminal bolt (arrowed).
12 Place the terminals of the low tension lead and the condenser over the terminal bolt.
13 Then fit the flanged nylon bush over the terminal bolt with the two leads immediately under its flange as shown.
14 Next fit a steel washer and then a 'star' washer over the nylon bush (see photo).
15 Then fit the nut over the terminal bolt and tighten it down as shown.
16 The points are now reassembled and the gap should be set as described in the previous section.
17 Finally replace the rotor arm and then the distributor cap.

4. Condenser - Removal, Testing and Replacement

1. The purpose of the condenser (sometimes known as a capacitor) is to ensure that when the contact breaker points open there is no sparking across them which would waste voltage and cause wear.
2. The condenser is fitted in parallel with the contact breaker points. If it develops a short circuit, it will cause ignition failure as the points will be prevented from interrupting the low tension circuit.
3. If the engine becomes very difficult to start or begins to miss after several miles running and the breaker points show signs of excessive burning, then the condition of the condenser must be suspect. A further test can be made by separating the points by hand with the ignition switched on. If this is accompanied by a flash it is indicative that the condenser has failed.

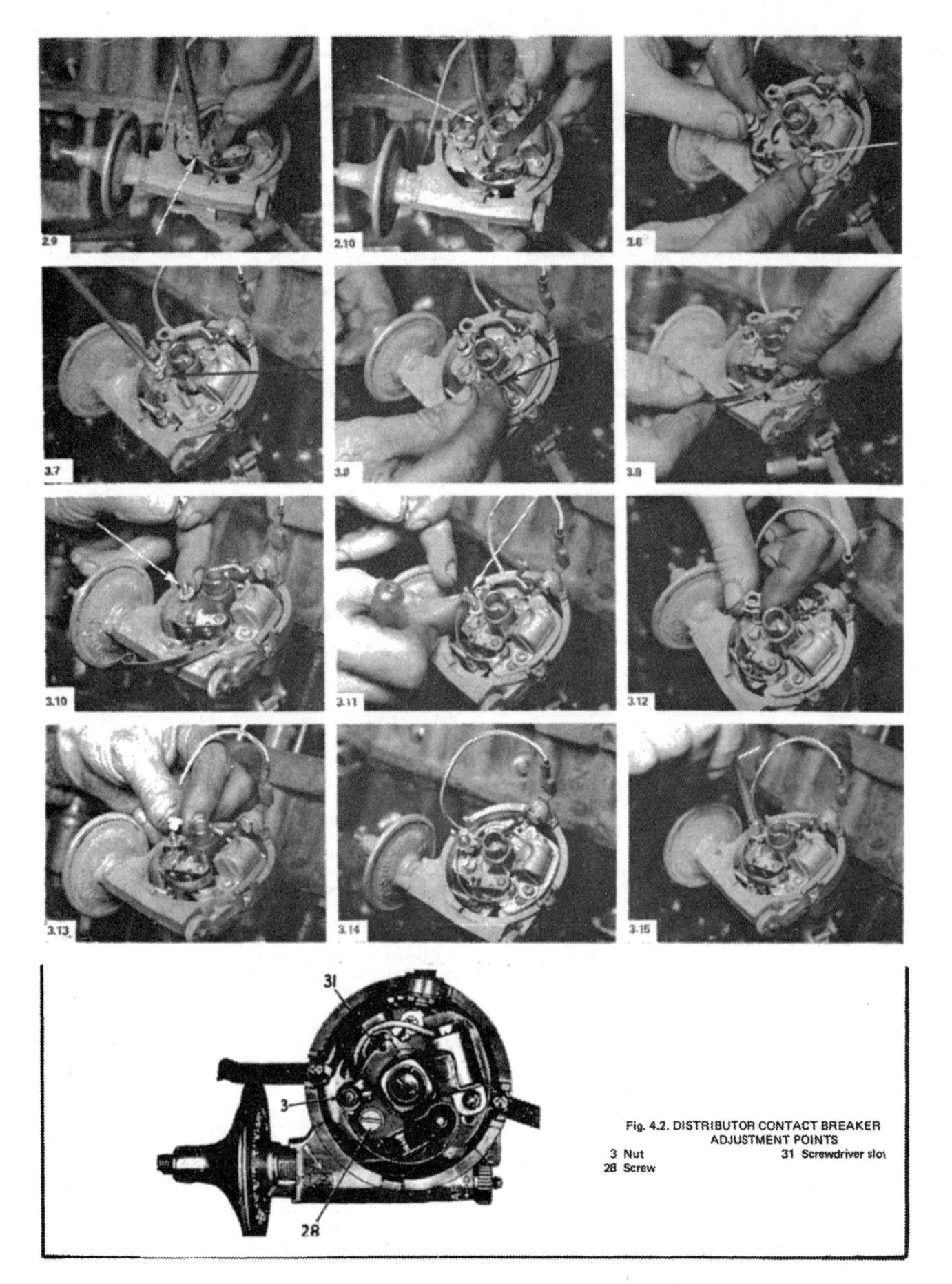

Fig. 4.2. DISTRIBUTOR CONTACT BREAKER
ADJUSTMENT POINTS
3 Nut
28 Screw
31 Screwdriver slot

97

Chapter 4/Ignition System

4. Without special test equipment the only sure way to diagnose condenser trouble is to replace a suspected unit with a new one and note if there is any improvement.
5. To remove the condenser from the distributor, remove the distributor cap and the rotor arm.
6. Loosen the outer nut from the contact stud and pull off the condenser lead.
7. Undo the mounting bracket screw and remove the condenser.
8. Replacement is simply a reversal of the removal process. Take particular care that the condenser lead does not short circuit against any portion of the breaker plate.

5. Distributor Lubrication

1. It is important that the distributor cam is lubricated with petroleum jelly at the specified mileages and that the breaker arm, governor weights, and cam spindle are lubricated with engine oil once every 1,000 miles. In practice it will be found that lubrication every 3,000 miles is adequate, though once every 1,000 miles is best.
2. Great care should be taken not to use too much lubricant, as any excess that finds its way into the contact breaker points could cause burning and misfiring.
3. To gain access to the cam spindle lift away the rotor arm. Drop no more than two drops of engine oil onto the screw head. This will run down the spindle when the engine is hot and lubricate the bearings.
4. To lubricate the automatic timing control allow a few drops of oil to pass through the hole in the contact breaker base plate through which the four sided cam emerges. Apply not more than one drop of oil to the pivot post and remove any excess.

6. Distributor - Removal

1. To remove the distributor from the engine, start by pulling the terminals off each of the sparking plugs. Release the Lucar connector or small nut which holds the low tension lead to the terminal on the side of the distributor and unscrew the high tension lead retaining cap from the coil and remove the lead.
2. Unscrew the union holding the vacuum tube to the distributor vacuum housing.
3. Remove the distributor body clamp bolts which hold the distributor clamp plate to the engine and remove the distributor. NOTE: If it is not wished to disturb the timing then under no circumstances should the clamp pinch bolt, which secures the distributor in its relative position in the clamp, be loosened. Providing the distributor is removed without the clamp being loosened from the distributor body, the timing will not be lost.
4. Replacement is a reversal of the above process, providing that the engine has not been turned in the meantime. If the engine has been turned it will be best to retime the ignition. This will also be necessary if the clamp pinch bolt has been loosened.

7. Distributor - Dismantling

1. With the distributor removed from the car and on the bench, remove the distributor cap and lift off the rotor arm. If very tight lever it off gently with a screwdriver.
2. Remove the points from the distributor as described in Section 3.
3. Remove the condenser from the contact breaker plate by releasing its securing screw.
4. Unhook the vacuum unit spring from its mounting pin on the moving contact breaker plate.
5. Remove the contact breaker plate.
6. Unscrew the two screws and lockwashers which hold the contact breaker base plate in position and remove the earth lead from the relevant screw. Remember to replace this lead on reassembly.
7. Lift out the contact breaker base plate.
8. NOTE the position of the slot in the rotor arm drive in relation to the offset drive dog at the opposite end of the distributor. It is essential that this is reassembled correctly as otherwise the timing may be 180º out.
9. Unscrew the cam spindle retaining screw which is located in the centre of the rotor arm drive and remove the cam spindle.
10 Lift out the centrifugal weights together with their springs.
11 To remove the vacuum unit, spring off the small circlip which secures the advance adjustment nut which should then be unscrewed. With the micrometer adjusting nut removed, release the spring and the micrometer adjusting nut lock spring clip. This is the clip that is responsible for the 'clicks' when the micrometer adjuster is turned, and it is small and easily lost as is the circlip, so put them in a safe place. Do not forget to replace the lock spring clip on reassembly.
11 It is only necessary to remove the distributor drive shaft or spindle if it is thought to be excessively worn. With a thin punch drive out the retaining pin from the driving tongue collar on the bottom end of the distributor drive shaft. The shaft can then be removed. The distributor is now completely dismantled.

8. Distributor - Inspection and Repair

1. Check the points as described in Section 3. Check the distributor cap for signs of tracking, indicated by a thin black line between the segments. Replace the cap if any signs of tracking are found.
2. If the metal portion of the rotor arm is badly burned or loose, renew the arm. If slightly burnt clean the arm with a fine file.
3. Check that the carbon brush moves freely in the centre of the distributor cover.
4. Examine the fit of the breaker plate on the bearing plate and also check the breaker arm pivot for looseness or wear and renew as necessary.
5. Examine the balance weights and pivot pins for wear and renew the weights or cam assembly if a degree of wear is found.
6. Examine the shaft and the fit of the cam assembly on the shaft. If the clearance is excessive compare the items with new units and renew either, or both, if they show excessive wear.
7. If the shaft is a loose fit in the distributor bush and can be seen to be worn, it will be necessary to fit a new shaft and bush. The single bush is simply pressed out. NOTE that before inserting a new bush it should be stood in engine oil for at least 24 hours.
8. Examine the length of the balance weight springs and compare them with new springs. If they have stretched they must be renewed.

9. Distributor - Reassembly

1. Reassembly is a straightforward reversal of the dismantling process but there are several points which should be noted in addition to those already given in the section on

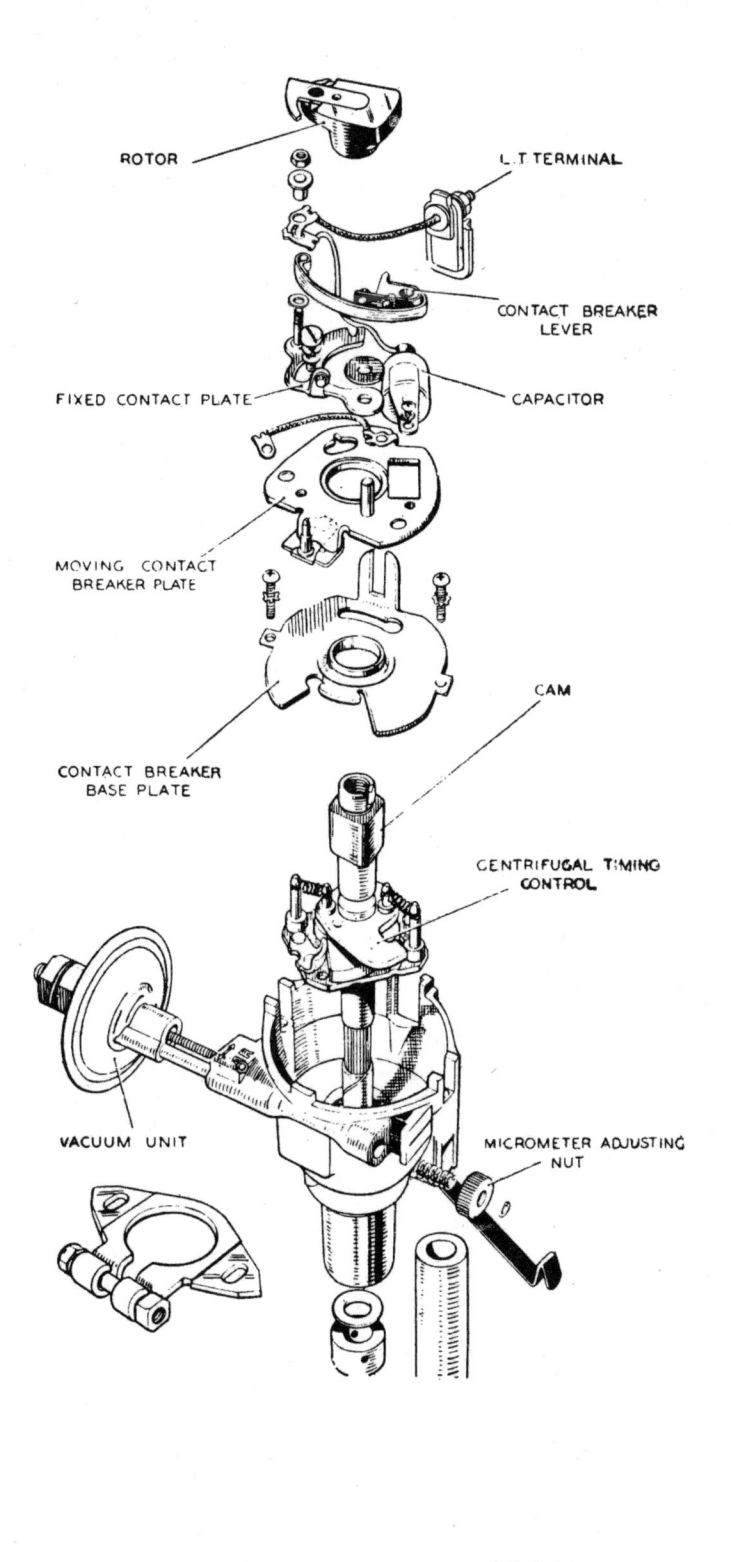

Fig. 4.3. Distributor Component Parts TR2, 3, 3A

Chapter 4/Ignition System

dismantling.

2. Lubricate with S.A.E. 20 engine oil the balance weights and other parts of the mechanical advance mechanism, the cam, the mainshaft, and the felts during assembly.

3. Always use a new upper and lower thrust washer and if fitting the original mainshaft and sleeve ensure they line up correctly. Check the mainshaft endfloat between the bottom thrust washer and the housing with a feeler gauge. The dimension should be between .002 and .005 inch if using new thrust washers.

4. Ensure the rivet holes are aligned and fit a new rivet. Also check that the endfloat is correct. Drill a rivet hole in the mainshaft using a No. 12 drill. If also fitting a new sleeve, drill the rivet hole at right angles to the slots and .44 inch from the sleeve bottom.

5. Always grease the tachometer drive gear and shaft and remember to stake over the housing plug in five or six places.

6. Finally set the contact breaker gap to the correct clearance.

10. Ignition Timing

1. If the clamp plate pinch bolt on the distributor has been loosened, or if a new or reconditioned distributor is being fitted it is necessary to set the ignition timing.

2. Turn the engine over so that No. 1 piston is coming up to T.D.C. on the compression stroke. (This can be checked by removing No. 1 sparking plug and feeling the pressure being developed in the cylinder.) If this check is not made it is all too easy to set the timing 180º out, as both No. 1 and 4 cylinders come up to T.D.C. at the same time, but only one is on the firing stroke. Continue turning the engine until the hole in the crankshaft pulley is in line with the timing pointer on the timing cover (Fig. 4.6). The engine is now at T.D.C.

3. Remove the distributor cover, slacken off the distributor body clamp bolt, and with the rotor arm pointing towards the No. 1 terminal (check this position with the distributor cap and lead to No. 1 sparking plug as shown in Fig. 4.5), insert the distributor into the distributor housing. The dog on the drive shaft should match up with the slot in the distributor driving spindle. Insert the two bolts holding the distributor in position.

4. Turn the knurled vernier adjuster screw clockwise to the fully retarded position indicated when the last division on the graduated scale can only just be seen.

5. Slowly and carefully turn the distributor body anti-clockwise until with the heel of the fibre rocker arm on the cam the points just begin to open. Check that with the heel on the peak of the cam the points gap does not exceed 0.016 inch.

6. Tighten the distributor clamp bolt with the distributor in this position. Check that the rotor arm is still pointing to the segment in the distributor cap which leads to No. 1 lead and plug.

7. Turn the knurled vernier adjuster screw anti-clockwise until the specified number of divisions appropriate to the model concerned are visible. Each complete division corresponds to 4 crankshaft degrees.

8. Difficulty is sometimes experienced in determining exactly when the contact breaker points open. This can be ascertained most accurately by connecting a 12 volt bulb in parallel with the contact breaker points (one lead to earth and the other from the distributor low tension terminal). Switch on the ignition and turn the advance and retard adjuster until the bulb lights up indicating that the points have just opened.

9. It must be noted that to get the very best setting the final adjustment should be made on the road. The distributor can be moved about ¼ of a division at a time until the best setting is obtained. The amount of wear in the engine, quality of petrol used, and amount of carbon in the combustion chambers all contribute to make the recommended settings no more than nominal ones. To obtain the best setting under running conditions first start the engine and allow to warm up to normal temperature and then accelerate in top gear from 30 to 50 m.p.h., listening for heavy pinking. If this occurs, the ignition needs to be retarded slightly until just the faintest trace of pinking can be heard under these operating conditions.

10 Since the ignition advance adjustment enables the firing point to be related correctly in relation to the grade of fuel used, the fullest advantage of any change of fuel will only be attained by re-adjustment of the ignition settings.

11. Sparking Plugs and Leads

1. The correct functioning of the sparking plugs is vital for the correct running and efficiency of the engine.

2. At intervals of 6,000 miles the plugs should be removed, examined, cleaned and, if worn excessively, replaced. The condition of the sparking plug will also tell much about the overall condition of the engine.

3. If the insulator nose of the sparking plug is clean and white, with no deposits, this is indicative of a weak mixture, or too hot a plug. (A hot plug transfers heat away from the electrode slowly - a cold plug transfers it away quickly.)

4. The plugs fitted as standard are either Lodge or Champion (see Specifications). If the top and insulator nose is covered with hard black looking deposits then this is indicative that the mixture is too rich. Should the plug be black and oily, then it is likely that the engine is fairly worn, as well as the mixture being too rich.

5. If the insulator nose is covered with light tan to greyish brown deposits then the mixture is correct and it is likely that the engine is in good condition.

6. If there are any traces of long brown tapering stains on the outside of the white portion of the plug, then the plug will have to be renewed, as this shows that there is a faulty joint between the plug body and the insulator, and compression is being allowed to leak away.

7. Plugs should be cleaned by a sand blasting machine, which will free them from carbon more thoroughly than cleaning by hand. The machine will also test the condition of the plugs under compression. Any plug that fails to spark at the recommended pressure should be renewed.

8. The sparking plug gap is of considerable importance, as, if it is too large or too small, the size of the spark and its efficiency will be seriously impaired. The sparking plug gap should be set to 0.025 inch for the best results.

9. To set it, measure the gap with a feeler gauge and then bend open, or close the outer plug electrode until the correct gap is achieved. The centre electrode should never be bent as this may crack the insulation and cause plug failure if nothing worse.

10 When replacing the plugs, remember to use new plug washers, and replace the leads from the distributor in the correct firing order (see Specifications), No. 1 cylinder being the one nearest the radiator.

11 The plug leads require no routine maintenance other than being kept clean and wiped over regularly. At intervals of 12,000 miles, however, pull each lead off the plug in turn and remove them from the distributor by unscrewing the knurled moulded terminal knobs. Water can seep down into these joints, giving rise to a white corrosive deposit which must be carefully removed from the brass washer at the end of each cable through which the ignition wires pass.

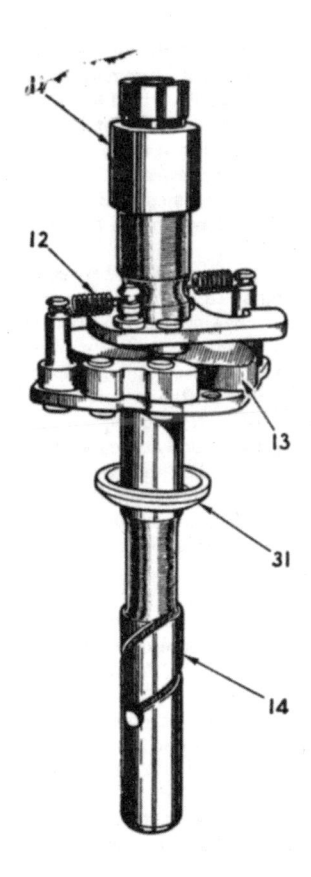

Fig. 4.4. CORRECT REASSEMBLY OF
CENTRIFUGAL WEIGHTS AND SPRINGS TO THE
ACTION PLATE
11 Cam assembly
12 Automatic advance springs
13 Weight assembly
14 Shaft and action plate
31 Nylon spacer

Fig. 4.5. IGNITION DISTRIBUTOR MOUNTED ON
ENGINE WITH ROTOR ARM SET TO NUMBER
1 CYLINDER FOR TIMING PURPOSES
1 Clamp bolt
2 Adjusting scale
3 Rotor arm
4 Thumbscrew

Fig. 4.6. Positioning of pointer on timing cover correctly aligned with the hole in the crankshaft pulley

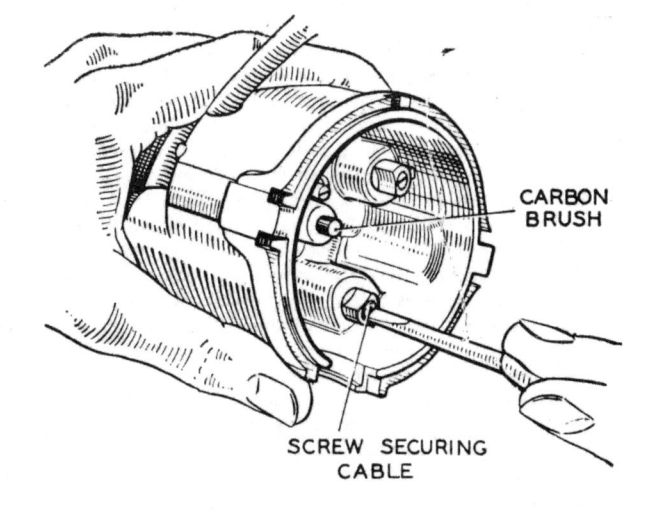

Fig. 4.7. Method of retaining high tension lead in the distributor cap.

CARBON BRUSH

SCREW SECURING CABLE

101

Chapter 4/Ignition System

12. Ignition System - Fault Finding

By far the majority of breakdown and running troubles are caused by faults in the ignition system either in the low or high tension circuits.

13. Ignition System - Fault Symptoms

There are two main symptoms indicating ignition faults. Either the engine will not start or fire, or the engine is difficult to start and misfires. If it is a regular misfire, i.e. the engine is only running on two or three cylinders the fault is almost sure to be in the secondary, or high tension, circuit. If the misfiring is intermittent, the fault could be in either the high or low tension circuits. If the car stops suddenly, or will not start at all, it is likely that the fault is in the low tension circuit. Loss of power and overheating, apart from faulty carburation settings, are normally due to faults in the distributor or incorrect ignition timing.

14. Fault Diagnosis - Engine Fails to Start

1. If the engine fails to start and the car was running normally when it was last used, first check there is fuel in the petrol tank. If the engine turns over normally on the starter motor and the battery is evidently well charged, then the fault may be in either the high or low tension circuits. First check the H.T. circuit. NOTE: If the battery is known to be fully charged the ignition light comes on and the starter motor fails to turn the engine CHECK THE TIGHTNESS OF THE LEADS ON THE BATTERY TERMINALS and also the secureness of the earth lead to its CONNECTION TO THE BODY. It is quite common for the leads to have worked loose, even if they look and feel secure. If one of the battery terminal posts gets very hot when trying to work the starter motor this is a sure indication of a faulty connection to that terminal.
2. One of the commonest reasons for bad starting is wet or damp sparking plug leads and distributor. Remove the distributor cap. If condensation is visible internally dry the cap with a rag and also wipe over the leads. Replace the cap.
3. If the engine still fails to start, check that current is reaching the plugs by disconnecting each plug lead in turn at the sparking plug end, and hold the end of the cable about 3/16 inch away from the cylinder block. Spin the engine on the starter motor by pressing the rubber button on the starter motor solenoid switch (under the bonnet).
4. Sparking between the end of the cable and the block should be fairly strong with a regular blue spark. (Hold the lead with rubber to avoid electric shocks.) If current is reaching the plugs, then remove them and clean and regap them to 0.025 inch. The engine should now start.
5. Spin the engine as before, when a rapid succession of blue sparks between the end of the lead and the block indicates that the coil is in order, and that either the distributor cap is cracked, the carbon brush is stuck or worn, the rotor arm is faulty, or that the contact points are burnt, pitted or dirty. If the points are in bad shape, clean and reset them as described in Section 2.
6. If there are no sparks from the end of the lead from the coil, then check the connections of the lead to the coil and distributor head, and if they are in order, check out the low tension circuit starting with the battery.
7. Switch on the ignition and turn the crankshaft so the contact breaker points have fully opened. Then with either a 20 volt voltmeter or bulb and length of wire check that current from the battery is reaching the starter solenoid switch. No reading indicates that there is a fault in the cable to the switch, or in the connections at the switch or at the battery terminals. Alternatively, the battery earth lead may not be properly earthed to the body.
8. If in order, check that current is reaching terminal 'A' (the one with the brown lead) in the control box by connecting the voltmeter between 'A' and an earth. If there is no reading this indicates a faulty cable or loose connections between the solenoid switch and the 'A' terminal. Remedy and the car will start.
9. Check with the voltmeter between the control box terminal A1 and an earth. No reading means a fault in the control box. Fit a new control box and start the car.
10 If in order, then check that current is reaching the ignition switch by connecting the voltmeter to the ignition switch input terminal (the one connected to the brown/blue lead) and earth. No reading indicates a break in the wire or a faulty connection at the switch or A1 terminals.
11 If the correct reading (approx. 12 volts) is obtained check the output terminal on the ignition switch (the terminal connected to the white lead). No reading means that the ignition switch is broken. Replace with a new unit and start the car.
12 If current is reaching the ignition switch output terminal, then check the SW terminal on the coil (it is marked 'SW'). No reading indicates loose connections or a broken wire from the ignition switch. If this proves to be the fault, remedy and start the car.
13 Check the CB terminal on the coil (it is marked CB) and if no reading is recorded on the voltmeter then the coil is broken and must be replaced. The car should start when a new coil has been fitted.
14 If a reading is obtained at the CB terminal then check the low tension terminal on the side of the distributor. If no reading then check the wire for loose connections, etc. If a reading is obtained then the final check on the low tension is across the breaker points. No reading means a broken condenser which, when replaced, will enable the car to finally start.

15. Fault Diagnosis - Engine Misfires

1. If the engine misfires regularly, run it at a fast idling speed, and short out each of the plugs in turn by placing a short screwdriver across from the plug terminal to the cylinder. Ensure that the screwdriver has a WOODEN or PLASTIC INSULATED HANDLE.
2. No difference in engine running will be noticed when the plug in the defective cylinder is short circuited. Short circuiting the working plugs will accentuate the misfire.
3. Remove the plug lead from the end of the defective plug and hold it about 3/16 inch away from the block. Restart the engine. If the sparking is fairly strong and regular the fault must lie in the sparking plug.
4. The plug may be loose, the insulation may be cracked, or the points may have burnt away giving too wide a gap for the spark to jump. Worse still, one of the points may have broken off. Either renew the plug, or clean it, reset the gap and then test it.
5. If there is no spark at the end of the plug lead, or if it is weak and intermittent, check the ignition lead from the distributor to the plug. If the insulation is cracked or perished, renew the lead. Check the connections at the distributor cap.
6. If there is still no spark, examine the distributor cap carefully for tracking. This can be recognised by a very thin black line running between two or more electrodes, or between an electrode and some other part of the

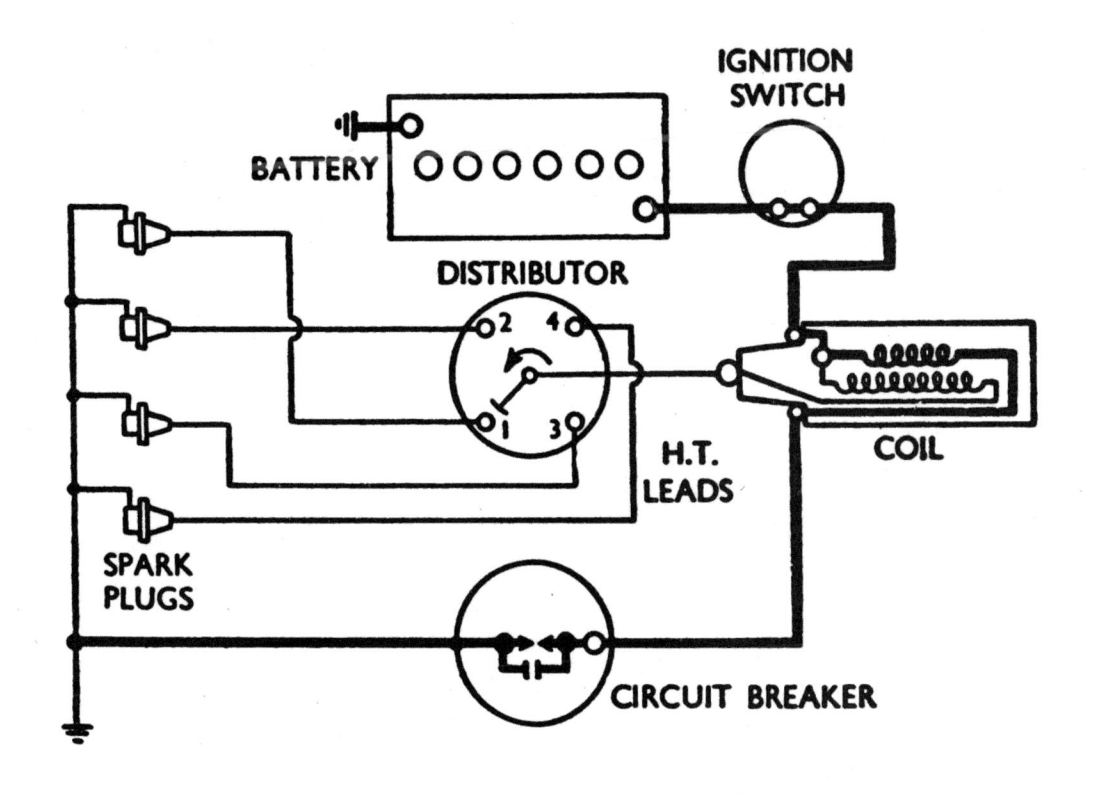

Fig.4.8. THE IGNITION CIRCUIT
The primary circuit is indicated by the heavier lines. (A full description is given in Section 1)

Chapter 4/Ignition System

distributor. These lines are paths which now conduct electricity across the cap thus letting it run to earth. The only answer is a new distributor cap.

7. Apart from the ignition timing being incorrect, other causes of misfiring have already been dealt with under the section dealing with the failure of the engine to start (Section 14).

8. If the ignition timing is too far retarded, it should be noted that the engine will tend to overheat and there will be a quite noticeable drop in power. If the engine is overheating and the power is down, and the ignition timing is correct, then the carburettors should be checked, as it is likely that this is where the fault lies. See Chapter 3 for details on this.

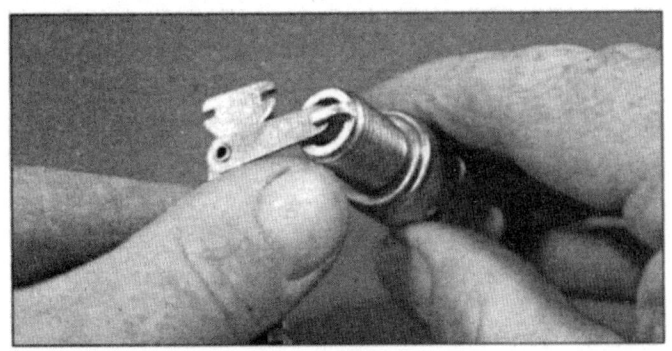

Measuring plug gap. A feeler gauge of the correct size (see ignition system specifications) should have a slight "drag" when slid between the electrodes. Adjust gap if necessary

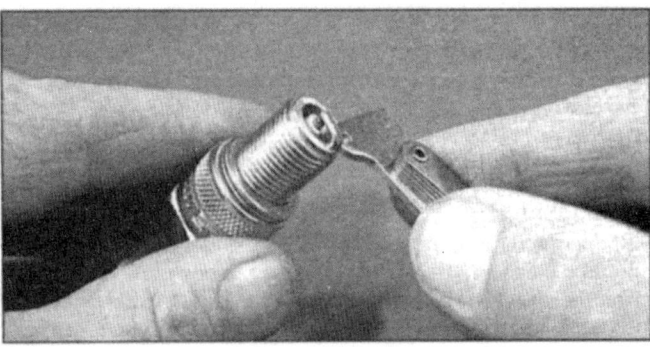

Adjusting plug gap. The plug gap is adjusted by bending the earth electrode inwards, or outwards, as necessary until the correct clearance is obtained. Note the use of the correct tool

Normal. Grey-brown deposits, lightly coated core nose. Gap increasing by around 0.001 in (0.025 mm) per 1000 miles (1600 km). Plugs ideally suited to engine, and engine in good condition

Carbon fouling. Dry, black, sooty deposits. Will cause weak spark and eventually misfire. Fault: over-rich fuel mixture. Check: carburettor mixture settings, float level and jet sizes; choke operation and cleanliness of air filter. Plugs can be re-used after cleaning

Oil fouling. Wet, oily deposits. Will cause weak spark and eventually misfire. Fault: worn bores/piston rings or valve guides; sometimes occurs (temporarily) during running-in period. Plugs can be re-used after thorough cleaning

Overheating. Electrodes have glazed appearance, core nose very white - few deposits. Fault: plug overheating. Check: plug value, ignition timing, fuel octane rating (too low) and fuel mixture (too weak). Discard plugs and cure fault immediately

Electrode damage. Electrodes burned away; core nose has burned, glazed appearance. Fault: pre-ignition. Check: as for "Overheating" but may be more severe. Discard plugs and remedy fault before piston or valve damage occurs

Split core nose (may appear initially as a crack). Damage is self-evident, but cracks will only show after cleaning. Fault: pre-ignition or wrong gap-setting technique. Check: ignition timing, cooling system, fuel octane rating (too low) and fuel mixture (too weak). Discard plugs, rectify fault immediately

Chapter 5/Clutch and Actuating Mechanism

Contents

General Description ...	1
Routine Maintenance ...	2
Clutch System - Bleeding ...	3
Clutch Pedal - Removal & Replacement ...	4
Clutch Removal ...	5
Clutch Replacement ...	6
Clutch Dismantling (TR2, 3, 3A, 4) ...	7
Clutch Inspection (TR2, 3, 3A, 4) ...	8
Clutch Reassembly (TR2, 3, 3A, 4) ...	9
Clutch Dismantling & Reassembly (TR4A) ...	10
Clutch - Inspection (TR4A) ...	11
Clutch Release Bearing & Cross Shaft - Removal & Reassembly ...	12
Clutch Slave Cylinder - Removal, Dismantling, Examination & Reassembly (TR2, 3, 3A) ...	13
Clutch Slave Cylinder - Adjustment (TR2, 3, 3A) ...	14
Clutch Slave Cylinder - Removal, Dismantling, Examination & Reassembly (TR4, 4A) ...	15
Clutch Slave Cylinder - Adjustment (TR4, 4A) ...	16
Clutch Master Cylinder - Removal & Refitting (TR2) ...	17
Clutch Master Cylinder - Dismantling, Overhaul & Reassembly (TR2) ...	18
Clutch Pedal Adjustment (TR2) ...	19
Clutch Master Cylinder - Removal & Refitting (TR3, 3A) ...	20
Clutch Master Cylinder - Dismantling, Overhaul & Reassembly (TR3, 3A) ...	21
Clutch Pedal Adjustment (TR3, 3A) ...	22
Clutch Master Cylinder - Removal & Refitting (TR4, 4A) ...	23
Clutch Master Cylinder - Dismantling, Overhaul & Reassembly (TR4, 4A) ...	24
Clutch Pedal Adjustment (TR4, 4A) ...	25
Clutch Faults ...	26
Clutch Squeal - Diagnosis & Cure ...	27
Clutch Slip - Diagnosis & Cure ...	28
Clutch Spin - Diagnosis & Cure ...	29
Clutch Judder - Diagnosis & Cure ...	30

Specifications

TR2, 3, 3A models
Up to engine number TS 7830E
Type ...	Borg and Beck model A.6.G
Diameter ...	9 inch
Thrust springs ...	9
Identification ...	Painted cream
Thrust pressure ...	120 to 130 lb.
Cushion springs ...	6
Identification ...	Painted grey
Free clutch pedal travel ...	¾ to 1 inch

From engine number TS 7830E
Type ...	As above but with following modifications
Driven plate ...	Improved design incorporating Belleville washer friction centre
Cushion springs ...	6
Identification ...	Painted white and light green

Hydraulic system up to chassis no. TS 13101
Type ...	Lockheed
Fluid ...	Lockheed hydraulic brake fluid
Slave cylinder end float ...	0.079 inch
Master cylinder plunger and pushrod clearance ...	0.030 inch

Hydraulic system from chassis no. TS 13101
Type ...	Girling
Fluid ...	Girling crimson clutch and brake fluid

TR4 models
Type ...	Borg and Beck model 9.A 6

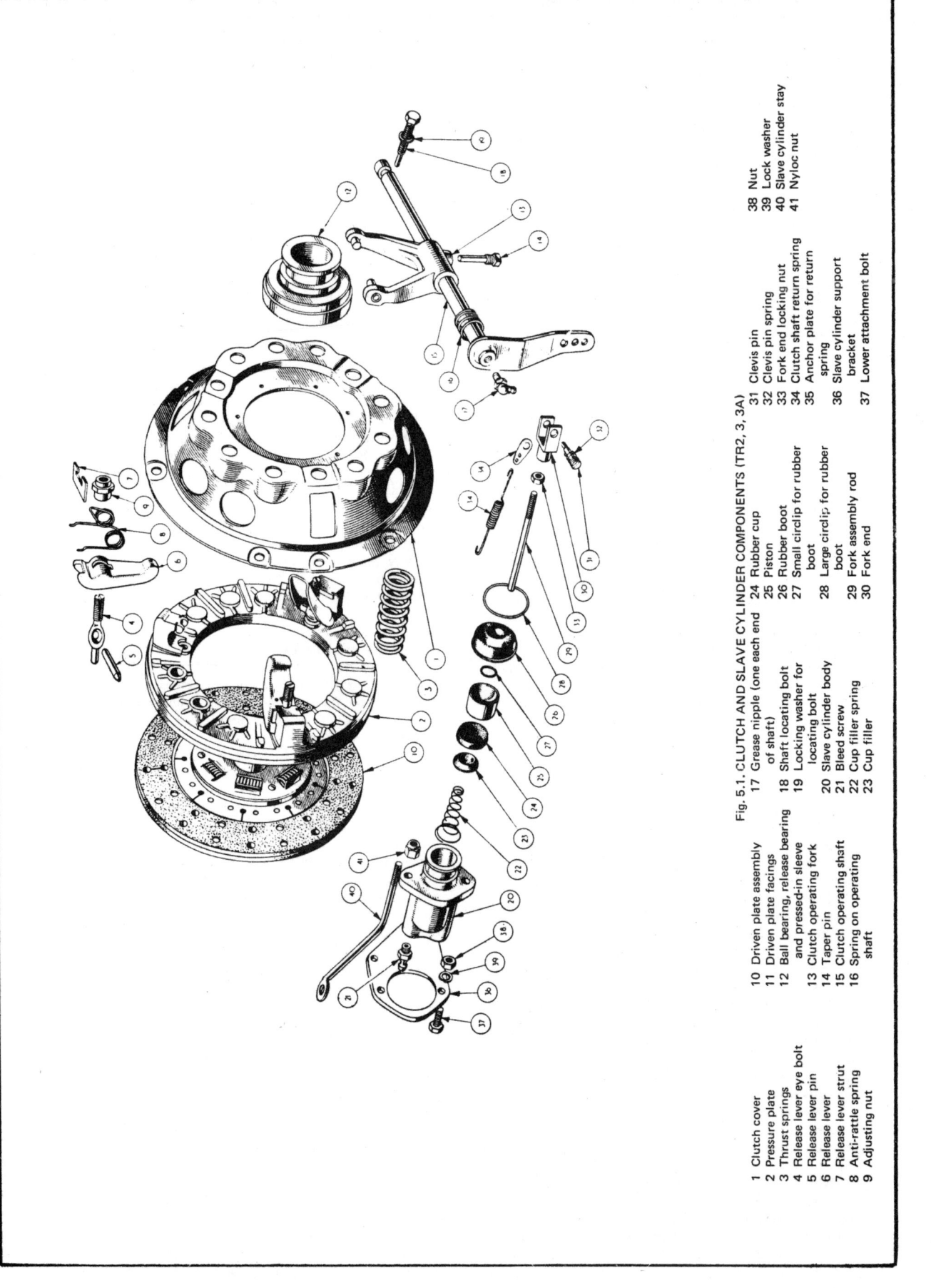

Fig. 5.1. CLUTCH AND SLAVE CYLINDER COMPONENTS (TR2, 3, 3A)

1 Clutch cover
2 Pressure plate
3 Thrust springs
4 Release lever eye bolt
5 Release lever pin
6 Release lever
7 Release lever strut
8 Anti-rattle spring
9 Adjusting nut
10 Driven plate assembly
11 Driven plate facings
12 Ball bearing, release bearing and pressed-in sleeve
13 Clutch operating fork
14 Taper pin
15 Clutch operating shaft
16 Spring on operating shaft
17 Grease nipple (one each end of shaft)
18 Shaft locating bolt
19 Locking washer for locating bolt
20 Slave cylinder body
21 Bleed screw
22 Cup filler spring
23 Cup filler
24 Rubber cup
25 Piston
26 Rubber boot
27 Small circlip for rubber boot
28 Large circlip for rubber boot
29 Fork assembly rod
30 Fork end
31 Clevis pin
32 Clevis pin spring
33 Fork end locking nut
34 Clutch shaft return spring
35 Anchor plate for return spring
36 Slave cylinder support bracket
37 Lower attachment bolt
38 Nut
39 Lock washer
40 Slave cylinder stay
41 Nyloc nut

Chapter 5/Clutch & Actuating Mechanism

Diameter	9 inch
Thrust springs	9
Identification	Painted cream
Cushion springs	6
Identification	Painted white and light green
TR4A models	
Type	Borg and Beck model DS
Diameter	8½ inch
Cushion springs	6
Identification	Painted yellow and light green
TR4 and 4A models hydraulic system	
Type	Girling
Fluid	Castrol Girling clutch and brake fluid to specification SAE 70 R3

1. General Description

All models except the TR4A covered by this manual are fitted with a conventional single dry plate clutch of 9 inch diameter whilst the TR4A is fitted with a diaphragm spring unit.

The conventional clutch comprises a steel cover which is bolted and dowelled to the rear face of the flywheel and contains the pressure plate, pressure plate springs, release levers and clutch disc or driven plate. The layout of the types of clutch are shown in Fig. 5.1 and Fig. 5.2.

The pressure plate, pressure springs and release levers are all attached to the clutch assembly cover. The clutch disc is free to slide along the splined input shaft of the gearbox and is held in position between the flywheel and pressure plate by the pressure of the pressure plate springs.

The friction lining material is riveted to the clutch disc and it has a spring cushioned hub to absorb transmission shocks and to help ensure a smooth take off.

The diaphragm spring clutch is shown in Fig. 5.3 and is similar to the conventional unit except that in place of the coil pressure springs there is just one diaphragm spring and this dispenses with the need for release levers.

The clutch is actuated hydraulically. The pendant clutch pedal is connected to the clutch master cylinder and hydraulic fluid reservoir by a short pushrod. The master cylinder and hydraulic reservoir are mounted on the engine side of the bulk head in front of the driver.

Depressing the clutch pedal moves the piston in the master cylinder forwards, so forcing hydraulic fluid through the clutch hydraulic pipe to the slave cylinder.

The piston in the slave cylinder moves forward on the entry of the fluid and actuates the clutch release arm by means of a short pushrod.

On the conventional clutch the release bearing is pushed forwards to bear against the release bearing thrust plate and three clutch release levers. These levers are pivoted so as to move the pressure plate backwards against the pressure of the pressure plate springs, in this way disengaging the pressure plate from the clutch disc.

When the clutch pedal is released, the pressure plate springs force the pressure plate into contact with the high friction linings on the clutch disc, at the same time forcing the clutch disc against the flywheel so taking up the drive.

With the diaphragm spring clutch the release arm pushes the release bearing forwards to bear against the release plate, so moving the centre of the diaphragm spring inwards. The spring is sandwiched between two annular rings which act as fulcrum points. As the centre of the spring is pushed in the outside of the spring is pushed out, so moving the pressure plate backwards and disengaging the pressure plate from the clutch disc.

When the clutch pedal is released the diaphragm spring forces the pressure plate into contact with the high friction linings on the clutch disc and at the same time pushes the clutch disc a fraction of an inch forwards on its splines so engaging the clutch disc with the flywheel. The clutch disc is now firmly sandwiched between the pressure plate and the flywheel so the drive is taken up.

As the friction linings on the clutch disc wear, the pressure plate automatically moves closer to the disc to compensate. There is therefore no need to periodically adjust either type of clutch.

2. Routine Maintenance

1. Routine maintenance consists of checking the level of the hydraulic fluid in the master cylinder every 1,000 miles and topping up with Lockheed or Girling hydraulic fluid if the level falls.
2. If it is noted that the level of the liquid has fallen then an immediate check should be made to determine the source of the leak.
3. Before checking the level of the fluid in the master cylinder reservoir, carefully clean the cap and body of the reservoir unit with clean rag so as to ensure that no dirt enters the system when the cap is removed. On no account should paraffin or any other cleaning solvent be used in case the hydraulic fluid becomes contaminated.
4. Check that the level of the hydraulic fluid is up to within ¼ inch of the filler neck and that the vent hole in the cap is clear. Do not overfill.

3. Clutch System - Bleeding

1. Gather together a clean jam jar, a 9 inch length of rubber tubing which fits tightly over the bleed nipple in the slave cylinder, a tin of hydraulic fluid and a friend to help.
2. Check that the master cylinder is full and if not fill it and cover the bottom two inches of the jar with hydraulic fluid.
3. Remove the rubber dust cap from the bleed nipple on the slave cylinder and with a suitable spanner open the bleed nipple one turn.
4. Place one end of the tube securely over the nipple and insert the other end in the jam jar so that the tube orifice is below the level of the fluid.
5. The assistant should now pump the clutch pedal up and down slowly until air bubbles rise to emerge from the end

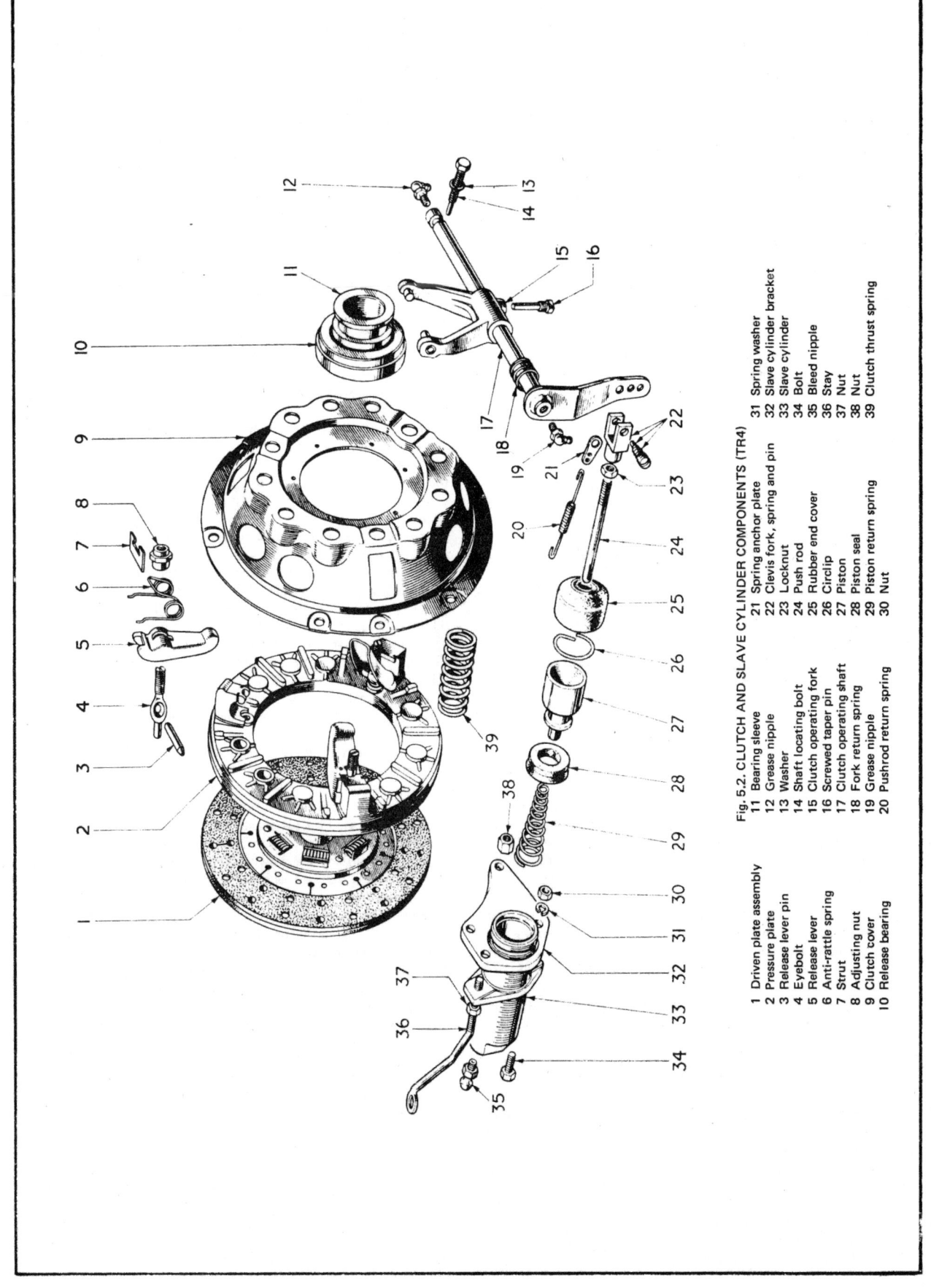

Fig. 5.2. CLUTCH AND SLAVE CYLINDER COMPONENTS (TR4)

1 Driven plate assembly
2 Pressure plate
3 Release lever pin
4 Eyebolt
5 Release lever
6 Anti-rattle spring
7 Strut
8 Adjusting nut
9 Clutch cover
10 Release bearing
11 Bearing sleeve
12 Grease nipple
13 Washer
14 Shaft locating bolt
15 Clutch operating fork
16 Screwed taper pin
17 Clutch operating shaft
18 Fork return spring
19 Grease nipple
20 Pushrod return spring
21 Spring anchor plate
22 Clevis fork, spring and pin
23 Locknut
24 Push rod
25 Rubber end cover
26 Circlip
27 Piston
28 Piston seal
29 Piston return spring
30 Nut
31 Spring washer
32 Slave cylinder bracket
33 Slave cylinder
34 Bolt
35 Bleed nipple
36 Stay
37 Nut
38 Nut
39 Clutch thrust spring

109

Chapter 5/Clutch & Actuating Mechanism

of the tubing. He should also check the reservoir frequently to ensure that the hydraulic fluid does not disappear so letting air into the system.

6. When no more air bubbles appear, tighten the bleed nipple on the downstroke.

7. Replace the rubber dust cap over the bleed nipple. Allow the hydraulic fluid in the jar to stand for at least 24 hours before using it to allow all the minute air bubbles to escape.

4. Clutch Pedal - Removal and Replacement

1. The clutch pedal is removed and replaced in exactly the same way as the brake pedal.
2. A full description of how to remove and replace the brake pedal can be found in Chapter 9.

5. Clutch - Removal

1. Remove the gearbox as described in Chapter 6, Section 3.
2. Remove the clutch cover assembly by undoing the six bolts holding the cover to the rear face of the flywheel (photo). Unscrew the bolts diagonally half a turn at a time so as to prevent distortion to the cover flanges.
3. Check that as the bolts are removed the cover moves up the two dowels so that when all the bolts are removed the cover does not suddenly fly off.
4. With all the bolts and spring washers removed lift the clutch assembly off the ends of the locating dowels. Do not touch the clutch driven plate. The driven plate or clutch disc will fall out at this stage as it is not attached to either the clutch cover assembly or the flywheel (photo).

6. Clutch - Replacement

1. It is important that no oil or grease gets on the clutch disc friction linings, or the pressure plate and flywheel faces. It is advisable to replace the clutch with clean hands and to wipe down the pressure plate and flywheel faces with a clean dry rag before assembly begins.
2. Place the clutch disc against the flywheel with the longer end of the hub facing outwards (photo) away from the flywheel. On no account should the clutch disc be replaced with the longer end of the centre hub facing into the flywheel as on reassembly it will be found quite impossible to operate the clutch with the friction disc in this position.
3. Replace the clutch cover assembly loosely on the dowels (one dowel is arrowed in the photo). Replace the six bolts and spring washers and tighten them finger tight so that the clutch disc is gripped but can still be moved.
4. The clutch disc must now be centralised so that when the engine and gearbox are mated the gearbox input shaft splines will pass through the splines in the centre of the driven plate hub.
5. Centralisation can be carried out quite easily by inserting a round bar or long screwdriver through the hole in the centre of the clutch, so that the end of the bar rests in the small hole in the end of the crankshaft containing the input shaft bearing bush. Ideally an old Triumph input shaft should be used.
6. Using the input shaft bearing bush as a fulcrum, moving the bar sideways or up and down will move the clutch disc in whichever direction is necessary to achieve centralisation.
7. Centralisation is easily judged by removing the bar and viewing the driven plate hub in relation to the hole in the release bearing. When the hub appears exactly in the centre of the release bearing hole all is correct. Alternatively the input shaft (arrowed) will fit the bush and centre of the clutch hub exactly, obviating the need for visual alignment (photo).

8. Tighten the clutch bolts firmly in a diagonal sequence to ensure that the cover plate is pulled down evenly (photo) and without distortion of the flange. Note how the flywheel is prevented from turning by a spanner located between the teeth of the starter ring and a bellhousing stud.

9. Mate the engine and gearbox, bleed the slave cylinder if the pipe was disconnected, and check the clutch for correct operation.

7. Clutch - Dismantling (TR2, 3, 3A, 4)

1. It is not very often that it is necessary to dismantle the clutch cover assembly, and in the normal course of events clutch replacement is the term used for simply fitting a new clutch disc. Under no circumstances must the diaphragm clutch unit be dismantled. If a fault develops in the unit an exchange replacement assembly must be fitted.
2. If a new clutch disc is being fitted it is a false economy not to renew the release bearing at the same time. This will preclude having to replace it at a later date when wear on the clutch linings is still very small.
3. It should be noted here that it is preferable to purchase an exchange clutch cover assembly unit, which will have been properly balanced rather than to dismantle and repair the existing cover.
4. Before beginning work ensure that either the Churchill clutch assembly gauging tool 99A or a press and a block of wood is available for compressing the clutch springs so that the three adjusting nuts can be freed.
5. Presuming that it is possible to borrow from your local Triumph agent clutch assembly tool 99A proceed as follows:-
6. Mark the clutch cover, release levers, and pressure plate lugs so that they can be refitted in the same relative positions.
7. Unhook the springs from the release bearing thrust plate and remove the plate and spring.
8. Place the three correctly sized spacing washers provided with the clutch assembly tool on the tool base plate in the positions indicated by the chart (found inside the lid of the assembly tool container).
9. Place the clutch face down on the three spacing washers so that the washers are as close as possible to the release levers, with the six holes in the cover flange in line with the six holes in the base plate.
10 Insert the six bolts provided with the assembly tool through the six holes in the cover flange, and tighten the cover down diagonally onto the base plate.
11 With a suitable punch, tap back the three tab washers and then remove the three adjusting nuts and bearing plates from the pressure plate bolts on early models and just unscrew the three adjusting nuts on later models.
12 Unscrew the six bolts holding the clutch cover to the base plate, diagonally, one turn at a time, so as to release the cover evenly. Lift the cover off and extract the six pressure spring retaining cups.

8. Clutch - Inspection (TR2, 3, 3A, 4)

1. Examine the clutch disc friction linings for wear and loose rivets and the disc for rim distortion, cracks, broken hub springs, and worn splines. Shown is a well worn friction plate (photo).

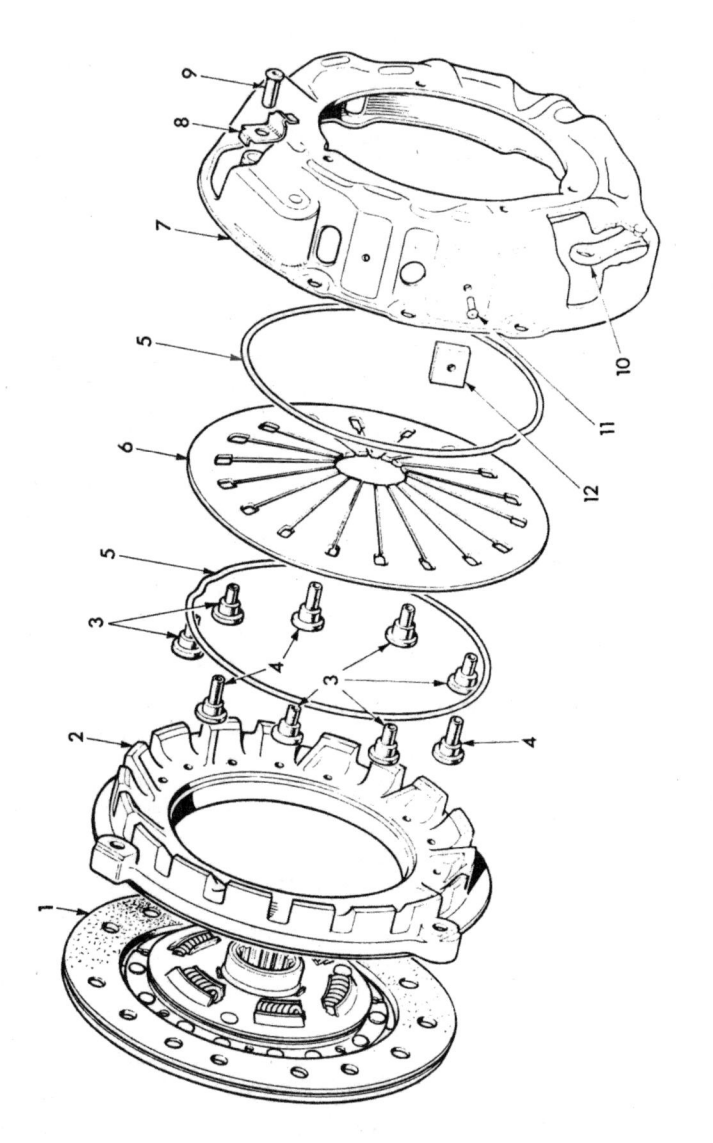

Fig. 5.3. DIAPHRAGM SPRING CLUTCH COMPONENTS

1 Driven plate
2 Pressure plate
3 Rivets
4 Locating pins
5 Fulcrum rings
6 Diaphragm spring
7 Cover pressing
8 Retractor clips
9 Rivet
10 Pressure plate strap
11 Rivet
12 Balance weight

Chapter 5/Clutch & Actuating Mechanism

2. It is always best to renew the clutch driven plate as an assembly to preclude further trouble, but, if it is wished to merely renew the linings, the rivets should be drilled out and not knocked out with a punch. The manufacturers do not advise that only the linings are renewed and personal experience dictates that it is far more satisfactory to renew the driven plate complete than to try and economise by only fitting new friction linings. Shown in the photo 8.1 is a new friction plate.

3. Check the machined faces of the flywheel and the pressure plate (photo). If either are badly grooved they should be machined until smooth. If the pressure plate is cracked or split it must be renewed, also if the portion on the other side of the plate in contact with the three release lever tips is grooved.

4. Check the release bearing thrust plate for cracks and renew it if any are found.

5. Examine the tips of the release levers which bear against the thrust plate, and renew the levers if more than a small flat has been worn on them (photo).

6. Renew any clutch pressure springs that are broken or shorter than standard.

7. Examine the depressions in the release levers which fit over the knife edge fulcrums and renew the levers if the metal appears badly worn.

8. Examine the clutch release bearing in the gearbox bell-housing and, if it turns or if it is roughly cracked or pitted, it must be removed and replaced.

9. Also check the clutch withdrawal lever for slackness. If this is evident, withdraw the lever and renew the bush.

9. Clutch - Reassembly (TR2, 3, 3A, 4)

1. During clutch reassembly ensure that the marked components are placed in their correct relative positions.

2. Place the three spacing washers on the clutch assembly tool base in the same position as for dismantling the clutch.

3. Place the clutch pressure plate face down on the three spacing washers.

4. Position the three release levers on the knife edge fulcrums (or release lever floating pins in the later clutches) and ensure that the anti-rattle springs are in place over the inner end of the levers.

5. Position the pressure springs on the pressure plate bosses.

6. Fit the flanged cups to the clutch cover and fit the cover over the pressure plate in the same relative position as it was originally.

7. Insert the six assembly tool bolts through the six holes in the clutch cover flange and tighten the cover down, diagonally, a turn at a time.

8. Replace the three bearing plates, tag washers and adjusting nuts over the pressure plate studs in the early units and just screw the adjusting nuts into the eyebolts in the later models.

9. To correctly adjust the clutch release levers use the clutch assembly tool as detailed below:-

a) Screw the actuator into the base plate and settle the clutch mechanism by pumping the actuator handle up and down a dozen times. Unscrew the actuator.

b) Screw the tool pillar into the base plate and slide the correctly sized distance piece (as indicated in the chart in the tool's box) recessed side downwards, over the pillar.

c) Slip the height finger over the centre pillar and turn the release lever adjusting nuts until the height fingers, when rotated and held firmly down, just contact the highest part of the clutch release lever tips.

d) Remove the pillar, replace the actuator and settle the clutch mechanism as in (a).

e) Refit the centre pillar and height finger and recheck the clutch release lever clearance and adjust if not correct.

10 With the centre pillar removed, lock the adjusting nuts found on early clutches by bending up the tab washers.

11 Replace the release bearing thrust plate and fit the retaining springs over the thrust plate hooks.

12 Unscrew the six bolts holding the clutch cover to the base plate, diagonally, a turn at a time and assembly is now complete.

10. Clutch - Dismantling and Reassembly (TR4A)

1. It is not very often that it is necessary to dismantle the clutch cover assembly and in the normal course of events clutch replacement is the term used for simply fitting a new clutch disc. Under no circumstances must the diaphragm clutch unit be dismantled. If a fault develops in the unit an exchange replacement assembly must be fitted.

2. If a new clutch disc is being fitted it is a false economy not to renew the release bearing at the same time. This will preclude having to replace it at a later date when wear on the clutch linings is still very small.

11. Clutch - Inspection (TR4A)

1. Examine the clutch disc friction linings for wear or loose rivets and the disc for rim distortion, cracks and worn splines.

2. It is always best to renew the clutch driven plate as an assembly to preclude further trouble, but, if it is wished to merely renew the linings the rivets should be drilled out and not knocked out with a centre punch. The manufacturers do not advise that only the linings are renewed and personal experience dictates that it is far more satisfactory to renew the driven plate complete than to try to economise by only fitting new friction linings.

3. Check the machined faces of the flywheel and the pressure plate. If either are badly grooved they should be machined until smooth. If the pressure plate is cracked or split it must be renewed.

12. Clutch Release Bearing and Cross Shaft - Removal and Reassembly

1. With the gearbox and engine separated to provide access to the clutch, attention can be given to the release bearing and cross shaft located in the gearbox bellhousing.

2. Refer to Fig. 5.4 and undo the cross shaft to fork taper bolt (10), having first removed the soft iron wire threaded through the bolt head (photo).

3. Carefully slide the cross shaft (8) from the bellhousing.

4. Lift away the fork (5) followed by the sleeve (2) and bearing (1). Note that there are two little end caps fitted to the fork fingers.

5. As the sleeve (2) is pressed into the bearing (1) the two parts may be separated by placing the bearing on the top of opened jaws of a firm bench vice and using a drift of suitable diameter tap out the sleeve (2).

6. Inspect the cross shaft (8), the fork (5), the end caps and sleeve (2) for signs of excessive wear and fit new parts as necessary. Hold the outer track of the release bearing (1) and rotate the inner track. If it feels rough during rotation fit a new bearing.

7. Reassembly is the reverse sequence to removal. Smear a little high melting point grease on the inside of the sleeve and also on the outer surface of the end caps and cross shaft

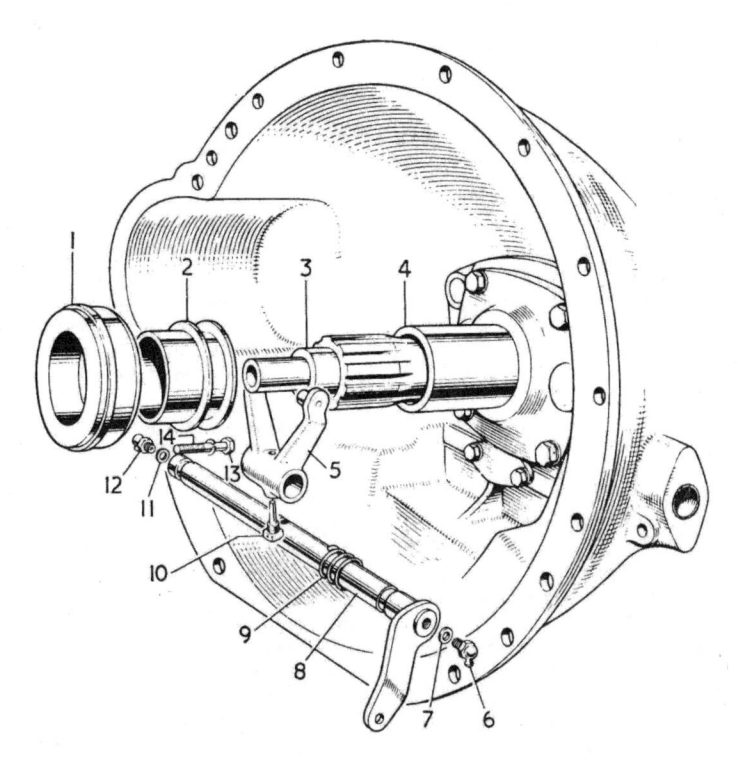

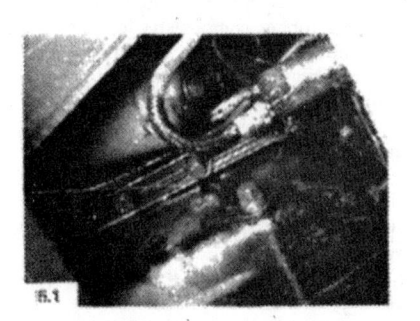

Fig. 5.4. CLUTCH RELEASE SYSTEM COMPONENTS
1 Release bearing
2 Bearing sleeve
3 Input shaft
4 Front cover
5 Fork
6 Grease nipple
7 Fibre washer
8 Cross-shaft
9 Anti-rattle spring
10 Tapered locking bolt
11 Fibre washer
12 Grease nipple
13 Locating bolt
14 Lockwasher

Chapter 5/Clutch & Actuating Mechanism

before refitting (photo).
8. Do not forget to lock the taper bolt (10) with soft iron wire (photo).

13. Clutch Slave Cylinder - Removal, Dismantling, Examination and Reassembly (TR2, 3, 3A)

1. The clutch slave cylinder is positioned on the left hand side of the bellhousing as shown in Fig. 5.1.
2. Before removing the slave cylinder it will be necessary to drain the hydraulic system by connecting a plastic tube to the bleed nipple, opening the nipple and operating the clutch pedal so passing the fluid through the plastic tube into a clean glass jar.
3. Using an open ended spanner hold the hexagon of the flexible hose and with a second open ended spanner undo the union to the Bundy pipe taking care not to twist the hose. Next remove the locknut and washer.
4. Disconnect the flexible hose from the wheel cylinder by rotating the complete hose until it is free.
5. Release the spring (34) (Fig. 5.5) and unscrew the shaped clevis pin (31). Lift away the spring (32) and the spring plate (35).
6. Undo the Nyloc nut (41) from the end of the slave cylinder stay (40).
7. Undo and remove the bottom slave cylinder securing nut (38) and bolt (37).
8. Carefully withdraw rearwards the slave cylinder from its support bracket (36).
9. Release the large diameter circlip (28) and extract the rod (29), fork (30) and rubber boot (26) from the slave cylinder body (20).
10 Separate the boot (26) from the rod (29) by undoing the small diameter circlip (27).
11 Using a compressed air jet or by gently tapping remove the remaining internal parts from the cylinder. The compressed air jet should be applied to the hydraulic hose connection but this must be done with care as they will fly out. We recommend placing a pad over the open end to catch the parts.
12 Wash all the internal parts with either brake fluid or methylated spirits and dry them using a non-fluffy rag.
13 Inspect the bore and piston for signs of deep scoring which, if evident, a new cylinder should be fitted.
14 Carefully examine rubber components for signs of swelling, distortion, splitting, hardening or other wear, although it is recommended new rubber parts are always fitted after dismantling.
15 During reassembly soak the parts with Lockheed brake fluid.
16 Fit the cup filler (23) onto the little end of the spring (22) and insert into the bore the spring being entered first.
17 Insert the rubber cup seal (24) with the lip first into the cylinder bore. This must be done with care as the lips must not be allowed to curl up when entering the seal into the bore.
18 Insert the piston (25) with the flat side leading into the bore.
19 Insert the rod (29) into the rubber boot (26) the correct way round and secure it in place with the small circlip (27).
20 Refit the rod assembly into the body (20) and secure the rubber boot (26) to the body with the large diameter circlip (28).
21 The clutch slave cylinder is refitted to the mounting bracket in the reverse sequence to removal. Ensure the bleed nipple is to the top.
22 Refill the reservoir of the twin master cylinders with Lockheed brake fluid and bleed the system as detailed in Section 3 of this Chapter.

14. Clutch Slave Cylinder - Adjustment (TR2, 3, 3A)

1. Slacken the locknut (33) (Fig. 5.1) on the fork assembly and screw out the rod (29) until all clearance has been removed by the end of the rod just being in contact with the piston (25) inside the cylinder.
2. Holding the rod firmly with a pair of pliers screw the locknut (33) along the rod (29) until a 0.079 inch feeler gauge can be correctly inserted between the nut (33) and the face of the fork end (30).
3. Screw the rod (29) back into the fork end (30) until the face of the locknut (33) just touches the face of the fork end (30). Tighten the locknut so locking the rod adjustment.
4. Periodically check this adjustment as it will alter as the clutch driven plate friction linings wear.

15. Clutch Slave Cylinder - Removal, Dismantling, Examination and Reassembly (TR4, 4A)

1. The clutch slave cylinder is positioned on the left hand side of the bellhousing (photo).
2. Before removing the slave cylinder take off the clutch master cylinder reservoir cap and place a piece of thin polythene over the top of the reservoir. Screw the cap down tightly over the polythene.
3. Extract the split pin, washer and clevis pin from the clutch pushrod yoke and withdraw the pushrod from the slave cylinder.
4. Undo the two bolts holding the slave cylinder to the bracket on the engine end plate.
5. Wipe the area clean of dust and dirt where the hydraulic pipes are connected to the slave cylinder and disconnect the hydraulic pipe from the slave cylinder by releasing the union with an open ended spanner and rotating the slave cylinder. Take care not to kink or twist the flexible hose. The polythene over the reservoir will prevent any loss of fluid when the hydraulic pipe is disconnected.
6. Clean the outside of the cylinder before dismantling.
7. Refer to Fig. 5.2., pull off the rubber dust cover (25) and by shaking hard the piston (27), seal (28) and the spring (29) should come out of the cylinder bore.
8. If they prove stubborn carefully use a compressed air jet on the hydraulic hose connection and this should remove the internal parts but do take care as they will fly out. We recommend placing a pad over the dust cover end to catch the parts.
9. Wash all the internal parts with either brake fluid or methylated spirits and dry using a non-fluffy rag.
10 Inspect the bore and piston for signs of deep scoring which, if evident, a new cylinder should be fitted.
11 Carefully examine the rubber components for signs of swelling, distortion, splitting, hardening or other wear, although it is recommended new rubber parts are always fitted after dismantling.
12 Reassembly is a straight reversal of the dismantling procedure but note the following points:-

a) As the component parts are refitted to the slave cylinder bore smear them with clean hydraulic fluid.
b) When refitting the piston seal ensure that it is positioned the correct way round as shown in Fig. 5.2.
c) On completion of refitting to its mounting bracket, top up the reservoir with the correct grade hydraulic fluid and bleed the system. Do not forget to remove the polythene.

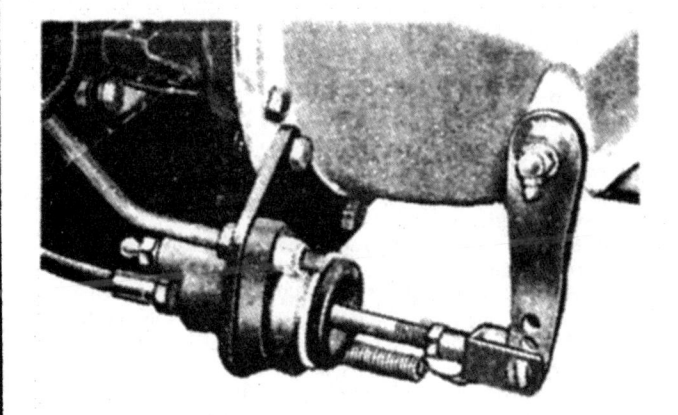

Fig. 5.5. Clutch slave cylinder mounted to clutch bellhousing

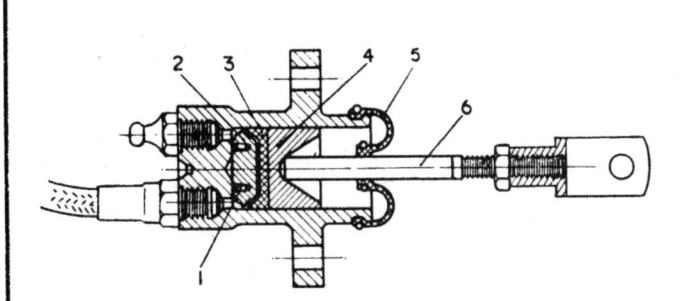

Fig. 5.6. CROSS SECTION VIEW OF CLUTCH SLAVE CYLINDER (TR2, 3, 3A)
1 Spring
2 Cup filler
3 Rubber cup
4 Piston
5 Rubber boot
6 Fork assembly

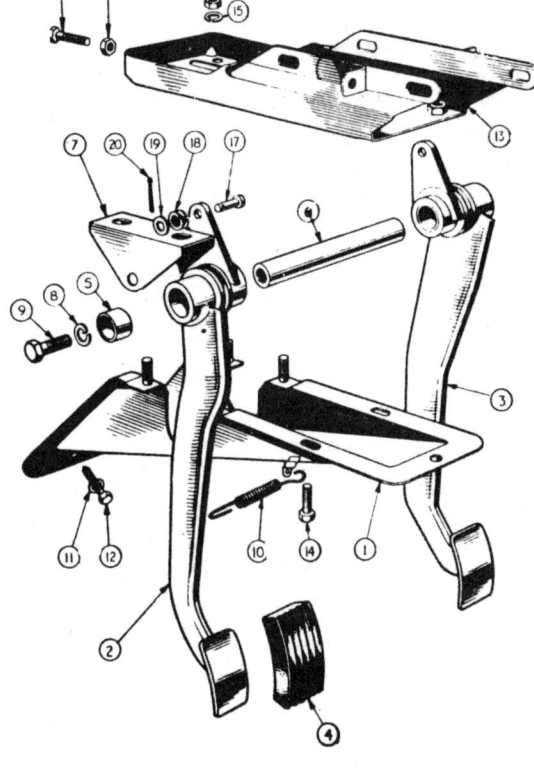

Fig. 5.7. CLUTCH AND BRAKE PEDAL ASSEMBLY
1 Pedal shaft cover assembly
2 Clutch pedal
3 Brake pedal
4 Rubber pad for pedals
5 Pedal pivot bush
6 Pedal shaft
7 Supporting bracket for pedal shaft
8 Lockwasher
9 Bolt securing brackets to shaft
10 Pedal return spring
11 Lockwasher
12 Bolt securing pedal assembly to bulkhead
13 Master cylinder support bracket
14 Bolt securing pedal assembly and master cylinder support bracket to bulkhead
15 Lockwasher
16 Nut securing pedal assembly and master cylinder support bracket to bulkhead
17 Clevis pin
18 Double coil spring washer
19 Plain washer
20 Split pin
21 Locknut
22 Pedal limit stop

115

Chapter 5/Clutch & Actuating Mechanism

16. Clutch Slave Cylinder - Adjustment (TR4, 4A)

1. Slacken the locknut (23) (Fig. 5.2) on the fork assembly (22) and screw out the rod (24) until all clearance has been removed by the end of the rod just being in contact with the piston (27) inside the cylinder.
2. Holding the rod firmly with a pair of pliers screw the locknut (23) along the rod (24) until a 0.010 inch feeler gauge can be correctly inserted between the nut (23) and the face of the fork end (22).
3. Screw the rod (24) back into the fork end (22) until the face of the locknut (23) just touches the face of the fork end (22). Tighten the locknut so locking the rod adjustment.
4. Periodically check this adjustment as it will alter as the clutch driven plate friction linings wear.

17. Clutch Master Cylinder - Removal and Refitting (TR2, 3, 3A)

Due to the master cylinder being of the twin bore design using the same body and reservoir for the brake master cylinder as well as the clutch master cylinder the unit should be removed in the manner described in Chapter 9, Section 16.

18. Clutch Master Cylinder - Dismantling, Overhaul and Reassembly (TR2, 3, 3A)

Full details of this operation are given in Chapter 9, Section 17.

19. Clutch Pedal Adjustment (TR2, 3, 3A)

1. It should not be necessary to adjust the pedal free movement unless the master cylinder assembly or the pedals have been removed for servicing.
2. The correct free movement of the pushrod should be adjusted to give between 1/2 to 5/8 inch free movement at the pedal. Should this movement not exist check that the reason is not something else such as a worn clutch or pedal pivots.
3. To adjust the pedal clearance slacken the locknuts (27) (Fig. 5.8) on the adjustment bracket (26). Also slacken the nuts (30) on the retaining bolts (28).
4. Slacken the locknut (21) (Fig. 5.7) and undo the adjusting bolt (22) about 1/8 inch. This will allow the combined master cylinder to be free to move in the support bracket.
5. Screw in the adjusting bolt (22) until the master cylinder assembly is pushed back and the pushrods are just in contact with the piston.
6. Hold the adjusting bolt (22) with a pair of pliers and screw in the locknut (21) until it just contacts the support bracket (13).
7. Unscrew the adjusting bolt (22) together with the previously set locknut (21) until a 0.030 inch feeler gauge can be correctly passed between the face of the locknut and the support bracket.
8. Tighten the locknut (21) without allowing the adjusting bolt (22) to rotate.
9. Move the master cylinder assembly forwards to its limit of movement and tighten the adjustment bracket locknuts to prevent it moving from its setting.
10 Finally tighten the attachment bolt nuts.

20. Clutch Master Cylinder - Removal and Refitting (TR3, 3A)

1. Connect a piece of plastic tubing to the clutch slave cylinder bleed nipple and by operating the clutch pedal several times with the bleed nipple open, drain the clutch hydraulic fluid in the reservoir into a clean glass container.
2. Undo the two pipes from the ports on the master cylinder and wrap the ends of the pipes in clean non-fluffy rag to stop dirt ingress and also to stop hydraulic fluid dripping onto the paintwork.
3. Extract the split pin from the clevis pin that holds the pedal to the push rod jaw end, lift away the plain washer and the clevis pin noting which way round the head of the clevis pin is fitted.
4. Carefully ease off the rubber boot retaining band and disconnect the rubber boot from the master cylinder body.
5. Push the clutch pushrod in slightly to relieve the pressure from the spring inside the master cylinder and, using a pair of long nose pliers, extract the circlip from its machined groove in the body of the master cylinder.
6. Lift out the pushrod assembly from the master cylinder together with the locating washer and the rubber boot.
7. Undo the two bolts which secure the master cylinder body to the mounting bracket and lift away the bolts and spring washers.
8. The master cylinder body may now be removed. Take care not to allow any hydraulic fluid to drop onto the paintwork.
9. Refitting is the reverse sequence to removal. The system will now have to be bled.

21. Clutch Master Cylinder - Dismantling, Overhaul and Reassembly (TR3, 3A)

1. If the clutch master cylinder has been removed from the car the rubber boot, pushrod, metal retaining washer and circlip will have been removed. If not carefully ease off the rubber boot retaining band and disconnect the rubber boot from the master cylinder body.
2. Push the clutch pushrod in slightly so as to relieve the pressure from the spring inside the master cylinder body and, using a pair of long nose pliers, extract the circlip from the machined groove in the body of the master cylinder.
3. Lift out the pushrod assembly from the master cylinder together with the locating washer and the rubber boot.
4. Pull the piston and valve assembly as one unit from the master cylinder.
5. Using a small screwdriver raise the leaf of the spring thimble to clear it from the shoulder on the plunger and pull the thimble from the plunger.
6. Compress the coil spring and slip the valve stem into the larger offset in the base of the thimble.
7. Slide the thimble off the head of the valve stem. Lift away the spacer and spring washer from the valve stem.
8. Remove the valve seal from the valve stem and the two seals from the plunger.
9. Clean and carefully examine all parts, especially the piston cup and rubber washers, for signs of distortion, swelling, splitting, or other wear and check the piston and cylinder for wear and scoring. Replace any parts that are faulty.
10 During the inspection of the piston seal it has been found advisable to maintain the shape of this seal as regular as possible and for this reason do not turn it inside out as slight distortion may be caused.
11 Rebuild the plunger and valve assembly in the following

Fig. 5.8. CLUTCH MASTER CYLINDER (LOCKHEED)

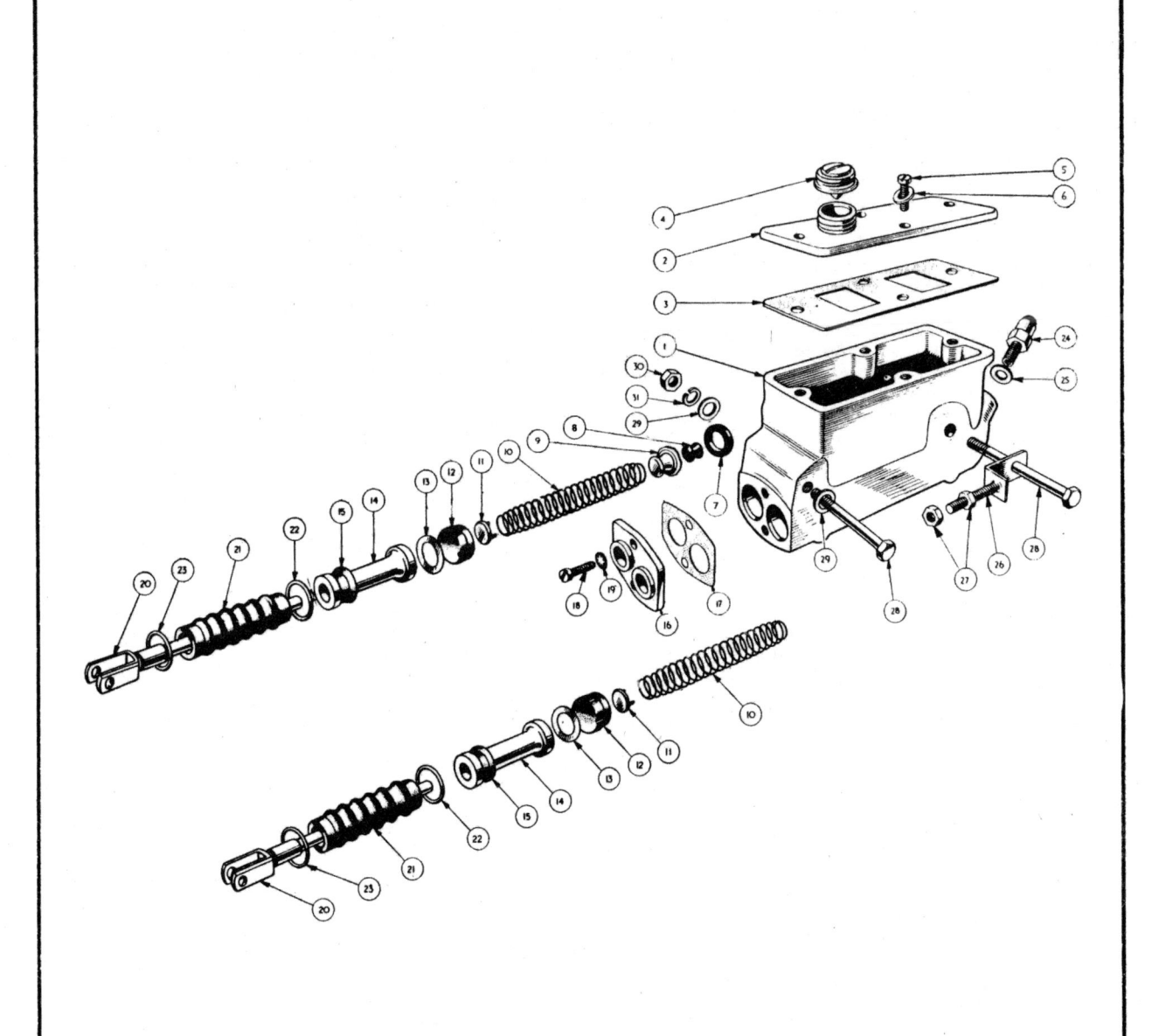

1 Body
2 Cover plate
3 Joint washer
4 Filler cap and baffle
5 Cover plate attachment screw
6 Shakeproof washer
7 Valve seal (brakes only)
8 Valve cup (brakes only)
9 Valve body (brakes only)
10 Valve return spring
11 Spring retainer
12 Main cup
13 Washer between main cup and piston
14 Piston
15 Piston secondary cup
16 Boot fixing plate
17 Gasket between plate and body
18 Plate attachment screw
19 Shakeproof washer
20 Pushrod assembly
21 Pushrod boot
22 Large clip (boot to fixing plate)
23 Small clip (boot to pushrod)
24 Slave cylinder pipe adaptor (clutch)
25 Gasket
26 Bracket assembly
27 Jam nut
28 Master cylinder attachment bolt
29 Plain washer (on front bolt only)
30 Nut
31 Lockwashers under nuts

Chapter 5/Clutch & Actuating Mechanism

manner:-

a) Fit the plunger seal to the plunger so that the larger circumference of the rubber lip will enter the cylinder bore first. The seal sits in the groove.
b) Then fit the valve seal to the valve in the same way.
c) Place the valve spring seal washer so its convex face abuts the valve stem flange and then fit the seal spacer and spring.
d) Fit the spring thimble to the spring which must then be compressed so the valve stem can be reinserted in the thimble.
e) Replace the front of the plunger in the thimble and then press down the thimble leaf so it locates under the shoulder at the front of the plunger.
f) Generously lubricate the assembly with hydraulic fluid and carefully replace it in the master cylinder body taking great care not to damage the rubber seals as they are inserted into the cylinder bore.
g) Fit the pushrod and washer in place and secure with the circlip. Replace the rubber boot.

22. Clutch Pedal Adjustment (TR3, 3A)

It is important that the plunger returns fully to the end of the stroke when the clutch pedal is released as otherwise the valve sealing the port from the reservoir may possibly not be fully opened, if at all.

Should the valve remain closed it may be found that pressure will build up in the hydraulic system which will cause the slave cylinder piston to remain extended so causing clutch slip.

The locknuts should always be adjusted on the pushrod so that there is between 1/2 to 5/8 inch free play on the pedal before it starts to operate.

23. Clutch Master Cylinder - Removal and Refitting (TR4, 4A)

1. It is not possible to remove the clutch master cylinder without removing the brake master cylinder.
2. Connect a piece of plastic tubing to one of the brake bleed nipples and by operating the brake pedal several times drain the brake hydraulic fluid in the reservoir into a clean glass container.
3. Next connect the piece of plastic tubing to the clutch slave cylinder bleed nipple and by operating the clutch pedal several times drain the clutch hydraulic fluid in the reservoir into a clean glass container.
4. Remove the brake light switch from its mounting on the master cylinder bracket. On earlier models a pressure operated switch is mounted on the five way connector of the hydraulic pipe system and need not be disturbed.
5. Refer to Fig. 5.9 and extract the split pins from the clevis pins (1) securing the pedals to the master cylinders. Take care to recover the springs and washers and then withdraw the clevis pins (1).
6. Carefully disconnect the clutch and brake master cylinder hydraulic pipe connections ensuring that the pipes are not twisted.
7. Undo the screws (4) and the four nuts from the studs (3). Lift the master cylinder support bracket (11) from the scuttle and then disconnect the clutch master cylinder from the bracket by undoing the two retaining nuts, bolts and spring washers.
8. Refitting the master cylinders is the reverse sequence to removal. It will be necessary to bleed both the brake and clutch hydraulic systems.

24. Clutch Master Cylinder - Dismantling, Overhaul and Reassembly (TR4, 4A)

1. Unscrew the filler cap (16) (Fig. 5.10) and drain the hydraulic fluid into a clean container.
2. Pull off the rubber boot (13) which exposes the circlip (12) which must be removed so the pushrod (10) complete with metal retaining washer (11) can be pulled out of the master cylinder.
3. Pull the piston (2) and valve assembly (8) as one unit from the master cylinder.
4. The next step is to separate the piston and valve assemblies. With the aid of a small screwdriver prise up the inner leg of the piston return spring retainer (4) which engages under a shoulder in the front of the piston and holds the retainer in place.
5. The retainer (4), spring (5) and valve assembly (8) can then be separated from the piston.
6. To dismantle the valve assembly compress the spring (5) and move the retainer (4) (which has an offset hole) to one side in order to release the valve stem (8) from the retainer (4).
7. With the seat spacer (6) and valve seal washer (7) removed the rubber seals can be taken off and inspected.
8. Clean and carefully examine all the parts, especially the piston cup and rubber washers, for signs of distortion, swelling, splitting, or other wear and check the piston and cylinder for wear and scoring. Replace any parts that are faulty.
9. During the inspection of the piston seal it has been found advisable to maintain the shape of this seal as regular as possible and for this reason do not turn it inside out as slight distortion may be caused.
10 Rebuild the piston and valve assembly in the following manner:-

a) Fit the piston seal (3) to the piston (2) so the larger circumference of the rubber lip will enter the cylinder bore first. The seal sits in the groove.
b) Then fit the valve seal (9) to the valve (8) in the same way.
c) Place the valve spring seal washer (7) so its convex face abuts the valve stem flange (8) and then fit the seat spacer (6) and spring (5).
d) Fit the spring retainer (4) to the spring (5) which must then be compressed so the valve stem (8) can be reinserted in the retainer (4).
e) Replace the front of the piston (2) in the retainer (4) and then press down the retaining leg so it locates under the shoulder at the front of the piston (2).
f) Generously lubricate the assembly with hydraulic fluid and carefully replace it in the master cylinder taking great care not to damage the rubber seals as they are inserted into the cylinder bore.
g) Fit the pushrod (10) and washer (11) in place and secure with the circlip (12). Replace the rubber boot (13).

25. Clutch Pedal - Adjustment (TR4, 4A)

To adjust the clutch pedal movement the slave cylinder must be set which will then give the desired free pedal travel. Refer to Section 16 of this Chapter for full information on this adjustment.

26. Clutch Faults

There are four main faults to which the clutch and

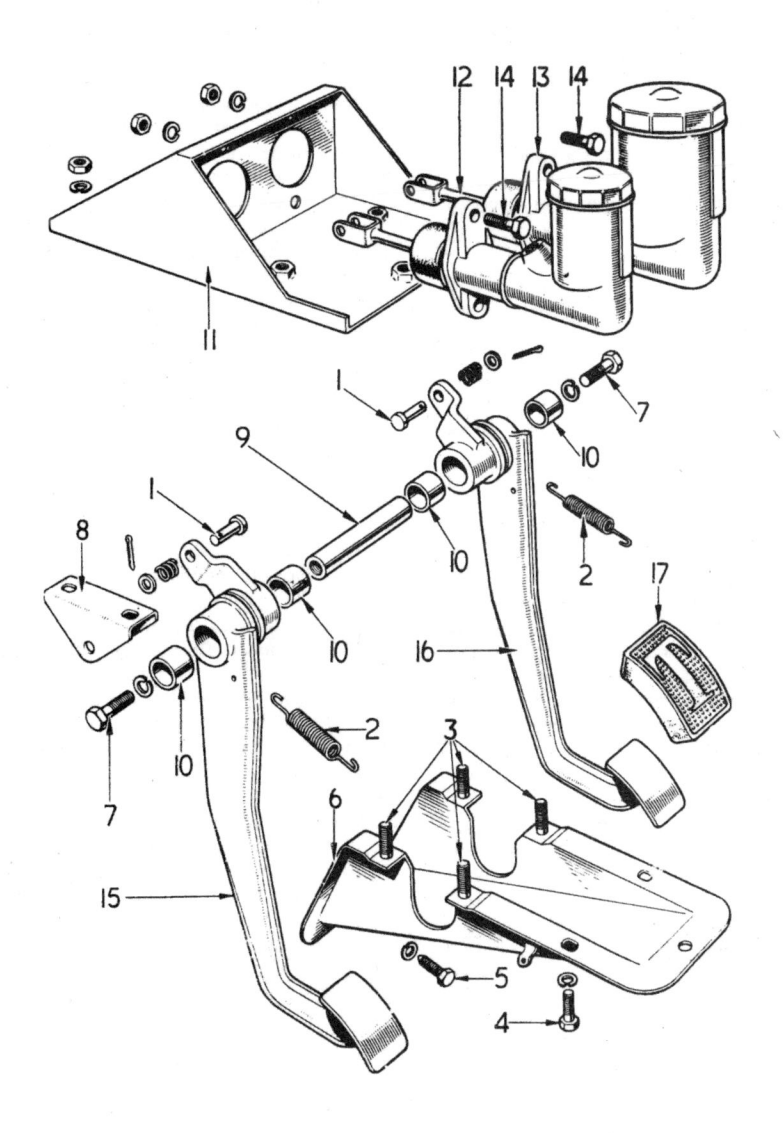

Fig. 5.9. CLUTCH AND BRAKE PEDAL AND MASTER CYLINDER BRACKET

1 Clevis pin
2 Pedal return spring
3 Bolts (pedal shaft cover assembly to master cylinder support bracket)
4 Bolts (pedal shaft cover assembly to master cylinder support bracket)
5 Setscrew (pedal shaft cover assembly to bulkhead)
6 Pedal shaft cover assembly
7 Setscrew (pedal stay to pedal shaft support bracket)
8 Pedal shaft support bracket
9 Pedal shaft
10 Pedal pivot bush
11 Master cylinder support bracket
12 Pushrod
13 Bracket master cylinder
14 Setscrew (master cylinder to support bracket)
15 Clutch pedal
16 Brake pedal
17 Pedal pad

119

Chapter 5/Clutch & Actuating Mechanism

release mechanism are prone. They may occur by themselves or in conjunction with any of the other faults. They are clutch squeal, slip, spin, and judder.

27. Clutch Squeal - Diagnosis and Cure

1. If, on taking up the drive or when changing gear, the clutch squeals, this is a sure indication of a badly worn clutch release bearing.
2. As well as regular wear due to normal use, wear of the clutch release bearing is much accentuated if the clutch is ridden or held down for long periods in gear, with the engine running. To minimise wear of this component the car should always be taken out of gear at traffic lights and for similar hold-ups.
3. The clutch release bearing is not an expensive item, but difficult to get at.

28. Clutch Slip - Diagnosis and Cure

1. Clutch slip is a self evident condition which occurs when the clutch friction plate is badly worn, oil or grease having got onto the flywheel or pressure plate faces, or the pressure plate itself is faulty.
2. The reason for clutch slip is that, due to one of the faults above, there is either insufficient pressure from the pressure plate, or insufficient friction from the friction plate to ensure solid drive.
3. If small amounts of oil get onto the clutch, they will be burnt off under the heat of clutch engagement and, in the process, gradually darkening the linings. Excessive oil on the clutch will burn off leaving a carbon deposit which can cause quite bad slip, or fierceness, spin and judder.
4. If clutch slip is suspected, and confirmation of this condition is required, there are several tests which can be made.
5. With the engine in second or third gear and pulling lightly up a moderate incline, sudden depression of the accelerator pedal may cause the engine to increase its speed without any increase in road speed. Easing off on the accelerator will then give a definite drop in engine speed without the car slowing.
6. In extreme cases of clutch slip the engine will race under normal acceleration conditions.

7. If slip is due to oil or grease on the linings a temporary cure can sometimes be effected by squirting carbon tetrachloride into the clutch. The permanent cure is, of course, to renew the clutch driven plate and trace and rectify the oil leak.

29. Clutch Spin - Diagnosis and Cure

1. Clutch spin is a condition which occurs when there is a leak in the clutch hydraulic actuating mechanism, there is an obstruction in the clutch either on the primary gear splines or in the operating lever itself, or the oil may have partially burnt off the clutch linings and have left a resinous deposit which is causing the clutch disc to stick to the pressure plate or flywheel.
2. The reason for clutch spin is that due to any, or a combination, of the faults just listed, the clutch pressure plate is not completely freeing from the centre plate even with the clutch pedal fully depressed.
3. If clutch spin is suspected, the condition can be confirmed by extreme difficulty in engaging first gear from rest, difficulty in changing gear, and very sudden take up of the clutch drive at the fully depressed end of the clutch pedal travel as the clutch is released.
4. Check the clutch master and slave cylinders and the connecting hydraulic pipe for leaks. Fluid in one of the rubber boots fitted over the end of either the master or slave cylinders is a sure sign of a leaking piston seal.
5. If these points are checked and found to be in order then the fault lies internally in the clutch, and it will be necessary to remove the clutch for examination.

30. Clutch Judder - Diagnosis and Cure

1. Clutch judder is a self evident condition which occurs when the gearbox or engine mountings are loose or too flexible, when there is oil on the face of the clutch friction plate, or when the clutch pressure plate has been incorrectly adjusted.
2. The reason for clutch judder is that due to one of the faults just listed, the clutch pressure plate is not freeing smoothly from the friction disc and is snatching.
3. Clutch judder normally occurs when the clutch pedal is released in first or reverse gears, and the whole car shudders as it moves backwards or forwards.

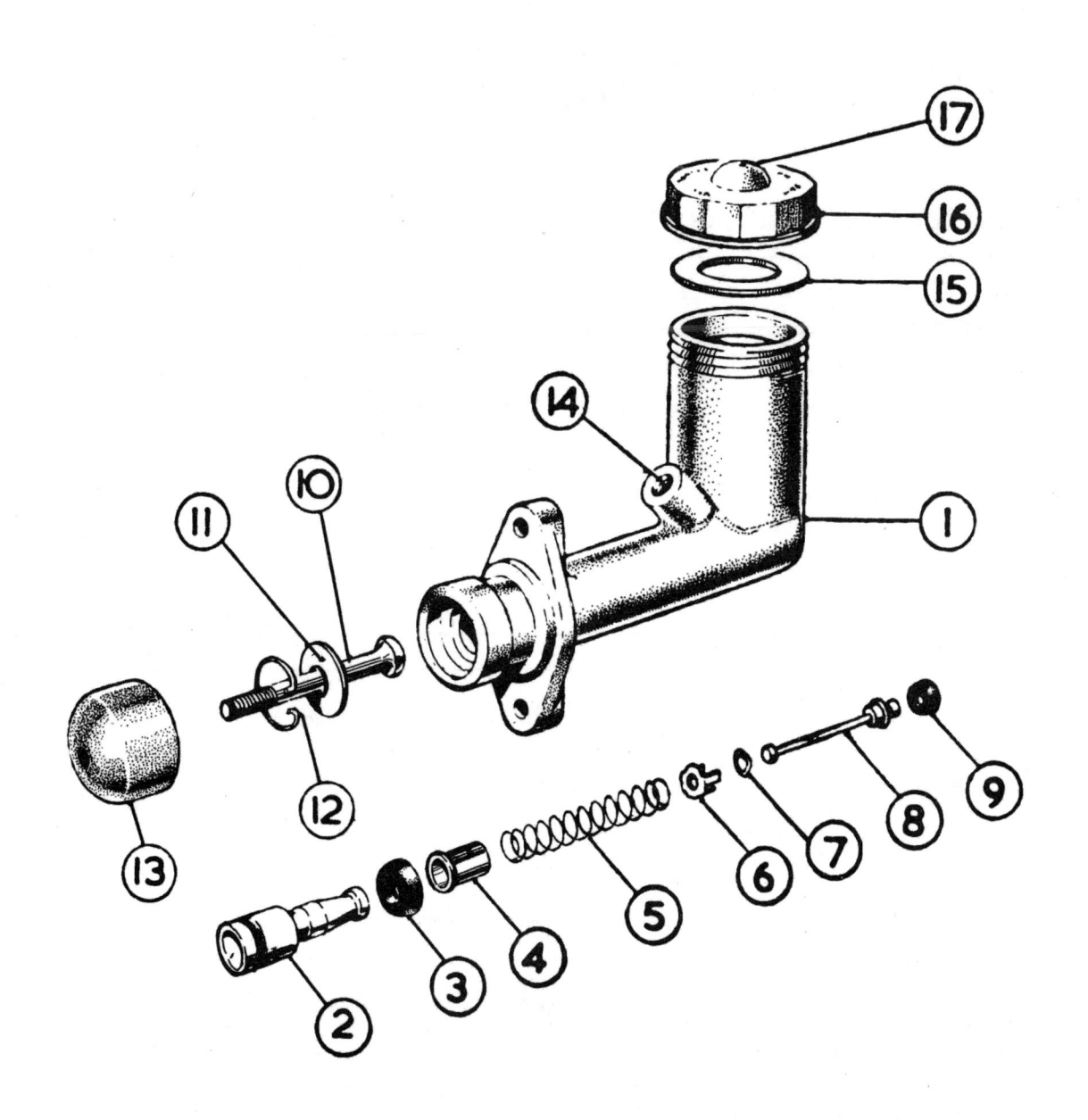

Fig. 5.10. CLUTCH MASTER CYLINDER COMPONENT
PARTS (TR4, 4A)

1 Master cylinder body
2 Plunger
3 Plunger seal
4 Spring retainer
5 Spring
6 Valve spacer
7 Spring washer
8 Valve stem
9 Valve seal
10 Pushrod
11 Retaining washer
12 Circlip
13 Dust cover
14 Outlet
15 Cap washer
16 Filler cap
17 Air vent

Chapter 6/Gearbox & Overdrive

Contents

General Description	...	1	Top Cover & Remote Control Assembly - Overhaul	10
Routine Maintenance	...	2	Overdrive - General Description	11
Gearbox - Removal & Refitting	...	3	Overdrive - Removal & Replacement	12
Gearbox Overhaul - General	...	4	Overdrive - Dismantling, Overhaul & Reassembly	13
Gearbox - Dismantling	...	5	Overdrive - Operating Lever Adjustment	14
Gearbox - Examination & Renovation	...	6	Overdrive - Operating Valve	15
First Motion Shaft - Dismantling & Reassembly	...	7	Overdrive - Non-return Valve - Removal & Replacement	16
Mainshaft - Dismantling & Reassembly	...	8	Overdrive - Pump Non-Return Valve	17
Gearbox - Reassembly	...	9		

Specifications

TR2, TR3, TR3A

Type	4 speed with synchromesh on 2nd, 3rd and 4th
Gearbox ratios:	
Overdrive top	.82
Top	Direct
Third	1.325
Second	2.00
First	3.38
Reverse	4.20
Bearings:	
Mainshaft rear and mainshaft centre	Fischer ball bearing MS12SG
	Hoffman ball bearing MS12K
Mainshaft rear	Fischer ball bearing 6206
	Hoffman ball bearing 130
Layshaft	Needle roller, 24 each set
Layshaft end float	.006 to .010 inch
Second speed constant gear float on bush	.004 to .006 inch
Third speed constant gear float on bush	.004 to .006 inch
Overall float of bush on mainshaft	.007 to .012 inch
Axial release load of 2nd speed synchromesh unit	25 to 27 lb.
Axial release load of 3rd speed synchromesh unit	19 to 21 lb.
Capacity:	
Gearbox	1½ pints
Gearbox plus overdrive	3½ pints
Drain and refill	2¾ pints

TR4, TR4A

Type	4 speed with synchromesh on all forward speeds
Gearbox ratios:	
Overdrive top	.82
Top	Direct
Overdrive third	1.09
Third	1.325
Overdrive 2nd	1.65
Second	2.01
First	3.139
Reverse	3.223
Countershaft diameter	.8125 - .0005 inch
Thrust washer thickness (front)	.068 - .002 inch
Thrust washer thickness (rear)	.105 + .002 inch

Fig. 6.1. GEARBOX INTERNAL MOVING PARTS TR2, 3, 3A

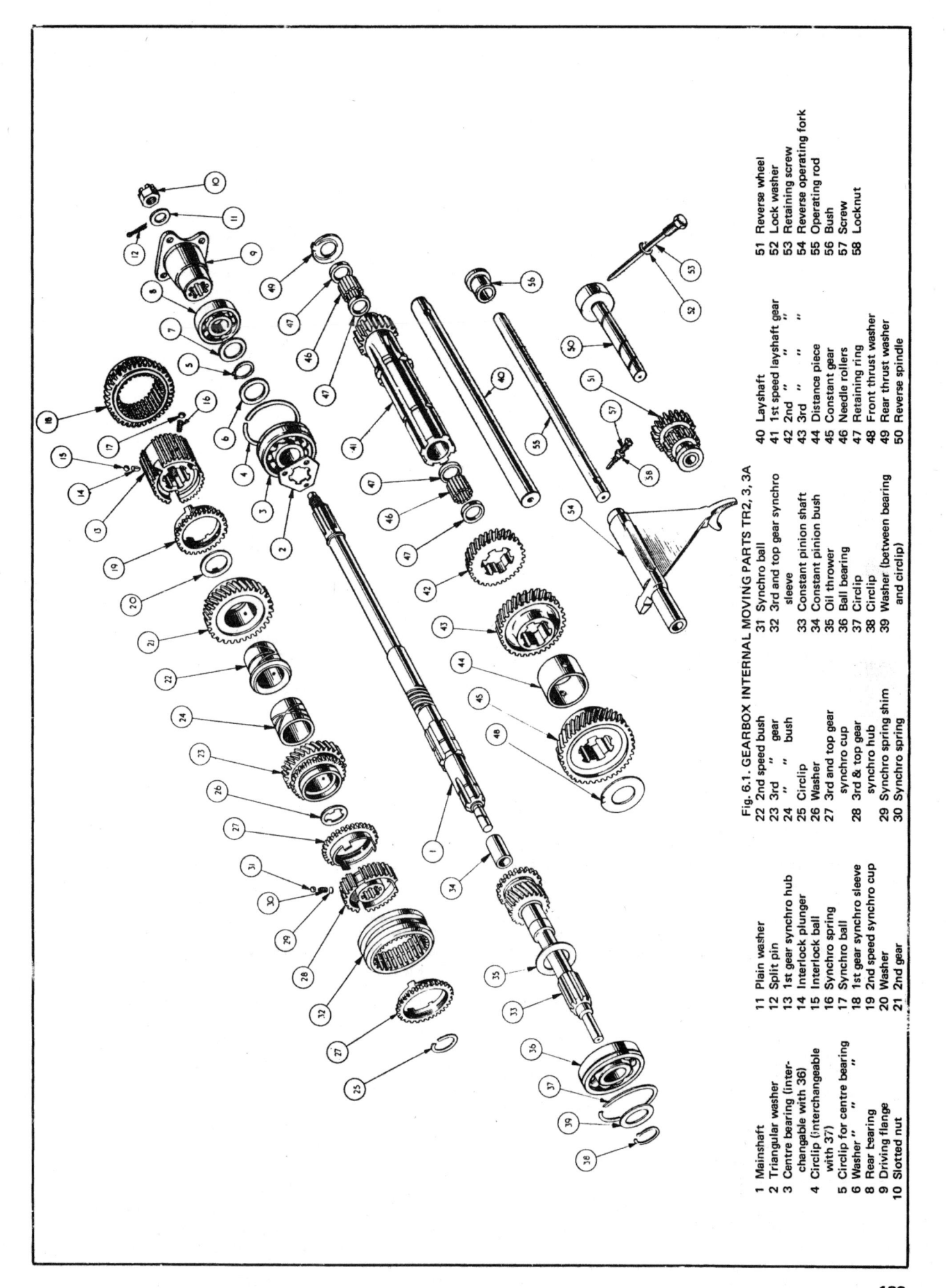

1 Mainshaft
2 Triangular washer
3 Centre bearing (interchangable with 37)
4 Circlip (interchangeable with 37)
5 Circlip for centre bearing
6 Washer "
8 Rear bearing
9 Driving flange
10 Slotted nut
11 Plain washer
12 Split pin
13 1st gear synchro hub
14 Interlock plunger
15 Interlock ball
16 Synchro spring
17 Synchro ball
18 1st gear synchro sleeve
19 2nd speed synchro cup
20 Washer
21 2nd gear
22 2nd speed bush
23 3rd " gear "
24 3rd " " bush
25 Circlip
26 Washer
27 3rd and top gear synchro cup
28 3rd & top gear synchro hub
29 Synchro spring shim
30 Synchro spring
31 Synchro ball
32 3rd and top gear synchro sleeve
33 Constant pinion shaft
34 Constant pinion bush
35 Oil thrower
36 Ball bearing
37 Circlip
38 Circlip
39 Washer (between bearing and circlip)
40 Layshaft
41 1st speed layshaft gear
42 2nd " " "
43 3rd " " "
44 Distance piece
45 Constant gear
46 Needle rollers
47 Retaining ring
48 Front thrust washer
49 Rear thrust washer
50 Reverse spindle
51 Reverse wheel
52 Lock washer
53 Retaining screw
54 Reverse operating fork
55 Operating rod
56 Bush
57 Screw
58 Locknut

123

Chapter 6/Gearbox & Overdrive

Countershaft end float	.007 + .005 inch	
Axial release load of 1st and 2nd synchromesh unit ...	25 - 27 lb.	
Axial release load of 3rd and 4th synchromesh unit ...	19 - 21 lb.	
Overall end float of 2nd/3rd gear bushes and thrust washers on mainshaft	.003 to .009 inch	
Overall end float of 1st gear bushes and thrust washers on mainshaft	.003 to .009 inch	
End float of 1st, 2nd and 3rd gear on bushes	.004 - .008 inch	
Thrust washer thickness:		
Part number	Thickness	Colour mark
129941	.120 to .118 inch	
129942	.128 to .121 inch	Green
129943	.126 to .124 inch	Blue
129944	.129 to .127 inch	Orange
134670	.132 to .006 inch	Yellow
Capacity:		
Gearbox	1½ pints	
Gearbox plus overdrive	3¼ pints	
Drain and refill	2¾ pints	

Torque Wrench Settings
TR2, TR3, TR3A

Front cover to gearbox	14 to 16 lb.ft. (1.936 to 2.212 Kg.m)
Extension to gearbox	14 to 16 lb.ft. (1.936 to 2.212 Kg.m)
Top cover to gearbox	14 to 16 lb.ft. (1.936 to 2.212 Kg.m)
Gearbox to engine	14 to 16 lb.ft. (1.936 to 2.212 Kg.m)
Rear mounting to gearbox extension	50 to 55 lb.ft. (6.913 to 7.604 Kg.m)
Propeller shaft flange nut	85 to 100 lb.ft. (11.752 to 13.826 Kg.m)

TR4, TR4A

Extension to gearbox	14 to 16 lb.ft. (1.936 to 2.212 Kg.m)
Gearbox to engine	8 to 10 lb.ft. (1.106 to 1.383 Kg.m)
Front cover to gearbox	14 to 16 lb.ft. (1.936 to 2.212 Kg.m)
Top cover to gearbox	14 to 16 lb.ft. (1.936 to 2.212 Kg.m)
Selector fork attachment	8 to 10 lb.ft. (1.106 to 1.383 Kg.m)
Propeller shaft flange nut	80 to 120 lb.ft. (11.060 to 16.590 Kg.m)

1. General Description

The manual gearbox fitted to TR2, 3, 3A models covered by this manual has four forward speeds and reverse with synchromesh action on the top three forward speeds. The manual gearbox fitted to the TR4 and 4A models has four forward speeds and reverse with synchromesh on all four forward speeds. Gears are selected by means of a remote control assembly mounted onto the top of the gearbox. A Laycock de Normanville overdrive unit operating on third and top gear is fitted to cars as an optional extra.

TR2, 3, 3A Gearbox

Fig. 6.1 shows the layout of the various moving parts whilst Fig. 6.2 shows the various fixed components and gear selection system. The clutch driven plate is splined to the first motion shaft (33) which is in constant mesh with the countershaft gear (45). The constant mesh gear (45) is splined to the countershaft hub (41) and is able to revolve at all times when no gears have been selected. It is supported at either end in needle roller bearings (46). Thrust washers (48, 49) are fitted at either end of the countershaft to take up excessive end float.

The mainshaft (1) carries the four forward gears and their respective synchromesh assemblies. The front of the shaft is supported in a bush (34) located in the rear of the first motion shaft (33). The rear end of the mainshaft is splined to the flange (9.) to which is connected the propeller shaft universal joint coupling flange. Various thickness thrust washers (20, 26) are fitted onto the mainshaft to control the end float of the bushes and gear assemblies on the mainshaft.

TR4, 4A models

The basic layout of the gearbox is identical to the one fitted to earlier models covered by this manual but there are differences which will affect the overhaul procedure. The moving parts of the gearbox are shown in Fig. 6.3 and Fig. 6.4 shows the fixed components and gear selection system.

Upon comparison between Fig. 6.1 and Fig. 6.3 it will be seen that the synchromesh unit for the first two speeds is different as is also the reverse wheel and selector system for reverse gear.

2. Routine Maintenance

This is confined to checking and topping up the oil level at 6,000 miles intervals with one of the recommended grade oils as listed on pages 11 of this manual. It is not recommended that the oil be drained except at overhaul periods as the gearbox and overdrive unit (if fitted) are filled with a special oil at the factory when new.

When topping up the oil level take care not to overfill

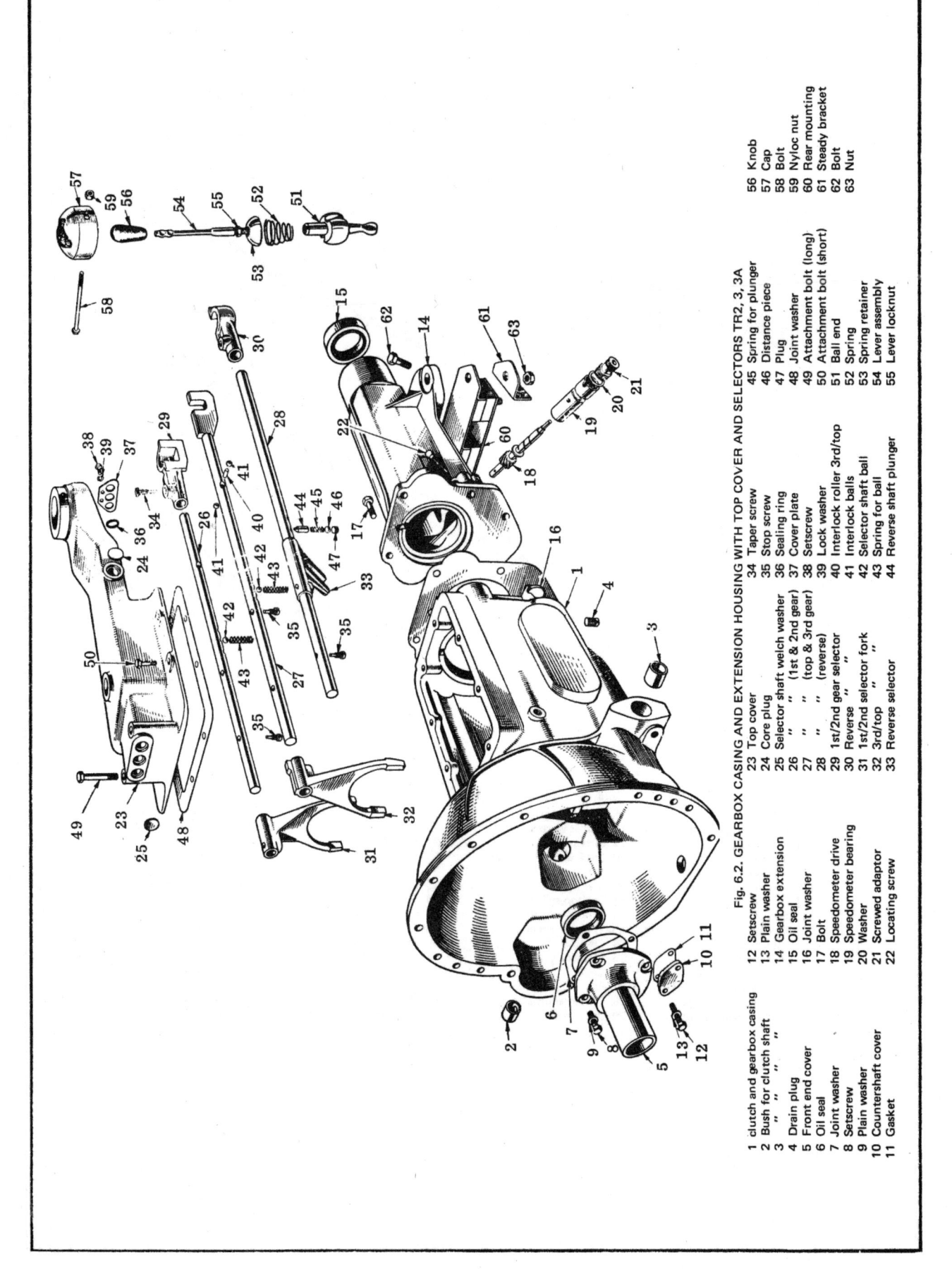

Fig. 6.2. GEARBOX CASING AND EXTENSION HOUSING WITH TOP COVER AND SELECTORS TR2, 3, 3A

1 clutch and gearbox casing
2 Bush for clutch shaft
3 " " "
4 Drain plug
5 Front end cover
6 Oil seal
7 Joint washer
8 Setscrew
9 Plain washer
10 Countershaft cover
11 Gasket
12 Setscrew
13 Plain washer
14 Gearbox extension
15 Oil seal
16 Joint washer
17 Bolt
18 Speedometer drive
19 Speedometer bearing
20 Washer
21 Screwed adaptor
22 Locating screw
23 Top cover
24 Core plug
25 Selector shaft welch washer
26 " " (1st & 2nd gear)
27 " " (top & 3rd gear)
28 " " (reverse)
29 1st/2nd gear selector
30 Reverse " "
31 1st/2nd selector fork
32 3rd/top " "
33 Reverse selector
34 Taper screw
35 Stop screw
36 Sealing ring
37 Cover plate
38 Setscrew
39 Lock washer
40 Interlock roller 3rd/top
41 Interlock balls
42 Selector shaft ball
43 Spring for ball
44 Reverse shaft plunger
45 Spring for plunger
46 Distance piece
47 Plug
48 Joint washer
49 Attachment bolt (long)
50 Attachment bolt (short)
51 Ball end
52 Spring
53 Spring retainer
54 Lever assembly
55 Lever locknut
56 Knob
57 Cap
58 Bolt
59 Nyloc nut
60 Rear mounting
61 Steady bracket
62 Bolt
63 Nut

125

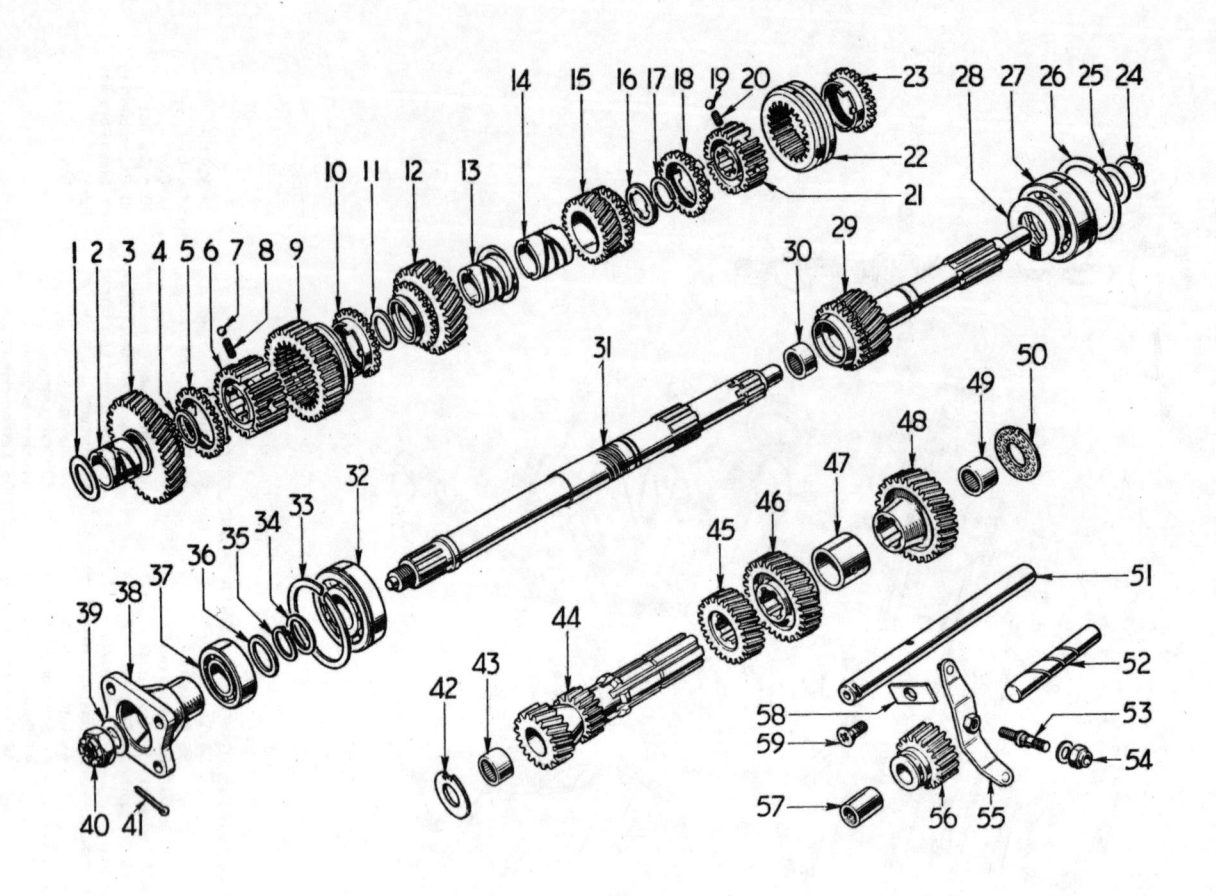

Fig. 6.3. GEARBOX INTERNAL MOVING PARTS (TR4, 4A)

1 Thrust washer	15 3rd speed gear	30 Needle roller bearing
2 Bush - 1st speed gear	16 Thrust washer	31 Mainshaft
3 1st speed gear	17 Circlip	32 Ball race
4 Thrust washer	18 3rd speed synchro cup	33 Circlip
5 1st speed synchro cup	19 Synchro ball	34 Distance washer
6 1st/2nd speed synchro hub	20 Spring	35 Circlip
7 Synchro ball	21 3rd/top synchro hub	36 Distance washer
8 Spring	23 Synchro sleeve	37 Rear ball race
9 Reverse mainshaft gear and synchro outer sleeve	23 Top gear synchro cup	38 Flange
	24 Circlip	39 Plain washer
10 2nd speed synchro cup	25 Distance washer	40 Slotted nut
11 Thrust washer	26 Circlip	41 Split pin
12 2nd speed gear	27 Ball race	42 Rear thrust washer
13 Bush - 2nd speed gear	28 Oil deflector plate	43 Needle roller bearing
14 Bush - 3rd speed gear	29 Input shaft	44 Layshaft hub

45 2nd speed layshaft gear	
46 3rd speed layshaft gear	
47 Distance piece	
48 Layshaft gear	
49 Needle roller bearing	
50 Front thrust washer	
51 Layshaft	
52 Reverse gear shaft	
53 Pivot stud	
54 Nyloc nut and washer	
55 Reverse gear operating lever	
56 Reverse gear	
57 Reverse gear bush	
58 Locating plate	
59 Screw	

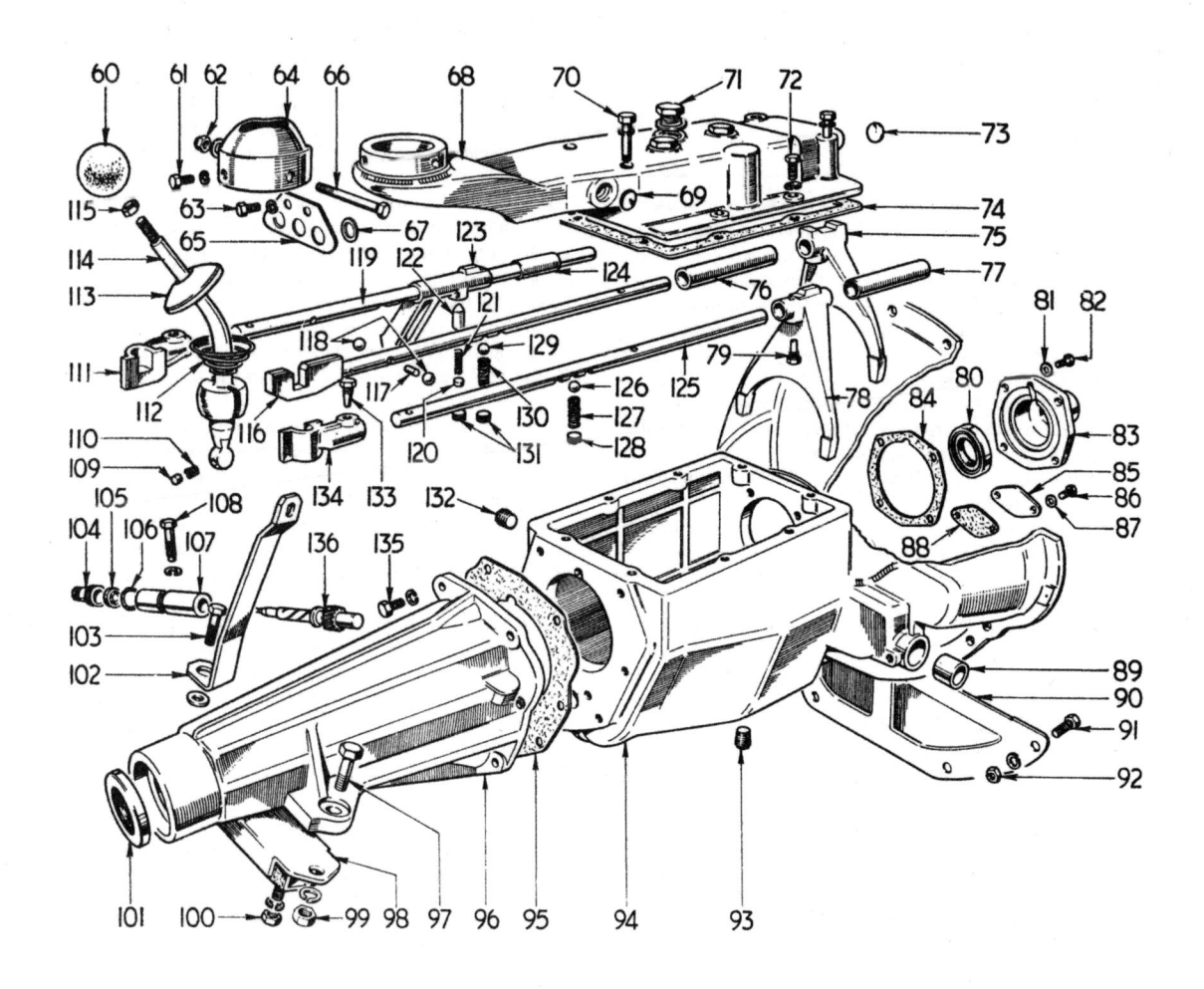

Fig. 6.4. GEARBOX CASING AND EXTENSION HOUSING WITH TOP COVER AND SELECTOR SYSTEM COMPONENTS (TR4, 4A)

60 Knob	80 Oil seal	100 Nut	120 Shim
61 Setscrew	81 Copper washer	101 Oil seal	121 Spring
62 Nyloc nut	82 Bolt	102 Stay	122 Plunger
63 Setscrew	83 Front cover	103 Bolt	123 Reverse actuator
64 Cap	84 Gasket	104 Speedometer cable adaptor	124 Distance piece
65 End plate	85 Countershaft end plate	105 Seal	125 2nd/1st selector shaft
66 Cross bolt	86 Setscrew	106 Rubber 'O' ring	126 Ball - detent
67 Rubber 'O' ring	87 Copper washer	107 Housing	127 Spring
68 Top cover	88 Gasket	108 Peg bolt	128 Plug
69 Welch plug	89 Bush	109 Plunger - anti-rattle	129 Ball - detent
70 Bolt	90 Cover plate	110 Spring	130 Spring
71 Plug	91 Setscrew	111 Selector - reverse	131 Plug
72 Bolt	92 Nut	112 Spring	132 Level/filler plug
73 Welch plug	93 Drain plug	113 Cap disc	133 Peg bolt
74 Gasket	94 Casing	114 Lever	134 Selector 1st/2nd
75 Top/3rd selector fork	95 Gasket	115 Nut	135 Bolt
76 Distance tube	96 Extension housing	116 Top/3rd selector shaft	136 Speedo drive gear
77 Distance tube	97 Bolt	117 Interlock plunger	
78 2nd/1st selector fork	98 Silentbloc mounting	118 Balls - interlock	
79 Peg bolt	99 Nut	119 Reverse selector shaft	

Chapter 6/Gearbox & Overdrive

the gearbox or overdrive otherwise leaks could occur at the various seals. Allow any excess oil to drain from the filler level plug before replacing the plug.

3. Gearbox - Removal and Refitting

1. The best method of removing the gearbox is to separate the gearbox bellhousing from the engine end plate and to lift the gearbox away from the inside of the car. It is recommended that during the final stages of removal the assistance of a second person is obtained especially if an overdrive unit is fitted to the rear of the gearbox. Where instructions are not common, the model to which the information applies will be given at the start of the paragraph.
2. Disconnect the battery earth terminal, raise the car and put on axle stands if a ramp is not available. The higher the car is off the ground the easier it will be to work underneath.
3. Lift away both seat cushions and also the carpeting from the front foot wells.
4. Undo the gearbox drain plug and drain the oil into a clean container. When all the oil has drained out replace the drain plug.
5. Undo and remove the eight nuts securing the seats to their seat runners. Lift away the front seats to give better access to the floor centre section.
6. TR4, 4A only — Make a note of the electrical cable connections at the rear of the switches and disconnect the electrical terminals. If a radio set is fitted this should be removed from its mounting (photo).
7. Slacken the gear change lever knob locknut and unscrew the knob. Also unscrew the locknut (photo).
8. Withdraw the gear change lever rubber boot from the gear change lever (photo).
9. Disconnect the two dip switch cables from their snap connectors (photo). and remove the dip switch.
10 Undo the two bolts holding the panel to the underside of the instrument panel switch console (photo).
11 TR4, 4A only — Undo the four bolts holding the facia support to the floor panels (photo).
12 TR4, 4A only — Disconnect the two heater control cables, one of which is shown in the photo.
13 TR4, 4A only — Withdraw the centre console from under the switch panel and lift away from the car (photo).
14 Undo the sixteen bolts with plain washers holding the floor centre section to the floor panels and lift away the complete centre section.
15 Undo the propeller shaft universal joint flange retaining nyloc nuts and bolts and washers from the flange at the rear of the gearbox extension housing (standard gearbox) or rear ofsthe overdrive unit (photo). Scribe a mark across the two flanges to ensure replacement in the same relative position.
16 Using a pair of pliers undo the speedometer drive cable knurled retainer from the gearbox extension housing (standard gearbox) or rear of the overdrive unit (photo).
17 Support the weight of the rear of the engine by placing a jack with a piece of wood on the saddle at the rear of the engine (photo).
18 Undo and remove the right hand overdrive or gearbox silencbloc mounting bolt followed by the nut and spring washer. Then undo the bracket to the chassis mounting nut and bolt (photo).
19 Lift away the bracket noting that the nut is welded to the underside to assist refitting (photo).
20 Remove the bolt and washer securing the gearbox remote control support stay to the silentbloc mounting (standard gearbox) or silentbloc mounting flange on the side of the overdrive unit (photo).
21 Lift away the little spacer from between the stay and overdrive unit mounting flange (photo).
22 Disconnect the clutch pedal return spring from the slave cylinder pushrod (photo).
23 Extract the clutch slave cylinder pushrod clevis split pin and withdraw the clevis to separate the linkage (photo).
24 Disconnect the heavy duty cable from the rear of the starter motor.
25 Undo the two starter motor retaining bolts and push the starter motor forwards so as to clear the clutch bellhousing.
26 Disconnect the two wires from their terminals of the reverse light switch and also the two wires from the solenoid if the overdrive unit is fitted.
27 Undo and remove the four bolts and nuts securing the clutch bellhousing cover plate to the bellhousing (photo).
28 Note the spring washers which are fitted between the nut and bellhousing flange.
29 Lift away the bellhousing cover plate (photo).
30 The clutch slave cylinder must next be removed from its location. The mounting nuts will have already been undone to remove the cover. Extract the pushrod from the end of the slave cylinder and put in a safe place. Tie the slave cylinder out of the way. It will not be necessary to disconnect the hydraulic hose from the rear of the slave cylinder (photo).
31 Turn the gearbox rear mounting through 90° and lift away from the underside of the unit (photo).
32 Undo the nuts and bolts holding the gearbox clutch bellhousing to the engine backplate.
33 The next operations must be done with care and the assistance of a second person is necessary. Pass a rope sling around the rear of the gearbox extension housing or overdrive unit so that one person can lift up the rear of the unit.
34 With the weight of the rear of the gearbox being taken by the rope sling held by a person standing at the rear of the front seat area carefully withdraw the gearbox taking care not to allow any weight to be taken by the gearbox input shaft otherwise it may bend.
35 When the input shaft is clear of the clutch swing the rear of the gearbox round to the left and withdraw through the front N/S door aperture (photo).
36 Before any work is to be carried out on the gearbox or overdrive unit it should be thoroughly washed in paraffin or 'Gunk' and dried using a non-fluffy rag (photo).
37 Replacement is the reverse sequence to removal. Do not forget to refill the gearbox with 1½ pints (3½ pints if gearbox is fitted with overdrive) of recommended grade oil. It will be easier to do this before the centre floor is refitted.

4. Gearbox Overhaul - General

Although the two gearboxes are similar in construction there are several major differences which require special attention and therefore the various procedures are described in detail for each gearbox. The following five sections are each divided into two parts, dealing with each gearbox in turn to avoid any confusion. Many of the photographs are common to each gearbox and adequate cross reference is made to these wherever possible.

5. Gearbox - Dismantling

NOTE: When dismantling or reassembling the gearbox carefully follow the photographs as well as the exploded diagrams.

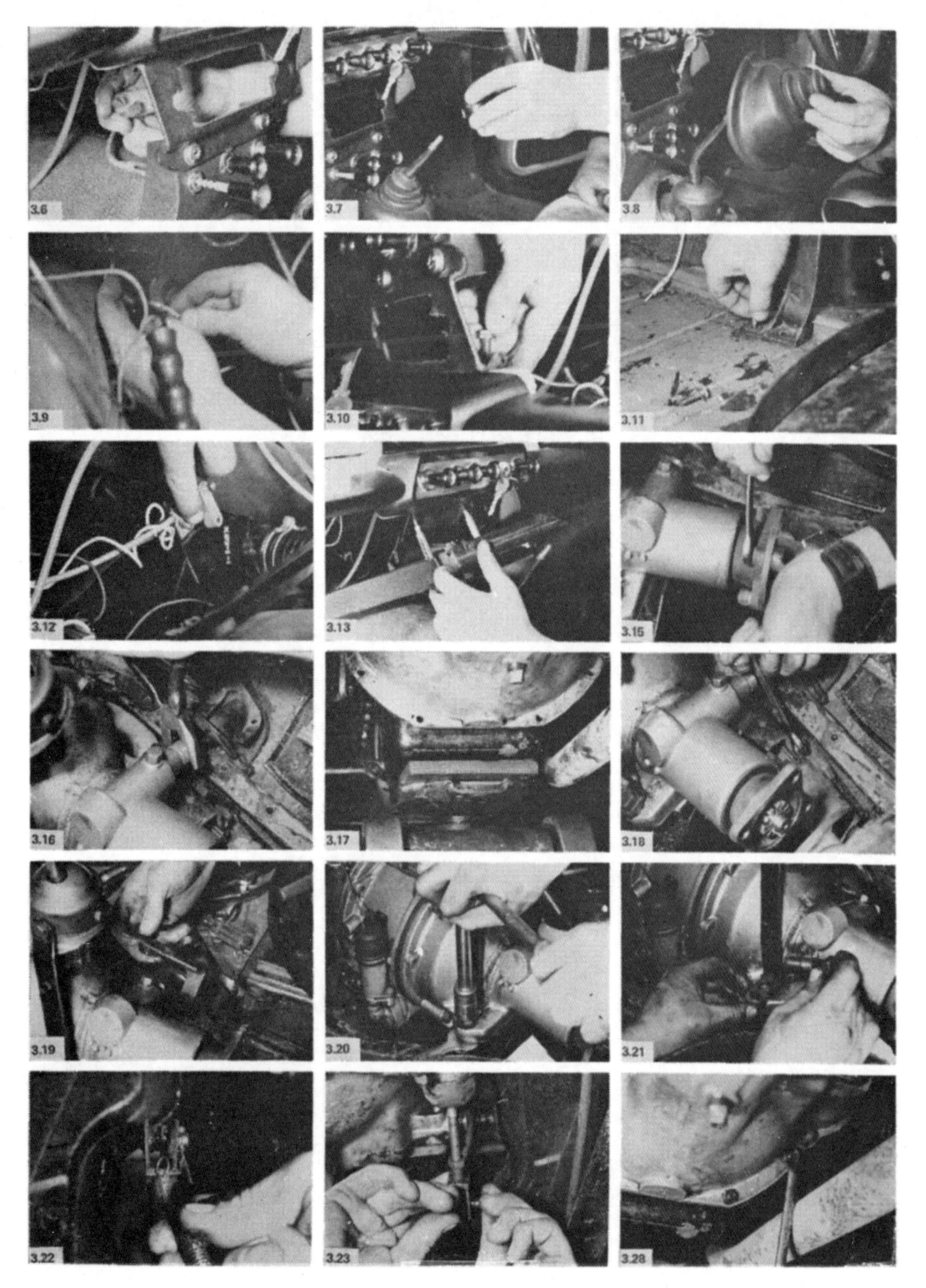

3.6 3.7 3.8
3.9 3.10 3.11
3.12 3.13 3.15
3.16 3.17 3.18
3.19 3.20 3.21
3.22 3.23 3.28

129

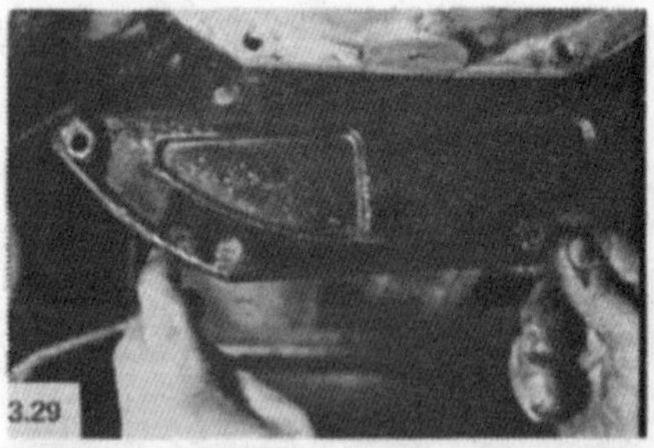
3.29

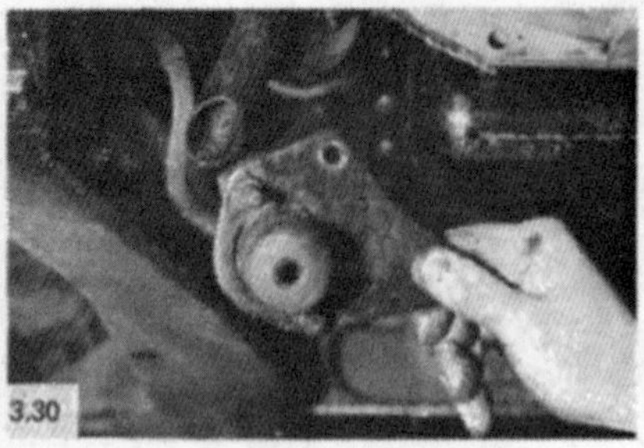
3.30

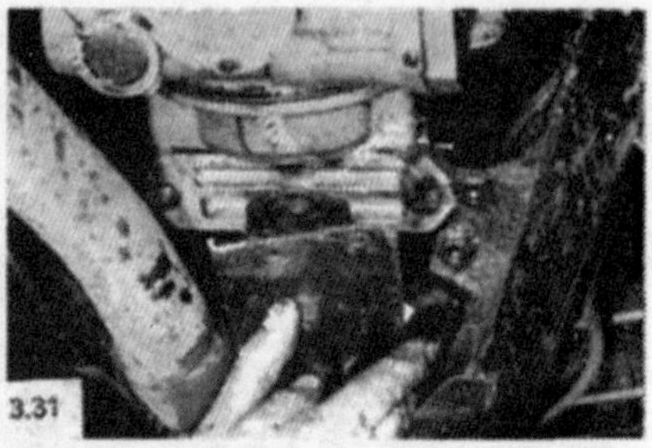
3.31

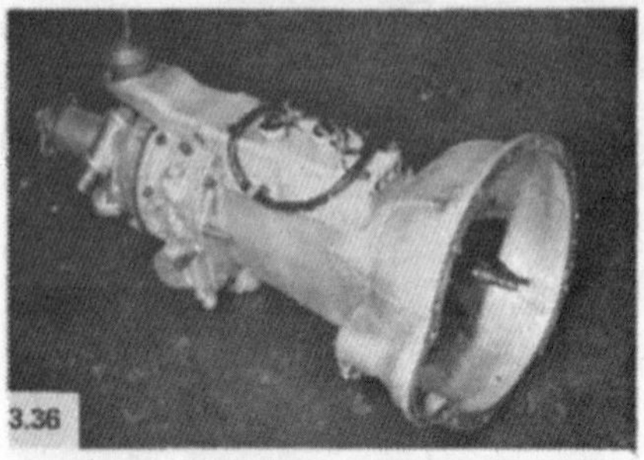
3.36

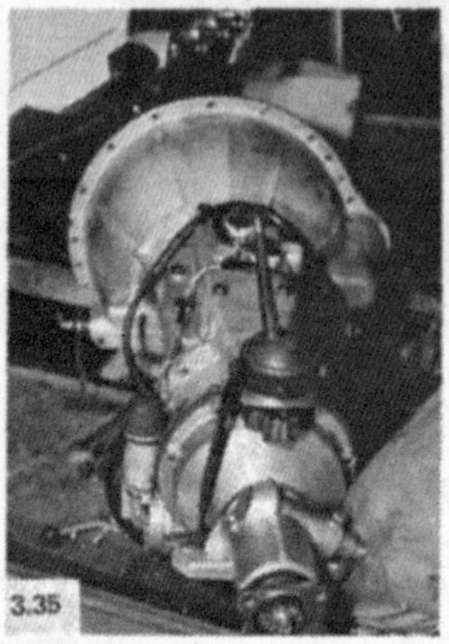
3.35

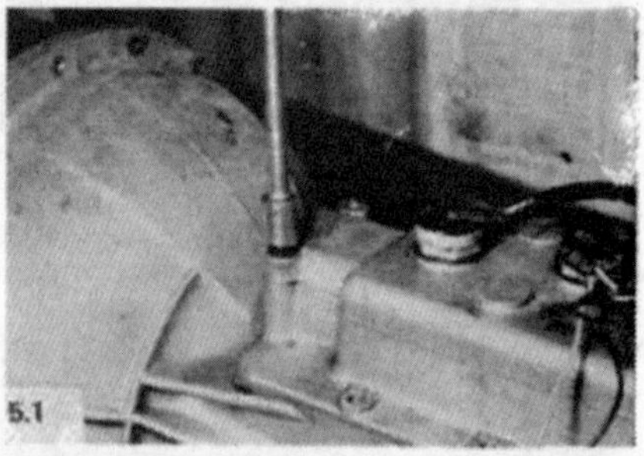
5.1

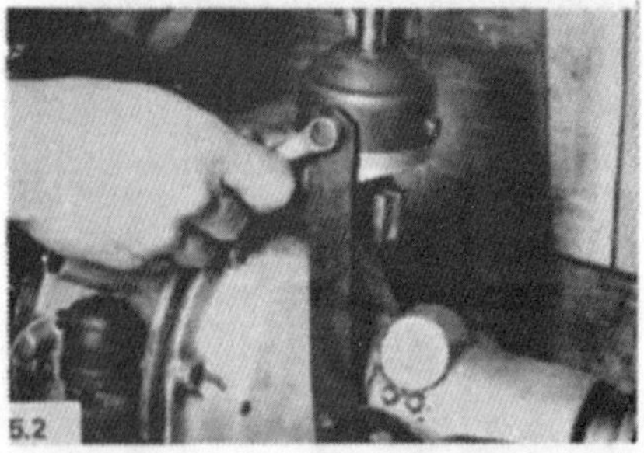
5.2

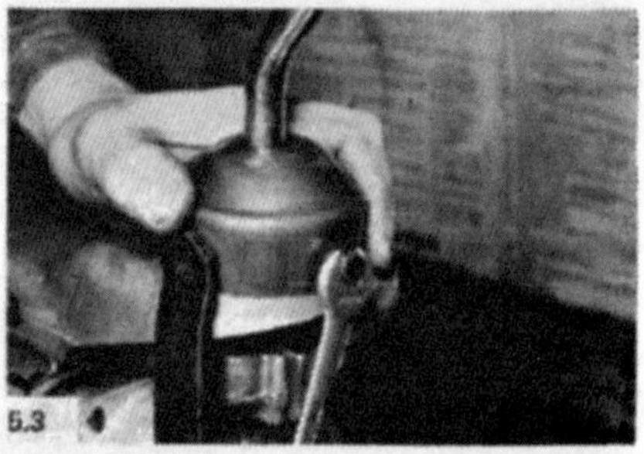
5.3

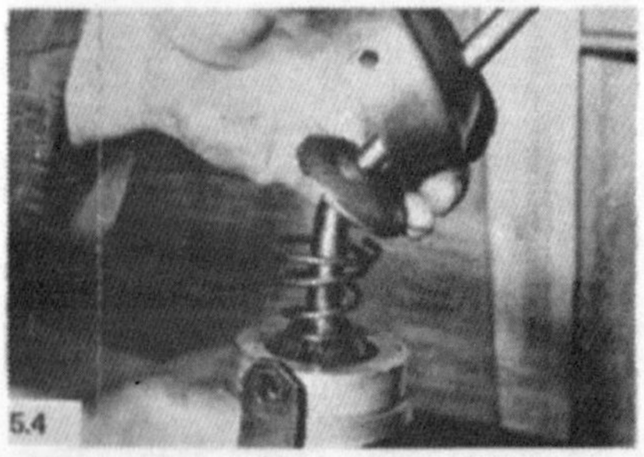
5.4

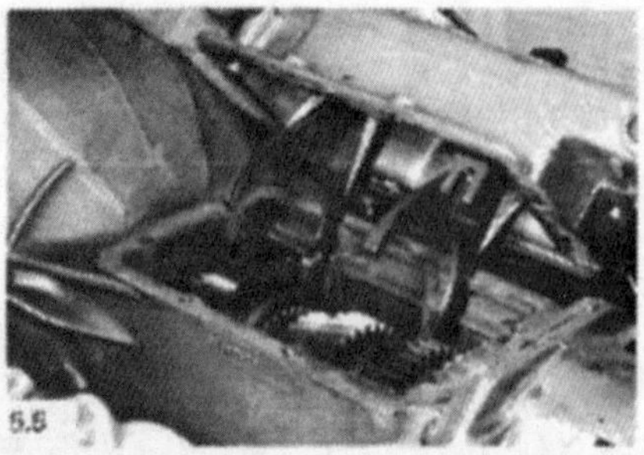
5.6

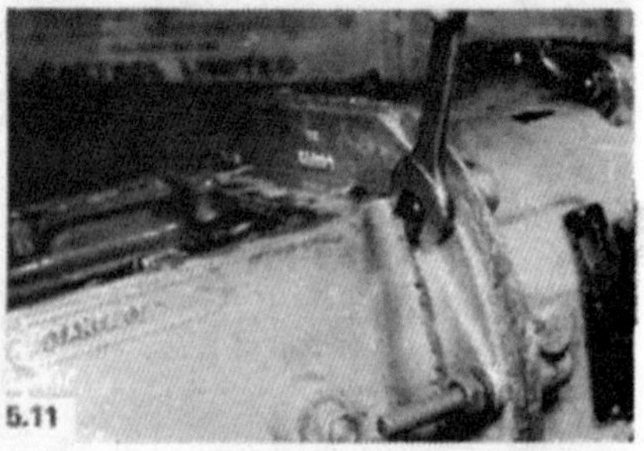
5.11

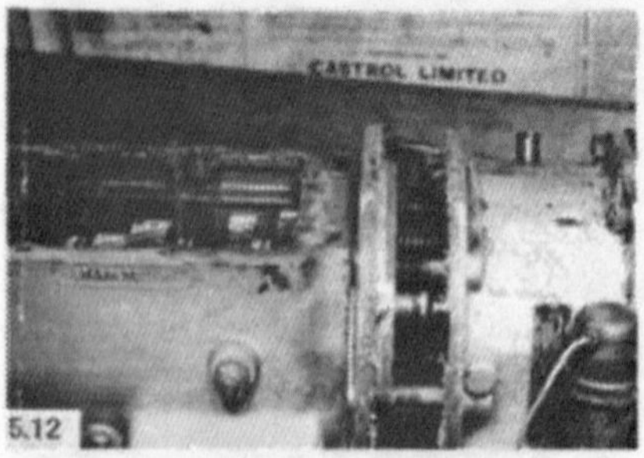

5.12

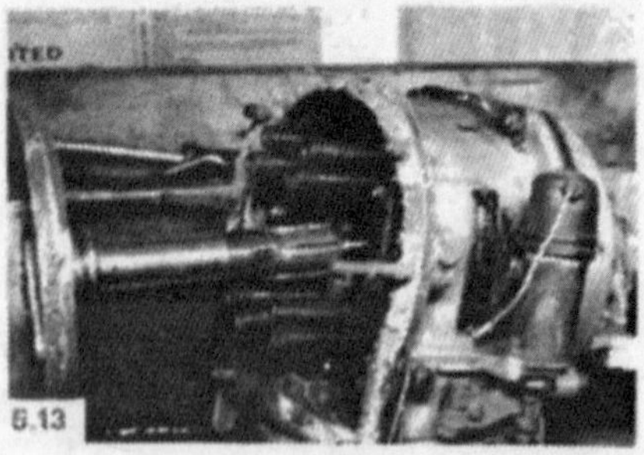
5.13

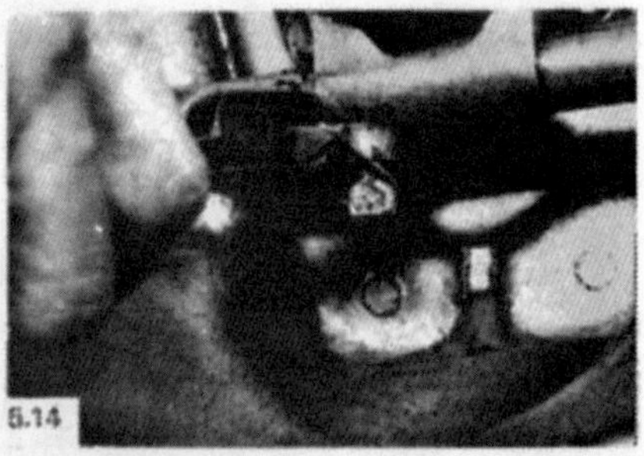
5.14

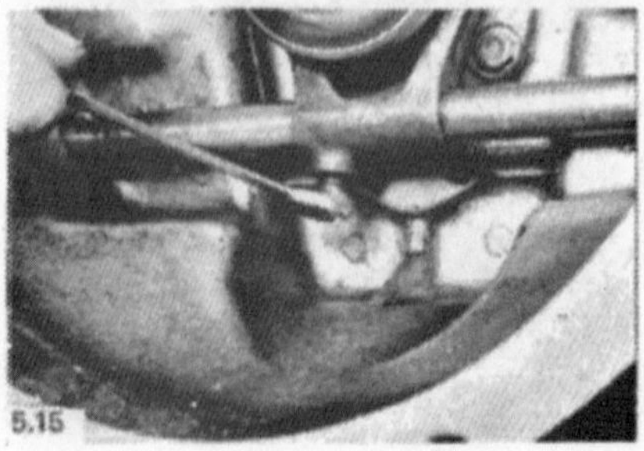
5.15

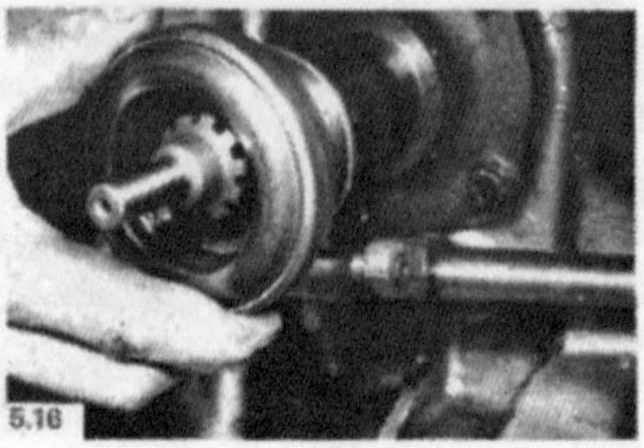
5.16

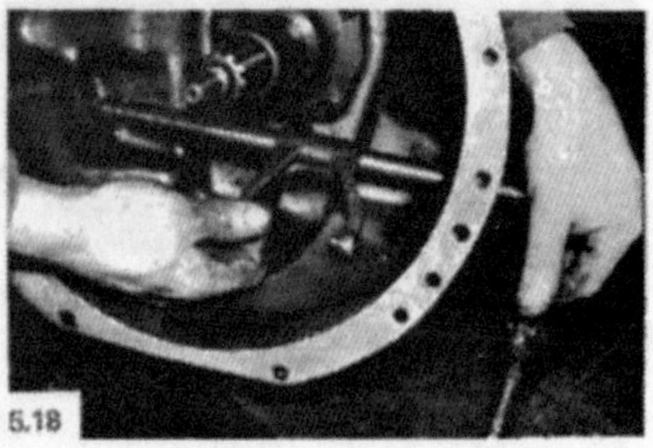
5.18

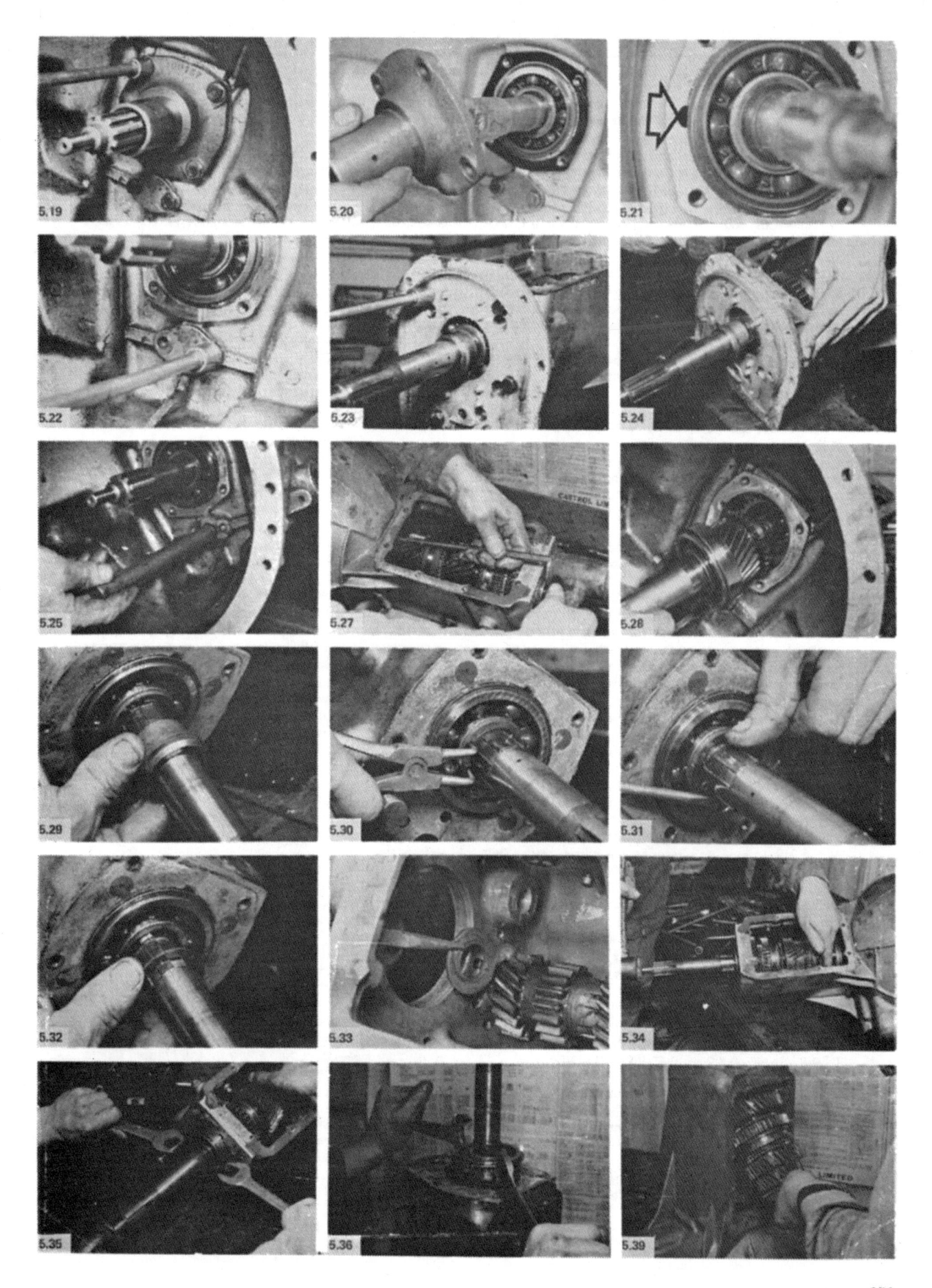

5.19 5.20 5.21
5.22 5.23 5.24
5.25 5.27 5.28
5.29 5.30 5.31
5.32 5.33 5.34
5.35 5.36 5.39

131

Chapter 6/Gearbox & Overdrive

TR2, 3, 3A

1. Undo the eight ½ inch AF bolts that hold the remote control and top cover onto the top of the gearbox (photo). Lift away the bolts and spring washers noting that the four longer bolts are to the front and rear of the top cover.
2. Undo and remove the nut and cross bolt that secures the remote control and top cover to the stay bracket as well as passing through the gear change lever cap (photo).
3. Remove the setscrew from the rear of the gear change lever cap. Note there is a spring washer under the head of the bolt (photo).
4. Lift the gear change lever cap up followed by the lever and lift away from the remote control housing (photo).
5. Lift away the remote control and top cover from the top of the gearbox noting the gasket placed between the two parts (photo).
6. Refer to Fig. 6.2 and remove the speedometer drive from the side of the extension housing (Items 18, 19, 20, 21).
7. Extract the split pin (12) from the slotted nut (10) (Fig. 6.1) and undo the nut from the end of the mainshaft (1). Lift away the nut (10) followed by the plain washer (11).
8. Carefully tap the flange (9) using a soft faced hammer from the rear of the gearbox extension.
9. Undo the bolt (17) (Fig. 6.2) holding the extension housing (14) to the rear of the gearbox and remove the bolts and spring washers.
10. Carefully tap the extension housing with a soft faced hammer to break the joint and withdraw the extension housing (14) and gasket (16).
11. If an overdrive unit is fitted to the gearbox undo the ½ inch AF nuts which hold the overdrive unit to the end of the gearbox casing. This should be done in a diagonal manner as there are strong springs which will automatically separate the two parts and if the pressure is not even the mating flanges could be strained. Remove the nuts and washers (photo).
12. Under the action of the strong springs in the front of the overdrive unit, the overdrive unit will automatically separate, this being controlled by the long studs situated on each side of the unit (photo).
13. Note there are eight springs in the front of the overdrive unit and that the upper and lowermost rows have springs of slightly greater length than the four in the centre which are mounted further forward (photo).
14. Cut the locking wire securing the square headed bolt which locates the clutch release fork to the cross shaft (photo).
15. Undo the square headed bolt and completely remove (photo).
16. Pull the release bearing forwards so disengaging it from the clutch release fork and completely remove it (photo).
17. To release the cross shaft undo the bolt which locks it in position, situated on the right hand side of the clutch housing on the cross shaft bush housing.
18. Pull the shaft from the side of the bell housing and at the same time pull the release fork from the shaft. The release fork can be a tight fit on the shaft (photo).
19. Undo the four bolts that hold the front cover to the front of the gearbox casing. Lift away the bolts and spring washers (photo).
20. Wrap some tape around the splines of the first motion shaft to protect the oil seal. Remove the front cover and its gasket (photo).
21. Note that there is a small cut out on the gasket and front cover which matches an oil hole in the gearbox casing by the ball race (photo).
22. Undo the two bolts that hold the layshaft cover plate to the front of the gearbox (photo). Lift away the bolts, spring washer, cover plate and gasket.
23. On gearboxes fitted with an overdrive unit an adaptor plate is fitted to the rear end. Undo the six adaptor plate retaining bolts (photo).
24. Gently tap the end of the adaptor plate to release it from the gearbox (photo).
25. Undo the countershaft retaining screw (53) (Fig. 6.1) and lift away with spring washer (52). Obtain a piece of metal rod of approximately the same diameter as the countershaft spindle but longer and push out the layshaft through the rear of the gearbox casing (photo).
26. Withdraw the metal rod that was used to remove the layshaft and allow the layshaft assembly to drop to the bottom of the gearbox.
27. The first motion shaft should next be removed. Using a metal drift gently tap the first motion shaft outwards through the front of the gearbox casing (photo).
28. Lift the first motion shaft complete with bearing from the front of the gearbox (photo).
29. Turning to the rear of the gearbox slide off the cam that drives the pump in the overdrive unit (if fitted) (photo).
30. Using a pair of circlip pliers extract the circlip from its groove in the mainshaft (photo).
31. With a screwdriver ease the circlip over the mainshaft splines (photo).
32. Slide the distance washer from the face of the bearing inner track and remove from the mainshaft (photo).
33. To remove the rear mainshaft bearing use a soft faced hammer and drive the mainshaft into the gearbox as shown in the photo until the bearing is at the rear of the mainshaft splines. Note the bearing circlip is still in position.
34. Carefully ease the bearing rearwards using two open ended spanners and tap at the same time the mainshaft into the gearbox. Continue this operation until the bearing is completely free of the splines and lift away the bearing (photo) and triangular shaped washer (2) (Fig. 6.1).
35. If difficulty is experienced in levering the bearing along the mainshaft place the gearbox on its end with the mainshaft vertical (photo).
36. The mainshaft assembly may now be lifted through the gearbox as shown in the photo.
37. Undo and remove the locknut (58) (Fig. 6.1) and screw (57) so that the reverse speed selector shaft and fork can be removed. Remove the selector shaft insert from the rear of the casing and the welch plug from the front.
38. Using a suitable diameter drift remove the reverse gear selector shaft (55) (Fig. 6.1) and the selector fork (54).
39. Tap out the reverse gear spindle (50) towards the rear of the gearbox casing and lift out the reverse gear wheel (51). Lift out the layshaft rear thrust washer (photo).
40. Lift out the layshaft front thrust washer (photo) and finally remove the layshaft assembly.
41. The countershaft may be dismantled by sliding off the gears and bushes from the splined countershaft hub (photo).

TR4, 4A

42. Follow the instructions given in Section 5, paras. 1 to 3.
43. Lift the gear change lever cap up followed by the lever and lift up away from the remote control housing (photo 5.4). Note that there is a spring and plunger located in the striker end of the gear lever and care must now be taken not to lose them.
44. Follow the instructions given in Section 5, paras. 5 to 8.
45. Using a pair of circlip pliers or a small screwdriver remove the circlip (35) in Fig. 6.3, from the end of the mainshaft. Follow this with the distance washer.
46. Now follow the instructions in Section 5, paras. 9 to 24.
47. Undo the large Phillips head screw which holds the keeper plate in position. The keeper plate locks the layshaft and reverse pinion shaft to the gearbox. Lift away the Phillips screw and slide out the keeper plate (photo).

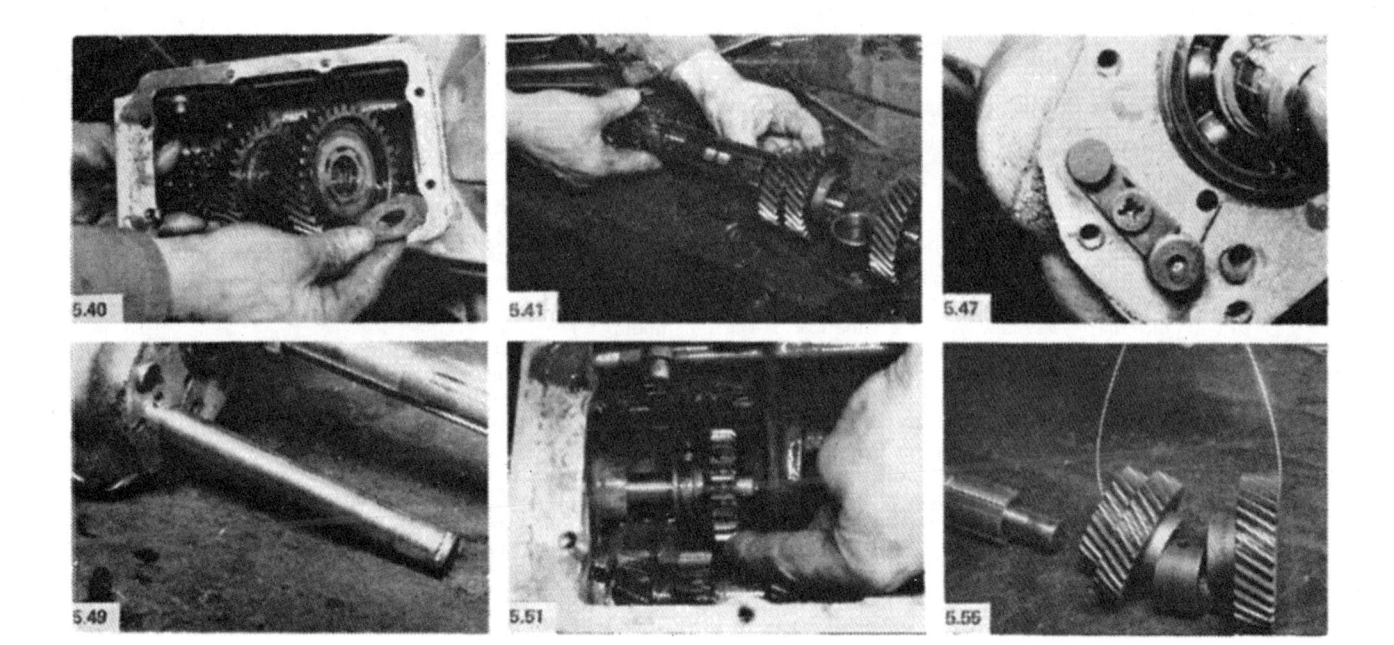

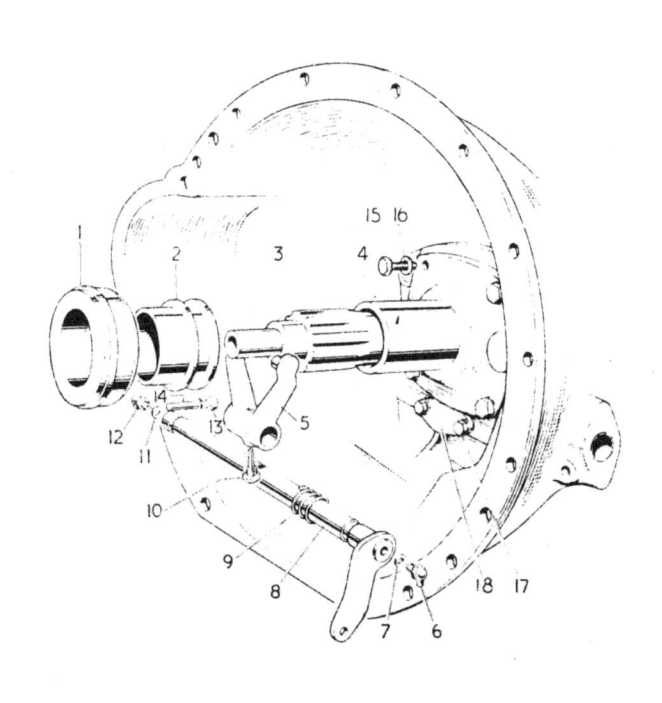

Fig. 6.5. CLUTCH RELEASE SYSTEM IN GEARBOX
BELLHOUSING

1 Release bearing
2 Sleeve
3 Input shaft
4 Front cover
5 Fork
6 Grease nipple
7 Fibre washer
8 Cross-shaft
9 Anti-rattle spring
10 Screwed taper pin
11 Fibre washer
12 Grease nipple
13 Cross-shaft locating bolt
14 Spring washer
15 Wedglok bolts
16 Washers
17 Bolts
18 Plate

133

Chapter 6/Gearbox & Overdrive

48 Obtain a piece of metal rod of approximately the same diameter as the layshaft spindle but longer and push out the layshaft spindle from the gearbox (photo 5.25).
49 Note that there is a milled slot in the layshaft spindle which must be to the rear during reassembly so that the keeper plate, which was previously removed, may engage in the slot (photo).
50 Follow the instructions given in paras 26 to 29 of this Section and in paras. 33 to 36.
51 Withdraw the reverse idler shaft from the rear of the gearbox (photo). Note the slot in the rear of the shaft into which the keeper plate engages.
52 Lift away the reverse idler gear having made a note of which way round it fits.
53 Lift out the laygear rear thrust washer (photo 5.39).
54 Lift out the laygear front thrust washer (photo 5.40) and finally remove the complate laygear assembly.
55 The laygear may be dismantled by sliding off the gears and bushes from the splined layshaft hub (photo 5.41). To keep them in their correct relative positions tie them together with a piece of string or wire (photo).

6. Gearbox - Examination and Renovation

1. Carefully clean and then examine all the component parts for general wear, distortion, slackness of fit, and damage to machined faces and threads.
2. Examine the gearwheel for excessive wear and chipping of the teeth. Renew them as necessary. If the laygear end float is above the permitted tolerance of 0.012 inch the thrust washers must be renewed. New thrust washers will almost certainly be required on any car that has completed more than 50,000 miles.
3. Examine the layshaft for signs of wear where the laygear needle roller bearings bear, and check the laygears on a new shaft for worn bearings. These are simply drifted out if new are to be fitted.
4. The four synchroniser rings are bound to be worn and it is a false economy not to renew them. New rings will improve the smoothness and speed of the gearchange considerably.
5. The needle roller bearing and cage located between the nose of the mainshaft and the annulus in the rear of the shaft is also liable to wear, and should be renewed as a matter of course.
6. Examine the condition of the three ball bearing assemblies, one on the first motion shaft, one on the mainshaft and the other in the tail of the gearbox extension. Check them for noisy operation, looseness between the inner and outer races, and for general wear. Normally they should be renewed on a gearbox that is being rebuilt.
7. Examine the mainshaft bushes and fit them on the mainshaft to check for overall endfloat.
8. Fit the inner thrust washer onto the mainshaft followed by the two bushes, and finally the circlip. With a feeler gauge measure the endfloat between the inner thrust washer and the adjacent bush. This should be between 0.003 and 0.009 inch. If outside these figures experiment with alternative thrust washers until the endfloat is correct.
9. To dismantle the synchromesh units, first wrap a length of clean rag completely round a unit and then pull off the outer synchro sleeve The cloth will catch the spring loaded balls and springs which are bound to fly out. Compare the length of the old springs with new and replace any that are worn. Note that an interlock plunger and ball is fitted to the second speed synchromesh hub.
10 Parts of the remote control gearchange are bound to be worn but this is dealt with in Section 10.

7. First Motion Shaft - Dismantling and Reassembly

TR2, 3, 3A

1. The first motion shaft may be dismantled by first removing the circlip from its groove in the shaft (photo).
2. Slide off the spacer washer from the face of the race inner track and place the first motion shaft on the top of the vice with the outer track of the race resting on soft faces (photo).
3. Using a soft faced hammer, drift the first motion shaft through the race inner track (photo).
4. Lift away the race from the first motion shaft followed by the oil deflector plate.
5. The component parts of the first motion shaft are shown in this photo.
6. To assemble the first motion shaft first fit the circlip to the new bearing outer track (photo).
7. Slide the oil deflector plate onto the first motion shaft and then the ball race with the circlip away from the constant mesh gear.
8. Place the race against soft metal on the top of the jaws of a vice and using a drift located in the spigot bearing hole drive the shaft into the bearing (photo).
9. Replace the spacer washer and finally the smaller circlip. Ensure that the circlip seats correctly in its groove.

TR4, 4A

The only difference in the first motion shaft fitted to this gearbox is that at the rear of the first motion shaft, a needle roller bearing is fitted (see Item 30, Fig. 6.3) instead of a plain phosphor bronze bush as shown in Fig. 6.1, Item 34.

8. Mainshaft - Dismantling and Reassembly

The mainshaft components of the earlier and later gearbox are basically identical with the exception of the first speed synchromesh unit which was not fitted to the earlier models. The following sequence is applicable to both early and late gearboxes.

1. Place two pieces of soft metal in the jaws of a firm bench vice ready for holding the mainshaft.
2. Place the end of the mainshaft between the soft faces of the vice so that it is parallel with the bench top.
3. Commence dismantling the mainshaft by sliding off the third and fourth gear synchromesh hub and the conical synchromesh ring. Note which way round it fits on the mainshaft (photo).
4. Using a pair of circlip pliers remove the circlip that holds the third gear in position (photo).
5. This can be a little difficult to remove so an assistant working with two screwdrivers will probably make this operation easier. With one end of the circlip released from the groove gradually work the way round until it is free of the groove and then ease it along the splines of the mainshaft (photo).
6. Remove the third gear thrust washer from the mainshaft. Note which way round it fits as there is a flange on one side (photo).
7. Slide the third speed gear and bush from the mainshaft. Note that in the recess of the third gear is a spline (photo).
8. Remove the second speed gear and second speed bush. Note that there is a little thrust washer inside the cone portion of the second speed gear (photo).
9. Remove the first and second gear synchronizer hub which also incorporates the reverse gear machined on its periphery. Also remove the two grooved synchromesh rings (photo).
10 Remove the mainshaft from the vice and slide off the

135

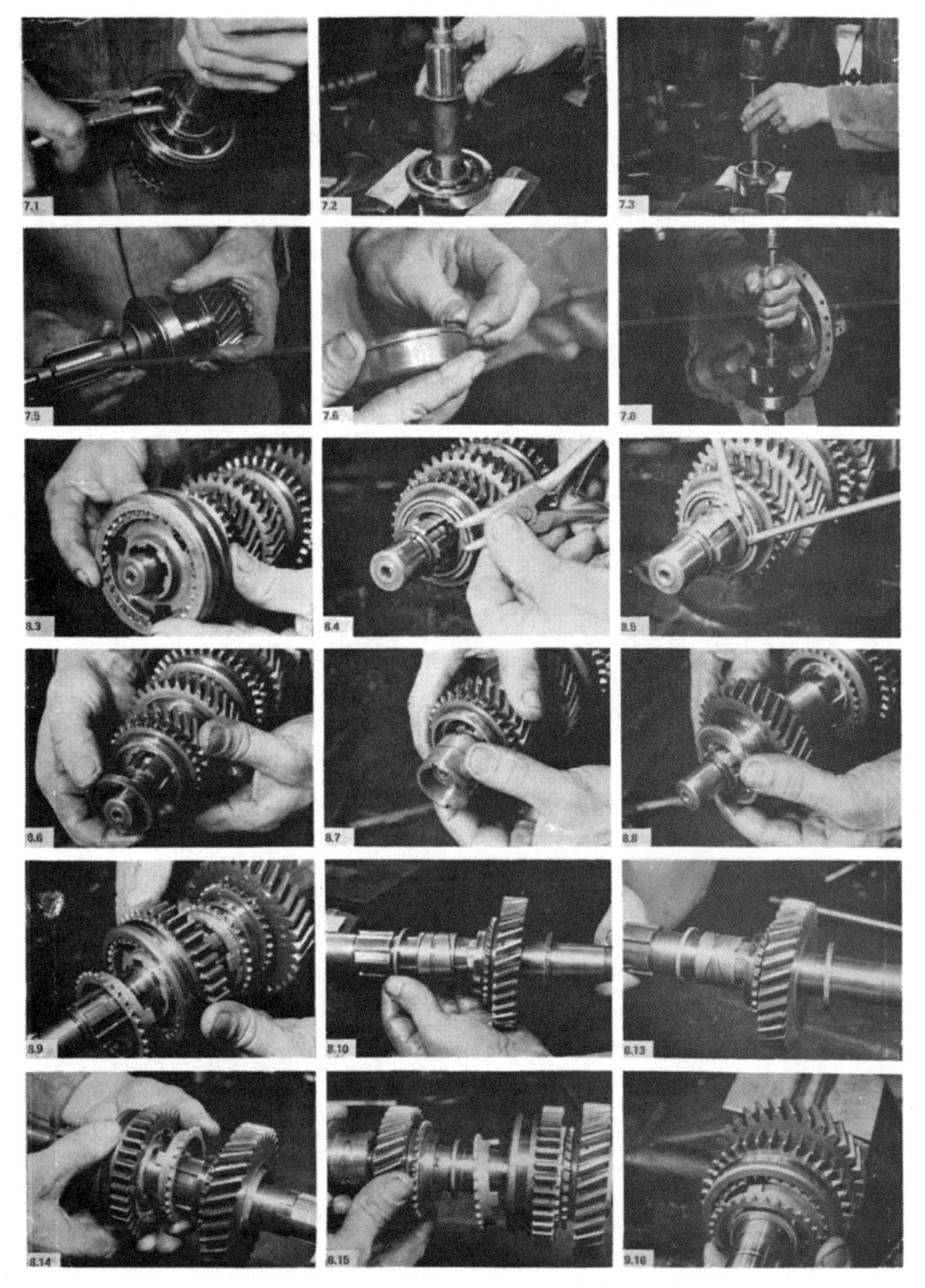

Chapter 6/Gearbox & Overdrive

first gear and bush from the longer end of the mainshaft. Note that there is a thrust washer between the mainshaft larger diameter splines and the first gear bush (photo).

11 Dismantling the mainshaft is now complete.

12 Before reassembling the components to the mainshaft it will be necessary to determine the overall end float of the bushes. To do this refer to Fig. 6.7 and assemble the thrust washer (11), bush (13), bush (14) and thrust washer (16) onto the mainshaft and hold the components in place with an old circlip (17). Using feeler gauges determine the total end float of both bushes. It should be between 0.003 and 0.009 inch and if necessary adjust the end float by selecting thrust washers (11, 16) of various thicknesses.

13 Assemble to the longer end of the mainshaft the thrust washer followed by the first gear bush, the first gear with the conical end towards the first thrust washer and then the second thrust washer (photo).

14 Next mount the longer end (tail end) of the mainshaft between soft jaws of a vice and fit from the shorter end the synchromesh ring followed by the first and second gear selector hub which incorporates on its forward periphery (part nearest the first gear) the reverse gear teeth (photo).

15 Continue building the front end of the mainshaft by fitting the synchromesh cone followed by a spacer, then second gear followed by the second gear bush which should be positioned with the raised lip on the end nearest to the front of the shaft (photo).

16 Ensure when refitting the synchromesh rings that the tongue on the ring mates with the recess in the synchromesh hub (photo).

17 Refit the third gear, the third gear bush and the thrust washer so that the end of the spacer abuts inside the recess in the forward end of the gear (photo).

18 Fit the spring circlip into position on the front of the mainshaft. Difficulty may be experienced in seating the circlip into its groove in the mainshaft but it is a lot easier than removal (photo).

19 The photo shows how the mainshaft looks when the front end is fully assembled with the two remaining synchromesh rings and the third and fourth gear synchromesh hub being placed in position. The protruding end of the hub must face the front of the mainshaft. Do not fit these last parts yet but leave until the mainshaft has been inserted into the gearbox casing.

9. Gearbox - Reassembly

TR2, 3, 3A

1. To reassemble the layshaft gear first refit the two needle bearing inner retaining rings (47) (Fig. 6.1).

2. Insert the layshaft (40) into the first speed layshaft gear (41) and pack some grease between the layshaft and layshaft gears at either end. Carefully replace the needle rollers to either end of the layshaft gear. Ensure that the layshaft does not slide out.

3. Retain the needle rollers by refitting the needle bearing outer retaining rings (47).

4. Refit the second speed layshaft gear to the first speed layshaft splines (42) followed by the third speed layshaft gear (43), distance piece (44) and constant mesh gear (45).

5. Fit the front thrust washer (48) for the layshaft gear in place in the gearbox casing having first coated the gearbox facing with grease to retain the thrust washer. Do not fit the rear thrust washer at this stage.

6. Obtain a piece of rod having a similar diameter to the layshaft (40) and of equal length to the first speed countershaft gear (41). Replace the layshaft (40) with this piece of rod; the reason for this is to retain the needle rollers within the first speed countershaft gear.

7. Carefully insert the layshaft into the bottom of the gearbox ensuring that the thrust washer (48) does not slip out. The largest gearwheel on the layshaft goes towards the bellhousing end of the gearbox casing.

8. Grease the smaller thrust washer (49) to the end of the gearbox casing ensuring that the tongue of the washer seats in the groove, at the same time it will be necessary to lift the layshaft up slightly.

9. Using feeler gauges check the end float of the laygear which should be 0.006 to 0.010 inch measured between the rear thrust washer (49) and the gear. Any excessive end float may be reduced by selective assembly of thrust washers and distance tubes.

10 Insert the reverse idler gear (51) into the casing and slide the reverse gear spindle (50) into position ensuring the drilled hole is in line with the hole in the casing so that when the countershaft retaining screw (53) is inserted it will pass through the hole in the end of the reverse gear spindle. The smaller diameter on the gear should face towards the front of the gearbox.

11 Replace the reverse gear selector fork (54) correctly engaging the end with the gear (51) and slide in the shaft (55). Lock the shaft in position with the retaining screw (57) and locknut (58).

12 Refit the selector shaft steel insert to the rear of the gearbox casing and the welch plug to the front.

13 Insert the tail end of the mainshaft through the large cut out for the bearing in the rear of the gearbox casing.

14 Position the third and top synchromesh unit (32, 28, 27) onto the front end of the mainshaft before the front end finally passes into the gearbox.

15 Fit the triangular washer (2) and push the centre bearing (3) onto the mainshaft as far as it will go. The circlip should be towards the rear of the bearing as shown in Fig. 6.1.

16 It is not possible to tap the rear bearing at the tail end of the mainshaft home without a support on the front end of the mainshaft because otherwise this gearwheel hits the third gear on the layshaft which could mean chipped gear teeth. Invert the gearbox so that the flange of the clutch bell housing is on the bench and position wood blocks under the end of the mainshaft so that it is well supported.

17 Using a soft metal drift, tap the rear main bearing down on the mainshaft by alternatively tapping the inner and outer tracks.

18 Continue tapping the bearing tracks until the bearing is fully positioned on the mainshaft so that there is approximately 3/16 inch between the inner race of the bearing on the tail end of the mainshaft and the groove which holds the circlip.

19 Once the bearing is fully on in this position then the supports inside the bell housing, which are supporting the front or nose of the mainshaft can be removed and the bell housing allowed to rest flange downwards on the bench. It is now necessary to drive the outer race of the bearing fully into the rear of the gearbox casing until the circlip on the outer race track is adjacent to the face of the casing.

20 With the gearbox still in the inverted position fit the spacer (6) and lock in position with the circlip.

21 Well lubricate the bush (34) in the rear face of the first motion shaft (33). Fit the top gear baulk ring (27) onto the end of the first motion shaft and insert into the casing.

22 Using a soft faced hammer drive the first motion shaft into position with the circlip hard up against the gearbox face.

23 Position the gearbox casing on the bench with a block of wood under the rear end of the gear casing in the inverted position. The countershaft gears should now drop into mesh with the mainshaft and first motion shaft gears. Insert the layshaft from the rear pushing out the previously inserted

8.17

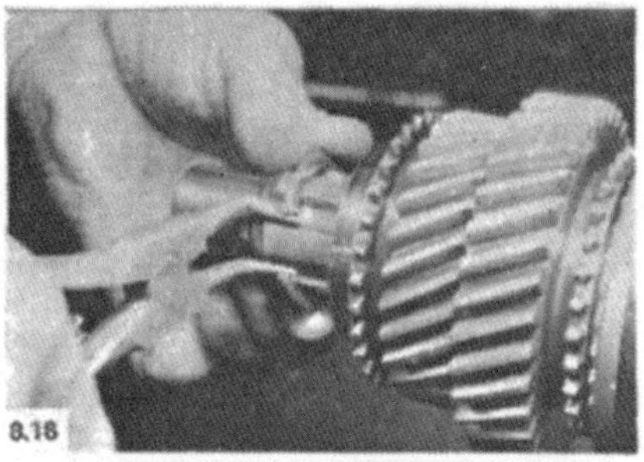

8.18

8.19

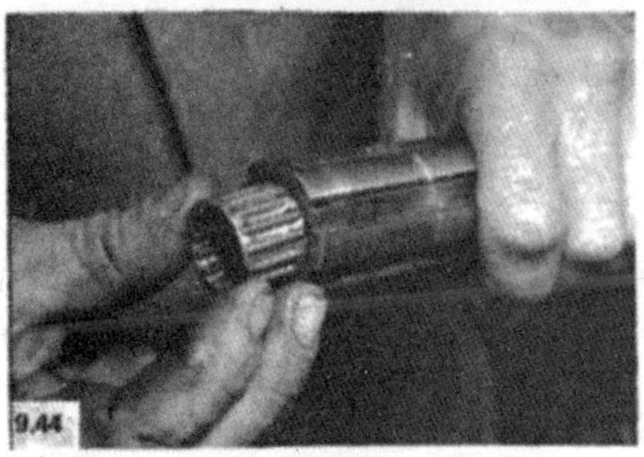

9.44

9.45

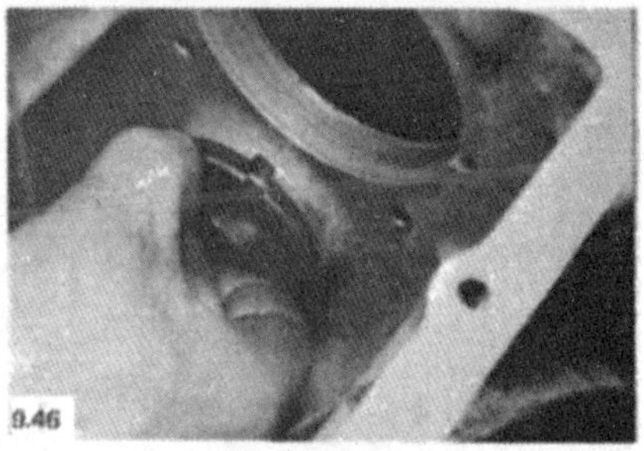

9.46

9.47

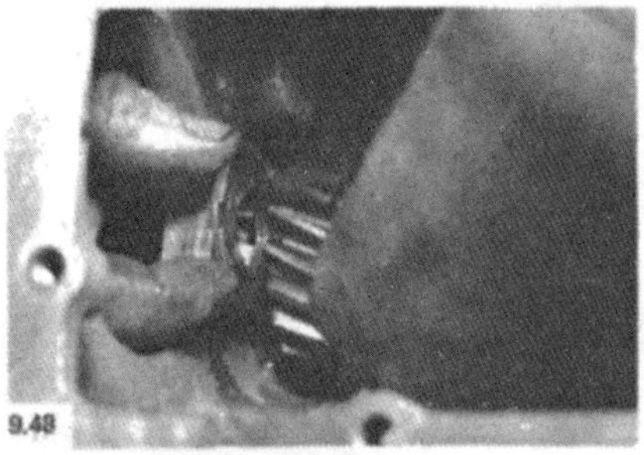

9.48

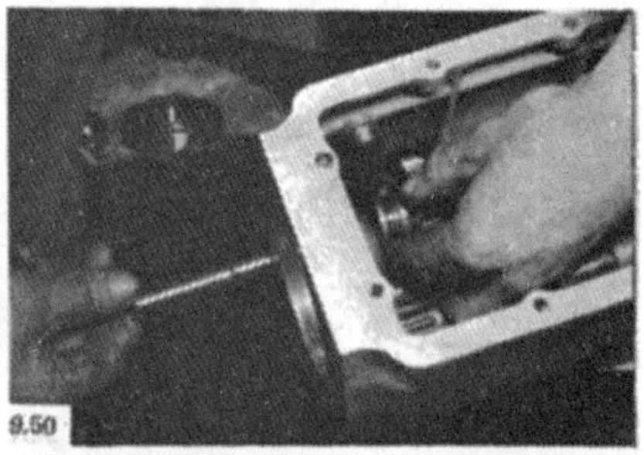

9.50

9.51

9.52

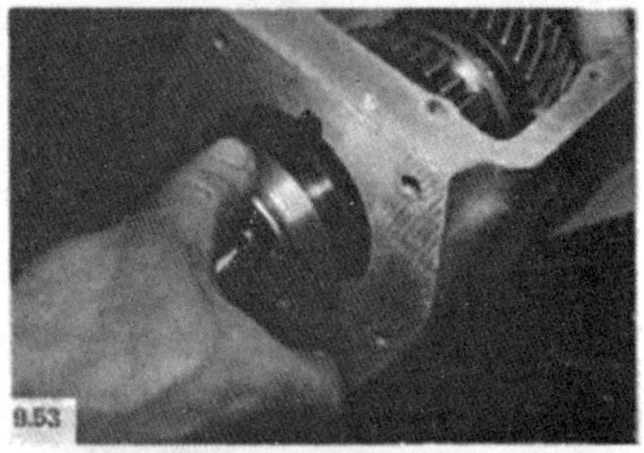

9.53

9.55

9.56

9.57

9.58

9.59

9.60

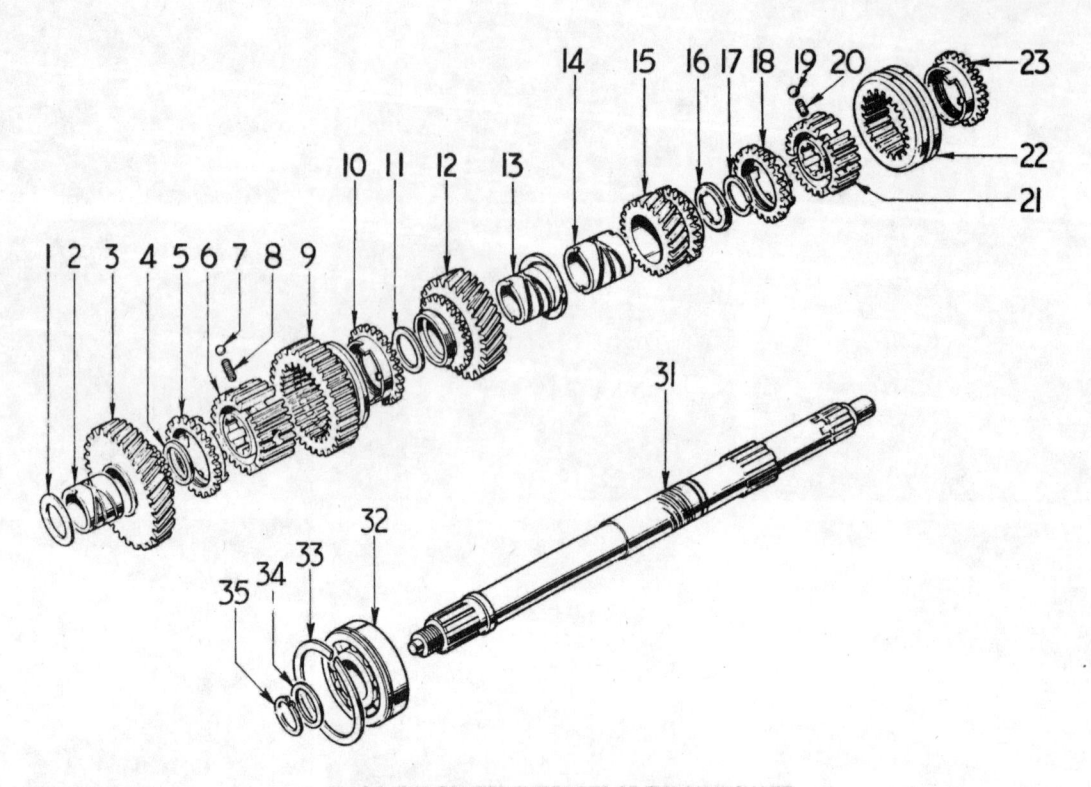

Fig. 6.6. THE COMPONENT PARTS OF THE MAINSHAFT

1 Thrust washer	8 Spring	15 3rd speed gear	22 Synchro sleeve
2 Bush 1st speed	9 Reverse mainshaft gear	16 Thrust washer	23 Top gear synchro cup
3 1st speed gear	10 2nd speed synchro cup	17 Circlip	31 Mainshaft
4 Thrust washer	11 Thrust washer	18 3rd speed synchro cup	32 Ball race
5 1st speed synchro cup	12 2nd speed gear	19 Synchro ball	33 Circlip
6 1st/2nd speed synchro hub	13 Bush 2nd speed	20 Spring	34 Distance washer
7 Synchro ball	14 Bush 3rd speed	21 3rd/top synchro hub	35 Circlip

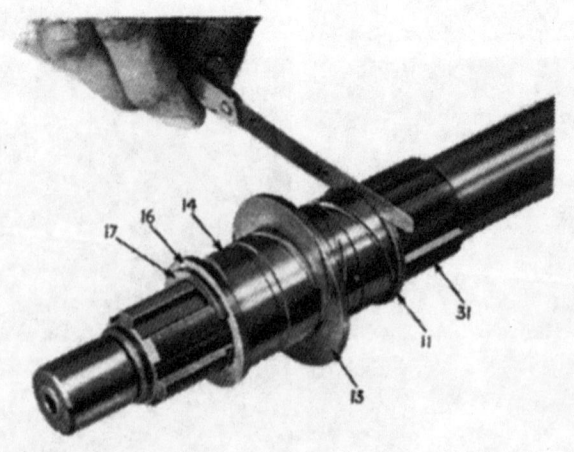

Fig. 6.7. USING FEELER GAUGE TO MEASURE BUSH ENDFLOAT

11 Thrust washer
13 Bush - second speed gear
14 Bush - third speed gear
16 Thrust washer
17 Circlip
31 Mainshaft

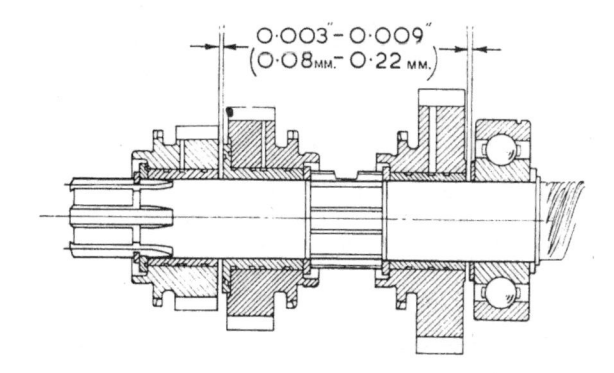

Fig. 6.8. Cross sectional view through mainshaft assembly. The arrows denote endfloat of mainshaft bushes

Fig. 6.9. Using feeler gauges to check second gear endfloat.

Fig. 6.10. The measurement of the gap between baulk ring teeth and cone

Chapter 6/Gearbox & Overdrive

bar.

24 Carefully align the hole in the countershaft with the drilling in the casing for the locking screw (53) and push home fully. Check with an electricians screwdriver that the blade will pass through the hole in the reverse shaft (50) and the hole in the countershaft (40). Lock the two shafts by inserting the screw (53) with a spring washer (52) and tighten securely.

25 Fit the layshaft cover plate (10) and a new gasket (11) to the front of the gearbox and secure with the two bolts (12) and copper washers (13). To assist the gasket to seal, coat with hermetite and also apply a little to the bolt threads.

26 The front cover (5) should be fitted next. Note that there is a cut out which should be positioned to the left when looking at the first motion shaft. Fit a new gasket (7) to the end cover (5).

27 Tighten the end cover bolt (8) fitted with spring washers (9).

28 Now fit the gasket (16) to the rear end of the gearbox using hermetite to ensure an oil tight joint. On overdrive models fit the overdrive adaptor plate whilst on ordinary models fit the gearbox extension.

29 Fit the six ½ inch AF bolts and flat washers and tighten securely.

30 Fit a new gasket to the rear end of the gearbox casing adaptor plate suitably coated with hermetite.

31 The splines on the mainshaft have to go through sets of splines inside the overdrive. It is therefore essential to line up their splines in relation to one another. A torch will assist here.

32 Secure the overdrive unit in the vertical position and insert the eight springs. It is important that these are correctly positioned whereby the four inner springs, although they are higher than the outer springs, are in fact shorter.

33 Place a piece of wire around the head of the plunger rod so that the spring can be compressed whilst the two units are being assembled. The reason for this is that the plunger rod for the hydraulic pump is spring loaded and will push the cam out of position before the mainshaft is finally fitted. Rotate the cam so that the plunger is positioned at the lowest part of the cam.

34 With an assistant to help gradually lower the gearbox to the overdrive unit. Pull on the wire so as to compress the spring and when the gearbox adaptor plate is nearly in position withdraw the wire.

35 Refit the ½ inch AF nuts and spring washers to the overdrive to adaptor plate studs and tighten in a diagonal manner so as to compress the eight springs.

36 For a conventional gearbox refit the circlip to the end of the mainshaft.

37 Carefully tap the flange (9) (Fig. 6.1) using a soft faced hammer until it is in position on the mainshaft.

38 Replace the plain washer (11) and the castellated nut (10) and tighten the nut securely. Lock the nut with a new split pin (12).

39 Replace the speedometer drive (Items 18, 19, 20, 21) on the side of the gearbox extension housing. (Fig. 6.2).

40 Ensure that all gears are in their neutral position and using an oil can lubricate all moving parts of the selector mechanism and synchromesh units.

41 Carefully lower the remote control and top cover with a new gasket fitted onto the top of the gearbox housing. Take care that all the selector forks are locating correctly, especially the reverse selector fork.

42 Refit the eight bolts with spring washers noting that the four longer bolts only go to the front and rear of the top cover. Tighten securely in a diagonal manner.

43 The unit is now ready for refitting to the car.

TR4, 4A

44 To reassemble the layshaft gear first grease the two needle roller bearings (43) (Fig. 6.3) and insert them into the ends of the hub (44) (photo).

45 Lubricate the hub splines and slide the second speed gear (45), third speed gear (46), distance tube (47) and layshaft gear (48) onto the splines (photo).

46 Fit the front thrust washer for the layshaft gear in place in the gearbox casing (photo) having first coated the gearbox facing with grease to retain the thrust washer. Do not fit the rear thrust washer at this stage.

47 Carefully insert the layshaft into the bottom of the gearbox ensuring that the thrust washer does not slip out. The largest gearwheel on the layshaft goes towards the bell housing end of the gearbox casing (photo).

48 Grease the smaller thrust washer to the end of the gearbox casing ensuring that the tongue in the washer seats in the groove, at the same time it will be necessary to lift the layshaft up slightly (photo).

49 Temporarily fit the layshaft spindle and using feeler gauges check the end float of the laygear which should be 0.007 to 0.012 inch, measured between the rear thrust washer (42) (Fig. 6.3) and the gear. Any excessive end float may be reduced by selective assembly of thrust washers and distance tubes. Remove the layshaft spindle again.

50 Insert the reverse idler gear into the casing locating the end of the actuating lever into its location groove on the rear of the gear. Slide the reverse gear shaft into position so that the milled notch is at the rear of the gearbox (photo).

51 Insert the tail end of the mainshaft through the large cut out for the bearing in the rear of the gearbox casing (photo).

52 Position the third and top synchromesh unit onto the front end of the mainshaft before the front end finally passes into the gearbox (photo).

53 Push the rear bearing onto the mainshaft as far as it will go. The circlip should be towards the rear of the bearing as shown in the photo.

54 It is not possible to tap the rear bearing on the tail end of the mainshaft home without a support on the front end of the mainshaft, because otherwise the front gearwheel hits third gear on the laygear which could mean chipped gear teeth. Invert the gearbox so that the flange of the clutch bell housing is on the bench and position wood blocks under the end of the mainshaft so that it is well supported.

55 Using a soft metal drift tap the rear main bearing down the mainshaft by alternatively tapping each side of the inner track (photo).

56 Continue tapping the bearing tracks until the bearing is fully positioned onto the mainshaft so that there is approximately 3/16 inch between the inner race of the bearing on the tail end of the mainshaft and the groove which holds the circlip (photo).

57 Once the bearing is fully on in this position then the supports inside the bellhousing which are supporting the front or the nose of the mainshaft can be removed and the bellhousing allowed to rest flange downwards on the bench. It is now necessary to drive the outer race of the bearing fully into the rear of the gearbox casing until the circlip on the outer race track is adjacent to the face of the casing (photo).

58 With the gearbox still in the inverted position fit the spacer and lock in position with the circlip (photo).

59 Well lubricate the needle roller bearing in the rear face of the first motion shaft. Fit the top gear baulk ring onto the end of the first motion shaft and insert into the casing (photo).

60 Using a soft faced hammer drive the first motion shaft into position with the circlip hard up against the gearbox face (photo).

Fig. 6.11. Using a straight edge and feeler gauges to check the end float between the mainshaft 3rd gear and its bush

Chapter 6/Gearbox & Overdrive

61 Position the gearbox casing on the bench as shown in the photo with a wood block under the rear end of the gear casing. The layshaft gears should now drop into mesh with the mainshaft and first motion shaft gears. Insert the layshaft spindle (photo) until the milled slot is flush with the machined face at the rear of the casing. Turn it until the slot faces the slot in the reverse idler shaft.

62 Locate the keeper plate in the milled slots of the layshaft spindle and reverse idler spindle and refit the Phillips head screw. This should be done up as tightly as possible (photo).

63 Fit the countershaft cover plate and new gasket to the front of the gearbox and secure with the two bolts and copper washers. To assist the gasket to seal coat with hermetite and also apply a little to the bolt threads (photo).

64 The front cover should be fitted next. Refer to the Fig. 6.4 and note that there is a cut out which should be positioned to the left (photo) when looking at the first motion shaft from the bellhousing. Fit a new gasket to the end cover.

65 Tighten the end cover bolts fitted with spring washers (photo).

66 Now fit the gasket to the rear end of the gearbox using hermetite ensure an oil tight joint. On overdrive models fit the overdrive adaptor plate whilst on ordinary models fit the gearbox extension. Fit the gearbox extension (photo).

67 Fit the six ½ inch AF bolts and flat washers and tighten securely.

68 Fit a new gasket to the rear end of the gearbox casing adaptor plate suitably coated with hermetite.

69 The splines on the mainshaft have to go through sets of splines inside the overdrive. It is therefore essential to line up their splines in relation to one another. A torch will assist here.

70 Secure the overdrive unit in the vertical position and insert the eight springs. It is important that these are correctly positioned whereby the four inner springs, although they look higher than the outer springs, are in fact shorter. The photo shows a finger pointing to one of the shorter springs.

71 Place a piece of wire around the head of the plunger rod so that the spring can be compressed whilst the two units are being assembled. The reason for this is that the plunger rod for the hydraulic pump is spring loaded and may baulk against the cam so preventing the gearbox and overdrive mating. The photo shows the cam removed from the mainshaft and positioned against the plunger to illustrate their relative positions when assembled. Ensure that the lowest part of the cam rests against the plunger head.

72 With an assistant to help gradually lower the gearbox to the overdrive unit. Pull on the wire so as to compress the spring and when the gearbox adaptor plate is nearly in position withdraw the wire.

73 Refit the nuts and spring washers to the overdrive to adaptor plate studs and tighten in a diagonal manner so as to compress the eight springs.

74 For a conventional gearbox refit the circlip (35) (Fig. 6.3) to the end of the mainshaft.

75 Carefully tap the flange (38) using a soft faced hammer until it is in position on the mainshaft.

76 Replace the plain washer (39) and the castellated nut (40) and tighten the nut securely. Lock the nut with a new split pin (41).

77 Replace the speedometer drive (Items 104, 105, 106, 107, 108, 136) on the side of the gearbox extension housing.

78 Ensure that all gears are in their neutral position and using an oil can well lubricate all moving parts of the selector mechanism and synchromesh units (photo).

79 Carefully lower the remote control and top cover with a new gasket fitted onto the top of the gearbox housing. Take care that all the selector forks are locating correctly, especially the reverse selector fork (photo).

80 Refit the eight ½ inch AF bolts with spring washers noting that the four longer bolts are to the front and rear of the top cover. Tighten securely in a diagonal manner (photo).

10. Top Cover and Remote Control Assembly - Overhaul

1. The components of the top cover and remote control assembly are shown in Fig. 6.12.

2. To remove the assembly undo the eight ½ inch AF bolts that hold the remote control and top cover onto the top of the gearbox. Lift away the bolts and spring washer noting that the four longer bolts are to the front and rear of the top cover.

3. Lift away the remote control and top cover from the top of the gearbox noting the gasket placed between the two parts.

4. Turn the cover over and unscrew the plugs (128, 131) and lift away the distance piece (120), springs (130, 121, 127), plunger (122) and ball bearings (126, 129).

5. Undo the peg bolts holding the selector forks to the selector rods.

6. Check that the selectors are in the neutral position and withdraw the third top gear selector shaft (116). As the shaft is being removed collect the interlock plunger (117) and ball bearings (118) as they are released.

7. Lift away the third/top selector fork and distance tube (76) from the top cover.

8. Repeat operations 6 and 7 for the first/second and also reverse gear selector shafts (119, 125).

9. Undo the two setscrews (63) and remove together with spring washers and lift away the retaining plate (65).

10 Lift away the three sealing rings (67) from their recess in the casing.

11 The selectors (111, 134) may be removed from their respective shafts by undoing the peg bolts (133).

12 Inspect all parts for signs of wear which, if evident, mean that new parts should be fitted. The seals (67) should be renewed every time the assembly is dismantled.

13 To reassemble first fit the selectors (111, 134) to their respective shafts and secure with peg bolts (133).

14 Replace new 'O' ring seals (67) into their recesses in the rear cover and fit the retaining plate (65). Replace the two bolts (63) and spring washers.

15 Place the interlock plunger (117) in the third/top selector shaft and insert the shaft into the top cover. Engage the selector fork (75), distance tube (76) and secure the fork with a peg bolt.

16 Replace the interlock ball bearing (118) between the reverse and third/top selector shaft bores retaining the ball with grease.

17 Insert the reverse selector shaft (119) into the top cover, engaging it with the reverse actuator (123) and distance tube (124). Fit the peg bolt to the selector fork.

18 Check that the reverse and third/top selector shafts are in neutral and fit the second interlock ball bearing (118) retaining the ball with grease.

19 Insert the first/second selector fork (78) and distance tube (77).

20 Lubricate all moving parts and refit to the top of the gearbox, preferably using a new gasket.

11. Overdrive - General Description

The overdrive unit is attached to the extension on the

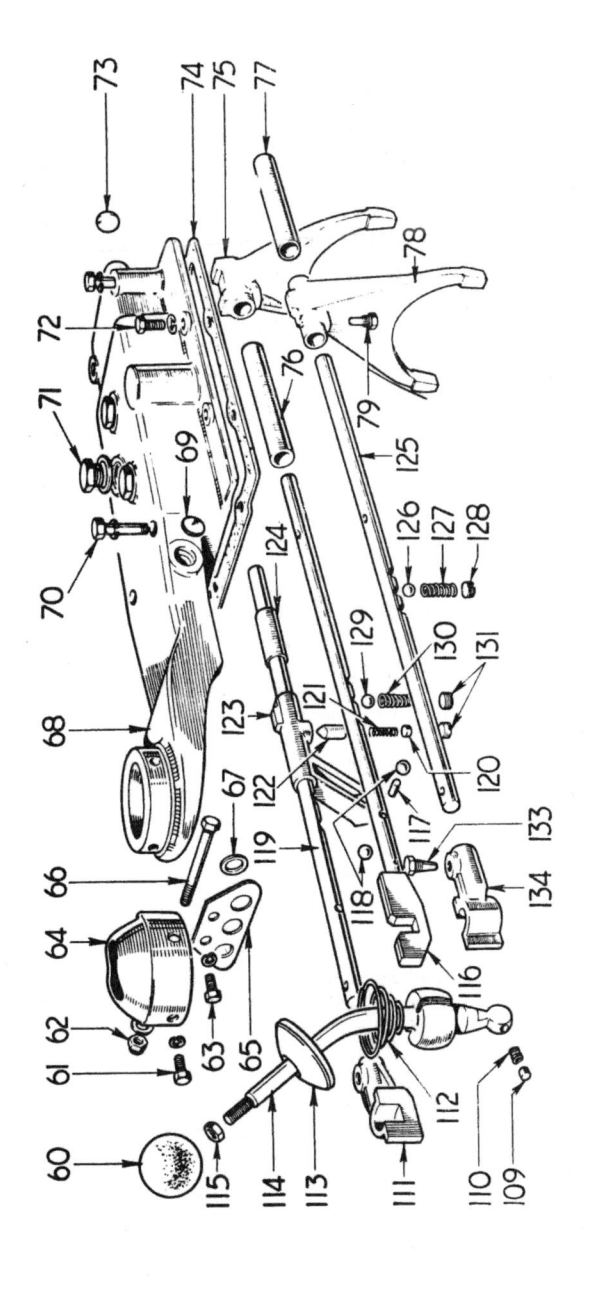

Fig. 6.12. GEARBOX TOP COVER AND SELECTOR COMPONENTS (TR4, 4A)

63 Setscrew	111 Selector (reverse)	123 Reverse actuator	130 Spring
65 Endplate	116 Top/3rd selector shaft	124 Distance piece	131 Plug
67 Rubber 'O' ring	118 Balls - interlock	125 2nd/1st selector shaft	133 Peg bolt
75 Top/3rd selector fork	119 Reverse selector shaft	126 Ball - detent	134 Selector 1st/2nd
76 Distance tube	120 Shim	127 Spring	
77 Distance tube	121 Spring	128 Plug	
78 2nd/1st selector fork	122 Plunger	129 Ball - detent	

143

Chapter 6/Gearbox & Overdrive

rear of the gearbox by eight studs and nuts, and takes the form of a hydraulically operated epicyclic gear. Overdrive operates on third and fourth speeds to provide fast cruising at lower engine revolutions. The overdrive 'in-out' switch on the right hand side of the steering wheel actuates a solenoid attached to the side of the overdrive unit. In turn the solenoid operates a valve which opens the hydraulic circuit which pushes the cone clutch into contact with the annulus when overdrive is engaged.

During high speed motoring the engine speed is decreased with the engagement of overdrive so that with continual use of the unit there will be a considerable increase in engine life.

A special switch called an inhibitor switch is incorporated in the electrical circuit and prevents the engagement of overdrive in reverse of first gears. The switch is located on the top of the gearbox top cover.

The normal minimum engagement speeds are top gear 40 m.p.h., third gear 30 m.p.h., whilst the minimum disengagement speed in top is under the control of the driver who must take care not to over rev the engine at high speeds and for third speed the disengagement should occur at a maximum of 70 m.p.h.

The overdrive unit operates in the following manner and numbers in brackets refer to Fig. 6.13. The operating gears in the overdrive are of epicyclic design and comprise a sunwheel (24) which meshes with three planet gears carried in a circular metal carrier (26). These planet gears mesh with an annulus (32) which has internal teeth. The planet carrier (26) is attached to the input shaft which is the output shaft of the gearbox and the annulus (32) is an integral part of the output shaft.

When the driver selects overdrive hydraulic pressure is built up by a plunger type pump (80, 81, 82) which operates from a cam (68) splined to the input shaft, i.e., the output shaft from the gearbox. The hydraulic pressure so built up by the pump forces the two pistons (66) against bridge pieces (6) which are themselves attached to the thrust ring (19). The thrust ring is pushed forwards by the pistons (66) so engaging the clutch (23) with the brake ring (83) with sufficient force so as to hold the sunwheel (24) firmly at rest.

The planet carrier (26) is now able to rotate with the input shaft allowing the planet wheels in the planet carrier assembly (26) to rotate about their own axis so driving the annulus (32) at a faster speed than the input shaft is rotating. Oil is drawn by the pump through a wire mesh filter (75) and delivers it to the operating valve (8-12) through an hydraulic accumulator, the amount of pressure being controlled by a pressure relief valve built into the accumulator. The oil is free to pass between the gearbox and overdrive unit and there is one common level for both units and this level is indicated by a level plug on the side of the gearbox.

Whenever the oil is drained the two drain plugs, one on the underside of the gearbox and the other on the underside of the overdrive unit, must be removed but it is usual practice not to change the oil during normal servicing but to top up. Only recommended grades of oil must be used and it is important that under no circumstances must oil anti-friction additives be used otherwise the overdrive unit will not operate correctly.

Cleanliness is very important so do not remove the drain plug without first wiping the surrounding area. Whenever the oil is drained for service/repair work on either the gearbox or the overdrive always clean the mesh filter (75).

The overdrive is normally a very reliable unit and trouble is usually due to either the solenoid sticking, a fault in the hydraulic system due to dirt ingress, insufficient oil, or incorrect solenoid operating lever adjustment.

12. Overdrive - Removal and Replacement

1. It is not necessary to remove the overdrive from the car in order to attend to the following:- The hydraulic lever setting, the relief valve, the non-return valve, the solenoid, and the operating valve.
2. If the unit as a whole requires overhaul it must be removed from the car together with the engine and gearbox as described in Chapter 1, Section 7.
3. To separate the overdrive from the gearbox undo the eight nuts from the ¼ inch (6.35 mm) diameter studs (noting the extra length of two of the studs) to separate the main overdrive casing from the gearbox rear extension. Carefully pull the overdrive off the end of the mainshaft.
4. To mate the overdrive and gearbox start by placing the overdrive in an upright position and then line up the splines of the clutch and planet carrier by eye turning them anti-clockwise only with the aid of a long thick screwdriver. Make certain that the spring clip is correctly positioned in the groove in the mainshaft and that it does not protrude above the mainshaft splines.
5. Under normal circumstances if everything is in line the gearbox mainshaft should enter the overdrive easily. If trouble is experienced do not try and force the components together but separate them and re-align the components. Place the gearbox in the top gear while refilling.
6. As the mainshaft is fed into the overdrive gently rotate the input shaft to and fro to help in making the mainshaft into the splines. At the same time make certain that the lowest portion of the cam on the mainshaft will rest against the pump plunger (82) and make certain as the gearbox extension and overdrive come together that the end of the mainshaft enters into the needle roller bearing in the tailshaft.
7. The remainder of the replacement procedure is a straight forward reversal of the removal sequence.

13. Overdrive - Dismantling, Overhaul and Reassembly

1. To enable a satisfactory overhaul to be completed there are several special tools that will be required. Full details of these are given as and where they are needed, and should be obtained before work commences. All numbers in brackets in this Section refer to Fig. 6.13 but for clarity there are several additional illustrations where a different code is used. Where this is the case the number in brackets at the end of each caption item denotes its equivalent number in Fig. 6.13.
2. It is recommended that, before the unit is dismantled, the exterior is thoroughly cleaned and dried as it is important that no dirt gets into the unit.
3. Place the unit on a clean bench and lift away the clutch return springs and place in a clean jam jar for sake keeping.
4. Bend back the tab washers (5) and unscrew the four nuts (4). Lift away the nuts, tab washers and bridge pieces (6).
5. Undo the six nuts (1) and lift away the nuts and spring washers from the studs (13, 14, 64).
6. The two casings may now be separated. Lift away the brake ring (83).
7. Working from the forward end of the sunwheel (24), first remove the steel thrust washer (17) followed by the phosphor bronze thrust washer (18). Lift out the clutch sliding member (23) complete with the thrust ring (19) and bearing (20).
8. Withdraw the sunwheel (24) and the planet carrier assembly (26).
9. Unscrew and remove the operating valve plug (8) and copper washer (7). Lift out the spring (9), plunger (10)

Fig. 6.13. OVERDRIVE UNIT COMPONENTS

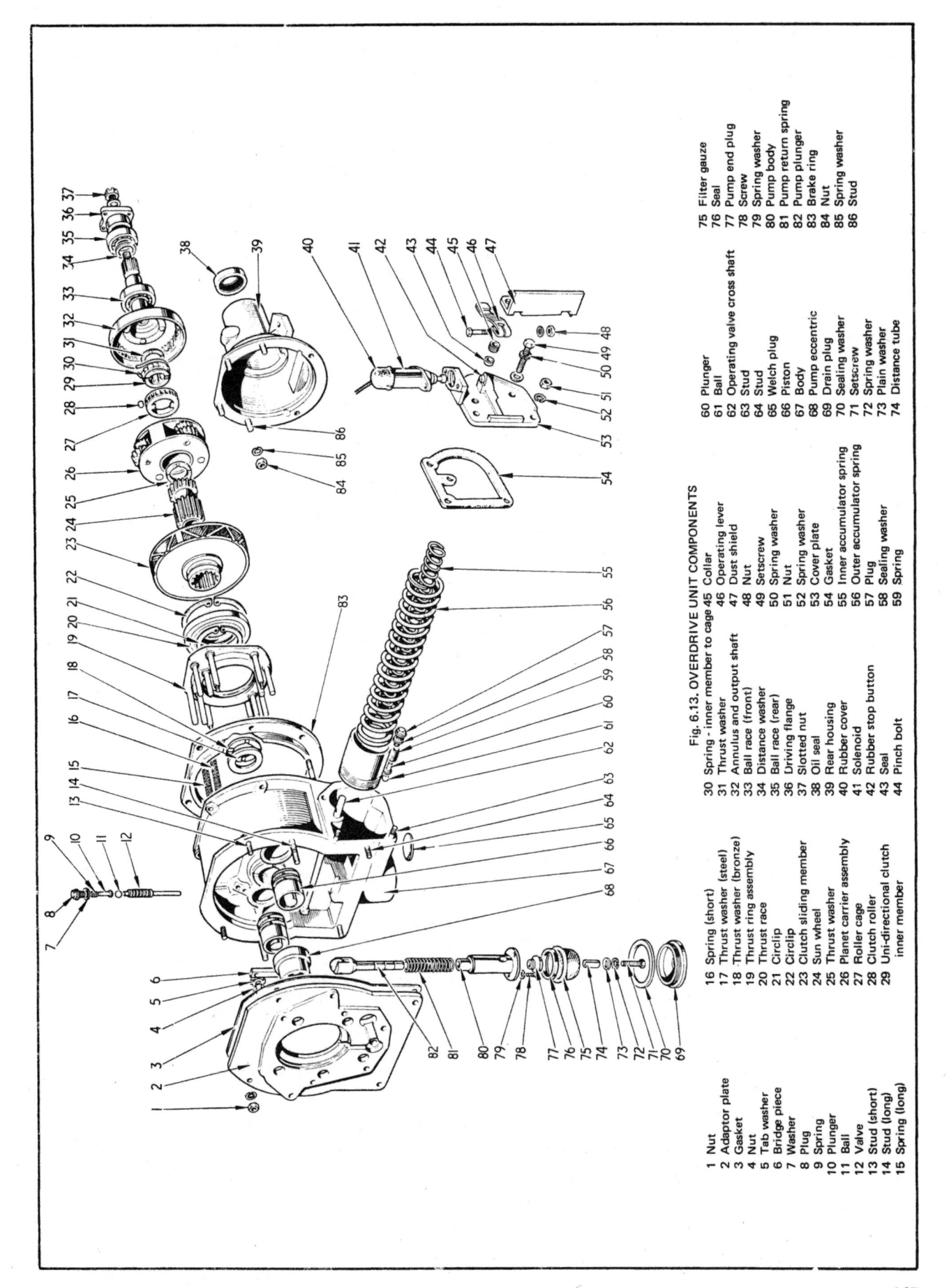

1 Nut	30 Spring - inner member to cage	45 Collar	75 Filter gauze
2 Adaptor plate	31 Thrust washer	46 Operating lever	76 Seal
3 Gasket	32 Annulus and output shaft	47 Dust shield	77 Pump end plug
4 Nut	33 Ball race (front)	48 Nut	78 Screw
5 Tab washer	34 Distance washer	49 Setscrew	79 Spring washer
6 Bridge piece	35 Ball race (rear)	50 Spring washer	80 Pump body
7 Washer	36 Driving flange	51 Nut	81 Pump return spring
8 Plug	37 Slotted nut	52 Spring washer	82 Pump plunger
9 Spring	38 Oil seal	53 Cover plate	83 Brake ring
10 Plunger	39 Rear housing	54 Gasket	84 Nut
11 Ball	40 Rubber cover	55 Inner accumulator spring	85 Spring washer
12 Valve	41 Solenoid	56 Outer accumulator spring	86 Stud
13 Stud (short)	42 Rubber stop button	57 Plug	
14 Stud (long)	43 Seal	58 Sealing washer	
15 Spring (long)	44 Pinch bolt	59 Spring	
16 Spring (short)		60 Plunger	
17 Thrust washer (steel)		61 Ball	
18 Thrust washer (bronze)		62 Operating valve cross shaft	
19 Thrust ring assembly		63 Stud	
20 Thrust race		64 Stud	
21 Circlip		65 Welch plug	
22 Circlip		66 Piston	
23 Clutch sliding member		67 Body	
24 Sun wheel		68 Pump eccentric	
25 Thrust washer		69 Drain plug	
26 Planet carrier assembly		70 Sealing washer	
27 Roller cage		71 Setscrew	
28 Clutch roller		72 Spring washer	
29 Uni-directional clutch inner member		73 Plain washer	
		74 Distance tube	

145

Chapter 6/Gearbox & Overdrive

and ball bearing (11) followed by the valve (12).

10 Using a pair of pliers carefully grip the operating pistons (66) on the centre bosses and rotate whilst pulling the pistons out of the front casing (67).

11 Undo the three cover plate retaining screws and lift away the screws, spring washers, cover plate and its joint washer.

12 Remove the two screws and spring washers that secure the solenoid (41) to the solenoid bracket assembly (53). Lift away the solenoid carefully easing the plunger from the yoke of the valve operating lever (46).

13 Slacken the clamp bolt (44) retaining nut (48) on the valve operating lever (46) and withdraw the lever (46) and distance collar (45) from the shaft (62).

14 Remove the nuts (51) and spring washers (52) from the two short studs that secure the solenoid bracket assembly (53) to the main casing (67). Also undo the two setscrews (painted red) (49) so as to release the accumulator springs (55, 56) tension. Do not remove the two setscrews first. Lift away the solenoid bracket (53) followed by the springs (55, 56) and the spacer tube assembly.

15 If it is necessary to remove the accumulator sleeve and piston assembly a special tool is required. Refer to Fig. 6.16 and insert tool number L.182 into the accumulator sleeve and tighten the lower wing nut. Withdraw the accumulator sleeve and piston assembly by applying a rotary pull to the upper wing bolt of the tool. There is no other way of removing these parts without causing damage to their very fine surface finish.

16 The next part to be removed is the pump return valve which is positioned in the cavity of the main body casing once the solenoid bracket assembly (53) is removed. Undo and lift out the hexagon plug (57) and washer (58) followed by the spring (59), plunger (60) and ball bearing (61). It is important that these parts are removed before the pump is removed from the main casing.

17 Undo and remove the drain plug (69). Lift away the filter (75). It will be seen that there are three magnetic rings positioned in the recess of the drain plug (69).

18 To remove the pump another special tool is required having a part number L.183A/1. Undo and remove the two retaining screws (78) and the base plug (77). Screw the short threaded portion of the spindle of the special tool into the pump body. Locate the adaptor in position against the casing and tighten the wing nut which will cause the body (80) to withdraw from the main casing (67) (Fig. 6.17). Lift out the plunger (82) and spring (81).

19 Using a pair of circlip pliers remove the circlip (21) from its groove in the forward end of the clutch hub (23) and taking great care not to damage the clutch member or friction lining, drive the clutch member from the thrust ring (19) and bearing (20) using a soft metal drift and hammer.

20 With a pair of circlip pliers remove the large diameter circlip (22) and using a vice and piece of suitable diameter tube press the bearing (20) from the thrust ring (19).

21 Should it be necessary to remove the uni-directional clutch special assembly ring tool number L.178 is necessary. Position the assembly ring over the front face of the annulus (32) and lift the inner member of the uni-directional clutch (29) up into it (Fig. 6.19).

22 Then remove the assembly ring and allow the rollers to come out followed by the hub so exposing the spring (30).

23 Lift away the phosphor bronze thrust washer (31) that is fitted between the uni-directional clutch (29) and the annulus (32).

24 Undo and remove the speedometer dowel screw and spring washer. Using special tool L.214 so as to prevent damage to the thread of the bearing assembly withdraw the speedometer drive bearing and pinion. Note the 'O' ring on the bearing centre outer circumference.

25 Extract the split pin securing the castellated nut (37) to the annulus (32). Undo the castellated nut and remove followed by the thick plain washer. Slide the coupling flange (36) from the splines on the annulus (32).

26 Using a press or a hammer and block of wood on the end of the annulus (32) with the castellated nut (37) replaced to protect the threads, remove the annulus from the rear casing (39).

27 The front bearing should remain in position on the annulus (32) but if it must be removed a suitable two leg puller or a press should be used. Note the position of the plain washer (34) which should be located on a shoulder in front of the annulus splines.

28 If the oil seal (38) has shown signs of leaking or the bearing (35) is to be renewed, prise the oil seal from the rear casing (39) making a note of which way round it fits. The bearing (35) may be drifted from the rear casing using a long soft metal drift.

29 Thoroughly clean all the component parts and then examine them carefully. Check that the oil pump plunger (82) and body (80) are not worn and that the spring has not contracted (free length should not be less than 2 inches). Examine the 'O' rings from the operating pistons and renew them if worn or if they are becoming hard, and check that the cylinder bores are free from score marks and wear. Check all the ball bearing races for roughness when turned and for looseness between the inner and outer races. Examine the splines for burrs and wear and the rollers of the uni-directional clutch for chips and flat spots.

30 Renew the clutch linings if they are burnt or worn and carefully examine the main (67) and rear (39) casings for cracks or other damage. Renew the steady bush if it is worn and examine the gear teeth for cracks, chips and general wear. Examine the sealing balls for ridges which will prevent them seating properly and check the free length of the springs.

31 Assembly of the unit can commence after any damaged or worn parts have been exchanged and new gaskets and seals obtained.

32 The first part to be refitted is the pump assembly for which tool number L.184 is required to ensure accurate refitment. This is shown in Fig. 6.20. Screw the two guide pegs of the tool into the two holes in the bottom pump face.

33 Refit the spring (81) to the pump plunger (82) and insert this into the pump body (80). Insert the pump assembly into the casing (67) positioning the flange of the body (80) over both guide pegs of the tool L.184 and locating the flat of the pump plunger against the guide peg in the front casing adjacent to the central guide bushes.

34 Drift the pump body home fully using the drift, this being part of tool L.184. Undo and remove the two guide pegs and fit the two retaining screws (78) and spring washers (79).

35 Refit the base plug (77). Reassemble the three magnetic rings and fibre sealing washer (70) onto the drain plug (69). Locate the filter (75) onto the central body of the drain plug (69) and screw into the body. Tighten fully to prevent subsequent oil leaks.

36 Insert the non-return valve ball bearing (61) into its drilling. Note that this ball bearing has a diameter of ¼ inch. Using a soft metal drift of diameter slightly less than ¼ inch, tap the ball bearing lightly so as to seat it in its drilling. Insert the plunger (60), spring (59) and plug (57) with a new copper washer (58) fitted under its head. Check that the copper washer seats on its location correctly to ensure no oil leaks.

37 Refit the piston into the sleeve taking care that the piston rings are not damaged. With the sleeve upright push

Fig. 6.14. Location of thrust springs (1) long springs (2) short springs

Fig. 6.15. Method of attaching gearbox to overdrive unit

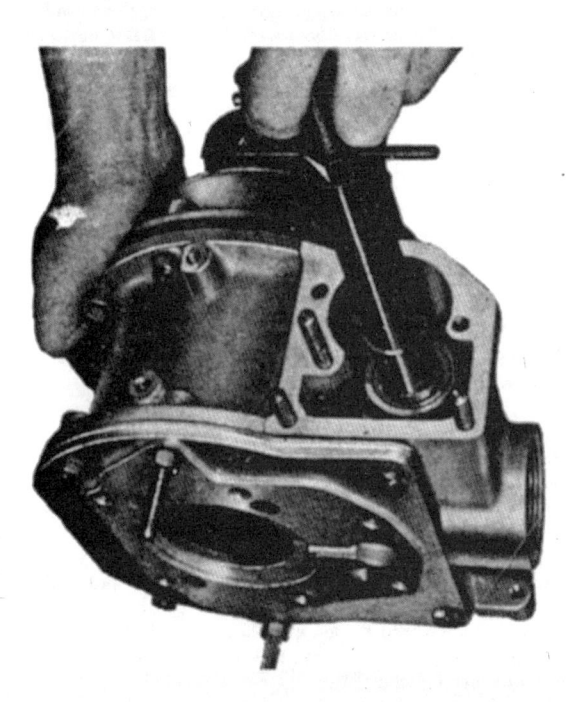

Fig. 6.16. Use of tool L182 to remove accumulator piston and sleeve assembly

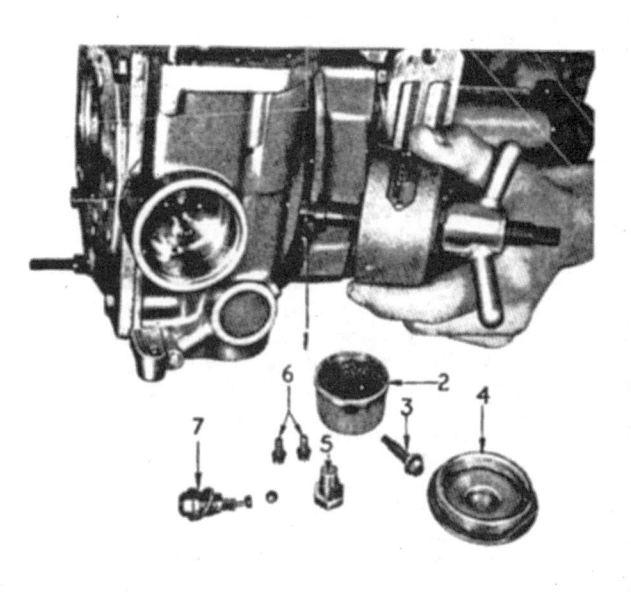

Fig. 6.17. TOOL L183A READY FOR SCREWING ITEM 1 INTO THE PUMP BODY
1 Screw of tool L183A/1
2 Filter
3 Bolt
4 Drain plug
5 Plug
6 Bolts
7 Pump non return valve

Chapter 6/Gearbox & Overdrive

the piston down until the rings are resting on the top of the bore. Using two thumbs compress each ring whilst a second person pushes the piston down.

38 Insert the springs (55, 56) into the tube and fit the accumulator tube into the recess in the accumulator sleeve and then carefully push into the casing, easing the sealing rings into the bore.

39 Fit a new 'O' ring over the operating shaft (62), if one was originally fitted, and using a new joint washer (54) refit the solenoid bracket (53) ensuring that the accumulator springs (55, 56) locate over a dowel in the brackets.

40 Tighten the two screws (49) with spring washers (50) evenly and then the nuts (51) with spring washers (52) onto the two short studs (63).

41 Fit new 'O' rings to the pistons (66) and lubricate with oil. Insert the pistons into their respective bores carefully easing the rubber 'O' rings into the bores in the casing. Note that the centre bosses of the pistons face outwards to the front of the casing.

42 Insert the operating valve (12) into its bore in the casing ensuring that it is the correct way up with the hemispherical end engaging on the flat of the small cam on the operating shaft (62).

43 Drop in the ball bearing (11), 5/16 inch diameter, followed by the plunger (10) with the larger diameter innermost and the spring (9). Fit a new copper washer (7) onto the operating valve plug (8) and refit the plug. Ensure the copper washer is sealing correctly on its location on the plug and tighten securely.

44 If any new parts are to be refitted to the rear casing or annulus a special tailshaft end float setting gauge will be necessary. This is numbered L.190A and will enable the thickness of the spacing washer (34) to be determined so that the bearings (33, 35) will not have excessive end float or pre-load. The gauge is shown in Fig. 6.21 and comprises an inner member which rests against the end of the annulus output shaft (32). The outer part rests on the rear bearing abutment in the rear casing (39).

45 Using a drift of suitable diameter to locate on the outer track of the front bearing (33) insert the bearing into the rear casing until the outer track abuts against a shoulder in the casing. Next, using a press or a drift of suitable diameter, insert the annulus (32) into the front bearing (33) which has been inserted into the casing.

46 Referring to Fig. 6.21 fit the gauge over the output shaft of the annulus until the outer member (1) contacts the rear bearing shoulder in the rear casing. Gently press down the inner member (2) and using feeler gauges determine dimension 'A'. Select a spacing washer (34) of the same thickness as the measurement just made using the feeler gauges. A range of washers are available in the following sizes: .146, .151, .156, .161, .166 inch. Remove the setting gauge.

47 Fit the previously selected washer (34) onto the annulus output shaft and using a drift of suitable diameter drive the rear bearing (35) into position in the rear casing. Also use the drift to refit the oil seal (38) ensuring that the lip is facing inwards. Lubricate the oil seal inner face.

48 Refit the rear coupling flange (36) into the splines of the annulus output shaft followed by the plain washer and castellated nut (37). Tighten the nut and secure with a new split pin.

49 Fit a new 'O' ring to the bearing and insert the speedometer pinion gear into the bearing. Insert the bearing and gear assembly into the casing and to ensure correct meshing rotate the annulus. Align the holes in the casing and bush and fit the dowel screw with a new copper washer under its head. Tighten the dowel screw securely.

50 Refit the spring (30) into the roller cage (27) of the uni-directional clutch. Insert the inner member (29) into the cage (27) and engage it into the other end of the spring (30). Also engage the slots of the inner member with the tongues on the roller cage ensuring that the spring is able to rotate the cage so moving the rollers (28) when they are refitted, up the inclined faces of the inner member (29). The cage should be spring loaded in an anti-clockwise direction when looking at it from the front.

51 Insert this assembly into the special assembly ring (tool number L.178) with its front end facing downwards and insert the rollers through the milled slot in the tool as shown in Fig. 6.19. It will be necessary to turn the uni-directional clutch in a clockwise direction until all rollers are in place.

52 Refit the uni-directional clutch assembly to the annulus (32) having first inserted the thrust washer (31). The assembly tool will allow the rollers to enter into the annulus without falling out or jamming. If the tool is not available a strong elastic band should be wrapped around the cage and then lifted to allow each roller to be inserted.

53 Before the planet carrier (26) is refitted the gears must be specially set. Turn each planet gear in turn until a dot mark on one of the teeth of the large gear is positioned radially outwards as shown in Fig. 6.23. Locate the phosphor bronze washer (25) in its recess in the planet carrier (26) and insert the sunwheel (24).

54 Ensure that the sunwheel meshes correctly with the planet gears at the same time keeping the dot marks in their original set position.

55 Insert the planet carrier and sunwheel assembly into the annulus (32).

56 Obtain a piece of metal bar the same diameter as the output shaft of the gearbox and insert it into the sunwheel (24) until the rod engages the planet carrier and uni-directional clutch splines.

57 The end float of the sunwheel must be checked to ensure that it is within the limits of between 0.008 and 0.014 inch. To do this slide an additional thrust washer of known thickness over the previously inserted metal rod until it rests on the top of the sunwheel (24) followed by the original phosphor bronze thrust washer (18) and the steel thrust washer (17).

58 Fit the thrust ring (19) into the front casing (67) and using a soft faced hammer tap it firmly into position. Carefully slide the front casing (67) over the metal rod and position it up the the rear casing assembly (39).

59 As an additional thrust washer has been fitted a gap between the two casings should now be evident. Using feeler gauges measure this gap as shown in Fig. 6.25. The thickness of the extra thrust washer MINUS the end float of the sunwheel is the correct measurement.

60 If this indicated end float is outside the limits specified in para. 57 it must be adjusted by replacing the STEEL thrust washer (17) at the front of the sunwheel (24) with a new one of greater or less thickness.

61 Remove the front casing (67) and thrust washers previously positioned as necessary.

62 Using a vice press the thrust bearing (20) into the thrust ring (19) and refit the large diameter circlip (22) into its groove in the thrust ring.

63 Next press the thrust ring assembly into the hub of the clutch sliding member (23) and lock in position using the smaller diameter circlip (21).

64 Carefully fit the clutch sliding member over the sunwheel splines (24) and engage the inner linings on the annulus assembly. Fit the phosphor bronze washer (18) on the top of the sunwheel and the steel washer (17) of suitable thickness as previously determined.

65 Lightly smear a little jointing compound onto both sides of the brake ring flange (83) and tap this home on the main casing (67).

66 Fit the main casing and brake ring to the rear casing,

Fig. 6.18. Removal of pump using tool L183A/1

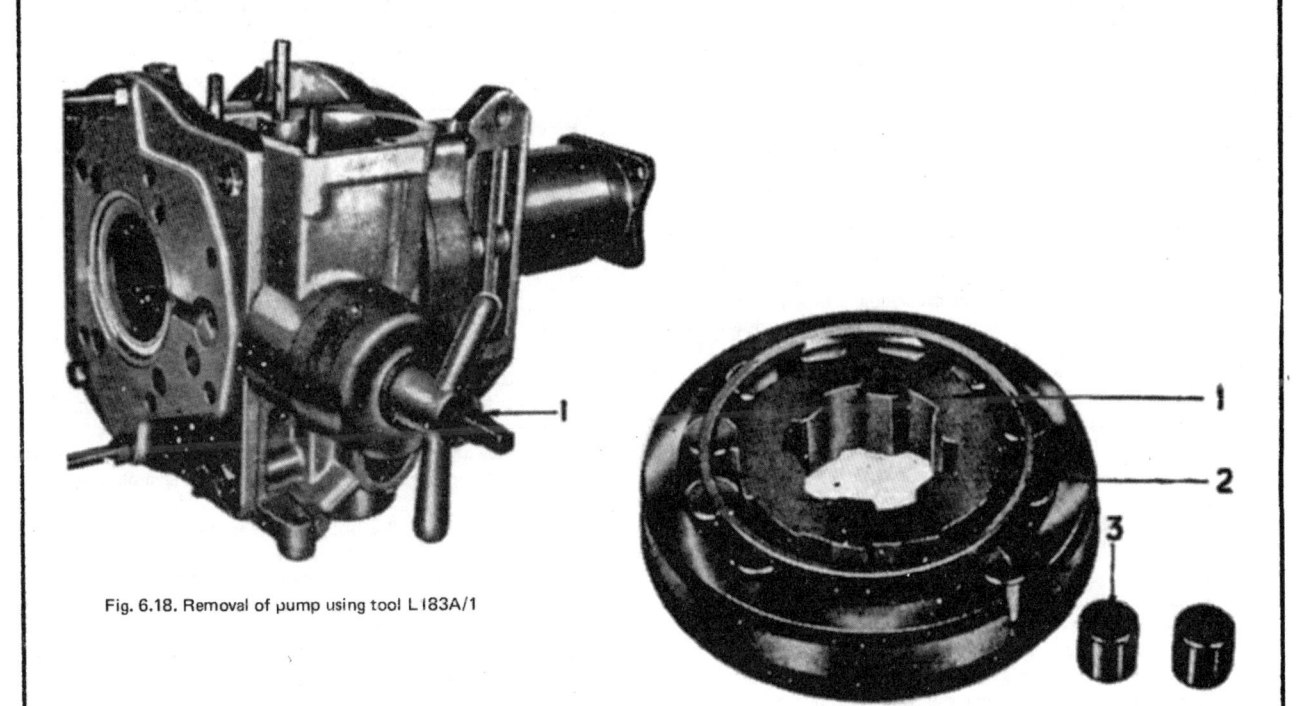

Fig. 6.19. Tool L178 being used to assemble roller clutch
(1) Inner member (2) Cage (3) Rollers

Fig. 6.20. Tool L184 being used to replace the pump body.
(1) Guide pins (2) Pump body

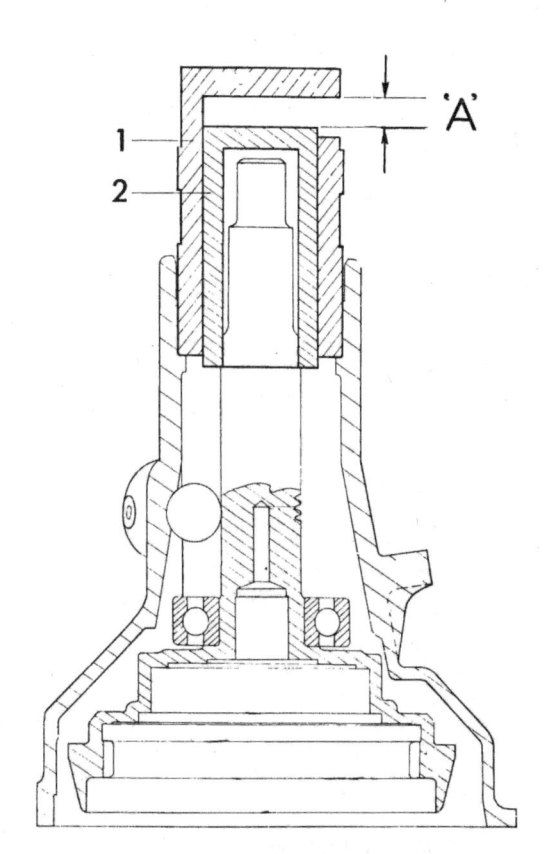

Fig. 6.21. Tool 190A being used to determine thickness of spacing washer

Chapter 6/Gearbox & Overdrive

taking care that the thrust ring pins are positioned through the four corresponding holes in the main casing. Fit spring washers into the six studs followed by the retaining nuts and tighten securely in a diagonal manner.

67 Replace the two operating piston bridge pieces (6) and secure on the studs using a new tab washer (5) and nuts (4). Bend over the locking tabs.

68 Slide the distance collar (45) onto the lever shaft (62).

69 Refit the operating lever (46) to the lever shaft (62) and lightly tighten the locknut (48).

70 Fit a new joint washer to the solenoid bracket (53) and insert the solenoid plunger into the yoke in the operating lever. Secure the solenoid (41) to the bracket with the two bolts and spring washer.

71 It will now be necessary to set the solenoid operating lever and full details of this are given in Section 14 of this Chapter.

72 Fit a new cover plate gasket and then the cover plate. Secure with three bolts and spring washers.

73 Reassembly is now complete. Do not forget to refill the gearbox and overdrive unit once the unit has been refitted.

14. Overdrive - Operating Lever Adjustment

1. If the overdrive does not engage, or will not release when it is switched out, providing the solenoid is not at fault, the trouble is likely to be that the operating lever is out of adjustment. Adjustment can be made without removing the overdrive.

2. To one end of a shaft passing through the overdrive casing is attached a setting lever having a 3/16 inch hole in its outer end as shown in Fig. 6.26 inset. The other end of the shaft is attached to the solenoid lever as shown in Fig. 6.26.

3. Switch on the ignition and set the overdrive switch to energise the solenoid. The hole in the setting lever should align with a similar hole in the casing which will indicate that the operating valve is fully open. To check this insert a 3/16 inch diameter rod (Fig. 6.26) through both holes. If it is not possible adjustment is necessary. Switch off the ignition.

4. Undo the three solenoid housing cover retaining bolts and lift away the cover.

5. Slacken the clamp bolt (44) on the operating lever (46) and rotate the shaft until the 3/16 inch diameter rod is able to pass into the hole in the casing.

6. Approximately 0.008 inch end float should be allowed for on the shaft. Push the solenoid plunger fully home at the same time holding the fork of the lever against the collar in the plunger.

7. Tighten the clamp bolt so securing the lever to the shaft.

8. Still continuing to push the plunger hard home in the solenoid set the rubber stop (6) (Fig. 6.26) until there is a gap of 0.150 to 0.155 inch between the end of the plunger and the stop.

9. Remove the 3/16 inch diameter rod and energise the solenoid. Check the alignment of the two setting holes with feeler gauges to the value of 0.150 to 0.155 inch between the stop and the plunger.

10 Operate the switch several times, checking with the test rod to ensure that the adjustment remains correct.

11 Measure the current consumed by the solenoid switch which, with the operating arm correctly set, should be about 2 amps. If a reading of 15 to 20 amps is obtained it is an indication that the solenoid plunger is not moving sufficiently to switch to the holding coil from the operating coil. If very fine adjustment will not remedy this condition, fit a new solenoid and plunger.

12 Replace the solenoid housing cover and tighten the three retaining bolts.

15. Overdrive - Operating Valve

Should the overdrive unit not function correctly and the fault diagnosed from the fault diagnosis chart as in the operating valve, the valve may be removed and checked as follows.

1. It will be seen that by referring to Fig. 6.13 the operating valve components (7-12) are located in the top of the main casing (67). To gain access to the valve with the unit in the car the floor panel must be removed as described in Section 3 paras. 3 to 37 inclusive.

2. Switch on the ignition but do not start the engine. Activate the overdrive control switch several times so as to operate the solenoid (41) (Fig. 6.13), thus releasing any residual oil pressure. Wipe the area around the valve plug free of dust.

3. Unscrew and remove the operating valve plug (8) and copper washer (7). Using a paper clip which has been straightened and the end bent to a small hook withdraw the spring (9). The plunger (10) may be removed using a small magnet or magnetised screwdriver. Also remove the ball bearing (11).

4. Using the other end of the paper clip with a slight kink in it carefully insert it into the centre of the valve (12) and withdraw the valve.

5. Clean the removed parts in petrol and allow to dry. Locate the small drilling near to the base of the valve (12) and check that it is free of dirt.

6. Inspect the ball bearing (11) for sign sof pitting which, if evident, mean that a new ball bearing should be obtained. It has a diameter of 5/16 inch.

7. If the ball bearing is satisfactory reset it by placing the ball bearing on a block of soft wood. Invert the valve and place on top of the ball bearing and lightly tap the end. If it is tapped too hard the drilling in the side of the valve or in the end may be closed.

8. Reassembling the valve is the reverse sequence to removal.

16. Overdrive Non-Return Valve - Removal and Replacement

1. Access to the relief and non-return valve located in the bottom of the overdrive is simply gained. First drain the oil from the gearbox and overdrive.

2. Cut through the locking wire, unscrew the plugs and remove and clean the components. Note that the valve cap and non-return valve body are unscrewed from the pump and that the relief valve body is removed with circlip pliers.

3. Examine the seatings for pits or chips and the balls for wear and ridges. The steel ball in the non-return valve is very hard and if the ball is undamaged and the seating is suspect tap the ball firmly into its seat with a soft metal drift.

4. Reassembly is a straightforward reversal of the removal sequence. Do not omit to fit the copper washer on the relief valve between the cap and main casing and hold the non-return valve ball to its spring with petroleum jelly during refitment.

5. Access to the operating valve can only be gained after removing the remote control assembly from the inside of the car. Undo the plug and check that the ball is lifted 1/32 inch when the solenoid is actuated. Failure to move points to a fault in the solenoid or operating arm.

6. The ball can be removed with a magnet and the valve with a piece of 1/8 inch wire. Check the ball and seat and clean out the small hole in the side of the valve tube. Check if the

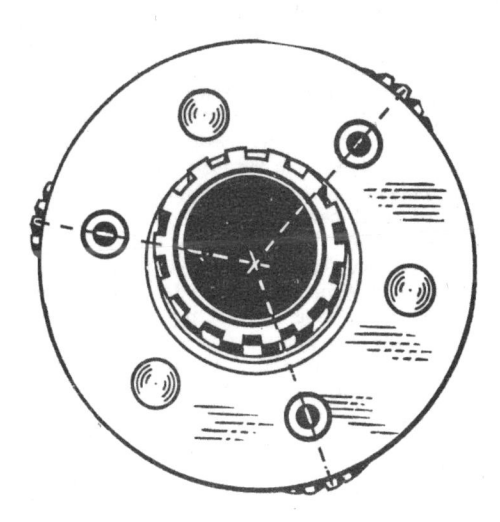

Fig. 6.22. Fitting the roller clutch to the annulus. The thrust washer (1) should be fitted first being held in place with grease.

Fig. 6.23. The position of the markings on the planet wheels when correctly fitted to sunwheel

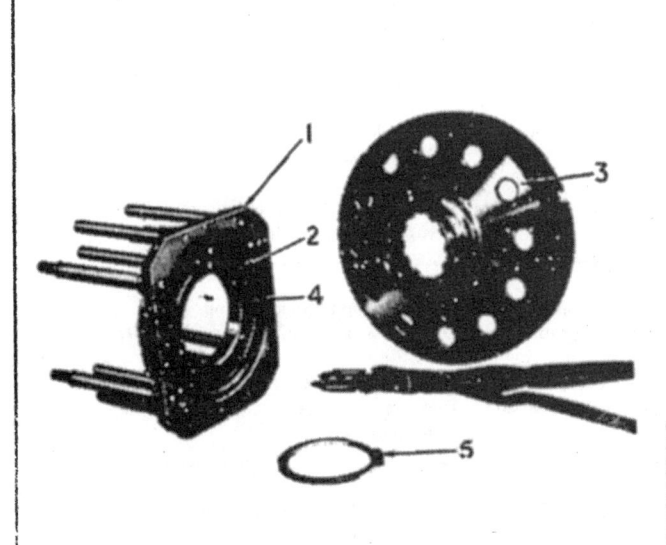

Fig. 6.24. CLUTCH SLIDING MEMBER
1 Thrust ring
2 Ball bearing
3 Cone clutch
4 Circlip
5 Circlip

Fig. 6.25. Use of feeler gauges to determine sun wheel endfloat

151

Chapter 6/Gearbox & Overdrive

oil pump is working by jacking the rear of the car off the ground, placing the car in top gear, engage overdrive and with the engine running watch if oil is being pumped into the valve chamber. Replacement is a reversal of the removal procedure.

17. Overdrive - Pump Non-Return Valve

If the overdrive unit does not function correctly, and the fault is diagnosed from the fault diagnosis chart that the pump non-return valve is not operating correctly, it may be removed and checked as follows.

1. It will be seen that by referring to Fig. 6.13 the pump non-return valve components (57-61) are situated in the solenoid side of the main casing (67). To gain access to the valve first drain the oil from the unit by undoing and removing the drain plug (69).
2. It is recommended that whenever the drain plug is removed the filter (75) and three magnetic plastic rings be cleaned before refitting.
3. Undo the three bolts, spring washers, cover plate and gasket.
4. Undo the solenoid retaining bolts and lift away the bolts, spring washers and the solenoid by disconnecting the solenoid plunger from the yoke of the operating valve lever (46).
5. Slacken the clamp bolt nut (48) and withdraw the operating lever (46) from the end of the valve operating shaft (62) followed by the distance collar (45).
6. Remove the nuts (51) and spring washers (52) from the two short studs that secure the solenoid bracket assembly (53) to the main casing (67). Also undo the two setscrews (painted red) (49) so as to release the accumulator springs (55, 56) tension. Do not remove the two setscrews first. Lift away the solenoid bracket (53) followed by the springs (55, 56) and spacer tube assembly.
7. The pump return valve is positioned in the cavity of the main body casing once the solenoid bracket assembly (53) is removed. Undo and lift out the hexagon plug (57) and washer (58) followed by the spring (59), plunger (60) and ball bearing (61).
8. Wash all valve parts in petrol and allow to dry. Ensure that the valve is clear of any foreign matter. Inspect the ball bearing for signs of pitting which, if evident, means a new bearing should be obtained. It has a diameter of ¼ inch.
9. Insert the ball bearing and tap using a soft metal drift and a hammer to reset it. Insert the plunger (60), spring (59) and plug (57) with a new copper washer (58) fitted under its head. Check that the copper washer seats on its location correctly to ensure no oil leaks.
10 Insert the accumulator springs (55, 56) into the tube and fit the accumulator into the recess in the accumulator sleeve still in the main casing.
11 Fit a new 'O' ring over the operating shaft (62), if one was originally fitted, and using a new joint washer (54) refit the solenoid bracket (53) ensuring that the accumulator springs (55, 56) locate over a dowel in the bracket.
12 Tighten the two screws (49) with spring washer (50) evenly and then the nuts (51) with spring washers onto the two short studs (63).
13 Slide the distance collar (45) onto the lever shaft (62).
14 Refit the operating lever (46) to the lever shaft (62) and lightly tighten the locknut (48).
15 Fit a new joint washer to the solenoid bracket (53) and insert the solenoid plunger into the yoke in the operating lever.
16 Secure the solenoid (41) to the bracket with the two bolts and spring washer.
17 It will now be necessary to set the solenoid operating lever and full details of this are given in Section 14 of this Chapter.
18 Fit a new cover plate gasket and then the cover plate. Secure with three bolts and spring washers.
19 Top up the level of oil in the gearbox and overdrive unit.

Fault Finding Chart - Gearbox & Overdrive

Cause	Trouble	Remedy
SYMPTOM: WEAK OR INEFFECTIVE SYNCHROMESH		
General wear	Synchronising cones worn, split or damaged.	Dismantle and overhaul gearbox. Fit new gear wheels and synchronising cones.
	Baulk ring synchromesh dogs worn, or damaged.	Dismantle and overhaul gearbox. Fit new baulk ring synchromesh.
SYMPTOM: JUMPS OUT OF GEAR		
General wear or damage	Broken gearchange fork rod spring	Dismantle and replace spring.
	Gearbox coupling dogs badly worn	Dismantle gearbox. Fit new coupling dogs.
	Selector fork rod groove badly worn	Fit new selector fork rod.
	Selector fork rod securing screw and locknut loose.	Remove side cover, tighten securing screw and locknut.
SYMPTOM: EXCESSIVE NOISE		
Lack of maintenance	Incorrect grade of oil in gearbox or oil level too low.	Drain, refill, or top up gearbox with correct grade of oil.
General wear	Bush or needle roller bearings worn or damaged.	Dismantle and overhaul gearbox. Renew bearings.
	Gearteeth excessively worn or damaged	Dismantle, overhaul gearbox. Renew gearwheels.
	Laygear thrust washers worn allowing excessive end play.	Dismantle and overhaul gearbox. Renew thrust washers.
SYMPTOM: EXCESSIVE DIFFICULTY IN ENGAGING GEAR		
Clutch not fully disengaging	Clutch pedal adjustment incorrect.	Adjust clutch pedal correctly.

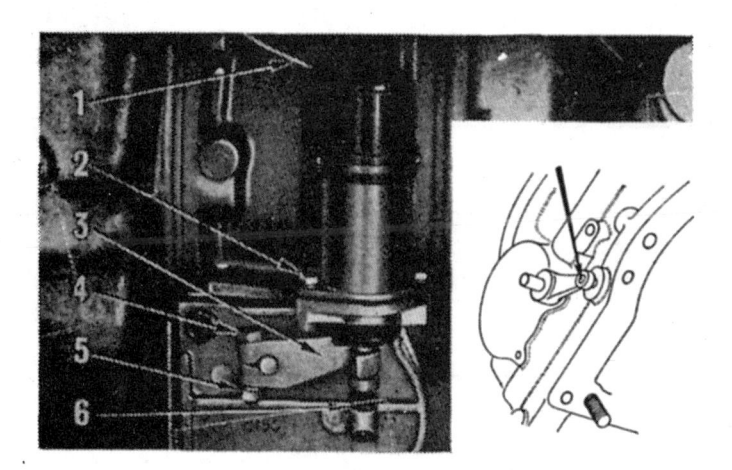

Fig. 6.26. THE OVERDRIVE SOLENOID AND OPERATING LEVER
1 Cable
2 Solenoid mounting bolt
3 Operating lever
4 Bolt
5 Nut
6 Rubber stop
(Inset shows 3/16 inch diameter rod in setting lever)

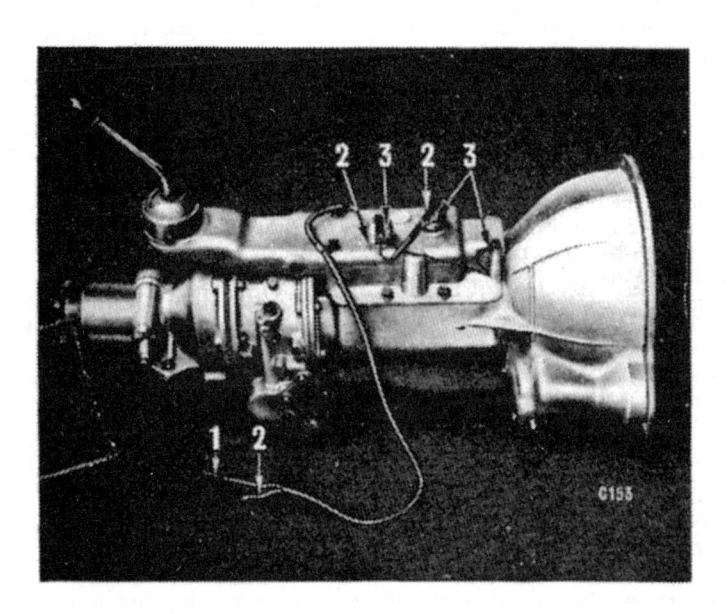

Fig. 6.27. COLOUR CODING OF OVERDRIVE CABLES
1 Yellow and Purple
2 Yellow
3 Black (Earth)

153

Chapter 7/Propeller Shaft and Universal Joints

Contents

General Description	1	Universal Joints - Inspection & Repair	4
Routine Maintenance	2	Universal Joints - Dismantling	5
Propeller Shaft - Removal & Replacement	3	Universal Joints - Reassembly	6

Specifications

Make	Hardy Spicer series 1300
Type	Tubular steel
Diameter	2 inches
Overall length	2' - 4 9/16"
Type of universal joints	Needle roller

1. General Description

Drive is transmitted from the gearbox to the rear axle by means of a finely balanced Hardy Spicer tubular propeller shaft.

Fitted at each end of the shaft is a universal joint which allows for vertical movement of the rear axle. Each universal joint comprises a four-legged centre spider, four needle roller bearings and two yokes.

Fore and aft movement of the rear axle is absorbed by a sliding spline in the front of the propeller shaft, which is splined and mates with a sleeve and yoke assembly. When assembled a dust cap, steel washer, and cork washer seal the end of the sleeve and sliding joint.

The yoke flange of the front universal joint is fitted to the gearbox mainshaft flange with four bolts, spring washers and nuts, and the yoke flange of the rear U.J. is secured to the pinion flange on the rear axle in the same way.

The propeller shaft is a relatively simple component and to overhaul and repair it is fairly easy.

2. Routine Maintenance

1. At intervals of 3,000 miles fill a grease gun with Castrolease I.M. or a similar recommended multi-purpose grease and thoroughly lubricate the following, through the three appropriate grease nipples which should first be wiped clean. Give 3 to 4 strokes of the grease gun:-

a) on the rear universal joint.
b) the sliding sleeve and yoke assembly at the front of the propeller shaft.
c) on the front universal joint.

3. Propeller Shaft - Removal and Replacement

1. Jack up the rear of the car, or position the rear of the car over a pit or a ramp.
2. If the rear of the car is jacked up supplement the jack with support blocks so that danger is minimised should the jack collapse.
3. If the rear wheels are off the ground place the car in gear or put the handbrake on to ensure that the propeller shaft does not turn when an attempt is made to loosen the four nuts on each flange.
4. The propeller shaft is carefully balanced to fine limits and it is important that it is replaced in exactly the same position it was in prior to its removal. Scratch a mark on the propeller shaft and rear axle flanges and the gearbox flanges to ensure accurate mating when the time comes for reassembly.
5. Unscrew and remove the four self locking nuts, bolts, and securing washers which hold the flange on the propeller shaft to the flange on the rear axle, and then unscrew and remove the four self locking nuts, bolts and washers which hold the front flange of the propeller shaft to the flange on the rear of the gearbox. Lower the propeller shaft to the ground.
6. Replacement of the propeller shaft is a reversal of the above procedure. Ensure that the mating marks scratched on the sides of the propeller shaft flanges line up with those on the gearbox and rear axle flanges.

4. Universal Joints - Inspection and Repair

1. Wear in the needle roller bearings is characterised by vibrations in the transmission, 'clonks' on taking up the drive, and in extreme cases of lack of lubrication, metallic squeaking, and ultimately grating and shrieking sounds as the bearings break up.
2. It is easy to check if the needle roller bearings are worn with the propeller shaft in position, by trying to turn the shaft with one hand, the other hand holding the rear axle flange when the rear universal is being checked, and the front gearbox coupling when the front universal is being checked. Any movement between the propeller shaft and

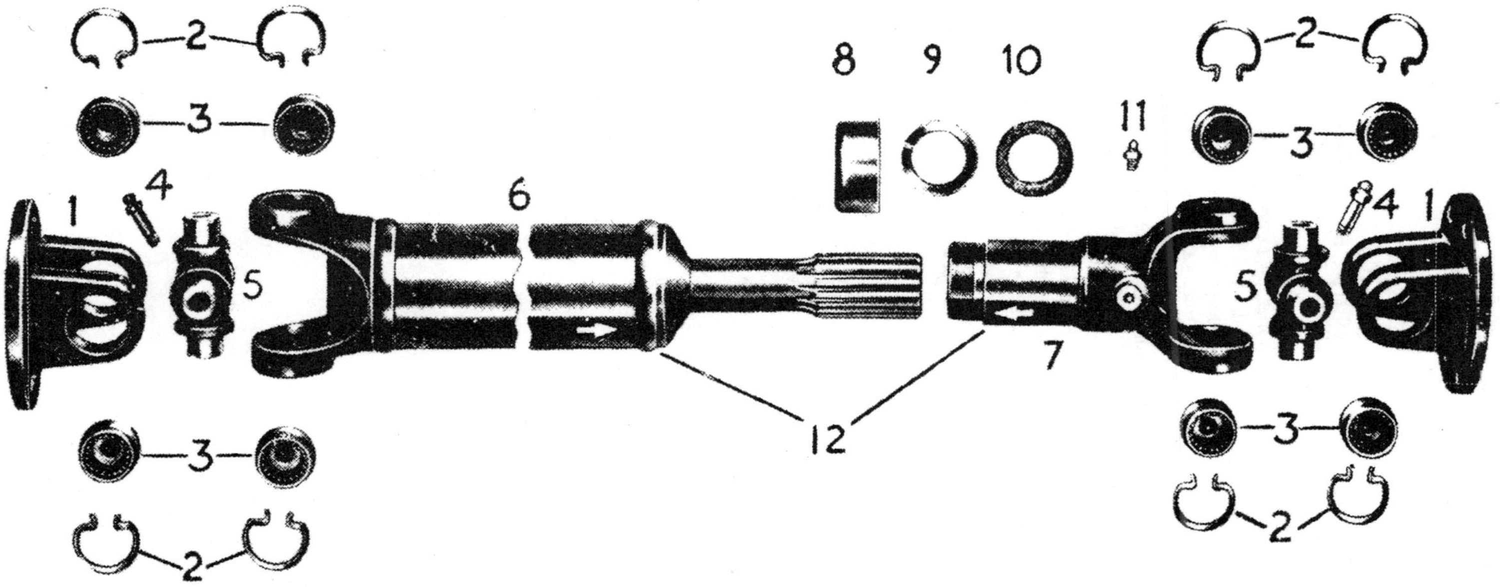

Fig. 7.1. PROPELLER SHAFT COMPONENT PARTS

1 Flange yoke	5 Spider	9 Steel washer
2 Circlips	6 Propeller shaft	10 Washer
3 Cups	7 Sliding yoke	11 Grease nipple
4 Grease nipple	8 Dust cap	

155

Chapter 7/Propeller Shaft & Universal Joints

the front and the rear half couplings is indicative of considerable wear.

3. If worn, the old bearings and spiders will have to be discarded and a repair kit, comprising new universal joint spiders, bearings, oil seals, and retainers purchased. Check also by trying to lift the shaft and noticing any movement in the joints.

4. Examine the propeller shaft splines for wear. To do this unscrew the dust cap from the sleeve, and then slide the sleeve from the shaft. Take off the steel washer and the cork washer. With the sleeve separated from the shaft assembly the splines can be inspected. If worn it will be necessary to purchase a new front sleeve assembly, or if the yokes are badly worn an exchange propeller shaft. It is not possible to fit oversize bearings and journals to the trunnion bearing holes.

5. Universal Joints - Dismantling

1. Clean away all traces of dirt and grease from the circlips located on the ends of the spiders, and remove the clips by pressing their open ends together with a pair of pliers and lever them out with a screwdriver. NOTE: If they are difficult to remove tap the bearing face resting on top of the spider with a mallet which will ease the pressure on the circlip (photo).

2. Hold the propeller shaft in one hand, as shown in Fig. 7.2, and remove the bearing cups and needle rollers by tapping the yoke at each bearing with a copper hide faced hammer. As soon as the bearings start to emerge they can be drawn out with your fingers. If the bearing cup refuses to move then place a thin bar against the inside of the bearing and tap it gently until the cup starts to emerge.

3. With the bearings removed it is relatively easy to extract the spiders from their yokes (Fig. 7.3). If the bearings and spider journals are thought to be badly worn this can easily be ascertained visually with the universal joints dismantled.

6. Universal Joints - Reassembly

1. Thoroughly clean out the yokes and journals. Make certain that the grease passages are quite clear.

2. Place the spider on the propeller shaft yoke and assemble the needle rollers in the bearing races with the assistance of some thin grease. NOTE: It is essential to fit the spiders in the yoke flanges so the lubricating nipples are facing the propeller shaft and not the yoke flanges. If fitted the wrong way round it will be impossible to lubricate the universal joints.

3. Refit the bearing cups on the spider and tap the bearings home so that they lie squarely in position.

4. Replace the circlips and lubricate the bearings well with lithium based grease.

5. Fit the dust cap, steel washer, and a new cork gasket over the splined part of the propeller shaft.

6. Grease the splines and then line up the arrow on the sleeve assembly with the arrow on the splined portion of the propeller shaft, and push the sleeve over the splines. Fit the washers to the sleeve and screw up the dust cap. The final assembly is shown in Fig. 7.5.

7. If correctly assembled the forked yokes on both shafts will have their axis parallel to each other. This is essential if vibration is to be eliminated.

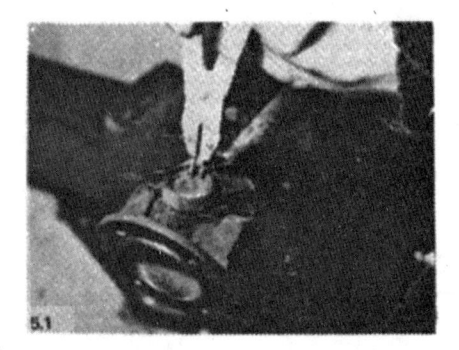

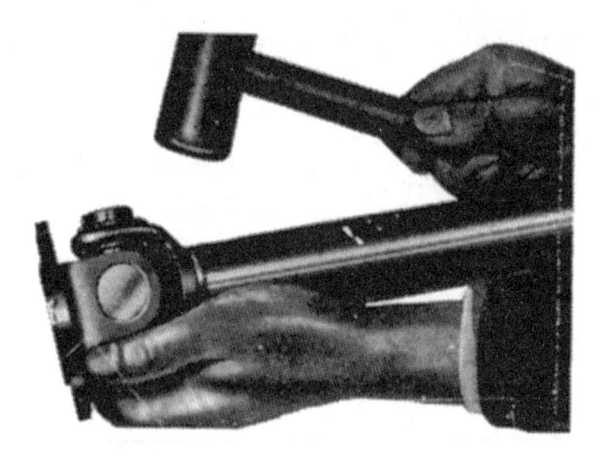

Fig. 7.2. Using a soft hammer to tap bearing cap from yoke

Fig. 7.3. Removal of spider from yoke

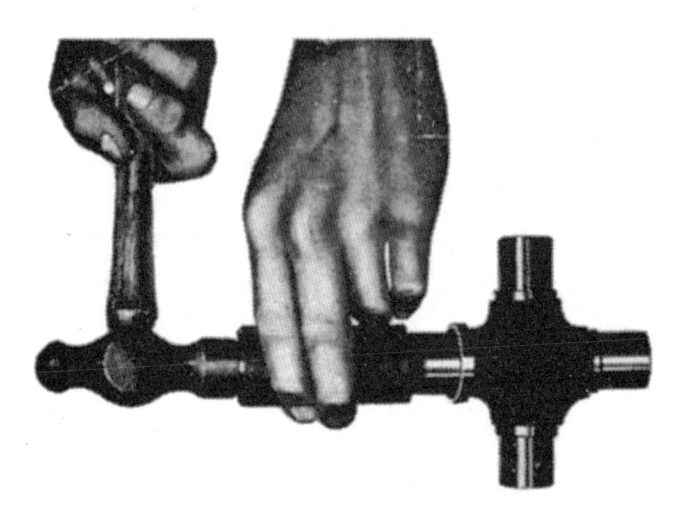

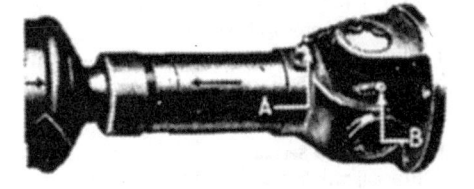

Fig. 7.4. Using a hammer and tubular drift to refit spider journal seal retainer

Fig. 7.5. Correct alignment of sliding yoke

157

Chapter 8/Rear Axle

Contents

General Description ... 1	Axle Shaft End Float Measurement & Adjustment
Rear Axle - Routine Maintenance ... 2	(TR2, 3, 3A) - Later Type ... 9
Rear Axle - Removal & Replacement (TR2, 3, 3A) ... 3	Differential Unit - Dismantling, Inspection, Reassembly
Rear Axle - Removal & Replacement (TR4, 4A standard) 4	& Adjustment (TR2, 3, 3A) - Early Type ... 10
Rear Hub - Removal & Refitting (TR2, 3, 3A) - Early	Differential Unit - Dismantling, Inspection, Reassembly
Type Standard Hub ... 5	& Adjustment (TR2, 3, 3A) - Later Type ... 11
Axle Shaft, Oil Seals & Bearings - Removal &	Differential Unit - Dismantling, Inspection, Reassembly
Refitting (TR2, 3, 3A) ... 6	& Adjustment (TR4, 4A) - Standard Rear Axle... 12
Rear Hub - Removal & Refitting (TR2, 3, 3A) -	Centre Lock Hubs (Wire Wheel) ... 13
Later Type ... 7	Differential Unit (I.R.S.) - Removal & Refitting ... 14
Axle Shaft, Oil Seals & Bearings - Removal &	Differential Unit (I.R.S.) - Dismantling, Inspection,
Refitting (TR2, 3, 3A) - Later type. ... 8	Reassembly & Adjustment ... 15

Specifications

Type ...	Semi floating
Final Drive ...	Hypoid
Differential carrier bearings...	Tapered roller
Bevel pinion bearings ...	Tapered roller
Rear hub bearings:	
TR2, TR3, TR3A ...	Ball
TR4, TR4A ...	Tapered roller
Crownwheel and pinion:	
Adjustment ...	Shims
Backlash ...	.004 to .006 inch
Carrier bearing pre-load ...	.002 to .004 inch pinch over both bearings
Pinion bearing pre-load ...	15 to 18 in./lb. without oil seal
Crownwheel run-out ...	.003 inch maximum
Final drive ratio:	
TR2, TR3, TR3A ...	3.7:1
TR4, TR4A ...	3.7:1 or 4.1:1
Number of crownwheel teeth ...	37 to 41
Number of pinion teeth ...	10
Lubricant capacity ...	1½ pints
Optional I.R.S. on TR4A ...	Same specification as TR4
Torque Wrench Settings	
Bearing caps to rear housing ...	34 to 36 lb.ft. (4.701 to 4.977 Kg.m)
Hub to axle shaft (live axle) early type. ...	110 to 125 lb.ft. (15.21 to 17.28 Kg.m)
Hub to axle shaft (live axle) later type. ...	125 to 145 lb.ft. (17.28 to 20.05 Kg.m)
Inner driving flange to inner axle (I.R.S. ...	100 to 110 lb.ft. (13.83 to 15.21 Kg.m)
Backing plate attachment ...	26 to 28 lb.ft. (3.595 to 3.871 Kg.m)
Rear cover attachment ...	16 to 18 lb.ft. (2.21 to 2.489 Kg.m)
Hypoid pinion flange (split pin) ...	85 to 100 lb.ft. (11.75 to 13.83 Kg.m)
Wheel studs and nuts...	44 to 55 lb.ft. (6.22 to 7.601 Kg.m)
Wire wheel adaptor nuts (TR3 only) ...	65 lb.ft. (8.987 Kg.m)
Hub extension studs for wire wheels ...	65 lb.ft. (8.987 (Kg.m)

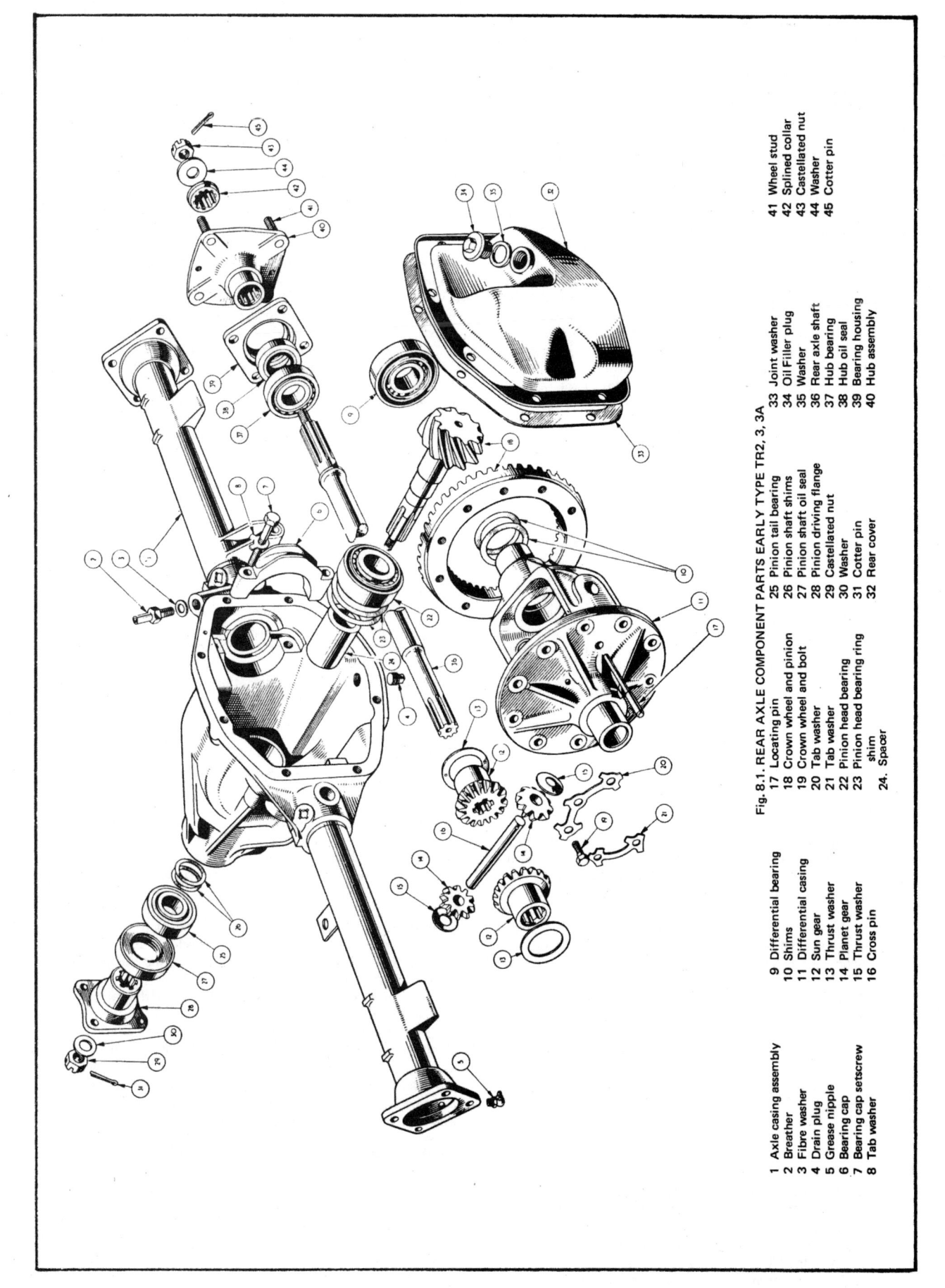

Fig. 8.1. REAR AXLE COMPONENT PARTS EARLY TYPE TR2, 3, 3A

1 Axle casing assembly
2 Breather
3 Fibre washer
4 Drain plug
5 Grease nipple
6 Bearing cap
7 Bearing cap setscrew
8 Tab washer
9 Differential bearing
10 Shims
11 Differential casing
12 Sun gear
13 Thrust washer
14 Planet gear
15 Thrust washer
16 Cross pin
17 Locating pin
18 Crown wheel and pinion
19 Crown wheel and bolt
20 Tab washer
21 Tab washer
22 Pinion head bearing
23 Pinion head bearing ring shim
24. Spacer
25 Pinion tail bearing
26 Pinion shaft shims
27 Pinion shaft oil seal
28 Pinion driving flange
29 Castellated nut
30 Washer
31 Cotter pin
32 Rear cover
33 Joint washer
34 Oil Filler plug
35 Washer
36 Rear axle shaft
37 Hub bearing
38 Hub oil seal
39 Bearing housing
40 Hub assembly
41 Wheel stud
42 Splined collar
43 Castellated nut
44 Washer
45 Cotter pin

159

Chapter 8/Rear Axle

1. General Description

The TR2, 3, 3A, 4 and 4A models covered by this manual have a three-quarter floating type rear axle fitted as standard although on the TR4A models independent rear suspension is fitted as an optional extra. This is dealt with separately at the end of this Chapter.

The standard rear axle is held in place by semi-elliptic springs which are constructed from a number of individual leaves of different lengths and are held together with a long bolt and clips. The semi-elliptic springs provide all the necessary lateral and longitudinal location of the axle. The rear axle incorporates a hypoid crown wheel and pinion and a two pinion differential.

All repairs to the differential unit must be carried out with the rear axle assembly removed from the car as special equipment is required to extract the differential unit. The pinions assembly is mounted to the front of the rear axle casing and is adjusted by means of shims. The crown wheel position may be altered by using shims so that the correct crown wheel and pinion mesh may be obtained.

Half shafts of the semi-floating design are fitted and at the hub end a single bearing is used.

A redesigned axle assembly was fitted on cars from commission number 13046 and modifications were made to the differential unit as well as the hubs. For simplicity reasons full overhaul details are given for each rear axle assembly that will be found on the models of cars covered by this manual.

There are several special tools that are necessary and mention of these tools together with the tool numbers is made, when and where applicable, so it is recommended that before work is commenced the section be studied and the tools if possible borrowed from the local agents.

2. Rear Axle - Routine Maintenance

1. Every 6,000 miles remove the filler plug in the rear axle casing end cover and top up with an S.A.E. 90 EP gear oil such as Castrol Hypoy. After topping up the axle do not replace the plug for five minutes to allow any excess to run out. If the axle is overfilled it is likely that oil will leak out of the ends of the axle casing and ruin the brake linings (standard axle) or with the optional independent rear suspension oil will seep past the oil seals.
2. On the later type axles there is a grease nipple fitted under the hub and this should receive six strokes only of a hand type grease gun. It is important that it is not over-greased.
3. Check the level of hydraulic fluid in the two shock absorbers and top up if necessary using the correct grade of fluid.
4. Spray or brush the rear springs with engine oil.
5. Every 12,000 miles drain the oil when hot, clean the drain plug and refill the axle with 1½ pints of S.A.E. 90 EP gear oil.

3. Rear Axle - Removal and Replacement (TR2, 3, 3A)

1. Undo the rear axle drain plug and allow the oil to drain into a container having a capacity of at least 1½ pints. When all the oil has drained out refit the drain plug.
2. Chock the front wheels and jack up the rear of the car as high as possible and place axle stands under the rear springs as near to the front spring eyes as possible.
3. Apply the handbrake, undo the wheel nut and remove the road wheels. Should centre lock wheels (wire spoke wheels) be fitted, remove the split collar from around the hub by inserting a wide blade screwdriver into the slit in the collar and expanding the collar, slide out the collar from the hub barrel. Unscrew the two countersunk screws, release the handbrake and withdraw the brake drum.
4. Release the handbrake (standard axle).
5. Fit a piece of plastic tube to one of the rear brake bleed nipples and place the other end in a clean glass jar. Undo the nipple and drain the brake hydraulic system.
6. Refer to Fig. 8.2 and disconnect the main brake hydraulic pipe union (4) from the support bracket on the chassis.
7. Undo the flexible hose locknut securing the hose to the support bracket and pull the threaded end of the hose through the bracket.
8. Extract the split pin securing the handbrake clevis pin (1) (Fig. 8.2) to the compensator lever. Lift away the washer and withdraw the clevis pin. Note that the head is on top of the fork end.
9. Undo the handbrake brake support bracket clamp bolt nut. Lift away the nut, plain washer and bolt and separate the cable from the support bracket.
10 Extract the split pin securing the handbrake cable fork end clevis pin to the handbrake lever at the rear of the backplate. Remove the plain washer and withdraw the clevis pin. Note the location of the clevis pin head. Repeat this for the other rear cable connection.
11 Using an open ended spanner very carefully undo the metal hydraulic pipe connecting union to the wheel cylinder. If it is tight take extreme caution not to twist the metal pipe. Well lubricate the union with penetrating oil and allow to soak before attempting to undo the union again. Repeat this for the other backplate wheel cylinder connection.
12 Using a screwdriver release the tab washers (later axle) and undo the six nuts and bolts (5) (Fig. 8.3) that hold the axle shaft assembly and the brake backplate assembly onto the flange of the sleeve of the rear axle casing. Repeat this for the other half shaft.
13 Very carefully withdraw the axle shaft assembly from the rear axle casing. On the later type of rear axle check if there are some shims fitted behind the backplate. Remove these and put in a safe place so that they will not be interchanged.
14 The rear axle movement check straps should next be removed by undoing the four retaining nuts (9) (Fig. 8.3). Remove the nuts, plain washers and the check straps.
15 Undo the four nyloc nuts (6) which secure the rear axle 'U' bolts to the spring. Remove the nuts.
16 Carefully swing the spring plate from under the spring but leave it attached to the damper arm by not undoing the nyloc nut (8).
17 Lift away the four 'U' bolts, two each side of the axle.
18 Undo the four nuts and bolts securing the propeller shaft rear flange to the final drive pinion companion flange and lower the rear end of the propeller shaft to the ground.
19 Check that all necessary connections have been disconnected and slide the rear axle unit towards the left of the car. Once the right hand end of the rear axle is clear of the right hand spring lower the right hand end to the ground.
20 Next move the axle to the right until the left hand end is free from the left hand spring and slide the axle from under the car as shown in Fig. 8.4.
21 Replacement is a straight forward reversal of the removal sequence. Do not forget to bleed the brake hydraulic system and refill the axle with 1½ pints of correct grade oil.

Fig. 8.2. Handbrake compensator linkage connections

Fig. 8.3. Rear axle spring mounting

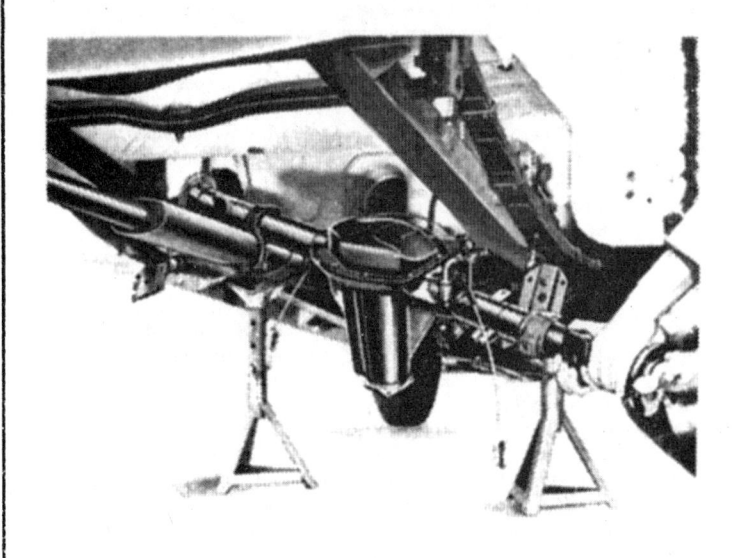

Fig. 8.4. Removal of axle from underside of car

161

Chapter 8/Rear Axle

4. Rear Axle - Removal and Replacement (TR4, 4A) - Standard

The removal of the rear axle is basically identical to that as described in Section 3. However, the rear exhaust pipe mounting must be released before the rear axle can be removed. Also it may be found that spacers are fitted between the spring and rear axle. These should be refitted in their original positions.

5. Rear Hub - Removal and Refitting (TR2, 3, 3A) - Early Type Standard Hub

1. Chock the front wheels to stop the car rolling forwards or backwards. Remove the rear wheel trim.
2. Extract the split pin (45) (Fig. 8.1) and slacken the castellated nut (43). DO NOT remove at this stage.
3. Jack up the rear of the car and support on axle stands. Undo the four wheel nuts and remove the nuts. Lift away the road wheel.
4. Remove the castellated nut (43) followed by the splined taper washer (42).
5. Apply the handbrake and undo the two countersunk screws securing the brake drum to the hub assembly. Release the handbrake and remove the brake drum. Should it be difficult to remove slacken off the brake adjustment and tap the circumference with a soft faced hammer.
6. It will now be necessary to use a special tool having a part number of M.86 or S.132/2. Fit the tool to the hub and withdraw the hub from the shaft. There is no other way of separating these two parts.
7. There is an alternative way of removing the hub but this entails removing the half shaft with the hub still attached. This method will necessitate the removal of the brake backplate and also the disconnection of the handbrake linkage and the hydraulic hose connection to the wheel cylinder. Further details of this method are given in Section 6 of this Chapter.
8. Reassembling is the reverse sequence to removal but on the later produced models covered by this section the axle shafts were modified giving an interference fit between the shaft and hub splines. A special tool having a number S125 will be necessary in order for the two parts to be assembled whether the axle shaft is still in the axle casing or not. As a last resort if the axle shaft is away from the axle casing a press may be used instead of the special tool.

Centre lock type (wire spoke wheels)

9. Chock the front wheels, raise the rear of the car and place on axle stands. Apply the handbrake.
10. Using a copper or hide faced hammer undo and remove the hub cap by tapping the hub cap lugs. Lift away the road wheel.
11. Extract the split pin (12) (Fig. 8.5) through the hole in the barrel of the hub (8). Undo and remove the castellated nut (11) from the axle shaft. This nut should not be excessively tight but if difficulty is experienced in undoing it refit the road wheel and lower the car to the ground so preventing the axle shaft from turning.
12. Lift away the washer (10) followed by the splined taper collar (9). Remove the split collar (15) from around the hub by inserting a wide blade screwdriver into the slit in the collar and expanding the collar. Undo the two countersunk screws (14), release the handbrake and withdraw the brake drum (13).
13. Fit the special tool numbered S132 and withdraw the hub. It should be noted that the hubs will have either a left hand or right hand thread depending on which side of the car the hub was fitted. Ensure that the correct removal ring is selected.
14. There is an alternative way of removing the hub but this entails removing the half shaft with the hub still attached. This method will necessitate the removal of the brake backplate and also the disconnection of the handbrake linkage and hydraulic hose connection to the wheel cylinder. Further details of this method are given in Section 6 of this Chapter.
15. Whilst the spoked wheels are away from the car it is recommended that the wheels and splines are thoroughly inspected.
16. Check for wear on the splines and if badly worn a new hub or wheel or both will have to be refitted.
17. Carefully examine the spokes for bending or rusting. Run a small spanner or screwdriver around the spokes and if the spokes are correctly fitted and tensioned they should give a clear metallic ring. A low tensioned or damaged spoke will give a flat note and conversely if the spoke is in too much tension a high metallic ring will be heard. Any faults with a wire wheel must be rectified by a person skilled in working with wire wheels.
18. Remove any signs of rust, and grease the splines before the wheels are refitted.
19. Reassembly is the reverse sequence to removal but on the later produced models covered by this section the axle shafts were modified giving an interference fit between the shaft and hub splines. A special tool having a number S12 will be necessary in order for the two parts to be assembled whether the axle shaft is still in the axle casing or not. As a last resort if the axle shaft is away from the axle casing a press may be used instead of the special tool.

6. Axle Shaft, Oil Seals and Bearings - Removal and Refitting (TR2, 3, 3A)

1. Check the front wheels, raise the rear of the car and place on axle stands. Apply the handbrake.
2. Undo the wheel nuts and remove the road wheels. Should centre lock wheels (wire spoke wheels) be fitted remove the split collar from around the hub by inserting a wide blade screwdriver into the slit in the collar and expanding the collar. Slide the collar from the hub barrel. Unscrew the two countersunk screws, release the handbrake and withdraw the brake drum.
3. Release the handbrake (standard type).
4. Fit a piece of plastic tube to one of the rear brake bleed nipples and place the other end in a clean glass jar. Undo the nipple and drain the brake hydraulic system.
5. Refer to Fig. 8.3 and disconnect the metal brake pipe from the rear of the wheel cylinder by using an open ended spanner and undoing the union. If it is tight take extreme caution not to twist the metal pipe. Well lubricate the union with penetrating oil and allow to soak before attempting to undo the union again.
6. Extract the split pin securing the handbrake cable fork end clevis pin to the handbrake lever at the rear of the backplate. Remove the plain washer and withdraw the clevis pin. Note the location of the clevis pin head.
7. Using a screwdriver release the tab washers (later axle) and undo the four or six nuts and bolts that hold the axle shaft assembly and the brake backplate assembly onto the flange of the sleeve of the rear axle casing.
8. Very carefully withdraw the axle shaft assembly from the rear axle casing. On the later type of rear axle check if there are some shims fitted behind the backplate. Remove these and put in a safe place so that they will not be interchanged.
9. Place some soft faced or wood blocks between the jaws

Fig. 8.5. CENTRE LOCK HUB COMPONENTS (EARLY TYPE)

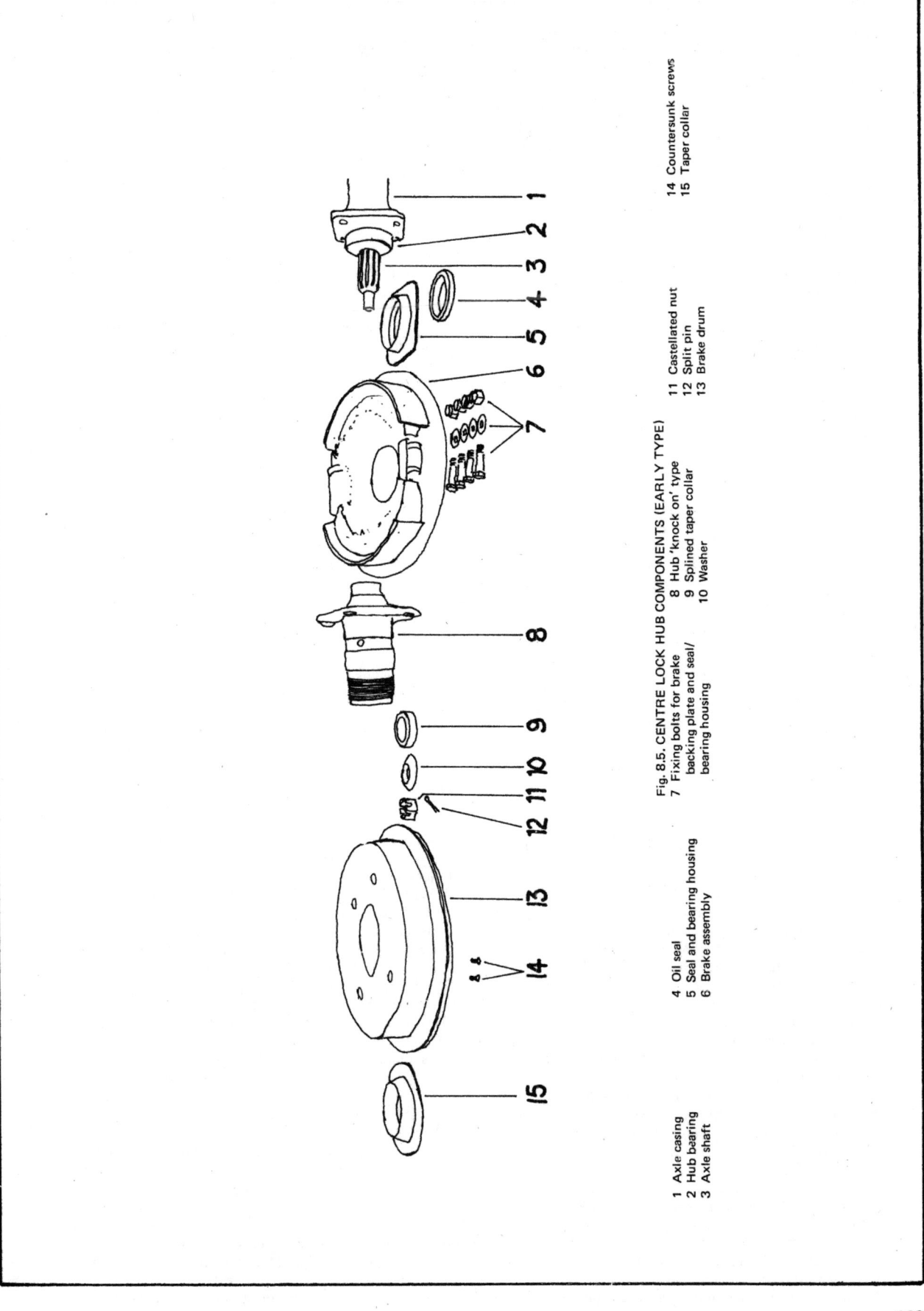

1 Axle casing
2 Hub bearing
3 Axle shaft
4 Oil seal
5 Seal and bearing housing
6 Brake assembly
7 Fixing bolts for brake backing plate and seal/bearing housing
8 Hub 'knock on' type
9 Splined taper collar
10 Washer
11 Castellated nut
12 Split pin
13 Brake drum
14 Countersunk screws
15 Taper collar

Chapter 8/Rear Axle

of a firm vice and hold the axle shaft vertically in the vice.

10 Refer to Fig. 8.1 and extract the split pin (45). Undo the castellated nut (43) and lift away the splined washer (42) and plain washer (44).

11 If the standard hub (40) is fitted it can be removed from the axle shaft by using special tool number M96 or S132/2.

12 If a centre lock hub Fig.8.5. (8) is fitted use a special tool number S132 to remove the hub from the axle shaft.

13 When either hub is removed from the axle shaft it will release the bearing housing (39) and the oil seal (38). The hub bearing (37) will however be still left on the axle shaft.

14 Inspect the oil seal and if it is unserviceable drift it out of the bearing housing.

15 The bearing may now be removed by placing the axle shaft in the vice with the bearing resting on the top of the jaws and, with the axle nut refitted, the axle shaft is knocked through the bearing using a soft faced hammer.

16 With all parts dismantled wash in petrol or paraffin and dry using a non fluffy rag.

17 Check the bearing for wear by rotating it using fingers to feel for signs of roughness or excessive movement.

18 Reassembly is the reverse sequence to dismantling. Refit the bearing and oil seal using a piece of tube of suitable diameter making sure that they are fitted squarely into position. Well lubricate the bearing once it has been refitted to the axle shaft.

19 On later produced models covered by this section, the axle shafts were modified giving an interference fit between the shaft and hub splines. A special tool having a number S125 will be necessary in order for the two parts to be assembled. As a last resort the hub may be fitted to the axle shaft using a press instead of the special tool.

7. Rear Hub - Removal and Refitting (TR2, 3, 3A) - Later Type

1. Check the front wheels to stop the car rolling forwards or backwards. Remove the rear wheel trim.
2. Extract the split pin (48) (Fig. 8.6) and slacken the castellated nut (46). DO NOT remove at this stage.
3. Jack up the rear of the car and support on axle stands. Undo the four wheel nuts and remove the nuts. Lift away the road wheel.
4. Remove the castellated nut (46) followed by the plain washer (47).
5. Apply the handbrake and undo the two countersunk screws securing the brake drum to the hub assembly. Release the handbrake and remove the brake drum. Should it be difficult to remove, slacken off the brake adjustment and tap the circumference with a soft faced hammer.
6. It will now be necessary to use a special tool having a part number of M86A. Fit the tool to the hub and withdraw the hub from the shaft. There is no other way of separating these two parts.
7. There is an alternative way of removing the hub but this entails removing the half shaft with the hub still attached. This method will necessitate the removal of the brake backplate and also the disconnection of the handbrake linkage and hydraulic hose connection to the wheel cylinder. Further details of this method are given in Section 8 of this chapter.
8. Reassembling is the reverse sequence to removal.

8. Axle Shaft, Oil Seals and Bearing - Removal and Refitting (TR2, 3, 3A) - Later Type

1. Chock the front wheels to stop the car rolling forwards or backwards. Remove the rear wheel trim.
2. Extract the split pin (48) (Fig. 8.6) and slacken the castellated nut (46). DO NOT remove at this stage.
3. Jack up the rear of the car and support on axle stands. Undo the four wheel nuts and remove the nuts. Lift away the road wheel.
4. Remove the castellated nut (46) followed by the plain washer (47).
5. Apply the handbrake and undo the two countersunk screws securing the brake drum to the hub assembly. Release the handbrake and remove the brake drum. Should it be difficult to remove, slacken off the brake adjustment and tap the circumference with a soft faced hammer.
6. It will now be necessary to use a special tool having a part number of M86A. Fit the tool to the hub and withdraw the hub from the shaft. There is no other way of separating these two parts.
7. Bend back the tab washer tabs (41) and undo the six bolts securing the hub bearing housing (38) and the brake backplate to the rear axle flange.
8. Remove the bearing housing (38) complete with the outer track of the bearing (37). Leave the brake backplate in place.
9. Withdraw the axle shaft (36) complete with the inner track of the bearing (37).
10. Lift away the rectangular key (45) from the axle shaft (36).
11. Using a two leg puller with reversible legs remove the inner and outer tracks of the bearing from the axle shaft (36) and bearing housing (38).
12. Wash all dismantled parts in petrol or paraffin and wipe dry using a non fluffy rag. Reassemble the parts of the bearing and rotate the inner and outer tracks whilst pressing them firmly together. If there are signs of roughness then the bearing should be renewed. Inspect the rollers and tracks for signs of cracking, rusting or pitting.
13. Inspect the oil seal (51) for signs of hardening or cracking and remove it from the axle sleeve if suspect. Note which way round the seal is fitted.
14. Using a piece of tube of suitable diameter fit a new oil seal to the axle sleeve so that the lips face inwards. Also use the same piece of tube to drive the inner track of the bearing (37) onto the axle shafts, the taper should face outwards.
15. Refit the outer track of the bearing (37) into the bearing housing making sure that it is fitted the correct way round. A soft metal drift may be used to refit this track. Make sure that it is fitted squarely and tap the drift on the track in a diagonal manner.
16. Refit the oil seal (39) into the bearing housing so that the lips of the seal face inwards.
17. Replace the rectangular key (45) to the axle shaft.
18. Refit the hub (43) followed by the plain washer (47) and the castellated nut (46).
19. Hold the axle shaft in a vertical position between soft faces or wood blocks in a firm bench vice.
20. Using a torque wrench set to read between 125 and 145 lb.ft., tighten the castellated nut (46) and lock using a new split pin (48).
21. If the brake backplate has been removed it would have been observed that there were shims (40) at the rear of the backplate. Refit the shims followed by the backplate.
22. Very carefully insert the axle shaft assembly taking care that the oil seal (51) is not damaged. Rotate the axle shaft until the splines on it line up with the internal splines of the sunwheel and, once located, push the axle shaft assembly in as far as it will go.
23. Replace the six bolts and nuts that secure the bearing housing, backplate and shims to the axle sleeve flange.
24. Replace the brake drum. If the backplate was removed it will be necessary to bleed the hydraulic system.
25. Refit the road wheel, adjust the brake shoe to drum

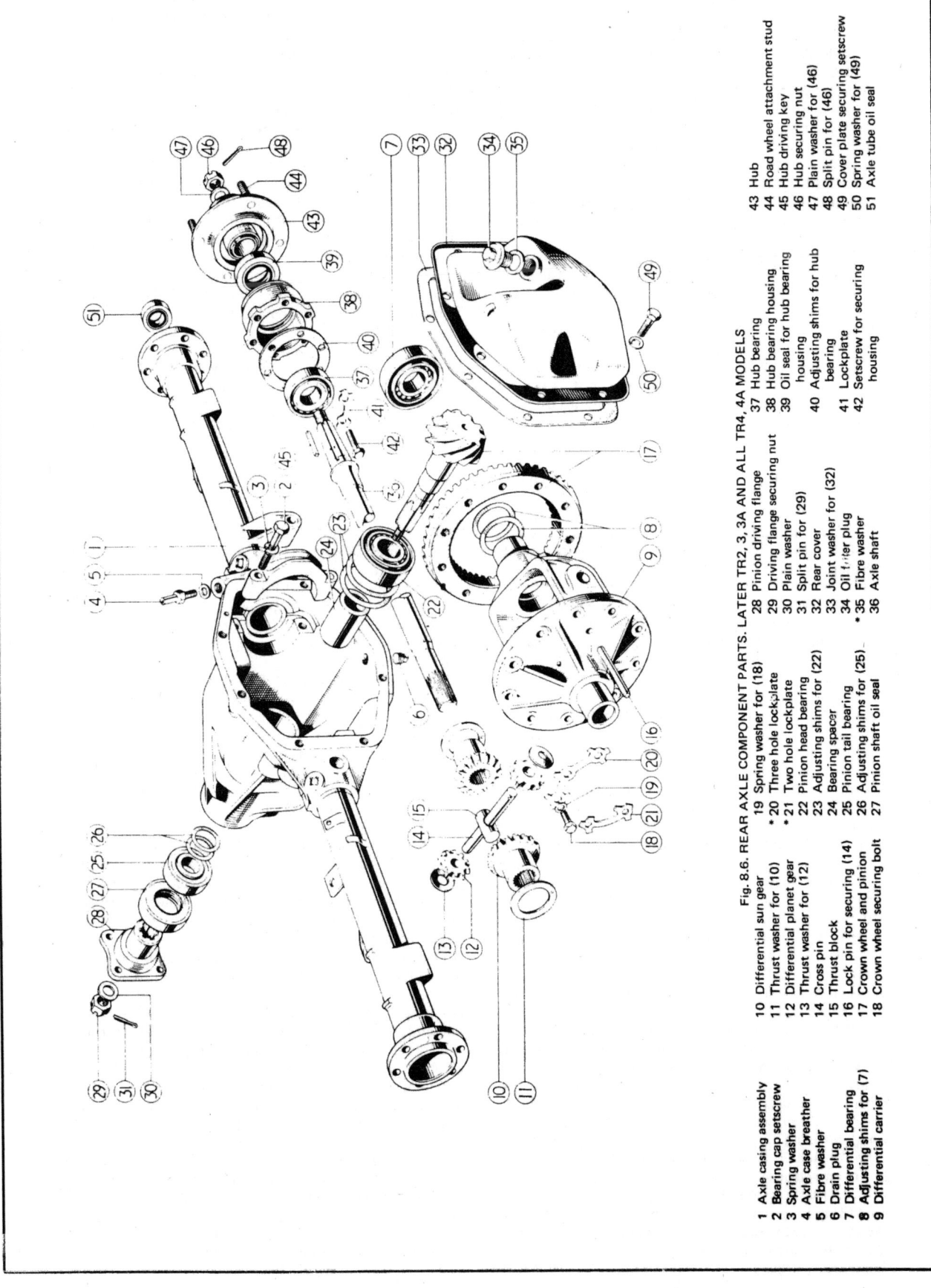

Fig. 8.6. REAR AXLE COMPONENT PARTS. LATER TR2, 3, 3A AND ALL TR4, 4A MODELS

1 Axle casing assembly
2 Bearing cap setscrew
3 Spring washer
4 Axle case breather
5 Drain plug
6 Fibre washer
7 Differential bearing
8 Adjusting shims for (7)
9 Differential carrier
10 Differential sun gear
11 Thrust washer for (10)
12 Differential planet gear
13 Thrust washer for (12)
14 Cross pin
15 Thrust block
16 Lock pin for securing (14)
17 Crown wheel and pinion
18 Crown wheel securing bolt
19 Spring washer for (18)
20 Three hole lockplate
21 Two hole lockplate
22 Pinion head bearing
23 Adjusting shims for (22)
24 Bearing spacer
25 Pinion tail bearing
26 Adjusting shims for (25)
27 Pinion shaft oil seal
28 Pinion driving flange
29 Driving flange securing nut
30 Plain washer
31 Split pin for (29)
32 Rear cover
33 Joint washer for (32)
34 Oil filler plug
35 Fibre washer
36 Axle shaft
37 Hub bearing
38 Hub bearing housing
39 Oil seal for hub bearing housing
40 Adjusting shims for hub bearing
41 Lockplate
42 Setscrew for securing housing
43 Hub
44 Road wheel attachment stud
45 Hub driving key
46 Hub securing nut
47 Plain washer for (46)
48 Split pin for (46)
49 Cover plate securing setscrew
50 Spring washer for (49)
51 Axle tube oil seal

165

Chapter 8/Rear Axle

clearance and lower the car.

9. Axle Shaft End Float Measurement and Adjustment (TR2, 3, 3A) - Later Type

It is important that the axle shaft end float is correctly adjusted on the later type rear axles as the differential unit cross pin has a thrust block on it whereas on the earlier axle it was not fitted.

The correct end float of each axle shaft should be between 0.004 and 0.006 inch and is adjusted by using shims placed between the brake backplate and the axle sleeve flange on each end of the axle casing.

By removing shims the end float may be decreased whilst the addition of shims will increase it. The amount of shims placed on one side should be approximately the same on the other side so as to ensure the thrust block on the differential unit cross shaft is centralised with an equal gap on either side.

To determine the axle shaft end float the brake should be removed and a dial indicator gauge fitted onto the brake backplate. The gauge plunger should rest on the hub flange as shown in Fig. 8.7.

The end float may be determined by alternatively pulling out and pushing in the axle shaft and it should be between 0.004 and 0.006 inch. If incorrect adjust by adding or removing shims.

10. Differential Unit - Dismantling, Inspection, Reassembly and Adjustment (TR2, 3, 3A) - Early Type

1. It is necessary to remove the rear axle assembly from the car if the final drive unit is to be dismantled. Remove the axle assembly as detailed in Section 3 or 4 of this Chapter. If the exterior is dirty wash in paraffin or Gunk and dry using an absorbent cloth.
2. Undo the eight bolts (49) (Fig. 8.6) securing the rear cover (32) to the axle casing assembly (1). Lift away the bolts (49), spring washers (50), rear cover (32) and its joint washer (33).
3. Look for identification marks on the two differential bearing end caps so that they may be refitted in their original positions upon reassembly. There should be marks on the cap, the side next to the abutting portion of the casing and also on the casing itself and are usually in number form.
4. A special tool having a part number of S101 is now required and is shown in Fig. 8.9. It is an axle case spreader and must be used to spread the axle casing so that the differential unit can be removed.
5. Fit the axle spreader to the axle casing and tighten the screw until it is just possible to lift out the differential unit.
6. Remove the differential unit and place on the bench. Make sure it does not roll onto the floor. It is important that the bearing outer races are not interchanged so suitably mark them for correct refitting in their original positions unless, of course, they are to be renewed.
7. Mark the relative position of the crown wheel (17) to the differential casing (1) to ensure correct refitting in its original position and knock back the tabs on the crown wheel retaining bolt tab washers. Undo the ten retaining bolts (18) and lift away the tab washers (20, 21).
8. The crownwheel retaining bolt size was changed from 5/16 inch UNF to 3/8 inch UNF starting at axle number TS 4731 as it was found that with the earlier size bolts they had a tendency to work loose after hard motoring conditions such as found in rallies and driving tests.
9. Extract the split pin (31) locking the castellated nut (29)

to the pinion shaft and undo the castellated nut. Lift away the nut followed by the plain washer (30). Withdraw the pinion driving flange (28) from the pinion shaft splines. If this is tight, tap with a soft faced hammer.
10 The pinion may now be removed from the axle casing by temporarily refitting the castellated nut and with a soft faced hammer tapping the pinion assembly rearwards.
11 Carefully recover the shims (26) that are placed between the race (25) and the spacer (24) for possible re-use during reassembly.
12 Remove the pinion head bearing inner cone. Using a soft metal drift carefully drive out the pinion outer track. It should be noted that when the outer track of the tail bearing is removed, the oil seal and tail bearing inner cone will also be released.
13 Upon removal of the pinion head bearing outer track, shims (23) will be released from between the outer track and the casing. Place these to one side for possible re-use during reassembly.
14 At this point refit the differential unit to the axle casing and release the tension of the axle case spreader.
15 Mount a dial indicator gauge onto the axle casing and place the probe onto the crownwheel mounting face. Rotate the differential unit and check that the run-out does not exceed 0.003 inch.
16 Tension the spreader and remove the differential unit. Release the tension again on the spreader.
17 Using a parallel pin punch very carefully drive out the cross shaft lock pin (16). It should be noted that on axles from number TS6260 the lock pin was made parallel instead of being stepped. Also remove the cross shaft (14) using a soft metal drift.
18 Rotate the sunwheels (10) which will in turn rotate the planet wheels, until the planet wheels (12), with their respective thrust washers (13) are opposite the cutaway portions of the differential casing (9) from which they can be lifted out.
19 Lift away the sunwheels (10) and the thrust washers (11).
20 The bearings (7) may be removed from the differential casing (9) by using a two leg puller and suitable thrust block. Note the shims (8) placed between the bearing track and the differential casing. Keep these for possible re-use during reassembly if new bearings are being used. If the original bearings are satisfactory there should be no reason for disturbing these bearings.
21 Check the rollers and races for general wear, score marks, and pitting and renew these components as necessary.
22 Examine the teeth of the crown wheel and pinion for pitting, score marks, chipping and general wear. If a new crown wheel and pinion are required, a mated crownwheel and pinion must be fitted. It is asking for trouble to renew one without the other.
23 Examine the thrust washers, sun and planet gears and cross shaft for signs of wear and, if evident, obtain new parts.
24 To reassemble first refit the two outer tracks of the two pinion bearings using a soft metal drift. Make sure that they are fitted squarely and they are the correct way round.
25 A special dummy pinion part of tool number M84 will now be required. Fit the dummy pinion with the pinion bearing inner cones attached and refit into the axle centre casing. Carefully tighten the flange nut until a correct pinion pre-load of between 15 to 18 lb. inch is obtained. A torque wrench may be used for this setting.
26 Zero the pinion setting gauge, part of tool number M84, using the little button held firmly on the gauge probe as the datum.
27 Fit the pinion setting gauge in position and tighten down the bearing caps making sure that they are correctly fitted in their original positions.

Fig. 8.7. Axle shaft end float measurement

Chapter 8/Rear Axle

28 The gauge may now be used to determine the shim thickness which is required under the pinion head bearing outer ring so as to bring the pinion into its correct datum position. It should be noted that as the bearing inner cones are a slide fit on the dummy pinion and a press fit on the actual pinion that is used, slight bearing expansion should be used with a total thickness of 0.002 to 0.003 inch BELOW the gauge reading to compensate for this expansion. Always select the shims using a micrometer gauge and check they are not bent or dirty before measurement.

29 Undo the bearing caps and lift away the pinion setting gauge, the dummy pinion and pinion bearing outer tracks.

30 Position the shims on the pinion head bearing outer track abutment face and refit the pinion bearing outer tracks using a soft metal drift or a piece of suitable diameter tube.

31 Refit the pinion head bearing inner cone onto the pinion shaft using a piece of suitable diameter tube.

32 The bearing spacer should be placed on the pinion shaft with the chamfer outwards (splined end of pinion shaft). The shims previously removed during dismantling of the unit should next be fitted to the pinion and the pinion assembly placed into the axle casing. The actual thickness of the last set of shims may have to be altered to correct the bearing pre-load.

33 Using a soft metal drift carefully tap the inner cone of the pinion tail bearing into position on the pinion and ensure that it is fitting against the shims (26) in front of the distance spacer (24).

34 Refit the driving flange (28) to the pinion shaft end followed by the plain washer (30) and the castellated nut (29). Tighten the nut using a torque wrench set to between 85 to 100 lb.ft. Use a large wrench to hold the pinion driving flange to stop the pinion rotating. NOTE: The oil seal is not fitted at this stage.

35 Using a torque wrench check that the bearing pre-load is between 15 and 18 lb. inch. If the pre-load is above this figure extra shims must be fitted to the shim pack (26) and conversely if the pre-load is not sufficient some shims must be removed.

36 Once the correct bearing pre-load is obtained, undo the castellated nut (29) and remove it followed by the plain washer (30) and the driving flange (28). Carefully fit the oil seal (27) ensuring that it is fitted with the lips inwards using a piece of suitable diameter tube. Lubricate the oil seal.

37 Refit the flange (28), plain washer (30) and castellated nut (29). Tighten the nut to a torque wrench setting of between 85 to 100 lb.ft., and lock using a new split pin (31).

38 Using a suitable diameter tube refit the differential case bearings (7) leaving out any shims that were positioned between the bearing inner track and the casing.

39 Expand the axle casing using the tool S101 just sufficiently for the differential unit to be inserted. When in position release the axle casing spreader tension and replace the bearing caps in their original positions.

40 Refit the cap and retaining bolts and tighten down the bolts. Slacken back by ¼ turn which will be sufficient for lateral movement of the bearing without it tilting.

41 Mount a dial indicator gauge on the axle casing with the probe resting on the crownwheel mounting flange. Using a lever move the differential assembly away from the dial indicator gauge. Zero the gauge needle.

42 Next lever the assembly towards the dial indicator gauge until the bearings are correctly seating. Note the reading on the dial indicator gauge (Dimension A).

43 Tension the axle case spreader and remove the differential carrier from the axle casing.

44 Refit the thrust washers (11) to the sun gears (10). Insert the sun gears (10) and thrust washers (11) into the differential carrier followed by the two planet gears (12) and thrust washers (13). Rotate the sun gears and the planet gears will automatically position themselves ready for the cross shaft (14) to be inserted. Note that the cross shaft has a hole drilled at one end for the lock pin (16) to pass through.

45 Insert the lock pin (16) into the differential casing and secure in position using a centre punch.

46 Wipe clean the mating faces of the crown wheel and the differential casing and refit the crownwheel in its original position by aligning the previously made marks.

47 Fit new lockplates and the retaining bolts to the crownwheel (see note in operation 9 of this section). Tighten the bolts in a diagonal manner using a torque wrench set to read between 22 and 24 lb.ft. Bend over the lockplate tabs.

48 Refit the differential unit to the axle casing and mount a dial indicator gauge on the axle casing with the probe resting onto the back of one of the crown wheel fixing bolts.

49 Using a lever move the differential assembly away from the dial gauge until the teeth of the crownwheel are fully in mesh with the teeth on the pinion. Zero the gauge needle.

50 Next lever the assembly towards the dial indicator as far as possible without forcing and note the reading on the dial indicator gauge. Let this be dimension B.

51 The lateral movement (dimension B) from which is subtracted the required crownwheel and pinion backlash of between 0.004 and 0.006 inch indicates the shim thickness (dimension C) required to be placed on the crownwheel side of the differential case. For calculation purposes take the average figure 0.005 inch.

52 To obtain the thickness for the shims required between the differential case bearing and the bearing on the opposite side to the crownwheel subtract dimension C from the toral lateral movement (dimension A) plus an allowance of 0.003 inch (dimension D) which will provide the required degree of bearing pre-load. This will give a total shim thickness so that the shims on the two bearings will be Dimension A for one bearing and the other will be Dimension A subtracted from the total shim thickness.

53 Once the necessary shims have been determined remove the differential unit again and remove the bearings from the differential case. Do not mix up the bearings. Fit the shims as previously determined to their respective sides, checking the shim thickness with a micrometer gauge. Refit the bearings in their original positions.

54 Fit the differential assembly back into the axle casing and release the axle case spreader. Remove the tool completely.

55 Replace the bearing caps in their original positions followed by the bolts and spring washers. Tighten the bolts using a torque wrench set to read between 34 and 36 lb.ft.

56 Using a dial indicator gauge check the crownwheel and pinion backlash which should be between 0.004 and 0.006 inch to be taken on several teeth throughout the circumference of the crownwheel.

57 Check the meshing of the crownwheel and pinion by smearing engineers' blue on the crownwheel and then turning the pinion. The contact mark on the teeth should appear as shown in Fig. 8.10A where it will be seen it is in the middle of the crownwheel teeth. If the mark appears on the toe or the heel of the crownwheel teeth then shims must be removed from one side of the differential bearings to the other side until the marks are in their correct position.

58 When all is correct, fit a new axle cover joint (33) and replace the axle cover. (Make sure that it is the correct way up.) Refit the cover retaining bolts (49) and spring washers (50) and tighten in a diagonal manner.

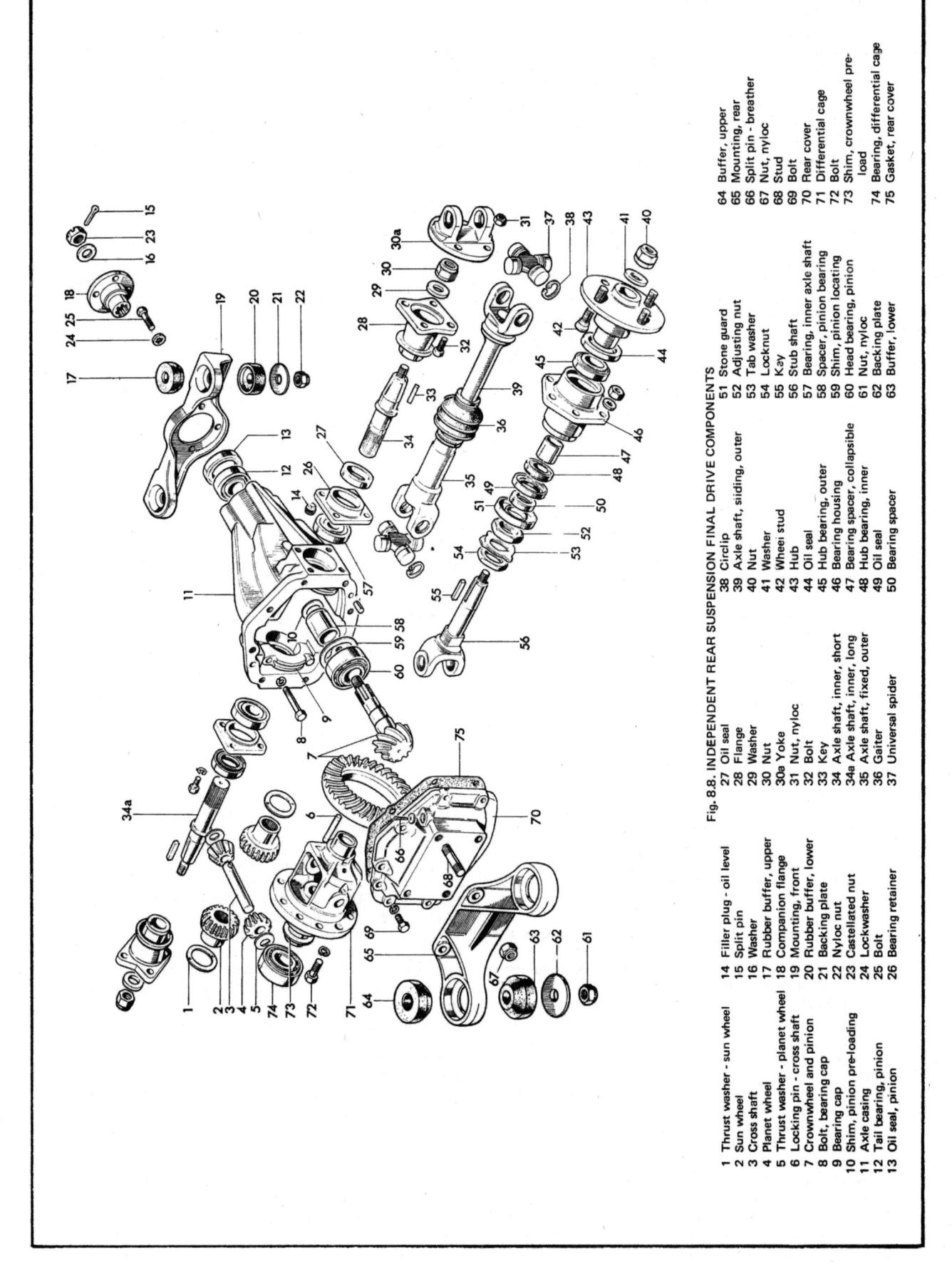

Fig. 8.8. INDEPENDENT REAR SUSPENSION FINAL DRIVE COMPONENTS

1 Thrust washer - sun wheel
2 Sun wheel
3 Cross shaft
4 Planet wheel
5 Thrust washer - planet wheel
6 Locking pin - cross shaft
7 Crownwheel and pinion
8 Bolt, bearing cap
9 Bearing cap
10 Shim, pinion pre-loading
11 Axle casing
12 Tail bearing, pinion
13 Oil seal, pinion
14 Filler plug - oil level
15 Split pin
16 Washer
17 Rubber buffer, upper
18 Companion flange
19 Mounting, front
20 Rubber buffer, lower
21 Backing plate
22 Nyloc nut
23 Castellated nut
24 Lockwasher
25 Bolt
26 Bearing retainer
27 Oil seal
28 Flange
29 Washer
30 Nut
30a Yoke
31 Nut, nyloc
32 Bolt
33 Key
34 Axle shaft, inner, short
34a Axle shaft, inner, long
35 Axle shaft, fixed, outer
36 Gaiter
37 Universal spider
38 Circlip
39 Axle shaft, sliding, outer
40 Nut
41 Washer
42 Wheel stud
43 Hub
44 Oil seal
45 Hub bearing, outer
46 Bearing housing
47 Bearing spacer, collapsible
48 Hub bearing, inner
49 Oil seal
50 Bearing spacer
51 Stone guard
52 Adjusting nut
53 Tab washer
54 Locknut
55 Key
56 Stub shaft
57 Bearing, inner axle shaft
58 Spacer, pinion bearing
59 Shim, pinion locating
60 Head bearing, pinion
61 Nut, nyloc
62 Backing plate
63 Buffer, lower
64 Buffer, upper
65 Mounting, rear
66 Split pin - breather
67 Nut, nyloc
68 Stud
69 Bolt
70 Rear cover
71 Differential cage
72 Bolt
73 Shim, crownwheel pre-load
74 Bearing, differential cage
75 Gasket, rear cover

Chapter 8/Rear Axle

11. Differential Unit - Dismantling, Inspection, Reassembly and Adjustment (TR2, 3, 3A) - Later Type

This unit is shown in Fig. 8.6 and when compared with Fig. 8.1 it will be seen that the final drive unit is basically identical with the exception of the thrust block on the cross pin which is fitted to the later axle. All other parts and settings are identical. Full service instructions are given in Section 10 of this Chapter.

12. Differential Unit - Dismantling, Inspection, Reassembly and Adjustment (TR4, 4A) - Standard Rear Axle

The rear axle and final drive unit fitted to the TR4 and 4A models as a standard specification item is identical to the later type of axle fitted to the TR2, 3, 3A models. Full service information is described in Section 10 of this Chapter using Section 11 as an introduction.

13. Centre Lock Hubs (Wire Wheel)

This section is applicable to all models covered by this manual fitted with the later type conventional live axle.

The centre lock wheels are fitted onto a splined extension which is bolted onto the four studs protruding from the brake drum. It is onto these studs that the conventional wheels are fitted.

The only point to watch is that, if the splined extension is fitted to hubs which previously had conventional wheels attached, the studs will have to be sawn down a little and the ends rounded to allow the wire wheels to be fitted. Conversely if conventional wheels are to be fitted to a hub which had wire wheels fitted longer studs must be fitted.

14. Differential Unit (I.R.S.) - Removal and Refitting

Independent rear suspension is fitted as an optional extra to TR4A models. In this layout design the differential unit is bolted onto the chassis and should be removed as follows:-
1. Chock the front wheels at the front and back, raise the rear of the car as high as possible and place on axle stands under the chassis members.
2. Disconnect the two silencer and tail pipe sections at the clips located in front of the silencers. Also release the two tail pipe straps and lift away the rear part of the twin pipe exhaust system.
3. Undo the four nyloc nuts securing the propeller shaft rear universal joint coupling to the differential unit companion flange (18) (Fig. 8.8). Lift away the nuts and bolts and lower the propeller shaft.
4. Undo the four nyloc nuts (30) securing the axle shaft yoke (30a) to the differential unit flange (28). Lift away the nuts, plain washers (29) and the bolts (32). Repeat this operation for the second shaft.
5. Undo the two nyloc nuts (61) securing the rear mounting (65) to the chassis frame. Lift away the backing plate (62) and lower buffer (63).
6. Support the weight of the rear axle using a hydraulic jack or other suitable means and undo the two nyloc nuts (22) securing the front mounting (19) to the chassis. Lift away the backing plate (21) and lower rubber buffer (20).
7. Carefully lower the differential unit axle casing and withdraw from under the car.
8. Recover the rear mounting upper rubber buffers (64) and front mounting upper rubber buffers (17).

9. Refitting is the reverse sequence to removal. If the unit has been dismantled do not forget to refill with 1½ pints of a recommended grade oil.

15. Differential Unit (I.R S.) - Dismantling, Inspection, Reassembly and Adjustment

1. If the exterior is dirty wash in paraffin or Gunk and dry using an absorbent cloth.
2. Undo the four nyloc nuts (67) (Fig. 8.3) from the studs (68) on the back of the rear cover (70). Lift away the nuts and the rear mounting. Note which way round the rear mounting is fitted, marking it if necessary to ensure correct refitting.
3. Unscrew and remove the eight bolts (69) with spring washers that secure the rear cover (70) to the axle casing (11) and lift away the rear cover. Note which way round the rear cover fits for correct refitting.
4. Carefully remove the joint (75) from the axle casing.
5. Undo and remove the four bolts and spring washers which secure the inner axle shaft (34), bearing retainer (26) to the axle casing. Mark the bearing retainer to ensure that it is refitted in its original position.
6. Carefully withdraw the inner axle shaft assembly from the axle casing (11) and keep separate so that the parts are not interchanged at any stage.
7. Undo and remove the nyloc nut (30) on the end of the inner axle shaft followed by the plain washer (29).
8. Using a two leg puller separate the flange (28) from the inner axle shaft. An alternative method is to place the flange (28) on the top of the jaws of a firm vice and with the shaft in a vertical position tap the end of the inner axle shaft with the nyloc nut refitted to ensure the thread is not damaged.
9. Lift away the rectangular key (33) and put in a safe place so that it is not lost.
10 Remove the bearing retainer (26) with the oil seal (27) in position.
11 Using an internal bearing puller or a soft metal drift remove the bearing (57) from the bearing retainer making a note of which way round the bearing is fitted.
12 Undo the four bearing cap bolts (8) and lift away the bolts (8) and spring washers. Mark the bearing caps (9) to ensure correct refitting in their original positions and lift away the bearing caps.
13 A special tool having a part number of S101 together with adaptors will now be required to spread the axle casing. Fit the axle spreader adaptor plates to the axle casing using four 3/8 inch UNF bolts 2¼ inch long. Next mount the spreader onto the adaptor plate ensuring that the pegs in the arms of the spreader fit into the large holes in the adaptor plates. Rotate the jacking screw until it is hand tight and then rotate a further half a turn using an open ended spanner. It should now just be possible to lift out the differential unit.
14 Remove the differential unit and place on the bench. Make sure it does not roll onto the floor. It is important that the bearing outer races are not interchanged so suitably mark them for correct refitting in their original positions unless, of course, they are to be renewed.
15 Mark the relative position of the crownwheel (7) to the differential casing (71) to ensure correct refitting in its original position and undo the crownwheel retaining bolts (72). Lift away the retaining bolts and spring washers.
16 Extract the split pin (15) locking the castellated nut (23) to the pinion shaft (7) and undo the castellated nut. Lift away the nut followed by the plain washer (16). Withdraw the pinion driving flange (18) from the pinion shaft splines. If this is tight, tap with a soft faced hammer.

170

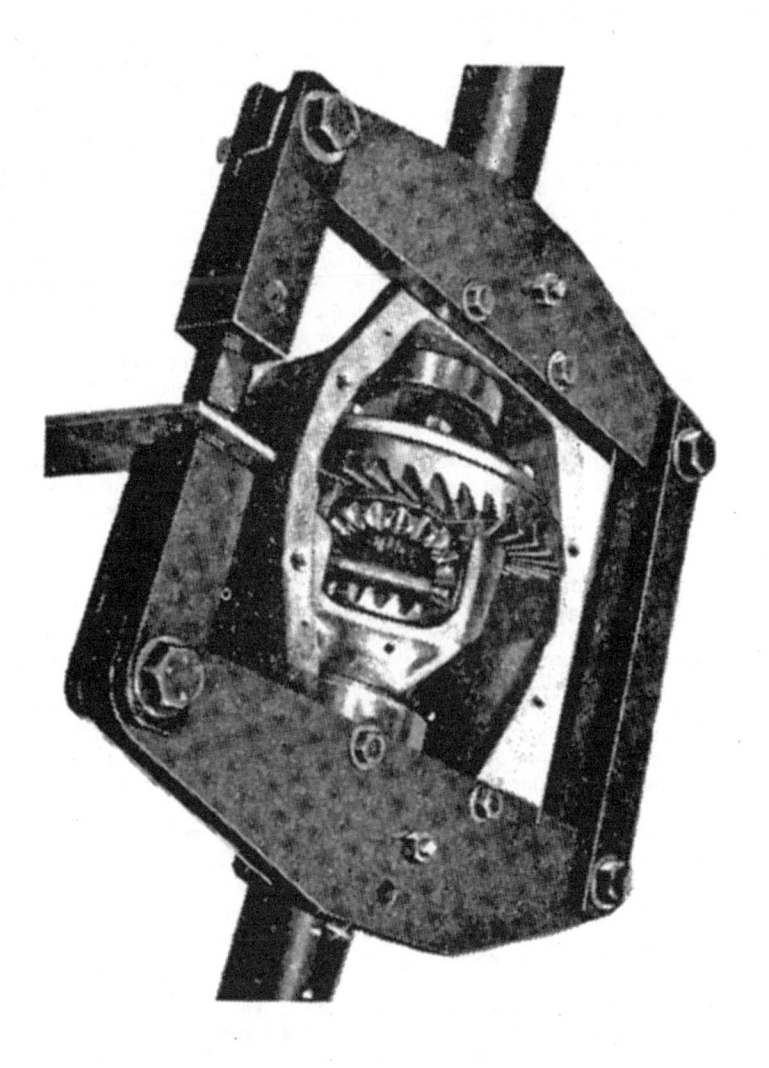

Fig. 8.9. Rear axle casing spreader tool S101 in position

Chapter 8/Rear Axle

17 Undo the four bolts (25) securing the front mounting (19) to the axle casing (11) and lift away the bolts and spring washers (24). The front mounting may now be removed.

18 The pinion may now be removed from the axle casing by temporarily refitting the castellated nut and, with a soft faced hammer, tapping the pinion assembly rearwards.

19 Carefully recover the shims (10) that are placed between the race (12) and the spacer (58) for possible re-use during reassembly.

20 Remove the pinion head bearing inner cone. Using a soft metal drift carefully drive out the pinion outer track. It should be noted that when the outer track of the tail bearing is removed the oil seal and tail bearing inner cone will also be released.

21 Upon removal of the pinion head bearing outer track, shims (59) will be released from between the outer track and the casing. Place these to one side for possible re-use during reassembly.

22 At this point refit the differential unit to the axle casing and release the tension of the axle case spreader.

23 Mount a dial indicator gauge onto the axle casing and place the probe onto the crownwheel mounting face. Rotate the differential unit and check that the run-out does not exceed 0.003 inch.

24 Tension the spreader and remove the differential unit. Release the tension again on the spreader.

25 Using a parallel pin punch very carefully to drive out the cross shaft lock pin (6). Also remove the cross shaft (3) using a soft metal drift.

26 Rotate the sun wheels (2) which will in turn rotate the planet wheels (4) until the planet wheels with their respective thrust washer (5) are opposite the cutaway portions of the differential casing (71) from which they can be lifted out.

27 Lift away the sunwheels (2) and the thrust washers (1).

28 The bearings (74) may be removed from the differential casing (71) by using a two leg puller and suitable thrust block. Note the shims (73) placed between the bearing rack and the differential casing. Keep these for possible re-use during reassembly if new bearings are being used. If the original bearings are satisfactory there should be no reason for disturbing these bearings.

29 Check the rollers and races for general wear, score marks, and pitting and renew these components as necessary.

30 Examine the teeth of the crownwheel and pinion for pitting, score marks, chipping and general wear. If a new crownwheel and pinion are required, a mated crownwheel and pinion must be fitted. It is asking for trouble to renew one without the other.

31 Examine the thrust washers, sun and planet gears and cross shaft for signs of wear and, if evident, obtain new parts.

32 To reassemble first refit the two outer tracks of the two pinion bearings using a soft metal drift. Make sure that they are fitted squarely and they are the correct way round.

33 A special dummy pinion, part of tool number M84 will now be required. Fit the dummy pinion with the pinion bearing inner cones attached and refit into the axle casing. Carefully tighten the flange nut until a correct pinion pre-load of between 15 to 18 lb. inch is obtained. A torque wrench may be used for this setting.

34 Zero the pinion setting gauge, part of tool number M84, using the little button held firmly on the gauge probe as the datum.

35 Fit the pinion setting gauge in position and tighten down the bearing caps making sure that they are correctly fitted in their original positions.

36 The gauge may now be used to determine the shim thickness which is required under the pinion head bearing outer ring so as to bring the pinion into its correct datum position. It should be noted that as the bearing inner cones are a slide fit on the dummy pinion and a press fit on the actual pinion that is used, slight bearing expansion will occur in the latter situation. A selection of shims should be used with a total thickness of 0.002 to 0.003 inch BELOW the gauge reading to compensate for this expansion. Always select the shims using a micrometer gauge and check they are not bent or dirty before measurement.

37 Undo the bearing caps and lift away the pinion setting gauge, the dummy pinion and pinion bearing outer tracks.

38 Position the shims on the pinion head bearing outer track abutment face and refit the pinion bearing outer tracks using a soft metal drift or a piece of suitable diameter tube.

39 Refit the pinion head bearing inner cone onto the pinion shaft using a piece of suitable diameter tube.

40 The bearing spacer should be placed on the pinion shaft with the chamfer outwards (splined end of pinion shaft). The shims previously removed during dismantling of the unit should next be fitted to the pinion, and the pinion assembly placed into the axle casing. The actual thickness of the last set of shims may have to be altered to correct the bearing pre-load.

41 Using a soft metal drift carefully tap the inner cone of the pinion tail bearing into position on the pinion and ensure that is fitting against the shims (10) in front of the distance spacer (58).

42 Refit the flange (18) to the pinion shaft end followed by the plain washer (16) and the castellated nut (23). Tighten the nut using a torque wrench set to between 85 to 100 lb.ft. Use a large wrench to hold the pinion driving flange to stop the pinion rotating. NOTE: The oil seal is not fitted at this stage.

43 Using a torque wrench check that the bearing pre-load is between 15 to 18 lb. inch. If the pre-load is above this figure extra shims must be fitted to the shim pack (10), and conversely if the pre-load is not sufficient, some shims must be removed.

44 Once the correct bearing pre-load is obtained, undo the castellated nut (23) and remove it followed by the plain washer (16) and driving flange (18). Carefully fit the oil seal (13) ensuring that it is fitted with the lips inwards using a piece of suitable diameter tube. Lubricate the oil seal.

45 Refit the front mounting (19) and secure in position with the four bolts (25) and spring washers (24).

46 Refit the flange (18), plain washer (16) and castellated nut (23). Tighten the nut to a torque wrench setting of between 85 and 100 lb.ft. and lock using a new split pin.

47 Using a suitable diameter tube refit the differential case bearings (74) leaving out any shims that were positioned between the bearing inner track and the casing.

48 Expand the axle casing using the tool S101 just sufficiently for the differential unit to be inserted. When in position release the axle casing spreader tension and replace the bearing caps in their original position.

49 Refit the cap retaining bolts and tighten down the bolts. Slacken back by ¼ turn which will be sufficient for lateral movement of the bearing without it tilting.

50 Mount a dial indicator gauge on the axle casing with the probe resting on the crownwheel mounting flange. Using a lever move the differential assembly away from the dial indicator gauge. Zero the gauge needle.

51 Next lever the assembly towards the dial indicator gauge until the bearings are correctly seating. Note the reading on the dial indicator gauge (Dimension A).

52 Tension the axle case spreader and remove the differential carrier from the axle casing.

53 Refit the thrust washers (1) to the sun gears (2). Insert the sun gears (2) and thrust washers (1) into the differential carrier followed by the two planet gears (4) and thrust

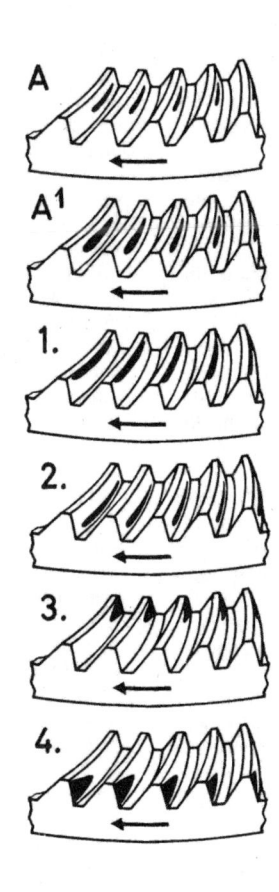

Fig. 8.10. CONTACT MARKING ON CROWNWHEEL

A
Correct contact marking picture without load.
A1
When subjected to load the contact picture is displaced somewhat toward the outside.
Displacement of the crownwheel changes primarily the backlash, in addition the contact picture is displaced in the axial direction of the teeth.
Displacement of the pinion primarily moves the contact marking in the direction of the tooth height, while the backlash changes only marginally.
In addition the four fundamentally **false** contact markings, which usually occur in conjunction with each other, but knowledge of which simplifies the actual adjustment work.

1. High, narrow contact marking (tip contact) on crownwheel. **Correction: displace the pinion toward the crownwheel axis** and, if necessary, correct backlash by moving the crownwheel away from the pinion.
2. Deep, narrow contact marking (roof contact) on crownwheel. **Correction: move the pinion away from the crownwheel axis** and, if necessary, correct backlash by pushing the crownwheel toward the pinion.
3. Short contact marking on smallest tooth end (toe contact) of the crownwheel. **Correction: move the crownwheel away from the pinion** and, if necessary, move the pinion closer toward the crownwheel axis.
4. Short contact marking on large tooth end (heel contact) of the crownwheel. **Correction: move the crownwheel toward the pinion** and, if necessary, move the pinion away from the crownwheel axis.

Chapter 8/Rear Axle

washers (5). Rotate the sun gears and the planet gears will automatically position themselves ready for the cross shaft (3) to be inserted. Note that the cross shaft has a hole drilled at one end for the lockpin (6) to pass through.

54 Insert the lock pin (6) into the differential casing and secure in position using a centre punch.

55 Wipe clean the mating faces of the crown wheel and the differential casing and refit the crownwheel in its original position by aligning the previously made marks.

56 Fit the retaining bolts (72) and spring washers to the crownwheel and tighten the bolts in a diagonal manner using a torque wrench to read between 22 and 24 lb.ft.

57 Refit the differential unit to the axle casing and replace the cap and retaining bolts and tighten down the bolts. Slacken them back by ¼ turn which will be sufficient for lateral movement of the bearing without it tilting.

58 Place the dial indicator gauge probe onto the back of one of the crownwheel fixing bolts.

59 Using a lever move the differential assembly away from the dial gauge until the teeth of the crownwheel are fully in mesh with the teeth on the pinion. Zero the gauge needle.

60 Next lever the assembly towards the dial indicator as far as possible without forcing and note the reading on the dial indicator gauge. Let this be dimension B.

61 The lateral movement (dimension B) from which is subtracted the required crown wheel and pinion backlash of between 0.004 and 0.006 inch indicates the shim thickness (dimension C) required to be placed on the crownwheel side of the differential case. For calculation purposes take the average figure 0.005 inch.

62 To obtain the thickness of the shims required between the differential case bearing and the bearing on the opposite side to the crownwheel subtract dimension C from the total lateral movement (dimension A) plus an allowance of 0.003 inch (dimension D) which will provide the required degree of bearing pre-load. This will give a total shim thickness so that the shims on the two bearings will be dimension A for one bearing and the other will be dimension A subtracted from the total shim thickness.

63 Once the necessary shims have been determined remove the differential unit again and remove the bearings from the differential case. Do not mix up the bearings. Fit the shims as previously determined to their respective sides, checking the shim thickness with a micrometer gauge. Refit the bearings in their original positions.

64 Fit the differential assembly back into the axle casing and release the axle case spreader. Remove the tool completely.

65 Replace the bearing caps in their original positions followed by the bolts and spring washers. Tighten the bolts using a torque wrench set to read between 34 to 36 lb.ft.

66 Using a dial indicator gauge check the crownwheel and pinion backlash which should be between 0.004 and 0.006 inch to be taken on several teeth throughout the circumference of the crownwheel.

67 Check the meshing of the crownwheel and pinion by smearing engineers' blue on the crownwheel and then turning the pinion. The contact mark on the teeth should appear as shown in Fig. 8.10 where it will be seen it is in the middle of the crownwheel teeth. If the mark appears on the toe or the heel of the crownwheel teeth then shims must be removed from one side of the differential bearings to the other side until the marks are in the correct position.

68 When all is correct, fit a new axle cover joint (75) and replace the axle cover (70) ensuring that it is the correct way up. Refit the cover retaining bolts (69) and spring washers and tighten in a diagonal manner.

69 Refit the rear mounting (65) to the studs on the axle cover and secure in place with the four nyloc nuts (67).

70 Replace the bearing (57) in the bearing retainer (26) making sure it is the correct way round. Using a piece of suitable diameter tube refit the oil seal (27), making sure that the lips are facing inwards. Lubricate the oil seal.

71 Refit the inner axle shaft to the bearing in the bearing retainer. Check that the correct inner axle shaft has been selected as they are of different lengths.

72 Locate the rectangular key in its slot in the inner axle shaft and fit the flange onto the shaft. Replace the plain washer (29) and secure the flange in place with the nyloc nut (30). Repeat this sequence for the second shaft.

73 Reassembly is now complete. Do not forget to fill the unit with 1½ pints of the correct grade oil.

Chapter 9/Braking System

Contents

Description	1
Brakes - Maintenance	2
Front Brakes - Adjustment (TR2 Lockheed System)	3
Rear Brakes - Adjustment (TR2 Lockheed System)	4
Rear Brakes - Adjustment (TR3, 3A, 4, 4A Girling System)	5
Drum Brake Shoe - Front - Inspection, Removal & Replacement (TR2 Lockheed System)	6
Drum Brake Shoe - Rear - Inspection, Removal & Replacement (TR2 Lockheed System)	7
Drum Brake Shoe - Rear - Inspection, Removal & Replacement (TR3, 3A, 4, 4A Girling System)	8
Flexible Hose - Inspection, Removal & Replacement	9
Bleeding the Hydraulic System	10
Drum Brake Wheel Cylinder Seals - Inspection & Overhaul (TR2 Lockheed System)	11
Drum Brake Wheel Cylinder Seals - Inspection & Overhaul (TR3, 3A, 4, 4A Girling System)	12
Drum Brake Front Wheel Cylinder - Removal & Replacement (TR2 Lockheed System)	13
Drum Brake Rear Wheel Cylinder - Removal & Replacement (TR2 Lockheed System)	14
Drum Brake Rear Wheel Cylinder - Removal & Replacement (TR3, 3A, 4, 4A Girling System)	15
Brake Master Cylinder - Removal & Replacement (TR2 Lockheed System)	16
Brake Master Cylinder - Dismantling, Examination & Reassembly (TR2 Lockheed System)	17
Brake Master Cylinder - Removal & Replacement (TR3, 3A Girling System)	18
Brake Master Cylinder - Dismantling, Examination & Reassembly (TR3, 3A Girling System)	19
Brake Pedal Adjustment (TR3, 3A Girling System)	20
Brake Master Cylinder - Removal & Replacement (TR4, 4A Girling System)	21
Brake Master Cylinder - Dismantling, Examination & Reassembly (TR4, 4A Girling System)	22
Brake Pedal Adjustment (TR4, 4A Girling System)	23
Handbrake Cables - Removal, Refitting and Adjustment (TR2)	24
Handbrake Cables - Removal & Refitting & Adjustment (TR3, 3A)	25
Handbrake Cables - Removal, Refitting & Adjustment (TR4)	26
Handbrake Cables - Removal, Refitting & Adjustment (TR4A)	27
Front Disc Brake Friction Pad - Removal, Inspection & Replacement (TR3, 3A)	28
Front Disc Brake Friction Pad - Removal, Inspection & Replacement (TR4, 4A)	29
Disc Brake Calliper - Removal, Dismantling & Reassembly (TR3, 3A)	30
Disc Brake Calliper - Removal, Dismantling & Reassembly (TR4, 4A)	31
Disc & Hub - Removal & Replacement	32
Brake Line Restrictor Valve	33
Vacuum Servo Unit	34

Specifications

TR2 plus several very early TR3 models up to chassis number TS. 13101

Make	Lockheed
Type	Hydraulic
Front	Drum, 2 leading shoe
Rear	Drum, leading and trailing shoe
Drum diameter:	
Front	10 inch diameter
Rear - early	9 inch diameter
- later	10 inch diameter
Lining width:	
10 inch drums	2¼ inch
9 inch drums	1¾ inch

Fig.9.1. FRONT DRUM BRAKE COMPONENTS (LOCKHEED)

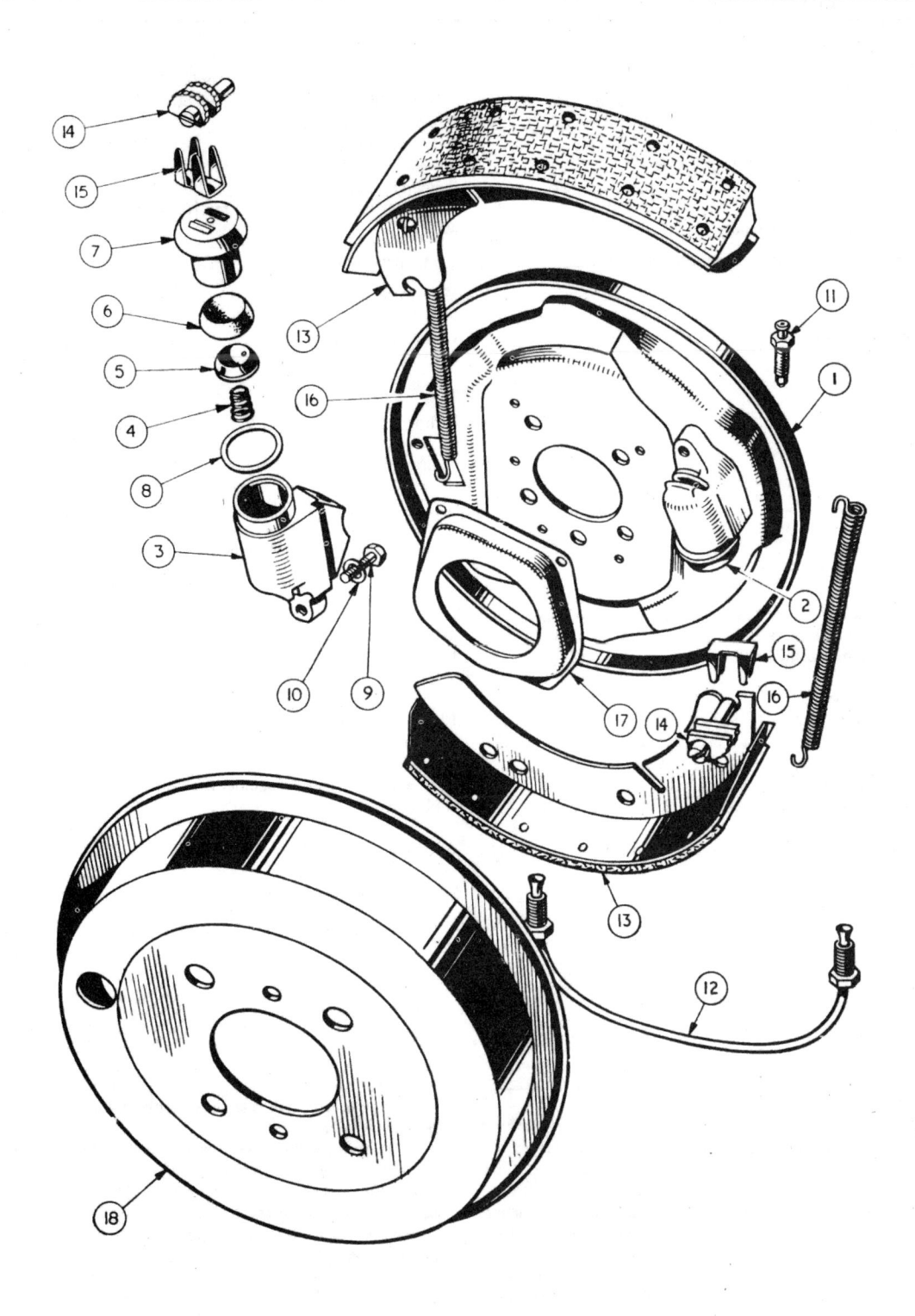

1. Front brake plate
2. Wheel cylinder
3. Wheel cylinder body
4. Spring in body
5. Cup filler
6. Cup
7. Piston assembly
8. Rubber seal
9. Wheel cylinder attachment bolt
10. Lock washer
11. Bleed screw
12. Bridge pipe
13. Brake shoe assembly
14. Micram adjuster
15. Micram adjuster mask
16. Brake shoe pull-off spring
17. Hub grease catcher
18. Brake drum

Chapter 9/Braking System

Linings:

Type	Identification	Application
DM7	3 narrow blue stripes	now obsolete
DM8	2 narrow, 1 wide blue stripe, remainder of edge aluminium colour	for 9 inch brakes
M20	5 green stripes, remainder bronze colour	for 10 inch brakes
Drum lining clearance	Minimum	

Brake pedal pushrod to piston clearance ... 0.030 inch minimum

Handbrake ... Mechanical on rear wheels

Hydraulic fluid ... Lockheed hydraulic fluid

TR3, 3A, 4, 4A

Make ... Girling

Type ... Hydraulic

Front ... Disc

Rear ... Drum, leading and trailing shoe

Disc Brakes:
- Diameter ... 11 inch
- Maximum disc run out ... .002 inch
- Minimum pad thickness ... 1/8 inch

Drum Brakes:
- Diameter (TR3, 3A) ... 10 inch
- (TR4, 4A) ... 10 inch
- Lining width ... 2¼ inch
- Lining identification ... M20 5 green stripes, remainder bronze
- Drum to lining clearance ... Minimum

Brake pedal pushrod to piston clearance ... .030 inch minimum

Handbrake ... Mechanical on rear wheels

Hydraulic fluid ... Girling Crimson Clutch & Brake Fluid

Vacuum servo unit (TR4, 4A) (optional extra) ... Mot-a-Vac

1. Description

The braking system fitted to the models covered by this manual vary considerably and as their operation and reliability is of utmost importance each system is dealt with separately. It should be emphasised that before starting work on overhaul or repair the correct parts should be obtained as the parts fitted to each system are not interchangeable and attempts to fit incorrect parts can cause brake failure. The hydraulic brake fluid cannot be interchanged or mixed as incorrect fluid will cause rapid deterioration of the seals which will certainly promote brake failure.

TR2 Braking System

The TR2 models are fitted with Lockheed drum brakes of the internal expanding shoe design to all four wheels. They are operated hydraulically by means of the brake pedal which is coupled to the brake master cylinder with an integral hydraulic fluid reservoir and separate wheel cylinders.

The handbrake linkage comprising a system of cables and levers operates on the rear brakes only and usually requires no separate adjustment.

The front brakes have two internally expanding shoes actuated by one hydraulic wheel cylinder to each brake unit. When the brake pedal is depressed hydraulic pressure is built up and transferred to the front wheel cylinders by a system of metal and flexible pipes and this causes the piston in the wheel cylinder to push each brake shoe outwards into contact with the internal circumference of the brake drum. Upon release of the brake pedal two strong springs, known as return springs, return the brake shoes to their resting position as well as retracting the wheel cylinder piston. The layout of each front drum brake unit is that of the two leading shoe designs so that as the brake drum rotates with the hub the brake shoes are pulled by a self servo action into contact with the drum as the brake pedal is depressed.

The rear brakes, like the front brakes, have two internally expanding shoes to each brake unit. However, only one wheel cylinder is used and, so that the operation is efficient as possible, the wheel cylinder is able to move in a slot in the backplate. When the brake pedal is depressed

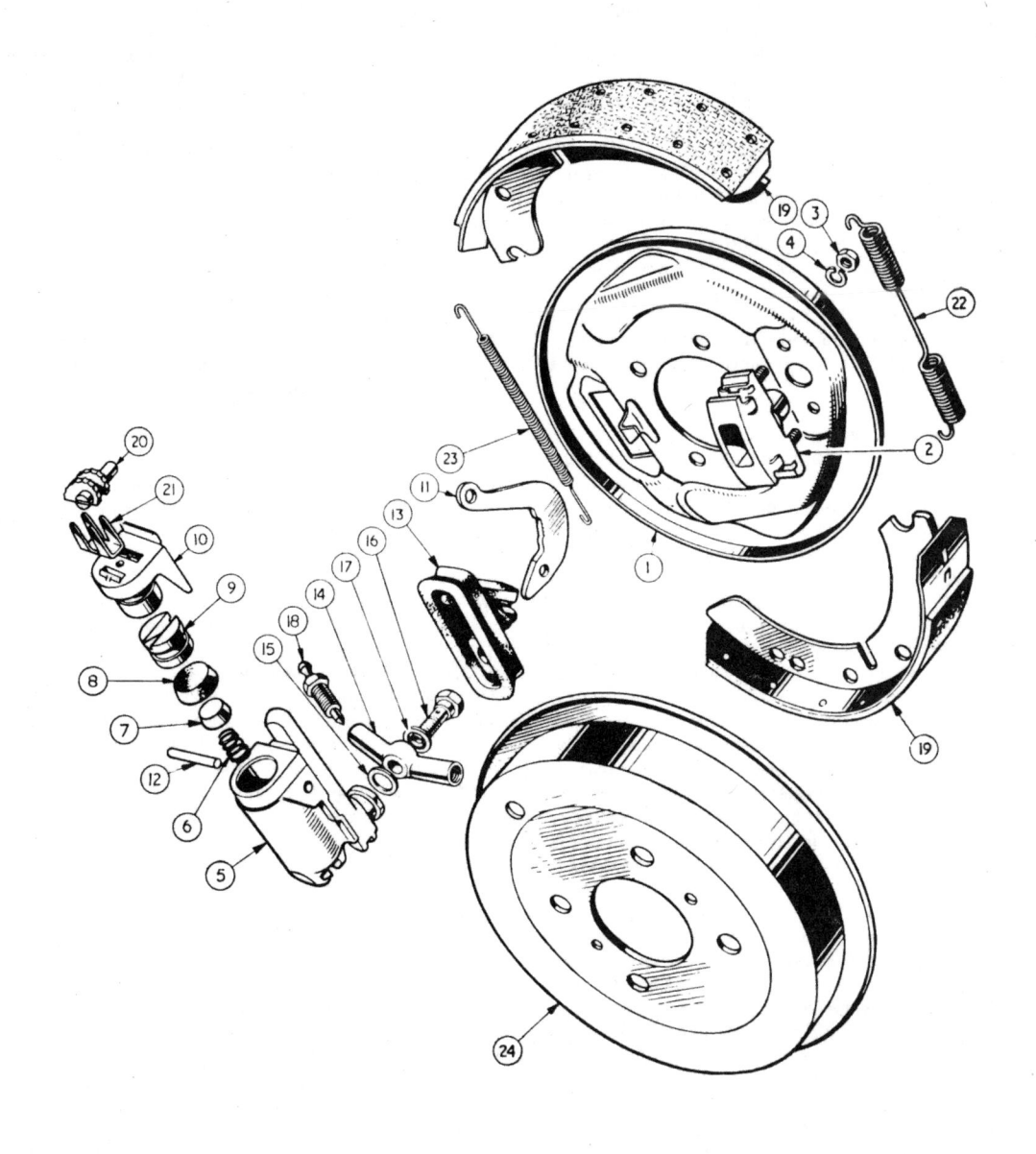

Fig. 9.2. REAR DRUM BRAKE COMPONENTS (LOCKHEED)

1 Rear brake plate	7 Cup filler	13 Rubber boot	19 Brake shoe assembly
2 Abutment assembly	8 Cup	14 Banjo connection	20 Micram adjuster
3 Abutment attachment nut	9 Hydraulic piston	15 Small copper gasket	21 Micram adjuster mask
4 Lockwasher	10 Handbrake piston assembly	16 Banjo bolt	22 Tension spring
5 Wheel cylinder body	11 Handbrake lever	17 Large copper gasket	23 Brake shoes pull-off spring
6 Spring in body	12 Handbrake lever pivot pin	18 Bleed nipple	24 Rear brake drum

179

Chapter 9/Braking System

hydraulic pressure is built up in the lines and this causes the piston to move outwards so pushing the brake shoes in contact with the piston to the internal circumference of the brake drum. As pressure continues to build up under normal brake operation the wheel cylinder will slide in its slot so pushing the second brake shoe into contact with the brake drum. At this point a state of equilibrium exists and both shoes will exert an equal pressure on the drum. The shoes and piston are retracted by two strong return springs. The layout of each rear drum brake unit is that of the one leading and one trailing shoe designs. The trailing shoe has a greater braking efficiency when the vehicle is being stopped in reverse or on hill parking whilst in normal forward motion the leading shoe is more efficient in operation due to the self servo action.

It will be observed that the brake and clutch hydraulic master cylinders are integral and it is recommended that the complete unit be serviced when either the clutch or brake is being overhauled.

TR3 and 3A Braking System

Models of cars up to chassis number TS 13101 had the same braking system but after this number the system was changed to that of the Girling design and disc brakes were fitted to the front with conventional drum brakes to the rear. They are operated hydraulically by means of the brake pedal which is coupled to the brake master cylinder and separate cylinders in the disc brake calliper or wheel cylinders in the drum brake unit.

The handbrake linkage comprising a system of cables and levers operates on the rear brakes only and usually requires no separate adjustment.

The front disc brakes are of the rotating disc and fixed calliper design whereby each calliper has two friction assemblies and it is between these that the disc rotates. When the brake pedal is depressed pressure is built up in the hydraulic fluid lines and transferred to the friction pads by one piston fitted to each side of the calliper. Due to the design of the calliper when the brake pedal pressure is released the friction pads automatically retract so that there is no need for separate adjustment. One of the characteristics of a hydraulic system is that the pressure is identical at all parts so equal pressure and piston movement with the calliper is identical.

The operating principles of the rear brakes is identical to that for the TR2 model with only slight modification in the design of the various components.

The hydraulic master cylinder is of the separate Girling CV type and is identical to the brake master cylinder. Both the master cylinders are connected to a single hydraulic fluid reservoir by means of pipes but should the level of fluid drop too far due to a leak on one or other system, there is a baffle in the reservoir so that enough fluid will be retained to operate the other system.

ONE WORD OF WARNING. A few TR3 cars were, in fact, fitted with the Lockheed system so if your car has a chassis number near to TS 13101 double check on which system is fitted and strictly adhere to the service instructions applicable to the system as detailed in this manual.

TR4 and 4A Braking System

The braking system fitted to the TR4 and 4A models covered by this manual is basically identical to that for the TR3 and 3A models with the exception of the fitting of an individual master cylinder and a restricter valve being fitted to the pipe from the master cylinder. This valve allows a slight back pressure to be retained in the pipes to prevent the front disc brake pads from retracting too far from the rotating disc which would otherwise cause excessive brake pedal travel.

A vacuum servo unit is fitted as an optional extra to assist the drivers' efforts in operating the brake pedal.

Certain minor modifications were made during the production of the TR4 models whereby the brake light switch was changed from the hydraulic pressure operated design to that of the mechanical type operating directly from the brake master cylinder pushrod. The bore of the brake master cylinder was reduced after commission number CT 5783 from 0.75 inch to 0.70 inch so care must be taken when obtaining spare parts.

2. Brakes - Maintenance

TR2 (Lockheed System)

1. Every 3,000 miles carefully clean the top of the combined clutch and brake master cylinder and undo the filler cap. Inspect the level of the fluid and top up until it is no higher than ½ inch from the underside of the cover plate. Check that the breathing holes in the cap are clear.
2. The level must not be allowed to fall below half full at any time.
3. If constant topping up becomes necessary, this indicates an hydraulic leak in either the clutch or braking system and must be investigated immediately the fault becomes apparent.
4. At intervals of 3,000 miles, or more frequently if the brake pedal travel becomes excessive, adjust the brake shoes to compensate for wear of the brake linings.

TR3, 3A, 4 and 4A (Girling System)

1. Every 3,000 miles carefully clean the top of the brake master cylinder reservoir, remove the cap, and inspect the level of the fluid in the reservoir. It should be over the top of the internal baffle yet still allowing some air space above the fluid. Check that the breathing holes in the cap are clear.
2. The level must not be allowed to fall below half at any time.
3. If constant topping up becomes necessary, this indicates a hydraulic leak in the braking hydraulic system and must be investigated immediately the fault becomes apparent.
4. As the front disc brake pads wear the level of the fluid in the reservoir will fall so if the level falls considerably and there are no signs of hydraulic fluid leaks inspect the state of wear of the disc brake pads.
5. At intervals of 3,000 miles, or more frequently if the brake pedal travel becomes excessive, adjust the rear brake shoes to compensate for wear of the linings.

3. Front Brakes - Adjustment (TR2 Lockheed System)

1. Place chocks on the rear wheels and firmly apply the handbrake. Jack up the front of the car and place on firm axle stands.
2. Firmly depress the brake pedal several times so that the shoes are centralised relative to the brake drum.
3. Remove the wheel trims and undo the wheel nuts. Lift away the two front wheels.
4. Rotate the brake drum (18) (Fig. 9.1) until the slot in one of the two Micram adjusters (14) can be seen through the hole in the wall of the brake drum.
5. Insert a wide blade screwdriver through the hole in the brake drum and rotate the Micram adjuster (14) until the brake shoe is in firm contact with the brake drum (18) without forcing it.
6. Turn the Micram adjuster back by one 'click'.
7. Rotate the brake drum half a turn and locate the second Micram adjuster. Repeat operations 5 and 6 for this adjuster.

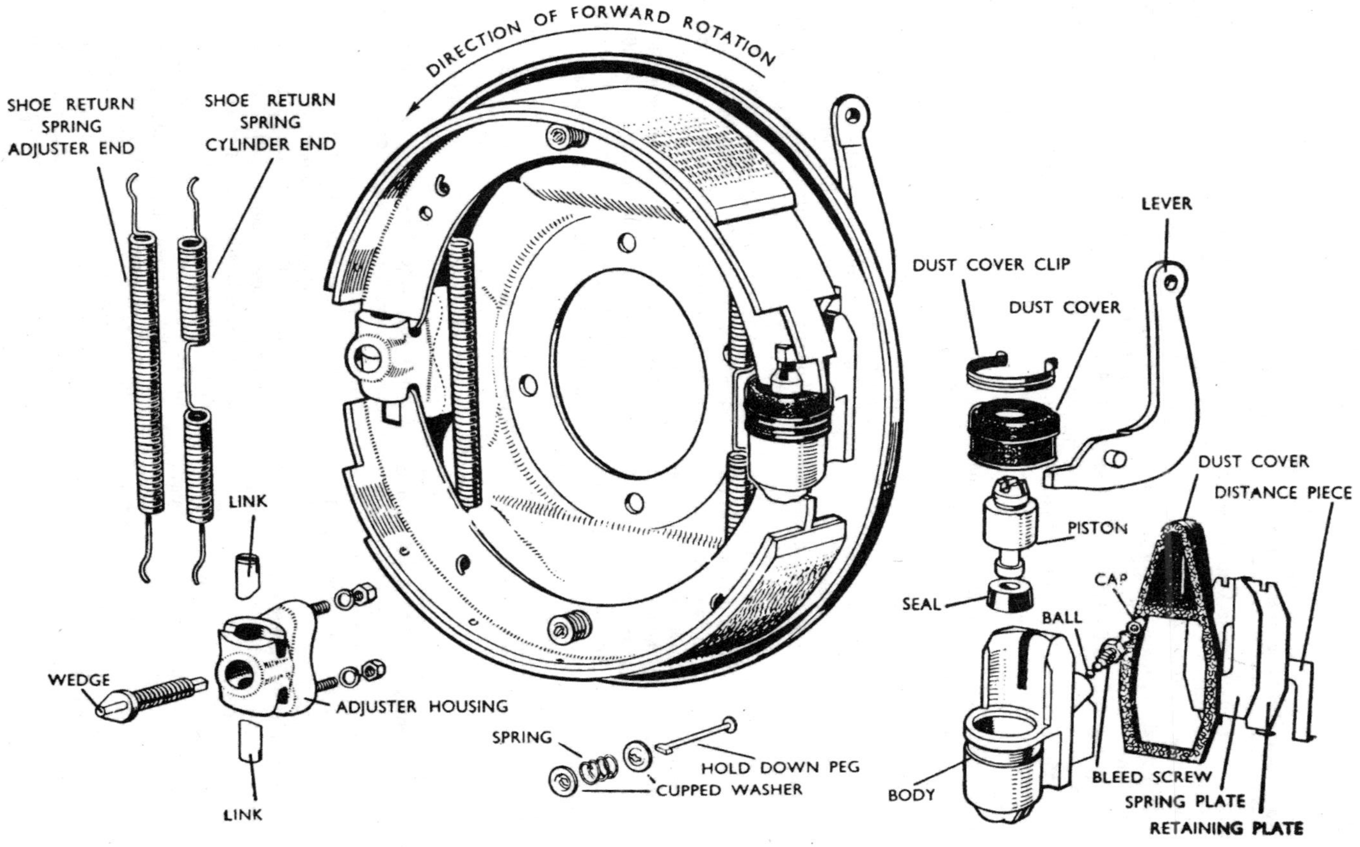

Fig.9.3. REAR DRUM BRAKE COMPONENTS (GIRLING)

Chapter 9/Braking System

8. Repeat operations 4, 5, 6 and 7 on the second front road wheel.
9. NOTE:- A rubbing noise when the wheel is spun is usually due to dust in the brake drum. If there is no obvious slowing of the wheel due to brake binding there is no need to slacken off the adjusters until the noise disappears. Better to remove the drum and blow out the dust.
10 Refit the road wheel, lower the car and road test.

4. Rear Brakes - Adjustment (TR2 Lockheed System)

1. Place chocks on the front wheels and jack up the rear of the car and place on firm axle stands.
2. Release the handbrake and firmly depress the brake pedal several times so that the shoes and wheel cylinder centralise relative to the brake drum.
3. Remove the wheel trims and undo the wheel nuts. Lift away the two rear wheels.
4. Rotate the brake drum (24) (Fig. 9.2) until the slot in the Micram adjuster (20) can be seen through the hole in the wall of the brake drum.
5. Insert a wide blade screwdriver through the hole in the brake drum and rotate the Micram adjuster (20) until the brake shoes are in firm contact with the brake drum (24).
6. Depress the brake pedal firmly several times so as to centralise the wheel cylinder and brake shoes relative to the drum and recheck the Micram adjuster movement.
7. Turn the Micram adjuster back by one 'click'.
8. Repeat operations 3, 4, 5, 6 and 7 on the second rear road wheel.
9. NOTE: A rubbing noise when the wheel is spun is usually due to dust in the brake drum. If there is no obvious slowing of the wheel due to brake binding there is no need to slacken off the adjuster until the noise disappears. Better to remove the drum and blow out the dust.
10 Refit the road wheels, lower the car and road test.
11 It should be observed that on adjusting the rear brakes the handbrake should automatically be adjusted as well. If there is still excessive handbrake movement and the brake shoe linings are found not to be badly worn the cables should be adjusted, details of this operation being given in Section 24 of this Chapter.

5. Rear Brakes - Adjustment (TR3, 3A, 4, 4A Girling System)

1. Place chocks on the front wheels, jack up the rear of the car and place on firm axle stands.
2. Release the handbrake and firmly depress the brake pedal several times so that the shoes and wheel cylinder are centralised relative to the brake drum.
3. It is not necessary to remove the rear wheels as the small headed adjuster will be found on the rear bottom of each backplate.
4. Soak the adjusters in penetrating oil before adjustment is attempted as the adjusters are very prone to rust.
5. As the edges of the adjusters are easily burred do not use an ordinary spanner, adjustable spanner, wrench or pliers but only use a square headed brake adjusting spanner.
6. Turn the adjuster clockwise a notch at a time until the wheel is locked. Then turn back the adjuster one notch or more so the wheel will rotate without binding.
7. Spin the wheel and apply the brakes hard to centralise the shoe and wheel cylinder or alternatively depress the brake pedal firmly several times.
8. Recheck that it is not possible to turn the adjuster further without locking the shoe.
9. NOTE: A rubbing noise when the wheel is spun is usually due to dust in the brake drum. If there is no obvious slowing of the wheel due to brake binding there is no need to slacken off the adjusters until the noise disappears. Better to remove the drum and blow out the dust.

6. Drum Brake Shoe - Front - Inspection, Removal and Replacement (TR2 Lockheed System)

1. After high mileages it will be necessary to fit replacement brake shoes with new linings. Refitting new brake linings to old shoes is not always satisfactory but if the services of a local garage or workshop with brake lining equipment are available, then there is no reason why your own shoes should not be successfully relined.
2. Remove the hub cap, loosen off the wheel nuts, chock the rear wheels and then securely jack up the front of the car and place on firm axle stands. Apply the handbrake and remove the road wheel.
3. Completely slacken off the brake adjustment and take out the two setscrews which hold the drum in place on the hub.
4. Remove the brake drum. If it proves obstinate tap the rim gently with a soft headed hammer. The shoes are now exposed for inspection.
5. The brake linings should be renewed if they are so worn that the rivet heads are flush with the surface of the lining. If bonded linings are fitted they must be removed when the material has worn down to $1/32$ inch at its thinnest point. If the shoes are being removed to give access to the wheel cylinders, then cover the linings with masking tape to prevent any possibility of their becoming contaminated with grease.
6. Rotate both the Micram adjusters fully anti-clockwise so slackening off the adjustment. Carefully disconnect one of the brake shoes from the adjuster by pulling against the action of the strong return springs and sliding out of the adjuster and metal mask.
7. Should the two brake shoe return springs still be in tension repeat the process in operation 6 to remove the second Micram adjuster and metal mask.
8. Lift away the two shoes and springs making a note of the holes in shoes to which the springs once engaged and which way round the springs are fitted. Place rubber bands over the wheel cylinders to prevent any possibility of the pistons dropping out.
9. Thoroughly clean all traces of dust from the shoes, backplates and brake drums with a dry paint brush and compressed air if available. Do not breathe in any dust as it will be of asbestos nature. Brake dust can cause squeal and judder and it is therefore important to clean out the brakes thoroughly.
10 Check that the pistons are free in their cylinders and that the rubber dust covers are undamaged and in position and that there are no hydraulic fluid leaks.
11 Prior to reassembly smear a trace of white brake grease to all sliding surfaces. The shoes should be quite free to slide on the closed end of the cylinder and the Micram adjuster. It is vital that no grease or oil comes into contact with the brake drums or the brake linings.
12 Replacement is a straight forward reversal of the removal procedure but note the following points:-

a) Check that when the Micram adjusters are refitted they are backed right off.
b) Ensure that the return springs are in their correct holes in the shoes and lie between them and the backplate.

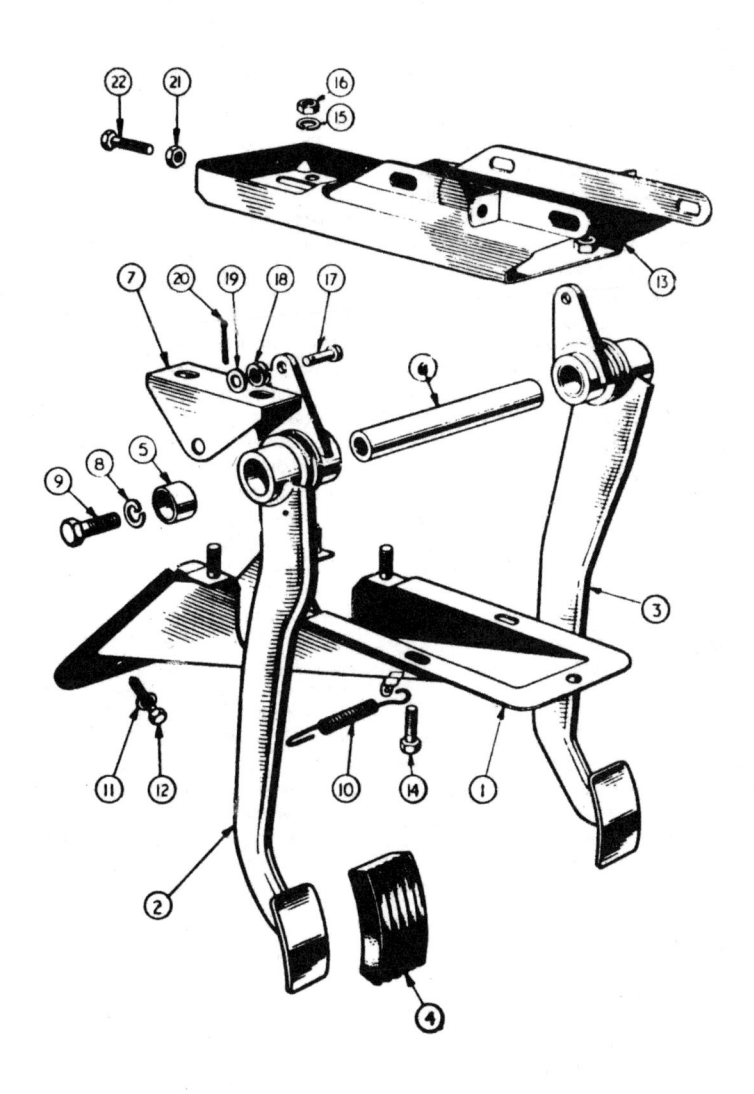

Fig. 9.4. BRAKE AND CLUTCH PEDAL ASSEMBLY
1 Pedal shaft cover assembly
2 Clutch pedal
3 Brake pedal
4 Rubber pad
5 Pivot bush
6 Pedal shaft
7 Bracket
8 Lockwasher
9 Bolt
10 Return spring
11 Lockwasher
12 Bolt (pedal assembly to bulkhead)
13 Master cylinder support bracket
14 Bolt
15 Lockwasher
15 Nut
17 Clevis pin
18 Double coil spring washer
19 Plain washer
20 Split pin
21 Locknut
22 Pedal limit stop

7. Drum Brake Shoe - Rear - Inspection, Removal and Replacement (TR2 Lockheed System)

1. After high mileages it will be necessary to fit replacement brake shoes with new linings. Refitting new brake linings to old shoes is not always satisfactory but if the services of a local garage or workshop with brake lining equipment is available, then there is no reason why your own shoes should not be successfully relined.
2. Remove the hub cap, loosen off the wheel nuts, chock the front wheels, then securely jack up the rear of the car and place on firm axle stands.
3. Release the handbrake and remove the road wheel.
4. Completely slacken off the brake adjustment and take out the two setscrews which hold the drum in place on the hub.
5. Remove the brake drum. If it proves obstinate tap the rim gently with a soft headed hammer. The shoes are now exposed for inspection.
6. The brake linings should be renewed if they are so worn that the rivet heads are flush with the surface of the lining. If bonded linings are fitted they must be removed when the material has worn down to 1/32 inch at its thinnest point. If the shoes are being removed to give access to the wheel cylinders, then cover the linings with masking tape to prevent any possibility of their becoming contaminated with grease.
7. Rotate the Micram adjuster fully anti-clockwise so slackening off the adjustment. Carefully disconnect one of the brake shoes from the adjuster by pulling against the action of the strong return springs and sliding out of the adjuster and metal mask.
8. Lift away the two shoes and springs making a note of the holes in shoes to which the springs once engaged and which way round the springs are fitted. Place rubber bands over the wheel cylinder to prevent any possibility of the pistons dropping out.
9. Thoroughly clean all traces of dust from the shoes, backplates and brake drums with a dry paint brush and compressed air if available. Do not breathe in any dust as it will be of an asbestos nature. Brake dust can cause squeal and judder and it is therefore important to clean out the brakes thoroughly.
10 Check that the piston is free in the wheel cylinder and that the rubber dust cover is undamaged and in position and that there are no hydraulic fluid leaks.
11 Prior to reassembly smear a trace of white brake grease to all sliding surfaces. The shoes should be quite free to slide on the closed end of the cylinder, the Micram adjuster and abutment assembly. It is vital that no grease or oil comes into contact with the brake drums of the brake linings.
12 Replacement is a straightforward reversal of the removal procedure but note the following points:-

a) Check that when the Micram adjusters are refitted they are backed right off.
b) Ensure that the return springs are in their correct holes in the shoes and lie between them and the backplate.

8. Drum Brake Shoe - Rear - Inspection, Removal and Replacement (TR3, 3A, 4, 4A Girling System)

1. After high mileages it will be necessary to fit replacement brake shoes with new linings. Refitting new brake linings to old shoes is not always satisfactory but if the services of a local garage or workshop with brake lining equipment are available, then there is no reason why your own shoes should not be successfully relined.
2. Remove the hub cap, loosen off the wheel nuts, then securely jack up the car and remove the road wheel. Ensure the handbrake is off.
3. Completely slacken off the brake drum. If it proves obstinate tap the rim.
3. Completely slacken off the brake adjustment and take out the two setscrews which hold the drum in place.
4. Remove the brake drum. If it proves obstinate tap the rim gently with a soft headed hammer. The shoes are now exposed for inspection.
5. The brake linings should be renewed if they are so worn that the rivet heads are flush with the surface of the lining. If bonded linings are fitted they must be removed when the material has worn down to ½ inch at its thinnest point. If the shoes are being removed to give access to the wheel cylinders, then cover the linings with masking tape to prevent any possibility of their becoming contaminated with grease.
6. Press in each brake shoe steady pin securing washer against the pressure of its spring.
7. Turn the head of the washer 90° so the slot will clear the securing bar on the steady pin and remove the spring and washer.
8. Detach the shoes and return springs by pulling one end of the shoes away from the slot in the closed end of one of the brake cylinders.
9. Disengage the brake shoe from the return spring carefully noting the holes into which the spring fits and then remove the remaining shoes in similar fashion. Place rubber bands over the wheel cylinders to prevent any possibility of the pistons dropping out.
10 Thoroughly clean all traces of dust from the shoes, backplates and brake drums with a dry paint brush and compressed air, if available. Brake dust can cause squeal and judder and it is therefore important to clean out the brakes thoroughly.
11 Check that the pistons are free in their cylinders and that the rubber dust covers are undamaged and in position and that there are no hydraulic fluid leaks.
12 Prior to reassembly smear a trace of white brake grease to all sliding surfaces. The shoes should be quite free to slide on the closed end of the cylinder and the piston anchorage point. It is vital that no grease or oil come into contact with the brake drums or the brake linings.
13 Replacement is a straight forward reversal of the removal procedure but note the following points:-

a) Check that when the Micram adjusters are replaced they are backed right off.
b) Do not omit to fit the steady pins and inner and outer washers if they were removed.
c) Ensure that the return springs are in their correct holes in the shoes and lie between them and the backplate.

9. Flexible Hose - Inspection, Removal and Replacement

1. Inspect the condition of the flexible hydraulic hoses leading from the chassis mounted metal pipes to the brake backplates. If any are swollen, damaged, cut or chafed they must be renewed.
2. Unscrew the metal pipe union nut from its connection to the hose and then holding the hexagon on the hose with a spanner, unscrew the attachment nut and washer.
3. The chassis end of the hose can now be pulled from the chassis mounting bracket and will be quite free.
4. Disconnect the flexible hydraulic hose at the backplate by unscrewing it from the brake cylinder. NOTE when releasing the hose from the backplate the chassis end must always be freed first.
5. Replacement is a straight forward reversal of the above procedure.

Fig. 9.5. BRAKE MASTER CYLINDER (LOCKHEED)

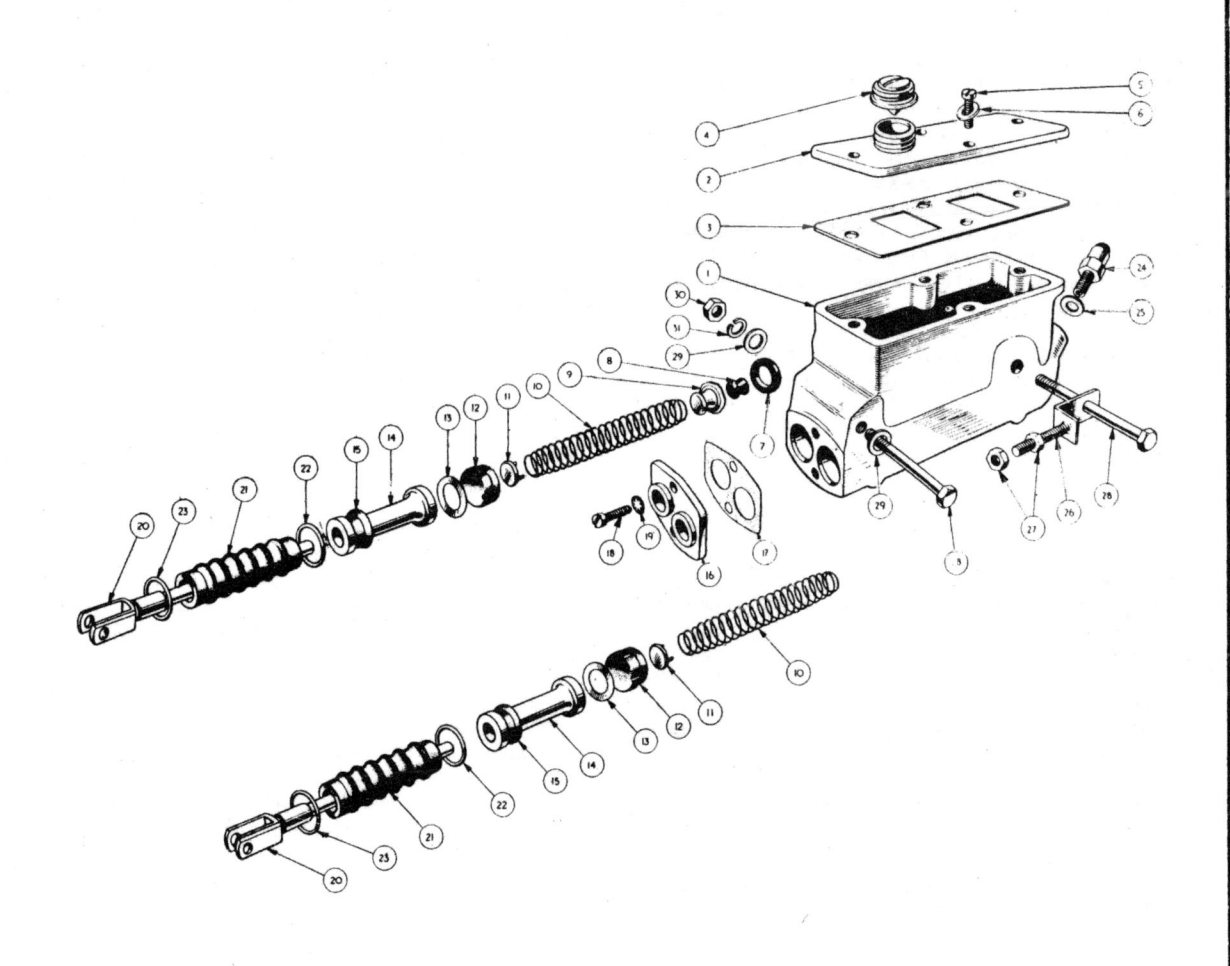

1 Body
2 Cover plate
3 Joint washer
4 Filler cap and baffle
5 Cover plate attachment screw
6 Shakeproof washer
7 Valve seal (brakes only)
8 Valve cup (brakes only)
9 Valve body (brakes only)
10 Valve return spring
11 Spring retainer
12 Main cup
13 Washer between main cup and piston
14 Piston
15 Piston secondary cup
16 Boot fixing plate
17 Gasket between plate and body
18 Plate attachment screw
19 Shakeproof washer
20 Pushrod assembly
21 Pushrod boot
22 Large clip (boot to fixing plate)
23 Small clip (boot to pushrod)
24 Slave cylinder pipe adaptor (clutch)
25 Gasket
26 Bracket assembly
27 Jam nut
28 Master cylinder attachment bolt
29 Plain washer (on front bolt only)
30 Nut
31 Lockwashers under nuts

Chapter 9/Braking System

10. Bleeding the Hydraulic System

1. Removal of all the air from the hydraulic system is essential to the correct working of the braking system, and before undertaking this examine the fluid reservoir cap to ensure that both vent holes, one on top and the second underneath but not in line, are clear, check the level of fluid and top up if required.
2. Check all brake line unions and connections for possible seepage and at the same time check the condition of the rubber hoses, which may be perished.
3. If the condition of the wheel cylinders is in doubt, check for possible signs of fluid leakage.
4. If there is any possibility of incorrect fluid having been put into the system, drain all the fluid out and flush through with methylated spirits. Renew all pistons, seal and cups since these may have been damaged and could possibly fail under pressure.
5. Gather together a clean jam jar, a 9 inch length of tubing which fits tightly over the bleed nipples and a tin of the correct brake fluid. (Girling amber brake fluid.)
6. To bleed the system clean the areas around the bleed valves and start on the rear brakes first by removing the rubber cup over the bleed valve and fitting a rubber tube in position.
7. Place the end of the tube in a clean glass jar containing sufficient fluid to keep the end of the tube underneath during the operation.
8. Open the bleed valve with a spanner and quickly press down the brake pedal. After slowly releasing the pedal, pause for a moment to allow the fluid to recoup in the master cylinder and then depress again. This will force air from the system. Continue until no more air bubbles can be seen coming from the tube. At intervals make certain that the reservoir is kept topped up, otherwise air will enter at this point again.
9. Repeat this operation on all four brakes and, when complete, check the level of the fluid in the reservoir and then check the feel of the brake pedal, which should be firm and free from any 'soongy' action normally associated with air in the system.
10 If the braking system is fitted with a servo unit see also Section 34 of this Chapter.

11. Drum Brake Wheel Cylinder Seals - Inspection and Overhaul (TR2 Lockheed System)

1. If hydraulic fluid is leaking from one of the brake cylinders it will be necessary to dismantle the cylinder and replace the dust cover and piston sealing rubber. If brake fluid is found running down the side of the wheel, or it is noticed that a pool of liquid forms alongside one wheel and the level in the master cylinder has dropped, and the hoses are all in good order, proceed as follows.
2. Remove the brake drums and brake shoes as described earlier in the chapter. Section 6 (front) or 7 (rear).
3. Ensure that all the other wheels and all the other brake drums are in place. Remove the piston, piston cup seal, cup filler and spring from the wheel cylinder by depressing the brake pedal. On rear drum brakes it will be necessary to remove the handbrake lever pivot pin from the wheel cylinder and withdraw the handbrake lever before the internal components of the wheel cylinder are removed.
3. Inspect the inside of the cylinder for score marks caused by impurities in the hydraulic fluid. If any are found the cylinder and piston will require renewal together as an exchange assembly.
4. If the cylinder is sound thoroughly clean it out with fresh hydraulic fluid.
5. The old rubber seal will probably be swollen and visibly worn. Smear the new rubber seal with hydraulic fluid and reassemble in the cylinder the spring, seal and piston, and then the rubber boot. The seal must be fitted with its lip towards the bottom of the cylinder.
6. Replenish the brake fluid, replace the brake shoes and brake drum and bleed the hydraulic system as previously described.

12. Drum Brake Wheel Cylinder Seals - Inspection and Overhaul (TR3, 3A, 4 and 4A Girling System)

1. If hydraulic fluid is leaking from one of the brake cylinders it will be necessary to dismantle the cylinder and replace the dust cover and piston sealing rubber. If brake fluid is found running down the side of the wheel, or it is noticed that a pool of liquid forms alongside one wheel and the level in the master cylinder has dropped, and the hoses are all in good order, proceed as follows.
2. Remove the brake drums and shoes as described earlier in this Chapter in Section 8.
3. Ensure that all the other wheels and the other brake drum is in place. Remove the dust cover clip and lift away the cover from the wheel cylinder. Disconnect the handbrake lever.
4. Using a screwdriver carefully prise apart the wheel cylinder retaining plate and the spring plate. Gently tap the retaining plate out from beneath the neck of the cylinder. Lift away the dust cover from the rear of the wheel cylinder and pull the wheel cylinder through the backplate towards the front.
5. Slowly depress the brake pedal so as to eject the piston with the seal attached.
6. Place a quantity of rag under the backplate or a tray to catch the hydraulic fluid as it pours out of the cylinder.
7. Inspect the inside of the cylinder for score marks caused by impurities in the hydraulic fluid. If any are found the cylinder and piston will require renewal together as an exchange assembly.
8. If the cylinder is sound thoroughly clean it out with fresh hydraulic fluid.
9. The old rubber seal will probably be swollen and visibly torn. Smear the new rubber seal with hydraulic fluid and reassemble the seal to the piston with the cup towards the closed end of the wheel cylinder. Insert the piston and seal assembly into the wheel cylinder and then the rubber dust cover and its clip.
10 Refit the wheel cylinder to the backplate in the reverse sequence to removal.
11 Replenish the brake fluid, replace the brake shoes and brake drum and bleed the hydraulic system as previously described.

13. Drum Brake Front Wheel Cylinder - Removal and Replacement (TR2 Lockheed System)

1. Remove the left or right hand brake drum and brake shoes as required, as described in Section 6.
2. To avoid having to drain the hydraulic system screw down the master cylinder reservoir cap tightly over a piece of polythene.
3. Free the hydraulic pipe from the wheel cylinder, details of which are given in Section 9.
4. Unscrew the two unions securing the metal pipe (12) (Fig. 9.1) to the wheel cylinders and remove the pipe. Note which way round it fits so that it is replaced in its original position.

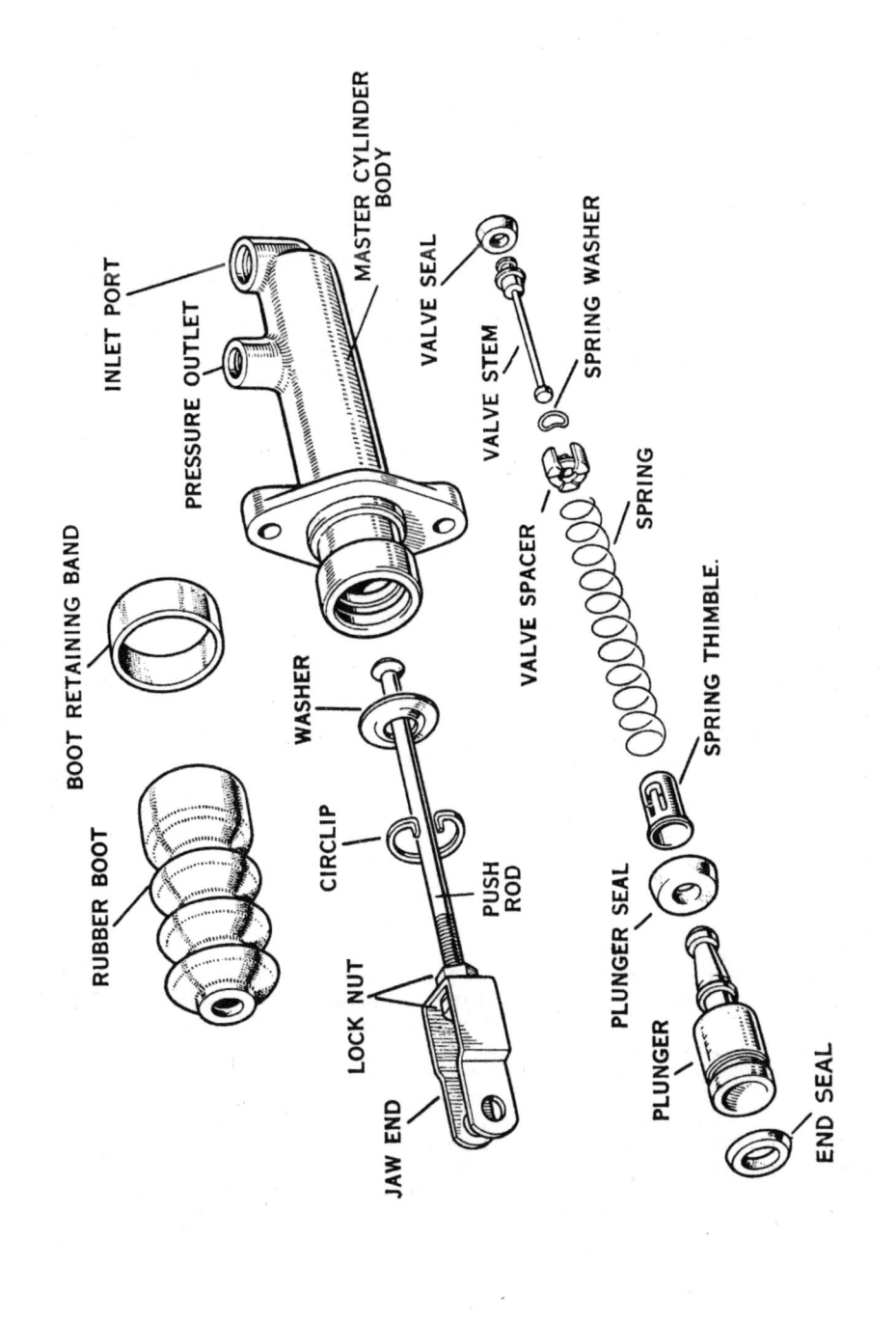

Fig. 9.6. BRAKE MASTER CYLINDER (GIRLING) TR3, 3A)

Chapter 9/Braking System

5. Undo the two bolts securing the wheel cylinder to the backplate and lift away the bolts and spring washers followed by the wheel cylinder itself (2).
6. Refitting the wheel cylinder is the reverse sequence to removal. The brake system must be bled when all parts have been reassembled.

14. Drum Brake Rear Wheel Cylinder - Removal and Replacement (TR2 Lockheed System)

1. Remove the left or right hand brake drum and brake shoes as required and as described in Section 7.
2. To avoid having to drain the hydraulic system screw down the master cylinder reservoir cap tightly over a piece of polythene.
3. Carefully undo the metal pipe from the banjo union connection (14) (Fig. 9.2).
4. Undo the banjo bolt (16) and lift it away together with the large copper gasket (17), banjo union connection (14) and small copper gasket (15). Retain these washers if new ones are not available.
5. Extract the split pin securing the handbrake cable clevis to the handbrake lever (11). Lift away the plain washer followed by the cotter. Note in which position the clevis pin head is placed for correct refitting.
6. Lift away the handbrake piston (10) followed by the rubber boot (13) from the rear of the backplate.
7. Swing the handbrake lever (11) until the shoulder is clear of the backplate (1). Gently slide the wheel cylinder body forwards and swing the cylinder about its forward end and swing the rear end clear of the backplate. Now slide the wheel cylinder back and at this point the forward end will be free of the backplate.
8. Refitting is the reverse sequence to removal. The brake system must be bled when all parts have been refitted. If the copper gaskets (15, 17) have to be re-used they should be softened by heating to red heat and then quenching in cold water.

15. Drum Brake Rear Wheel Cylinder - Removal and Replacement (TR3, 3A, 4, 4A Girling System)

1. Remove the left or right hand brake drum and brake shoes as required, as described in Section 8. To avoid having to drain the hydraulic system screw down the master cylinder reservoir cap tightly over a piece of polythene.
2. Free the hydraulic pipe from the wheel cylinder at the union and disconnect the handbrake cable clevis from its lever (Fig. 9.3).
3. Take off the dust excluder, the retaining plate and the spring clip and remove the cylinder from the backplate.
4. On replacement smear the slot in the backplate and the cylinder neck with Girling white brake grease. The rest of the replacement process is a straight forward reversal of the removal sequence. Bleed the brakes on completion of reassembly.

16. Brake Master Cylinder - Removal and Replacement (TR2 Lockheed System)

1. As the brake and clutch master cylinder are of an integral unit design, the two systems will be affected when one or other part of the master cylinder is overhauled. It is therefore recommended that when one system is being worked upon and the master cylinder is involved it should be completely overhauled at that time. It is for this reason the clutch master cylinder overhaul details are incorporated in this Chapter and not the clutch Chapter as usually brake master cylinder overhaul is more frequent than the overhaul of clutch master cylinder. This method of presentation also avoids confusion that could otherwise arise.
2. Connect a piece of plastic tube to the clutch slave cylinder bleed nipple. Insert the free end of the tube in a clean glass jam jar and open the bleed nipple.
3. Unscrew the combined master cylinder filler cap and pump the clutch pedal so draining the clutch portion of the master cylinder.
4. Connect the piece of plastic tube to a bleed nipple on one of the front wheel cylinders. Insert the free end of the tube in the clean glass jam jar and open the bleed nipple. Pump the brake pedal so draining the brake portion of the master cylinder.
5. From inside the car remove the square shaped panel behind the rear wall of the master cylinder pocket.
6. Remove the rubber grommet from the inside wall of the pocket so that it will be easier to remove the rear master cylinder retaining bolt.
7. Disconnect the clutch and brake system hydraulic pipes from the rear of the master cylinder body. It will be observed that the pipe to the clutch outlet is connected to the master cylinder via an adaptor. The pipe must be freed from the adaptor before removing the adaptor from the outlet.
8. Extract the split pins locking the clevis pins at the push rod to pedal joint. Lift away the plain washer followed by the double coil spring washers and finally the celvis pin. Note the position of the head of the clevis pin so that it may be refitted the correct way.
9. Undo the two nuts from the bolts securing the master cylinder. Lift away the nuts, spring and plain washers and withdraw the two bolts. It will be necessary to remove the bolt through the hole in the wall and out into the car.
10 Obtain some absorbent rags and place by the master cylinder so that when it is lifted away any hydraulic fluid spilled may immediately be wiped up.
11 Lift away the master cylinder assembly.
12 Wrap the ends of the two exposed pipes in clean non fluffy rag to stop dirt ingress.
12 To refit the master cylinder assembly first replace the clutch adaptor to the clutch cylinder outlet.
14 Place the master cylinder assembly in the master cylinder support bracket and refit the front mounting bolt, with a spring washer next to the head. On the other end of the bolt fit a plain, spring washer and secure with the nut.
15 The rear master cylinder mounting bolt also passes through the support bracket (13) (Fig. 9.4) as well as the adjusting brackets (26) (Fig. 9.5). Undo but do not remove the locknuts on the adjusting brackets and also leave the nut on the rear mounting bolt finger tight so that the master cylinder assembly is free to slide backwards and forwards for pedal adjustment.
16 Connect the two hydraulic system pipe unions to the outlets on the front of the master cylinder body. Do not forget that the clutch pipe is connected to the adaptor on the clutch master cylinder whilst the brake master cylinder is connected directly to the cylinder body.
17 Refit the brake and clutch pedals to the master cylinder pushrods. Insert the clevis pins with the heads in their original positions, pointing inwards. Refit the double spring washer, plain washer and secure with a new split pin.
18 The pedal clearance must next be adjusted, details of which are given in Section 19 of Chapter 5.
19 Refill the reservoir with the correct grade of hydraulic fluid and bleed the two systems, details of the clutch system being given in Section 3 of Chapter 5, and of the brake system in Section 10 of this Chapter.
20 Refit the rubber grommet and cover to the master

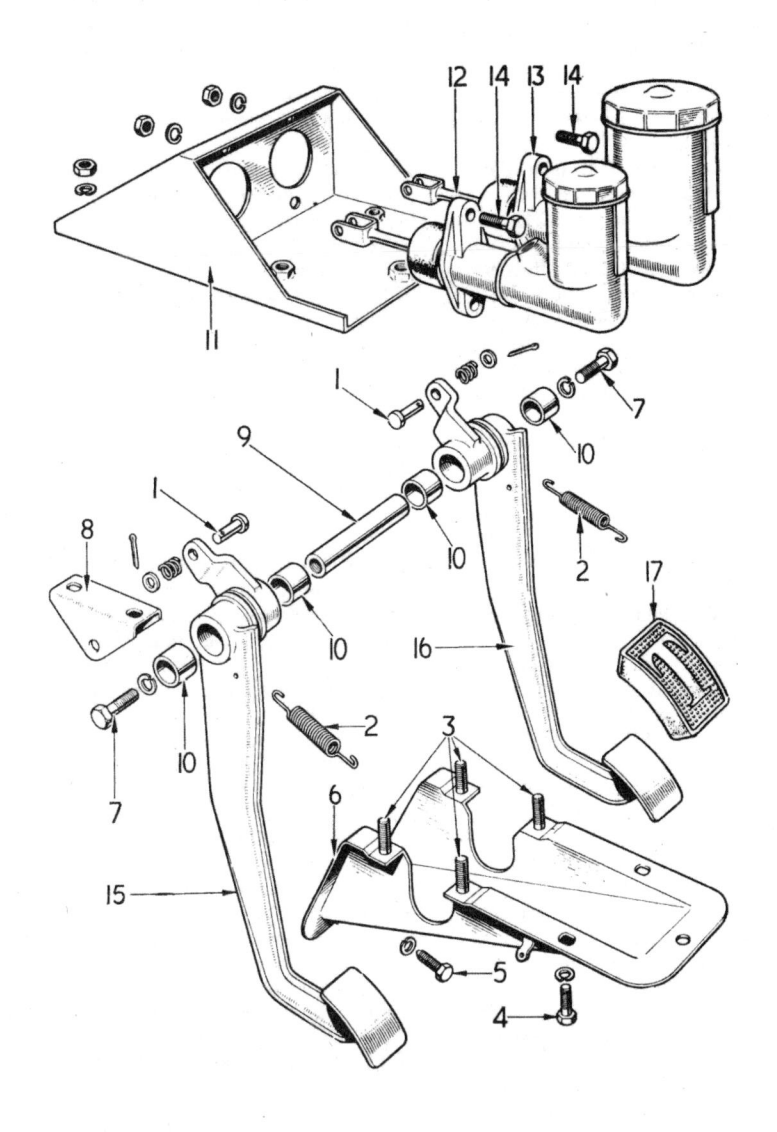

Fig. 9.7. BRAKE PEDAL AND MASTER CYLINDER
MOUNTING BRACKET

1 Clevis pin
2 Pedal return spring
3 Studs
4 Screws
5 Setscrew
6 Pedal shaft cover assembly
7 Setscrew
8 Pedal support bracket
9 Pedal shaft
10 Pedal pivot bush
11 Master cylinder support bracket
12 Pushrod
13 Master cylinder
14 Setscrew
15 Clutch pedal
16 Brake pedal
17 Pedal pad

Chapter 9/Braking System

cylinder pocket.

21 Thoroughly road test the car, bearing in mind that the clutch system as well as the brake system must be tested. Recheck for hydraulic fluid leaks.

17. Brake Master Cylinder - Dismantling, Examination and Reassembly (TR2 Lockheed System)

1. Refer to Item 1 of the previous Section which acts as an introduction to this Section as well.
2. All numbers in brackets refer to Fig. 9.5. Remove the circlips (22) from the master cylinder body and withdraw the pushrod assemblies (20) and the rubber boots (21).
3. Release the rubber boots (21) from the pushrods (20) after having first undone the two clips (23). As the parts are removed place them in order on a clean non fluffy rag or newspaper so that the parts are not accidently interchanged.
4. Undo the two screws (18) that secure the plate (16) to the master cylinder body (1) and remove the screws (18) shakeproof washers (19), plate (16) and gasket (17) from the body (1).
5. Carefully withdraw the pistons (14) which will have the secondary seals (15) attached.
6. Place a pad over the pushrod end of the master cylinder and apply a compressed air jet to the outlet drillings of the master cylinder. Collect the washers (13), cup seals (12), spring retainers (11) and springs (10).
7. Extract the check valve body (9), valve cup (8) and valve seats (7), from the brake cylinder bore. These are omitted from the clutch cylinder bore.
8. To enable the hydraulic fluid reservoir to be cleaned undo the four cover retaining screws (5). Lift away the screws (5), spring washer (6), the cover (2) and gasket (3).
9. Remove the secondary cup seal (15) from the piston (14) noting which way round the cup seal fits.
10 Clean and carefully examine all parts especially the piston cup seal and rubber washers for signs of distortion, swelling, splitting or other wear and check the piston and cylinder for wear and scoring. Replace any parts that are faulty.
11 During the inspection of the piston seal it has been found advisable to maintain the state of this seal as regular as possible and for this reason do not turn it inside out as slight distortion may be caused.
12 With all parts clean and new parts obtained where required soak the seals in correct grade fluid and assemble wet.
13 Replace the secondary seals (15) to the pistons (14) fitting the lip on each cup face towards the head of the piston using the fingers only. Ensure that the seals fit in their grooves correctly.
14 Insert the valve seal (7) into the bottom of the brake cylinder bore ensuring that it lies flat. To avoid confusion the brake cylinder bore is the one on the left when the master cylinder is held the correct way up and looking down the bores (the position shown in Fig. 9.5).
15 Refit the valve cup (8) onto the valve body (9).
16 Insert the valve assembly into one end of the spring (10) and to the other end of the spring fit the retainer (11).
17 Carefully insert the complete spring assembly into the brake cylinder bore with the valve entered first.
18 Fit the retainer (11) to the spring (10) and insert this into the clutch cylinder bore so that the retainer is outwards.
19 With the main cup seals (12) well wetted, insert them into the bores, taking extreme care not to turn over the lips or damage the cups, as they are entered into the bore.
20 Place the master cylinder on end so the open ends of the bores are upwards and gently lay the washers (13) onto the cup seals (12).

21 Insert the two pistons (14) into the bores again, taking care not to damage the secondary seals (15) as they are being entered into the bores. As with the main cup seals they should be well wetted first.
22 Push the pistons down the bores and retain them in place with the endplate (16) and a new gasket (17). Tighten the two retaining screws (18) with shakeproof washers (19) fitted under the heads.
23 Replace the pushrods (20) with the rubber boots (21) fitted and secure either end of the boots with the clips (22, 23).
24 Half fill the reservoir with clean brake fluid of the correct grade and push the pistons inwards. They ought to return on their own accord. Continue pushing and releasing the pistons and after several strokes it should be observed that fluid is ejected from the outlets.
25 Refit the top cover (2) with a new gasket (3) positioning the top cover so that the filler cap is nearest to the outlet connections of the master cylinder. Secure in place with the four bolts and spring washers.
26 The master cylinder assembly is now ready for refitting.

18. Brake Master Cylinder - Removal and Replacement (TR2, 3A Girling System)

1. Connect a piece of plastic tubing to the brake wheel cylinder bleed nipple and by operating the brake pedal several times with the bleed nipple open, drain the brake hydraulic fluid from the reservoir into a clean glass container.
2. Undo the two pipes from the ports on the master cylinder and wrap the ends of the pipes in clean non fluffy rag to stop dirt ingress and also to stop hydraulic fluid dripping onto the paintwork.
3. Extract the split pin from the clevis pin that holds the pedal to the pushrod jaw end, lift away the plain washer and the clevis pin, noting which way round the head of the clevis pin is fitted.
4. Carefully ease off the rubber boot retaining band and disconnect the rubber boot from the master cylinder body.
5. Push the brake pushrod in slightly to relieve the pressure from the spring inside the master cylinder and, using a pair of long nosed pliers, extract the circlip from its machined groove in the body of the master cylinder.
6. Lift out the pushrod assembly from the master cylinder together with the locating washer and the rubber boot.
7. Undo the two bolts which secure the master cylinder body to the mounting bracket and lift away the bolts and spring washers.
8. The master cylinder body may now be removed but take care not to allow any hydraulic fluid to drop onto the paintwork.
9. Refitting is the reverse sequence to removal. The system will now have to be bled.

19. Brake Master Cylinder - Dismantling, Examination and Reassembly (TR3, 3A Girling System

1. If the brake master cylinder has been removed from the car the rubber boot, pushrod, metal retaining washer and circlip will have been removed. If not carefully ease off the rubber boot retaining band and disconnect the rubber boot from the master cylinder body (Fig. 9.6).
2. Push the brake pushrod in slightly so as to relieve the pressure from the spring inside the master cylinder body and, using a pair of long nosed pliers, extract the circlip from the machined groove in the body of the master cylinder.
3. Lift out the pushrod assembly from the master cylinder

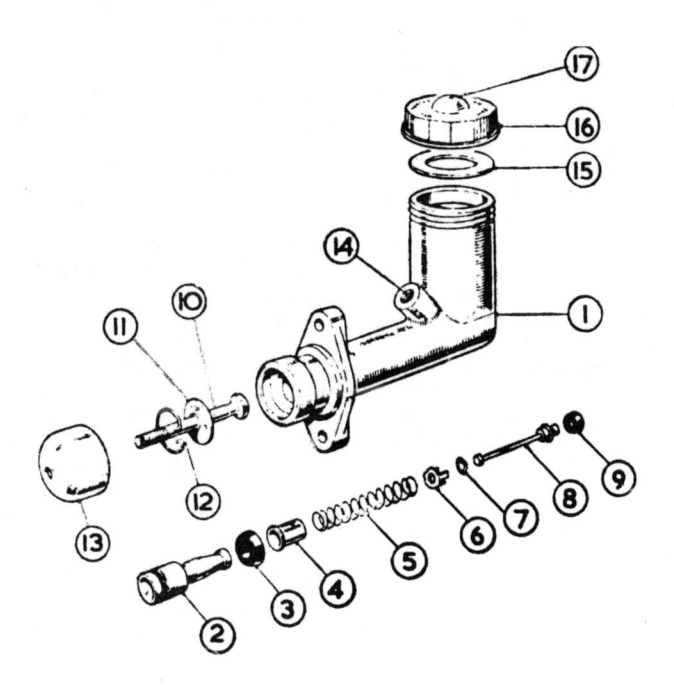

Fig. 9.8. BRAKE MASTER CYLINDER —
GIRLING (TR4A)

1 Master cylinder body
2 Plunger
3 Plunger seal
4 Spring retainer
5 Spring
6 Valve spacer
7 Spring washer
8 Valve stem
9 Valve seal
10 Pushrod
11 Retaining washer
12 Circlip
13 Dust cover
14 Outlet
15 Cap washer
16 Filler cap
17 Air vent

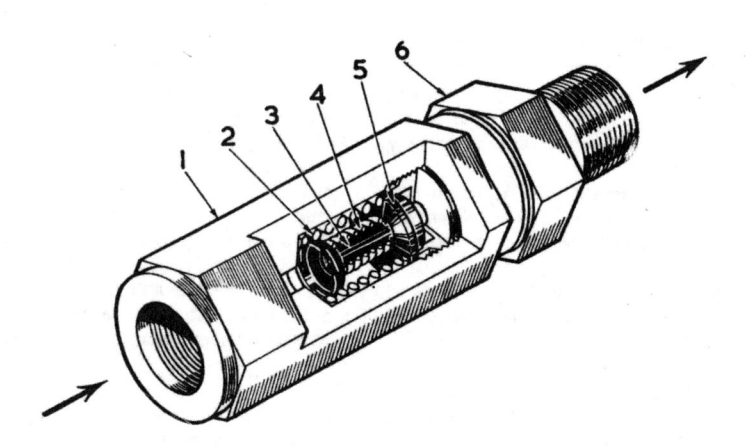

Fig. 9.9. CROSS SECTION THROUGH BRAKE
RESTRICTER VALVE

1 Body
2 Spring
3 Valve
4 Spring
5 Disc
6 End cap

Chapter 9/Braking System

together with the locating washer and the rubber boot.
4. Pull the piston and valve assembly as one unit from the master cylinder.
5. Using a small screwdriver raise the leaf of the spring thimble to clear it from the shoulder on the plunger and pull the thimble from the plunger.
6. Compress the coil spring and slip the valve stem into the larger offset in the base of the thimble.
7. Slide the thimble off the head of the valve stem. Lift away the spacer and spring washer from the valve stem.
8. Remove the valve seal from the valve stem and the two seals from the plunger.
9. Clean and carefully examine all parts, especially the piston cup and rubber washers, for signs of distortion, swelling, splitting, or other wear and check the piston and cylinder for wear and scoring. Replace any parts that are faulty.
10 During the inspection of the piston seal it has been found advisable to maintain the shape of this seal as regular as possible and for this reason do not turn it inside out as slight distortion may be caused.
11 Rebuild the plunger and valve assembly in the following manner:-

a) Fit the plunger seal to the plunger so that the larger circumference of the rubber lip will enter the cylinder bore first. The seal sits in the groove.
b) Then fit the valve seal to the valve in the same way.
c) Place the valve spring seal washer so its convex face shuts the valve stem flange and then fit the seal spacer and spring.
d) Fit the spring thimble to the spring which must then be compressed so the valve stem can be reinserted in the thimble.
e) Replace the front of the plunger in the thimble and then press down the thimble leaf so it is located under the shoulder at the front of the plunger.
f) Generously lubricate the assembly with hydraulic fluid and carefully replace it in the master cylinder body, taking great care not to damage the rubber seals as they are inserted into the cylinder bore.
g) Fit the pushrod and washer in place and secure the circlip. Replace the rubber boot.

20. Brake Pedal Adjustment (TR3, 3A Girling System)

It is important that the plunger returns fully to the end of the stroke when the brake pedal is released as otherwise the valve sealing the port from the reservoir may possibly not be fully opened, if at all.

Should the valve remain closed it may be found that pressure will build up in the hydraulic system which will cause the slave cylinder piston to remain extended, so causing brake pedal slip.

The locknuts should always be adjusted on the pushrod so that there is between 1/2 to 5/8 inch free play on the pedal before it starts to operate.

21. Brake Master Cylinder - Removal and Replacement (TR4, 4A Girling System)

1. It is possible to remove the brake master cylinder without removing the clutch master cylinder.
2. Connect a piece of plastic tubing to one of the brake bleed nipples and by operating the brake pedal several times drain the brake hydraulic fluid in the reservoir into a clean glass container.
3. Next connect the piece of plastic tubing to the clutch slave cylinder bleed nipple and by operating the clutch pedal several times drain the clutch hydraulic fluid in the reservoir into a clean glass container.
4. Remove the brake light switch from its mounting on the master cylinder bracket. On earlier models a pressure operated switch is mounted on the five way connector of the hydraulic pipe system and need not be disturbed.
5. Refer to Fig. 9.7 and extract the split pins from the clevis pins (1) securing the pedals to the master cylinders. Take care to recover the springs and washers and then withdraw the clevis pin (1).
6. Carefully disconnect the clutch and brake master cylinder hydraulic pipe connections ensuring that the pipes are not twisted.
7. Undo the screws (4) and the four nuts from the studs (3). Lift the master cylinder support bracket (11) from the scuttle then disconnect the clutch master cylinder from the bracket by undoing the two retaining nuts, bolts and spring washers.
8. Refitting the master cylinders is the reverse sequence to removal. It will be necessary to bleed both the brake and clutch hydraulic systems.

22. Brake Master Cylinder - Dismantling, Examination and Reassembly (TR4, 4A Girling System)

1. Unscrew the filler cap (16) (Fig. 9.8) and drain the hydraulic fluid into a clean container.
2. Pull off the rubber boot (13) which exposes the circlip (12) which must be removed so the pushrod complete with metal retaining washer (11) can be pulled out of the master cylinder.
3. Pull the piston (2) and valve assembly (8) as one unit from the master cylinder.
4. The next step is to separate the piston and valve assemblies. With the aid of a small screwdriver prise up the inner leg of the piston return spring retainer (4) which engages under a shoulder in the front of the piston and holds the retainer (4) in place.
5. The retainer (4), spring (5), and valve assembly (8) can then be separated from the piston.
6. To dismantle the valve assembly compress the spring (5) and move the retainer (4) which has an offset hole to one side in order to release the valve stem (8) from the retainer (4).
7. With the seat spacer (6) and valve seal washer (9) removed, the rubber seals can be taken off and inspected.
8. Clean and carefully examine all the parts, especially the piston cups and rubber washers, for signs of distortion, swelling, splitting or other wear and check the piston and cylinder for wear and scoring. Replace any parts that are faulty.
9. During the inspection of the piston seal it has been found advisable to maintain the shape of this seal as regular as possible and for this reason do not turn it inside out as slight distortion may be caused.
10 Rebuild the piston and valve assembly in the following manner:-

a) Fit the piston seal (3) to the piston (2) so the larger circumference of the rubber lip will enter the cylinder bore first. The seal sits in the groove.
b) Then fit the valve seal (9) to the valve (8) in the same way.
c) Place the valve spring seal washer (7) so its convex face abuts the valve stem flange (8) and then fit the seat spacer (6) and spring.
d) Fit the spring retainer (4) to the spring (5) which must then be compressed so the valve stem (8) can be reinserted in

Fig. 9.10. HANDBRAKE SYSTEM TR2

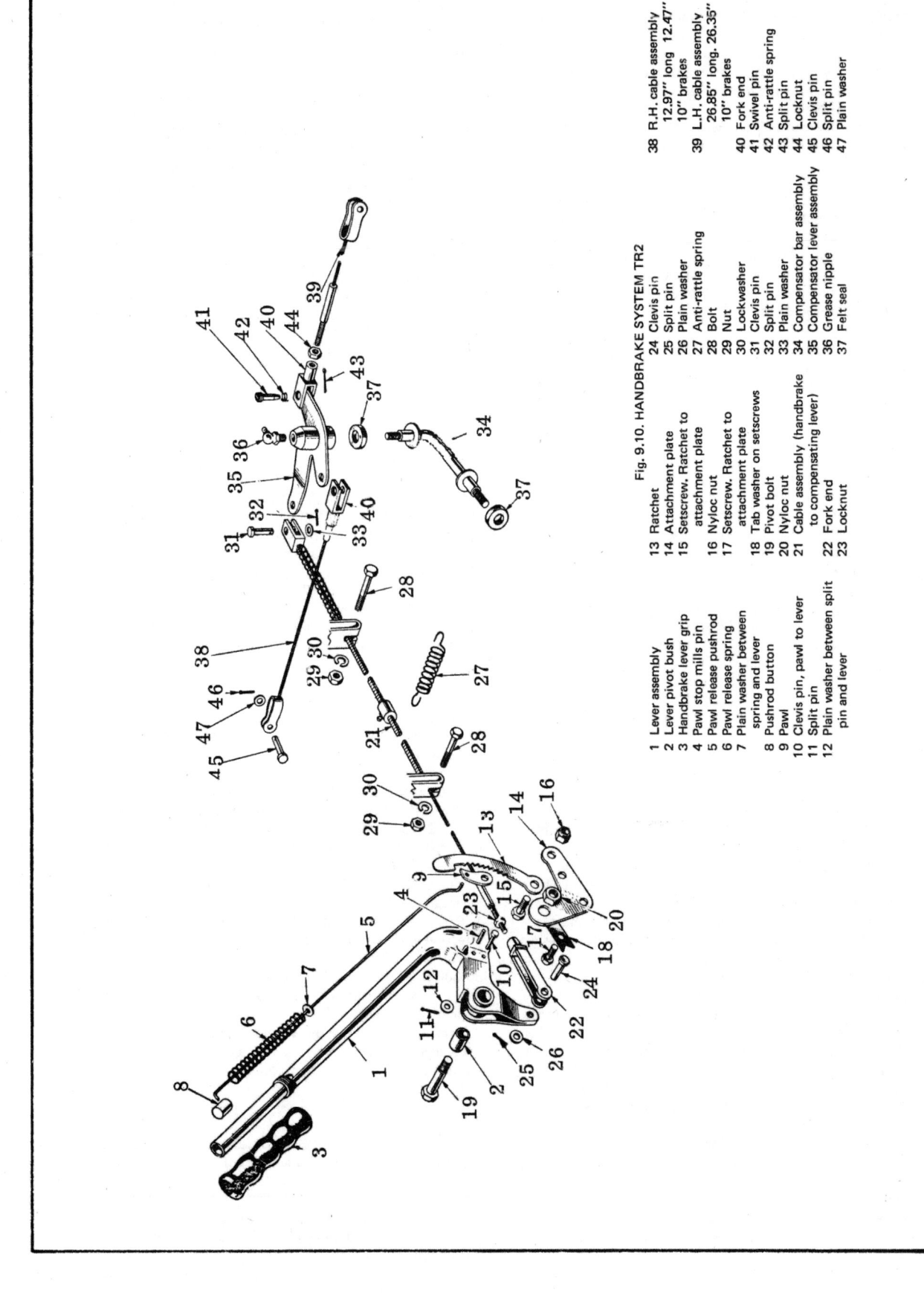

1 Lever assembly
2 Lever pivot bush
3 Handbrake lever grip
4 Pawl stop mills pin
5 Pawl release pushrod
6 Pawl release spring
7 Plain washer between spring and lever
8 Pushrod button
9 Pawl
10 Clevis pin, pawl to lever
11 Split pin
12 Plain washer between split pin and lever
13 Ratchet
14 Attachment plate
15 Setscrew, Ratchet to attachment plate
16 Nyloc nut
17 Setscrew, Ratchet to attachment plate
18 Tab washer on setscrews
19 Pivot bolt
20 Nyloc nut
21 Cable assembly (handbrake to compensating lever)
22 Fork end
23 Locknut
24 Clevis pin
25 Split pin
26 Plain washer
27 Anti-rattle spring
28 Bolt
29 Nut
30 Lockwasher
31 Clevis pin
32 Split pin
33 Plain washer
34 Compensator bar assembly
35 Compensator lever assembly
36 Grease nipple
37 Felt seal
38 R.H. cable assembly 12.97" long. 12.47" 10" brakes
39 L.H. cable assembly 26.85" long. 26.35" 10" brakes
40 Fork end
41 Swivel pin
42 Anti-rattle spring
43 Split pin
44 Locknut
45 Clevis pin
46 Split pin
47 Plain washer

Chapter 9/Braking System

the retainer (4).

e) Replace the front of the piston (2) in the retainer (4) and then press down the retaining leg so it locates under the shoulder at the front of the piston (2).

f) Generously lubricate the assembly with hydraulic fluid and carefully replace it in the master cylinder, taking great care not to damage the rubber seals as they are inserted into the cylinder bore.

g) Fit the pushrod (10) and washer (11) in place and secure with the circlip (12). Replace the rubber boot (13).

23. Brake Pedal Adjustment (TR4, 4A Girling System)

There is no provision for the individual adjustment of the brake pedal. Excessive movement before brake operation indicates that the brakes require adjusting or new linings and/or pads need to be fitted.

24. Handbrake Cables - Removal, Refitting and Adjustment (TR2)

Removal

1. The handbrake cable system is shown in Fig. 9.10 and it will be observed that there are three individual cables which can be separately removed if required.

2. To remove the main handbrake cable first undo the nuts (29) from the clamp bolts (28) securing the cable to the clamps. Lift away the nuts (29), spring washers (30) and bolts (28).

3. Undo the locknut (23) securing the inner cable to the fork end connected to the handbrake lever assembly.

4. Extract the split pin (25) from the clevis pin (24) securing the fork end (22) to the handbrake lever assembly. Lift away the plain washer (26) followed by the clevis pin (24). Note the position of the clevis pin head for correct refitting.

5. Extract the split pin (32) from the clevis pin (31) securing the rear main cable fork end to the compensator lever assembly (35). Lift away the washer (33) followed by the clevis pin, noting the head of the clevis pin is to the top of the fork.

6. Lift away the main handbrake cable.

7. To remove the right hand cable extract the split pin (46) from the fork end clevis pin at the handbrake lever on the rear brake backplate. Lift away the plain washer (47) followed by the clevis pin (45). Note the head of the clevis pin is towards the front.

8. Extract the split pin from the clevis pin on the compensator lever assembly (35), lift away the plain washer followed by the clevis pin. Note the head of the clevis pin is to the top of the fork end (40).

9. To remove the adjustable left hand cable extract the split pin (46) from the fork end clevis pin at the handbrake lever on the rear brake backplate. Lift away the plain washer (47) followed by the clevis pin (45). Note the head of the clevis pin is towards the front.

10 Slacken the locknut (44) on the compensator lever fork end. Extract the split pin (43) from the compensator lever fork end clevis swivel pin (41) and lift away the clevis pin (41) and anti-rattle spring (42). Note the head of the clevis swivel pin is on the top of the fork end.

Refitting

1. Before refitting handbrake cables the length of the transverse cables must be checked against the information below.

Cable	Length 10 inch diameter Drum brakes	Length 9 inch diameter Drum brakes
Right hand	12.47 inch	12.97 $\pm$ 0.06 inch
Left hand	26.35 inch	26.85 $\pm$ 0.06 inch

2. Refitting is the reverse sequence to removal but it is recommended that the compensator assembly be first removed from the back axle and new felt seals (37) (Fig. 9.10) be fitted. The bar on the axle should be screwed fully home and then turned back one complete turn. Refit the compensator lever (35) in exactly the same manner as the bar assembly (34).

3. Thoroughly grease all cables and pivot points during refitting.

Adjustment

1. Normally if the rear brakes have been correctly adjusted there is no need for the handbrake cables to be separately adjusted unless they have either been incorrectly fitted or the cables have stretched due to a longer service life.

2. Adjust the rear brakes until the shoes are hard against the drums.

3. Release the handbrake.

4. Extract the split pin (25) (Fig. 9.10) from the clevis pin (24) securing the fork end (22) to the handbrake lever (1). Lift away the plain washer (26) followed by the clevis pin (24).

5. Slacken the locknut (23) and screw the fork end (22) along the cable (21) until all the slack has been taken out of the cable. Refit the clevis pin (24) with the head to the right followed by the plain washer (26) and secure with a new split pin (25).

6. Tighten the locknut (23) and slacken the rear brake adjusters by one 'click'.

7. It should not be necessary to adjust the left hand cable unless the compensator lever is not at an angle of 17 degrees.

25. Handbrake Cables - Removal, Refitting and Adjustment (TR3, 3A)

The layout of the handbrake system is shown in Fig. 9.11 and it will be seen that it is practically the same as for the TR2 models. Removal and refitting of the three cables is straight forward provided the general instructions of the previous section are followed.

The cable adjustment is slightly different and the following sequence should be followed:-

1. Screw the rear brake shoe adjusters in a clockwise direction until the shoes are in firm contact with the drum.

2. Pull on the handbrake lever one notch.

3. Adjust the length of the cables so that the cables are free of slack and the compensator lever assembly is at an angle of 17 degrees.

4. Back off the rear brake shoe adjusters two 'clicks' and once this has been done the rear brakes and handbrake should now be correctly adjusted.

26. Handbrake Cables - Removal, Refitting and Adjusting (TR4)

This system is identical to that for the TR2 models and full service information may be found in Section 24 of this Chapter.

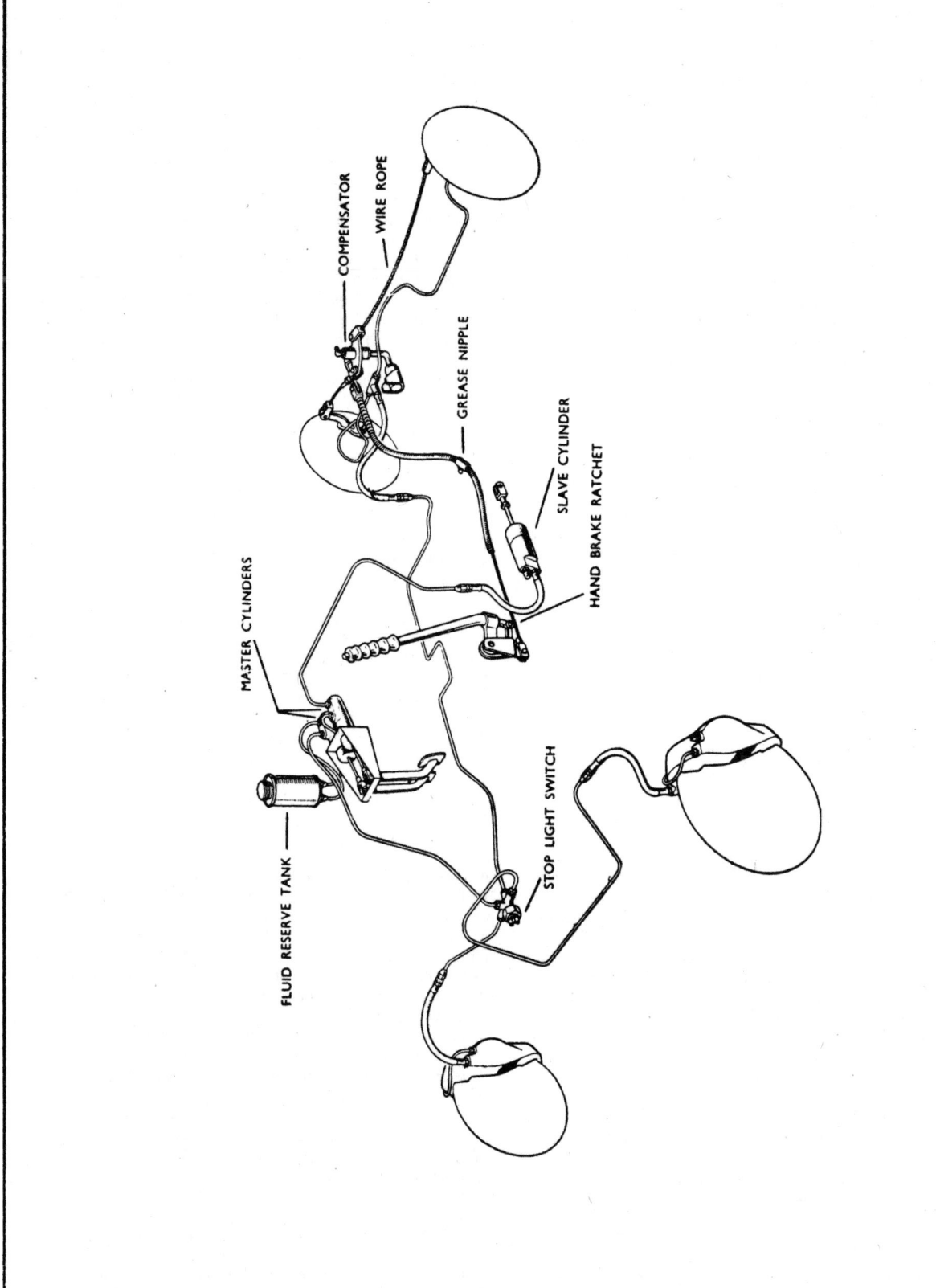

Fig. 9.11. Handbrake system TR3, 3A

Chapter 9/Braking System

27. Handbrake Cables - Removal, Refitting and Adjustment (TR4A)

Removal

1. The handbrake cable system is shown in Fig. 9.12 and it will be observed that there are two individual cables which can be separately removed if required.
2. Chock the front wheels, raise the rear of the car and place on firmly based stands.
3. Remove the rear wheels.
4. Undo the eight self tapping screws (13) (Fig. 9.12) securing the cardboard cover (12) to the floor panel. Lift away the cover easing it over the handbrake lever assembly (1).
5. Release the handbrake and pull the outer cable towards the rear and disconnect it from the tunnel mounting by pivoting it forwards and vertically.
6. Lift the ball on the end of the inner cable from its location hole in the top of the compensator (18).
7. Extract the split pin (31) from the fork end (26) clevis pins (29), lift away the washer (30) followed by the clevis pin (29).
8. Undo the nut (24) securing the outer cable holder from its mounting. Lift away the nut (24) followed by the spring washer (25). Remove the holder and the rubber cover.
9. Withdraw the cable from the underside of the car.
10 Repeat operations 5, 6, 7, 8 and 9 to remove the second cable.

Refitting

1. Refitting is the reverse sequence to removal.
2. Thoroughly grease all cables and pivot points during refitting. Always use new clevis pins if they show signs of wear and also never use a split pin twice.

Adjustment

1. Chock the front wheels, raise the rear of the car and place on firmly based axle stands.
2. Remove the rear wheels and adjust the rear brakes.
3. Undo the eight self tapping screws (13) (Fig. 9.12) securing the cardboard cover (12) to the floor panel. Lift away the cover easing it over the handbrake lever assembly (1).
4. Extract the split pins (31) securing the fork end clevis pin at the handbrake lever on the backplate. Lift away the plain washer followed by the clevis pin (20). Note that the head of the clevis pin is on the top of the fork end (26).
5. Undo the locknut (28) and screw each fork end (26) along the inner cable so as to bring the compensator (18) lever and the handbrake lever tight when pulled onto the fifth notch of the ratchet.
6. When this adjustment is obtained tighten the locknuts (28). Refit the clevis pin with the head uppermost followed by the plain washer (30) and a new split pin (31).
7. Refit the handbrake lever cover assembly (12) and secure with the eight self tapping screws (13).
8. Replace the road wheel and thoroughly road test.

28. Front Disc Brake Friction Pad - Removal, Inspection and Replacement (TR3, 3A)

1. Chock the rear wheels, apply the handbrake firmly, raise the front of the car from the ground and place on firmly based stands. Remove the front wheels.
2. Refer to Fig. 9.13 and undo but not remove the two set bolts holding the triangular retaining plates onto the calliper body. Once the triangular plates can be lifted sufficiently to disengage the peg on the plate from its slot in the calliper body swing the plates around through 180 degrees.
3. The friction pads may now be removed from the calliper body. Note their location for correct refitting if they have not badly worn.
4. Inspect the amount of friction material left on the friction pads and if it has worn down to less than $1/8$ inch new pads must be fitted.
5. Remove the cap from the hydraulic fluid reservoir if new pads are to be fitted and wrap absorbent cloth around the reservoir so that any fluid spilt in the subsequent operations will be immediately absorbed and not spilt onto the paintwork.
6. Carefully clean the recesses in the calliper in which the friction pad assemblies lie and also the exposed face of each piston from all traces of dirt and rust. A cloth soaked in methylated spirits is good for this cleaning operation.
7. Press each pad back into its cylinder so as to allow new pads to be fitted.
8. Fit the new friction pads, or the original ones if they are not badly worn, and check that they are able to slide freely in their recesses.
9. Return the triangular plates to their original position with the pegs engaged in their slots in the body. Tighten the two retaining set bolts.
10 Pump the brake pedal several times to adjust the pad to disc clearance and check the level of hydraulic fluid in the reservoir. Top up if necessary using correct grade fluid.
11 Replace the road wheels, lower the car and road test for correct brake efficiency.

29. Front Disc Brake Friction Pad - Removal, Inspection and Replacement (TR4, 4A)

1. Remove the front wheels and inspect the amount of friction material left on the friction pads. The pads must be renewed when the thickness of the material has worn down to $1/8$ inch.
2. Referring to Fig. 9.14 pull out the wire clips (9) which secure the pad retaining pins (10) in place and remove the pins.
3. The friction pads (4) and anti-squeal shims (5) can now be lifted from the calliper.
4. Carefully clean the recesses in the calliper in which the friction pad assemblies lie and the exposed face of each piston from all traces of dirt and rust.
5. Remove the cap from the hydraulic fluid reservoir and place a large rag underneath the unit. Press the pistons in half of the calliper right in; this will cause the fluid level in the reservoir to rise and possibly to spill over the brim onto the protective rag.
6. Fit new pads and refit the anti-squeal shims with the arrow towards the direction of rotation as shown in Fig. 9.15. Insert the pad retainer pins (10) and secure them with the retainer clips (9).

30. Disc Brake Calliper - Removal, Dismantling and Reassembly (TR3, 3A)

1. Jack up the front of the car and place on firmly based stands. Apply the handbrake firmly and chock the rear wheels. Remove the road wheel and disconnect the flexible hydraulic pipe as previously detailed in Section 9 of this Chapter. Have a pad of absorbent cloth ready to catch hydraulic fluid as it drips from the end of the exposed pipe.
2. Remove the two friction linings as detailed in Section 28 of this Chapter.

Fig. 9.12. HANDBRAKE SYSTEM - TR4A

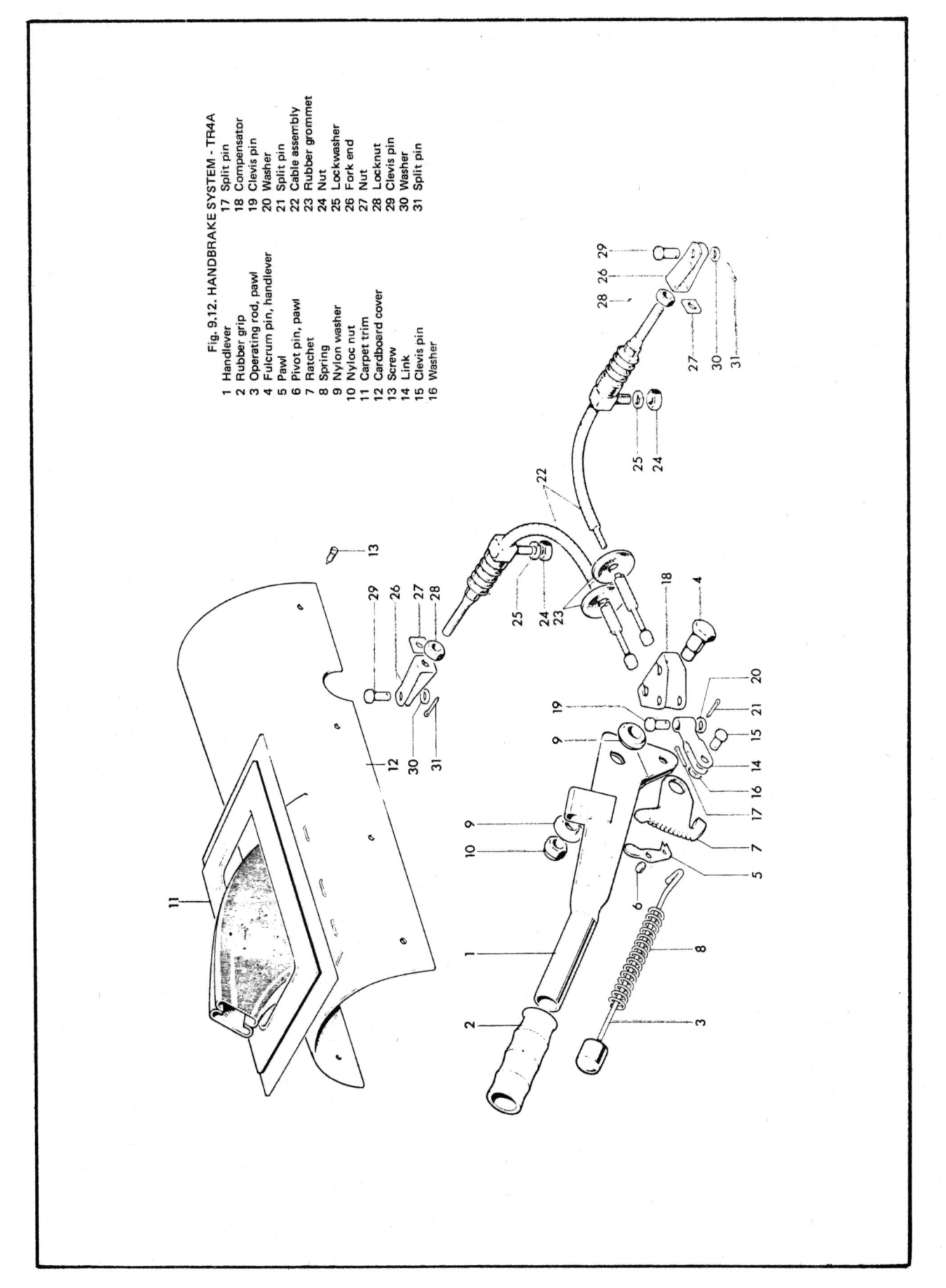

1 Handlever
2 Rubber grip
3 Operating rod, pawl
4 Fulcrum pin, handlever
5 Pawl
6 Pivot pin, pawl
7 Ratchet
8 Spring
9 Nyloc washer
10 Nyloc nut
11 Carpet trim
12 Cardboard cover
13 Screw
14 Link
15 Clevis pin
16 Washer
17 Split pin
18 Compensator
19 Clevis pin
20 Washer
21 Split pin
22 Cable assembly
23 Rubber grommet
24 Nut
25 Lockwasher
26 Fork end
27 Nut
28 Locknut
29 Clevis pin
30 Washer
31 Split pin

3. Undo and remove the two bolts which secure the calliper to the vertical swivel link of the front suspension and lift away the calliper from the disc.
4. Remove the dust covers from their locating grooves in the cylinder bores (Fig. 9.13). Very carefully remove the pistons from their cylinders ensuring that they are kept separate so that they are not interchanged and fitted back in the wrong bores. Whilst removing the pistons do not scratch the bore or the piston, otherwise new parts will have to be fitted.
5. Do not under any circumstances attempt to undo the plug retainers as an easy way to remove the pistons. The plug retainers are very tightly fitted into their locations and without the use of special equipment they cannot be removed.
6. Should difficulty be experienced in removing the pistons reconnect the flexible hose to the calliper and depress the brake pedal whilst holding one of the pistons with a G clamp. Remove the sealing ring from the displaced piston and refit the piston. Clamp this piston and eject the second piston by repeating the brake pedal pumping operation.
7. The correct method of removing the old seals from the pistons and the cylinder is to use a blunt tool and ease off the old seal, taking extreme care not to damage the recesses into which the seals fit.
8. Thoroughly wash all the metal parts in methylated spirits and wipe dry using a clean rag.
9. Examine the components carefully, renew the rubbers as a matter of course, and replace the pistons if slightly grooved or otherwise worn.
10 As each internal part is refitted it should be well wetted in clean hydraulic fluid.
11 Start reassembling by refitting the sealing ring to each piston carefully working the seal into its groove until it is correctly seated.
12 Fit the sealing ring to the inner groove of the cylinder bore again carefully working the seal into its groove until it is correctly seated.
13 Next fit the projecting lip of the dust cover into the outer groove in the cylinder bore.
14 With the pistons well wetted insert the closed end into the cylinder bore squarely so that the seals are not tilted and push the piston down as far as it will go.
15 Carefully fit the outer lip of the dust cover into the special groove of the piston.
16 Fit the calliper over the disc insert the two calliper securing bolts and fully tighten.
17 Replace the two pads and secure in position with the two triangular shaped retaining plates.
18 Reconnect the brake flexible hose and bleed the hydraulic system.

31. Disc Brake Calliper - Removal, Dismantling and Reassembly (TR4, 4A)

1. Jack up the car, remove the road wheel and disconnect the flexible hydraulic pipe as previously detailed in Section 9.
2. Remove the disc brake friction pads and anti-squeal shims as previously described.
3. Unscrew the two calliper mounting bolts and lockwashers and remove the calliper assembly from the disc.
4. Referring to Fig. 9.14 pull off the dust covers (8) and remove the pistons from the calliper body (3).
5. Very carefully remove the rubber piston sealing rings (7) from their recesses in the calliper. The pistons, cylinders, and rubbers should be cleaned only with clean brake fluid.
6. Examine the components carefully, renew the rubbers as a matter of course and replace the pistons if slightly grooved or otherwise worn.
7. Reassembly commences by carefully fitting new piston sealing rings into the recesses in the calliper cylinders.
8. Fit the larger diameter lip of the rubber dust cover (8) to the groove on the outside of the top of the cylinder.
9. Slide the pistons closed end first into the cylinders, with great care, and then fit the outer lip of the dust excluder into the groove in the outer end of the piston.
10 Fit the calliper over the disc, insert the two securing bolts, replace the anti-squeal shims and the pads. Reconnect the flexible brake hose and bleed the system as described in Section 10.

32. Disc and Hub - Removal and Replacement

1. Jack up the front of the car and place on axle stands. Chock the rear wheels and apply the handbrake firmly.
2. Remove the road wheel on whichever side the disc and hub are to be serviced.
3. The grease cap or sometimes called the dust cover (35) (Fig. 11.1) is a very tight fit and is removed by levering with a screwdriver or tapping the flange with a hammer.
4. Extract the split pin (34) from the castellated nut (32). Undo the castellated nut and remove the nut followed by the washer (33). If a grease nipple (30) is fitted to the end of the stub axle (22) this should next be removed.
5. Undo the two calliper retaining bolts securing the calliper to the vertical swivel link of the front suspension (12) and carefully lift away from the disc. Hang the calliper out of the way using a piece of wire or string. Remember not to depress the brake pedal as otherwise the pistons could be ejected.
6. Withdraw the hub and disc assembly from the stub axle (22). If this is difficult to remove use a 2 or 3 leg universal puller as sometimes it can be a tight fit.
7. Before separating the disc and hub, make an alignment mark so an identical position can be regained upon reassembly.
8. To free the brake disc from the hub undo the four bolts and spring washers and separate the two parts.
9. Inspect the discs for signs of excessive scoring and, if evident, the discs may be reground but no more than a maximum total of 0.060 inch may be removed from the disc. The desirable finish should be 32 micro inch maximum when measured circumferentially and 50 micro inch when measured radially.
10 Refitting is the reverse sequence to removal. The hub will require adjusting as detailed in Chapter 11.
11 Measure the run out at the outer periphery of the disc by means of a feeler gauge positioned between the inside of the calliper and the disc. If the run out on the friction faces of the disc exceeds 0.002 inch remove the disc and reposition it on the hub casing. If the run out is really bad the disc is probably distorted due to overheating and a new one should be fitted.

33. Brake Line Restrictor Valve

A restrictor valve is fitted into the hydraulic line from the brake master cylinder on TR4 and 4A models so that there is always a slight pressure in the hydraulic system. This pressure maintains the disc pads in near contact with the disc at all times when the brakes are not actually applied.

The valve is shown in Fig. 9.9. and operates as follows:-

When the brake pedal is depressed the hydraulic pressure will compress the spring (4) and also lift the valve (3) from its seat on the disc (5) allowing hydraulic fluid to pass

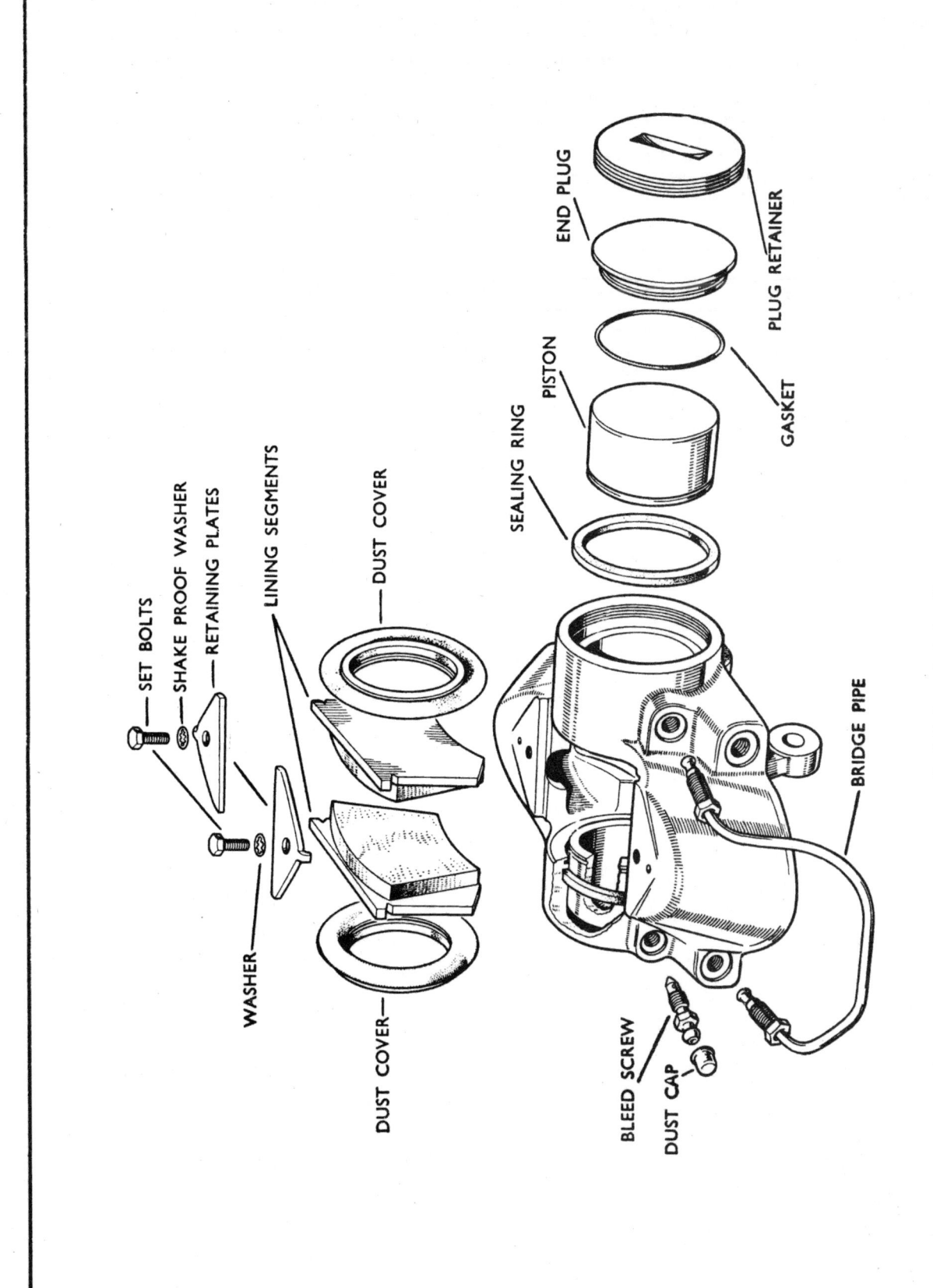

Fig. 9.13. Front disc brake calliper - Girling

Chapter 9/Braking System

through the valve and operate the brake system. Braking having been completed and the pedal is released, the newly created difference in pressure between one side of the valve and the other will act on the disc (5) and compress the spring (2). When the pressure of the spring (2) is greater than the difference in pressure within the valve, the disc (5) will be returned to its seating and will maintain a small pressure in the pipe line of the hydraulic system.

During initial production of the TR4 models the hydraulically operated brake light switch was fitted to the brake line restrictor valve until the mechanically operated switch was introduced.

34. Vacuum Servo Unit

A vacuum servo unit was offered as an optional extra to TR4 and 4A models. This supplements the driver's effort required to apply the brakes. It is reliable in operation and should not require service attention except for the filter to be cleaned regularly every 3,000 miles or less in dusty climates.

The vacuum required to operate the unit is obtained from a connection on the inlet manifold. Should for any reason there be a failure in the vacuum side of the system the brake will operate normally but without the additional assistance.

The sequence of bleeding the braking system with a servo unit fitted is slightly different and the additional notes below should be observed.

1. To bleed the brakes it is not necessary for the engine to be running as vacuum is not required.
2. When operating the brake pedal press the pedal down sharply and allow the pedal to slowly return. Wait five seconds at the end of each return stroke. Whenever the pedal is released tighten the applicable bleed screws.
3. Commence the bleed operation at the nipple on the servo unit and then follow round the car starting on the pipe with the shortest run and progressing so finishing up with the pipe having the longest run.
4. Should air have entered the system from the master cylinder slacken the hydraulic outlet pipe connection and press the pedal down several times to expel the air. When fluid flows from the union tighten the union and start the bleed operation.

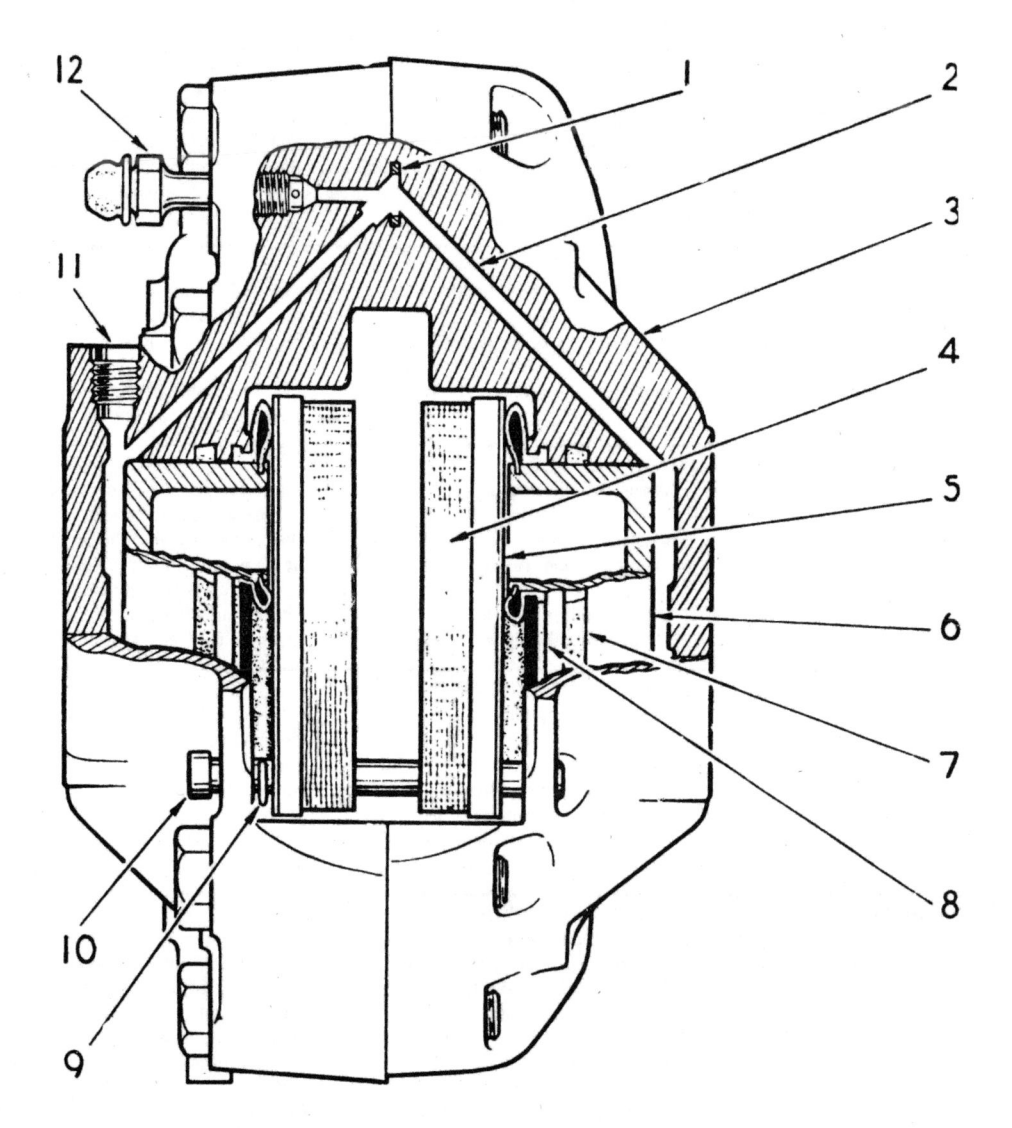

Fig. 9.14. DISC BRAKE CALLIPER COMPONENT
PARTS (TR4, 4A)

1 Rubber 'O' ring
2 Fluid transfer channels
3 Calliper body
4 Friction pad
5 Anti-squeal shim
6 Piston
7 Piston sealing ring
8 Dust cover
9 Retaining clip
10 Retaining pin
11 Flexible hose connection
12 Bleed nipple

Fault Finding Chart - Braking System

Cause	Trouble	Remedy
SYMPTOM: PEDAL TRAVELS ALMOST TO FLOORBOARDS BEFORE BRAKES OPERATE		
Leaks and air bubbles in hydraulic system.	Brake fluid level too low.	Top up master cylinder reservoir. Check for leaks.
	Wheel cylinder leaking.	Dismantle wheel cylinder, clean, fit new rubbers and bleed brakes.
	Master cylinder leaking (bubbles in master cylinder fluid).	Dismantle master cylinder, clean, and fit new rubbers. Bleed brakes.
	Brake flexible hose leaking.	Examine and fit new hose if old hose leaking. Bleed brakes.
	Brake line fractured.	Replace with new brake pipe. Bleed brakes.
	Brake system unions loose.	Check all unions in brake system and tighten as necessary. Bleed brakes.
Normal wear	Linings over 75% worn.	Fit replacement shoes and brake linings.
Incorrect adjustment	Brakes badly out of adjustment	Jack up car and adjust brakes.
	Master cylinder push rod out of adjustment causing too much pedal free movement.	Reset to manufacturer's specification.
SYMPTOM: BRAKE PEDAL FEELS SPRINGY		
Brake lining renewal	New linings not yet bedded-in.	Use brakes gently until springy pedal feeling leaves.
Excessive wear or damage	Brake drums badly worn and weak or cracked.	Fit new brake drums.
Lack of maintenance	Master cylinder securing nuts loose.	Tighten master cylinder securing nuts. Ensure spring washers are fitted.
SYMPTOM: BRAKE PEDAL FEELS SPONGY AND SOGGY		
Leaks or bubbles in hydraulic system	Wheel cylinder leaking.	Dismantle wheel cylinder, clean, fit new rubbers and bleed brakes.
	Master cylinder leaking (bubbles in master cylinder reservoir).	Dismantle master cylinder, clean, and fit new rubbers and bleed brakes. Replace cylinder if internal walls scored.
	Brake pipe line or flexible hose leaking.	Fit new pipeline or hose.
	Unions in brake system loose.	Examine for leaks, tighten as necessary.
SYMPTOM' EXCESSIVE EFFORT REQUIRED TO BRAKE CAR		
Lining type or condition	Linings badly worn.	Fit replacement brake shoes and linings.
	New linings recently fitted - not yet bedded-in.	Use brakes gently until braking effort normal.
	Harder linings fitted than standard causing increase in pedal pressure.	Remove linings and replace with normal units.
Oil or grease leaks	Linings and brake drums contaminated with oil, grease, or hydraulic fluid.	Rectify source of leak, clean brake drums, fit new linings.
SYMPTOM: BRAKES UNEVEN AND PULLING TO ONE SIDE		
Oil or grease leaks	Linings and brake drums contaminated with oil, grease or hydraulic fluid.	Ascertain and rectify source of leak, clean brake drums, fit new linings.
Lack of maintenance	Tyre pressures unequal.	Check and inflate as necessary.
	Radial ply tyres fitted at one end of car only.	Fit radial ply tyres of the same make to all four wheels.
	Brake backplate loose.	Tighten backplate securing nuts and bolts.
	Brake shoes fitted incorrectly.	Remove and fit shoes correct way round.
	Different type of linings fitted at each wheel.	Fit the linings specified by the manufacturers all round.
	Anchorages for front suspension or rear axle loose.	Tighten front and rear suspension pick-up points including spring anchorage.
	Brake drums badly worn, cracked or distorted.	Fit new brake drums.
SYMPTOM: BRAKES TEND TO BIND, DRAG, OR LOCK-ON		
Incorrect adjustment	Brake shoes adjusted too tightly.	Slacken off brake shoe adjusters two clicks.
	Handbrake cable over-tightened.	Slacken off handbrake cable adjustment.

Fig. 9.15. Removal of brake pad TR4, 4A. Note. The arrow on the anti-squeal plate is pointing in the direction of forward rotation of the road wheel

Fault Finding Chart - Braking System

Cause	Trouble	Remedy
Wear or dirt in hydraulic system or incorrect fluid.	Master cylinder push rod out of adjustment giving too little brake pedal free movement.	Reset to manufacturer's specifications.
	Reservoir vent hole in cap blocked with dirt.	Clean and blow through hole.
	Master cylinder by-pass port restricted - brakes seize in 'on' operation.	Dismantle, clean and overhaul master cylinder. Bleed brakes.
	Wheel cylinder seizes in 'on' position.	Dismantle, clean and overhaul wheel cylinder. Bleed brakes.
Mechanical wear.	Brake shoe pull off springs broken, stretched or loose.	Examine springs and replace if worn or loose.
Incorrect brake assembly.	Brake shoe pull off springs fitted wrong way round, omitted, or wrong type used.	Examine and rectify as appropriate.
Neglect	Handbrake system rusted or seized in the 'on' position.	Apply 'Plus Gas' to free, clean and lubricate.

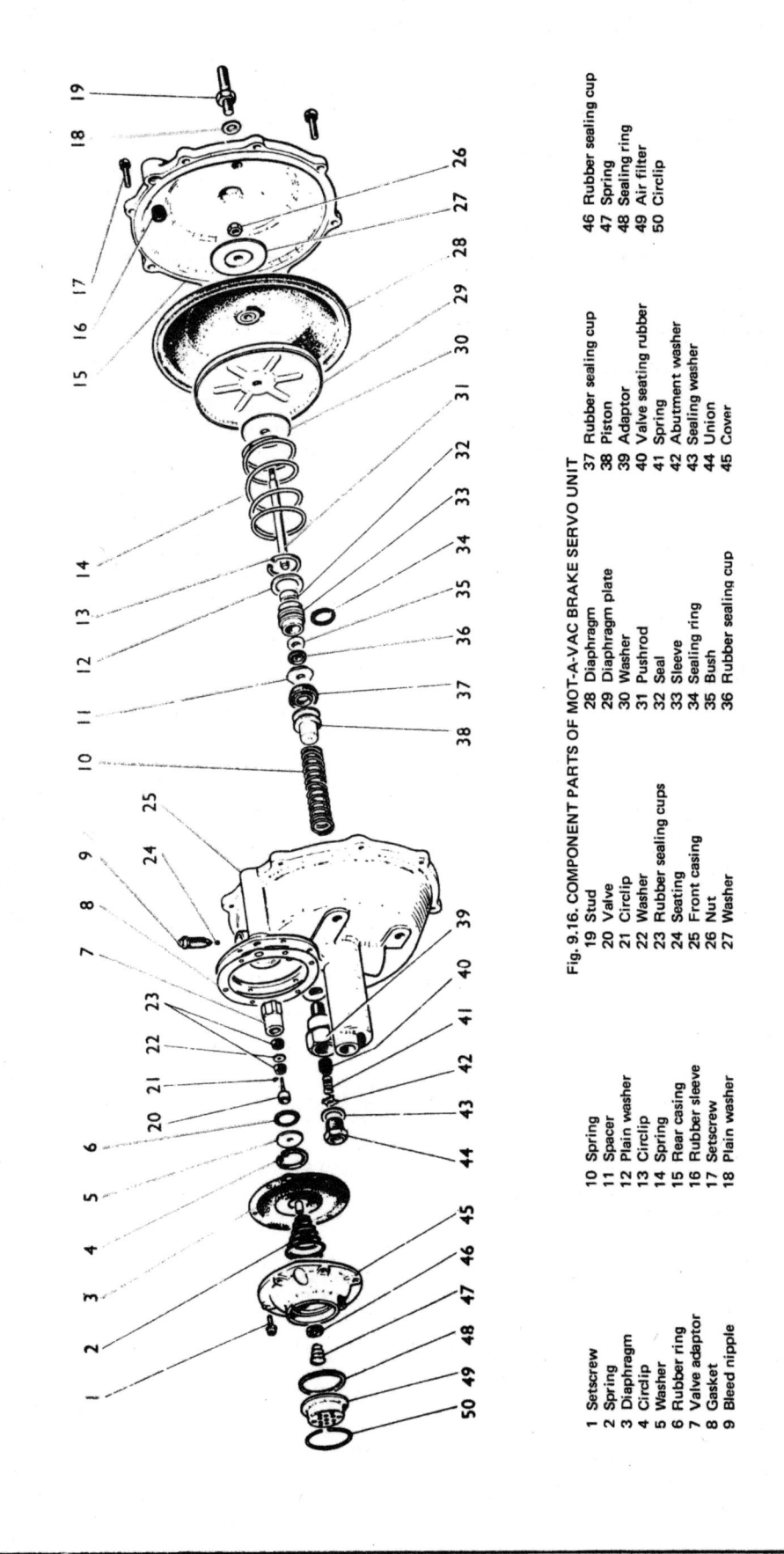

Fig. 9.16. COMPONENT PARTS OF MOT-A-VAC BRAKE SERVO UNIT

1 Setscrew	14 Spring	27 Washer	40 Valve seating rubber
2 Spring	15 Rear casing	28 Diaphragm	41 Spring
3 Diaphragm	16 Rubber sleeve	29 Diaphragm plate	42 Abutment washer
4 Circlip	17 Setscrew	30 Washer	43 Sealing washer
5 Washer	18 Plain washer	31 Pushrod	44 Union
6 Rubber ring	19 Stud	32 Seal	45 Cover
7 Valve adaptor	20 Valve	33 Sleeve	46 Rubber sealing cup
8 Gasket	21 Circlip	34 Sealing ring	47 Spring
9 Bleed nipple	22 Washer	35 Bush	48 Sealing ring
10 Spring	23 Rubber sealing cups	36 Rubber sealing cup	49 Air filter
11 Spacer	24 Seating	37 Rubber sealing cup	50 Circlip
12 Plain washer	25 Front casing	38 Piston	
13 Circlip	26 Nut	39 Adaptor	

205

Chapter 10/Electrical System

Contents

General Description	1
Battery - Removal and Replacement	2
Battery - Maintenance & Inspection	3
Electrolyte Replenishment	4
Battery - Charging	5
Dynamo - Routine Maintenance	6
Dynamo - Testing in Position	7
Dynamo - Removal & Replacement	8
Dynamo - Dismantling & Inspection	9
Dynamo - Repair & Reassembly	10
Starter Motor - General Description	11
Starter Motor - Removal & Replacement	12
Starter Motor & Drive Gear - Dismantling & Reassembly (TR2, 3, 3A)	13
Starter Motor & Drive Gear - Dismantling & Reassembly (TR4, 4A)	14
Starter Motor Solenoid	15
Control Box - General Description	16
Cut-Out & Regulator Contacts - Maintenance	17
Voltage Regulator - Adjustment	18
Cut-Out - Adjustment	19
Fuses	20
Flasher Circuit - Fault Tracing & Rectification	21
Windscreen Wiper Mechanism - Maintenance	22
Windscreen Wiper Blades - Removal & Replacement	23
Windscreen Wiper Arms - Removal & Replacement (TR2, 3, 3A)	24
Windscreen Wiper Arms - Removal & Replacement (TR4, 4A)	25
Windscreen Wiper Mechanism - Fault Diagnosis & Rectification (TR2, 3, 3A)	26
Windscreen Wiper Motor & Rack - Removal & Replacement (TR2, 3, 3A)	27
Windscreen Wiper Motor - Dismantling, Inspection, & Reassembly (TR2, 3, 3A)	28
Windscreen Wiper Mechanism - Fault Diagnosis & Rectification (TR4, 4A)	29
Windscreen Wiper Motor, Gearbox & Wheelbox - Removal & Replacement (TR4, 4A)	30
Windscreen Wiper Motor - Dismantling, Inspection & Reassembly (TR4, 4A)	31
Horns - Fault Tracing & Rectification	32
Horns - Servicing & Adjustment (TR2, 3, 3A)	33
Horns - Servicing & Adjustment (TR4, 4A)	34
Headlamps (TR2, 3, 3A)	35
Headlamps (TR4, 4A)	36
Fuel Gauge - Fault Finding & Rectification	37
Temperature Gauge - Fault Tracing & Recitifcation (TR2, 3, 3A)	38
Temperature Gauge - Fault Tracing & Rectification (TR4, 4A)	39

Specifications

	TR2, 3, 3A	TR4, 4A
Battery		
Type	Lucas lead acid 12 volt	Lucas lead acid 12 volt
Model: (Home)	GTW 7 A - 2	BT 9 A
(Export)	GTW 9 A - 2	BTZ 9 A
Earthed terminal	Positive	Positive
Capacity at 10 hour rate (ampere hours)	38 (home) 51 (export)	51
Capacity at 20 hour rate (ampere hours)	43 (home) 58 (export)	58
Number of plates per cell	7 (home) 9 (export)	9
Electrolyte to fill one cell	¾ pint (Home) 1 (export)	1
Specific gravity charged:		
Climates below 32ºC	1.270 to 1.290	1.270 to 1.290
Climates above 32ºC	1.130 to 1.150	1.130 to 1.150
Charging current (amperes)	4 (home) 5 (export)	5
Dynamo		
Model	Lucas C39PV2	Lucas C40-1
Type	Two pole, compensated voltage	Two pole, compensated voltage
Rotation	Clockwise	Clockwise
Field resistance	6.1 ohms	6 ohms
Maximum output	19 amperes	22 amperes
Number of bushes	2	2
Minimum bush length	11/32"	11/32"
Brush tension	22 to 25 oz. (min. 15 oz)	22 to 25 oz. (min. 15 oz)
Cut in speed	1050 to 1200 r.p.m.	1050 to 1200 r.p.m.

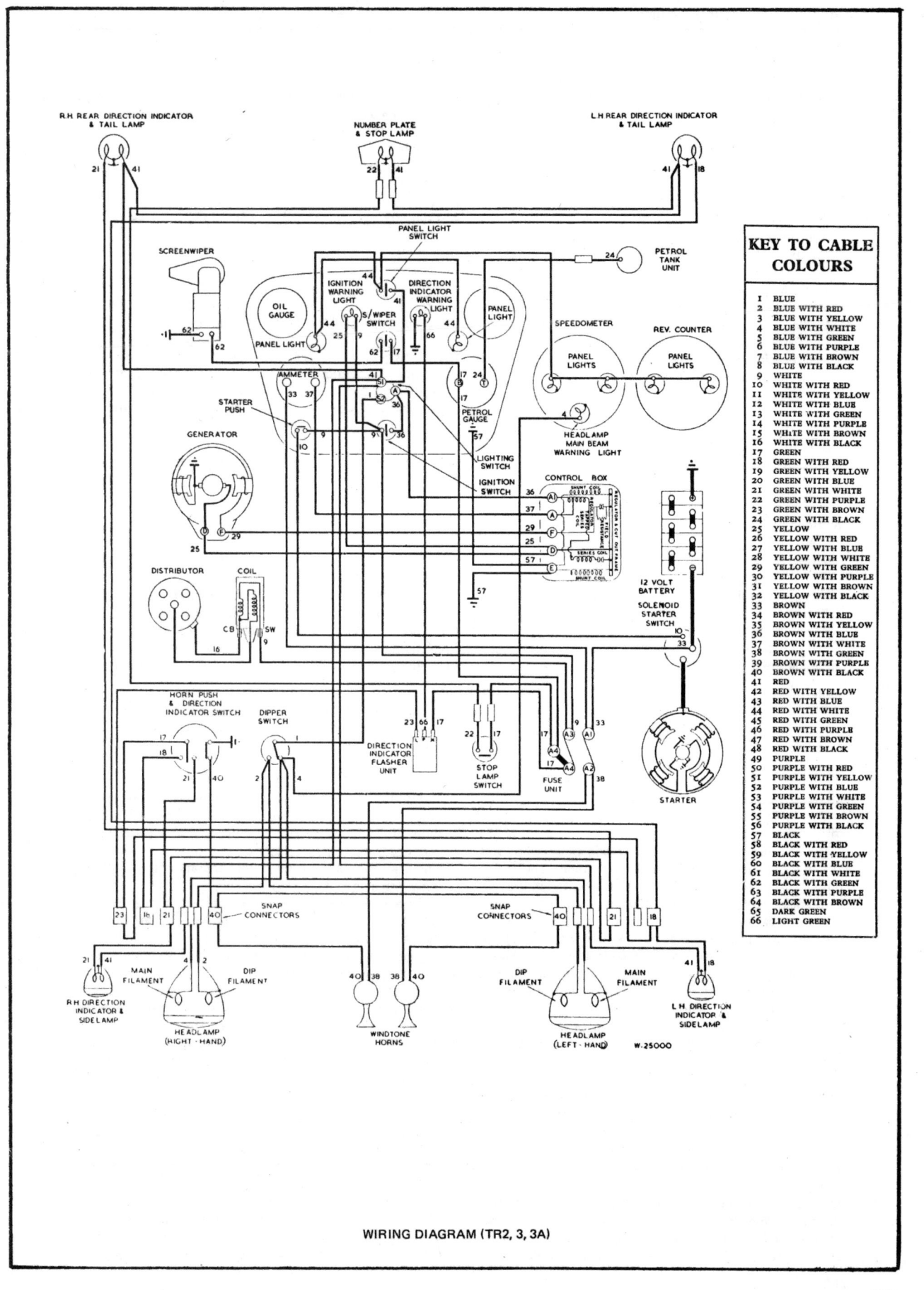

WIRING DIAGRAM (TR2, 3, 3A)

	KEY TO CABLE COLOURS
1	BLUE
2	BLUE WITH RED
3	BLUE WITH YELLOW
4	BLUE WITH WHITE
5	BLUE WITH GREEN
6	BLUE WITH PURPLE
7	BLUE WITH BROWN
8	BLUE WITH BLACK
9	WHITE
10	WHITE WITH RED
11	WHITE WITH YELLOW
12	WHITE WITH BLUE
13	WHITE WITH GREEN
14	WHITE WITH PURPLE
15	WHITE WITH BROWN
16	WHITE WITH BLACK
17	GREEN
18	GREEN WITH RED
19	GREEN WITH YELLOW
20	GREEN WITH BLUE
21	GREEN WITH WHITE
22	GREEN WITH PURPLE
23	GREEN WITH BROWN
24	GREEN WITH BLACK
25	YELLOW
26	YELLOW WITH RED
27	YELLOW WITH BLUE
28	YELLOW WITH WHITE
29	YELLOW WITH GREEN
30	YELLOW WITH PURPLE
31	YELLOW WITH BROWN
32	YELLOW WITH BLACK
33	BROWN
34	BROWN WITH RED
35	BROWN WITH YELLOW
36	BROWN WITH BLUE
37	BROWN WITH WHITE
38	BROWN WITH GREEN
39	BROWN WITH PURPLE
40	BROWN WITH BLACK
41	RED
42	RED WITH YELLOW
43	RED WITH BLUE
44	RED WITH WHITE
45	RED WITH GREEN
46	RED WITH PURPLE
47	RED WITH BROWN
48	RED WITH BLACK
49	PURPLE
50	PURPLE WITH RED
51	PURPLE WITH YELLOW
52	PURPLE WITH BLUE
53	PURPLE WITH WHITE
54	PURPLE WITH GREEN
55	PURPLE WITH BROWN
56	PURPLE WITH BLACK
57	BLACK
58	BLACK WITH RED
59	BLACK WITH YELLOW
60	BLACK WITH BLUE
61	BLACK WITH WHITE
62	BLACK WITH GREEN
63	BLACK WITH PURPLE
64	BLACK WITH BROWN
65	DARK GREEN
66	LIGHT GREEN

Chapter 10/Electrical System

	TR2, 3, 3A	TR4, 4A
Starter Motor		
Type	Lucas four pole, four bush, series wound, 12 volt	Lucas four pole, four bush, series wound, 12 volt
Model	M418G	M418G
Minimum brush length	5/16 inch	5/16 inch
Brush spring tension	30 to 40 ounces	30 to 40 ounces
Lock torque	17 ft/lb.	17 ft/lb.
Lock voltage	7.4 to 7	7.4 to 7
Lock current draw	440 to 460 amperes	440 to 460 amperes
Number of teeth on ring gear	90	90
Number of teeth on pinion	10	10
Control Box		
Make	Lucas	Lucas
Model	RB106/1: Later cars RB106/2	RB106/2
Regulator settings:		
Open circuit 68ºF and 1500 generator r.p.m.	15.6 to 16.2 v.	16.0 to 16.6 v.
Temperature variation allowance	Each 18ºF above 68ºF subtract .3 volt	Each 18ºF above 68ºF subtract .3 volt
	Each 18ºF below 68ºF add .3 volt	Each 18ºF below 68ºF add .3 volt
Cut-out:		
Cut-in voltage	12.7 to 13.3 v.	12.7 to 13 v.
Drop-off voltage	8.5 to 10.0	11 to 8.5
Reverse current	3.5 to 5 amperes	—
Windscreen Wiper Motor		
Make	Lucas	Lucas
Model	CRT15	DR3A
Current consumption	2 to 3.5	2 to 3.5
Drive to wheelboxes	Rack and pinion	Rack and pinion
Armature end float	.008 to .012 inch	.008 to .012 inch
Armature resistance	.29 to .352 ohms	.29 to .352 ohms
Field resistance	8 to 9.5 ohms	8 to 9.5 ohms
Wiping speed	44 to 48 cycles per minute	44 to 48 cycles per minute
Horns		
Type	Lucas WT614 or WT618	Lucas 9H
Maximum current consumption	WT614: 6½ amps per horn WT618: 8 amps per horn	3½ amps per horn

1. General Description

The electrical system fitted to all models covered by this manual is of the conventional 12 volt type. The major components consist of: a 12 volt battery located in the rear of the engine compartment with its positive terminal earthed, a control box, cut-out and fuse unit, a dynamo which is fitted to the engine and driven by a 'V' belt from the engine crankshaft, and a starter motor which is fitted and forward of the gearbox bellhousing. The ignition system is also part of the electrical system but because of its importance and complexity is covered separately in Chapter 4.

Included in this Chapter are the electrical system wiring diagrams to assist the owner driver to trace and correct some of the simpler electrical faults.

Cars produced for the U.K. market have headlamp units fitted with double filament, pre-focus, dipping bulbs fitted to the rear of reflectors that are sealed to the headlamp glass.

There is a good supply of instruments to assist the driver in the operation of the car. A petrol gauge is connected to a fuel tank sender unit and the gauge operates by measuring the varying resistance of a rheostat in the tank unit as the fuel level rises and falls. An ammeter is also fitted and it indicates the rate of flow of current from or to the battery. It does not however indicate the flow of current to the starter motor or horns. Besides showing if the battery charging circuit is in good working order it will also show the correct operation of other circuits such as the side and headlamps, brake lights or electrical accessories and, when switched on or brought into operation, the needle will show a change in its original reading.

Two fuses are to be found protecting the electrical system on the TR2, 3, and 3A models and these protect the horns and all other circuits operated by switching on the ignition system switch. The ignition system itself is not protected by one of these fuses.

On the later models a third fuse is fitted and besides protecting all the previously mentioned circuits also protects the side, tail and number plate lights.

Full specifications of the electrical system to be found on the models covered by this Chapter and servicing details of the major electrical items are to be found elsewhere in this Chapter.

2. Battery - Removal and Replacement

1. The earthed battery terminal should always be removed first. Therefore, on later negative earth cars, remove the negative lead before the positive and replace the negative lead last. On positive earth models disconnect the positive and then the negative leads from the battery terminals by

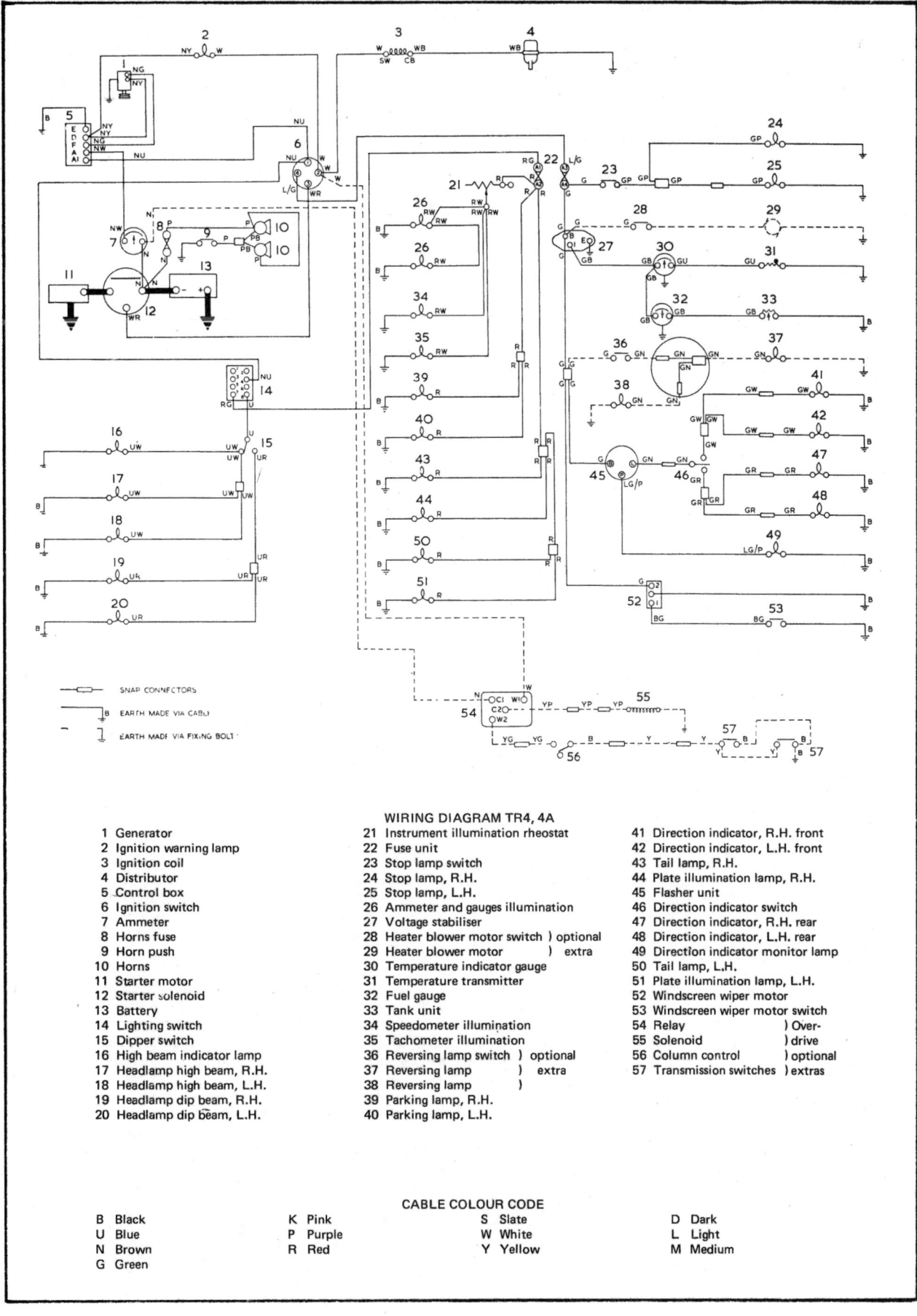

WIRING DIAGRAM TR4, 4A

1. Generator
2. Ignition warning lamp
3. Ignition coil
4. Distributor
5. Control box
6. Ignition switch
7. Ammeter
8. Horns fuse
9. Horn push
10. Horns
11. Starter motor
12. Starter solenoid
13. Battery
14. Lighting switch
15. Dipper switch
16. High beam indicator lamp
17. Headlamp high beam, R.H.
18. Headlamp high beam, L.H.
19. Headlamp dip beam, R.H.
20. Headlamp dip beam, L.H.
21. Instrument illumination rheostat
22. Fuse unit
23. Stop lamp switch
24. Stop lamp, R.H.
25. Stop lamp, L.H.
26. Ammeter and gauges illumination
27. Voltage stabiliser
28. Heater blower motor switch) optional
29. Heater blower motor   ) extra
30. Temperature indicator gauge
31. Temperature transmitter
32. Fuel gauge
33. Tank unit
34. Speedometer illumination
35. Tachometer illumination
36. Reversing lamp switch) optional
37. Reversing lamp   ) extra
38. Reversing lamp   )
39. Parking lamp, R.H.
40. Parking lamp, L.H.
41. Direction indicator, R.H. front
42. Direction indicator, L.H. front
43. Tail lamp, R.H.
44. Plate illumination lamp, R.H.
45. Flasher unit
46. Direction indicator switch
47. Direction indicator, R.H. rear
48. Direction indicator, L.H. rear
49. Direction indicator monitor lamp
50. Tail lamp, L.H.
51. Plate illumination lamp, L.H.
52. Windscreen wiper motor
53. Windscreen wiper motor switch
54. Relay   ) Over-
55. Solenoid   ) drive
56. Column control   ) optional
57. Transmission switches) extras

CABLE COLOUR CODE

B	Black	K	Pink	S	Slate	D	Dark
U	Blue	P	Purple	W	White	L	Light
N	Brown	R	Red	Y	Yellow	M	Medium
G	Green						

Chapter 10/Electrical System

slackening the retaining nuts and bolts, or by unscrewing the retaining screws, if these are fitted.

2. Remove the battery clamp and carefully lift the battery out of its compartment. Hold the battery vertical to ensure that none of the electrolyte is spilled.

3. Replacement is a direct reversal of this procedure. NOTE: Replace the negative lead before the earth (positive) lead and smear the terminals with petroleum jelly (vaseline) to prevent corrosion. NEVER use an ordinary grease as applied to other parts of the car.

3. Battery - Maintenance and Inspection

1. Normal weekly battery maintenance consists of checking the electrolyte level of each cell to ensure that the separators are covered by ¼ inch of electrolyte. If the level has fallen top up the battery using distilled water only. Do not overfill. If a battery is overfilled or any electrolyte spilled, immediately wipe away the excess as electrolyte attacks and corrodes any metal it comes into contact with very rapidly.

2. As well as keeping the terminals clean and covered with petroleum jelly, the top of the battery, and especially the top of the cells, should be kept clean and dry. This helps to prevent corrosion and ensures that the battery does not become partially discharged by leakage through dampness and dirt.

3. Once every three months remove the battery and inspect the battery securing bolts, the battery clamp plate, tray, and battery leads for corrosion (white fluffy deposits on the metal which are brittle to touch). If any corrosion is found, clean off the deposits with ammonia and paint over the clean metal with an anti-rust/anti-acid paint.

4. At the same time inspect the battery case for cracks. If a crack is found, clean and plug it with one of the proprietary compounds marketed by firms such as Holts for this purpose. If leakage through the crack has been excessive it will be necessary to refill the appropriate cell with fresh electrolyte as detailed later. Cracks are frequently caused to the top of a battery case by pouring in distilled water in the middle of winter **after** instead of **before** a run. This gives the water no chance to mix with the electrolyte and so the former freezes and splits the battery case.

5. If topping up the battery becomes excessive and the case has been inspected for cracks that could cause leakage, but none are found, the battery is being overcharged and the voltage regulator will have to be checked and reset.

6. With the battery on the bench, at the three monthly interval check, measure its specific gravity with a hydrometer to determine the state of the charge and condition of the electrolyte. There should be very little variation between the different cells and, if a variation in excess of 0.025 is present, it will be due to either:-

a) Loss of electrolyte from the battery at some time caused by spillage or a leak resulting in a drop in the specific gravity of the electrolyte, when the deficiency was replaced with distilled water instead of fresh electrolyte.

b) An internal short circuit caused by a buckled plate or a similar malady pointing to the likelihood of total battery failure in the near future.

7. The specific gravity of the electrolyte for fully charged conditions at the electrolyte temperature indicated is listed in Table A. The specific gravity of a fully discharged battery at different temperatures of the electrolyte is given in Table B.

8. Specific gravity is measured by drawing up into the body of a hydrometer sufficient electrolyte to allow the indicator to float freely (see Fig. 10.1). The level at which the indicator floats indicates the specific gravity.

Table A

Specific Gravity - Battery Fully Charged

1.268 at 100°F or 38°C electrolyte temperature
1.272 at 90°F or 32°C   "   "
1.276 at 80°F or 27°C   "   "
1.280 at 70°F or 21°C   "   "
1.284 at 60°F or 16°C   "   "
1.288 at 50°F or 10°C   "   "
1.292 at 40°F or 4°C   "   "
1.296 at 30°F or -1.5°C   "   "

Table B

Specific Gravity - Battery Fully Discharged

1.098 at 100°F or 38°C electrolyte temperature
1.102 at 90°F or 32°C   "   "
1.106 at 80°F or 27°C   "   "
1.110 at 70°F or 21°C   "   "
1.114 at 60°F or 16°C   "   "
1.118 at 50°F or 10°C   "   "
1.122 at 40°F or 4°C   "   "
1.126 at 30°F or -1.5°C   "   "

4. Electrolyte Replenishment

1. If the battery is in a fully charged state and one of the cells maintains a specific gravity reading which is 0.025 or more lower than the others, and a check of each cell has been made with a voltage meter to check for short circuits (a four to seven second test should give a steady reading of between 1.2 to 1.8 volts), then it is likely that electrolyte has been lost from the cell with the low reading at some time.

2. Top the cell up with a solution of 1 part sulphuric acid to 2.5 parts of water. If the cell is already fully topped up draw some electrolyte out of it with a pipette. The total capacity of each cell is ¾ pint.

3. When mixing the sulphuric acid and water NEVER ADD WATER TO SULPHURIC ACID - always pour the acid slowly onto the water in a glass container. IF WATER IS ADDED TO SULPHURIC ACID IT WILL EXPLODE.

4. Continue to top up the cell with the freshly made electrolyte and then recharge the battery and check the hydrometer readings.

5. Battery - Charging

1. In winter time when heavy demand is placed upon the battery, such as when starting from cold, and much electrical equipment is continually in use, it is a good idea to occasionally have the battery fully charged from an external source at the rate of 3.5 to 4 amps.

2. Continue to charge the battery at this rate until no further rise in specific gravity is noted over a four hour period.

3. Alternatively, a trickle charger charging at the rate of 1.5 amps can be safely used overnight.

4. Specially rapid 'boost' charges, which are claimed to restore the power of the battery in 1 to 2 hours, are most dangerous as they can cause serious damage to the battery plates through overheating.

5. While charging the battery note that the temperature

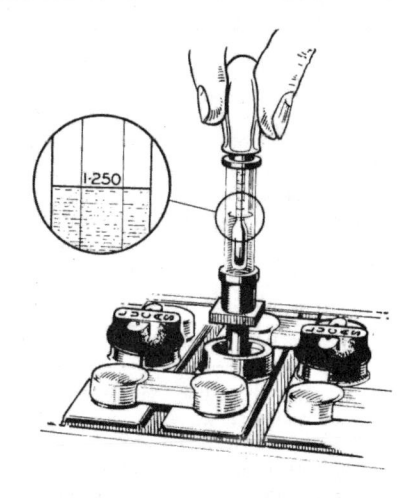

Fig. 10.1. Measuring specific gravity

Fig. 10.2. Generator Mountings

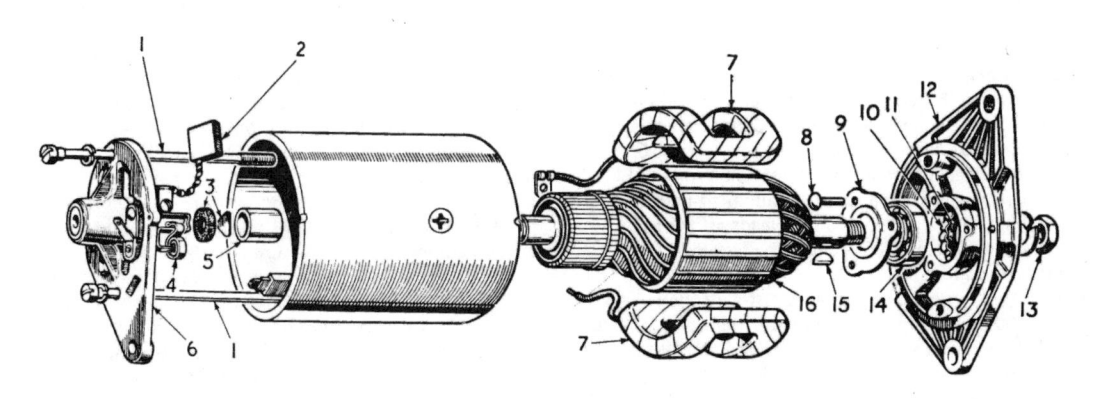

Fig. 10.3. EXPLODED VIEW OF DYNAMO (C40–1)
1 Bolts
2 Brush
3 Felt ring and aluminium sealing disc
4 Brush spring
5 Bearing bush
6 Commutator end bracket
7 Field coils
8 Rivet
9 Bearing retainer plate
10 Corrugated washer
11 Felt washer
12 Driving end bracket
13 Pulley retainer nut
14 Bearing
15 Woodruff key
16 Armature

211

Chapter 10/Electrical System

of the electrolyte should never exceed 100°F.

6. Dynamo - Routine Maintenance

1. Routine maintenance consists of checking the tension of the fan belt, and lubricating the dynamo rear bearing once every 12,000 miles.
2. The fan belt should be tight enough to ensure no slip between the belt and the dynamo pulley. If a shrieking noise comes from the engine when the unit is accelerated rapidly, it is likely that it is the fan belt slipping. On the other hand, the belt must not be too taut or the bearings will wear rapidly and cause dynamo failure or bearing seizure. Ideally ½ inch of total free movement should be available at the fan belt midway between the fan and the dynamo pulley.
3. To adjust the fan belt tension slightly slacken the three dynamo retaining bolts and swing the dynamo on the upper two bolts outwards to increase the tension, and inwards to lower it.
4. It is best to leave the bolts fairly tight so that considerable effort has to be used to move the dynamo, otherwise it is difficult to get the correct setting. If the dynamo is being moved outwards to increase the tension and the bolts have only been slackened a little, a long spanner acting as a lever placed behind the dynamo with the lower end resting against the block works very well in moving the dynamo outwards. Retighten the dynamo bolts and check that the dynamo pulley is correctly aligned with the fan belt.
5. Lubrication of the dynamo consists of inserting three drops of S.A.E. 30 engine oil in the small oil hole in the centre of the commutator end bracket. This lubricates the rear bearing. The front bearing is pre-packed with grease and requires no attention.

7. Dynamo - Testing in Position

1. If, with the engine running, no charge comes from the dynamo, or the charge is very low, first check that the fan belt is in place and is not slipping. Then check that the leads from the control box to the dynamo are firmly attached and that one has not come loose from its terminal.
2. The lead from the larger 'D' terminal on the dynamo should be connected to the 'D' terminal on the control box and similarly the 'F' terminals on the dynamo and control box should also be connected together. Check that this is so and that the leads have not been incorrectly fitted. Ensure that a good connection exists to control box terminal 'E'.
3. Make sure none of the electrical equipment (such as the lights or radio) is on and then pull the leads off the dynamo terminals marked 'D' and 'F' and join the terminals together with a short length of wire.
4. Attach to the centre of the length of wire the negative clip of a 0-20 volts voltmeter and run the other clip to earth on the dynamo yoke. Start the engine and allow it to idle at approximately 750 r.p.m. At this speed the dynamo should give a reading of about 15 volts on the voltmeter. There is no point in raising the engine speed above a fast idle as the reading will then be inaccurate.
5. If no reading is recorded then check the brushes and brush connection. If a very low reading of approximately 1 volt is observed then the field winding may be suspect.
6. If a reading of between 4 to 6 volts is recorded it is likely that the armature winding is at fault.
7. If the voltmeter shows a good reading then, with the temporary link still in position, connect both leads from the control box to 'D' and 'F' on the dynamo ('D' to 'D' and 'F' to 'F'). Release the lead from the 'D' terminal at the control box end and clip one lead from the voltmeter to the end of the cable, and the other lead to a good earth. With the engine running at the same speed as previously, an identical voltage to that recorded at the dynamo should be noted on the voltmeter. If no voltage is recorded then there is a break in the wire. If the voltage is the same as recorded at the dynamo then check the 'F' lead in similar fashion. If both readings are the same as at the dynamo then it will be necessary to test the control box.

8. Dynamo - Removal and Replacement

1. Slacken the two dynamo retaining bolts, and the nut on the sliding link, and move the dynamo in towards the engine so that the fan belt can be removed.
2. Disconnect the two leads from the dynamo terminals.
3. Remove the nut from the sliding link bolt and remove the two upper bolts. The dynamo is then free to be lifted away from the engine.
4. Replacement is a reversal of the above procedure. Do not finally tighten the retaining bolt and the nut on the sliding link until the fan belt has been tensioned correctly. See Fig. 10.2 for details of the mountings.

9. Dynamo - Dismantling and Inspection

1. As will be seen from the dynamo specifications two types were fitted. They are both basically identical with the exception on the later dynamo on which the yoke was of windowless design and the two end brackets had larger openings. Mount the dynamo in a vice and unscrew and remove the two through bolts from the commutator end bracket (see photo).
2. Mark the commutator end bracket and the dynamo casing so the end bracket can be replaced in its original position. Pull the end bracket off the armature shaft. NOTE: Some versions of the dynamo may have a raised pip on the end bracket which locates in a recess on the edge of the casing. If so, marking the end bracket and casing is not necessary. A pip may also be found on the drive end bracket at the opposite end of the casing (see photo).
3. Lift the two brush springs and draw the brushes out of the brush holders (arrowed).
4. Measure the brushes and, if worn down to 9/32 inch or less, unscrew the screws holding the brush leads to the end bracket. Take off the brushes complete with leads. Old and new brushes are compared in the photographs.
5. If no locating pip can be found, mark the drive end bracket and the dynamo casing so the drive end bracket can be replaced in its original position. Then pull the drive end bracket complete with armature out of the casing.
6. Check the condition of the ball bearing in the drive end plate by firmly holding the plate and noting if there is visible side movement of the armature shaft in relation to the end plate. If play is present the armature assembly must be separated from the end plate. If the bearing is sound there is no need to carry out the work described in the following two paragraphs.
7. Hold the armature in one hand (mount it carefully in a vice if preferred) and undo the nut holding the pulley wheel and fan in place. Pull off the pulley wheel and fan.
8. Next remove the Woodruff key (arrowed) from its slot in the armature shaft and also the bearing locating ring.
9. Place the drive end bracket across the open jaws of a vice with the armature downwards and gently tap the armature shaft from the bearing in the end plate with the aid of a suitable drift.
10 Carefully inspect the armature and check it for open or

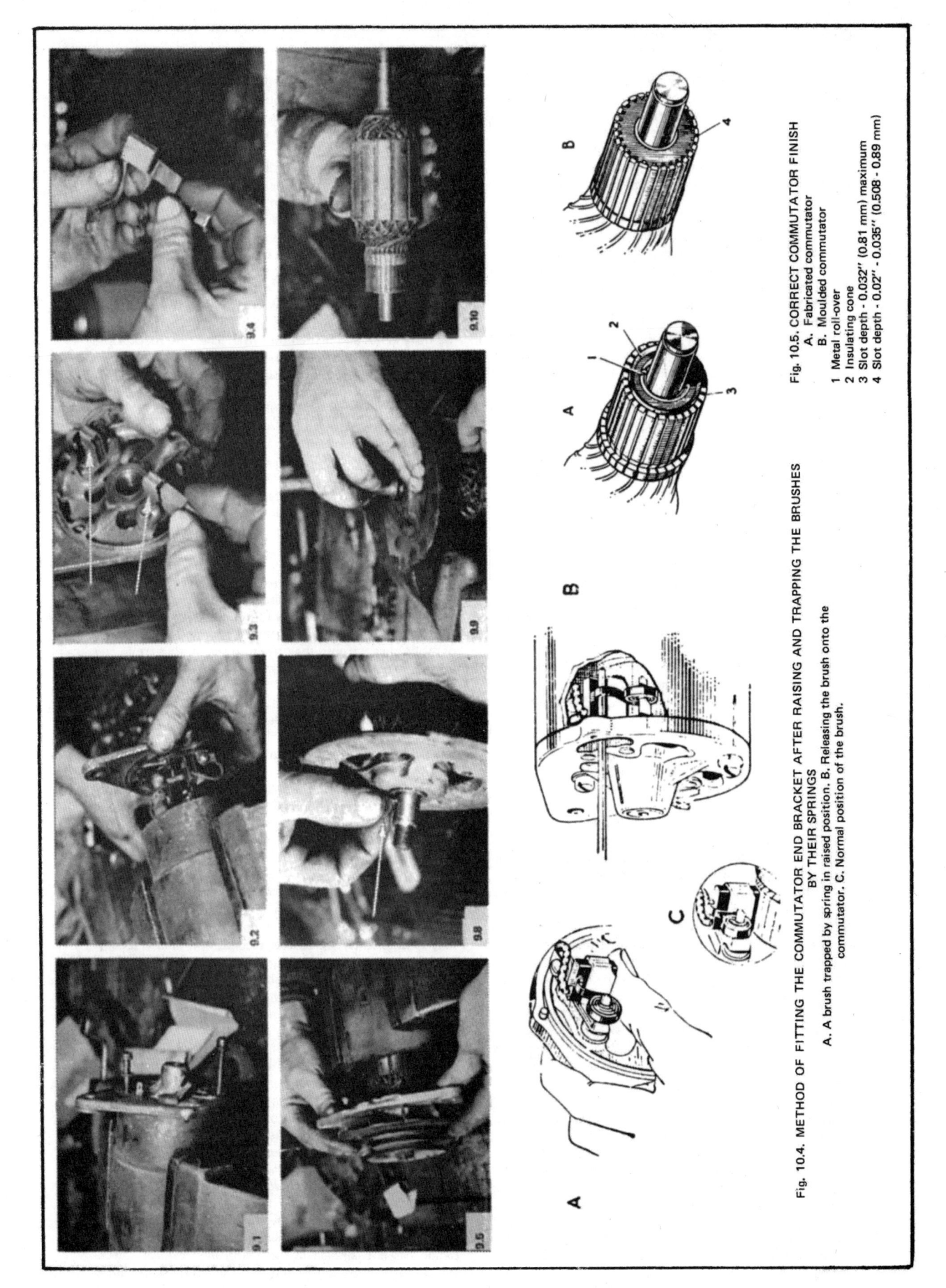

Fig. 10.4. METHOD OF FITTING THE COMMUTATOR END BRACKET AFTER RAISING AND TRAPPING THE BRUSHES BY THEIR SPRINGS
A. A brush trapped by spring in raised position. B. Releasing the brush onto the commutator. C. Normal position of the brush.

Fig. 10.5. CORRECT COMMUTATOR FINISH
A. Fabricated commutator
B. Moulded commutator
1 Metal roll-over
2 Insulating cone
3 Slot depth - 0.032'' (0.81 mm) maximum
4 Slot depth - 0.02'' - 0.035'' (0.508 - 0.89 mm)

213

Chapter 10/Electrical System

short circuited windings. It is a good indication of an open circuited armature when the commutator segments are burnt. If the armature has short circuited the commutator segments will be very badly burnt, and the overheated armature windings badly burnt, and the overheated armature windings badly discoloured. If open or short circuits are suspected then test by substituting the suspect armature for a new one.

11 Check the resistance of the field coils. To do this, connect an ohmmeter between the field terminals and the yoke and note the reading which should be about 6 ohms. If the ohmmeter reading is infinity this indicates an open circuit in the field winding. If the reading is below 5 ohms this indicates that one of the field coils is faulty and must be replaced.

12 Field coil replacement involves the use of a wheel operated screwdriver, a soldering iron, caulking and riveting and this operation is considered to be beyond the scope of most owners. Therefore, if the field coils are at fault, either purchase a rebuilt dynamo, or take the casing to a Triumph dealer or electrical engineering works for new field coils to be fitted.

13 Next check the condition of the commutator (arrowed). If it is dirty and blackened as shown, clean it with a petrol dampened rag. If the commutator is in good condition the surface will be smooth and quite free from pits or burnt areas, and the insulated segments clearly defined.

14 If, after the commutator has been cleaned, pits and burnt spots are still present, wrap a strip of glass paper round the commutator, taking great care to move the commutator ¼ of a turn every ten rubs till it is thoroughly clean.

15 In extreme cases of wear the commutator can be mounted in a lathe and, with the lathe turning at high speed, a very fine cut may be taken off the commutator. If the commutator has worn so that the insulators between the segments are level with the top of the segments, then undercut the insulators to a depth of 1/32 inch (.8 mm). The best tool to use for this purpose is half a hacksaw blade ground to a thickness of the insulator and the handle end of the blade covered in insulating tape to make it comfortable to hold. This is the sort of finish the surface of the commutator should have when finished (see photo).

16 Check the bush bearing (arrowed) in the commutator end bracket for wear by noting if the armature spindle rocks when placed in it. If worn it must be renewed.

17 The bush bearing can be removed by a suitable extractor or by screwing a 5/8 inch tap four or five times into the bush. The tap complete with bush is then pulled out of the end bracket.

18 NOTE: Before fitting a new bush bearing that it is of the porous bronze type and it is essential that it is allowed to stand in S.A.E. 30 engine oil for at least 24 hours before fitment. In an emergency the bush can be immersed in hot oil (100°C) for 2 hours.

19 Carefully fit the new bush into the end plate, pressing it in until the end of the bearing is flush with the inner side of the endplate. If available press the bush in with a smooth shouldered mandrel the same diameter as the armature shaft.

10. Dynamo - Repair and Reassembly

1. To renew the ball bearing fitted to the drive end bracket drill out the rivets, which hold the bearing retainer plate to the end bracket, and lift off the plate.
2. Press out the bearing from the end bracket and remove the corrugated and felt washers from the bearing housing.
3. Thoroughly clean the bearing housing, and the new bearing and pack with high melting point grease.
4. Place the felt washer and corrugated washer in that order in the end bracket bearing housing.
5. Then fit the new bearing as shown.
6. Gently tap the bearing into place with the aid of a suitable drift.
7. Replace the bearing plate and fit three new rivets.
8. Open up the rivets with the aid of a suitable cold chisel.
9. Finally peen over the open end of the rivets with the aid of a ball hammer as illustrated.
10 Refit the drive end bracket to the armature shaft. Do not try and force the bracket on but, with the aid of a suitable socket abutting the bearing, tap the bearing in gently so pulling the end bracket down with it.
11 Slide the spacer up the shaft and refit the Woodruff key.
12 Replace the fan and pulley wheel and then fit the spring washer and nut and tighten the latter. The drive bracket end of the dynamo is now fully assembled as shown.
13 If the brushes are little worn and are to be used again then ensure that they are placed in the same holders from which they were removed. When refitting brushes, either new or old, check that they move freely in their holders. If either brush sticks clean with a petrol moistened rag and, if still stiff, lightly polish the sides of the brush with a very fine file until the brush moves quite freely in its holder.
14 Tighten the two retaining screws and washers which hold the wire leads to the brushes in place.
15 It is far easier to slip the end piece with brushes over the commutator if the brushes are raised in their holders as shown and held in this position by the pressure of the springs resting against their flanks (arrowed).
16 Refit the armature to the casing and then the commutator end plate and screw up the two through bolts.
17 Finally, hook the ends of the two springs off the flanks of the brushes and onto their heads so the brushes are forced down into contact with the armature.

11. Starter Motor - General Description

The starter motor is mounted on the right hand lower side of the engine backplate and is held in position by two bolts which also clamp the bellhousing flange. The motor is of the four field coil, four pole piece type and utilizes four spring loaded commutator bushes. Two of these bushes are earthed, and the other two are insulated and attached to the field coil ends.

Starter Motor - Testing in Engine

1. If the starter motor fails to operate then check the condition of the battery by turning on the headlamps. If they glow brightly for several seconds and then gradually dim, the battery is in an uncharged condition.
2. If the headlamps glow brightly and it is obvious that the battery is in good condition then check the tightness of the battery wiring connections (and in particular the earth lead from the battery terminal to its connection on the body frame). Check the tightness of the connections at the relay switch and at the starter motor. Check the wiring with a voltmeter for breaks or shorts.
3. If the wiring is in order then check that the starter motor switch is operating. To do this press the rubber button in the centre of the relay switch under the bonnet. If it is working the starter motor will be heard to 'click' as it tries to rotate. Alternatively check it with a voltmeter.
4. If the battery is fully charged, the wiring in order, and the switch working and the starter motor fails to operate then it will have to be removed from the car for examination. Before this is done, however, ensure that the starter pinion has not jammed in mesh with the flywheel. Check this by turning the square end of the armature shaft with a

9.13

9.14

9.15

9.16

10.4

10.5

10.6

10.7

10.8

10.9

10.10

10.11

10.12

10.14

10.15

215

Chapter 10/Electrical System

spanner. This will free the pinion if it is stuck in engagement with the flywheel teeth.

12. Starter Motor - Removal and Replacement

1. Disconnect the battery earth terminal for safety reasons.
2. Disconnect the starter motor cable from the terminal on the starter motor endplate.
3. Unscrew and remove the two bolts that hold the starter motor to the engine backplate and the flywheel housing flange.
4. Lift the starter motor out of engagement with the teeth on the flywheel ring gear and remove the engine from the engine compartment.
5. Refitting is a straightforward reversal of the removal procedure.

13. Starter Motor and Drive Gear - Dismantling and Reassembly (TR2, 3, 3A)

1. With the starter motor on the bench, loosen the screw on the cover band and slip the cover band off.
2. With a piece of wire bent into the shape of a hook, lift back each of the brush springs in turn and check the movement of the brushes in their holders by pulling on the flexible connectors.
3. If the brushes are so worn that their faces do not rest against the commutator or if the ends of the brush heads are exposed on their working face, they must be renewed.
4. If any of the brushes tend to stick in their holders then wash them with a petrol moistened cloth and, if necessary, lightly polish the sides of the brushes with a very fine file until the brushes move quite freely in their holders.
5. If the surface of the commutator is dirty or blackened clean it with a petrol moistened rag. Secure the starter motor in a vice and check it by connecting a heavy gauge cable between the starter motor terminal and a 12 volt battery.
6. Connect the cable from the other battery terminal to earth on the starter motor body. If the motor turns at high speed it is in good order.
7. If the starter motor still fails to function or if it is wished to renew the brushes, then it is necessary to further dismantle the motor.
8. Start by lifting the brush spring, with the aid of a wire hook, and then take off the brushes from their holders one at a time.
9. Undo the terminal nuts from the field coil terminal post which protrudes through the commutator end bracket.
10. Unscrew and remove the two through bolts and spring washers.
11. The commutator end bracket, the drive end bracket and the armature can now be separated.
12. At this stage, if the brushes are to be renewed, the flexible connectors must be unsoldered and the connectors of new brushes soldered in their place. Check that the new brushes move freely in their holders as detailed in paragraph 4. If cleaning the commutator with petrol fails to remove all burnt areas and spots then wrap a piece of glass paper round the commutator and rotate the armature.
13. If the commutator is very badly worn, remove the drive assembly as detailed later in this Section and mount the armature in a lathe. With the lathe turning at high speed, take a very fine cut out of the commutator and finish the surface by polishing with glass paper. DO NOT UNDERCUT THE MICA INSULATORS BETWEEN THE COMMUTATOR SEGMENTS.
14. With the starter motor dismantled, test the four field coils for an open circuit. Connect a 12 volt battery with a 12 volt bulb in one of the leads between the field terminal post and the topping point of the field coils to which the brushes are connected. An open circuit is proved by the bulb not lighting.
15. If the bulb lights it does not necessarily mean that the field coils are in order, as there is a possibility that one of the coils will be earthing to the starter yoke or pole shoes. To check this, remove the lead from the brush connector and place it against a clean portion of the starter yoke. If the bulb lights the field coils are earthing.
16. Replacement of the field coils calls for the use of a wheel operated screwdriver, a soldering iron, caulking and riveting operations and is considered to be beyond the majority of owners. The starter yoke should be taken to a reputable electrical engineering works for new field coils to be fitted. Alternatively, purchase an exchange Lucas starter motor.
17. If the armature is damaged this will be evident after visual inspection. Look for signs of burning, discoloration and for conductors that have been lifted away from the commutator. Ensure that if any parts of the drive gear are worn or damaged they are renewed.
18. Fig. 10.7 shows the component parts of the starter motor drive and it will be seen that there is a rubber torsion member (N) incorporated into the drive. This member is designed to take up the shock of drive engagement with the starter ring gear on the flywheel. Friction washers (M) are also fitted so that in extreme conditions the drive is able to slip so preventing overloading of the starter motor causing damage to the drive assembly or the electrical parts.
19. To dismantle the drive assembly first remove the locating ring cover (A) and lift away the locating ring (B) from the end of the starter armature shaft.
20. Next remove the retaining ring (C) using a screwdriver and remove the pinion and barrel assembly (D).
21. If a peg (E) is fitted this should be removed using a small parallel pin punch. Alternatively the nuts (F) are caulked to the thread and do not require the use of a peg to lock them. To remove the nuts hold the square end of the starter armature in a vice and unscrew the locating nut (F).
22. The friction washer (G) restraining spring (H) should be removed next and then slide the sleeve (J) and control nut (K) off the splined shaft.
23. Remove the coupling plate (L), the friction washer (M) and the rubber unit assembly (N).
24. Wash all parts except the rubber unit assembly (N) in petrol and wipe dry with a non fluffy rag. Inspect the parts for wear or signs of fracture and obtain new parts as required.
25. The front and rear end brackets are fitted with phosphor bronze bushes in which the armature revolves. If excessive side movement of the armature is evident they should be renewed.
26. To remove the old bushes use a stepped drift having a diameter equal to that of the armature shaft and drive out the old bushes. Soak the new bushes in oil for at least 24 hours or, as an alternative, place in oil at 100°C for at least two hours and allow to cool.
27. Refit the new bearings with the stepped drift bearing in mind that the bushes must not be reamed otherwise their self lubricating properties will be lost.
28. Reassembling the starter motor and drive assembly is the reverse sequence to removal. If the locating nut (F) was caulked over it will be necessary to fit a new nut. Do not lubricate the drive assembly as it will only pick up dust and cause the drive to stick.

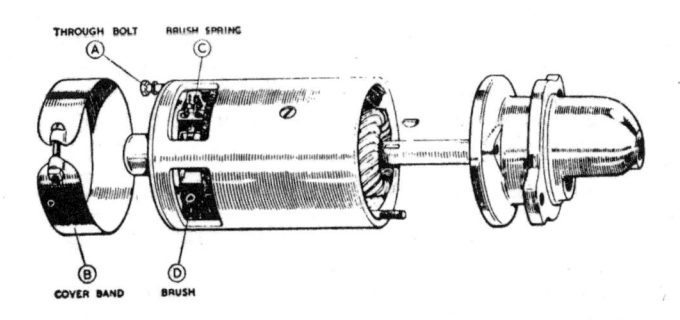

Fig. 10.6. Components of starter motor TR2, 3, 3A

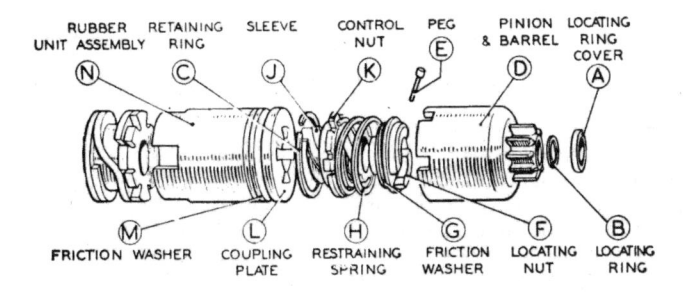

Fig. 10.7. Starter motor drive assembly TR2, 3, 3A

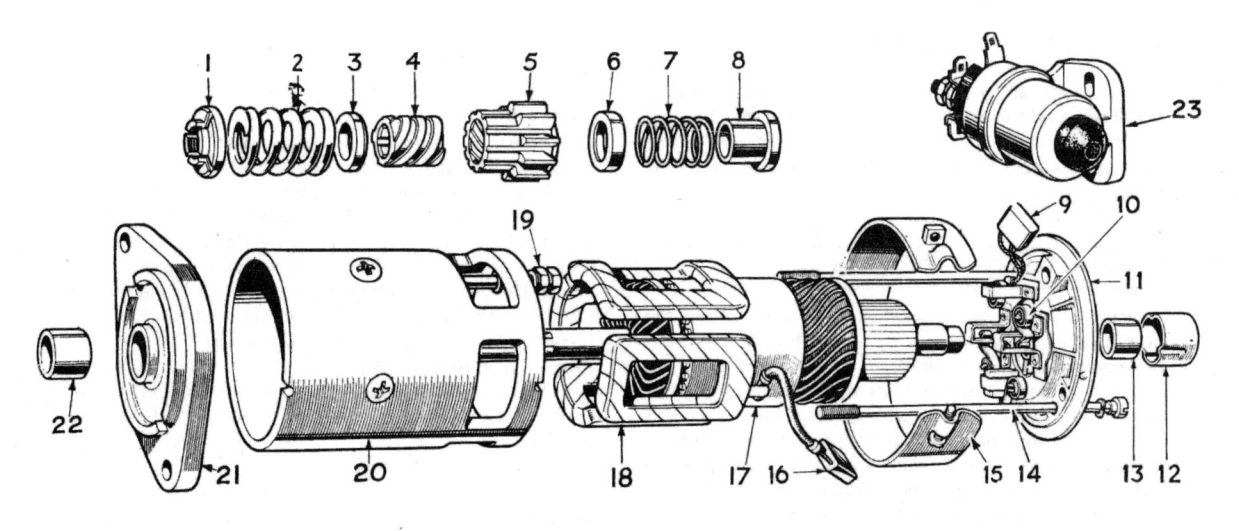

Fig. 10.8. EXPLODED VIEW OF STARTER MOTOR (TR4, 4A)

1 Starter drive nut
2 Starter drive spring
3 Thrust washer
4 Screwed sleeve
5 Pinion
6 Thrust washer
7 Spring
8 Collar
9 Brush
10 Brush spring
11 Commutator end bracket
12 Cover
13 Bush
14 Bolt
15 Brush cover
16 Brush
17 Field coil connection
18 Field coil
19 Terminal
20 Yoke
21 Drive end cover
22 Bush
23 Starter solenoid

Chapter 10/Electrical System

14. Starter Motor and Drive Gear - Dismantling and Reassembly (TR4, 4A)

The starter motor is basically identical to that as used for the TR2, 3, 3A models with the exception that the front end cover is flat and does not have a hood shielding part of the drive gear. This starter motor is shown in Fig. 10.8.

The starter motor drive has been modified to that of the simple inertia type as illustrated in Fig. 10.8. To dismantle the drive proceed as follows:-

1. Using a pair of pliers extract the split pin from the end of the armature shaft and undo the nut (1).
2. Slide off the spring (2), thrust washer (3), noting which way round it fits, screwed sleeve and pinion (4, 5), thrust washer (6), noting which way round it fits, spring (7) and the collar (8).
3. Unscrew the sleeve (4) from the pinion (5).
4. Wash all parts in petrol and dry using a non fluffy rag. Inspect for wear or signs of fracture and obtain new parts as required.
5. Reassembly of the starter motor drive is the reverse sequence to removal. Do not lubricate the drive assembly as it will only pick up dust and cause the drive to stick. Fit a new split pin to retain the nut (1).

15. Starter Motor Solenoid

The starter motor solenoid is shown in Fig. 10.8. It operates from the starter button or switch and comprises a solenoid which opens and closes heavy duty copper contacts so completing the circuit to the starter motor. To test a solenoid disconnect the heavy duty cable to the starter motor at the solenoid. Operate the starter motor switch or button whereupon a click should be heard from the solenoid. After a time the contacts in the solenoid will become burnt so creating a high resistance across the contacts rendering the switch inoperative. To test this situation reconnect the starter motor lead and, with the ignition switched off, bridge the two terminals at the rear of the solenoid and the starter motor should turn. Do not use a piece of thin wire but a pair of pliers is ideal for this test. As the solenoid is a sealed unit should the contacts become burnt or the solenoid itself fail a new unit must be obtained and fitted. It will be noted that most switches fitted to models covered by this manual have a rubber button at the rear of the solenoid to enable the engine to be started from under the bonnet.

16. Control Box - General Description

The control box comprises the voltage regulator and the cut-out. The voltage controls the output from the dynamo depending on the state of the battery and the demands of the electrical equipment and ensures that the battery is not overcharged. The cut-out is really an automatic switch and connects the dynamo to the battery when the dynamo is turning fast enough to produce a charge. Similarly it disconnects the battery from the dynamo when the engine is idling or stationary so that the battery does not discharge through the dynamo.

17. Cut-Out and Regulator Contacts - Maintenance

1. Every 12,000 miles check the cut-out and regulator contacts. If they are dirty or rough or burnt, place a piece of fine glass paper (DO NOT USE EMERY PAPER OR CARBORUNDUM PAPER) between the cut-out contacts, close them manually and draw the glass paper through several times.
2. Clean the regulator contacts in exactly the same way but use emery or carborundum paper and not glass paper. Carefully clean both sets of contacts from all traces of dust with a rag moistened in methylated spirits.

18. Voltage Regulator - Adjustment

1. If the battery is in sound condition, but is not holding its charge, or is being continually overcharged and the dynamo is in sound condition, then the voltage regulator in the control box must be adjusted.
2. Check the regulator setting by removing and joining together the cables from the control box terminals A1 and A. Then connect the negative lead of a 20 volt voltmeter to the 'D' terminal on the dynamo and the positive lead to a good earth. Start the engine and increase its speed until the voltmeter needle flicks and then steadies. This should occur at about 2,000 r.p.m. If the voltage at which the needle steadies is outside the limits listed below, then remove the control box cover and turn the adjusting screw (1) in Fig. 10.11, clockwise a quarter of a turn at a time to raise the setting and a similar amount, anti-clockwise, to lower it.

Air Temperature	Open Circuit Voltage
10ºC or 50ºF	16.1 to 16.7
20ºC or 68ºF	16.0 to 16.6
30ºC or 86ºF	15.9 to 16.5
40ºC or 104ºF	15.8 to 16.4

3. It is vital that the adjustments be completed within 30 seconds of starting the engine as otherwise the heat from the shunt coil will affect the readings.

19. Cut-Out - Adjustment

1. Check the voltage required to operate the cut-out by connecting a voltmeter between the control box terminals 'D' and 'E'.
2. Remove the control box cover, start the engine and gradually increase its speed until the cut out closes. This should occur when the reading is between 12.7 to 13.3 volts.
3. If the reading is outside these limits turn the cut-out adjusting screw (2) (Fig. 10.11) a fraction at a time clockwise to raise the voltage, and anti-clockwise to lower it. To adjust the drop off voltage bend the fixed contact blade carefully. The adjustment to the cut-out should be completed within 30 seconds to starting the engine as otherwise heat build up from the shunt coil will affect the readings.
4. If the cut-out fails to work, clean the contacts and, if there is still no response, renew the cut-out and regulator unit.

20. Fuses

TR2, 3, 3A

Two fuses are fitted into the electrical system and are situated next to the control box in a fuse holder. The fuse situated between the A1 and A2 terminals in the fuse box protects the horns. The second fuse, fitted between the A3 and A4 terminals, protects the circuits that are controlled by the ignition switch with the exception of the

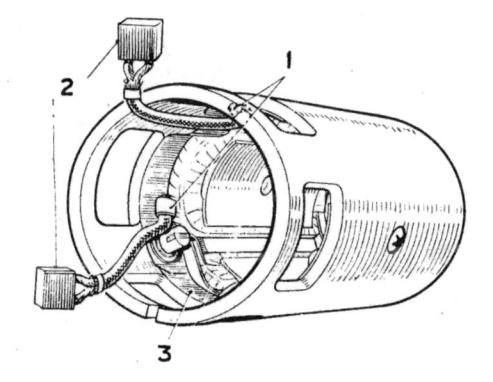

Fig. 10.9. STARTER MOTOR BRUSH CONNECTIONS
1 Field coil connections 3 Yoke
2 Brushes

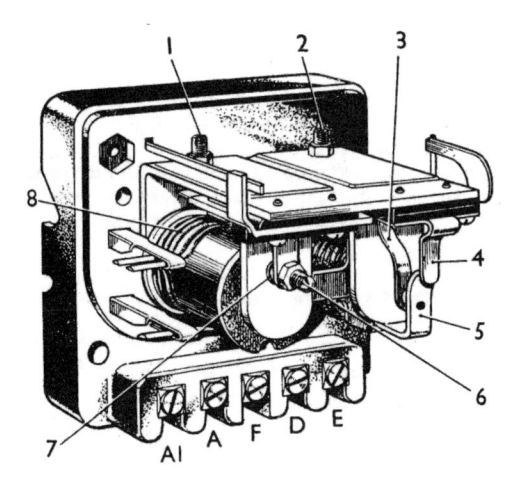

Fig.10.10. EARLY TYPE CONTROL BOX
1. Regulator adjusting screw
2. Cut-out adjusting screw
3. Fixed contact blade
4. Stop arm
5. Armature tongue & moving contact
6. Regulator moving contact
7. Fixed contact
8. Regulator series windings

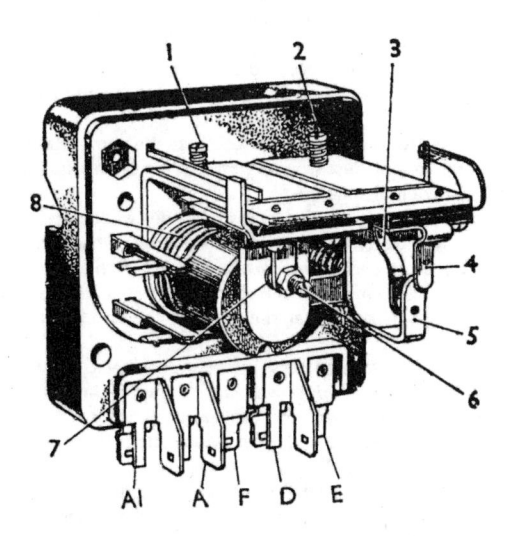

Fig.10.11. LATER TYPE CONTROL BOX (LUCAR TERMINALS)
1. Regulator adjusting screw
2. Cut-out adjusting screw
3. Fixed contact blade
4. Stop arm.
5. Armature tongue & moving contact
6. Regulator fixed contact screw
7. Regulator moving contact
8. Regulator series winding

Chapter 10/Electrical System

ignition circuit itself. If either of the two 25 amp fuses blow due to a short circuit or other similar trouble, trace and rectify the cause before renewing the fuse. Two spare fuses are held in the fuse box. If one of these spare fuses is used remember to fit a replacement at the earliest opportunity.

TR4, 4A

The fuse holder is situated next to the control box and contains two 25 amp fuses plus two spare fuses for replacement purposes. The left hand fuse protects the side and number plate lights and the right hand fuse protects the circuits that are controlled by the ignition switch with the exception of the ignition circuit itself. There is a third fuse in a line holder positioned below the fuse box. This has a rating of 35 amps and protects the horn circuit. To remove the old fuse simply hold one end of the tubular container. If any of the three fuses blow due to a short circuit or similar trouble trace and rectify the cause before renewing the fuse. Do not forget to replace any spare fuses used as soon as possible.

21. Flasher Circuit - Fault Tracing and Rectification

1. The actual flasher unit is enclosed in a small cylindrical metal container and is brought into operation by a switch on the steering column. A warning light is situated on the instrument panel to show when the direction indicators are working.
2. If the flasher unit fails to operate, or works very slowly or very rapidly, check out the flasher circuit as detailed below, before assuming there is a fault in the unit itself:-

a) Examine the direction indicator bulbs, front, and rear for broken filaments.
b) If the external flashers are working but the internal flasher warning light has ceased to function check the filament of the warning bulb and replace as necessary.
c) With the aid of the wiring diagram check all the flasher circuit connections if a flasher bulb is sound but does not work.
d) In the event of total direction indicator failure check the A3—A4 fuse.
e) With the ignition switched on check that current is reaching the flasher unit by connecting a voltmeter between the 'plus' or 'B' terminal and the 'L' terminal and operate the flasher switch. If the flasher bulbs light up the flasher unit itself is defective and must be replaced as it is not possible to dismantle and repair it.

22. Windscreen Wiper Mechanism - Maintenance

1. Renew the windscreen wiper blades at intervals of 12,000 miles, or more frequently if the screen is not efficiently cleared of water.
2. The cable which drives the wiper blades from the gearbox attached to the windscreen wiper motor is pre-packed with grease and requires no maintenance.
3. The washer round the wheelbox spindle can be lubricated with several drops of glycerine every 6,000 miles.

23. Windscreen Wiper Blades - Removal and Replacement

1. Lift the wiper arm away from the windscreen and remove the old blade by turning it towards the arm and then disengaging the arm from the slot in the blade.
2. To fit a new blade slide the end of the wiper arm into the slotted spring fastening in the centre of the blade. Push the blade firmly onto the arm until the raised portion of the arm is fully home in the hole in the blade.

24. Windscreen Wiper Arms - Removal and Replacement (TR2, 3, 3A)

1. Before removing a wiper arm turn the windscreen wiper switch to the fully off position, with the ignition switch on, to ensure that the arms are in their normal parked position parallel with the bottom of the windscreen.
2. To remove an arm pivot the arm and, using an open ended spanner, carefully slacken the collet nuts. Then continue to undo the collet nuts until the arm is free from the spindle.
3. When replacing an arm position it so that it is in the correct relative parked position and then tighten the collet nut securely.

25. Windscreen Wiper Arms - Removal and Replacement (TR4, 4A)

1. Before removing a wiper arm turn the windscreen wiper switch to the fully off position, with ignition switch on, to ensure that the arms are in their normal parked position parallel with the bottom of the windscreen.
2. To remove an arm pivot the arm and, using a screwdriver, ease back the clip in the hub of the arm. Pull the arm from the splines on the drive spindle.
3. When replacing an arm position it so it is in the correct relative parked position and then press the arm head onto the splined drive till the retaining clip clicks into place.

26. Windscreen Wiper Mechanism - Fault Diagnosis and Rectification (TR2, 3, 3A)

1. Should the windscreen wipers fail or work very slowly then check the current the motor is taking by connecting up a 1-20 ammeter in series in the circuit and turning on the wiper switch. Consumption should be approximately 3 amps.
2. If no, or a very small, current is being taken by the motor first check that the battery is fully charged. Also, using a voltmeter, check that the wiper motor circuit is free of dirty or broken connections.
3. Disconnect the electrical connections at the rear of the motor and undo the three end cover retaining screws. Lift away the end cover so exposing the brushes and commutator.
4. Blow away any dust and check that the commutator is clean and free of dust from in between the segments. Clean with a petrol moistened rag.
5. Check that the two brushes are firmly in contact with the commutator and that they are not loose or badly worn. Check the brush spring tension and, if weak, fit new springs. The brush levers must be free to pivot and may be eased by moving to and fro several times. Refit the end cover and retest.
6. If the wiper takes a very high current check the wiper blades for freedom of movement. If this is satisfactory check the gearbox cover and gear assembly for damage and measure the armature end float which should be approximately .010 inch (.254 mm).
7. The end float is set by the adjusting screw in the end cover. Check that excessive friction in the outer cable, connecting the wheelboxes, caused by too small a curvature is not the cause of the high current consumption.

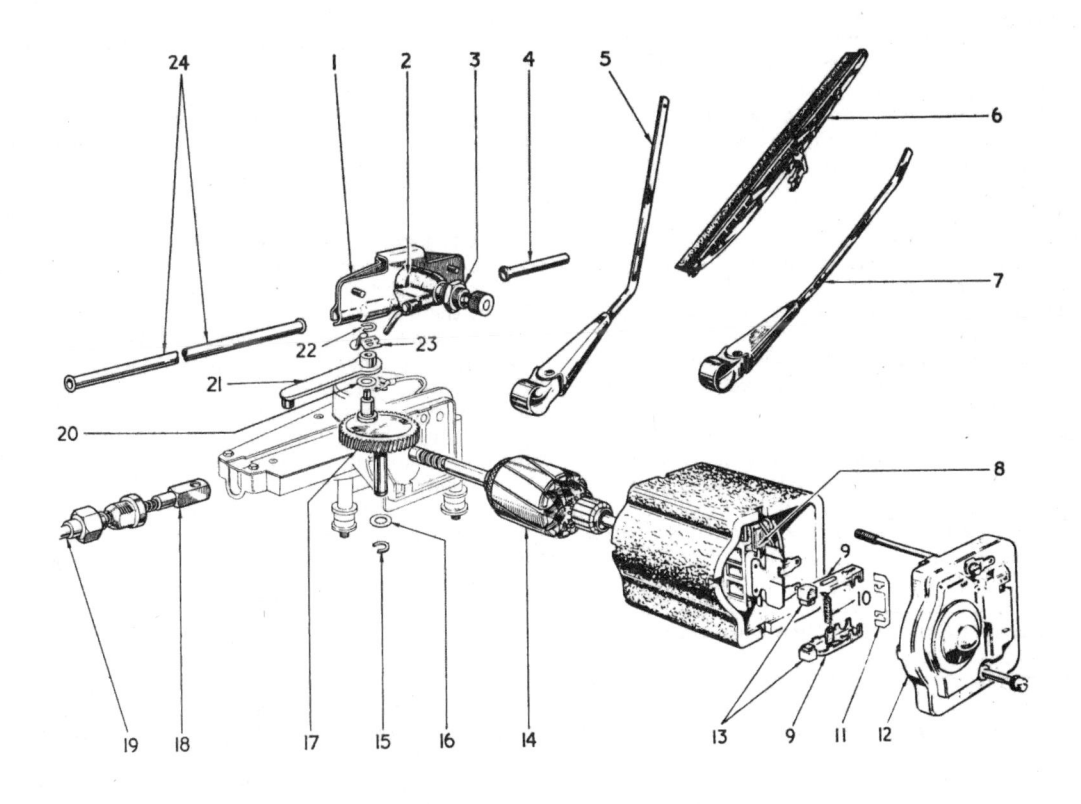

Fig. 10.13. EXPLODED VIEW OF WINDSCREEN WIPER MOTOR (TR4, 4A)

1 Wheel box
2 Jet and bush assembly
3 Nut
4 Rigid tubing - right hand side
5 Wiper arm
6 Blade
7 Wiper arm
8 Field coil assembly
9 Brush gear
10 Tension spring & retainers
11 Brush gear retainer
12 End cover
13 Brushes
14 Armature
15 Circlip
16 Washer
17 Final drive wheel
18 Cable rack
19 Rigid tubing - left hand side
20 Spacer
21 Connecting rod
22 Circlip
23 Parking switch contact
24 Rigid tubing - centre section

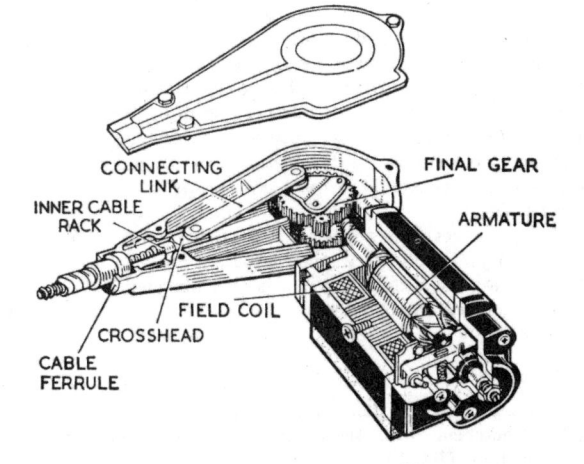

Fig. 10.12. Windscreen wiper motor with gearbox cover removed TR2, 3, 3A

221

Chapter 10/Electrical System

27. Wiper Motor and Rack - Removal and Replacement (TR2, 3, 3A)

1. Should it be necessary to remove the motor first disconnect the battery earth terminals.
2. Undo the three screws securing the gearbox cover in place on the gearbox and lift away the cover.
3. Disconnect the electrical cables from the rear of the wiper motor.
4. Carefully lift off the connecting link (Fig. 10.12) from the crosshead and final gear.
5. Disconnect the rack outer casing, cable rack and crosshead from the gearbox casing.
6. The wiper motor may now be removed from its mounting on the bulkhead.
7. To detach the cable rack from the wheelbox remove the wiper arms by undoing the collet nuts and lifting the arms off the spindles.
8. Carefully withdraw the cable rack from the outer casing.
9. Before refitting the cable rack inspect the wheelbox gears for wear. Thoroughly lubricate the cable rack with Duckham's HBB or an equivalent grease.
10 Refitting the cable rack or wiper motor is the reverse sequence to removal.

28. Windscreen Wiper Motor - Dismantling, Inspection and Reassembly (TR2, 3, 3A)

1. Due to the motor being of simple design and in a conveniently mounted position it can be serviced whilst still in the car. The only exception of course is when the motor requires major overhaul or renewal.
2. Disconnect the electrical connections at the rear of the wiper motor and undo the three end cover retaining screws. Lift away the end cover so exposing the brushes and commutator.
3. Blow away any dust and check that the commutator is clean and free of dust from in between the segments. Clean with a petrol moistened rag.
4. Check that the two brushes are firmly in contact with the commutator and they are not loose or badly worn. Check the brush spring tension and if it appears weak fit new springs. The brush levers must be free to pivot and may be eased by moving to and fro several times.
5. Should the operation of the motor now prove satisfactory but there is no drive to the wheelboxes, first undo the three screws securing the gearbox cover in place. Remove the gearbox cover. If the crosshead moves sluggishly between its gearbox, lightly smear a small amount of medium grade engine oil in the groove formed in the die cast housing.
6. Remove traces of old grease from the gearbox and repack with fresh, preferably of a Zinc Oxide base.
7. If there are any other faults it is recommended that a service exchange unit be fitted.
8. Reassembly is the reverse sequence to dismantling.

29. Windscreen Wiper Mechanism - Fault Diagnosis and Rectification (TR4, 4A)

1. Should the windscreen wipers fail to park, or park badly, then check the limit switch on the gearbox cover.
2. Loosen the four screws which retain the gearbox cover and place the projection close to the rim of the limit switch in line with the groove in the gearbox cover.
3. Rotate the limit switch anti-clockwise 25º and tighten the four screws retaining the gearbox cover. If it is wished to park the windscreen wipers on the other side of the windscreen rotate the limit switch 180º clockwise.
4. Should the windscreen wipers fail, or work very slowly, then check the current the motor is taking by connecting up a 1-20 ammeter in the circuit and turning on the wiper switch. Consumption should be between 2.7 to 3.4 amps.
5. If no current is passing through check the wiring for breaks and loose connections.
6. If the wiper motor takes a very high current check the wiper blades for freedom of movement. If this is satisfactory check the gearbox cover and gear assembly for damage and measure the armature endfloat which should be between .008 and .012 inch (.20 to .30 mm).
7. The endfloat is set by the adjusting screw. Check that excessive friction in the cable connecting tubes caused by too small a curvature is not the cause of the high current consumption.
8. If the motor takes a very low current ensure that the battery is fully charged. Check the brush gear after removing the commutator end bracket or cover and ensure that the brushes are bearing on the commutator. If not, check the brushes for freedom of movement and, if necessary, renew the tension spring.
9. Check the armature by substitution if this unit is suspected.

30. Windscreen Wiper Motor, Gearbox and Wheelbox - Removal and Replacement (TR4, 4A)

1. Remove the windscreen wiper arms by lifting the blades, carefully raising the retaining clip with a screwdriver, and then pulling the arms off the splined driveshaft.
2. Disconnect the electrical cables from the wiper motor and release the outer cable from the gearbox housing.
3. Undo the large nut that secures the outer tubing (19) (Fig. 10.13).
4. Undo and remove the three bolts that hold the wiper motor mounting bracket. It should be noted that two of these bolts can be reached from the inside of the car. The third bolt is accessible through the engine compartment.
5. Remove the motor complete with its mounting bracket and at the same time withdrawing the cable rack (18).
6. Disconnect the battery earth terminal and working under the fascia panel disconnect the two demister hoses from the nozzles and undo the two nozzle securing nuts and spring washers. Remove the two nuts and washers and remove the demister nozzles. The parts are shown in Fig. 12.27.
7. Undo and remove the cover plates which are positioned underneath the wiper system wheelboxes. Each cover plate is held in position with two screws.
8. Undo and remove the nut (3) (Fig. 10.13) from each wheelbox and lift up the jet and bush assembly (2) for about two inches.
9. Disconnect the washer water pipes at the jets. If it recommended that a piece of electrical cable is placed around the right hand rigid tubing (4) so as to keep it in place.
10 Remove the wheelbox backplate by undoing the two screws and lifting away the backplate. Ease out the rigid tubing so disengaging it from the wheelbox body.
11 Use a pair of long nosed pliers to grip the rear of the wheelbox and lift it out of the aperture.
12 Reassembly of the wheel boxes, motor and cable is the reverse sequence to removal. It may be necessary to rotate the rack cable so as to engage it with the gear in the wheelboxes.

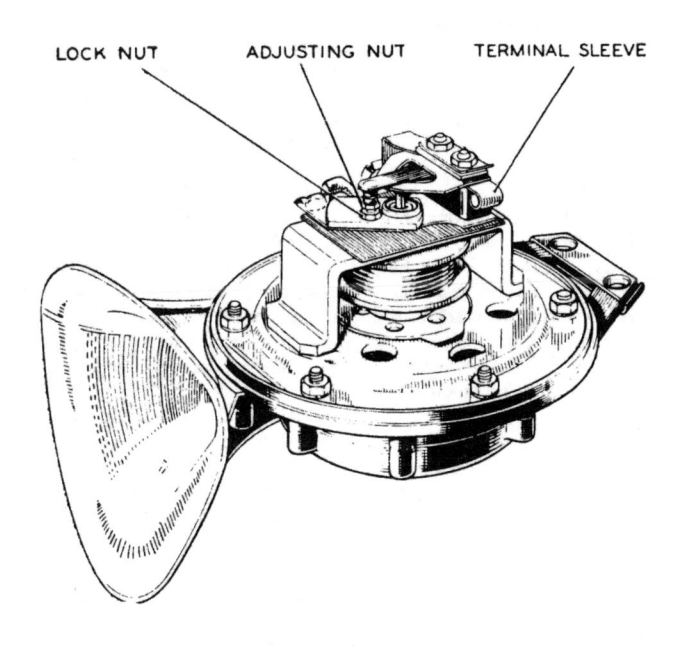

Fig. 10.14. Horn type WT 618 with cover removed TR2, 3, 3A

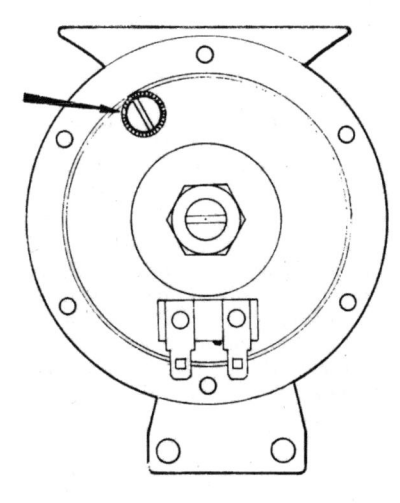

Fig. 10.15. Location of horn adjusting screw TR4, 4A

Chapter 10/Electrical System

31. Windscreen Wiper Motor - Dismantling, Inspection and Reassembly (TR4, 4A)

1. Mark the domed cover in relation to the flat gearbox lid, undo the four screws holding the gearbox lid in place and lift off the lid and domed cover.
2. Pull off the small circlip (22) (Fig. 10.13) and remove the limit switch wiper (23). The connecting rod (21) and cable rack (18) can now be lifted off. Take particular note of the spacer (20) located between the final drive wheel (17) and the connecting rod (21).
3. Undo and remove the two through bolts from the commutator end cover (12). Pull off the end cover.
4. Lift out the brush gear retainer (11) and then remove the brush gear (9). Clean the commutator and brush gear and, if worn, fit new brushes. The resistance between adjacent commutator segments should be .34 to .41 ohm.
5. Carefully examine the internal wiring for signs of chafing, breaks or chafing which would lead to a short circuit. Insulate or replace any damaged wiring.
6. Measure the value of the field resistance which should be between 12.8 and 14 ohms. If a lower reading than this is obtained it is likely that there is a short circuit and a new field coil should be fitted.
7. Renew the gearbox gear teeth if they are damaged, chipped or worn.
8. Reassembly is a straightforward reversal of the dismantling sequence, but ensure the following items are lubricated:-

a) Immerse the self aligning armature bearing in S.A.E. 20 engine oil for 24 hours before assembly.
b) Oil the armature bearings in S.A.E. 20 engine oil.
c) Soak the felt lubricator in the gearbox with S.A.E. 20 engine oil.
d) Grease generously the wormwheel bearings, crosshead, guide channel, connecting rod, crankpin, worm, cable rack and wheelboxes and the final gear shaft.

32. Horns - Fault Tracing and Rectification

1. If a horn works badly or fails completely first check the wiring leading to it for short circuits, blown fuse or loose connections. Also check that the horn is firmly secured and that there is nothing lying on the horn body.
2. Twin horns are fitted and are of two different notes. The high note has a letter H on the inside of the trumpet and the low note horn has a letter L similarly positioned on the trumpet.
3. If a horn loses its adjustment it will not alter the pitch as the tone of a horn depends on the vibration of an air column. It will however give a softer and more harsh sound. Also excessive current will be required which is one cause for fuses to blow. The correct method of adjusting horns is to measure the current and not to use feeler gauges.
4. Further information on servicing is given in the section applicable to model of car.

33. Horns - Servicing and Adjustment (TR2, 3, 3A)

1. On earlier models Lucas horns type WT 614 were fitted but on the later cars type WT 618 were fitted instead.
2. To check the horn adjustment connect a 0 to 30 ammeter into series with the horns at some convenient point.
3. Operate the horns and note the current consumption for both horns. The WT 614 type horn should have a current consumption of 13 amps. and the WT 618 type should have a current consumption of 16 amps.
4. If the consumption exceeds this amount disconnect the horns from each other and test each of them in turn. A single WT 614 horn should require 6½ amps. to operate correctly and a WT 618 horn requires 8 amps.
5. If a horn is to be adjusted away from the car make sure it is made secure in a bench vice with good electrical connections.
6. Remove the cover by undoing the centre screw and lifting off.
7. Remove the fuse from the A1-A2 terminals and replace with a piece of stout wire. Using a suitable size open ended spanner undo the adjusting nut locknut (Fig. 10.14). Turn the adjusting nut in a clockwise direction until the contact points are just apart. Test this setting by closing the horn circuit and the horn should not operate.
8. Turn the adjusting nut half a turn in an anti-clockwise direction and tighten the locknut whilst holding the adjusting nut. Insert a 0-30 ammeter into the circuit in series and by very carefully rotating the adjusting nut in a clockwise direction decrease the current or anti-clockwise to increase the current; adjust the nut accordingly until the figures in operation 4 of this Section are achieved.
9. When correct adjustment is achieved tighten the locknut and replace the cover.
10 If the contacts are badly worn they should be removed but before fitting the new set check the steel pushrod for freedom of movement and, if excessive, a new pushrod can be obtained. If movement is still excessive a new horn will have to be fitted. Lubricate the pushrod with a little grease.
11 The armature should not touch the base plate but have a clearance of 0.020 inch between them. To adjust this slacken the screws that secure the armature and move it centrally in the base plate. Use feeler gauges to set the gap when retightening the screws.
12 Generally inspect the horn wiring for loose or broken connections of chafed insulation. On WT 614 type horns a resistance was fitted across the horn coil but on the WT 618 type the contact breaker terminal was made of a resistance material. If the resistance is inoperative excessive arcing will occur between the two contact points.
13 If there are any other faults with the horn it is recommended that a new horn be fitted.

34. Horns - Servicing and Adjustment (TR4, 4A)

1. The horn should never be dismantled but it is possible to adjust it. This adjustment is to compensate for wear only and will not affect the tone. At the rear of the horn is a small adjustment screw on the broad rim, nearly opposite the two terminals. Do not confuse this with the large screw in the centre.
2. Turn the adjustment screw anti-clockwise until the horn just fails to sound. Then turn the screw a quarter of a turn clockwise, which is the optimum setting.

35. Headlamps (TR2, 3, 3A)

1. To remove a headlight first undo and remove the self tapping screw located as shown in Fig. 10.16.
8. Using a wide blade screwdriver, or stout knife, spring the front rim off the mounting flange. Lift away the rim and the rubber dust excluder noting which way round it is fitted.
3. Using the palms of the hands press on the light unit glass and rotate in an anti-clockwise direction. The heads of the beam adjustment screws will pass into the larger holes in the seating rim so releasing the unit and allowing it to be

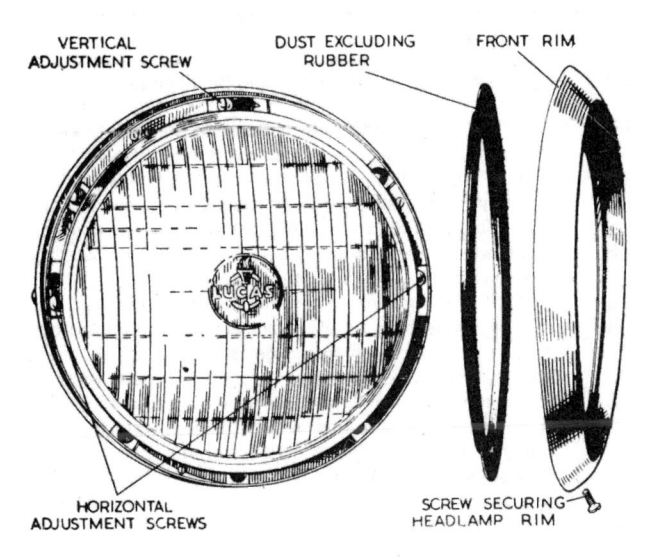

Fig. 10.16. Headlamp with front rim and dust excluder rubber removed TR2, 3, 3A

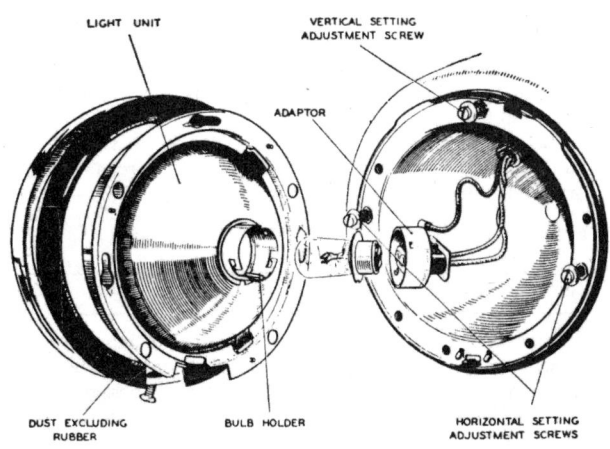

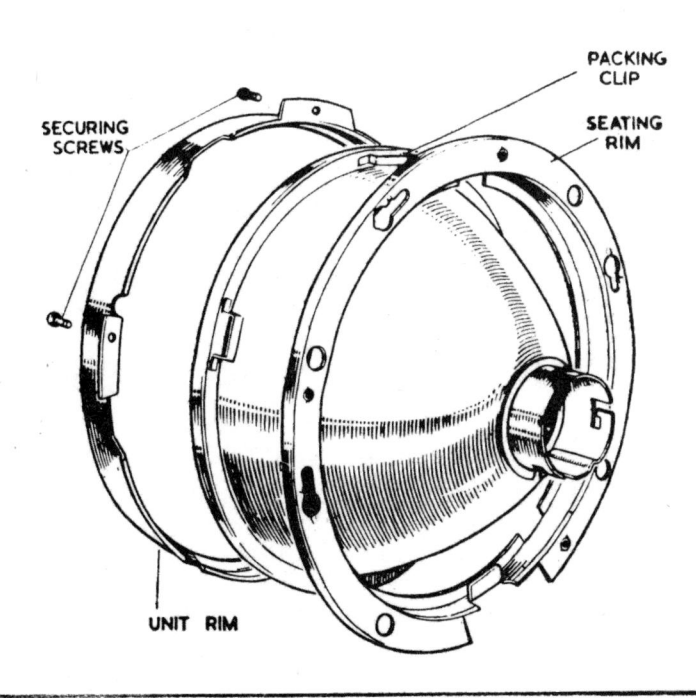

Fig. 10.17. Headlamp bulb and bulb holder TR2, 3, 3A

Fig. 10.18. Light unit position relative to seating rim

225

Chapter 10/Electrical System

drawn forwards.

4. To remove the bulb refer to Fig. 10.17 and press the adaptor in lightly against the reflector and turn it in an anti-clockwise direction to release the adaptor. Do not allow the bulb to drop out once the adaptor is free.

5. Lift out the old bulb if a new one is to be fitted and insert the new bulb positioning it so that the indent in the rim fits into the indent in the bulb holder. This will ensure that its focus will be correct as the filaments will be in their correct positions.

6. Should it be necessary to fit a new light unit undo the three small self tapping screws and remove the light unit from the unit rim and the seating rim.

7. Reassembly is the reverse sequence to removal.

8. Do not turn any of the three spring loaded screws as these are for adjusting the headlight beam. The one at the top of the headlamp unit rim is for vertical adjustment and the ones on each side of the rim for adjustment to the left and right.

9. In the author's experience the best method of focusing the headlights is to remove the rims at home and then set the lights up at night to give the best results, on a long straight flat road. Always lower the beam of the lights a little from their optimum position so as not to dazzle other road users and to compensate for those occasions when there is weight in the back.

10 Bear in mind that M.O.T. regulations demand that when on main beam the beams must be parallel with the road and with each other.

36. Headlamps (TR4, 4A)

The sequence for removal of the headlamp bulb and renewal of the light is basically identical to that for the earlier models, the only differences being in the design of the bulb holder but it is still separated from the light unit in the same manner. Also the method of attaching the headlamp rim is different whereby it is simply sprung into position and not retained with a self tapping screw as shown in Fig. 10.16. The component parts to the headlights fitted to these models is shown in Fig. 10.19.

37. Fuel Gauge - Fault Finding and Rectification

A fuel gauge sender unit is fitted to the petrol tank so that a float connected to an arm and a rheostat as shown in Fig. 10.20 (TR2, 3, 3A) or Fig. 10.21 (TR4, 4A) is able to vary the resistance of the gauge circuit depending on the amount of petrol in the tank. The gauge which is mounted on the instrument panel is able to measure the resistance and indicate the tank contents.

The fuel gauge can mis-read in four different ways. There can be no reading at all, there can be an intermittent reading, the needle on the gauge can read too high or too low. If there is no reading at all check for loose electrical connections. Providing the wiring is in order check the components one at a time by substitution. Unfortunately, if any of these items prove faulty they must be renewed as they are sealed and cannot be repaired. It will be observed that in Fig. 10.21, applicable to TR4 and 4A models, a voltage stabiliser unit is also fitted into the circuit.

38. Temperature Gauge - Fault Tracing and Rectification (TR2, 3, 3A)

The temperature gauge is connected to the transmitter by a capillary tube and the three parts cannot be separated. If a fault should occur a complete new assembly must be fitted as it cannot be repaired without specialist equipment.

39. Temperature Gauge - Fault Tracing and Rectification (TR4, 4A)

1. If the temperature gauge fails to work or works incorrectly, it will be necessary to test for circuit continuity using an ohmmeter. Alternatively, units can be tested by substitution.

2. The system comprises a temperature transmitter, located in the thermostat housing, a voltage stabiliser and the temperature gauge itself.

3. None of these units can be repaired and if any are defective they must be exchanged for replacement parts.

Fig. 10.19. HEADLAMP AND SIDELAMP COMPONENTS

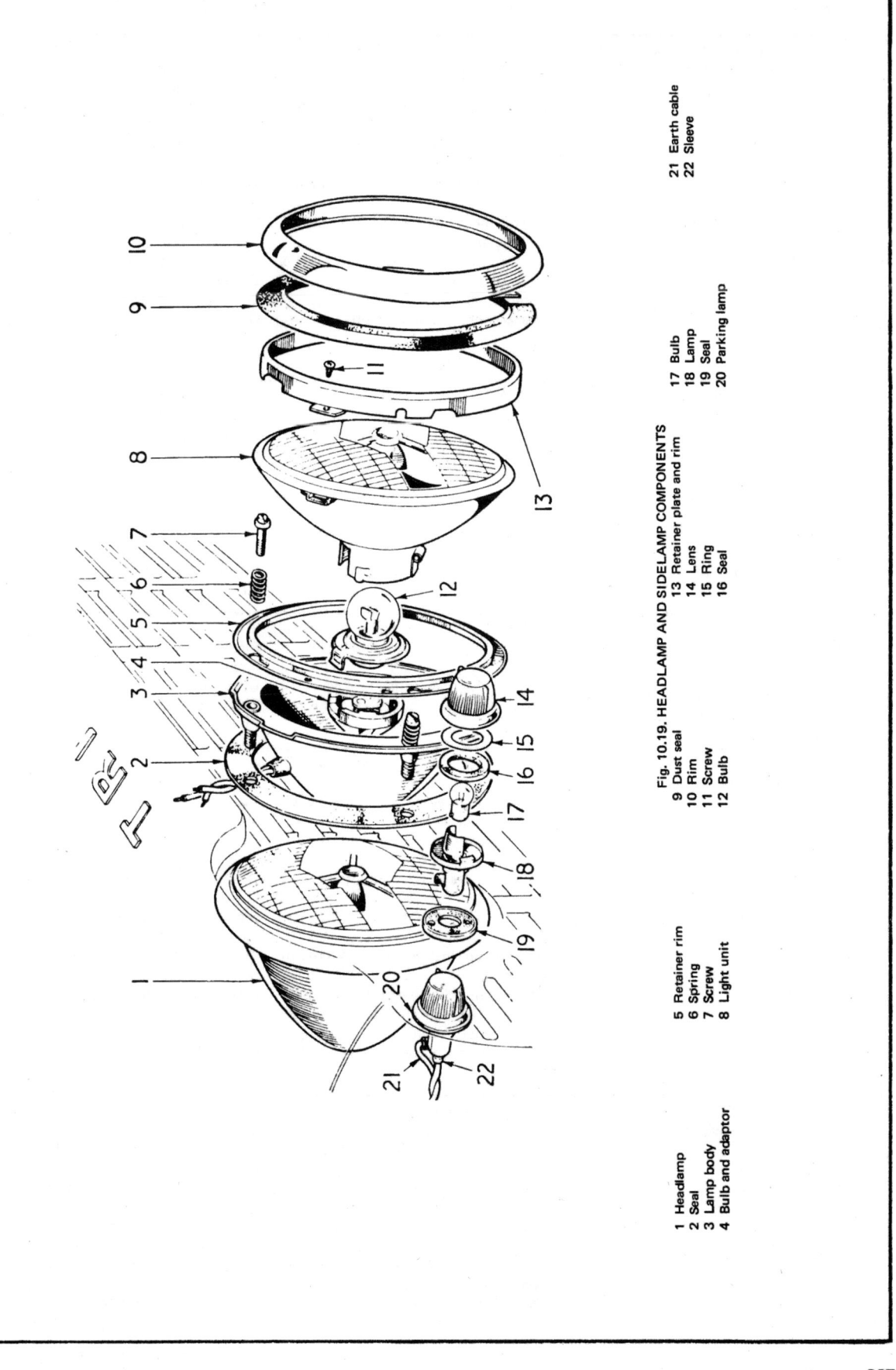

1 Headlamp	5 Retainer rim	9 Dust seal	13 Retainer plate and rim	17 Bulb	21 Earth cable
2 Seal	6 Spring	10 Rim	14 Lens	18 Lamp	22 Sleeve
3 Lamp body	7 Screw	11 Screw	15 Ring	19 Seal	
4 Bulb and adaptor	8 Light unit	12 Bulb	16 Seal	20 Parking lamp	

Fault Finding Chart - Electrical System

Cause	Trouble	Remedy
SYMPTOM: STARTER MOTOR FAILS TO TURN ENGINE		
No electricity at starter motor	Battery discharged.	Charge battery.
	Battery defective internally.	Fit new battery.
	Battery terminal leads loose or earth lead not securely attached to body.	Check and tighten leads.
	Loose or broken connections in starter motor circuit.	Check all connections and tighten any that are loose.
	Starter motor switch or solenoid faulty	Test and replace faulty components with new.
Electricity at starter motor: faulty motor	Starter motor pinion jammed in mesh with flywheel gear ring.	Disengage pinion by turning squared end of armature shaft.
	Starter brushes badly worn, sticking, or brush wires loose.	Examine brushes, replace as necessary, tighten down brush wires.
	Commutator dirty, worn or burnt.	Clean commutator, recut if badly burnt.
	Starter motor armature faulty.	Overhaul starter motor, fit new armature.
	Field coils earthed.	Overhaul starter motor.
SYMPTOM: STARTER MOTOR TURNS ENGINE VERY SLOWLY		
Electrical defects	Battery in discharged condition.	Charge battery.
	Starter brushes badly worn, sticking, or brush wires loose.	Examine brushes, replace as necessary, tighten down brush wires.
	Loose wires in starter motor circuit.	Check wiring and tighten as necessary.
SYMPTOM: STARTER MOTOR OPERATES WITHOUT TURNING ENGINE		
Dirt or oil on drive gear	Starter motor pinion sticking on the screwed sleeve.	Remove starter motor, clean starter motor drive.
Mechanical damage.	Pinion or flywheel gear teeth broken or worn.	Fit new gear ring to flywheel, and new pinion to starter motor drive.
SYMPTOMS: STARTER MOTOR NOISY OR EXCESSIVELY ROUGH ENGAGEMENT		
Lack of attention or mechanical damage	Pinion or flywheel gear teeth broken or worn.	Fit new gear teeth to flywheel, or new pinion to starter motor drive.
	Starter drive main spring broken.	Dismantle and fit new main spring.
	Starter motor retaining bolts loose.	Tighten starter motor securing bolts. Fit new spring washer if necessary.
SYMPTOM: BATTERY WILL NOT HOLD CHARGE FOR MORE THAN A FEW DAYS		
Wear or damage	Battery defective internally.	Remove and fit new battery.
	Electrolyte level too low or electrolyte too weak due to leakage.	Top up electrolyte level to just above plates.
	Plate separators no longer fully effective.	Remove and fit new battery.
	Battery plates severely sulphated.	Remove and fit new battery.
Insufficient current flow to keep battery charged	Fan/dynamo belt slipping.	Check belt for wear, replace if necessary, and tighten.
	Battery terminal connections loose or corroded.	Check terminals for tightness, and remove all corrosion.
	Dynamo not charging properly.	Remove and overhaul dynamo.
	Short in lighting circuit causing continual battery drain.	Trace and rectify.
	Regulator unit not working correctly.	Check setting, clean and replace if defective.
SYMPTOM: IGNITION LIGHT FAILS TO GO OUT, BATTERY RUNS FLAT IN A FEW DAYS		
Dynamo not charging	Fan belt loose and slipping, or broken.	Check, replace and tighten as necessary.
	Brushes worn, sticking, broken or dirty	Examine, clean, or replace brushes as necessary.
	Brush springs weak or broken.	Examine and test. Replace as necessary.
	Commutator dirty, greasy, worn or burnt.	Clean commutator and undercut segment separators.
	Armature badly worn or armature bent.	Fit new or reconditioned armature.
	Commutator bars shorting.	Undercut segment separators.

Fig. 10.20. Electrical circuit for fuel gauge and tank sender unit (TR2, 3, 3A)

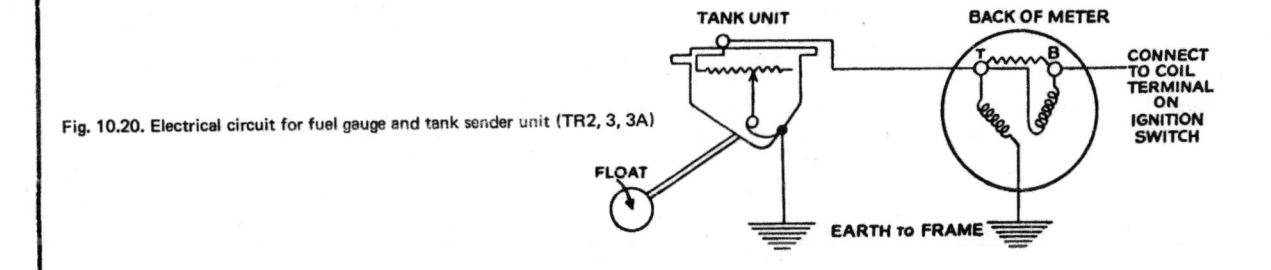

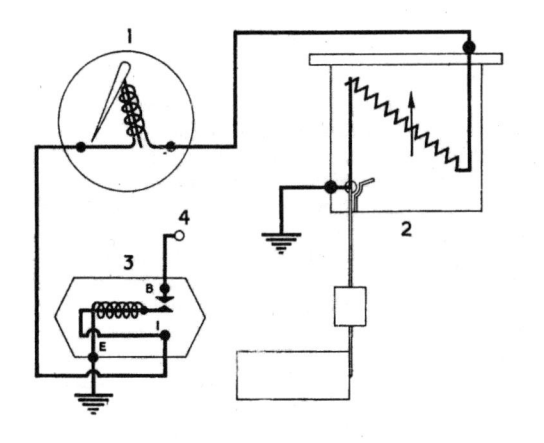

Fig. 10.21. ELECTRICAL CIRCUIT FOR FUEL GAUGE, TANK SENDER UNIT AND VOLTAGE STABILISER (TR4, 4A)
1 Fuel indicator gauge
2 Tank unit
3 Voltage stabiliser
4 To 'A4' terminal on fuse unit

Fig. 10.22. Temperature gauge circuit TR4, 4A

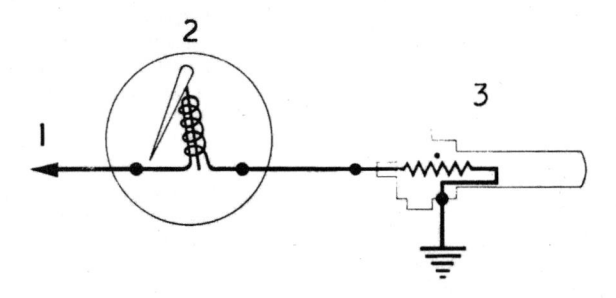

229

Fault Finding Chart - Electrical System

Cause	Trouble	Remedy
	Dynamo bearings badly worn	Overhaul dynamo, fit new bearings.
	Dynamo field coils burnt, open, or shorted.	Remove and fit rebuilt dynamo.
	Commutator no longer circular.	Recut commutator and undercut segment separators.
	Pole pieces very loose.	Strip and overhaul dynamo. Tighten pole pieces.
Regulator or cut-out fails to work correctly.	Regulator incorrectly set.	Adjust regulator correctly.
	Cut-out incorrectly set.	Adjust cut-out correctly.
	Open circuit in wiring of cut-out and regulator unit.	Remove, examine and renew as necessary.

Failure of individual electrical equipment to function correctly is dealt with alphabetically, item by item, under the headings listed below:

FUEL GAUGE

Cause	Trouble	Remedy
Fuel gauge gives no reading	Fuel tank empty!	Fill fuel tank.
	Electric cable between tank sender unit and gauge earthed or loose.	Check cable for earthing and joints for tightness.
	Fuel gauge case not earthed.	Ensure case is well earthed.
	Fuel gauge supply cable interrupted.	Check and replace cable if necessary.
	Fuel gauge unit broken.	Replace fuel gauge.
Fuel gauge registers full all the time	Electric cable between tank unit and gauge broken or disconnected.	Check over cable and repair as necessary.

HORN

Cause	Trouble	Remedy
Horn operates all the time	Horn push either earthed or stuck down.	Disconnect battery earth. Check and rectify source of trouble.
	Horn cable to horn push earthed.	Disconnect battery earth. Check and rectify source of trouble.
Horn fails to operate	Blown fuse.	Check and renew if broken. Ascertain cause.
	Cable or cable connection loose, broken or disconnected.	Check all connections for tightness and cables for breaks.
	Horn has an internal fault.	Remove and overhaul horn.
Horn emits intermittent or unsatisfactory noise	Cable connections loose.	Check and tighten all connections.
	Horn incorrectly adjusted.	Adjust horn until best note obtained.

LIGHTS

Cause	Trouble	Remedy
Lights do not come on	If engine not running, battery discharged.	Push-start car, charge battery.
	Light bulb filament burnt out or bulbs broken.	Test bulbs in live bulb holder.
	Wire connections loose, disconnected or broken.	Check all connections for tightness and wire cable for breaks.
	Light switch shorting or otherwise faulty.	By-pass light switch to ascertain if fault is in switch and fit new switch as appropriate.
Lights come on but fade out	If engine not running battery discharged.	Push-start car, and charge battery.
Lights give very poor illumination	Lamp glasses dirty.	Clean glasses.
	Reflector tarnished or dirty.	Fit new reflectors.
	Lamps badly out of adjustment.	Adjust lamps correctly.
	Incorrect bulb with too low wattage fitted.	Remove bulb and replace with correct grade.
	Existing bulbs old and badly discoloured.	Renew bulb units.
	Electrical wiring too thin not allowing full current to pass.	Rewire lighting system.
Lights work erratically - flashing on and off, especially over bumps.	Battery terminals or earth connection loose.	Tighten battery terminals and earth connection.
	Lights not earthing properly.	Examine and rectify.
	Contacts in light switch faulty.	By-pass light switch to ascertain if fault is in switch and fit new switch as appropriate.

Fault Finding Chart - Electrical System

Cause	Trouble	Remedy
	WIPERS	
Wiper motor fails to work	Blown fuse.	Check and replace fuse if necessary.
	Wire connections loose, disconnected, or broken.	Check wiper wiring. Tighten loose connections.
	Brushes badly worn.	Remove and fit new brushes.
	Armature worn or faulty.	If electricity at wiper motor remove and overhaul and fit replacement armature.
	Field coils faulty.	Purchase reconditioned wiper motor.
Wiper motor works very slowly and takes excessive current	Commutator dirty, greasy or burnt.	Clean commutator thoroughly.
	Drive to wheelboxes too bent or unlubricated.	Examine drive and straighten out severe curvature. Lubricate.
	Wheelbox spindle binding or damaged.	Remove, overhaul or fit replacement.
	Armature bearings dry or unaligned.	Replace with new bearings correctly aligned.
	Armature badly worn or faulty.	Remove, overhaul or fit replacement armature.
Wiper motor works slowly and takes little current.	Brushes badly worn.	Remove and fit new brushes.
	Commutator dirty, greasy or burnt.	Clean commutator thoroughly.
	Armature badly worn or faulty.	Remove and overhaul armature or fit replacement.
Wiper motor works but wiper blades remain static	Driving cable rack disengaged or faulty	Examine and if faulty replace.
	Wheelbox gear and spindle damaged or worn.	Examine and if faulty replace.
	Wiper motor gearbox parts badly worn	Overhaul or fit new gearbox.

Chapter 11/Suspension - Dampers - Steering

Contents

General Description	1
Front & Rear Suspension - Maintenance	2
Cam & Peg Steering - Maintenance	3
Rack & Pinion Steering - Maintenance	4
Front Hubs - Removal, Dismantling, Inspection Reassembly & Refitting (TR2)	5
Front Hubs - Removal, Dismantling, Inspection Reassembly & Refitting (TR3, 3A, 4, 4A)	6
Stub Axle - Removal & Refitting	7
Front Suspension Coil Spring - Removal & Refitting	8
Front Suspension Shock Absorbers - Removal & Refitting	9
Front Suspension Top Ball Joint - Removal & Refitting (TR2, 3, 3A)	10
Front Suspension Top Ball Joint - Removal & Refitting (TR4, 4A)	11
Front Suspension Top Wishbones - Removal & Refitting (TR2, 3, 3A)	12
Front Suspension Top Wishbones - Removal & Refitting (TR4, 4A)	13
Front Suspension Vertical Link & Lower Wishbone - Removal & Refitting (TR2)	14
Front Suspension Vertical Link & Lower Wishbone - Removal & Refitting (TR3, 3A, 4)	15
Front Suspension Vertical Link & Lower Wishbone - Removal & Refitting (TR4A)	16
Rear Spring - Removal & Refitting (Conventional Suspension)	17
Rear Shock Absorbers - Removal & Refitting (Conventional Suspensions)	18
Rear Spring - Removal & Refitting (Independent Rear Suspension - TR4A)	19
Rear Suspension Arm - Removal & Refitting (Independent Rear Suspension - TR4A)	20
Outer Axle Shaft & Hub Assembly - Removal & Refitting (Independent Rear Suspension - TR4A)	21
Stub Axle Shaft & Hub Assembly - Dismantling & Reassembly (Independent Rear Suspension - TR4A)	22
Outer Axle Shaft - Dismantling & Reassembly (Independent Rear Suspension - TR4A)	23
Rear Shock Absorbers - Removal & Refitting (Independent Rear Suspension - TR4A)	24
Steering Wheel - Removal & Refitting (Cam & Peg System)	25
Steering Wheel (Adjustable Type) - Description	26
Adjustable Steering Wheel - Removal & Refitting (Cam & Peg System)	27
Cam & Peg Steering - Removal & Replacement (TR2, 3, 3A)	28
Cam & Peg Steering - Dismantling, Overhaul & Reassembly	29
Cam & Peg Steering - Adjustment in Car	30
Cam & Peg Steering - Idler Unit Removal & Refitting	31
Modifications - Steering (TR2, 3, 3A)	32
Steering Wheel - Removal & Refitting (Rack & Pinion System)	33
Steering Column - Removal, Dismantling & Refitting (Rack & Pinion System)	34
Rack & Pinion Steering - Removal & Replacement (TR4)	35
Rack & Pinion Steering - Removal & Replacement (TR4A)	36
Rack & Pinion Steering - Dismantling, Reassembly & Adjustment	37
Rack & Pinion Backlash - Adjustment	38
Outer Ball Joint - Removal & Replacement	39

Specifications

Front Suspension

Type	Independent		
Type of spring	Coil		
Spring specifications:			
	TR2, 3, 3A Standard	TR4, 4A up to CT 29984 Standard	TR4, 4A after CT 29984 Standard
Number of working coils	6¾	6¾	5¾
Mean diameter of coils	3.5 inch	3.5 inch	3.5 inch
Rate	310 in.lb.	310 in.lb.	310 in.lb.
Free length (approx.)	9.75 inch.	9.75 inch.	11.1 inch.
Fitted length	6.75 ± 3/32 in.	6.75 ± 3/32 in.	8.12 ± 3/32 in.
Fitted load	925 lb.	925 lb.	925 lb.

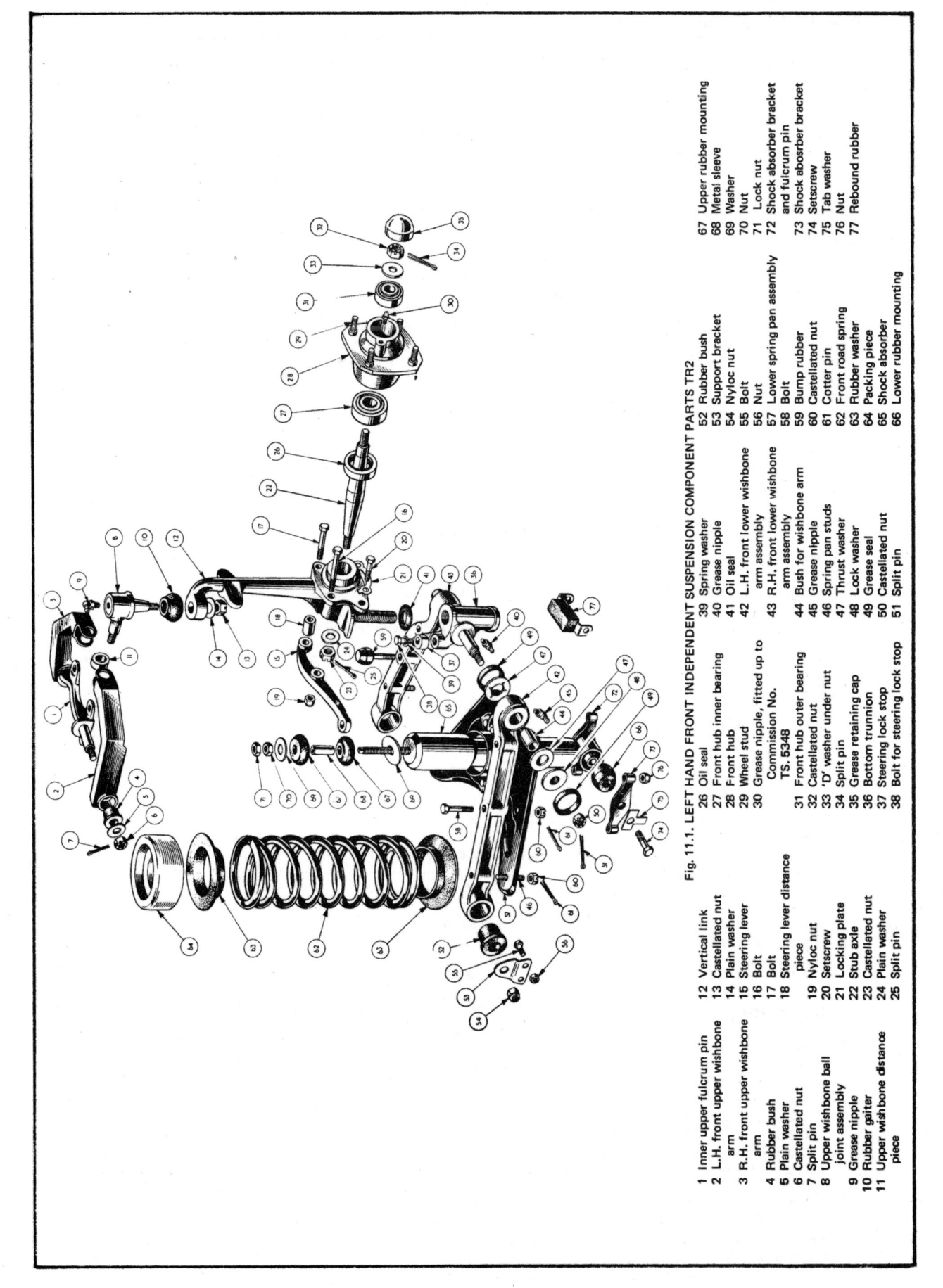

Fig. 11.1. LEFT HAND FRONT INDEPENDENT SUSPENSION COMPONENT PARTS TR2

1 Inner upper fulcrum pin
2 L.H. front upper wishbone arm
3 R.H. front upper wishbone arm
4 Rubber bush
5 Plain washer
6 Castellated nut
7 Split pin
8 Upper wishbone ball joint assembly
9 Grease nipple
10 Rubber gaiter
11 Upper wishbone distance piece
12 Vertical link
13 Castellated nut
14 Plain washer
15 Steering lever
16 Bolt
17 Bolt
18 Steering lever distance piece
19 Nyloc nut
20 Setscrew
21 Locking plate
22 Stub axle
23 Castellated nut
24 Plain washer
25 Split pin
26 Oil seal
27 Front hub inner bearing
28 Front hub
29 Wheel stud
30 Grease nipple, fitted up to Commission No. TS.5348
31 Front hub outer bearing
32 Castellated nut
33 'D' washer under nut
34 Split pin
35 Grease retaining cap
36 Bottom trunnion
37 Steering lock stop
38 Bolt for steering lock stop
39 Spring washer
40 Grease nipple
41 Oil seal
42 L.H. front lower wishbone arm assembly
43 R.H. front lower wishbone arm assembly
44 Bush for wishbone arm
45 Grease nipple
46 Spring pan studs
47 Thrust washer
48 Lock washer
49 Grease seal
50 Castellated nut
51 Split pin
52 Rubber bush
53 Support bracket
54 Nyloc nut
55 Bolt
56 Nut
57 Lower spring pan assembly
58 Bolt
59 Bump rubber
60 Castellated nut
61 Cotter pin
62 Front road spring
63 Rubber washer
64 Packing piece
65 Shock absorber
66 Lower rubber mounting
67 Upper rubber mounting
68 Metal sleeve
69 Washer
70 Nut
71 Lock nut
72 Shock absorber bracket and fulcrum pin
73 Shock absorber bracket
74 Setscrew
75 Tab washer
76 Nut
77 Rebound rubber

233

Chapter 11/Suspension - Dampers - Steering

	TR2, 3, 3A Standard	TR4, 4A up to CT 29984 Standard	TR4, 4A after CT 29984 Standard
Hand of helix	Right	Right	Right
Static deflection (approx.)	3 inch.	3 inch.	3 inch.
Wire diameter	.5 ± .002 inch.	.5 ± .002 inch.	.5 ± .002 inch.
Front lock	28½°	29°	28½°
Back lock	31°	30½°	31°
Front damper	Telescopic sealed unit non adjustable		

Rear Suspension

Type .... Live axle with semi-floating axle shafts
Optional TR4A only ... Independent rear suspension

Spring specifications:

	TR2, TR3	TR4 Standard Pre CT 23883	TR4, 4A Standard Post CT 23383
Number of leaves	6	6	6
Width	2 inch	2 inch	2 inch
Thickness:			
Main	7/32 inch	main 7/32 inch	7/32 inch
2 to 5	3/16 inch	2. 3/16 inch	3/16 inch
6	11/64 inch	3-6 11/64 inch	11/64 inch
Rate ± 5%	128 in./lb.	128 in./lb.	128 in./lb.
Static deflection	4.04 inch	4.04 inch	4.04 inch
Laden camber	7/8 in. negative	.38-.63 negative	3.0-3.255 positive
Static load	515 lb.	515 lb.	515 lb.
Inside diameter of spring eye			
Front	1.313 inch	1.313 inch	1.313 inch
Rear	.875 to .880 in.	.875 to .880 in.	.875 to .880 in.
Distance centre of front eye to centre of centre bolt hole (static laden)	18.63 ± .063 in.	18.63 ± .063 in.	18.63 ± .063 in.

Rear dampers:
Type .... Two piston with filler plug
Fluid .... Armstrong shock absorber fluid 624

Steering

TR2, 3, 3A

Type .... High gear cam and lever
Steering wheel:
   Diameter .... 17 inch
   Number of spokes .... 3 sets
   Standard column .... T spoke layout
   Telescopic column .... Y spoke layout
   Number of turns, lock to lock 2¼
Angles:
   Toe-in .... 0 to 1/8 inch
   Castor 0
   Camber .... 2°
   K.P.I. .... 7°
Centre tie-rod length .... 19.44 inch
Outer tie-rod length .... 7.68 inch
Steering box:
   Adjustment .... Shims and locked setscrew
   Ratio .... 12 to 1
Turning circle .... 32 feet

TR4, 4A

Type .... Rack and pinion with telescopic column
Angles:
   Toe-in (standard) .... 0 to 1/8 inch
   Toe-in (Special types) .... 0 to 1/16 inch
   Castor (up to CT 6389 & CT 6343 wire wheels) .... 0°
   Castor (after previous chassis numbers) .... 3° positive
   Castor (all TR4A) .... 2° 40 min. ± ½°
   Camber .... 2°
   K.P.I. (TR4) .... 7°
   K.P.I. (TR4A) .... 9° ± ¾
Pinion end float adjustment .... Shims
Rock damper adjustment .... Shims
Inner ball joint pin adjustment .... Shims
Turning circle .... 33 feet

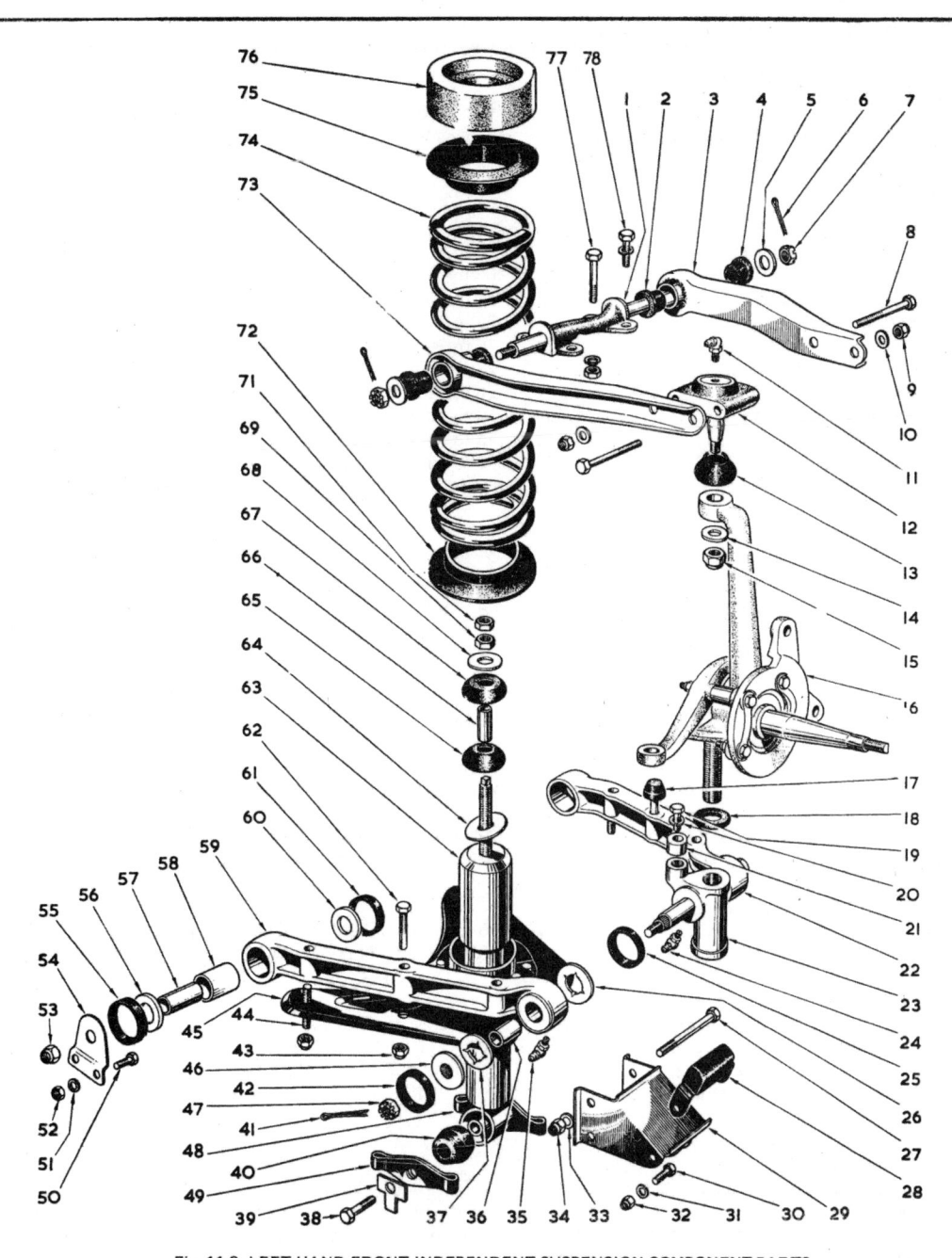

Fig. 11.2. LEFT HAND FRONT INDEPENDENT SUSPENSION COMPONENT PARTS
(TR3, 3A, 4, 4A)

1 Upper inner fulcrum	20 Spring washer	40 Rubber bush	58 Nylon bush
2 Rubber bush	21 Lock stop collar	41 Split pin	59 Lower wishbone - front
3 Upper wishbone arm - rear	22 Lower wishbone arm - rear	42 Rubber seal	60 Thrust washer
4 Rubber bush	23 Lower trunnion bracket	43 Nyloc nut	61 Rubber seal
5 Washer	24 Grease nipple	44 Stud	62 Bolt
6 Split pin	25 Rubber seal	45 Spring pan	63 Damper
7 Slotted nut	26 Thrust washer	46 Serrated washer	64 Washer
8 Bolt	27 Bolt	47 Slotted nut	65 Rubber bush
9 Nyloc nut	28 Rebound rubber	48 Damper attachment bracket - rear	66 Sleeve
10 Plain washer	29 Bracket		67 Rubber bush
11 Grease nipple	30 Bolt	49 Damper attachment bracket - front	68 Washer
12 Upper ball joint	31 Spring washer		69 Nut
13 Rubber gaiter	32 Nyloc nut	50 Bolt	71 Locknut
14 Plain washer	33 Plain washer	51 Spring washer	72 Rubber collar
15 Nyloc nut	34 Nyloc nut	52 Nut	73 Upper wishbone arm - front
16 Calliper bracket and vertical link	35 Grease nipple	53 Nyloc nut	74 Spring
	36 Bush - nylon	54 Fulcrum bracket	75 Rubber collar
17 Bump rubber	37 Thrust washer	55 Rubber seal	76 Distance piece
18 Rubber seal	38 Bolt	56 Thrust washer	77 Bolt
19 Bolt	39 Tab washer	57 Steel sleeve	78 Bolt

235

Chapter 11/Suspension - Dampers - Steering

Rear Suspension Geometry (TR4A I.R.S.)
- Toe-in ... 0 to 1/16 inch
- Camber ... 1° negative ± ½°

Torque Wrench Settings

Front Suspension (TR2, 3, 3A)
- Backplate and steering levers to vertical link ... 24 to 26 lb.ft. (3.318 to 3.595 Kg.m)
- Ball pin to vertical link ... 55 to 65 lb.ft. (7.604 to 8.987 Kg.m)
- Top wishbone to fulcrum pin ... 26 to 40 lb.ft. (3.595 to 5.53 Kg.m)
- Spring pan to wishbone ... 26 to 28 lb.ft. (3.595 to 3.871 Kg.m)
- Tie-rod to idler lever and drop arm ... 26 to 28 lb.ft. (3.595 to 3.871 Kg.m)
- Top inner fulcrum to chassis ... 26 to 28 lb.ft. (3.595 to 3.871 Kg.m)
- Lower wishbone to fulcrum pin ... 26 to 28 lb.ft. (3.595 to 3.871 Kg.m)
- Lower fulcrum bracket to chassis ... 16 to 18 lb.ft. (2.212 to 2.489 Kg.m)
- Stub axle to vertical link ... 55 to 60 lb.ft. (7.604 to 8.295 Kg.m)
- Wheel studs and nuts... 45 to 55 lb.ft. (6.221 to 7.604 Kg.m)
- Wire wheel adaptor nuts (TR3 only) ... 65 lb.ft. (8.987 Kg.m)

Front Suspension (TR4, 4A)
- Ball pin to vertical link ... 55 to 65 lb.ft. (7.604 to 8.987 Kg.m)
- Lower fulcrum bracket to chassis ... 16 to 18 lb.ft. (2.212 to 2.489 Kg.m)
- Stub axle to vertical link ... 55 to 60 lb.ft. (7.604 to 8.295 Kg.m)
- Lower wishbone to fulcrum ... 26 to 28 lb.ft. (3.595 to 3.871 Kg.m)
- Top wishbone to fulcrum ... 26 to 40 lb.ft. (3.595 to 5.530 Kg.m)
- Top inner fulcrum to chassis ... 26 to 28 lb.ft. (3.595 to 3.871 Kg.m)
- Brake disc attachment ... 32 to 35 lb.ft. (4.424 to 4.839 Kg.m)
- Calliper attachment ... 50 to 55 lb.ft. (6.913 to 7.604 Kg.m)

Rear Suspension (TR2, 3, 3A)
- Spring front end to frame ... 28 to 30 lb.ft. (3.871 to 4.148 Kg.m)
- Spring to rear axle ... 28 to 30 lb.ft. (3.871 to 4.148 Kg.m)
- Spring shackle ... 26 to 28 lb.ft. (3.595 to 3.871 Kg.m)
- Damper to frame ... 26 to 28 lb.ft. (3.595 to 3.871 Kg.m)

Rear Suspension (TR4, 4A live axle)
- Spring to axle 'U' bolts (TR4) ... 28 to 30 lb.ft. (3.871 to 4.148 Kg.m)
- Spring to axle 'U' bolts (TR4A) ... 26 to 28 lb.ft. (3.595 to 3.871 Kg.m)

Rear Suspension (TR4A I.R.S.)
- Inner driving flange to rear hub and axle shaft ... 28 to 30 lb.ft. (3.871 to 4.148 Kg.m)
- Rear hub assembly ... 100 to 110 lb.ft. (13.826 to 15.209 Kg.m)
- Trailing arm to mounting bracket ... 45 to 50 lb.ft. (6.221 to 6.913 Kg.m)
- Trailing arm mounting brackets to frame ... 28 to 30 lb.ft. (3.871 to 4.148 Kg.m)

1. General Description

The two independent front suspension units are of the wishbone design and each unit is mounted independent to the other on the chassis. The inboard ends of the wishbones are mounted in special rubber bushes so that vertical movement can be accommodated. A ball joint is attached to the outer end of the top wishbones whilst attached to the lower wishbone is a trunnion bearing. Connecting the upper and lower wishbones is the vertical link onto which is attached the stub axle.

The vertical link is controlled by tie rods connected to the steering gearbox. The maximum lock of the front wheels is limited by an eccentric collar which is bolted onto the upper face of the trunnion.

The bushed ends of the wishbones are fitted with white metal washers so as to provide a positive location as well as to take any end thrust. To prevent rapid wear due to road dust and dirt rubber seals are fitted to protect the moving parts.

Upon the introduction of the TR3 models certain modifications were incorporated into the front suspension. The rubber bushes on the ends of the wishbones were replaced by nylon bushes. Also, as detailed in Chapter 9, the braking system was changed from drum brakes for the front wheels to disc brakes. This meant changes in hub design, full details of which are given where applicable.

The suspension vertical link is so designed to act as a mounting for the drum brake backplate whereas for the TR3 models a bracket is fitted to the vertical link and this carries the disc brake calliper.

The stub axle mounting is tapered and mates with a similar taper in the vertical link. It is pressed into position and secured with a large nut. It is onto the stub axle that the front hub is attached using taper roller bearings. Attached to the hub is the brake drum or disc and the road wheel.

Positioned between the lower wishbone and the chassis is a coil spring to absorb road shocks. Spring damping is achieved by using a non adjustable telescopic shock absorber positioned in the centre of the coil spring.

The TR4 models use the same design of front suspension as the TR3 models although upon the introduction of the TR4A certain minor modifications were incorporated in the design. The main difference is in the method of attaching the lower wishbone arms whereby the inner pivot brackets

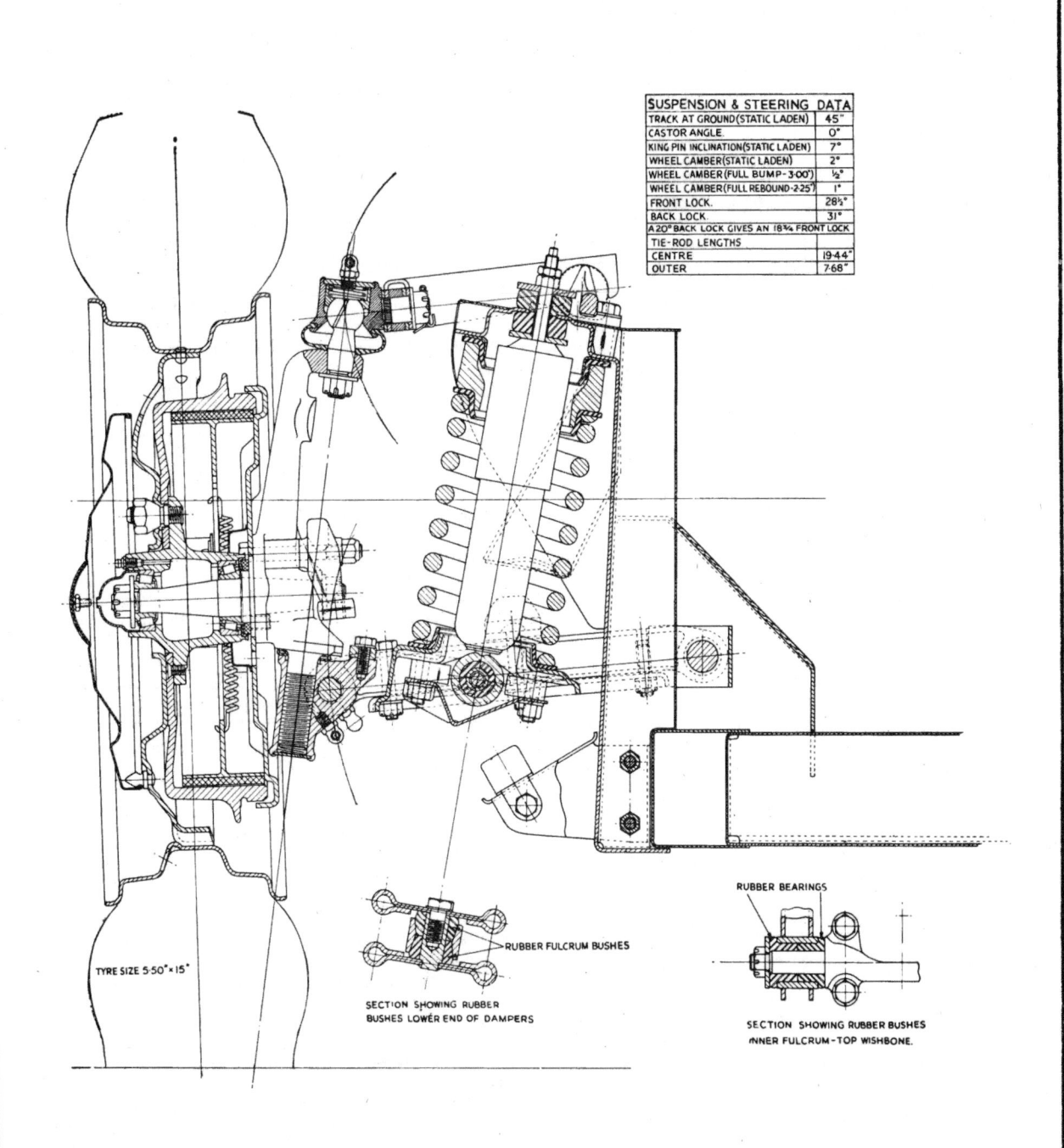

SUSPENSION & STEERING DATA	
TRACK AT GROUND (STATIC LADEN)	45"
CASTOR ANGLE.	0°
KING PIN INCLINATION (STATIC LADEN)	7°
WHEEL CAMBER (STATIC LADEN)	2°
WHEEL CAMBER (FULL BUMP -3·00")	½°
WHEEL CAMBER (FULL REBOUND -2·25")	1°
FRONT LOCK.	28½°
BACK LOCK.	31°
A 20° BACK LOCK GIVES AN 18¾° FRONT LOCK	
TIE-ROD LENGTHS	
CENTRE	19·44"
OUTER	7·68"

TYRE SIZE 5·50" × 15"

RUBBER FULCRUM BUSHES

SECTION SHOWING RUBBER BUSHES LOWER END OF DAMPERS

RUBBER BEARINGS

SECTION SHOWING RUBBER BUSHES INNER FULCRUM - TOP WISHBONE.

Fig. 11.3A. Front suspension arrangement nearside wheel TR2, 3, 3A

237

Chapter 11/Suspension - Dampers - Steering

are shimmed and vertically positioned on the chassis. The brackets are retained to the chassis with Nyloc nuts positioned behind the chassis.

The outer mounting for the trunnion bracket has also been modified and the lower trunnion brackets can now be removed from the wishbone without disturbing the lower inboard fulcrum brackets and their shims.

The rear axle fitted as standard to the models covered by this manual is the conventional live axle which is attached slightly forwards of the centre of the semi-elliptical laminated leaf springs. To control spring movement piston type shock absorbers are positioned between the chassis and axle mountings. The rear axle assembly was modified from commission number 13046 and full details of this are given in Chapter 8.

Independent rear suspension is offered as an optional extra on TR4A models whereby the differential unit is bolted to the chassis and the rear wheels are driven by two drive shafts incorporating splined joints to accommodate vertical wheel movement. The wheels are mounted on trailing suspension arms that pivot on the chassis and a coil spring is positioned between the suspension arm and the chassis. A piston type damper is used to control spring movement.

For the conversion enthusiast it is not possible to fit independent rear suspension to the TR4 or previous models without considerable modifications as the TR4A chassis design is entirely different. However to improve car stability with the conventional live axle special recambered rear road springs are available together with distance pieces and may be obtained from local agents.

The steering unit fitted to TR2 and TR3 models is that of the cam and lever type and has an operating ratio of 12 to 1. The movement of the rocker shaft should be limited to 33° on either side of the mid point of the cam by steering lock stops. When correctly adjusted the steering wheel should turn 2¼ turns from one lock to the other lock. The cam is of a spiral form and a conical shaped peg connected to the steering lever engages with the cam. The conical peg and cam are designed so that the peg does not reach the bottom face of the cam so that depth of engagement is adjustable by using a hardened steel setscrew mounted on the top cover. When this screw is turned clockwise it contacts the steering levers upper face and holds the conical peg in contact with the cam.

The steering unit fitted to TR4 and 4A models is that of the rack and pinion design with adjustable tie rods interconnecting the rack ends with the swivel arms. The rack is fitted with a special adjustable damper and an adjustable ball joint at the inner end of each tie rod. The pinion shaft end float is controlled by shims situated at the upper pinion bush. The steering column is attached to the pinion via universal couplings.

2. Front and Rear Suspension - Maintenance

1. There are four grease nipples situated on each independent front suspension unit. They are located on the lower wishbone outer bushes (2) and steering swivel (2). A further one grease nipple will be found on the outer tie-rod ball joint. These should be greased with four strokes of the grease gun every 1,500 miles (cars produced up to July, 1963) or 3,000 miles on models produced since this date.
2. On TR4A models the lower steering swivel should be lubricated by removing the plug and fitting a grease nipple. Using a Hypoy gear oil lubricate until oil seeps out from around the swivel. This should be done every 6,000 miles.
3. On the early TR2 and 3 models a further three grease nipples should be lubricated every 1,000 miles. They are located on the outer tie rod ball joints (2) and the slave drop arm pivot (1).
4. On early TR2 models the front wheel hub should be lubricated every 6,000 miles by applying a grease gun at the grease nipple exposed when the wheel trim is removed.
5. Later TR2 and TR3 models should have the hubs stripped out and cleaned of old grease and repacked every 12,000 miles. This interval should be increased to 24,000 miles for TR4 and 4A models except where competition work is involved.
6. On models produced before July 1963, apply five strokes of the grease gun to the rear hub grease nipples every 6,000 miles. Cars produced after this date may have the mileage intervals increased to 12,000 miles. This operation is not applicable to TR4A models.
7. On TR4A models fitted with independent rear suspension check for grease nipples on the outer axle shaft universal joints and, if evident, apply the grease gun every 6,000 miles.
8. The securing nuts on the rear spring 'U' bolts should be checked for tightness at intervals of 6,000 miles and the springs wiped with an oily rag. Check for broken leaves, loose shackles and worn shackle bushes at the same time.

3. Cam and Peg Steering - Maintenance

1. Every 6,000 miles check the level of oil in the steering gearbox (TR2, 3 and 3A models) and top up to the level of the filler orifice.
2. Have your local Triumph agent check the front wheel toe-in every 6,000 miles.

4. Rack and Pinion Steering - Maintenance

1. Every 12,000 miles remove the plug from the top of the rack and pinion steering unit (TR4) and fit a grease nipple and lubricate with five strokes of the grease gun. Remove the nipple and refit the plug. On TR4A models this mileage interval may be increased to 24,000 miles.
2. Check the rubber gaiters for damage and leaks and keep the securing clips tight. The oil also lubricates the tie rod inner ball joints.
3. Check the rack and pinion housing bellows for signs of lubricant leaks or for splitting and tighten the clips or fit new rubber bellows as necessary.
4. Have your local Triumph agent check the front wheel toe in every 6,000 miles.

5. Front Hubs - Removal, Dismantling, Inspection, Reassembly and Refitting (TR2)

1. Chock the rear wheels and apply the handbrake. Slacken the road wheel nuts, jack up the front of the car and place on axle stands positioned under the chassis frame. Remove the road wheel.
2. Remove the grease cap (35) (Fig. 11.1) from the hub using a wide blade screwdriver. It may be found that on some early cars produced before chassis number TS 5348 a grease nipple (30) may be fitted and this should be removed.
3. Undo the two brake drum to hub retaining countersunk screws and withdraw the brake drum.
4. Extract the split pin (34) from the castellated nut and undo this nut (32) and washer (33).
5. Remove the hub assembly from the stub axle (22). If this is tight use a two leg puller with a thrust pad over the end of the stub axle so preventing damage to the threads.
6. With the hub removed the outer bearing (31) will have

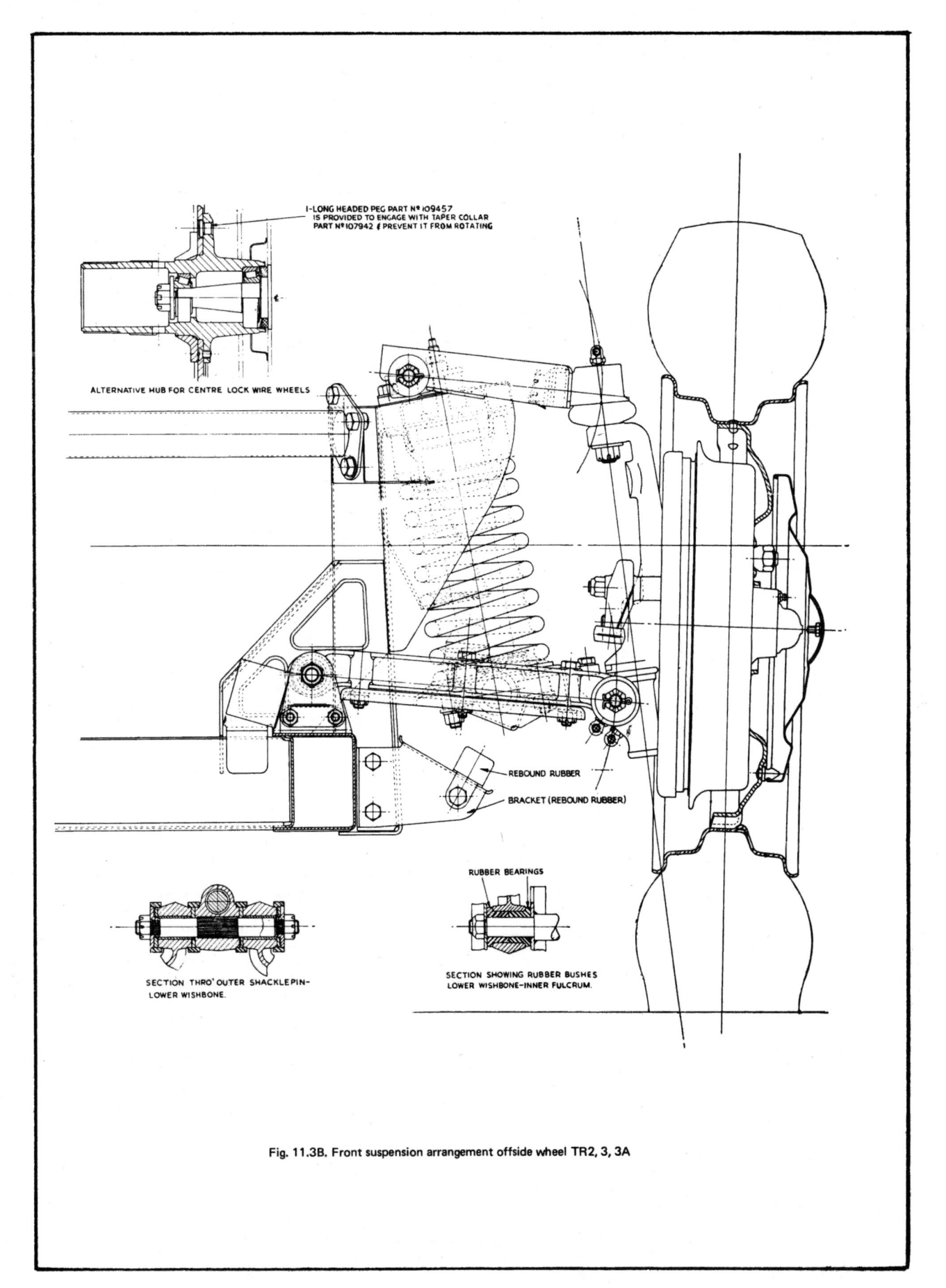

Fig. 11.3B. Front suspension arrangement offside wheel TR2, 3, 3A

Chapter 11/Suspension - Dampers - Steering

also been removed. The inner bearing (27) may be left on the stub axle or may be loose so be careful not to allow it to drop on the floor as the hub is being withdrawn.

7. Using a soft metal drift carefully remove the two bearing outer tracks from the hub (28) making a note of which way round they are fitted.

8. With a universal two leg puller remove the inner track of the bearing (27) from the stub axle (22).

9. Remove the four nuts, spring washers and bolts which secure the hub grease catcher to the brake backplate. Lift away the grease catcher.

10 Thoroughly wash all dismantled parts in clean petrol and dry using a non-fluffy rag. Inspect the oil seal (26) for signs of deterioration which, if evident, the oil seals should be renewed.

11 Carefully examine both races for signs of wear or overheating. The rollers should show no signs of pitting or grooving and when each bearing is assembled in the hand and rotated between the fingers their operation should be smooth. Fit new bearings if any part is suspect.

12 If the oil seal (26) is to be renewed, remove the old felt from the backing washer and affix a new piece using a jointing compound. When dry, soak the felt in clean engine oil and squeeze out any surplus oil.

13 Seat the grease seal on its spigot of the vertical link with the felt pad facing towards the centre of the car. Refit the inner wheel bearing (27).

14 Replace the hub grease catcher so that the shaped end of the pressing is below the vent hole in the brake backplate. Refit the grease catcher retaining nuts, bolts and spring washers.

15 If the bearing outer tracks have been removed from the hub these or new ones should be refitted to the hub using a soft faced hammer and a soft metal drift. Ensure that the tracks are fitted the correct way round.

16 Repack the hub and bearings with grease working it well into the bearings and refit the hub to the stub axle. Replace the 'D' washer (33) and the castellated nut (32).

17 It will now be necessary to adjust the hub bearings by first tightening the castellated nut (32) to a torque wrench setting of 10 lb.ft. and then turning back by between 1½ to 2 flats until a new split pin (34) can be inserted into the stub axle end.

18 The grease cap (35) should not be packed with grease but refitted dry. If a grease nipple (30) was originally fitted this should be replaced and the hub greased with a grease gun.

19 Refit the road wheel and remove the axle stands.

6. Front Hubs - Removal, Dismantling, Inspection, Reassembly and Refitting (TR3, 3A, 4, 4A)

The procedure for dismantling and overhaul of the hubs is identical to that for TR2 models with the exception of the disc brake calliper. This should be removed by undoing and removing the two bolts that secure the calliper to the vertical link. It is not necessary to disconnect the hydraulic flexible hose. Suspend the calliper using wire or string so as not to strain the flexible hose. Refer to Section 5 of this Chapter for full service information.

7. Stub Axle - Removal and Refitting

1. Refer to Section 5 or Section 6 of this Chapter and remove the hub assembly.

2. To remove the stub axle from the vertical link refer to Fig. 11.1 and extract the split pin (25). Undo the castellated nut (23) and remove together with the plain washer (24).

3. The stub axle (22) may be removed from the vertical link (12) by placing a soft wood block on the threaded end of the stub axle (22) and tapping the wood block so as to release the stub axle.

4. Refitting the stub axle is the reverse sequence to removal.

8. Front Suspension Coil Spring - Removal and Refitting

1. Chock the rear wheels and apply the handbrake. Slacken the road wheel nuts, jack up the front of the car and place on axle stands positioned under the chassis frame. Remove the road wheels.

2. Place a small jack under the spring pan (57) (Fig. 11.1) and partially compress the road spring (62). Ensure that the jack is firmly positioned on the ground and well located on the spring pan otherwise it may fly out.

3. Undo and remove the upper shock absorber retaining lock nut (71) and nut (70) from the stud on the end of the shock absorber. Lift away the plain washer (69) and upper rubber mounting (67).

4. Undo and remove the two long bolts, nuts and spring washers that secure the suspension rebound rubber (77) and its bracket from the side of the chassis frame. Lift away the rebound rubber and bracket.

5. Carefully lower the small jack from under the spring pan.

6. Undo and remove the four nuts and lock washers from the underside and centre of the spring pan. Lift away the rebound rubber abutment plate and the shock absorber may then be withdrawn through the spring plate.

7. Extract the six split pins (61) (Fig. 11.1) from the castellated nuts (60) on the underside of the lower wishbones (42, 43).

8. Remove the bump rubber (59) from the rear wishbone (43) and also the bolt (58) from the front wishbone (42). At this stage do not remove the four remaining nuts (60).

9. Insert two pieces of 3/8 inch threaded metal rod six inches long into the holes left by the bolt (58) and bump rubber (59) to act as a guide and place the small jack under the spring pan (57) and compress the spring again.

10 Undo and remove the four remaining nuts (60) and very carefully lower the jack ensuring that the spring pan slides down the two previously positioned guide pins. When all tension on the spring has been released, remove the jack and lift away the spring (62) together with rubber washers (63) and packing piece (64).

11 Inspect the coil spring for signs of excessive corrosion or cracking and, if evident, the coil springs must be renewed as a pair otherwise the stability of the car can be affected.

12 Check that the length of the spring is within the limits specified at the beginning of this Chapter. Examine the rubber washers (63) for oil contamination or deterioration and obtain new ones if suspect.

13 To refit the coil spring a length of high tensile steel threaded rod will be required together with two high tensile steel nuts and a selection of thick washers.

14 Refit the spring by first assembling the rubber washers (63) at either end and the packing piece (64) with its spigot facing downwards onto the top of the spring.

15 Position the spring assembly up into the suspension unit with the packing piece to the top.

16 Slide the spring pan (57) onto the guide pins which were previously placed in the centre holes of the wishbones for spring removal purposes.

17 Using the high tensile steel rod, washers and nuts with the rod positioned through the centre of the coil spring, screw up the lower nut until the spring pan (57) is in position and secure in place with the four nuts (60) and the two bolts at the outer ends of the wishbones. At this point

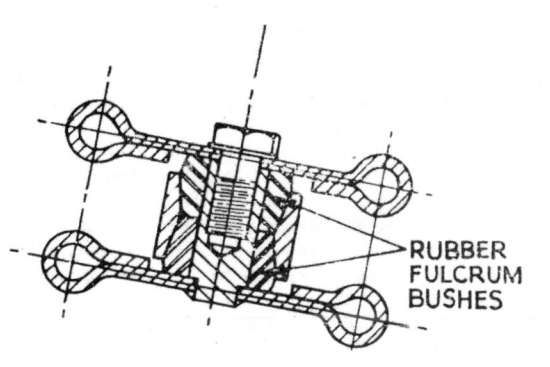

Fig. 11.4. Cross section of lower mounting brackets and bushes for damper (TR2, 3, 3A)

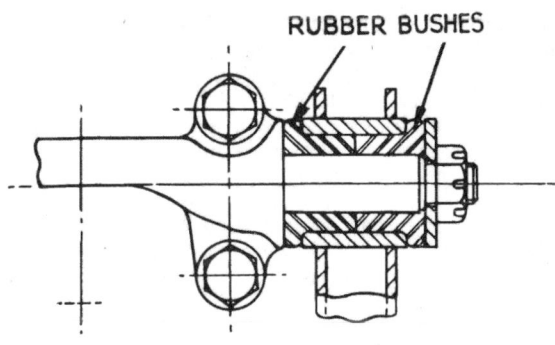

Fig. 11.5. Cross section of upper inner wishbone fulcrum showing location of rubber bushes (TR2, 3, 3A)

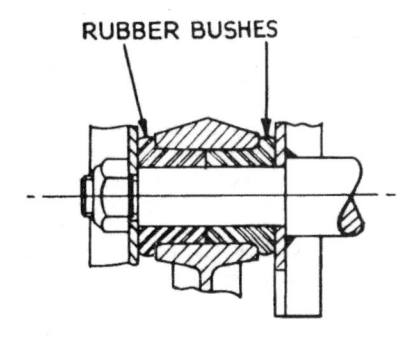

Fig. 11.6. Cross section through lower inner wishbone fulcrum. (TR2, 3, 3A)

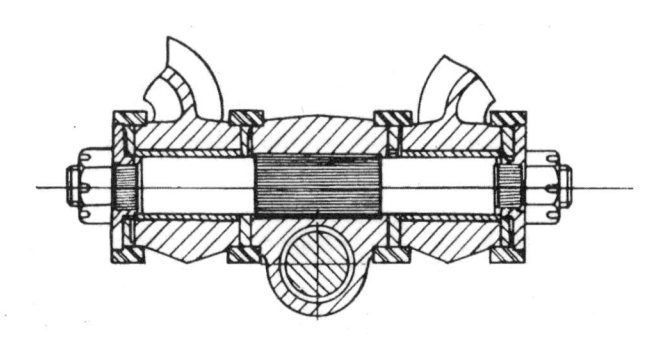

Fig. 11.7. Cross section through outer shackle pin and lower wishbone bearing. The bearings must be free to rotate and should have an endfloat of between 0.004 to 0.012 inch (TR2, 3, 3A)

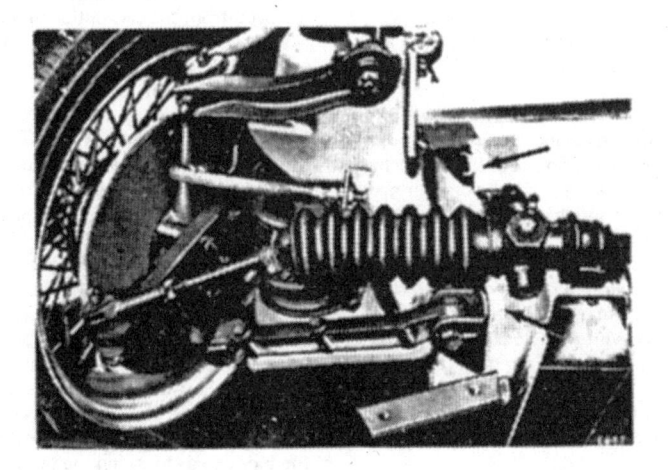

Fig. 11.8. Position of inner fulcrum brackets and shims (TR4, 4A)

Chapter 11/Suspension - Dampers - Steering

the high tensile steel rod and the two guide rods may be removed.

18 Refit the bump stop (59) onto the rear wishbone. Also refit the bolt (58) to the front wishbone.

19 Tighten all six nuts (60) in a diagonal manner and lock in position using new split pins (61).

20 The shock absorber may now be refitted by inserting it through the hole in the spring pan until the two retaining brackets locate on the studs of the spring pan assembly and, at the same time, the upper part of the shock absorber passes through the spring abutment on the chassis spring. The spring will have to be compressed slightly using the small jack to achieve the correct shock absorber fitting position.

21 Refit the second rubber mounting (67) with its spigot facing downwards onto the metal sleeve (68) followed by the plain washer (69) and nut (70). Tighten the nut until it just nips the plain washer and metal sleeve and lock this nut with the locknut (71).

22 Position the rebound rubber abutment plate onto the lower mounting studs, these being welded to the spring pan. Ensure that the apex of the wedge is pointing towards the centre of the car and retain in position using nuts and spring washers.

23 Refit the rebound rubber and its bracket (77) onto the chassis frame using two long bolts and secure with nuts and spring washers.

24 Remove the small jack and refit the road wheel. Lift the car from the axle stands and lower to the ground.

9. Front Suspension Shock Absorber - Removal and Refitting

1. Chock the rear wheels and apply the handbrake. Slacken the road wheel nuts, jack up the front of the car and place on axle stands positioned under the chassis frame. Remove the road wheels.

2. Place a small jack under the spring pan (57) (Fig. 11.1) and partially compress the road spring (62). Ensure that the jack is firmly positioned on the ground and well located on the spring pan otherwise it may fly out.

3. Undo and remove the upper shock absorber retaining locknut (71) and nut (70) from the stud on the end of the shock absorber. Lift away the plain washer (69) and upper rubber mounting (67).

4. Undo and remove the two long bolts, nuts and spring washers that secure the suspension rebound rubber (77) and its bracket from the side of the chassis frame. Lift away the rebound rubber and bracket.

5. Carefully lower the small jack from under the spring pan.

6. Undo and remove the four nuts and lock washers from the underside and centre of the spring pan. Lift away the rebound rubber abutment plate and the shock absorber may then be withdrawn through the spring plate.

7. Once the shock absorber has been removed from the car, bend back the locking plate tabs (75) and undo the setscrew (74). Lift away the setscrew followed by one of the brackets (73). The other bracket (72) may be withdrawn from the shock absorber eye together with the two part rubber bush (66). This second bracket has the fulcrum pin attached to it.

8. Check the rubber bushes for signs of deterioration due to oil contamination. Also check that the fulcrum pin is firmly attached to its bracket (72).

9. Inspect the external part of the damper for signs of hydraulic fluid leaks, denting or a bent ram which if any of these points are evident fit a new shock absorber.

10 The easiest way to test a shock absorber is to place the lower mounting eye between the soft faces of a firm bench vice and the shock absorber vertically positioned. Very slowly compress and extend the shock absorber for its full movement range twelve times and it should be observed that an equal and constant resistance is felt on the upward and downward strokes. If unequal resistance is felt on either or both strokes the shock absorber must be renewed as it is not possible to dismantle it.

11 To refit the shock absorber first press one rubber bush onto the fulcrum pin bracket (72) and insert the bush into the eye of the shock absorber. Fit the second part of the rubber bush onto the fulcrum pin. Fit the second bracket (73) followed by the tab washer (75) and secure with the setscrew (74). Lock the setscrew head by bending over the tab washer tabs.

12 With the shock absorber held vertically slide the plain washer (69) onto the upper mounting stud followed by the rubber mounting (67) with its spigot uppermost and the metal sleeve (68).

13 The shock absorber may now be refitted by inserting it through the hole in the spring pan until the two retaining brackets locate on the studs of the spring pan assembly and at the same time the upper part of the shock absorber passes through the spring abutment on the chassis spring. The spring will have to be compressed slightly using the small jack to achieve the correct shock absorber fitting position.

14 Refit the second rubber mounting (67) with its spigot facing downwards onto the metal sleeve (68) followed by the plain washer (69) and nut (70). Tighten the nut until it just nips the plain washer and metal sleeve and lock this nut with the lock nut (71).

15 Position the rebound rubber abutment plate onto the lower mounting studs, these being welded to the spring pan. Ensure that the apex of the wedge is pointing towards the centre of the car and retain in position using nuts and spring washers.

16 Refit the rebound rubber and its bracket (77) onto the chassis frame using two long bolts and secure with nuts and spring washers.

17 Remove the small jack and refit the road wheel. Lift the car from the axle stands and lower to the ground.

10. Front Suspension Top Ball Joint - Removal and Refitting (TR2, 3, 3A)

It is difficult to test a ball joint for wear once it has been removed from the car. Better to do this by rocking the road wheel with the hands placed in the 6 and 12 o'clock positions whilst a second person watches for movement of the top ball joint. To remove the ball joint proceed as follows:-

1. Chock the rear wheels, apply the handbrake and jack up the front of the car. Place the car on axle stands placed on the main chassis members. Remove the road wheel.

2. Using a small jack support the weight of the suspension unit under the spring pan.

3. Refer to Fig. 11.1 and extract the split pin from the castellated nut (13). Undo and remove the nut followed by the plain washer (14).

4. Using a small ball joint separator disconnect the ball joint (8) from the vertical link (12). Should a ball joint separator not be available place a metal block or large hammer on one side of the tapered eye of the vertical link. Using a second hammer tap the opposite side of the eye to the block so as to spring the tapers.

5. Take the weight of the brake and hub assembly and undo the nut that secures the ball joint to the wishbones. Lift away the ball joint (8) and distance piece (11).

6. Refitting a new ball joint is the reverse sequence to removal. Always use a new split pin to secure the ball

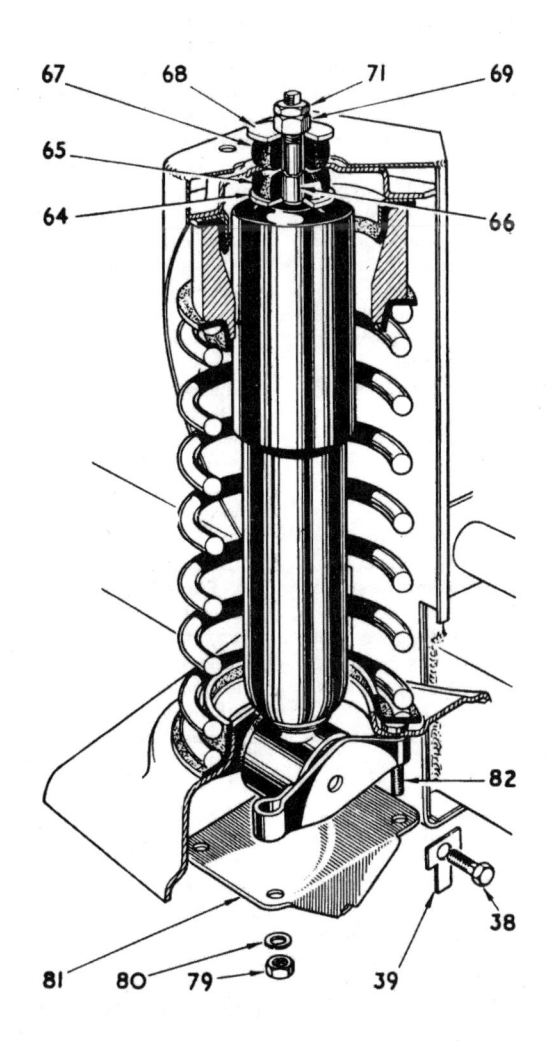

Fig. 11.9. FRONT SHOCK ABSORBER MOUNTING

38 Bolt	66 Washer	71 Locknut	82 Stud
39 Lockplate	67 Rubber bush	79 Bush	
64 Washer	68 Plain washer	80 Spring washer	
65 Rubber bush	69 Nut	81 Rebound stop plate	

Chapter 11/Suspension - Dampers - Steering

joint castellated nut.

11. Front Suspension Top Ball Joint - Removal and Refitting (TR4, 4A)

It is difficult to test a ball joint for wear once it has been removed from the car. Better to do this by rocking the road wheel with the hands placed in the 6 and 12 o'clock positions whilst a second person watches for movement of the top ball joint.

NOTE: A modified ball joint and upper wishbone assembly was fitted to TR4 cars after commission number CT 6390 and CT 6344 (fitted with wire wheels). This new type of ball joint was fitted as standard to all TR4A models. The service overhaul procedure for cars produced before the above quoted numbers is similar to details given in Section 10 of this Chapter.

1. Chock the rear wheels, apply the handbrake and jack up the front of the car. Place the car on axle stands placed on the main chassis members. Remove the road wheel.
2. Using a small jack support the weight of the suspension unit under the spring pan.
3. Refer to Fig. 11.2 and undo the nyloc nuts (15). Remove the nut followed by the plain washer (14).
4. Using a small ball joint separator disconnect the ball joint (12) from the vertical link (16). Should a ball joint separator not be available place a metal block or large hammer on one side of the tapered eye of the vertical link. Using a second hammer tap the opposite side of the eye to the block so as to spring the tapers.
5. Undo the two nyloc nuts (9) securing the upper ball joint retaining bolts (8) and lift away the nuts, bolts and plain washers (10). Note the positioning of the two bolts. The upper ball joint may now be removed.
6. Refitting the upper ball joint is the reverse sequence to removal.

12. Front Suspension Top Wishbones - Removal and Refitting (TR2, 3, 3A)

1. Chock the rear wheels, apply the handbrake and jack up the front of the car. Place the car on axle stands positioned on the main chassis members. Remove the road wheel.
2. Using a small jack support the weight of the suspension unit under the spring pan.
3. Extract the split pins (7) (Fig. 11.1) and undo the nuts (6). Lift away the nuts and plain washers (5).
4. Undo the nut which secures the top ball joint to the wishbones. Lift away the ball joint (8) and distance piece (11).
5. Carefully pull the two upper wishbones (2, 3) away from the fulcrum pin (1) together with the rubber bushes (4).
6. Remove the rubber bushes (4) and inspect for signs of oil contamination or deterioration and, if evident, new bushes should be fitted.
7. Reassembly is the reverse sequence to removal. Do not however tighten the nuts (6) fully until the car has been lowered to the ground and with two people sitting in the car so as to allow the suspension to be set at normal working height. Then tighten the nuts and lock using new split pins (7).

13. Front Suspension Top Wishbones - Removal and Refitting (TR4, 4A)

NOTE: A modified upper wishbone assembly was fitted to TR4 cars after commission number CT 6390 and CT 6344 (fitted with wire wheels). This new upper wishbone was fitted as standard to all TR4A models. The service overhaul procedure for cars produced before the above quoted numbers is similar to details given in Section 12 of this Chapter.

1. Chock the rear wheels, apply the handbrake and jack up the front of the car. Place the car on axle stands positioned on the main chassis member. Remove the road wheel.
2. Using a small jack support the weight of the suspension unit under the spring pan.
3. Undo the two nyloc nuts (9) (Fig. 11.2) securing the upper ball joint retaining bolts (8) and lift away the nuts, bolts and plain washers (10). Note the positioning of the two bolts.
4. Extract the split pins (6) and undo the nuts (7). Lift away the nuts and plain washers (5).
5. Carefully pull the two upper wishbones (3, 73) away from the fulcrum pin (1) together with the rubber bushes (2.4).
6. Remove the rubber bushes (2, 4) and inspect for signs of oil contamination or deterioration and, if evident, new bushes should be fitted.
7. Reassembly is the reverse sequence to removal. Do not however tighten the nuts (7) fully until the car has been lowered to the ground and with two people sitting in the car so as to allow the suspension to be set at its normal working height. Then tighten the nyloc nuts (7) fully.

14. Front Suspension Vertical Link and Lower Wishbones - Removal and Refitting (TR2)

1. Chock the rear wheels, apply the handbrake and jack up the front of the car. Place the car on axle stands positioned on the main chassis members. Remove the road wheel.
2. Refer to Section 8 and remove the coil spring and shock absorber.
3. It will now be necessary to drain part of the brake hydraulic system. Fit a piece of plastic tubing to the bleed nipple on the wheel cylinder on the side of the suspension which is to be dismantled. Put the other end of the tube in a clean glass jar. Open the bleed nipple and depress the brake pedal several times. Close the bleed nipple and remove the plastic tube.
4. Refer to Section 5 and remove the hub.
5. Refer to Fig. 11.1 and bend back the tabs on the locking plate (21). Undo and remove the two bolts (16, 17) and nuts (19), which secure the steering lever (15) to the vertical link (12). Collect the distance piece (18).
6. Undo the two setscrews (20) that secure the brake backplate to the vertical link once the tab washer (21) tabs have been bent back. The backplate may now be withdrawn.
7. Remove the nuts (56) and bolts (55) that secure the bracket (53). Next remove the nyloc nut (54) and lift away the brackets (53).
8. Withdraw the split pin (51) and remove the nuts followed by the seal washers and bush (49, 48, 47, 44). Carefully remove the two lower wishbones (42, 43) and this will leave the remainder of the suspension only attached to the two top wishbones.
9. To remove the remainder of the suspension system undo the two bolts that secure the fulcrum pin (1) in position and then lift away the remaining suspension system.
10 If it is not required to disturb the upper wishbones or top ball joint the vertical link may be separated at the ball joint by extracting the split pin from the castellated nut (13). Undo and remove the nut followed by the plain washer (14).
11 Using a small ball joint separator disconnect the ball joint (8) from the vertical link (12). Should a ball joint

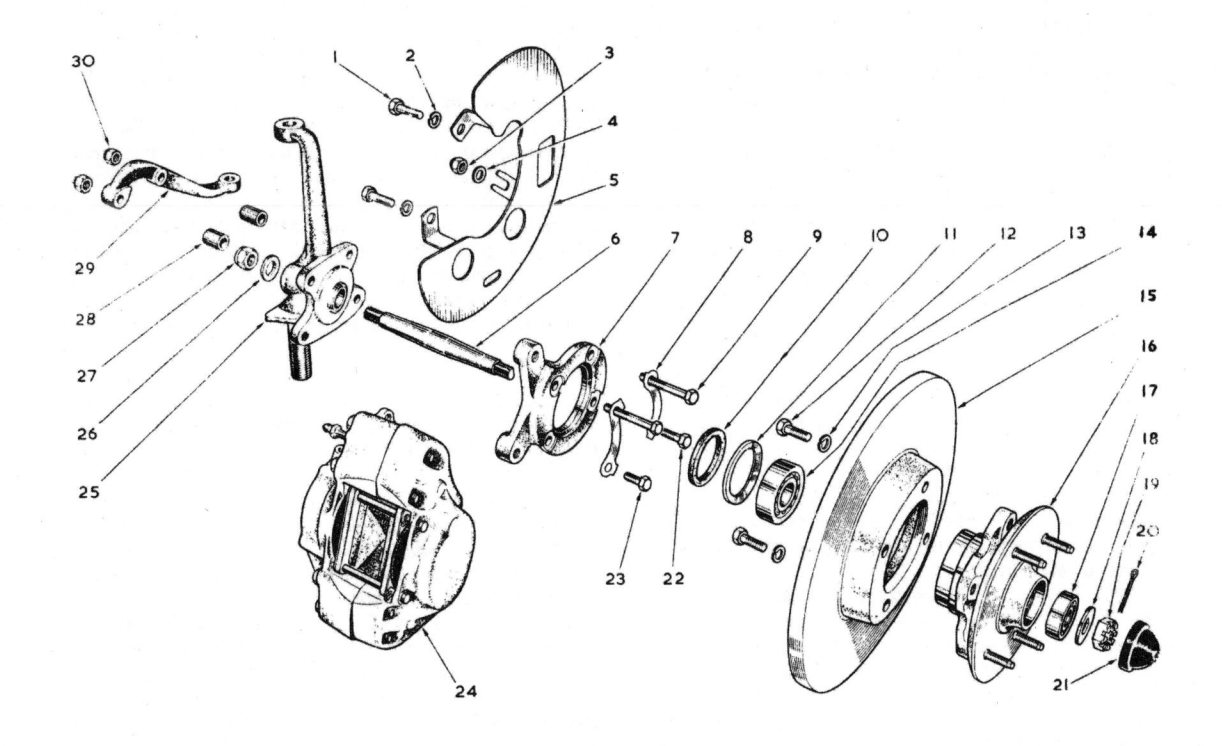

Fig. 11.10. DISC BRAKE AND HUB COMPONENTS (TR3, 3A, 4, 4A)

1 Bolt	9 Bolt	17 Outer taper race	25 Vertical link
2 Spring washer	10 Felt seal	18 Washer	26 Plain washer
3 Nyloc nut	11 Seal retainer	19 Slotted nut	27 Nyloc nut
4 Plain washer	12 Bolt	20 Split pin	28 Distance pieces
5 Dust shield	13 Spring washer	21 Hub cap	29 Steering arm
6 Stub axle	14 Inner taper race	22 Bolt	30 Nyloc nut
7 Calliper bracket	15 Disc	23 Bolt	
8 Tab plate	16 Hub	24 Calliper unit	

Chapter 11/Suspension - Dampers - Steering

separator not be available place a metal block or large hammer on one side of the tapered eye of the vertical link. Using a second hammer tap the opposite side of the eye to the block so as to spring the tapers.

12 Undo the bolt (38) and lift away the eccentric collar (37). This will allow the bottom trunnion (36) to be unscrewed from the vertical link (12). Lift away the oil seal (41).

13 Thoroughly wash all parts in paraffin and wipe dry using a non fluffy rag.

14 Inspect the trunnion (36) and the vertical link (12) for signs of wear especially the threads in the lower trunnion and on the end of the vertical link. If these are worn a new trunnion and vertical link must be fitted as a pair and not singly.

15 Carefully examine all pivoting parts for wear. Also inspect the rubber bushes for signs of deterioration or oil contamination and, if evident, a new set of bushes should be fitted. Inspect the oil seal (41) similarly and fit new if suspect.

16 Generally inspect the wishbone for signs of twisting or bending and obtain new parts if suspect. Do not attempt to straighten them.

17 With all parts ready for reassembly and new items obtained where required the method of reassembling will depend to a certain extent on how far the unit was dismantled. Instructions are given assuming that the upper wishbone members are still in position.

18 First fit the ball pin taper into the vertical link with the rubber gaiter (10) in position. Refit the plain washer (14) and secure with the castellated nut (13). Lock the castellated nut with a new split pin.

19 Check that the pin in the trunnion assembly (36) is a tight fit as it should be a press fit being held in position by splines. Also ensure that it is centralised with the ends equidistant from the centre of the trunnion. If it is not central refit one nut and tap the end with a soft faced hammer.

20 Replace the rubber sealing ring (41) to the lower threaded end of the vertical link and screw on the bottom trunnion (36). It should be screwed home, without forcing and then turned back one complete turn, and then positioned so that the shackle pin lies parallel to the body of the car, but inwards, between the base of the vertical link and the chassis frame as the shackle pin is offset.

21 Refit the locking spring washer (39) and steering lock stop bush (37) onto the steering stop securing bolt (38) and replace on the bottom trunnion assembly. Do not tighten fully at this stage.

22 Replace the rubber bushes (52) to the inner lower fulcrum pin located on the upper face of the chassis frame.

23 Fit the two thrust washers (47) and grease seals (49) onto the shackle pin, one to each side of the shackle pin.

24 Replace the lower wishbone arms (42, 43) onto the rubber bushes already positioned on the inner fulcrum pin and onto the bottom trunnion shackle pin. Fit the second pair of rubber bushes (52) onto the inner fulcrum pin and into the lower wishbone arm. Next refit the support bracket (53) with the two holes lower most. Secure the brackets in position using the nyloc nuts (54) but do not tighten fully at this stage.

25 Attach the support brackets (53) to the brackets welded to the chassis frame using nuts (56), bolts (55) and spring washers. Now is the time to tighten the nyloc nuts (54) securely.

26 Fit onto each end of the trunnion shackle a thrust washer (47), lockwasher with collar facing inwards (48) and the rubber grease seals (49). Refit the castellated nuts (50) onto each end of the shackle pin.

27 To give the required end float, tighten the two castellated nuts (50) equally until the assembly feels solid. Next turn back the nuts between ½ to 2 flats until the split pin holes are visible. Lock the nut (50) with a new split pin (51). By these means the required end float of between 0.004 and 0.012 inch should be obtained.

28 Using a soft faced hammer carefully tap the lower wishbones outwards so as to set the lockwashers (48) correctly.

29 Refer to Section 8 and refit the coil spring and shock absorber.

30 Refer to Section 5 and refit the front hub assembly.

31 The braking system must next be bled as detailed in Chapter 9, Section 10.

32 Replace the road wheel and lower the car to the ground. By bouncing the front of the car up and down check that the front suspension unit is able to move vertically freely without signs of binding.

33 The steering lockstop collar (37) should be adjusted to 31 degrees back lock and 28½ degrees front lock, and to make this adjustment correctly a specialist calibrated turntable as used to check front wheel alignment will be required. This is therefore a job to be left to the local garage.

15. Front Suspension, Vertical Link and Lower Wishbone - Removal and Refitting (TR3, 3A, 4)

Certain modifications were introduced on the TR3 and subsequent models, fitted with front disc brakes, as well as slight differences in design. As the disc brake calliper is bolted directly to the vertical link it must be removed every time the hub is to be withdrawn from the stub axle.

In place of the brake drum a disc is bolted to the hub. Due to the difference in brake design there is no backplate but instead a dust cover is bolted in its place.

The bottom wishbone rubber bushes were changed to steel and nylon bushes with rubber sealing rings to prevent wear on the nylon bushes. Also white metal thrust washers were changed to nylon.

For full service information the procedure is basically identical to that in the previous section, but bearing in mind the above detailed modifications, the following additional information should assist and is applicable only to the models covered by this Section.

1. It is not necessary to disconnect the hydraulic flexible hose but instead, remove the calliper retaining bolts, and suspend the calliper using string or wire so that the flexible hose is not strained.

2. When assembling the lower wishbone first fit the rubber sealing rings to the nylon washers and insert the nylon bushes into the ends of the lower wishbone arms. Next smear the fulcrum pin with a little grease and slide the bushes into place on the fulcrum pin. Smear the outside of the steel bushes and fit one pair of nylon washers complete with sealing rings. Also smear the lower trunnion shackle pin with a little grease and slide the lower wishbone onto the steel bushes on the fulcrum pin and the shackle pin of the trunnion at the same time. When in position place the outer pair of nylon washers and sealing rings over the fulcrum pin and shackle pin. Refit the nuts securing the lower wishbone arms in place and set the end float as detailed in Section 14, Item 27. Thereafter reassembly procedures are identical.

16. Front Suspension Unit, Vertical Link and Lower Wishbone - Removal and Refitting (TR4A)

The basic design of the front suspension unit is identical to that for the TR3, 3A and 4 models and is serviced in the main as described in Section 15. However there were several

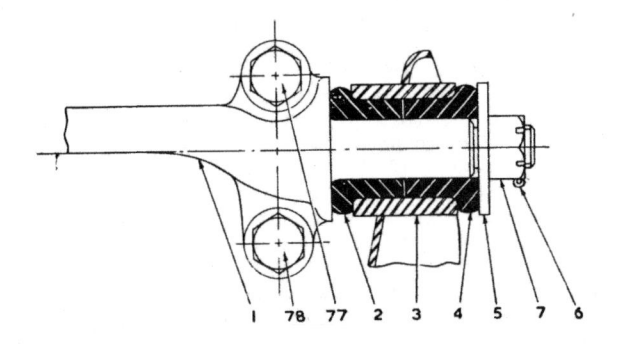

Fig. 11.11. Cross section through upper inner fulcrum (TR4, 4A)

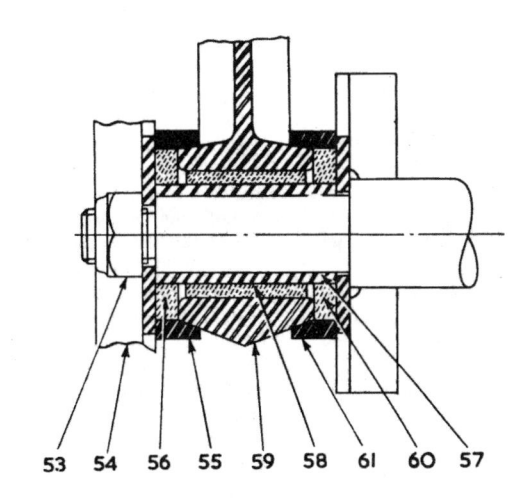

Fig. 11.12. Cross section through bottom inner fulcrum

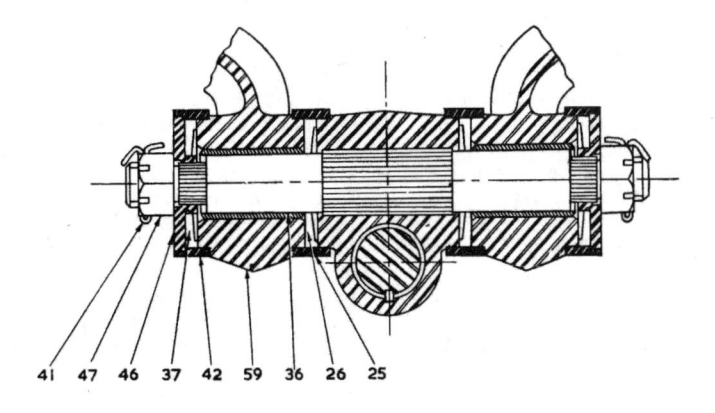

Fig. 11.13. Cross section through lower outer fulcrum

Chapter 11/Suspension - Dampers - Steering

minor modifications which will be apparent as work proceeds. These will probably include the following slight changes.

1. The inner fulcrum brackets of the lower wishbone arms are shimmed and positioned vertically to the chassis. Fig. 11.8 shows this modification arrowed.
2. The inner fulcrum brackets are secured to the chassis with nyloc nuts and not conventional nuts and spring washers.
3. The outer mounting for the lower trunnion bracket has been modified so that now the trunnion bracket can be removed from the lower wishbones without disturbing the lower inner fulcrum brackets and their shims.

17. Rear Spring - Removal and Refitting (Conventional Suspension)

1. Chock the front and rear of the front wheels and raise the rear end of the car as high as possible and place on axle stands positioned on the chassis members.
2. Remove the road wheel and also, to give better working space, the rear wing stay that is positioned behind the rear wheel between the wing and the chassis, this being held by nuts, bolts, plain and spring washers.
3. Refer to Fig. 11.14 and hold the bottom damper link (16) hexagon mounting and undo the nyloc nut (20). Push the damper link (16) upwards out of the way of the working area.
4. Undo and remove the two nuts (10) and spring washers followed by the shackle assembly plate (9) from the rear end of the spring.
5. Withdraw the other part of the shackle, the shackle pin and plate (7) from the spring eye and chassis mounting. Also remove the rubber bushes (8) from the spring eye and chassis mounting.
6. Screw a 5/16 inch x 24 UNF bolt into the head of the front fulcrum bolt (3) to a depth of approximately ½ inch. Extract the split pin (6), undo the nut (4) and remove followed by the 'D' washer (5).
7. Using a tyre lever positioned under the head of the 5/16 inch bolt carefully withdraw the fulcrum bolt (3).
8. With a small jack positioned under the spring to support its weight, and packing under the axle to take its weight, undo the four nyloc nuts (13) that hold the two 'U' bolts (11) onto the mounting plate (12). Lift away the nuts (13) and plain washers (14).
9. Remove the 'U' bolts (11) followed by the mounting plate (12) and at this point the spring (1) may be withdrawn from the underside of the car.
10 Remove the silentbloc bush (2) from the front spring eye using a suitable size drift.
11 Should it be necessary the spring may be dismantled by holding securely in a bench vice. Using a chisel bend open the clips by a sufficient amount to allow the leaves to be lifted out later.
12 Undo and remove the centre bolt whereupon the leaves may be separated.
13 The parts of the spring should be thoroughly cleaned in either petrol or paraffin and wiped dry using a non fluffy rag. Do not, of course, wash the rubber parts in petrol or paraffin but wipe clean with a rag.
13 Inspect the spring for wear especially where each leaf ends and rubs on the lower leaf. Check for cracks, particularly around the centre bolt hole. If the spring is unserviceable, rear springs must be fitted in pairs otherwise stability of the car could be affected.
14 Check the bushes for deterioration or oil contamination and, if evident, new bushes should be fitted.
15 Whilst reassembling the spring leaves coat each leaf with a graphite grease to ensure silent operation and long life.
16 To assemble the spring place the head of the centre bolt vertically in a vice and refit each spring leaf in turn until all are in place and then secure with the bolt.
17 With the spring leaf clips in position bend the clips back so as to hold the leaves firmly. Squeezing the clip using the vice will give satisfactory results.
18 Press the forward silent bloc bush (2) into the front eye of the spring.
19 Position the spring under the car, with the shorter end forward, so that it is above the rear shackle bracket of the chassis and yet below the axle.
20 Using a small jack support the weight of the spring assembly and loosely attach the spring plate (12) to the shock absorber link (16) and fit the nyloc nut (20).
21 Position the 'U' bolts (11) over the axle on either side of the spring and carefully insert the threaded part of the 'U' bolt through the holes in the spring plate (12). Do not damage the threads. Refit the four nyloc nuts (13) and plain washers (14).
22 Tighten the shock absorber link mounting nyloc nut (20) securely.
23 Insert the front bolt (3) from the inner side of the chassis frame through its support tube into the silentbloc bush of the road spring and position the machined flat on the head of the bolt against its abutment on the inner side of the chassis frame. Refit the 'D' washer (5) followed by the castellated nut (4). Tighten the nut securely and lock with a new split pin (6).
24 Refit the two rubber half bushes (7, 8) to the eye at the rear end of the road spring. Next fit the second pair of half bushes (7, 8) into the shackle eye on the chassis frame.
25 Carefully push the shackle pins of the shackle assembly (7) through the rubber bushes (7, 8) and once in position refit the shackle plate (9) to the exposed ends of the shackle pins. Fit spring washers and secure with nuts (10).
26 Refit the rear wing stay by positioning it behind the rear wheel in the wing valance and the chassis bracket. Secure it using nuts, bolts, plain and spring washers.
27 Remove the axle stands from the rear of the car and lower to the ground.

18. Rear Shock Absorber - Removal and Refitting (Conventional Suspension)

1. Chock the front and rear of the front wheels and raise the rear end of the car as high as possible and place on axle stands positioned on the chassis members. Remove the road wheel.
2. Refer to Fig. 11.14 and undo the nyloc nut (20) that secures the link (16) to the mounting plate (12).
3. Undo and remove the nut (19) that secures the shock absorber arm to the link (16).
4. It may be necessary to use a small universal ball joint separator to disconnect the arm from the link as it is a taper fit. Should a universal ball joint separator not be available place a metal block of heavy hammer against one side of the tapered eye on the steering arm. Using a second hammer, shock the taper apart by tapping on the opposite side of the eye to the metal block or hammer.
5. Undo the two nuts (18) and lift away followed by the bolts (17) and the shock absorber itself.
6. Thoroughly clean the exterior of the shock absorber and place in a vertical position in a vice so that the arm can be moved up and down.
7. Undo the filler plug (25) (Fig. 11.15) and top up the oil level, using correct grade oil, to the base of the filler plug boss. Refit the filler plug.
8. Move the arm up and down about ten times so as to expel

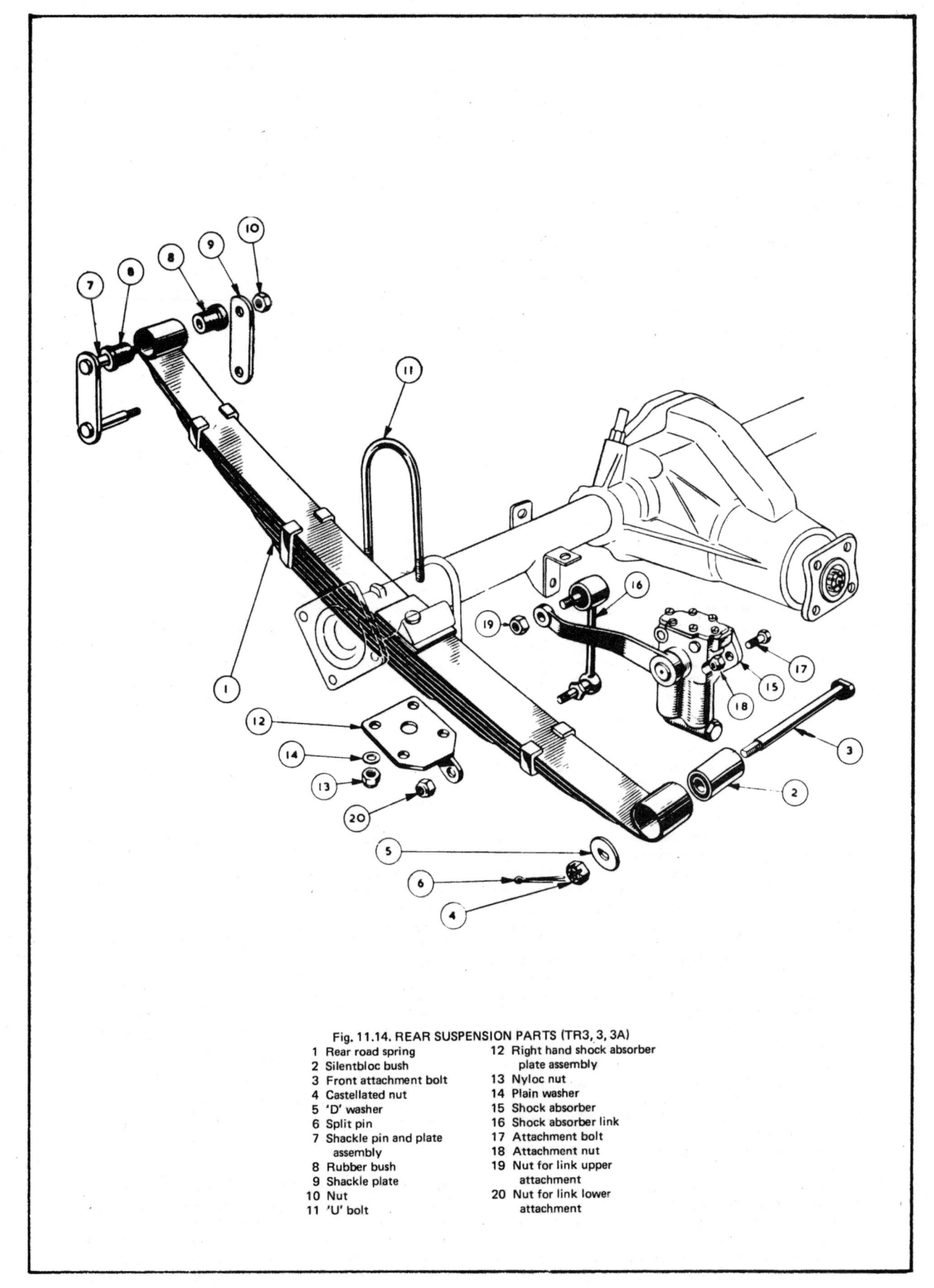

Fig. 11.14. REAR SUSPENSION PARTS (TR3, 3, 3A)
1 Rear road spring
2 Silentbloc bush
3 Front attachment bolt
4 Castellated nut
5 'D' washer
6 Split pin
7 Shackle pin and plate assembly
8 Rubber bush
9 Shackle plate
10 Nut
11 'U' bolt
12 Right hand shock absorber plate assembly
13 Nyloc nut
14 Plain washer
15 Shock absorber
16 Shock absorber link
17 Attachment bolt
18 Attachment nut
19 Nut for link upper attachment
20 Nut for link lower attachment

Chapter 11/Suspension - Dampers - Steering

any air that might be in the system. It should be found that on the final strokes an equal and constant resistance should be felt on both the upwards and downwards strokes. If unequal resistance is felt on either stroke a replacement shock absorber should be obtained.

9. Refitting the shock absorber is the reverse sequence to removal.

19. Rear Spring - Removal and Refitting (Independent Rear Suspension - TR4A)

1. Chock the front and rear of the front wheels and raise the rear end of the car as high as possible and place on axle stands positioned on the chassis members. Remove the road wheel. Place a small jack under the suspension arm.
2. Refer to Fig. 11.16 and undo the locknut (28). Remove the locknut followed by the nut (27), backing plate (26), rubber buffer (24) and separate the shock absorber link (21) from the suspension arm. Recover the upper rubber buffer (24) and backing plate (26).
3. Thread some wire through the two universal joints to stop the two halves separating. Undo the four nyloc nuts and bolts that secure the inner universal joint coupling flange to the final drive unit.
4. Carefully lower the small jack under the suspension arm keeping a check on the flexible hose to make sure that it is not strained. The spring (15) may now be lifted out followed by the lower rubber insulator (17) and upper rubber insulator (16).
5. Inspect the spring for signs of excessive rusting or cracking and, if evident, a new pair of springs must be fitted. If only one new spring is fitted the stability of the car can be affected. Check the height of the spring against dimensions given in the specifications, at the beginning of this Chapter. Check that the rubber insulators (16, 17) are in good order and should be renewed if suspect.
6. Refitting the spring is the reverse sequence to removal.

20. Rear Suspension Arm - Removal and Refitting (Independent Rear Suspension - TR4A)

1. Refer to Section 19 and remove the rear spring.
2. Using a small jack raise the suspension arm so as to relieve the weight from its mountings.
3. Place a piece of plastic hose onto the rear brake bleed nipple. Insert the free end of the plastic hose into a clean glass jar and open the bleed nipple. Drain the brake hydraulic system by operating the brake pedal. Close the bleed nipple and remove the plastic hose.
4. Remove the brake drum from the hub assembly. If difficulty is experienced in withdrawing the drum slacken off the brake adjustment and tap the back flange of the drum using a soft faced hammer.
5. Thread some wire through the two universal joints to hold the two halves of the axle shaft together and, using a socket wrench passed through the holes in the driving flange (43) (Fig. 8.8) remove the six nuts securing the hub assembly (46) to the suspension arm.
6. Undo the four nuts (31) and bolts (32) which secure the inboard coupling to the flange (28) on the final drive unit.
7. Carefully withdraw the axle shaft through the boss in the suspension.
8. Disconnect the handbrake cable from the handbrake lever at the rear of the brake backplate.
9. Refer to Chapter 9, Section 9 and disconnect the brake hydraulic flexible hose.
10 Undo the nyloc nuts (10) and lift away followed by the plain washers (9). Withdraw the bolts (8) and lift the suspension arm from the underside of the car Fig. 11.16

11 Inspect the rubber bushes (5) for signs of deterioration and, if evident, the bushes should be renewed. To remove the bushes they may be pressed out using a socket of suitable diameter between the jaws of a vice. When new bushes are being fitted insert a bolt into the centre bush to protect the bush against distortion and lubricate the bush with rubber grease.

12 Normally it should not be necessary to remove the two brackets (6, 7) but should this be required take great care of the shims (14) and refit them in their original position. Also ensure that the brackets are fitted in their original position and are identified with four grooves to be fitted uppermost on the outside bracket and the inside bracket has two grooves which again must be fitted uppermost.

13 Refitting the suspension arm is the reverse sequence to removal but the following additional points should be noted.

14 Do not fully tighten the nuts (10) until all is assembled and the car is back on the ground. With two people sitting in the car to give it a normal ride condition then tighten the nuts.

15 Whenever the suspension arm is removed it is recommended that the car be taken to the local agent so that the rear wheel alignment may be checked, otherwise if it is incorrect car stability and tyre wear will be affected.

21. Outer Axle Shaft and Hub Assembly - Removal and Refitting (Independent Rear Suspension - TR4A)

1. The drive shafts and hubs are removed from the suspension arm and this will be necessary if the universal joints or hub bearings require service attention.
2. Working on one side of the car, remove the hub cap and loosen the wheel nuts. Chock the front wheels, jack up the rear of the car and support on stands. Take off the road wheel.
3. Undo the two countersunk screws holding the brake drum to the hub drive flange (43) (Fig. 8.8).
4. Carefully pull off the brake drum. If it is tight slacken off the brake adjustment, full details of which are given in Chapter 9, Section 8. Using a soft faced hammer tap the flange on the circumference of the brake drum to free it from the studs.
5. Upon close inspection it will be found that there is a hole in the hub flange (43) which is sufficiently large to allow a socket to pass through. Undo and remove the six nyloc nuts which hold the bearing housing (46) to the boss on the suspension arm boss.
6. Undo the four nuts and bolts (31, 32) holding the inboard universal coupling (30a) to the inner axle shaft flange (28).
7. Using a piece of wire threaded through the two universal joints of the axle shaft to stop the halfshafts (35, 39) from separating.
8. Carefully withdraw the axle shaft through the suspension arm boss.
9. It will be noted that it is not necessary to disturb the braking system.
10 Refitting is the reverse procedure to removal. Do not forget to remove the wire holding the two universal joints together.

22. Stub Axle Shaft and Hub Assembly - Dismantling and Reassembly (Independent Rear Suspension - TR4A)

1. To dismantle this shaft three special tools numbered S. 109A, S. 318 and S. 4221A16 are required as well as a torque wrench capable of being set to give a reading of

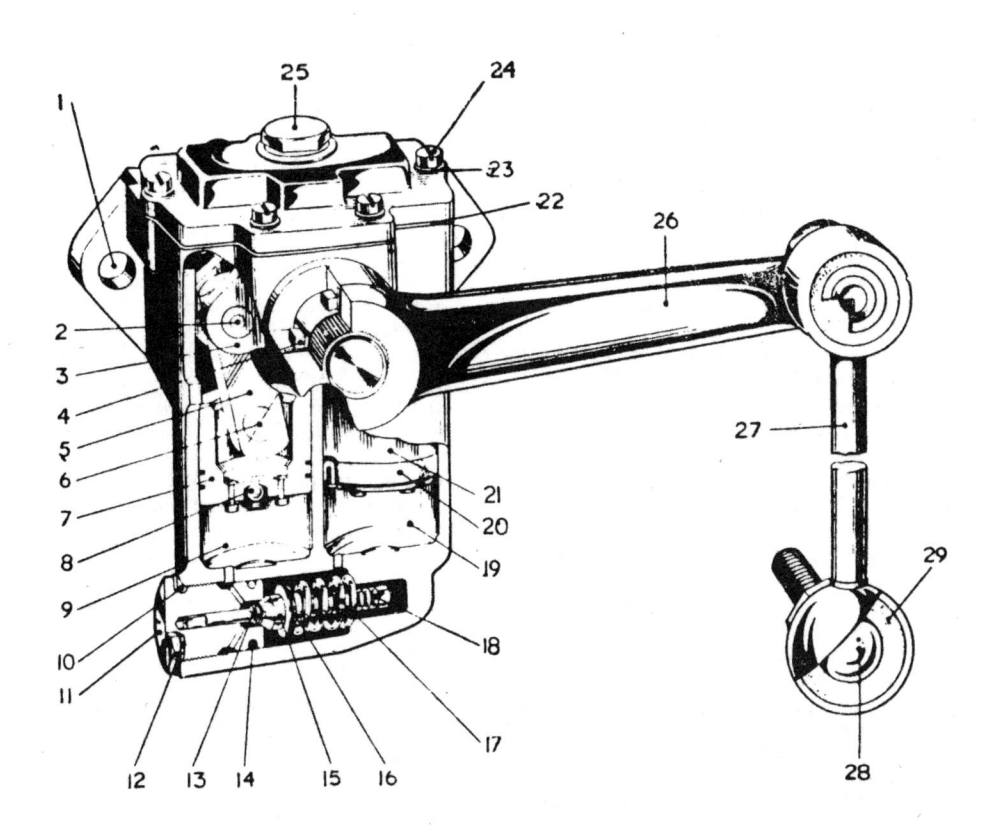

Fig. 11.15. REAR SHOCK ABSORBER COMPONENTS

1 Mounting holes	9 Compression or bump cylinder	16 Compression washer	24 Lid screw
2 Crank pin		17 Compression spring	25 Filler plug
3 Crank plat	10 Ring seal	18 Rebound spring	26 Arm
4 Oil seal	11 Valve screw	19 Rebound cylinder	27 Connecting link
5 Connecting rod	12 Valve screw washer	20 Rebound piston seal	28 Ball end bolt
6 Piston pin	13 Rebound valve	21 Rebound piston	29 Rubber cushion
7 Compression or bump piston	14 Ring seal	22 Gasket	
8 Recuperating valve	15 Compression valve	23 Shakeproof washer	

Chapter 11/Suspension - Dampers - Steering

90 - 100 lb.ft., and a dial indicator gauge. If these can be borrowed from a local Triumph agent so well and good but if not then we would recommend that the following work be left to the local agents.

2. Place a shaft in the holder S. 318 as shown in Fig. 11.17 which should be mounted in a good size vice.

3. Using a socket wrench undo and remove the nut (40) (Fig. 8.8). Lift away the washer (41) and with tool S. 109A withdraw the hub. Unfortunately there is no safe alternative method of removing the hub because of the high pressures required (see Fig. 11.17).

4. Whilst the hub is being removed, the bearing housing (46) will also come away with the hub.

5. Lift away the rectangular key (55) and throw away the collapsible spacer (47) as it must not be used again. Lift away the inner hub bearing cone (48) followed by the bearing spacer (50) and stone guard (51) making sure to take note which way round it fits.

6. Undo the lockwasher tabs (53) and turn the adjustment nut (52) and locknut (54) one complete revolution towards the universal joint.

7. Support the housing (46) under its mounting face and, using a soft metal drift, carefully drive out the bearing outer race (45).

8. It will now be necessary to use tool number S. 4221A16 to extract the outer hub bearing cone (45) from the hub. A large three leg puller can do this operation provided the feet are such that they can locate at the rear of the bearing inner track.

9. Thoroughly wash all displaced components in paraffin and dry using a clean rag.

10 Inspect the bearing rollers for signs of wear, pitting or cracking and, if evident, the bearing must be renewed. Also inspect the stub shaft (56) and the hub (46) for wear or damage especially around the inner hub bearing seat. If any part is suspect it should be renewed.

11 To reassemble first press the outer hub bearing cone (45) up to the shoulder on the hub (46). A metal tube of suitable diameter may be used to drift the bearing cone into place if a press is not available. Be careful not to tilt the cone when refitting to the hub.

12 Press the outer and inner hub bearing outer races up to the shoulder in the bearing housing (46). Alternatively a soft metal drift may be used. As in the previous operation be careful not to tilt the cone when refitting the hub.

13 Refit the inner and outer oil seals (44, 49).

14 Replace the stone guard (51), bearing spacer (50), the inner cone of the inner hub bearing and a new collapsible spacer (47) onto the stub shaft and fit the rectangular key (55) into the stub shaft. The inner end of the key should be in line with the two indentations on the shoulders of the keyway.

15 The bearing housing should be well packed with the correct grade grease. Ensure that there is plenty of grease in the spacer between the two roller bearings.

16 Fit the bearing housing over the stubshaft until the inner hub bearing outer race engages with its mating cone. Special care must be taken not to damage the lip of the inner oil seal.

17 Refit the hub onto the stubshaft followed by the plain washer (41) and nut (40). Using a torque wrench set to a reading of between 90 - 100 lb.ft. tighten the stubshaft nut.

18 It will now be necessary to reset the bearing end float first with the axle shaft assembled to the holding tool as shown in Fig. 11.17 tighten the nut (52) to the stoneguard (51) until it is finger tight.

19 Attach a dial indicator gauge onto the hub flange with the stylus touching the bearing housing flange as shown in Fig. 11.18.

20 Firmly pull the bearing housing as far as possible downwards away from the dial indicator gauge. Use a rocking motion to ensure correct contact of the bearing parts and set the dial to zero.

21 Push the bearing housing towards the dial indicator gauge once more using a rocking motion to ensure correct contact of the bearing parts and this time note the reading on the dial.

22 Slowly tighten the large nut (52) one flat at a time. At each flat repeat operations 20 and 21 above until an end float reading of between 0.004 - 0.002 inch is obtained and lock the adjustment nut (52) with the nut (54) and tab washer (53).

23 Should for any reason insufficient care have been taken and the end float is accidentally reduced to below 0.002 inch the collapsible spacer (47) must be renewed. It will not spring back to its original dimensions.

23. Outer Axle Shaft - Dismantling and Reassembly (Independent Rear Suspension - TR4A)

1. Wash the exterior of the shaft and joints in paraffin and dry using a clean non fluffy rag.

2. Place the assembly on a clean bench top and remove the wire that was previously threaded through the two universal joints.

3. Undo the clips holding the two ends of the rubber gaiter (36) (Fig. 8.8) to the inner and outer axle shafts (35, 39).

4. Carefully withdraw the outer sliding axle shaft (39) from the fixed shaft (35). Lift away the gaiter and clips.

5. Inspect the gaiter for signs of cracking, splitting or hardening especially the area around the two clips and obtain a new gaiter if necessary.

6. Dismantling of the universal joints is identical to that for the propeller shaft universal joints, full details of which are given in Chapter 7, Section 5.

24. Rear Shock Absorber - Removal and Refitting (Independent Rear Suspension - TR4A)

1. Chock the front and rear of the front wheels and raise the rear end of the car as high as possible and place on axle stands positioned on the chassis members. Remove the road wheel.

2. Using a small jack raise the suspension arm so as to relieve the weight from its mountings.

3. Refer to Fig. 11.16 and undo the locknut (28). Remove the locknut followed by the nut (27), backing plate (26), rubber buffer (24) and separate the shock absorber link (21) from the suspension arm (1). Recover the upper rubber buffer (24) and backing plate (26).

4. Undo and remove the two nuts and bolts that secure the shock absorber to the chassis and lift away the nuts, bolts (19) and spring washers followed by the shock absorber itself.

5. Undo and remove the nut (22) that secures the shock absorber arm to the link (21).

6. It may be necessary to use a small universal ball joint separator to disconnect the arm from the link as it is a taper fit. Should a universal ball joint separator not be available place a metal block or heavy hammer against one side of the tapered eye on the steering arm. Using a second hammer, shock the taper apart by tapping on the opposite side of the eye to the metal block or hammer.

7. Thoroughly clean the exterior of the shock absorber and place in a vertical position in a vice so that the arm can be moved up and down.

8. Undo the filler plug (25) (Fig. 11.15) and top up the oil

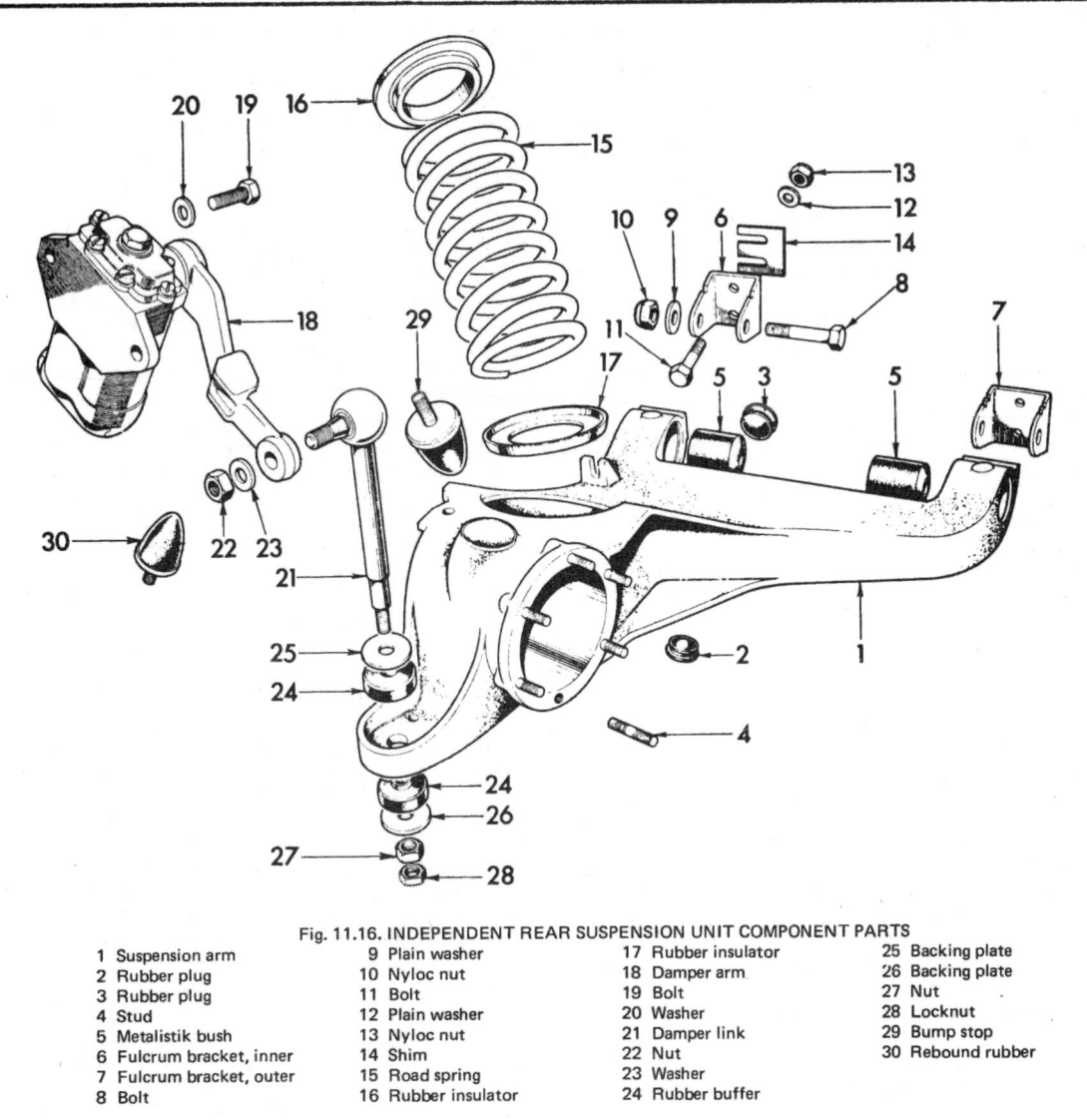

Fig. 11.16. INDEPENDENT REAR SUSPENSION UNIT COMPONENT PARTS

1 Suspension arm	9 Plain washer	17 Rubber insulator	25 Backing plate
2 Rubber plug	10 Nyloc nut	18 Damper arm	26 Backing plate
3 Rubber plug	11 Bolt	19 Bolt	27 Nut
4 Stud	12 Plain washer	20 Washer	28 Locknut
5 Metalistik bush	13 Nyloc nut	21 Damper link	29 Bump stop
6 Fulcrum bracket, inner	14 Shim	22 Nut	30 Rebound rubber
7 Fulcrum bracket, outer	15 Road spring	23 Washer	
8 Bolt	16 Rubber insulator	24 Rubber buffer	

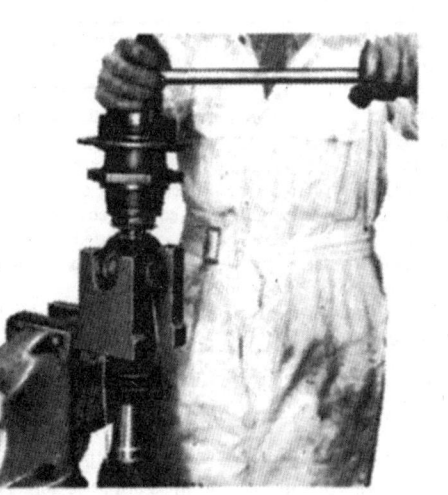

Fig. 11.17. Drive shaft installed in tool S318

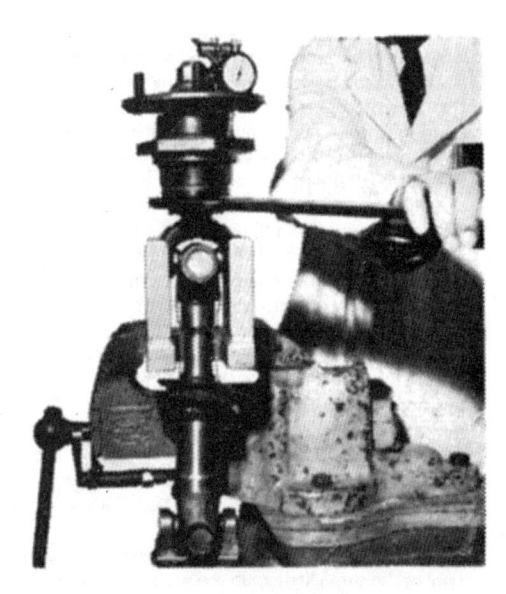

Fig. 11.18. Adjustment of bearing endfloat

253

Chapter 11/Suspension - Dampers - Steering

level, using correct grade oil, to the base of the filler plug boss. Refit the filler plug.

9. Move the arm up and down about ten times so as to expel any air that might be in the system. It should be found that on the final strokes an equal and constant resistance should be felt on both the upwards and downwards strokes. If unequal resistance is felt on either stroke a replacement shock absorber should be obtained.

10 Refitting the shock absorber is the reverse sequence to removal.

25. Steering Wheel - Removal and Refitting (Cam and Peg System)

1. Disconnect the positive terminal from the battery for safety reasons.
2. Locate the horn and direction indicator electric cable snap connectors on the wing valance and clean any dirt from the cables so that their colour coding may be determined. If the cables are badly faded or colours indistinguishable, label the cables using various coloured tapes wrapped around the cables.
3. Separate the horn and direction indicator cables from the snap connectors.
4. Place an absorbent cloth under the end of the steering box and slacken the gland nut (14) (Fig. 11.19).
5. Undo the three little grub screws situated radially around the hub of the steering wheel.
6. Carefully withdraw the control head and stator tube from the steering column, taking care not to bend the stator tube. If required the stator tube may be slid out from the control head.
7. To remove the steering wheel, using a socket or box spanner, undo the steering wheel retaining nut (52).
8. Using a centre punch mark the top of the inner column and the steering wheel hub so that the steering wheel may be correctly positioned upon refitting.
9. With the palms of the hands thump the underside of the spokes to separate the steering wheel from the inner column.
10 To refit the steering wheel and stator assembly first replace the steering wheel onto the inner column aligning the previously made centre punch marks.
11 If the centre punch marks have been omitted or a new wheel or column has been fitted set the front wheels to the straight ahead position and refit the steering wheel with the two sets of spokes horizontal to each other. Replace the steering wheel retaining nut and tighten securely.
12 With the front wheels in the straight ahead position refit the stator tube with the anti-rattle springs in position. The slot in the stator tube should be facing uppermost in the 12 o'clock position in the inner column.
13 Replace the brass olive onto the end of the stator tube protruding from the end of the steering box. Refit the nut (14) and screw on until it is fully home and then turn back one complete turn.
14 Insert the electric cables from the control head into the stator tube and ease down until the control head is in position on the end of the stator tube. The direction indicator switch lever should be in the 12 o'clock position and the vertical lever of the stator tube is at the 6 o'clock position. This positioning is important otherwise the self cancelling system of the direction indicators will not operate correctly.
15 Without moving the steering wheel or control head, tighten the three little grub screws in the hub of the steering wheel so securing the control head in place.
16 Turning to the bottom of the steering box tighten the gland nut (14).
17 Reconnect the electric cables to the connectors on the side of the wing valance taking care that the cable colours or previously positioned coloured identification tapes are matched. Also reconnect the positive terminal of the battery.
18 Top up the steering box with the correct grade oil.

26. Steering Column (Adjustable Type) - Description

An adjustable steering column was fitted to some TR2, 3 and 3A models and enables the steering wheel to have a movement range of 2½ inches. The external component parts are shown in Fig. 11.20 and, upon inspection, it will be observed that a three spoke steering wheel is used instead of a two spoke wheel.

The inner column and steering box are identical to the non adjustable type with the exception that there are longer top splines and not steering wheel retaining nut threads. The outer column is slightly shorter in length.

The operation of the adjustable steering column is such that the steering wheel hub is able to slide up and down on long splines situated at the top end of the inner column. A circlip is placed in a groove at the top of the inner column so stopping the steering wheel coming off the end.

An internally splined steel tube is positioned firmly in the aluminium hub of the steering wheel and protrudes from the lower end of the hub. The protruding part is split and tapered so as to match the internal taper on the locking sleeve (D) (Fig. 11.20). By screwing up the locking sleeves the two tapers are brought together so locking the steel tube onto the splines of the inner column by a drill chuck type action.

A telescopic metal shroud (B) covers the lower exposed portion of the inner column splines. Inside the inner column is a two part stator tube of which the lower section is longer and it has a slot in its upper end into which indentations on the upper and shorter section fit. The stator tube is therefore telescopic as the steering wheel is adjusted and yet it will not rotate with it.

Service overhaul procedures are identical to that for the conventional steering system with a fixed steering wheel with the exception of the removal and refitting of the steering wheel and control head.

27. Adjustable Steering Wheel - Removal and Refitting (Cam and Peg System)

1. Disconnect the positive terminal from the battery for safety reasons.
2. Locate the horn and direction indicator electric cable snap connectors on the wing valance and clean any dirt from the cables so that their colour coding may be determined. If the cables are badly faded or colours indistinguishable label the cables using various coloured tapes wrapped around the cables.
3. Separate the horn and direction indicator cables from the snap connectors.
4. Undo the three little grub screws situated radially around the hub of the steering wheel.
5. Carefully withdraw the control head and cables from the stator tube.
6. Slacken off the locking sleeve (D) (Fig. 11.20) and push on the rim of the steering wheel until the hub is at its lowest point of adjustment. This operation will expose the circlip (Fig. 11.21) which may next be removed using a small electrical screwdriver.
7. Using a centre punch mark the top of the inner column and the steering wheel hub so that the steering wheel may be correctly positioned upon refitting.

Fig. 11.19. CAM AND STEERING PEG BOX

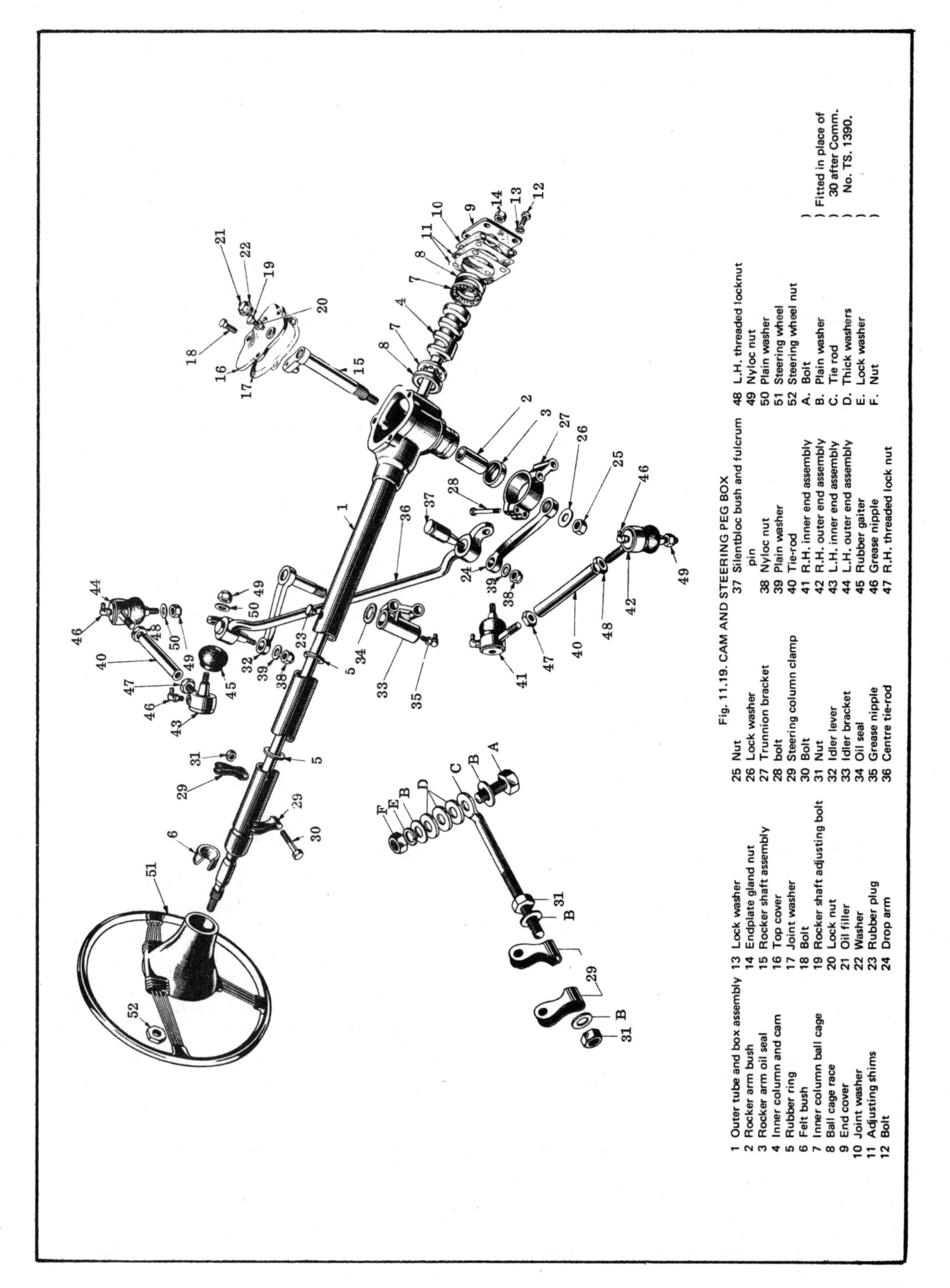

1 Outer tube and box assembly	13 Lock washer	25 Nut	37 Silentbloc bush and fulcrum pin
2 Rocker arm bush	14 Endplate gland nut	26 Lock washer	38 Nyloc nut
3 Rocker arm oil seal	15 Rocker shaft assembly	27 Trunnion bracket	39 Plain washer
4 Inner column and cam	16 Top cover	28 bolt	40 Tie-rod
5 Rubber ring	17 Joint washer	29 Steering column clamp	41 R.H. inner end assembly
6 Felt bush	18 Bolt	30 Bolt	42 R.H. outer end assembly
7 Inner column ball cage	19 Rocker shaft adjusting bolt	31 Nut	43 L.H. inner end assembly
8 Ball cage race	20 Lock nut	32 Idler lever	44 L.H. outer end assembly
9 End cover	21 Oil filler	33 Idler bracket	45 Rubber gaiter
10 Joint washer	22 Washer	34 Oil seal	46 Grease nipple
11 Adjusting shims	23 Rubber plug	35 Grease nipple	47 R.H. threaded lock nut
12 Bolt	24 Drop arm	36 Centre tie-rod	

48 L.H. threaded locknut
49 Nyloc nut
50 Plain washer
51 Steering wheel
52 Steering wheel nut
A. Bolt
B. Plain washer
C. Tie rod
D. Thick washers
E. Lock washer
F. Nut

) Fitted in place of
) 30 after Comm.
) No. TS. 1390.

255

Chapter 11/Suspension - Dampers - Steering

8. With the hand hold the shroud (B) (Fig. 11.20) so as to prevent it pushing the parts off the column and remove the steering wheel from the inner column.

9. Lift away the cup shaped washer (C) followed by the shroud (B) and the bakelite washer (A).

10 To refit the steering wheel first position the front wheels in the straight ahead position.

11 Refit the bakelite washer (A) over the inner column splines and position it so that it is on the top of the outer column and the little spigot on the washer faces towards the top of the column.

12 Smear a little grease onto the splines and replace the telescopic metal shroud (B) onto the inner column until the smaller diameter end engages with the little spigot on the bakelite washer (A).

13 Place the steering wheel on the passenger's seat and, using one hand, hold down the larger diameter end of the telescopic metal shroud and place the cupped washer (C) into the shroud.

14 Check that the locking sleeve (D) is in the slackened position and fit the steering wheel onto the inner column so that the single spike is pointing downwards and the other two spikes horizontal. Gently press the steering wheel rim downwards until it is at its lowermost position. Tighten the locking sleeve (D).

15 Replace the circlip into its seating at the top of the inner column splines. Double check that the circlip is seating correctly.

16 The control lead may next be refitted. Check that the direction indicator lever (F) is in the 12 o'clock position and the lever on the stator tube plate is in the 6 o'clock position. Lightly grease all moving parts of the control head and stator tube.

17 Reconnect the electrical cables to the connectors on the side of the wing valance taking care that the cable colours or previously positioned colour identification tapes are matched. Also reconnect the positive terminal of the battery. Check that there is sufficient cable slack at the bottom of the steering box so as to allow the steering wheel to be adjusted to its fully extended position.

28. Cam and Peg Steering - Removal and Replacement (TR2, 3, 3A)

1. Loosen the front wheel securing nuts on the wheel adjacent to the steering box, jack up the front of the car and place supports under the coil spring pins between the wishbones and revolve the front wheel.

2. Disconnect the positive terminal from the battery for safety reasons.

3. Refer to Chapter 12, Sections 9 and 31 and remove the front bumper and front apron.

4. Refer to Section 25 of this Chapter and remove the steering wheel from the column assembly.

5. Locate and slacken the outer steering column clamp or clamps securing the column to the fascia and body.

6. Refer to Fig. 11.19 and undo the nyloc nut (38). Lift away the nut and plain washer (39) securing the drop arm (24) to the centre tie rod.

7. Using a long tyre lever separate the drop arm from the centre tie rod.

8. Undo and remove the clip securing the draught excluder to the lower end of the steering outer column.

9. Undo the two bolts (28) that secure the trunnion bracket (27) to the chassis member. Lift away the two bolts.

10 Rotate the inner column until the drop arm is lying parallel with the outer column and carefully withdraw the steering box and column forwards and downwards.

11 The outer column should slide through the draught excluder.

12 Wipe clean the drop arm and rocker shaft end and ensure that there are two scribe lines, one on the rocker shaft end and the other on the face of the drop arm. These are marks to ensure correct refitting but if not evident, make suitable identification marks using a file or scriber.

13 Undo and remove the nut (25) and plain lock washer (26) and, using a two leg puller or ball joint separator, disconnect the drop arm from the rocker shaft. It is important that this joint is not hammered otherwise damage on the cam or bearings could result.

14 If the unit is to be dismantled thoroughly wash in paraffin and dry using a non fluffy rag.

15 To refit the steering box and column assembly first assemble the trunnion bracket to the steering box so that the chassis mounting part is facing forwards. Replace the two bolts but do not tighten at this stage.

16 If the drop arm has not been left attached to the rocker shaft, carefully align the scribe marks on the drop arm face and rocker shaft and replace the plain lock washer. Replace the nut and tighten securely. Bend part of the plain lock washer over the flat machined face on the drop arm and bend another part of the plain lock washer over one side of the nut.

17 Refit the screw clip onto the draught excluder.

18 Carefully insert the end of the column into the hole in the draught excluder and push the column up until the steering box is in approximately the correct position. Ensure that, as the column moves towards the rear of the fascia, it is not allowed to damage any cables or trim.

19 Position the trunnion bracket into the chassis bracket and replace the two locating bolts and lockwashers. Note that the longer bolt will also accommodate the bumper stiffening bracket and must be fitted to the lower of the two holes. Leave both bolts loose at this stage.

20 Attach the outer column to the mounting bracket located under the fascia panel and tighten the two nuts on the lower support stay. Note that on early produced models a nut and bolt were used instead of the two nuts.

21 Now is the time to tighten the two bolts that secure the trunnion bracket to the chassis bracket. Once these are tight secure the two bolts that hold the trunnion bracket to the steering unit.

22 Reconnect the centre tie rod to the drop arm and secure with the plain washer (39) and nyloc nut (38). Ensure that the nut is really tight as it must pull the tapers together.

23 Tighten the screw clip that secures the draught excluder to the outer steering column.

24 Refer to Section 25 of this Chapter and replace the steering wheel.

25 Replace the front apron and bumper assembly as detailed in Chapter 12, Section 9 and 31

26 If the steering box has not yet been filled with oil it should be done so now. Use a high pressure oil in a squirt can or old but clean washing up liquid polythene container with a nozzle in the cap. This way the oil is not splashed everywhere.

27 Reconnect the positive terminal of the battery and lower the car to the ground, having first removed the axle stands.

29. Cam and Peg Steering - Dismantling, Overhaul and Reassembly

1. If the exterior is dirty wash in paraffin and dry using a non fluffy rag.

2. The drop arm should first be removed. Ensure that there are two scribe marks, one on the rocker shaft and the other on the face of the drop arm. These are marks to ensure

Fig. 11.20. ADJUSTABLE STEERING COLUMN

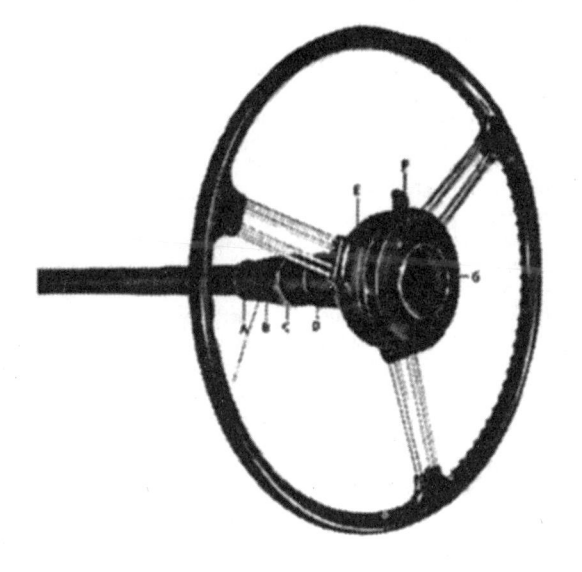

A Spigotted bakelite washer
B Metal telescopic shroud
C Plated steel cup washer
D Locking sleeve
E Telescopic steering wheel
F Flasher control
G Control head

Fig. 11.21. Circlip positioned on the end of inner column. To gain access the steering wheel has been pushed down the inner column splines.

Chapter 11/Suspension - Dampers - Steering

correct refitting but, if not evident, make suitable identification marks using a file or scriber.

3. Undo and remove the nut (25) (Fig. 11.19) and plain lockwasher and, using a two leg puller or ball joint separator, disconnect the drop arm from the rocker shaft. It is important that this joint is not hammered otherwise damage to the cam or bearings could result.

4. Place the steering box over a drop tray and remove the three bolts (18). Lift away the top cover (16) and the gasket (17).

5. With extreme care withdraw the rocker shaft assembly as the splines on the bottom of the rocker shaft can easily damage the lips of the oil seal (3). If the oil seal is not to be renewed it is recommended that the splines are packed with a thick grease to help the splines slide over the seal.

6. Undo the four bolts (12) and lift away together with the spring washers (13). Remove the cover (9), its gasket (10) and shims (11).

7. Lift away the bottom bearing ball cage race (8) and ball cage (7).

8. The inner column and cam assembly (4) may now be withdrawn through the steering box and it will be noted that the rubber rings (5) will also come away with the inner column.

9. If necessary the bearing bush (2) and oil seal (3) may be removed from the outer column by using a long metal rod to act as a drift.

10 The upper inner column ball cage (7) and ball cage race (8) may be lifted away from the column.

11 Thoroughly wash all component parts in petrol and wipe dry using a non fluffy rag.

12 Assemble the bearings and check for signs of wear, roughness of damaged race tracks. Check the oil seal for signs of hardening.

13 Carefully examine the inner column to ensure that it is not bent. Inspect the cam profile to ensure that it has not worn especially in the centre portions where most contact with the peg occurs.

14 Inspect the splines on the end of the rocker shaft and interior of the drop arm to ensure that they have not rounded due to a slack joint.

15 Any parts that are suspect should be renewed. Also it is recommended that new gaskets be obtained and fitted.

16 To reassemble first carefully insert the bearing bush (6) into the outer column and press into position using the hand or a block of soft wood.

17 Place the trunnion bracket (27) in position on the rocker shaft housing so that the chassis mounting points point forwards and downwards. Screw up the two bolts (28) but do not tighten fully.

18 Position the upper ball race in the steering box and very carefully insert the inner column (4) with the two rubber rings (5) positioned equidistant along the column. The ball cage should also have been positioned the correct way round on the shaft.

19 Place the second ball cage in position on the lower bearing face of the cam and then followed by the race.

20 Put a little grease on the joint washer (10) and the old shims (11) and place on the end cover (9). Refit the end cover to the steering box and secure in place with the four bolts (12) and spring washers (13).

21 There should not be any end float on the inner column and cam assembly and a little amount of pre-load is desirable. This end float is adjusted easily by removing or adding shims between the steering box and end cover gasket. It will be found that adding shims increases the end float and conversely by subtracting shims decreases the end float.

22 When the end float has been eliminated the oil seal (3) should be refitted, if the original was removed, to the rocker shaft body.

23 Pack the splines on the end of the rocker shaft with grease to protect the fine surface edge of the seal and carefully insert the rocker shaft through the aperture in the top of the steering box. The conical pins should settle in the groove of the cam.

24 Undo the adjusting bolt (19) by first releasing the lock nut (20) and fit a new gasket (17) holding it in place with a little grease. Replace the cover (16) and secure with the three bolts (18) and lock washers.

25 Locate the scribe marks on the drop arm and splined rocker shaft end and fit the drop arm into position. Secure with the nut (25) and lockplate (26). Bend over one side of the lockplate to secure it to the flat on the side of the drop arm and the other side bend up to lock the nut.

26 Once operations 21 and 22 have been completed satisfactorily the end float will have been removed and the second adjustment may now be made. The depth of the rocker shaft peg and cam is adjusted by means of the bolt (19). Rotate this screw in a clockwise direction to increase the depth of engagement or anti-clockwise to reduce the depth until correct engagement is obtained and this point is reached when slight resistance is felt with the rocker shaft in the central or straight ahead position.

26 Carefully refit the graphite impregnated bush (6) into the upper end of the outer column (1).

28 Refit the steering wheel retaining nut (52) to ensure that the threads on the top of the inner column (4) are not accidentally damaged when the steering box and column assembly are refitted.

30. Cam and Peg Steering - Adjustment in Car

1. It is possible to adjust the mesh and end float that may become evident as the parts within the steering box start to wear.

2. Before the rocker arm pin and cam mesh is adjusted it is important that there is no end float on the inner column. It is adjusted by shims (11) (Fig. 11.19). To gain access to the shims the electrical cables and stator tube should be disconnected as detailed in Section 28 of this Chapter.

3. Undo the four bolts (12) and remove together with the spring washers (13). Place a wad of absorbent cloth under the end of the steering box to catch the oil which will drain out in the next operation.

4. Separate the end cover (9) from the end of the steering box and lift away the shims (11) and joint washer (10).

5. The end float may now be adjusted by removing or adding shims until there is no end float movement and just a little pre-load which may be determined by refitting the end cover and tightening the four bolts with spring washers. Lift the front wheels clear of the ground and check the resistance to movement of the steering wheel. Now slacken the four bolts and recheck the steering wheel resistance which should be slightly less than in the first test.

6. With all end float eliminated the mesh of the rocker shaft peg and the cam may now be adjusted by undoing the locknut (20) and turning the adjusting bolt (19) in a clockwise or anti-clockwise direction. It should be understood that the cam has a slightly larger diameter in the centre than at its ends and that, as the steering wheel is turned from one lock to the other, the rocker shaft has more left at either end of its prescribed arc than at the centre.

7. Carefully adjust the bolt (19) until slight resistance is felt on the steering wheel as it passes through the centre of the arc when the front wheels are in the straight ahead position. When the required adjustment has been made lock the nut (20) to secure the bolt (19).

8. Refill the steering box with recommended grade oil and road test preferably in a quiet road where several three

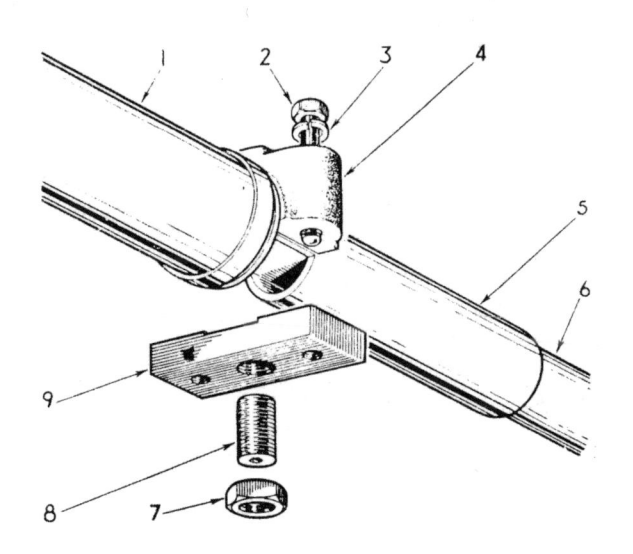

Impact clamp on steering column

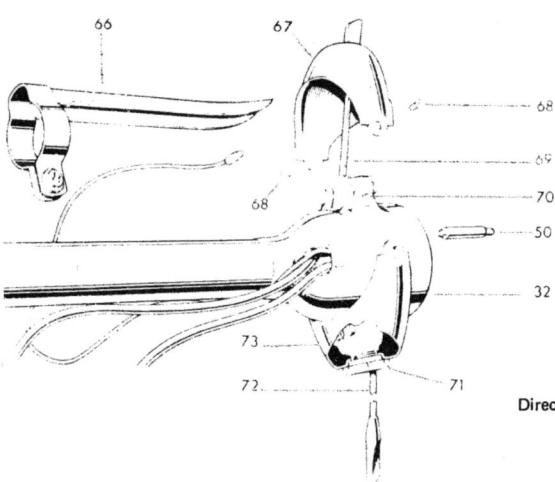

Direction indicator and overdrive switch mounted to upper column

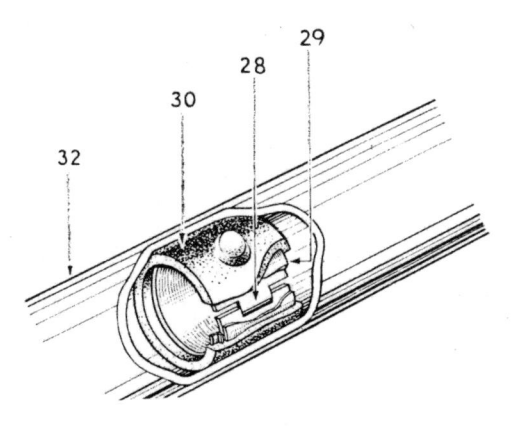

Correct fitting of steering column bush assembly.

259

Chapter 11/Suspension - Dampers - Steering

point turns may be made to check full steering wheel movement and the degree of resistance felt whilst on full lock.

31. Cam and Peg Steering - Idler Unit - Removal and Refitting

The idler unit is situated on the opposite side of the chassis to the steering box and is bolted onto a bracket which is welded to the chassis. The centre tie rod end opposite the steering box is attached to the idler unit lever as shown in Fig. 11.19. To remove the idler unit proceed as follows:-

1. Chock the rear wheels and apply the handbrake. Slacken the wheel nuts on the wheel opposite to the steering box and jack up the front of the car and place on axle stands. Remove the road wheel.
2. Undo the nyloc nut (38) (Fig. 11.19) and lift away together with the plain washer (39).
3. Using a tyre lever separate the centre tie rod (36) from the idler unit lever (32). Should difficulty be experienced in separating the two parts place a metal block or heavy hammer against one side of the tapered eye on the idler lever. Using a second hammer shock the taper apart by tapping on the opposite side of the eye to the metal block or hammer.
4. Slacken and remove the two bolts that secure the idler unit body (33) to the bracket welded on the chassis.
5. Lift away the idler unit and, if it is to be dismantled further, wash the exterior in paraffin and wipe dry using a non fluffy rag.
6. Unscrew the lever (32) from the idler unit body (33) followed by the grease nipple (35) and the seal (34). With the unit dismantled and free of grease and road dust inspect the threads in both the body and lever for signs of slackness and, if evident, a new unit must be fitted.
7. Inspect the seal for hardening and distortion and, if suspect, a new seal must be obtained. Check the grease nipple for blockage by using a grease gun on the end and pumping grease through it. When all parts have been inspected and the necessary new parts obtained the unit may now be reassembled.
8. Replace the seal (34) onto the threaded section of the idler unit lever (32). Smear grease onto the threads of the lever. Refit the grease nipple (35) to the idler unit body (33).
9. Fit the lever (32) into the idler unit body (33) and screw up fully. Turn the lever back one complete turn.
10 Refit the idler unit on to its chassis mounting bracket and secure in position with the two bolts. Check that the lever is able to turn through a complete arc, without stopping, indicating that operation 9 is satisfactory.
11 Assemble the centre tie rod (36) onto the idler unit lever (32) ensuring that the centre tie rod is able to move freely on the silentbloc bush and fulcrum pin assembly (37). Refit the plain washer (39) and nyloc nut (38) and tighten the nut securely.
12 With the front end of the car still off the ground check that the steering wheel can be turned from one lock to the other and if satisfactory replace the road wheel, remove the axle stands and lower the car.

32. Modifications - Steering (TR2, 3, 3A models)

1. A modified steering column clamp was fitted to cars produced from commission number TS. 1390 so providing better rigidity of the steering column.
2. Refer to Fig. 11.19. The bolt (30) was replaced with a tie rod (C). The other end of the tie rod is attached to the fascia - battery compartment stay by a bolt (A) which is 1½ inch long. Three thick washers (D) act as packing pieces between the stay and the tie rod. This modification was incorporated at the same time as 1 above.
3. An additional steering column support bracket was fitted on cars produced since commission number TS. 5777 and this bracket is clamped to the steering column using two nuts and bolts. It is also held onto the front suspension system by a further one nut and bolt. When the steering column and box is being removed it will be necessary to slacken the two clamping nuts and bolts on the steering column.

33. Steering Wheel - Removal and Refitting (Rack and Pinion System)

1. Disconnect the positive terminal from the battery for safety reasons.
2. Using a screwdriver or a knife remove the horn push from the centre of the steering wheel.
3. Lift out the horn brush from the inside of the steering wheel hub.
4. Using a centre punch mark the inner column and the hub of the steering wheel to ensure correct reassembly. Undo the steering wheel retaining nut using a socket or box spanner.
5. The steering wheel may now be removed from the inner column by using the palms of the hands and thumping on the underside of the steering wheel rim.
6. To refit the steering wheel replace the wheel on the inner column carefully aligning the previously made centre punch marks. With the steering wheel in position refit the retaining nut and tighten securely. It is advisable to peen the metal of the nut to the inner column to prevent the nut working loose.
7. Insert the horn brush into its hole in the steering wheel hub and replace the horn button assembly making sure the emblem is the correct way up relative to the spokes.
8. Reconnect the positive terminal of the battery.

34. Steering Column - Removal, Dismantling and Refitting (Rack and Pinion System)

1. Disconnect the positive terminal from the battery for safety reasons.
2. Refer to Fig. 11.22 and undo the pinch bolt (4) which secures the coupling adaptor to the steering unit pinion.
3. Undo the two bolts (55) securing the impact clamp (54) to the upper inner column (24). Lift away the two bolts, spring washers (53) followed by the clamp (54) and the clamp plate (23).
4. Carefully push the lower column (20) into the upper column (24) so as to disengage the coupling (5) and adaptor plate (2) from the steering unit pinion.
5. Push the coupling (5) and adaptor plate (2) to one side and pull from the column. Lift away the nylon washer.
6. Now, working inside the car, first undo and remove the nuts (58) and spring washers which will release the lower bracket and clamp and felt.(33) Next undo and remove the two nuts (61) and spring washers from the two bolts (34) in the upper clamp (40).
7. Undo the two nuts (62) and remove the nuts and spring washers (63). This will release the stay (59) and the bracket (65). Remove the felt (44).
8. Wipe the cables free of dust at the connectors for the horn direction indicator, and overdrive unit (if fitted), cables to enable the colour coding to be seen. If the cables are faded mark the cables for correct refitting during

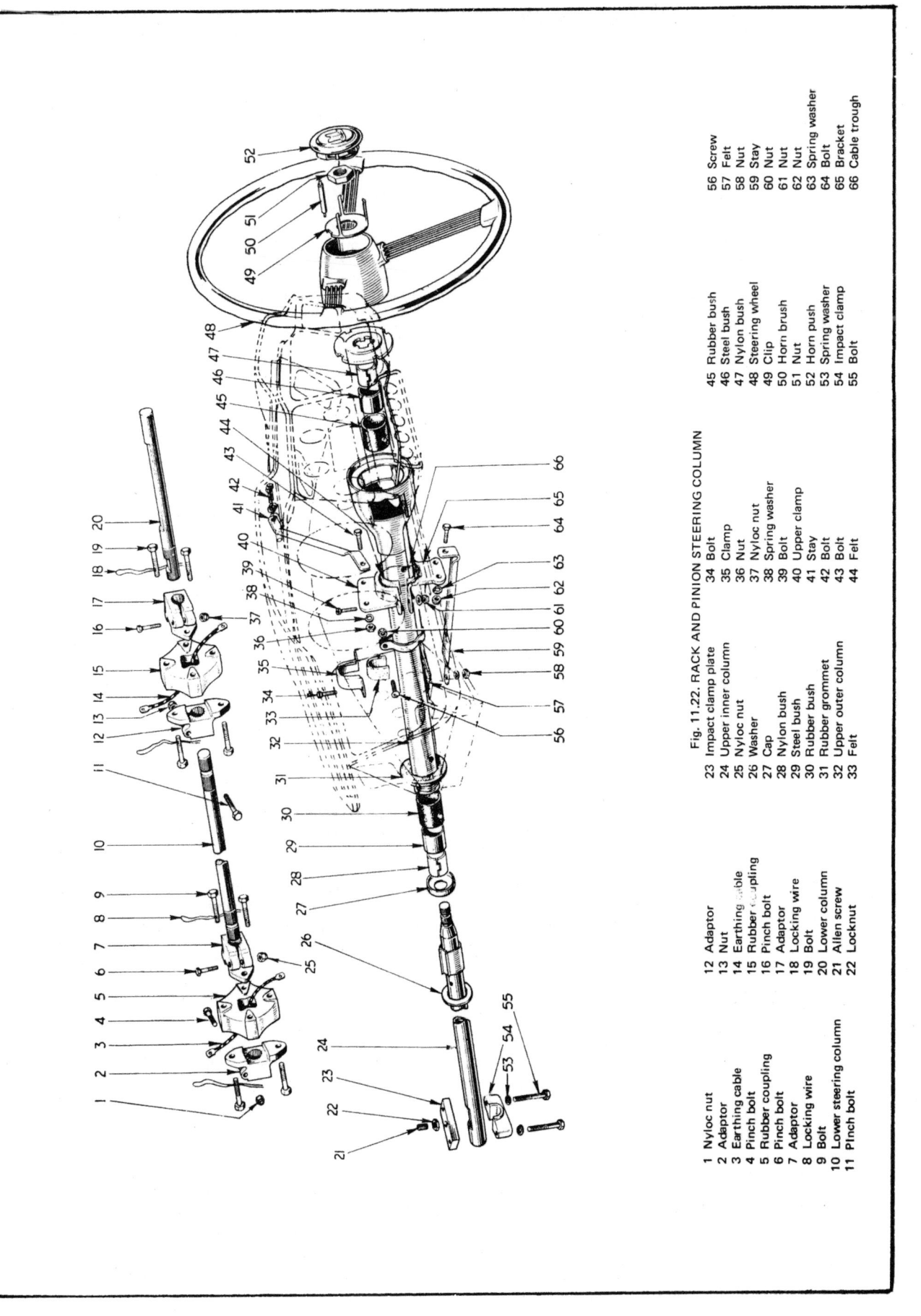

Fig. 11.22. RACK AND PINION STEERING COLUMN

1 Nyloc nut
2 Adaptor
3 Earthing cable
4 Pinch bolt
5 Rubber coupling
6 Pinch bolt
7 Adaptor
8 Locking wire
9 Bolt
10 Lower steering column
11 Pinch bolt
12 Adaptor
13 Nut
14 Earthing cable
15 Rubber coupling
16 Pinch bolt
17 Adaptor
18 Locking wire
19 Bolt
20 Lower column
21 Allen screw
22 Locknut
23 Impact clamp plate
24 Upper inner column
25 Nyloc nut
26 Washer
27 Cap
28 Nylon bush
29 Steel bush
30 Rubber bush
31 Rubber grommet
32 Upper outer column
33 Felt
34 Bolt
35 Clamp
36 Nut
37 Nyloc nut
38 Spring washer
39 Bolt
40 Upper clamp
41 Stay
42 Bolt
43 Bolt
44 Felt
45 Rubber bush
46 Steel bush
47 Nylon bush
48 Steering wheel
49 Clip
50 Horn brush
51 Nut
52 Horn push
53 Spring washer
54 Impact clamp
55 Bolt
56 Screw
57 Felt
58 Nut
59 Stay
60 Nut
61 Nut
62 Nut
63 Spring washer
64 Bolt
65 Bracket
66 Cable trough

261

Chapter 11/Suspension - Dampers - Steering

reassembly. Disconnect the cables from the connectors.
9. Undo and remove the bolt which secures the cable trough clip (66).
10 Carefully pull on the steering wheel and column upwards ensuring that the outer column slides through the bulkhead rubber grommet (31). Check that the cable trough (66) slides off the column. The steering wheel and column assembly may now be lifted away from the car.
11 Should it be necessary to dismantle the steering column and wheel assembly further, first the universal couplings (5, 15) may be removed. Note the earthing cables (3, 14) and to which bolts they are attached.
12 Remove the switch cover retaining screws and lift away the cover. Undo and remove the two direction indicator switch retaining screws on the flanges on the top of the outer column head and withdraw the switch and the cables by feeding the cables through the slot in the column head. Repeat this operation for the overdrive unit switch if an overdrive is fitted.
13 The inner column (24) and steering wheel (48) may now be separated from the outer column.
14 To separate the steering wheel from the upper inner column using a screwdriver or knife carefully prise off the horn push (52) from the centre of the steering wheel.
15 Lift out the horn brush (50) from inside the steering wheel hub. Note the position of steering wheel spokes relative to the direction indicator self cancel lugs on the upper inner column.
16 Using a socket or box spanner undo the steering wheel retaining nut (51) from the upper inner column (24). If necessary holding the column between soft faces in a firm vice. Lift away the clip (49).
16 Separate the steering wheel from the upper inner column by thumping with the palms of the hands on the underside of the steering wheel rim.
17 Remove the end cap (27) from the lower end of the outer column and whilst depressing the protrusions on the rubber bush (30) with a piece of suitable diameter rod placed in the hole in the outer column, use a piece of long rod and push at the rubber bush (30). Separate the metal sleeve (29) and the nylon bush (28) from the flexible end of the rubber bush (30).
18 The bushes in the upper end of the outer column may be removed from the column using the same method as detailed in the previous operation.
19 With the assembly completely dismantled inspect the bushes for signs of wear or deterioration. Also check the rubber couplings for wear or softening caused by oil contamination. The upper and lower inner column should be inspected for worn splines as well as the adaptors for the universal couplings. Test the two inner columns for straightness.
20 To reassemble first fit the nylon bush (28) and steel sleeve (29) into the rubber bush (30).
21 Lubricate the outer surface of the rubber bush (30) with a little rubber grease and push it into the bottom of the outer column ensuring that the rubber bush locating lugs correctly seat into the hole in the outer column. Also ensure that the metal reinforcement ring at the end of the bush is positioned towards the lower end of the column.
22 Repeat the previous operations to refit the upper bush assembly to the upper part of the column.
23 Replace the metal cap (27) onto the lower end of the outer column.
24 The steering wheel may next be fitted to the upper inner column carefully aligning the direction indicator self cancel system lugs on the column with the steering wheel spokes. With the steering wheel in position refit the retaining nut (51) and tighten securely. It is advisable to peen the metal of the nut to the inner column to prevent the nut working loose.
25 Slide the upper column into the outer column ensuring that the upper and lower bush assemblies are not dislodged.
26 Feed the direction indicator switch cables through the hub and slot in the upper end of the outer column and also the cables for the overdrive switch if an overdrive unit is fitted. Replace the switch retaining screws followed by the lock ring.
27 Refit the switch covers and secure in position with the retaining screws.
28 Insert the horn brush (50) into its hole in the steering wheel hub and replace the horn button assembly making sure the emblem is the correct way up relative to the spokes.
29 Refit the universal coupling adaptors and the earthing cables and secure the latter to one of the coupling adaptor retaining bolts. It is recommended that the adaptor bolts are wired together in pairs.
30 To refit the steering wheel and column assembly first pass the lower end of the column through the fascia and rubber grommet (31) in the bulkhead.
31 Replace the electric cable trough (66) and secure it in position with the retaining nuts, bolts and spring washers.
32 Refit the felt and upper half of the upper support clamp and the tie stay with their respective nuts, bolts and spring washers but do not at this stage tighten fully. Attach the other end of the tie stay and secure it with a nut and spring washer.
33 Refit the felt and lower clamp bracket and, like the previous operation, do not tighten fully.
34 Reconnect the lower column to the universal coupling adaptors and secure with bolts and nyloc nuts. Also refit the nylon washer to the inner column.
35 Insert the lower column assembly in the inner column. Then refit the impact clamp by first slackening the locknut (22) and undoing the Allen screw (21) two complete turns. Rotate the lower inner column until the machined flat is in line with the machined aperture in the upper inner column. The impact clamp may now be fitted and secured with the two bolts and spring washers.
36 Check that the front wheels are in the straight ahead position and the steering wheel spokes horizontal and refit the lower coupling to the steering unit pinion shaft. Refit the coupling adaptor clamp nut and bolt and tighten fully.
37 The steering column may now be adjusted to the desired height by either pushing on the rim of the steering wheel to lower, or pulling on the outer column to raise, the position of the steering wheel. When the desired position has been reached tighten the Allen screw and lock with the locknut.
38 Tighten all nuts and bolts on the upper and lower clamps.
39 Reconnect the horn, direction indicator and overdrive unit control cables to the snap connectors ensuring that they are correctly fitted.
40 Reconnect the battery positive terminal and road test the car for correct steering control.

35. Rack and Pinion Steering - Removal and Replacement (TR4)

1. Loosen the front wheel securing nuts, jack up the front of the car, place on supports under the coil spring pans between the wishbones and remove the front wheels.
2. Remove the radiator filler cap and undo the radiator drain tap. Drain the coolant into a container of suitable size for re-use if anti-freeze has been added.
3. Slacken the bottom radiator hose clips and remove the bottom hose completely.
4. Undo and remove the bolt (1) (Fig. 11.25) from the steering column coupling.
5. Undo and remove the nyloc nuts securing the two tie

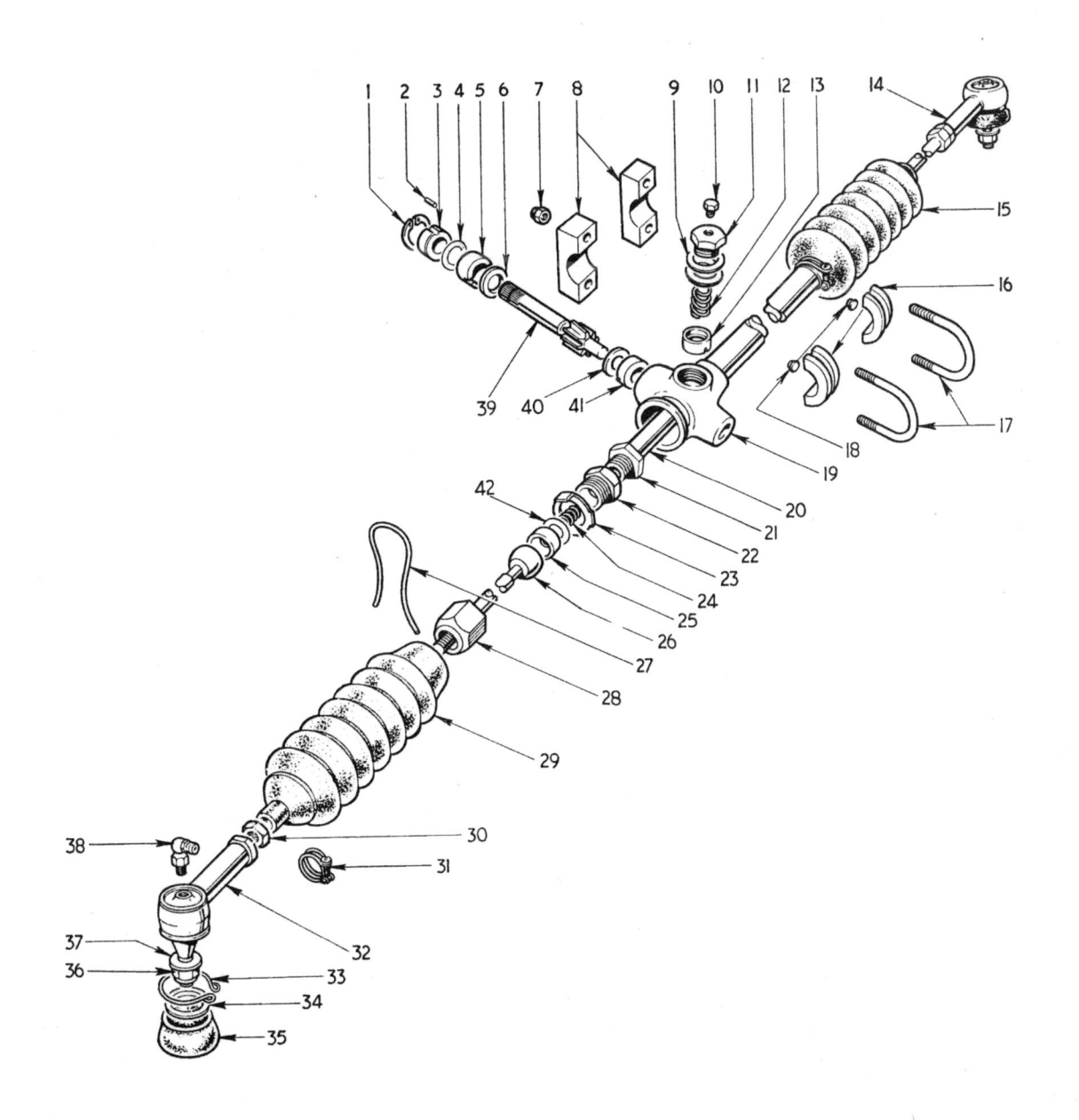

Fig. 11.24. RACK AND PINION UNIT WITH COMPONENT PARTS

1 Circlip	12 Spring	23 Lockplate	34 Washer
2 Peg	13 Thrust button	24 Spring	35 Rubber gaiter
3 Retainer	14 Tie rod ends	25 Cup	36 Nyloc nut
4 Shim	15 Rubber gaiter	26 Outer tie-rod	37 Washer
5 Bush	16 Packing pieces - front	27 Locking wire	38 Grease nipple
6 Thrust washer	17 'U' bolts	28 Cup nut	39 Pinion
7 Nyloc nut	18 Dowels	29 Rubber gaiter	40 Thrust washer
8 Packing pieces - rear	19 Rack tube	30 Locknut	41 Bush
9 Shim	20 Rack	31 Wire clip	42 Shim
10 Plug	21 Locknut	32 Outer tie rod end	
11 Cap	22 Sleeve nut	33 Clip	

Chapter 11/Suspension - Dampers - Steering

rod ends to the steering arms and, using a small universal ball joint separator, disconnect the tie rod ends from the steering arms on the vertical links. Should a universal ball joint separator not be available place a metal block or heavy hammer against one side of the tapered eye on the steering arm. Using a second hammer, shock the taper apart by tapping on the opposite side of the eye to the metal block or hammer.

6. Remove the nyloc nuts (7) (Fig. 11.24) from the steering rack retaining 'U' bolts (17) followed by the 'U' bolts (17) and aluminium packing pieces (16).

7. Carefully move the steering rack assembly forwards so as to disengage the pinion splined coupling and then withdraw through the wheel arch. Take great care not to split the rubber bellows.

8. If the unit is to be dismantled for overhaul thoroughly wash in paraffin and dry using a non fluffy rag.

9. Refitting is the reverse procedure to removal but certain precautions must be taken to simplify the form. It is advisable to check the length of the two tie rods and adjust as necessary until they are of exact equal length. The tie rod ball joints have nylon inserts which do not require lubrication service. Should the rubber boots have become damaged or perished in service a complete new joint must be fitted. If the rubber boot has been damaged only during lifting away the steering rack assembly then the rubber boot only may be renewed. There should be no exception to this rule.

10 Test the rack for freedom of movement by rotating the pinion from one lock to the other and back again.

11 It will be necessary to centralise the unit by counting the number of turns the pinion requires to move the rack from one end to the other. Divide the number in half and turn the pinion back by this amount. Using an accurate steel rule check the rack dimensions with those given in Fig. 11.26.

12 Carefully insert the steering rack unit through the wheel arch taking care that the pinion position is not disturbed.

13 Position the steering wheel in the correct straight ahead position and reconnect the universal coupling. Replace the lock bolt.

14 Secure the rack housing in position by refitting the aluminium packing pieces, 'U' bolts and nyloc nuts.

15 Reconnect the ball joints to the steering arms and check that the steering wheel turns easily from one lock to the other. Tighten the nuts to a torque wrench setting of 55 - 60 lb.ft.

16 Replace the road wheel and remove the axle stands.

17 Position the front wheels so that they are in the straight ahead position. Tighten the universal coupling pinch bolt.

18 Refer to Fig. 11.22 and undo the pinch bolt (16). With the steering wheel spokes in the horizontal position pull upwards on the spokes so as to compress the spring.

19 A second person should move the intermediate shaft towards the rear and engage the splines of the rack pinion with the universal joint. Retighten the pinch bolt (16).

20 Check and adjust the front wheel alignment.

36. Rack and Pinion Steering - Removal and Replacement (TR4A)

1. Although the rack and pinion assembly is the same for TR4A models the method of mounting is different and a different method employed.

2. Loosen the front wheel securing nuts, jack up the front of the car and place supports under the coil spring pans between the wishbones and remove the front wheels.

3. Undo and remove the bolt that secures the universal joint coupling to the pinion.

4. Refer to Chapter 2, Section 16 and remove the engine cooling fan assembly.

5. Undo and remove the nyloc nuts securing the two tie rod ends to the steering arms and using a small universal ball joint separator disconnect the tie rod ends from the steering arms on the vertical links. Should a universal ball joint separator not be available place a metal block or heavy hammer against one side of the tapered eye on the steering arm. Using a second hammer, shock the taper apart by tapping on the opposite side of the eye to the metal block or hammer.

6. Undo and remove the nuts (17) (Fig. 11.23) and plain washers (18) that secure the 'U' bolts (7) to the locating plate (16).

7. Lift away the two locating plates (16) followed by the two 'U' bolts complete with metal shrouds (7).

8. Carefully move the steering rack assembly forwards so as to disengage the pinion splined coupling and then withdraw through the wheel arch. Take great care not to split the rubber bellows.

9. If the unit is to be dismantled for overhaul thoroughly wash in paraffin and dry using a non fluffy rag.

10 Refitting is the reverse procedure to removal but certain precautions must be taken to simplify the form. It is advisable to check the length of the two tie rods and adjust as necessary until they are exactly equal length. The tie rod ball joints have nylon inserts which do not require lubrication. Should the rubber boots have become damaged or perished in service a complete new joint must be fitted. If the rubber boot has been damaged only during lifting away the steering rack assembly then the rubber boot only may be renewed. There should be no exception to this rule.

11 Before the steering rack assembly is finally fitted to the car it will facilitate installation if the rack is brought to its central position. This position is easily obtained by turning the pinion from one stop to the other and measure the complete distance the rack has travelled at one end. The rack will be in its central position when it is moved back through half the measurement made.

12 Carefully insert the rack assembly making sure that the setting in operation 11 is not distorted, locate and insert the pinion splines with the universal joint couplings, checking that the steering wheel spokes are correctly positioned for the straight ahead position.

13 Refit the 'U' bolts (17), metal rubber mounting covers, locating plates (16), washers (18), and nyloc nuts (7) . Lightly tighten the nuts.

14 Slide one of the 'U' bolts outwards as far as possible to the ends of the elongated holes in the crossmember brackets. Ease the locating plate (16) inwards until the edge of 'B' (see Fig. 11.23) completely contacts the side of the bracket. Should this not be possible file the elongated holes further so that this position may be obtained.

15 Tighten the two 'U' bolt nyloc nuts (17) using a torque wrench set to between 14 16 lb.ft. and compress the mounting rubbers (8) to give a clearance of $1/8$ inch between the flange plates on the rack tube 'A' and the 'U' bolts retainer flange 'A'.

16 Refit the second 'U' bolt mounting and position in the same manner.

17 Reconnect the two tie rod ends to the steering arms and tighten the nuts to a torque wrench setting of between 55 - 60 lb.ft. Fit new split pins.

18 Replace the road wheel and remove the axle stands.

19 Position the front wheels so that they are in the straight ahead position. Tighten the universal coupling pinch bolt.

20 Refit the engine cooling fan as detailed in Chapter 8, Section 16.

21 Refer to Fig. 11.22 and undo the pinch bolt (16). With the steering wheel spokes in the horizontal position pull

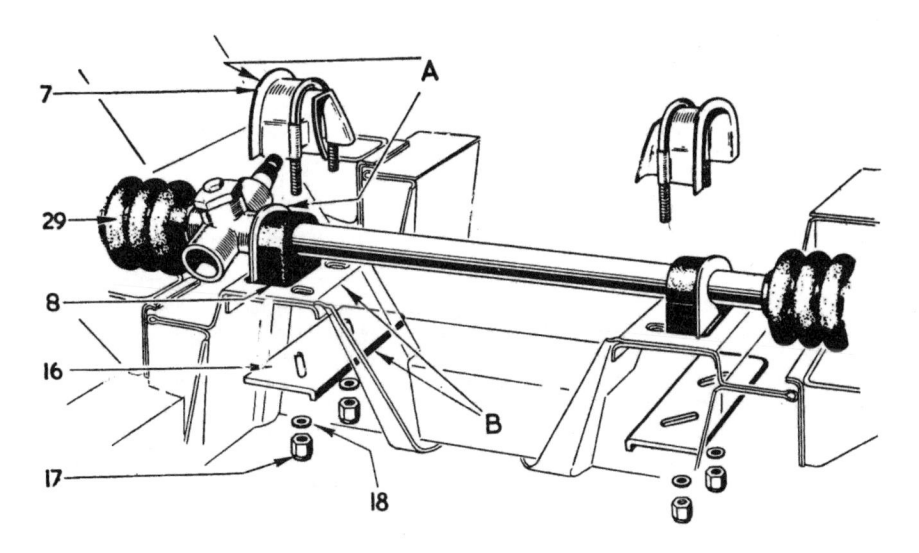

Fig. 11.23. STEERING RACK AND PINION MOUNTING TR4A
A. Distance between flanges must be 1/8" (3.17 mm). B. Flange of item (16) must contact innermost flange of frame.

- 7 'U' bolt
- 8 Rubber bush
- 16 Locating plate
- 17 Nyloc nut
- 18 Plain washer
- 29 Rubber gaiter

Fig. 11.25. RACK AND PINION UNIT UNIVERSAL COUPLING AND MOUNTINGS

- 1 Bolt
- 2 'U' bolt
- 3 Circlip
- 4 Cross tube

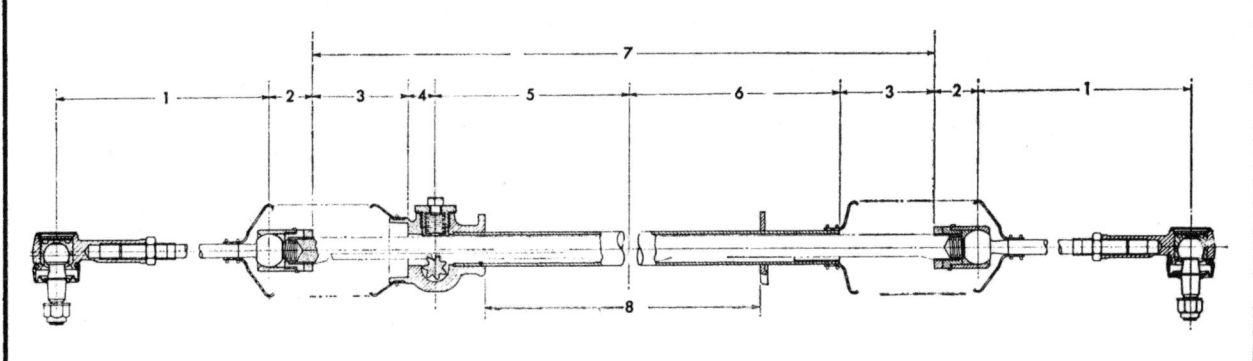

Fig. 11.26. RACK AND PINION STEERING UNIT DIMENSIONS

TR4A
1 8.42" (213.87 mm)
8 12.65" (321.31 mm)

TR4
1 8.55" (217.17 mm)
2 1.42" (36.06 mm)
3 3.09" (78.5 mm)
4 0.88" (22.35 mm)
5 8.00" (203.2 mm)
6 8.88" (225.55 mm)
7 23.94" (60.81 cm)

Chapter 11/Suspension - Dampers - Steering

upwards on the spokes so as to compress the spring.
22 A second person should move the intermediate shaft towards the rear and engage the splines of the rack pinion with the universal joint. Retighten the pinch bolt (16).
23 Check and adjust the front wheel alignment.

37. Rack and Pinion Steering - Dismantling, Reassembly and Adjustment

1. All numbers in brackets refer to Fig. 11.24. Undo the clips (27, 31) on the rubber gaiters (15, 29) and pull the gaiters back to expose the inner ball joint assemblies.
2. Loosen the locknuts (28) and completely unscrew both the tie rod assemblies (26) from the rack (20).
3. Pull out the coil springs (24), free the tab washer (23), unscrew the nut (22) and take off the shim (42) and cup (25).
4. Mark the positions of the locknuts (30) on the tie rods (14, 32) so the toe-in is approximately correct on reassembly, undo the locknuts (30) and screw off the ball joints.
5. Pull off the rubber gaiter (15, 29) and undo the cup nut (28) from the tie rods, and then remove the locknuts (21).
6. Unscrew and remove the damper cap (10), spring (12), plunger (13) and shims (9). Fig. 11.24 refers.
7. The pinion can be removed after taking out the circlip (1). Take great care not to lose the small locating peg (2).
8. The rack can now be pulled from the housing tube and the thrust washer (40) and bush (41) taken from the pinion housing (19).
9. Clean all the parts thoroughly and examine the teeth of the rack and pinion for wear or damage. Also examine the pinion thrust washer and bushes, thrust pad, and inner and outer ball joints and replace as necessary.
10 Reassembly commences by sliding the rack (20) into place. Then fit the bush (41) and thrust washer (40) and adjust the pinion endfloat after assembling the thrust washer (6), bush (5) and retaining ring (3) to the pinion, and fitting and securing the pinion to the housing with the circlip (1).
11 By trial and error fit a different number of shims (4) (available in thicknesses of 0.004 inch and 0.016 inch) until the minimum amount of end float exists when the pinion is pushed in and out commensurate with free rotation of the pinion.
12 When the correct shim thickness has been ascertained fit a new rubber 'O' ring to the retaining ring and, after the assembly has been fitted, fit the dowel (2) and circlip (1).
13 Then adjust the rack and pinion backlash as described in Section 38. Reassembly is now a straightforward reversal of the dismantling sequence. Check that the rack ball joints fit tightly but are free to move. If they are excessively loose or tight adjustment can be made by varying the number and thickness of the shims (42) between the ball joint cup (25) and the ball housing.
14 After fitting the rack and pinion in place fill it with the recommended lubricant.

38. Rack and Pinion Backlash - Adjustment

Backlash between the pinion and the rack can be taken up by means of an adjustment between the rack damper cap and the rack housing. If backlash is present adjust the rack damper in the following manner. Numerical references in brackets refer to Fig. 11.24.
1. Disconnect the outer ends of the steering tie rods (26) by knocking out the tie rod ball joint shanks from the holes in the steering arms.
2. Unscrew the damper cap (11) and remove the spring (12) and shims (9).
3. Refit the damper cap together with the plunger (13) but without the spring and shims.
4. Tighten the damper cap until it requires about a 2lb pull at the steering wheel rim to turn the wheel.
5. Measure the gap between the underside of the damper cap and the rack housing with a feeler gauge and add to this figure a clearance figure of .002 inch to .005 inch (.05 to .127 mm). The total figure represents the thickness of the shims that must be fitted under the cap. Shims are available in thicknesses of .003 inch and .010 inch (.76 and .254 mm).
6. Remove the cap, replace the spring, fit the necessary shims and tighten the cap down firmly. Reconnect the tie rod ball joints to the steering arms and note the improvement when the car is taken on the road.

39. Outer Ball Joint - Removal and Replacement

If the tie rod outer ball joints are worn it will be necessary to renew the whole ball joint assembly as they cannot be dismantled and repaired. To remove a ball joint, free the ball joint shank from the steering arm and mark the position of the locknut on the tie rod accurately to ensure near accurate 'toe-in' on reassembly.

Slacken off the ball joint locknut and, holding the tie rod by the flat with a spanner to prevent it from turning, unscrew the complete ball assembly from the rod. Replacement is a straightforward reversal of this process. Visit your local Triumph agent to ensure that toe-in is correct.

Fault Finding Chart - Suspension - Dampers - Steering

Before diagnosing faults from the following chart check that irregularities are not caused by:-
1. Binding brakes.
2. Incorrect 'mix' of radial and cross-ply tyres.
3. Incorrect tyre pressures.
4. Misalignment of the body frame.

Symptoms	Reason	Remedy
Steering wheel can be moved considerably before any sign of movement is apparent at the road wheels.	Wear in steering linkage, gear and column coupling.	Check all joints and gears. Renew as necessary.
Vehicle difficult to steer in a straight line - 'Wanders'	As above.	As above.
	Wheel alignment incorrect (shown by uneven front tyre wear)	Check wheel alignment.
	Front wheel bearings loose.	Adjust or renew.
	Worn suspension unit swivel joints.	Renew as necessary.
Steering stiff and heavy.	Incorrect wheel alignment (uneven or excessive tyre wear)	Check and adjust.
	Wear or seizure in steering linkage joints	Grease or renew.
	Wear or seizure in suspension linkage joints.	Grease or renew.
	Excessive wear in steering gear unit.	Adjust or renew.
Wheel wobble and vibration.	Road wheels out of balance.	Balance wheels.
	Road wheels buckled.	Check for damage.
	Wheel alignment incorrect.	Check.
	Wear in steering and suspension linkages.	Check or renew
	Broken front spring.	Renew.
Excessive pitching and rolling on corners and during braking.	Defective damper and/or broken spring	Renew.

Chapter 12/Bodywork and Underframe

Contents

General Description ...	1
Maintenance - Body & Chassis ...	2
Maintenance - Upholstery & Carpets ...	3
Maintenance - Hoods & Tonneau Covers ...	4
Minor Body Repairs ...	5
Major Chassis & Body Repairs ...	6
Chassis & Body Interchangeability ...	7
Maintenance - Hinges & Locks ...	8
Front Bumper & Brackets - Removal, Dismantling & Refitting (TR2, 3, 3A) ...	9
Front Bumper & Brackets - Removal, Dismantling & Refitting (TR4, 4A) ...	10
Rear Overriders & Brackets - Removal & Refitting (TR2, 3, 3A) ...	11
Rear Bumper & Brackets - Removal, Dismantling & Refitting (TR3, 3A) ...	12
Front Wing - Removal & Refitting (TR2, 3, 3A) ...	13
Front Wing - Removal & Refitting (TR4, 4A) ...	14
Rear Wing - Removal & Refitting (TR2, 3, 3A) ...	15
Rear Wing - Removal & Refitting (TR4, 4A) ...	16
Bonnet Lid - Removal & Refitting (TR2, 3, 3A) ...	17
Bonnet Lock - Adjustment (TR2, 3, 3A) ...	18
Bonnet Lid - Removal & Refitting (TR4, 4A) ...	19
Bonnet Lock & Striker - Adjustment (TR4, 4A) ...	20
Luggage Compartment Lid - Removal, Dismantling & Refitting (TR2, 3, 3A) ...	21
Luggage Compartment Lid - Removal, Dismantling & Refitting (TR4, 4A) ...	22
Spare Wheel Compartment Lid - Removal & Refitting (TR2, 3, 3A) ...	23
Door - Removal & Refitting (TR2, 3, 3A) ...	24
Door Lock - Removal & Refitting (TR2, 3, 3A) ...	25
Door - Sealing (TR2, 3, 3A) ...	26
Door - Removal & Refitting (TR4, 4A) ...	27
Door Lock & Remote Control - Removal & Refitting (TR4, 4A) ...	28
Door Glass & Regulator - Removal & Refitting (TR4, 4A) ...	29
Door Exterior Handle - Removal, Refitting & Adjusting (TR4, 4A) ...	30
Front Apron - Removal & Refitting (TR2) ...	31
Front Moulding & Grille - Removal & Refitting (TR3, 3A) ...	32
Front Grille - Removal & Refitting (TR4, 4A) ...	33
Sidescreen - Adjustment (TR2, 3, 3A) ...	34
Aero Screens - Fitting (TR2, 3, 3A) ...	35
Windscreen - Removal & Refitting (TR2, 3, 3A) ...	36
Windscreen - Removal & Refitting (TR4, 4A) ...	37
Windscreen Glass - Refitting (TR4, 4A) ...	38
Occasional Rear Seat - Fitting (TR3, 3A) ...	39
Hardtop Kit - Fitting (TR2, 3, 3A) ...	40
Instrument - Removal & Refitting (All Models) ...	41
Heater & Demister Unit - Removal & Refitting (All Models) ...	42
Heater & Demister Unit Kit - Fitting (TR2, 3, 3A) ...	43
Heater & Demister Unit - Fitting (TR4, 4A) ...	44
Fascia Panel - Removal & Refitting (TR4, 4A) ...	45

1. General Description

The all steel welded body for models covered by this manual is bolted to a separate box section chassis of the form shown in Fig. 12.1. It comprises two longitudinal members joined by crossmembers at the front and rear. In the centre of the two longitudinal members is a cruciform bracing system which gives the chassis frame the required rigidity.

Short brackets extended from the two longitudinal members provide the necessary mountings for the extremities of the body.

Although a relatively straightforward operation, it is possible for the body to be removed from the chassis but in normal circumstances this is not necessary except for accident damage repair and, as this should be left to the specialist body repairer, the details of this are outside the limits of this manual.

The front and rear wings are easily detachable from the body and full details of these operations are given in this Chapter.

The body for the TR3 and 3A series is basically the same as that of the TR2 with, of course, the obvious differences in the styling of the grille and radiator air intake. Stainless steel mouldings are fitted between the front and rear wings and the body on the later models.

It is possible to fit occasional rear seats to the TR3 and 3A models and is well within the capabilities of the do-it-yourself motorist.

The body of the TR4 and 4A models again differs in detail from the earlier models due, of course, to the

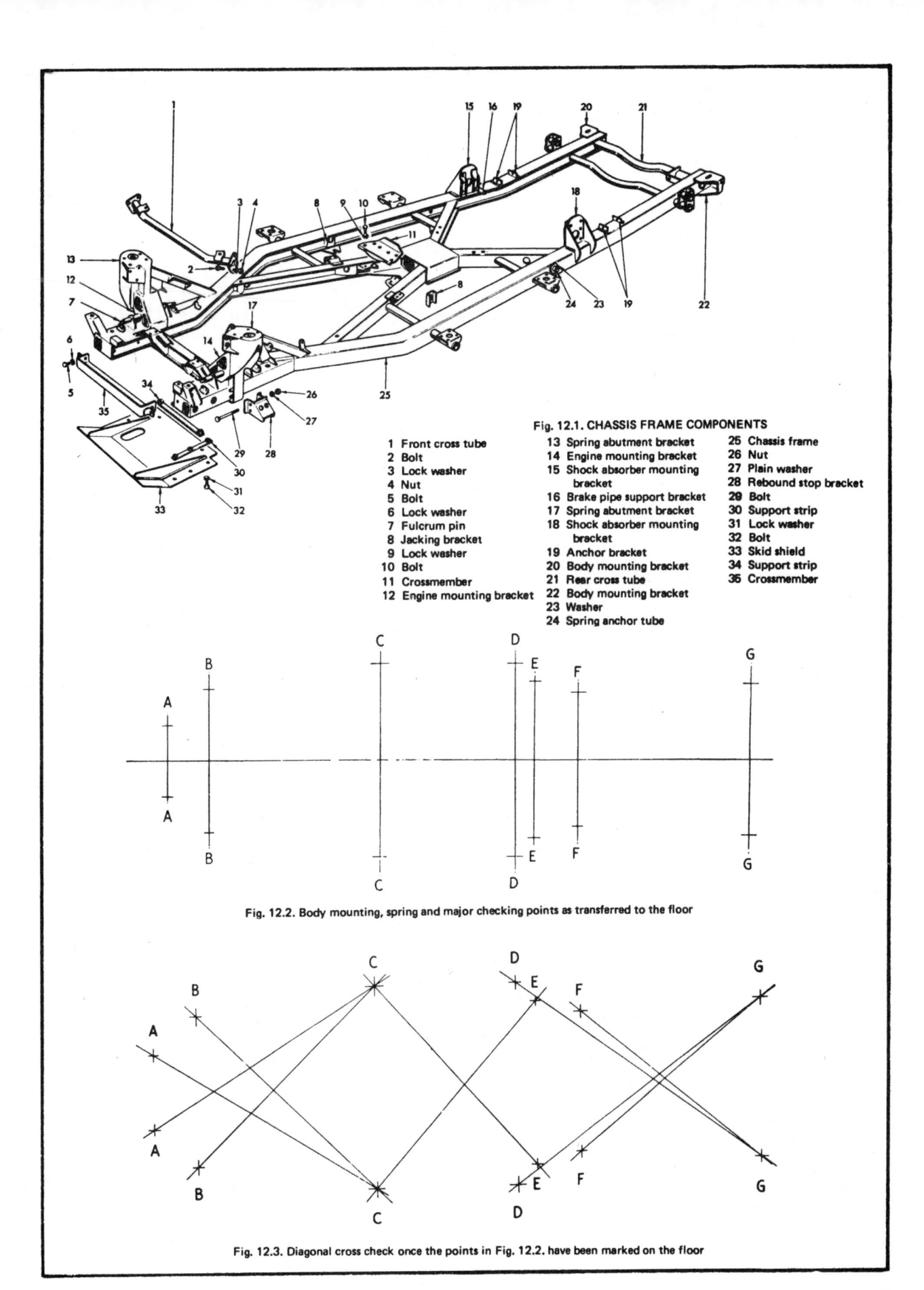

Fig. 12.1. CHASSIS FRAME COMPONENTS

1 Front cross tube	13 Spring abutment bracket	25 Chassis frame
2 Bolt	14 Engine mounting bracket	26 Nut
3 Lock washer	15 Shock absorber mounting bracket	27 Plain washer
4 Nut	16 Brake pipe support bracket	28 Rebound stop bracket
5 Bolt	17 Spring abutment bracket	29 Bolt
6 Lock washer	18 Shock absorber mounting bracket	30 Support strip
7 Fulcrum pin	19 Anchor bracket	31 Lock washer
8 Jacking bracket	20 Body mounting bracket	32 Bolt
9 Lock washer	21 Rear cross tube	33 Skid shield
10 Bolt	22 Body mounting bracket	34 Support strip
11 Crossmember	23 Washer	35 Crossmember
12 Engine mounting bracket	24 Spring anchor tube	

Fig. 12.2. Body mounting, spring and major checking points as transferred to the floor

Fig. 12.3. Diagonal cross check once the points in Fig. 12.2. have been marked on the floor

269

1

This photographic sequence shows the steps taken to repair the dent and paintwork damage shown above. In general, the procedure for repairing a hole will be similar; where there are substantial differences, the procedure is clearly described and shown in a separate photograph.

2

First remove any trim around the dent, then hammer out the dent where access is possible. This will minimise filling. Here, after the large dent has been hammered out, the damaged area is being made slightly concave.

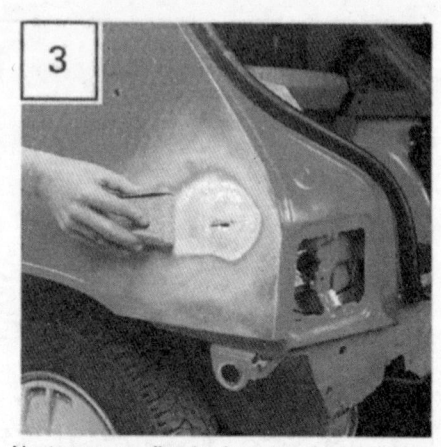

3

Next, remove all paint from the damaged area by rubbing with course abrasive paper or using a power drill fitted with a wire brush or abrasive pad. 'Feather' the edge of the boundary with good paintwork using a finer grade of abrasive paper.

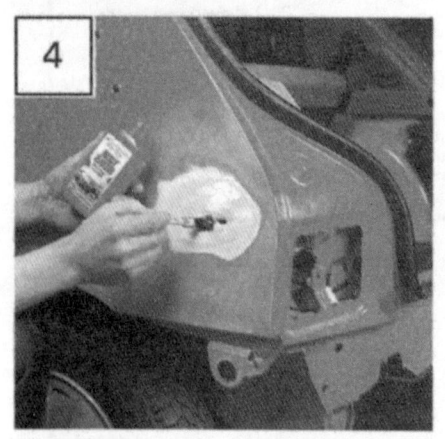

4

Where there are holes or other damage, the sheet metal should be cut away before proceeding further. The damaged area and any signs of rust should be treated with Turtle Wax Hi-Tech Rust Eater, which will also inhibit further rust formation.

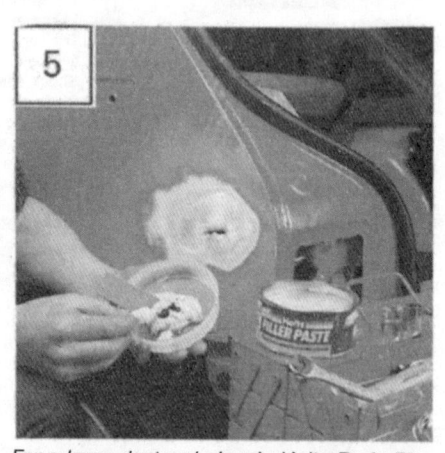

5

For a large dent or hole mix Holts Body Plus Resin and Hardener according to the manufacturer's instructions and apply around the edge of the repair. Press Glass Fibre Matting over the repair area and leave for 20-30 minutes to harden. Then ...

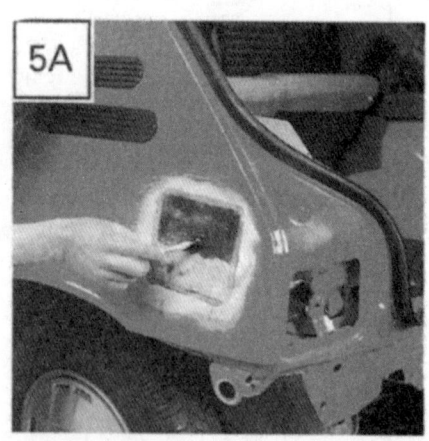

5A

... brush more Holts Body Plus Resin and Hardener onto the matting and leave to harden. Repeat the sequence with two or three layers of matting, checking that the final layer is lower than the surrounding area. Apply Holts Body Plus Filler Paste as shown in Step 5B.

5B

For a medium dent, mix Holts Body Plus Filler Paste and Hardener according to the manufacturer's instructions and apply it with a flexible applicator. Apply thin layers of filler at 20-minute intervals, until the filler surface is slightly proud of the surrounding bodywork.

5C

For small dents and scratches use Holts No Mix Filler Paste straight from the tube. Apply it according to the instructions in thin layers, using the spatula provided. It will harden in minutes if applied outdoors and may then be used as its own knifing putting.

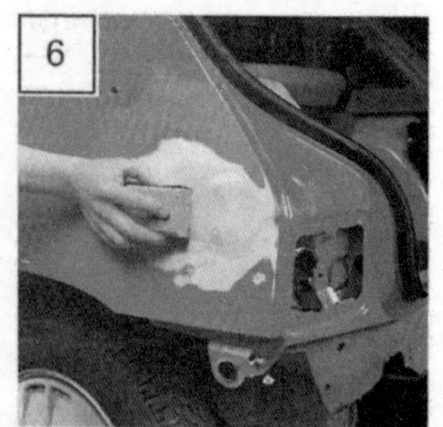

6

Use a plane or file for initial shaping. Then, using progressively finer grades of wet-and-dry paper, wrapped around a sanding block, and copious amounts of clean water, rub down the filler until glass smooth. 'Feather' the edges of adjoining paintwork.

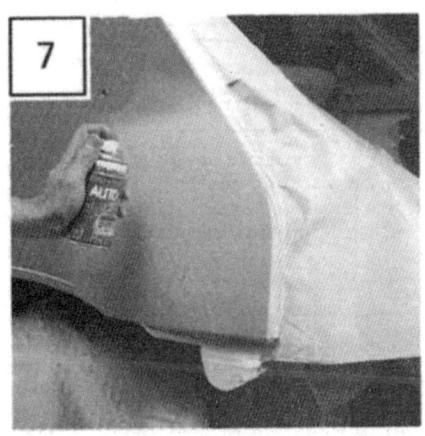

7 Protect adjoining areas before spraying the whole repair area and at least one inch of the surrounding sound paintwork with Holts Dupli-Color primer.

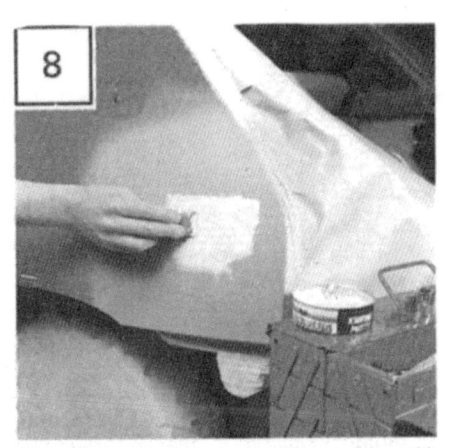

8 Fill any imperfections in the filler surface with a small amount of Holts Body Plus Knifing Putty. Using plenty of clean water, rub down the surface with a fine grade wet-and-dry paper - 400 grade is recommended - until it is really smooth.

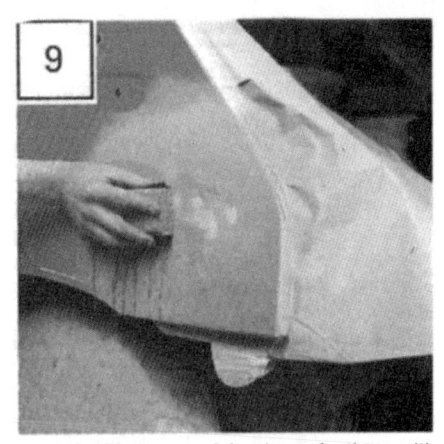

9 Carefully fill any remaining imperfections with knifing putty before applying the last coat of primer. Then rub down the surface with Holts Body Rubbing Compound to ensure a really smooth surface.

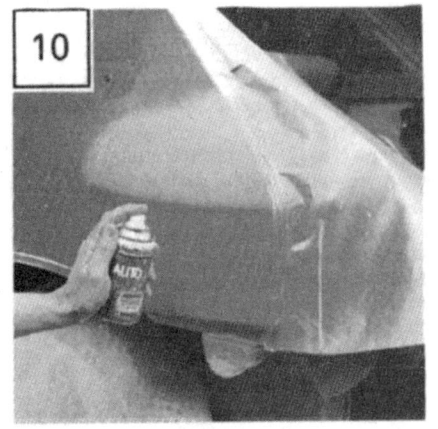

10 Protect surrounding areas from overspray before applying the topcoat in several thin layers. Agitate Holts Dupli-Color aerosol thoroughly. Start at the repair centre, spraying outwards with a side-to-side motion.

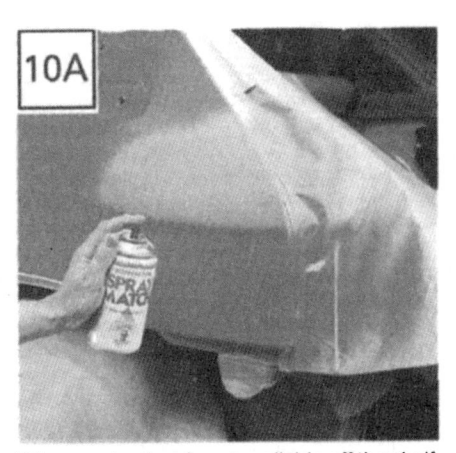

10A If the exact colour is not available off the shelf, local Holts Professional Spraymatch Centres will custom fill an aerosol to match perfectly.

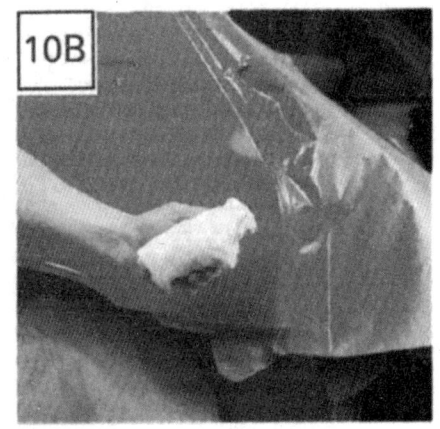

10B To identify whether a lacquer finish is required, rub a painted unrepaired part of the body with wax and a clean cloth.

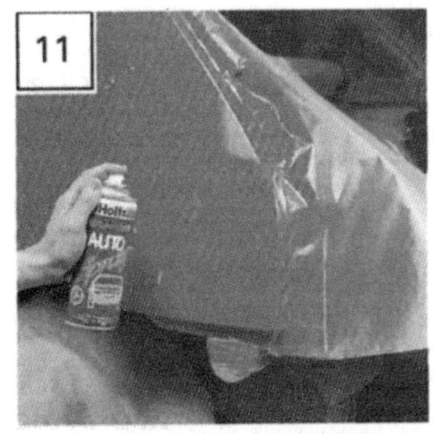

11 If *no* traces of paint appear on the cloth, spray Holts Dupli-Color clear lacquer over the repaired area to achieve the correct gloss level.

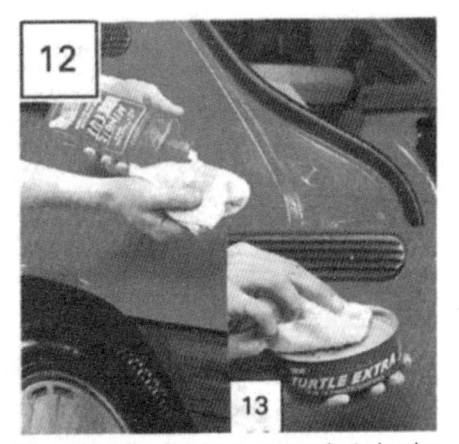

12 The paint will take about two weeks to harden fully. After this time it can be 'cut' with a mild cutting compound such as Turtle Wax Minute Cut prior to polishing with a final coating of Turtle Wax Extra.

14 When carrying out bodywork repairs, remember that the quality of the finished job is proportional to the time and effort expended.

Chapter 12/Bodywork & Underframe

restyling but full servicing information covering these models is given in this Chapter.

TR2, 3, 3A models were available in either a soft top or hard top version whilst the TR4, 4A also included a Surrey top in the range with a fixed rear section of a hard top and a soft top for the roof section.

2. Maintenance - Body and Chassis

1. The condition of your car's bodywork is of considerable importance as it is on this that the secondhand value of the car will mainly depend. It is much more difficult to repair neglected bodywork than to renew mechanical assemblies. The hidden portions of the body, such as the wheel arches and the underframe and the engine compartment are equally important, though obviously not requiring such frequent attention as the immediately visible paintwork.

2. Once a year or every 12,000 miles it is a sound scheme to visit your local main agent and have the underside of the body steam cleaned. This will take about 1½ hours and cost about £4. All traces of dirt and oil will be removed and the underside can then be inspected carefully for rust, damaged hydraulic pipes, frayed electrical wiring and other faults.

3. At the same time the engine compartment should be cleaned in the same manner. If steam cleaning facilities are not available then brush 'Gunk' or a similar cleanser over the whole engine and engine compartment with a stiff paintbrush, working it well in where there is an accumulation of oil and dirt. Do not paint the ignition system but protect it with oily rags when the 'Gunk' is washed off. As the 'Gunk' is washed away it will take with it all traces of oil and dirt, leaving the engine looking clean and bright.

4. The wheel arches should be given particular attention as undersealing can easily come away here and stones and dirt thrown up from the road wheels can soon cause the paint to chip and flake, and so allow rust to set in. If rust is found, clean down the bare metal with wet and dry paper, paint on an anti-corrosive coating such as Kurust or, if preferred, red lead, and renew the paintwork and undercoating.

5. The bodywork should be washed once a week or when dirty. Thoroughly wet the car to soften the dirt and then wash the car down with a soft sponge and plenty of clean water. If the surplus dirt is not washed off very gently, in time it will wear the paint down as surely as wet and dry paper. It is best to use a hose if this is available. Give the car a final wash down and then dry using a soft chamois leather to prevent the formation of spots.

6. Spots of tar and grease thrown up from the road can be removed with a rag dampened with petrol.

7. Once every six months, or every three months if wished, give the bodywork and chromium trim a thoroughly good wax polish. If a chromium cleaner is used to remove rust on any of the plated parts remember that the cleaner also removes part of the chromium so use sparingly.

3. Maintenance - Upholstery and Carpets

1. Remove the carpets or mats and thoroughly vacuum clean the interior of the car every three months or more frequently if necessary.

2. Beat out the carpets and vacuum clean them if they are very dirty. If the upholstery is soiled apply an upholstery cleaner with a damp sponge and wipe off with a clean dry cloth.

4. Maintenance - Hoods and Tonneau Covers

Under no circumstances try to clean hoods and tonneau covers with detergents, caustic soaps, or spirit cleaners. Plain soap and water is all that is required with a soft brush to clean dirt that may be ingrained. Wash the hood as frequently as the rest of the car.

5. Minor Body Repairs

There comes a time in the life of a car when rust appears on some part or other of the many exterior body panels. To the do-it-yourself motorist even the most formidable looking rust patches or panels that have corroded through can be repaired provided that their condition has not been allowed to become so bad necessitating a new panel or section to be fitted.

Many of the motorists' accessory shops stock body repair and filler kits and it was by using one of these kits that a TR4, having bad rust patches, was given a new lease of life. By following the maker's instructions very satisfactory results may be obtained as will be seen once this section has been studied.

1. The offside rear wing panel had bad rust marks and in several places there were actual holes, as can be seen in this photo.

2. The first stage of repair is to knock the loose pieces of metal away until firm metal surrounds the hole. To enable an adequate depth of filler to be used so that the body panel curves may be reproduced the area around the hole should be hammered in by about ½ inch (photo).

3. Any stainless steel or chrome trim near to the area being repaired should be removed otherwise it could be damaged or impair the work. In this case the finisher on the top of the wing is being removed (photo).

4. Using a wire brush, remove all paintwork and rust from around the area to be repaired. Care must be taken at this stage to remove as much as possible so that a good bond between the filler and the body panel will be obtained (photo).

5. Either supplied with the repair kit, or offered as an extra, will be a piece of gauze. Cut a piece just a little bigger than the size of the hole (photo).

6. Bend over the edges of the gauze and shape it so that it will catch on the inside of the hole. If it is found that the hole is in place where the gauze will fall out, retain it in place with bent paper clips (photo).

7. Follow the instructions given on the filler pack and mix the filler accordingly. Mix only sufficient for immediate needs as it hardens quickly and will only be wasted (photo).

8. Apply a little filler to each corner of the gauze to give additional support to it and then work around the outside of the hole. Allow the filler to dry (photo).

9. Using a wide spreader fill up the remainder of the hole and the surrounding, if possible keeping to the contour of the body panel so making the subsequent operations easier (photo).

10 If necessary build up the contour in several stages (photo).

11 Using a very coarse file, or Dreadnought milling file, carefully shape the hardened filler so that it blends in with the panel shape. Ensure that not too much is removed otherwise it will have to be built up again (photo).

12 To stop any paint spray in subsequent operations finding its way onto the surrounding panels use newspaper and Sellotape to mask off the area under repair.

13 With a little 'wet or dry' rubbing paper, backed with a piece of wood, remove the teeth marks and scratches left from the previous operation. If it is found that the grain

Chapter 12/Bodywork & Underframe

clogs, the rubbing paper may be thoroughly wetted (photo).

14 The edges of existing paintwork should be feathered so that no ridges will be evident when the repaired section is finally resprayed.

15 If there are any chrome fittings such as letters or badges which are in the area of repair and may be difficult to mask from paint spray, then coat them with a little grease so that the paint spray does not adhere to the chrome work.

16 When the surface is perfectly smooth it is now time to put on the first coat of paint. This should be a primer coat and may be obtained in an aerosol tin. Before spraying for the first time read the instructions and then practice on a piece of flat metal or wood.

17 Holding the jet about six inches away from the surface spray the area taking care that runs are not allowed to form. This is usually caused by holding the jet too near to the area being painted.

18 Very carefully inspect the dry primer coat for signs of imperfections of the paint feathering or flatting sequences previously completed. Any imperfections should be attended to at this stage. Respray with primer.

19 When the surface is really flat and smooth lightly rub the primer to give a key for the top coat.

20 Just before the top coat is applied try a little of the paint on a less prominent part of the bodywork to ensure a good colour match. If the colours vary considerably due to weathering it will be better to have some matching paint mixed at the local garage and the affected parts sprayed otherwise results could look very patchy.

21 When the final coat is dry remove the newspaper and tape. Allow the paint to harden before replacing any chrome trim. Leave the repainted surfaces for about seven days before using any polish.

22 Where the paintwork has blistered due to rust forming behind the paint as shown in this photograph the area affected must be rubbed down well with emery paper (photo).

23 Do not confine the area to the paint blisters alone but increase it to about 1½ inches around the affected area (photo).

24 When the extent of rust has been determined use a wire brush to derust any deeply rusted areas. Tap in any holes to give a key for the filler (photo).

25 Using a wide spreader apply some prepared filler to the area under repair (photo).

26 Allow the filler to dry and then prepare the surface as previously described in this Section.

27 This is what the finished panel should look like (photo).

6. Major Chassis and Body Repairs

1. Major chassis and body repair work cannot successfully be undertaken by the average owner. Work of this nature should be entrusted to a competent body repair specialist who should have the necessary jigs, welding and hydraulic straightening equipment as well as skilled panel beaters to ensure that a proper job is done.

2. If the damage is severe it is vital that on completion of repair the chassis is in correct alignment. Less severe damage may also have twisted or distorted the chassis although this may not be visible immediately. It is therefore always best on completion of repair to check for twist and squareness to ensure that all is correct.

3. To check for twist, position the car on a clean level floor, place a jack under each jacking point, raise the car, and take off the wheels. Raise or lower the jacks until points C and D (Fig. 12.2) are exactly equidistant from the floor.

4. With the points C and D correctly set, should it prove impossible to obtain equal height measurements at A and G, then the chassis is twisted.

5. If the previous test proved satisfactory the next check should be for squareness by taking a series of measurements on the floor. Drop a plumb line and bob weight from the lettered points on the chassis frame (Fig. 12.2) to the floor and mark these points with a sharpened piece of chalk. Letter them to correspond with the letters in Fig. 12.2.

6. When all datum marks have been made carefully remove the car from the area.

7. Connect the letters in pairs, i.e., AA, DD, GG together by drawing a line between them using a straight edge (Fig. 12.2).

8. Draw a centre line through the previously made lines so that the floor pattern is similar to that shown in Fig. 12.2 and measure each line from the centre line to the lettered end. Obviously each corresponding line from the centre line outwards should measure the same.

9. A further check may be made by joining diagonals as shown in Fig. 12.3. The points of intersection of the diagonals should also be on the centre line of the floor pattern.

7. Chassis and Body Interchangeability

Due to the fact that the chassis and bodies of the models covered by this manual differ slightly from one model to another it is not possible to interchange these two major items. Modifications which are not considered within the scope of the do-it-yourself motorist would be required.

8. Maintenance - Hinges and Locks

Once every six months, or every 6,000 miles, the door, bonnet and boot hinges should be oiled, using a few drops of engine oil from an oil can. The door striker plates should be given a thin smear of grease to reduce wear and ensure free movement.

9. Front Bumper and Brackets - Removal, Dismantling and Refitting (TR2, 3, 3A)

1. If it is only necessary to remove the bumper blade, it may be separated from the four support brackets whilst the latter remain mounted on the car.

2. Slacken the two nuts located behind the inner support brackets and lift the over riders free from the heads of the bolts. Recover the four mouldings positioned between the overriders and the bumper blade.

3. Remove the nuts and plain washers which secure the overrider to the blade.

4. Loosen and remove the nuts, plain washers and bolts that secure the bumper blade to the outer support brackets.

5. Lift the bumper blade from its four support brackets. Recover the four packing pieces that locate between the bumper blade and the brackets.

6. If it is necessary to remove the four brackets it should be noted that the two brackets nearest to the steering box have an additional support from the lower bolt on the steering trunnion bracket.

7. Remove the two bolts from each pair of support brackets and chassis frame. Slacken the lower bolt on the steering trunnion bracket and remove all four brackets.

8. It is recommended that although it is possible to assemble the bumper blade and support brackets and then fit them to the car, it is better to assemble the brackets to the car first and then refit the bumper blade.

9. Reassembly is the reverse sequence to removal but the

Chapter 12/Bodywork & Underframe

following point should be noted. There is an additional support in the form of a short plate with holes at each end. One end should be fitted under the head of the lower steering column trunnion bracket bolt and the other end fitted under the head of the front bumper support bracket bolt.

10 Do not forget to fit the spacers between the bumper blade and the support brackets and the four strips of moulding that are positioned between the overrider and the bumper blade.

10. Front Bumper and Brackets - Removal, Dismantling and Refitting (TR4, 4A)

1. Refer to Fig. 12.4. Undo and remove the two bolts (57) that secure the overrider support stay (56) to the inner valance.
8. Undo and remove the two bolts (41) which secure the bumper bar support brackets to the mounting bracket (61).
3. Carefully lift away the bumper (52) complete with the overriders (51) and support stays (4, 9, 56).
4. If necessary the overrider (51) can be separated from the bumper bar (52) by undoing the retaining bolts (36) and removing them together with plain (38) and spring (37) washers. Recover the two P.V.C. mouldings (50).
5. The support brackets may be removed from the bumper bar by undoing the nuts (47) and lifting away the nuts, spring washers (46), plain washers (45) and distance pieces (44).
6. To remove the bumper support brackets (35, 61) from the body loosen the securing nuts (34), remove the nuts, spring washers (33) and plain washers (32), then withdraw the clamp plates with studs (31).
7. Refitting is the reverse sequence to removal. Do not tighten fully any nuts or bolts until all have been correctly positioned and loosely fitted.

11. Rear Overriders and Brackets - Removal and Refitting (TR2, 3, 3A)

1. The rear overriders may be removed from their support brackets by slackening the retaining nuts and sliding the overriders away.
2. To remove the brackets use a ring spanner to hold the head of the lower attachment bolt, working under the car undo and remove the nut, lock washer, plain washer and then extract the bolt.
3. Using the ring spanner hold the nut of the upper attachment bolt and undo the bolt. Withdraw the bolt through the distance piece and support bracket.
4. Lift away the nut, plain washer and distance piece.
5. To refit first attach the overrider support bracket to the chassis frame at its lowermost point by inserting the retaining bolt through the chassis frame and into the bracket. Replace the plain washer, lock washer and nut but do not fully tighten the nut yet.
6. Locate the distance piece and feed the bolt through the support bracket and a plain washer and then through the distance piece followed by a second plain washer. Replace the nut and tighten securely.
7. Tighten the first nut which was originally left slack.
8. Position the overrider retaining bolts in the brackets together with the plain washers and lock washers and nuts. Do not tighten the nuts yet.
9. Slide the keyhole in the overrider over the head of the bolt and when in position tighten the nut securely.

12. Rear Bumper and Brackets - Removal, Dismantling and Refitting (TR4, 4A)

1. Disconnect the battery earth terminal for safety reasons.
2. Locate the rear number plate illumination light cable connectors within the rear luggage compartment and disconnect the cables. Withdraw the cables through the luggage compartment to the underside of the car.
3. Refer to Fig. 12.4 and remove the bolts (63) that secure the two overrider support brackets (10, 67) to the chassis.
4. Slacken but do not remove the nuts (25) and remove the stud (29). As the inner end of the stud has a slot it is possible to remove the stud.
5. On later models it will be found that the nuts and washers shown in the dotted part of the illustration are superseded by a distance piece (26).
6. Undo and remove the two bolts (8) that secure the two overriders (6, 9) to the bumper and support brackets (5).
7. Remove the two nuts (15) that secure the bumper to the support brackets (4).
8. Carefully lift away the bumper from the rear of the car noting the position of the two distance pieces (12).
9. To remove the two support brackets (4, 5) from the body undo and remove the four bolts (1) and lift away the support brackets.
10 Refitting is the reverse sequence to removal but the following additional points should be noted.
11 Do not completely tighten any nuts and bolts until all have been positioned and loosely fitted.
12 There should be a clearance of 0.75 inch between the bumper and body panels which may be adjusted by positioning the support and outrigger brackets.

13. Front Wing - Removal and Refitting (TR2, 3, 3A)

1. The removal of a front wing is a very easy procedure which should present no difficulties except in extreme cases of corrosion. It is recommended that all nuts and bolts likely to be rusted be soaked in penetrating oil overnight prior to removal.
2. Chock the rear wheels, apply the handbrake, and remove the wheel trim on the side that is to be worked on. Slacken the wheel nuts, jack up the front of the car and support it on axle stands. Remove the road wheel.
3. Undo and remove the six bolts that secure the front wing to the apron and the five bolts whose heads are facing the tyre treads.
4. Undo and remove the six bolts from the top of the wing. The bolts heads will be found just beneath the side of the bonnet lid location.
5. Remove the nut and bolt that secures the door check strap to the front door post. Using a pencil, outline the hinge position to assist refitting.
6. Slacken and remove the seven bolts securing the door hinges to the door post. During this operation, which requires two people, one person should take the weight of the door while the other removes the bolts. Attempts to do the operation single handed will probably result in damage. After removing the bolts lift away the complete door.
7. The six bolts that secure the rear of the wing will now be exposed and these should next be undone.
8. Carefully extract the rubber grommet from the inside of the car and using a socket or box spanner remove the bolt from the inside of the hole exposed by the removal of the grommet.
9. Undo and remove the five bolts that secure the bulkhead sealer plate. The bolts are located under the wing at the rear of the arch. Lift away the sealer plate.

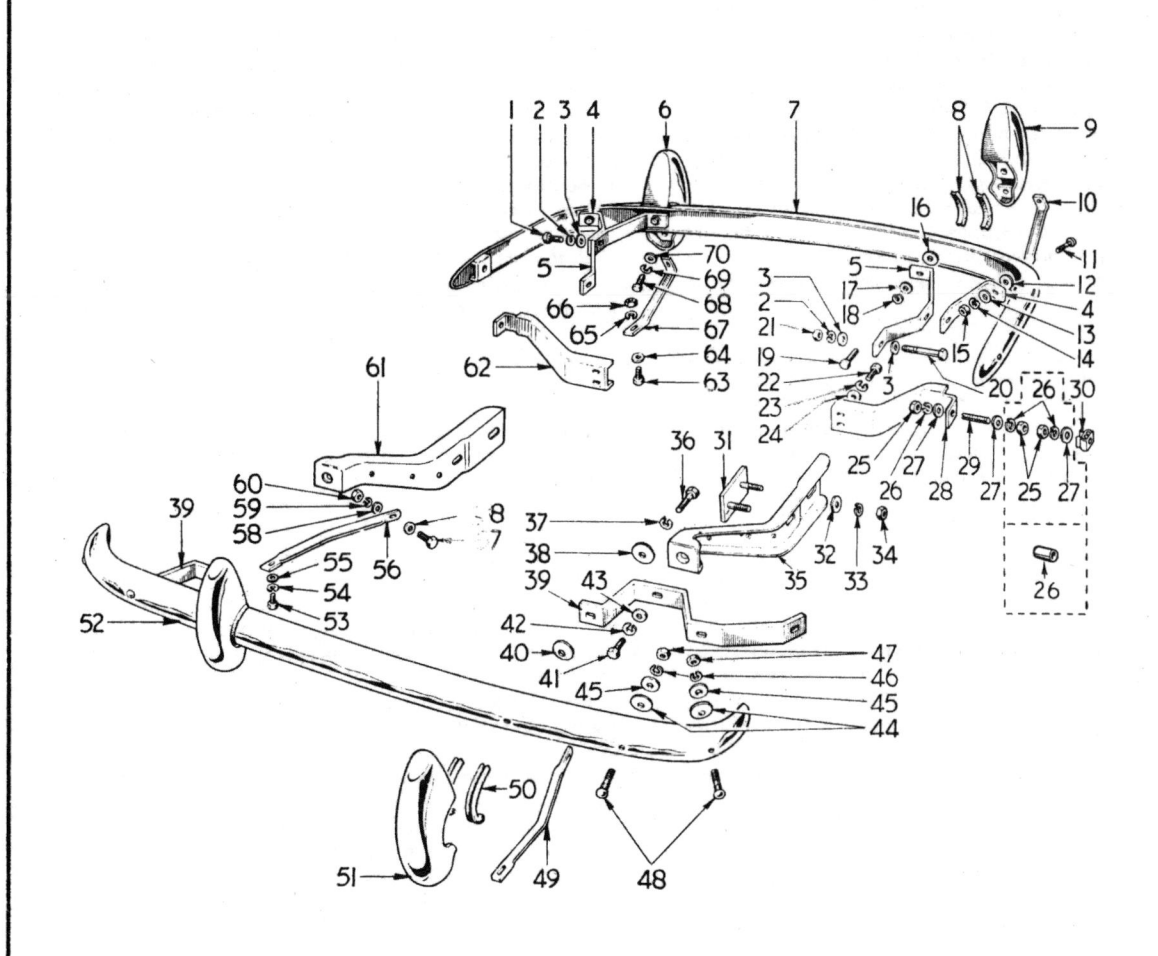

Fig. 12.4. FRONT AND REAR BUMPER AND BRACKET ASSEMBLIES TR4, 4A

1 Bolt	19 Bolt	37 Washer	55 Washer
2 Washer	20 Bolt	38 Washer	56 Overrider support bracket
3 Washer	21 Nut	39 Bumper support bracket	57 Bolt
4 Support bracket	22 Bolt	40 Distance piece	58 Washer
5 Support bracket	23 Washer	41 Bolt	59 Washer
6 Overrider	24 Washer	42 Washer	60 Nut
7 Rear bumper bar	25 Nut	43 Washer	61 Bumper support bracket
8 P.V.C. moulding	26 Washer	44 Distance piece	62 Rear bumper outrigger
9 Overrider	27 Washer	45 Washer	63 Bolt
10 Overrider support bracket	28 Rear bumper outrigger	46 Washer	64 Washer
11 Bolt	29 Stud	47 Nut	65 Washer
12 Distance piece	30 Nut	48 Bolts	66 Nut
13 Washer	31 Clamp plate	49 Overrider support bracket	67 Overrider support bracket
14 Washer	32 Washer	50 P.V.C. moulding	68 Bolt
15 Nut	33 Washer	51 Overrider	69 Washer
16 Distance piece	34 Nut	52 Front bumper bar	70 Washer
17 Washer	35 Bumper support bracket	53 Bolt	
18 Washer	36 Bolt	54 Washer	

Chapter 12/Bodywork & Underframe

10 Remove the three bolts situated underneath the sill panel and behind the arch opening.
11 Carefully free the lower end of the wing by pulling outwards and then lift upwards to disengage the flange of the wing adjacent to the dash panel.
12 The wing may then be lifted away from the body.
13 Refitting the wing is the reverse sequence to removal. Care should be taken to ensure that all the joints are well sealed, using a Bostik sealer.
14 The sealing bead strip fitted between the wing and the apron should be positioned with its hole uppermost.
15 Any bolts that protrude into the wheel arch should be well greased to prevent thread corrosion.
16 When the door is refitted check that it opens and closes freely.

14. Front Wing - Removal and Refitting (TR4, 4A)

1. The removal of a front wing is a very easy procedure and should present no difficulties except in extreme cases of corrosion. It is recommended that all nuts and bolts likely to be rusted be soaked in penetrating oil overnight prior to removal.
2. Refer to Fig. 12.4 and remove the two bolts (57) that secure the overrider support stay (56) to the inner valance.
3. Undo and remove the two bolts (41) and lift the front bumper assembly (52) away from the front of the car.
4. The location of the front wing retaining screws is shown in Fig. 12.5 and these should be undone and removed in a diagonal manner so as to provide support to the front wing.
5. When all screws have been removed the front wing may be removed. Undo the two screws securing each of the bonnet side buffer rubbers and lift away the rubbers. Also remove the chromium beading that is sandwiched between the wing and the body.
6. Refitting the wing is the reverse sequence to removal but the following additional points should be noted.
7. Carefully remove all traces of the old sealing compound before reassembly and when refitting seal the joint between the wing and the body with a non setting sealing compound.
8. The retaining lugs on the chromium beading should be straightened before it is refitted between the wing and body. As the wing retaining screws (A) are tightened press the chromium beading down into position and once they are tight bend over the retaining tags.

15. Rear Wing - Removal and Refitting (TR2, 3, 3A)

1. It is recommended that before the rear wing is removed all nuts and bolts likely to be corroded be soaked overnight in penetrating oil.
2. For safety reasons disconnect the battery earth terminal.
3. Locate the rear light cluster electric cable terminals and check whether the colours have faded making identification of the cables difficult for correct reconnection. If necessary place some tape around each cable pair in a different manner for identification purposes. Disconnect the cables from the terminal connectors.
4. Undo and remove the two screws that secure the light cluster to the wing panel. Lift away the light cluster.
5. Chock the front wheels and remove the rear wheel trim on the side that is to be worked on. Slacken the wheel nuts, jack up the rear of the car, and support on axle stands. Remove the road wheel.
6. Undo and remove the nine bolts from the inside of the wing running from the top of the wing to the lower front edge.
7. Next remove the five bolts from the inside of the rear luggage compartment.
8. Undo the nut that secures the wing to the chassis stay and lift away the nut, lock washer, plain washer and bolt.
9. Slacken the three bolts located on the fixing flange of the wing at its rearmost end. It is not necessary to completely remove the three bolts.
10 By drawing the wing panel rearwards the fixing flange will be disconnected from the bolts. When free lift away the panel. Recover the sealing strip.
11 Refitting the wing is the reverse sequence to removal.
12 Any bolts protruding into the wheel arch should be well greased to prevent thread corrosion.
13 Reconnect the electrical cables to the rear light cluster in the same positions noted before disconnection. Reconnect the battery earth cable.

16. Rear Wing - Removal and Refitting (TR4, 4A)

1. It is recommended that all nuts and bolts likely to be rusted be soaked in penetrating oil overnight prior to removal.
2. Disconnect the battery earth terminal for safety reasons.
3. Locate the cable terminal connectors for the rear lights and check that the cable colour coding can be readily identified. If the colouring has faded use tape to identify each pair of cables to assist reconnection. Also disconnect the flasher and number plate light cables from the snap connectors positioned in the upper corners of the luggage compartment.
4. From inside the luggage compartment undo and remove the rear light cluster four securing nuts and spring washers. Lift away the rear light cluster.
5. Refer to Section 12 of this Chapter and remove the rear bumper and support brackets.
6. Undo and remove the four retaining screws that secure the interior trim panel at the rear of the fuel tank.
7. Cars fitted with the soft top should have the soft top and hoodstick assembly removed.
8. Undo the six screws that secure the quarter trim panel in place, lift away the screws and the trim panel.
9. Refer to Fig. 12.6 and remove the fifteen screws that hold the wing panel to the body. Lift away the wing and chrome beading from the body.
10 Refitting the wing is the reverse sequence to removal but the following additional points should be noted.
11 Carefully remove all traces of the old sealing compound before reassembly and when refitting seal the joint between the wing and the body with a non setting sealing compound.
12 The retaining tags on the chromium beading should be straightened before it is refitted between the wing and body. As the wing retaining screws (A) are tightened press the chromium beading down into position and once they are tight bend over the retaining tags.
13 Once the rear lights and battery have been reconnected check that all the lights function correctly.

17. Bonnet Lid - Removal and Refitting (TR2, 3, 3A)

1. Operate the bonnet release catch, if a cable operated lock system is fitted, or turn the Dzuz fastener with the special key so releasing the bonnet. Do not open fully at this stage.
2. Mark the outline of the hinge under the dash to assist in refitting in its original position.
3. Undo and remove the two nuts and washers that secure each hinge to the under dash panel.
4. With the assistance of a second person lift the bonnet up squarely and then away over the front of the car.

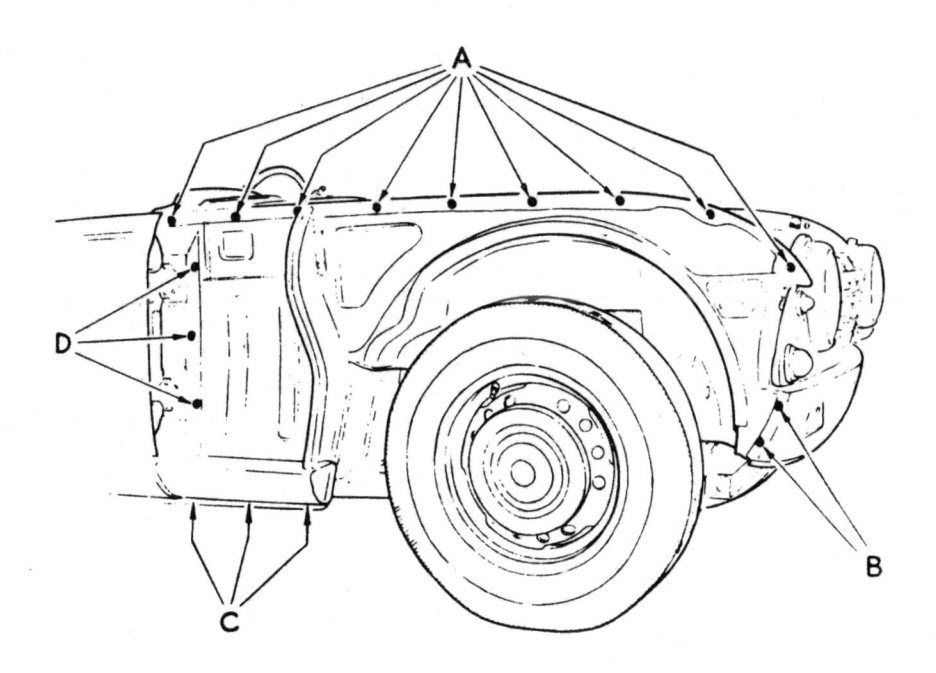

Fig. 12.5. Front wing attachment points TR4, 4A

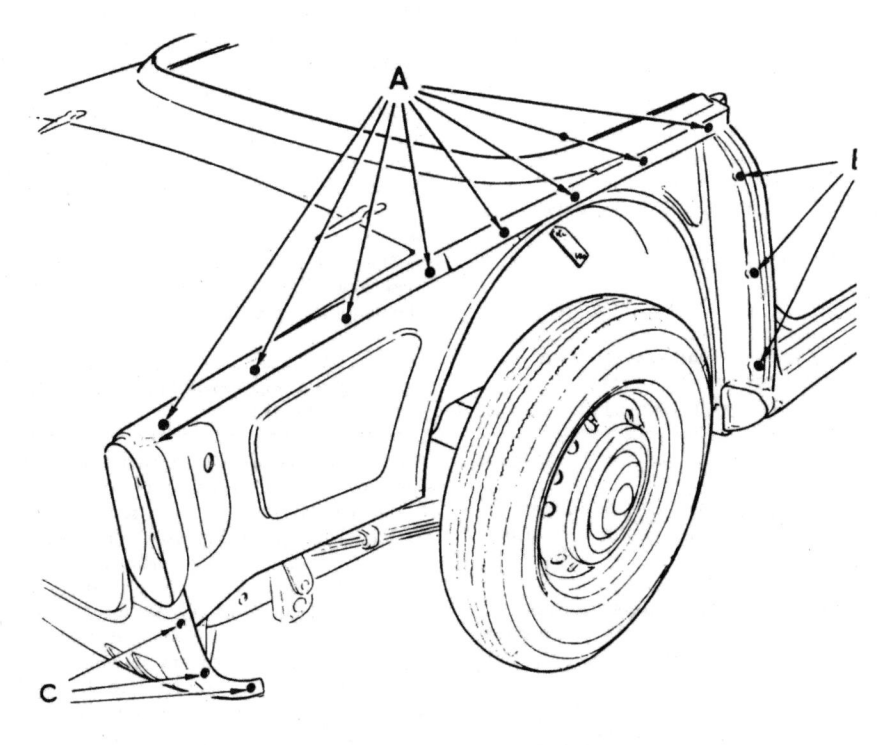

Fig. 12.6. Rear wing attachment points TR4, 4A

277

Chapter 12/Bodywork & Underframe

5. Refitting the bonnet is the reverse sequence to removal. If a cable operated bonnet release catch is fitted it may be necessary to adjust the locks as detailed in Section 18.

18. Bonnet Lock - Adjustment (TR2, 3, 3A)

1. On cars produced before commission number TS 4229 cable operated locks were fitted and it is important that the locks are checked for correct alignment if the bonnet lid or front apron has been removed.
2. With the assistance of a second person check that the release levers of the locks are pulled clear of the plunger apertures when the bonnet release knob is operated. If this condition does not exist the cable must be adjusted accordingly.
3. For correct lock operation the plunger centres and apertures must be identical. Set the plungers approximately in the centre of the apertures, and with a second person operating the bonnet release, gradually lower the bonnet lid.
4. If the plungers are not correctly set fouling will be felt; this should be adjusted to eliminate any misalignment.

19. Bonnet Lid - Removal and Refitting (TR4, 4A)

1. Operate the bonnet release catch and open the bonnet fully.
2. It is recommended that the assistance of a second person be obtained to assist by taking the weight of the bonnet as the hinges are released.
3. To give a guide as to the location of the hinges for adjustment after refitting outline the hinges on the wing valance with a pencil before removal.
4. Undo the two bolts that secure each hinge to the wing valance. Lift away the bolts, spring and plain washers; the bonnet may now be lifted away over the front of the car.
5. Refitting is the reverse sequence to removal. If hinge adjustment from the original setting is necessary the release catch and bonnet striker mechanism may require adjustment, details of which are given in Section 20.

20. Bonnet Lock and Striker - Adjustment (TR4, 4A)

1. Once the bonnet has been refitted and adjusted the lock and strikers should be checked for correct adjustment.
2. Refer to Fig. 12.8. Undo but not remove the clamping ferrule screw (23).
3. A second person should push and hold the bonnet lock control situated inside the car until it is within 1/8 inch of its 'fully in' position.
4. Tighten the clamping ferrule screw.
5. Lubricate the cable and lock moving plate and lever.
6. The bonnet striker mechanism may be adjusted by slackening the locknut on the fastener assembly (10) (Fig. 12.9).
7. Turn the dovetail centre bolt with a wide blade screwdriver in a clockwise direction to take up movement at the catch plate or in an anti-clockwise direction to increase movement at the catch plate. This adjustment is made by trial and error. When correct tighten the locknut.
8. Provision is made for adjusting the rubber buffer (3) located at the rear corner of the engine compartment if excessive movement is evident with correct lock adjustment.

21. Luggage Compartment Lid - Removal, Dismantling and Refitting (TR2, 3, 3A)

1. Open the luggage compartment lid and mark the hinges and locks for correct identification as they are not interchangeable.
2. It is recommended that an assistant be requested to support the lid so that when the hinge nuts are released it does not slip and damage the paintwork.
3. Undo and remove the two nuts and shakeproof washers from each hinge. Note that the right hand hinge also accommodates the stay rod for the lid.
4. Carefully lift away the lid.
5. To remove the hinges from the luggage compartment first detach the forward edge of the trim within the luggage compartment, so giving access to the hinge retaining nuts.
6. Undo and remove the two nuts and shakeproof washers from each hinge. Lift away the hinge.
7. To remove the two carriage type locks undo the two securing screws and lift away the screws, spring washers and the lock.
8. To remove the carriage lock escutcheon plates undo the two retaining screws and lift away together with the spring washers and the plate itself.
9. The lock fitted to the centre of the luggage compartment lid is easily removed by undoing and removing the bolt that secures the lock latch to the lock shaft. Under the head of the bolt is a shakeproof washer to stop it working loose.
10 Undo and remove the nuts securing the lock barrel to the luggage compartment lid, using a socket or box spanner.
11 Refitting the luggage compartment locks, hinges and the lid itself is the reverse sequence to removal. The following additional points should be noted.
12 The hinges and carriage type locks are not interchangeable and therefore must be fitted in their original positions.
13 Do not fully tighten the lid to hinge securing nuts until the lid has been centralised within its aperture.
14 Whilst working on the boot lid it is recommended that the surrounding rubber seal is checked for signs of permanent distortion or perishing. If its condition has deteriorated a new seal should be fitted or water leaks will develop causing corrosion or damage to the contents of the luggage compartment.
15 There are two drain pipes at the rearmost corners and these should be checked for blockage by threading a piece of wire through the pipes.

22. Luggage Compartment Lid - Removal, Dismantling and Refitting (TR4, 4A)

1. Open the luggage compartment lid; referring to Fig. 12.10 undo the restrainer (47) securing bolt from the bonnet lid. It will now be necessary for a second person to take the weight of the lid so that when the hinges are released it does not slip and damage the paintwork.
2. Undo the single nut (2) on each hinge (6) securing the front half of the hinge to the body panel. Recover the spring washer and nut from the hinge stud.
3. The luggage compartment lid may now be removed towards the rear of the car when the hinge studs have been released from their holes in the body panel.
4. To remove the lock handle (16) undo the nut (20) and lift away the nut, spring washer (19). The handle can then be withdrawn from the lid.
5. The lock (23) can be removed by undoing the two nuts (21). Lift away the nuts, spring washers (22), bolts (25) and second spring washer (24) followed by the lock assembly (23).

278

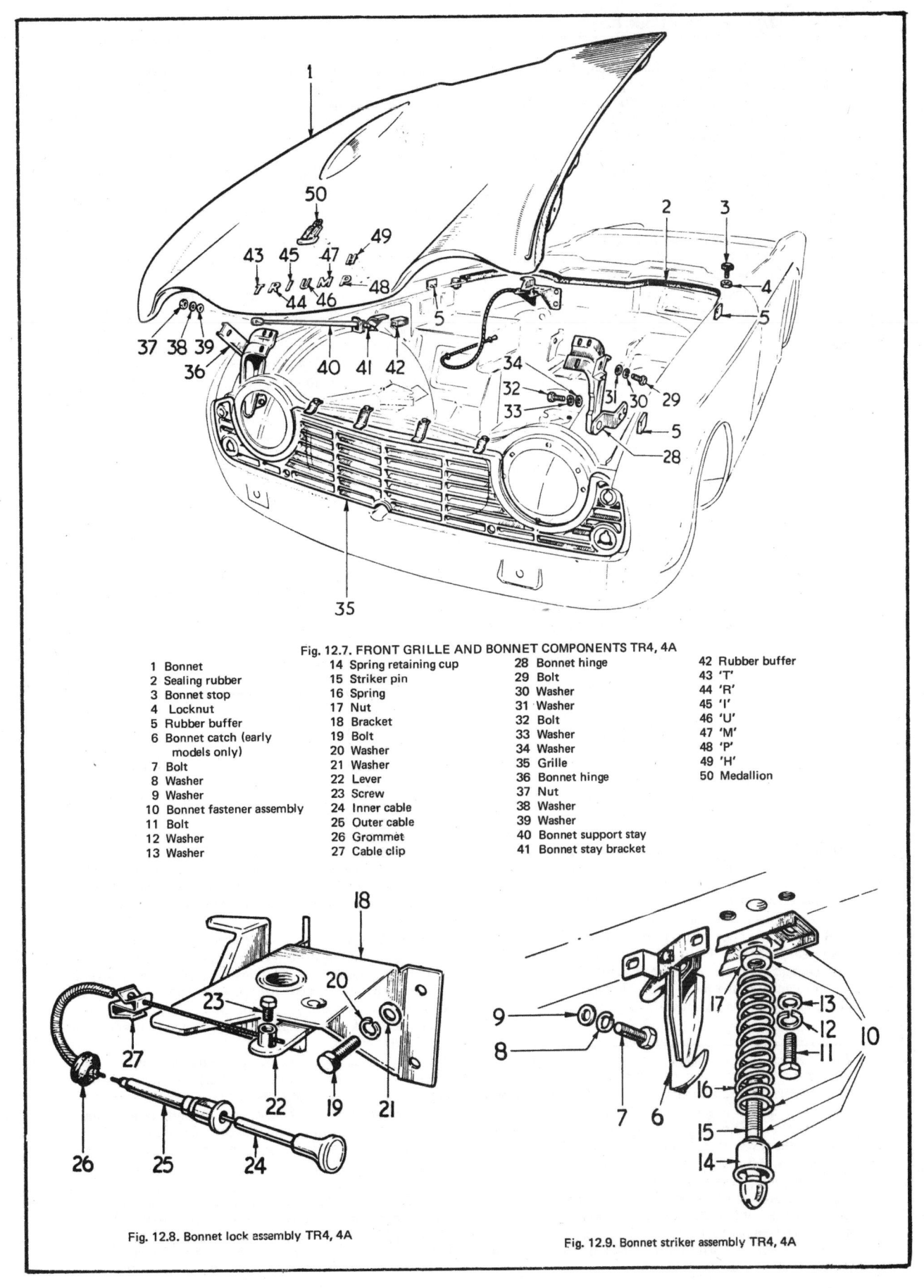

Fig. 12.7. FRONT GRILLE AND BONNET COMPONENTS TR4, 4A

1 Bonnet
2 Sealing rubber
3 Bonnet stop
4 Locknut
5 Rubber buffer
6 Bonnet catch (early models only)
7 Bolt
8 Washer
9 Washer
10 Bonnet fastener assembly
11 Bolt
12 Washer
13 Washer
14 Spring retaining cup
15 Striker pin
16 Spring
17 Nut
18 Bracket
19 Bolt
20 Washer
21 Washer
22 Lever
23 Screw
24 Inner cable
25 Outer cable
26 Grommet
27 Cable clip
28 Bonnet hinge
29 Bolt
30 Washer
31 Washer
32 Bolt
33 Washer
34 Washer
35 Grille
36 Bonnet hinge
37 Nut
38 Washer
39 Washer
40 Bonnet support stay
41 Bonnet stay bracket
42 Rubber buffer
43 'T'
44 'R'
45 'I'
46 'U'
47 'M'
48 'P'
49 'H'
50 Medallion

Fig. 12.8. Bonnet lock assembly TR4, 4A

Fig. 12.9. Bonnet striker assembly TR4, 4A

279

Chapter 12/Bodywork & Underframe

6. The hinges (6) may be removed from the lid (14) by undoing the nuts (10) and removing the nuts and washers (11, 12, 13). Next undo the nuts (8) and lift away the nuts and spring washers (9). The hinge may then be separated from the lid and the shaped fibre pad removed.

7. It is important to note that the hinges are not interchangeable and must be refitted in their original position.

8. Reassembling the components to the lid is the reverse sequence to removal as is also the refitting of the lid to the rear of the body.

9. Should adjustment of the lock be necessary, provision is made at the striker, but further adjustment may be made by elongating the holes further. However, first check that the surround sealing rubber (36) is not permanently distorted or perished; this is the usual cause for poor lid fitting.

10 Lubricate the lock cylinder and hinges with a light machine oil.

23. Spare Wheel Compartment Lid - Removal and Refitting (TR2, 3, 3A)

1. To remove the spare wheel compartment lid use the special key to release the two carriage locks. Lift away the lid.

2. Each lock is secured with two screws which should be removed to release the lock from the lid. Mark both locks for correct identification as they are not interchangeable.

3. The lock escutcheon plates are removed by undoing the two retaining screws and lifting away the screws, lock washers and plates.

4. If the spare wheel and tool straps have broken they may be removed by undoing the two screws retaining each strap within the luggage compartment.

5. Refitting the various parts of the spare wheel compartment and lid is the reverse sequence to removal.

24. Door - Removal and Refitting (TR2, 3, 3A)

1. Remove the nut and bolt that secures the door check strap to the front door post.

2. Using a pencil outline the hinge positions to assist refitting.

3. Undo and remove the seven bolts that secure the door hinges to the door post and lift away the complete door. An assistant to take the weight of the door whilst the hinge securing bolts are being undone would be an advantage to save any damage by one person trying to take the weight of the door while undoing the bolts.

4. Refitting the door is the reverse sequence to removal. Take care to ensure that it is hung correctly and that the lock engages smoothly with the dovetail on the rear post. Before tightening the hinge retaining bolts check that the hinges align with the previously made pencil marks.

25. Door Lock - Removal and Refitting (TR2, 3, 3A)

1. Undo the four screws that secure the front side screen retaining brackets. Make a note of the location of the screws and the position of the bracket for correct reassembly.

2. Undo the screw that secures the upper end of the trim covered lock pull strap.

3. Remove the screws securing the rear side screen bracket making notes of the location of the screws and which way round the bracket fits. Lift away the bracket.

4. Undo and remove the dome headed nut on the door lever.

5. Remove the two screws that retain the lock plate in position and lift away the lock plate.

6. Undo and remove the self tapping screws and cup washers that are positioned around the edge of the door trim. Lift away the interior trim.

7. The lock is secured to the door frame by four screws which should now be removed. Lift away the lock from the door interior.

8. If it is desired the door check strap can be removed by first undoing the nut and bolt securing it to the door post. Then remove the two retaining screws from the door and lift away the check strap.

9. Refitting is the reverse sequence to removal. It is recommended that the door lock components are greased before finally refitting to the door.

10 Do not fit the interior trim panel until the lock and striker dovetail on the door post have been correctly adjusted.

11 When the side screen retaining brackets have been refitted, with the heads of the locking screws facing inwards, check that the side screens fit correctly.

26. Door - Sealing (TR2, 3, 3A)

Because of water entry problems, cars produced since commission number TS 5251 have an additional moulded rubber sealing strip fitted to the top forward end of the doors.

It is possible to fit the moulded rubber sealing strip to earlier produced cars and to do so refer to Fig. 12.11 which shows the position of the six clips inserted into ¼ inch diameter holes drilled 0.19 inch from the edge. Note that the seventh clip is fitted into the outward face of the pillar above the top of the hinge.

27. Door - Removal and Refitting (TR4, 4A)

1. Undo the five screws that retain the kick pad to the 'A' post and remove the pad from the car.

2. Release the clip (26) (Fig. 12.12) retaining the pin (25) in the door check arm (27). Extract the pin (25) noting that the head is uppermost.

3. Using a pencil outline the position of the door hinge (19) relative to the body to assist correct refitting.

4. Undo and remove the six bolts that secure the hinges (19) to the body and lift away the complete door. An assistant to take the weight of the door whilst the hinge securing bolts are undone would be an advantage to save any damage by one person trying to take the weight of the door while undoing the bolts.

5. If required, with the door removed, the hinges can be removed by undoing the three hinge retaining bolts (17).

6. Refitting the door is the reverse sequence to removal. Take care to ensure that it is hung correctly and that the lock engages smoothly. Before the hinges are finally tightened check that the hinges align with the previously made pencil marks.

7. Should it be necessary to adjust the position of the hinges, vertical movement can be adjusted by means of the bolts securing the hinges to the 'A' post. In and out movement can be adjusted by means of the bolts securing the hinge to the door. Adjustment is considered correct when the door is evenly fitted into the door aperture when closed.

28. Door Lock and Remote Control - Removal and Refitting (TR4, 4A)

1. Before removing the door lock first wind up the door

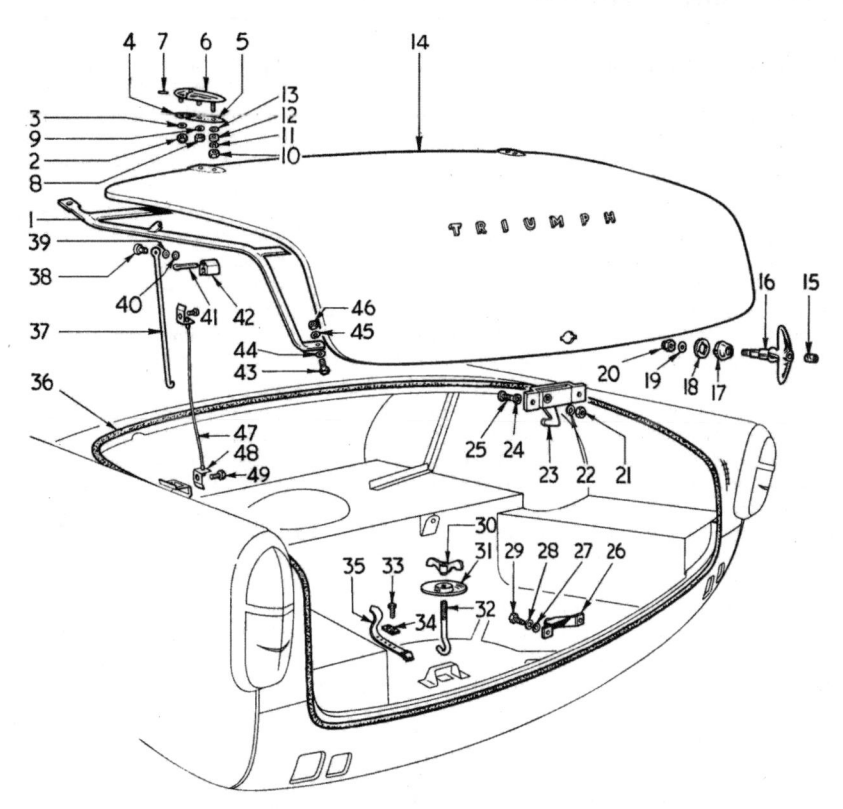

Fig. 12.10. LUGGAGE COMPARTMENT LID COMPONENTS TR4, 4A

1 Lid reinforcement tube	14 Locker lid assembly	27 Washer	40 Clip
2 Nut	15 Lock cylinder	28 Washer	41 Split pin
3 Washer	16 Handle	29 Screw	42 Retainer
4 Fibre washer	17 Escutcheon	30 Wing nut	43 Screw
5 Fibre washer	18 Washer	31 Disc plate	44 Washer
6 Hinge	19 Washer	32 Hook bolt	45 Washer
7 Hinge pin	20 Nut	33 Screw	46 Nut
8 Nut	21 Nut	34 Plate	47 Restrainer
9 Washer	22 Washer	35 Strap	48 Bracket
10 Nut	23 Lock	36 Sealing rubber	49 Screw
11 Washer	24 Washer	37 Lid support	
12 Washer	25 Screw	38 Pivot pin	
13 Washer	26 Striker	39 Washer	

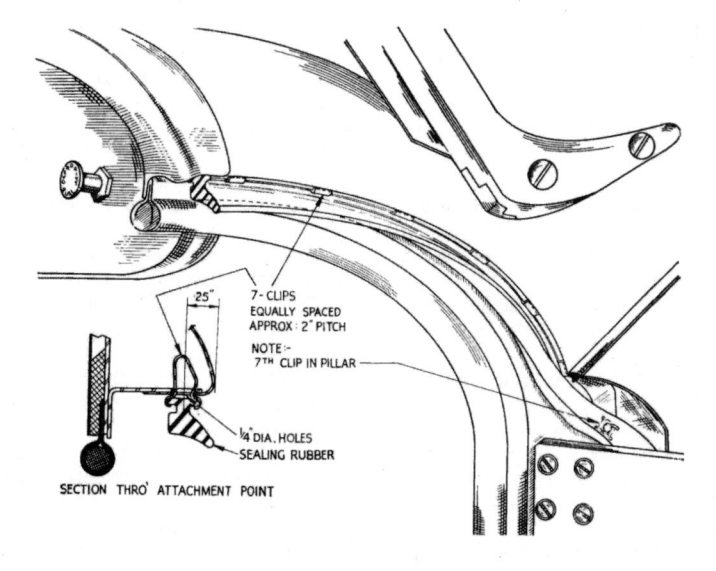

Fig. 12.11. Front door water sealing Early TR2 modification

281

Chapter 12/Bodywork & Underframe

glass and make a note of the position of the handles for correct refitting.

2. Using a small electrician's size screwdriver push in the door handle escutcheon and push out the small tapered pin (36) (Fig. 12.12). The door handle (37) can then be removed from the remote control unit (61).

3. Repeat the previous operation for the window winder regulator handle and remove the handle (40) from the regulator (55).

4. Undo the two screws (39) that secure the interior handle (38) to the door panel.

5. Undo the screw (45) having first removed the cover button (44) that secures the rear edge of the trim panel to the door. Lift away the screw and special cover button retaining washer (46). Repeat this procedure on the forward positioned screw of the trim pocket.

6. Using a wide blade screwdriver or a knife carefully ease the trim panel clips from their holes in the door panel. When they are all free lift away the trim panel.

7. Release the spring clip (64) and wave washer (65) and then disconnect the remote control link (61) from the lock assembly (76).

8. Carefully disconnect the link (93) connecting the exterior door handle control to the lock at the lock end of the link.

9. Undo the three screws (98, 78) that secure the door glass channel to the door at the rear of the lock and lift away the channel.

10 Undo and remove the four screws (67, 69) and spring washers that secure the lock to the door and lift away the lock assembly.

11 The remote control assembly can be removed by undoing the three screws (62) and removing the screws and spring washers. Lift away the remote control assembly.

12 Refitting is the reverse sequence to removal. It is recommended that all moving parts be well greased before refitting to ensure long and reliable service.

13 The lock is not adjustable in any way but if difficulty is experienced in closing or opening the door the cause could well be the striker dovetail and door restraint device. The position of the two parts are easily adjusted by slackening the mounting screws and adjusting the position accordingly until the correct setting is found by trial and error. Do not slam the door when adjusting either or both parts.

---

29. Door Glass and Regulator - Removal and Refitting (TR4, 4A)

1. To remove the door glass and regulator first wind up the door glass and make a note of the position of the handles for correct refitting.

2. Using a small electrician's size screwdriver push in the door handle escutcheon and push out the small tapered pin (36) (Fig. 12.12). The door handle (37) can then be removed from the remote control unit (61).

3. Repeat the previous operation for the window winder regulator handle and remove the handle (40) from the regulator (55).

4. Undo the two screws (39) that secure the interior handle (38) to the door panel.

5. Undo the screw (45) having first removed the cover button (44) that secures the rear edge of the trim panel to the door. Lift away the screw and special cover button retaining washer (46). Repeat this procedure on the forward positioned screw of the trim pocket.

6. Using a wide blade screwdriver or a knife carefully ease the trim panel clips from their holes in the door panel. When they are all free lift away the trim panel.

7. Lower the glass until it is in its midway position.

8. Refer to Fig. 12.13 and disconnect the arms (L) from the channel (M) located at the base of the door glass by removing the spring clips (102) with leather washers (103) and then springing the arms (L) clear of the channel.

9. Raise the glass to give better access and support with a piece of wood.

10 Undo the nut (F) and remove together with the spring washer securing the pivot (56) to the door inner panel.

11 Remove the pivot (56) and the double coil spring washer (53) placed between the regulator and the inner panel of the door.

12 Undo and remove the four screws (H) that secure the regulator mechanism to the door inner panel and lift away the assembly (55) through the largest cut out in the rear of the inner door panel.

13 Next remove the inner weatherstrip (6) by pushing its lower edge upwards from inside the door panels using a screwdriver. It will be observed that the weatherstrip is held in position by seven small spring clips (7).

14 The glass may now be removed from the door but take care that the water deflector panel (85) is not damaged.

15 Refitting the glass and regulator assembly is the reverse sequence to removal but care must be taken when replacing the weatherstrip. For this a special tool should be used as shown in Fig. 12.14 so that when pushing in the weatherstrip the clips do not fall out. The inset in this illustration shows the tool in use.

---

30. Door Exterior Handle - Removal, Refitting and Adjusting (TR4, 4A)

1. To remove the door exterior handle first wind up the door glass and make a note of the position of the handles for correct refitting.

2. Using a small electrician's size screwdriver push in the door handle escutcheon and push out the small tapered pin (36) (Fig. 12.12). The door handle (37) can then be removed from the remote control unit (61).

3. Repeat the previous operation for the window winder regulator handle and remove the handle (40) from the regulator (55).

4. Undo the two screws (39) that secure the interior handle (38) to the door panel.

5. Undo the screw (45) having first removed the cover button (44) that secures the rear edge of the trim panel to the door. Lift away the screw and special cover button retaining washer (46). Repeat this procedure on the forward positioned screw of the trim pocket.

6. Using a wide blade screwdriver or a knife carefully ease the trim panel clips from their holes in the door panel and when all are free lift away the trim panel.

7. Disconnect the interconnecting link (93) placed between the lock and the exterior handle at the lock end.

8. Undo and remove the two screws (4, 95) and take off the handle (1) and seating washers (97, 5).

9. To refit the handle, and adjust it, hold the handle, with its seating washers in position, firmly in position on the door panel. Check the clearance between the push button plunger and the lock contactor through the hole in the inner door panel. It is recommended that the clearance is not checked by simply depressing the push button as by this method it can be deceptive. The correct clearance should be 0.0625 inch and should be checked with feeler gauges.

10 Rotate the plunger operating lever to the unlocked position so that when the push button is depressed the plunger moves through the housing.

11 Release the locknut (1) (Fig. 12.15) and screw the plunger bolt (2) in or out until the required setting is obtained, then tighten the locknut before releasing the

Fig.12.12. FRONT DOOR COMPONENTS (TR4.4A)

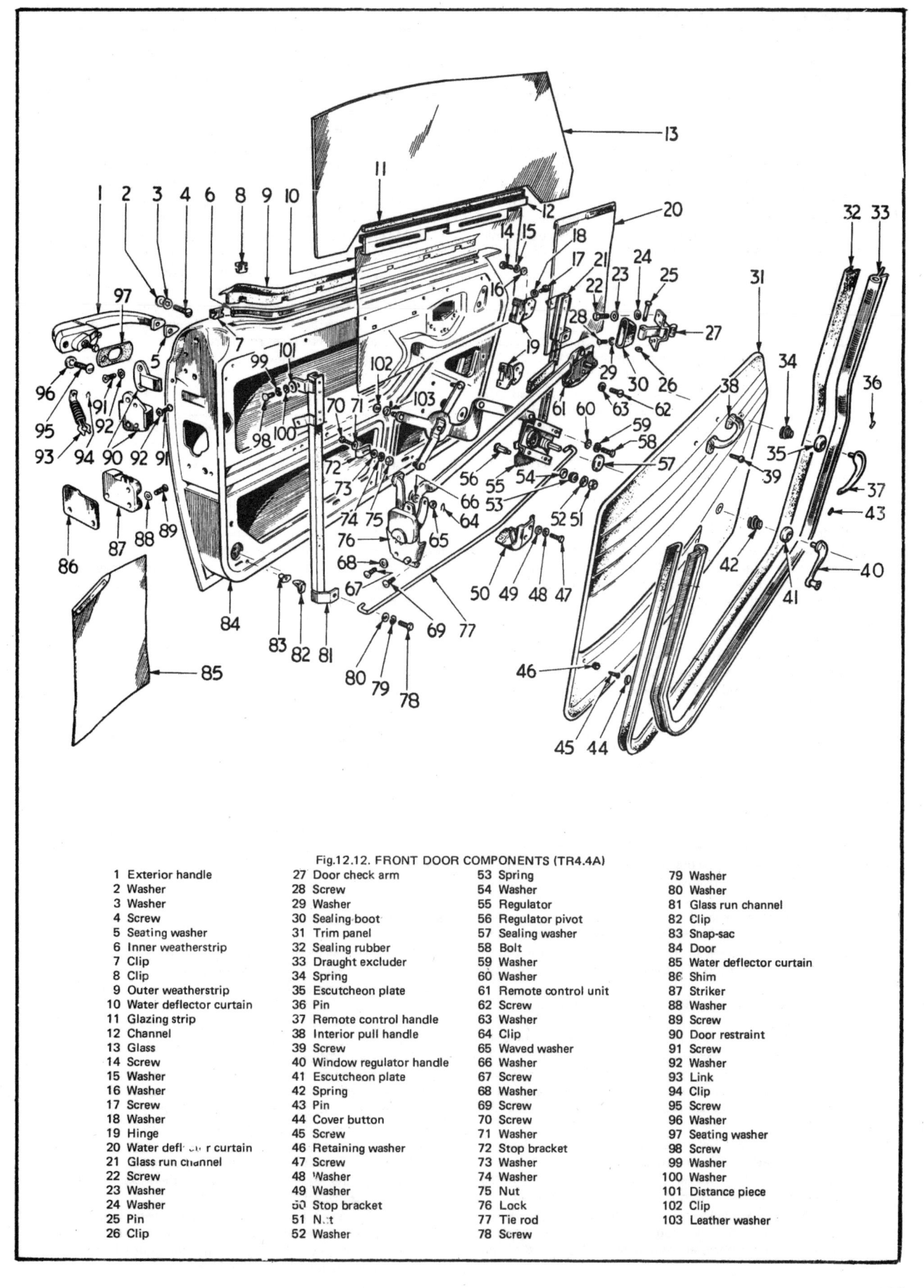

1 Exterior handle	27 Door check arm	53 Spring
2 Washer	28 Screw	54 Washer
3 Washer	29 Washer	55 Regulator
4 Screw	30 Sealing boot	56 Regulator pivot
5 Seating washer	31 Trim panel	57 Sealing washer
6 Inner weatherstrip	32 Sealing rubber	58 Bolt
7 Clip	33 Draught excluder	59 Washer
8 Clip	34 Spring	60 Washer
9 Outer weatherstrip	35 Escutcheon plate	61 Remote control unit
10 Water deflector curtain	36 Pin	62 Screw
11 Glazing strip	37 Remote control handle	63 Washer
12 Channel	38 Interior pull handle	64 Clip
13 Glass	39 Screw	65 Waved washer
14 Screw	40 Window regulator handle	66 Washer
15 Washer	41 Escutcheon plate	67 Screw
16 Washer	42 Spring	68 Washer
17 Screw	43 Pin	69 Screw
18 Washer	44 Cover button	70 Screw
19 Hinge	45 Screw	71 Washer
20 Water deflector curtain	46 Retaining washer	72 Stop bracket
21 Glass run channel	47 Screw	73 Washer
22 Screw	48 Washer	74 Washer
23 Washer	49 Washer	75 Nut
24 Washer	50 Stop bracket	76 Lock
25 Pin	51 Nut	77 Tie rod
26 Clip	52 Washer	78 Screw
79 Washer		
80 Washer		
81 Glass run channel		
82 Clip		
83 Snap-sac		
84 Door		
85 Water deflector curtain		
86 Shim		
87 Striker		
88 Washer		
89 Screw		
90 Door restraint		
91 Screw		
92 Washer		
93 Link		
94 Clip		
95 Screw		
96 Washer		
97 Seating washer		
98 Screw		
99 Washer		
100 Washer		
101 Distance piece		
102 Clip		
103 Leather washer		

Chapter 12/Bodywork & Underframe

push button.

12 Refit the connecting link (93) to the plunger operating lever and secure with a circlip. The link should be fitted so that the bent section at the top is inclined away from the handle.

13 Rotate the plunger operating lever to the locked position so that the location holes in the operating lever and plunger housing are lined up. Insert a short length of 1/8 inch diameter rod cranked to a right angle and carefully manipulate the connecting rod (B) through the handle aperture so that they hang downwards in the door when the handle and seating washers are finally secured to the door with the two screws (95, 4).

14 Refitting the remaining parts is the reverse sequence to removal.

31. Front Apron - Removal and Refitting (TR2)

1. Operate the bonnet release catch, if a cable operated lock system is fitted, or turn the Dzuz fasteners with the special key so releasing the bonnet. Support the lid in its open position.
2. For safety reasons disconnect the battery earth terminals.
3. Undo and remove the two bolts which secure each of the two top apron reinforcement bars to the 'U' shaped brackets positioned on the top of the front wing panels.
4. Locate the electric cable terminal connectors and check whether the colours have faded making identification of the cables difficult for correct reconnection. If necessary place some tape around each cable pair in a different manner for identification purposes. Disconnect the cables from the terminal connectors.
5. On cars produced before commission number TS 4229 having cable operated locks, locate the clip fitted to the centre of and forward of the apron reinforcement bar and release the cable connecting the two locks together.
6. Undo and remove the twelve bolts which secure the outer edges of the apron to the wings. There are six bolts each side of the apron. The correct bolts are those which are fitted horizontally when seen from the inside of the wheel arches. Do not confuse these with the bolts that are fitted vertically in the wheel arch.
7. Undo and remove the nut, lock washer and bolt securing the chassis frame/front apron steady stay at the apron end.
8. Undo and remove the bolt from the starting handle guide bracket but do not remove the bracket itself as it is not necessary.
9. With the assistance of a second person the apron may now be removed by lifting the lower section upwards and forwards so as to break the water seal. Lift the apron out of its brackets on the top of the wing and then away from the front of the car.
10 Recover the beadings which fit between the apron and front wings.
11 Refitting the apron is the reverse sequence to removal but there are several additional points to be noted.
12 The beading should be attached to the front apron in such a way that the hole is adjacent to the uppermost hole of the apron and the remaining slotted holes adjacent to the lower holes.
13 Bolts protruding into the wheel arch should be well greased to prevent thread corrosion.
14 Reconnect the electrical cables in the positions noted before disconnection. Reconnect the battery earth cable.
15 If the bonnet locks are cable operated lower the lid gently to check that the plungers and locks are correctly aligned. Adjust if necessary as detailed in Section 18 of this Chapter.

32. Front Moulding and Grille - Removal and Refitting (TR3, 3A)

1. Undo and remove the self tapping screws, one at each end of the two horizontally positioned grille bars.
2. Carefully ease the upper section of the grille into the air intake and turn it through an angle of approximately 30°. The grille assembly may now be lifted away.
3. Undo the nuts and lockwashers holding the moulding in place. The nuts will be found behind the front cowling.
4. Undo and remove the nuts and lock washers from the stud plates that secure the moulding to the air intake and lift away the two half mouldings. As in the previous operation the nuts will be found behind the front cowling.
5. The stud plates themselves may be removed by sliding them to the end of each half moulding.
6. Refitting the front moulding and grille is the reverse sequence to removal.

33. Front Grille - Removal and Refitting (TR4, 4A)

1. Before the front grille is removed the parking and direction indicator lamps must be removed.
2. Open the bonnet and disconnect the battery earth terminal for safety reasons.
3. Locate the cable terminal connectors for the parking and direction indicator lamps and check that the cable colour coding can be suitably identified and is not faded or discoloured. Mark the cables if necessary using tape and disconnect the terminal connectors.
4. Remove the chromium plated lens retaining ring followed by the lens and the bulb.
5. Unscrew the three self tapping screws that secure the lamp body in position. Remove the screws and gently ease the lamp body and cables from the aperture in the front grille.
6. Remove the two bolts that secure the overrider support stay to the inner valance. Undo the bolt that secures the overrider to the front bumper and lift away the bolt, plain washer and spring washer followed by the overrider and two pieces of P.V.C. moulding positioned between the overrider and bumper blades.
7. Locate and remove the eight front grille retaining screws. There are four screws in the upper edge and four screws in the lower edge.
8. The front grille may now be lifted away from the front of the car.
9. Refitting the front grille is the reverse sequence to removal.
10 When the electrical cables and battery have been reconnected check that the parking light and direction indicator light operate satisfactorily.

34. Sidescreen - Adjustment (TR2, 3, 3A)

Should it be necessary to adjust the position of the sidescreen, upon inspection it will be seen that there is an aluminium wedge attached to each of the sidescreen support stays by a single screw, which in turn fits in a slotted aperture, giving all the required adjustment.

By moving the wedges up or down on the support stays adjustment is achieved by trial and error.

Once adjustment has been completed check that the press-studs on the side screen curtain align with the fasteners on the door panel. Check that the knurled screws retain the support stays in their sockets firmly.

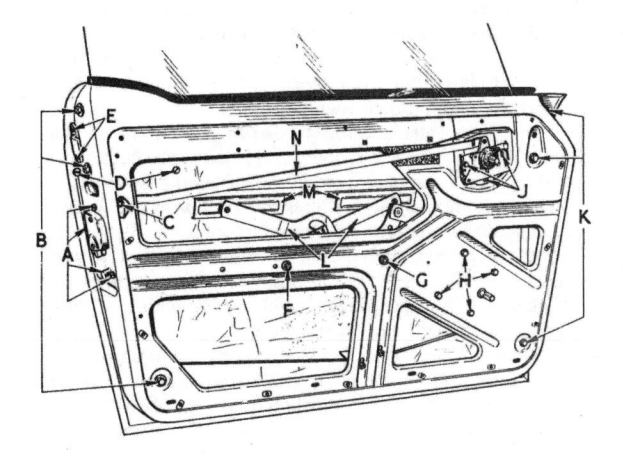

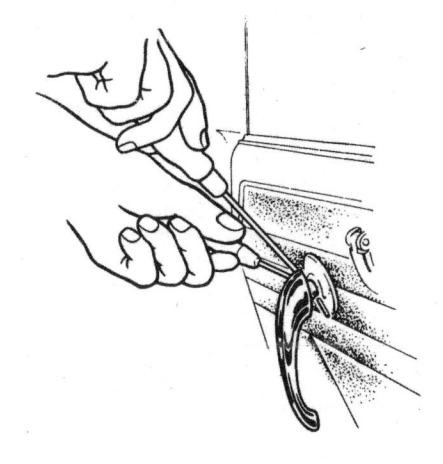

Fig. 12.13. Door assembly

Fig. 12.13A. Removing interior door handles TR4, 4A

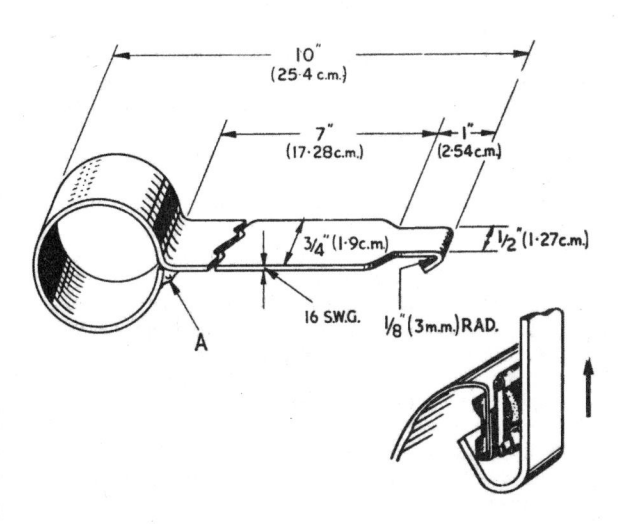

Fig. 12.14. Details of hooked tool for fitting spring clips

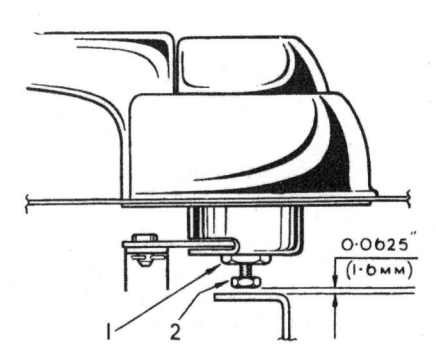

Fig. 12.15. Correct adjustment of exterior door handle

Chapter 12/Bodywork & Underframe

35. Aero Screens - Fitting (TR2, 3, 3A)

1. To fit aero screens first remove the windscreen and the steady bracket.
2. Undo the two chromium plated bolts on each side of the scuttle panel.
3. Position the aero screens with the toe of the mounting bracket facing forwards. Fix the aero screens with the chromium plated bolts previously removed.
4. Once the aero screens have been fitted the conventional screen can be refitted with the aero screens still in position.

36. Windscreen - Removal and Refitting (TR2, 3, 3A)

1. If either a hard top or soft top is fitted release it from the top of the windscreen surround.
2. Using a screwdriver release the windscreen wiper arms and blades from the wiper linkage spindles.
3. Using a wide blade screwdriver turn the spring loaded windscreen stanchion retaining screws 90º in an anti-clockwise direction. Check that the heads of the screws are protruding under the action of the springs.
4. With the assistance of a second person carefully ease the windscreen assembly forwards and allowing the rubber draught excluder to ride over the wiper arm spindles.
5. The windscreen may now be lifted over the bonnet and away from the car.
6. Refitting is the reverse sequence to removal but there are two additional points to be noted.
7. The stanchion guides should be smeared with grease to prevent corrosion. Grease the spring loaded stanchion screws as well.
8. When the windscreen is in position check that the rubber draught excluder is fitting correctly to avoid subsequent water leaks.

37. Windscreen - Removal and Refitting (TR4, 4A)

1. To remove the complete windscreen assembly first slacken the mounting bracket securing bolts (16, 17) (Fig. 12.16). It is not necessary to remove the bolts completely.
2. Undo the two nuts (24) and remove together with their spring washers (25). These will be found under the fascia panel.
3. Using an open ended spanner undo and remove the three bolts (22) which secure plates (21) at the lower part of the windscreen frame (11).
4. With the assistance of a second person the windscreen may be lifted away from the car.
5. Refitting is the reverse sequence to removal. Grease the nuts (24) to ensure that they can be easily undone in the future.
6. Ensure that the rubber seal (23) is fitted correctly and is a watertight joint in adverse weather conditions.

38. Windscreen Glass - Refitting (TR4, 4A)

1. It is more simple to fit the glass with the windscreen frame in position on the car. As it is not normally necessary to remove the windscreen glass instructions for refitting are given only to replace a broken glass screen. Should removal of an unbroken screen be necessary simply reverse the refitting sequence. On cars fitted with a hard top the rear glass may be refitted or removed in a similar manner to the windscreen.

2. Taking care not to damage the frame remove the old rubber weather strip (9) (Fig. 12.16). Discard the old rubber weather strip as a new one should be fitted.
3. Using a vacuum cleaner remove any traces of the shattered glass from the interior. Lift up the carpeting as particles often find their way underneath it.
4. Turn the heater controls to demist and switch on the boost motor to blow out any glass lodged in the ducting. If rattling noises are heard disconnect the flexible hoses to the heater unit and collect any glass that may be in the hose or ducting not blown out by the booster motor.
5. Fit the rubber weatherstrip (9) onto the glass (10) and insert the mouldings (1, 8) in position in the weatherstrip. If difficulty is experienced in this operation use a little concentrated soap solution as a lubricant.
6. Obtain a length of cord longer than the circumference of the weatherstrip and position it in the outer channel of the weatherstrip. The two ends should overlap about twelve inches and be located at the top of the weatherstrip.
7. Position the glass and weatherstrip in the frame and get a second person to push hard on the glass to assist it seating.
8. From the inside of the car hold one end of the cord firmly and pull on the other end so that the inner lip is pulled over the metal edge of the frame.
9. When the lip has been pulled into position seat the weatherstrip correctly in the frame using the palm of your hand.
10 Use a non setting sealant such as Seelastick to seal the joints between the rubber, glass and frame.

39. Occasional Rear Seat - Fitting (TR3, 3A)

An occasional rear seat is offered as an optional extra and may be fitted without major body modification, especially as the front seats are already hinged to give better access to the rear luggage space. To fit the occasional rear seat kit proceed as follows:-
1. Move the front seats on their runners as far forward as possible.
2. Lift out the carpeting placed on the floor behind the front seats.
3. On the floor behind the front seats are two large bolts and washers. These should be removed.
4. Using a sharp knife or scissors make two small holes in the carpeting where the two holes are once the two bolts in the floor have been removed. Replace the carpet.
5. Undo and remove the two chromium plated bolts and plain washers from the trim at the rear of the passenger compartment.
6. Lift and place the occasional seat in position behind the front seats and secure in position using the four bolts and plain washers.
7. Removing the rear occasional seat is the reverse sequence to fitting. Always return the bolts to their original positions to avoid losing them.

40. Hardtop Kit - Fitting (TR2, 3, 3A)

The hardtop is offered as an optional extra during manufacture but may be purchased as a kit for later fitment. The kit includes the hard top fully trimmed but the rubber sections and the rear window glass are not fitted. These parts are included in the kit for subsequent fitting once the hardtop is in position. When the kit is ordered for TR2 models the sliding side windows must be ordered as additional items.

When fitting the hardtop kit to the earlier models it should be appreciated that slight additional work may have

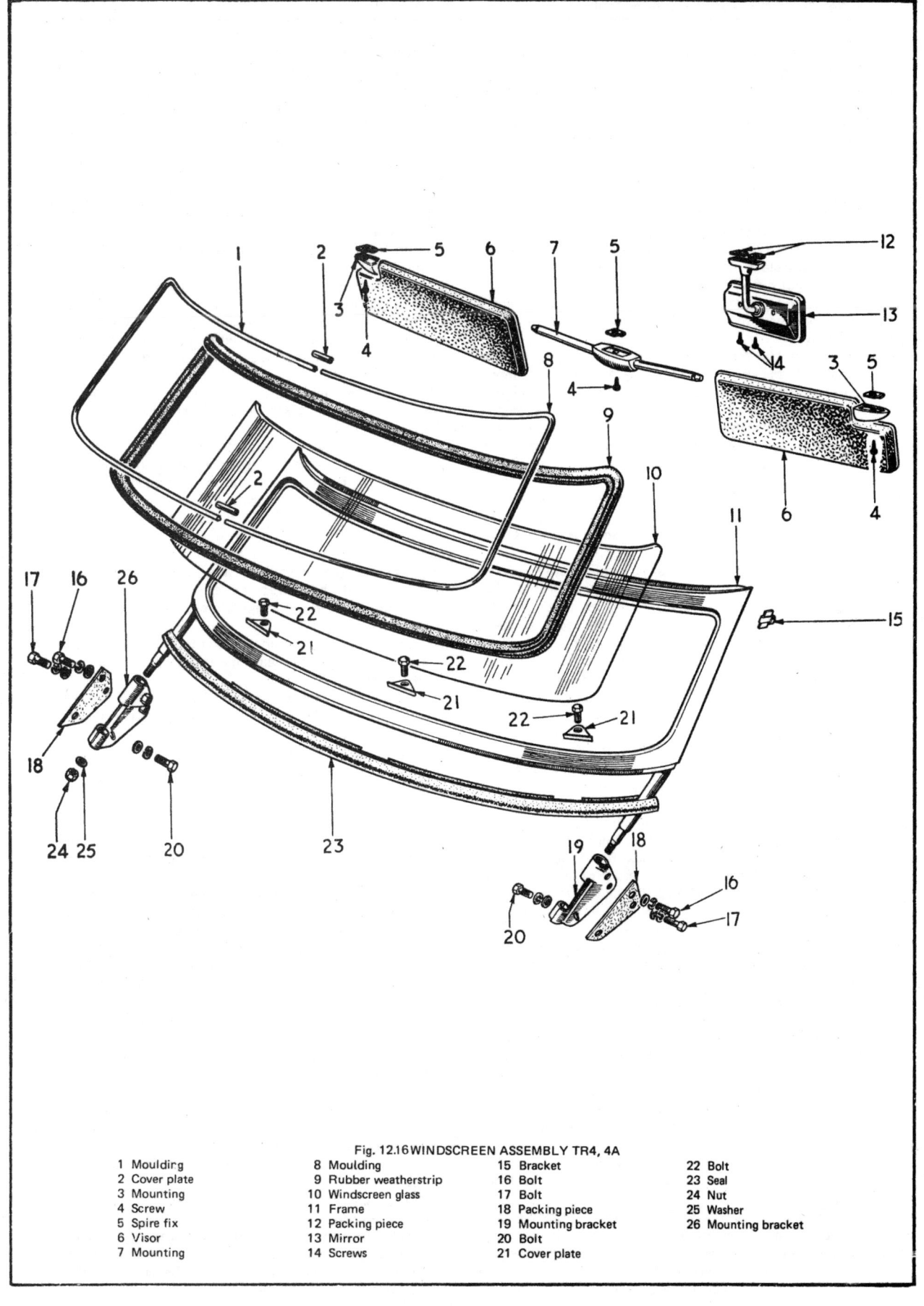

Fig. 12.16 WINDSCREEN ASSEMBLY TR4, 4A

1 Moulding
2 Cover plate
3 Mounting
4 Screw
5 Spire fix
6 Visor
7 Mounting
8 Moulding
9 Rubber weatherstrip
10 Windscreen glass
11 Frame
12 Packing piece
13 Mirror
14 Screws
15 Bracket
16 Bolt
17 Bolt
18 Packing piece
19 Mounting bracket
20 Bolt
21 Cover plate
22 Bolt
23 Seal
24 Nut
25 Washer
26 Mounting bracket

Chapter 12/Bodywork & Underframe

to be undertaken to accommodate any discrepancies in the bodies as they were not jig but individually built. One further point to note is that if heavy drivers or passengers have used the windscreen as a support for climbing in or out of the car the windscreen pillars could be distorted. It is important that no distortion has occurred as the windscreen pillar acts as a location for the hardtop fitting and the rear part will not position correctly if distortion has occurred. To fit the kit proceed as follows:-

1. The hood should first be removed by lifting the fasteners from around the edge of the body.
2. Undo and remove the two flat headed screws and the two hood fastener screws to release the hood webbing from the rear. For further information see Fig. 12.17.
3. Undo and remove the four countersunk screws securing the hood frame to the body and lift the frame away from the body.
4. Remove the self tapping screws that secure the five cappings to the elbow rail and detach the cappings. Remove the two wooden blocks from the elbow rail (see Fig. 12.18).
5. Undo and remove the self tapping screws that secure the millboard panel in front of the petrol tank. The screws at the bottom of the panel will be exposed once the rear carpet has been folded back. With all the screws removed the millboard panel can be removed.
6. Open the kit container and lay out all the parts on a blanket to ensure that they are not scratched. Loosely assemble the three windscreen attachment brackets onto the hardtop front rail.
7. Next insert the three shorter angle brackets through the slots in the stiffener rail at the rear of the hardtop. The longer brackets should be fitted, one each side, to the stiffener rail. The brackets should be retained in position with the short flat head screws and spring washers (Fig. 12.19). Use a sharp knife to cut the trim fabric to allow entry of the brackets into the slots in the stiffener channel.
8. It is recommended that masking tape be used to protect the paintwork on the body which will be in contact with the hardtop during its fitting.
9. With the assistance of a second person place the hardtop on the car and position the brackets previously assembled onto it under the top rail of the windscreen.
10. The hardtop should then be centralised relative to the passenger compartment with both doors closed. Take time over this otherwise the finished result will be disappointing.
11. Using a pencil or scriber mark the position of the attachment bracket holes in the underside of the windscreen top rail. This is shown in Fig. 12.20. Once the marks are made slacken off the brackets and with the assistance of a second person lift off the hardtop again.
12. Using a pencil or scriber mark the top side of the screen surround exactly opposite to the pencil marks previously made.
13. With a No. 11 size drill carefully drill the six holes by holding the drill downwards to the top of the screen surround. The holes should be $3/16$ inch from the edge as shown in Fig. 12.20. Take extreme care not to touch the glass with the drill.
14. Remove the windscreen attaching brackets from the hardtop and fix to the underside of the screen surround. Secure with the six chromium plated screws and spring washers as shown in Fig. 12.17.
15. Fit and loosely retain the five bridge pieces to the angled brackets that were previously fitted to the rear stiffener rail.
16. With the assistance of a second person replace the hard top onto the car and attach it to the windscreen surround brackets previously fitted. Check that the bridge pieces are now resting on the elbow rail channel.
17. Using a pencil, mark for subsequent identification the position of the bridge pieces on the elbow rail. Again remove the hardtop from the car.
18. Using a number 11 size drill make ten holes through the markings on the elbow rail.
19. Undo and remove the bridge pieces from the hardtop and secure to the elbow rail channel using flat headed screws which screw into tapping plates positioned under the channel as shown in Fig. 12.19.
20. Using a pencil make a mark opposite to the centre of each bridge piece on the masking tape. Attach the cappings to the body and loosely retain with self tapping screws.
21. With the pencil extend the previously made marks and then remove the cappings from the body.
22. Mark the inside of the cappings exactly in line with the marks on the inside.
23. With a $3/8$ inch drill, drill the cappings at the points marked on the inside. Check when all holes have been drilled that the holes correctly align with those on the bridge pieces.
24. Replace the millboard panel to the front of the petrol tank and secure in place with the self tapping screws. Replace the carpet.
25. Replace the three narrow protection caps onto the rear cappings and align the centre holes with the threaded centres of the bridge pieces. Drill the capping through the protection caps and secure with self tapping screws. The two larger caps are fitted in a similar manner to the side elbow rails.
26. Insert the four countersunk screws and chromium plated washers into the holes that were previously used to accommodate the hood bracket screws.
27. Carefully remove the masking tape used to protect the paintwork of the car.
28. The drip channels should next be fitted. Using a file or a pair of tin snips carefully shape the ends of the drip channel as shown in Fig. 12.21.
29. Position the channels and draught rubbers (C) on the hard top as shown in Fig. 12.22 and secure with small self tapping screws (B and C).
30. The rubber moulding (D) (Fig. 12.23) should next be secured, using Seelastick, to the rear lower edge and the rubber section (E) (Fig. 12.24) to the front top end of the hardtop.
31. The hardtop should be refitted to the body and this time loosely assemble all its attachment bolts. Gradually tighten the fastenings until all are secure. The hard top is now in position.
32. The rear window glass should now be fitted and for this a special tool will be required. Most body repair shops have one and it should not be too difficult to borrow for a few hours. To make a good weatherproof seal between the hardtop and the outer lip of the glazing rubber 'Seelastick' or other similar non setting sealant should be used. Endeavour to borrow a Seelastick gun or obtain a tube of similar sealant with a nozzle fitted to the end of the container.
33. Carefully fit the rubber moulding around the glass with the filler section facing towards the rear of the car.
34. Position the glass with the surround in position in the aperture in the hardtop and push hard with the palms of the hand.
35. A second person inside the car using a very blunt knife or screwdriver should ease the inner lip into position inside the car.
36. Using a special tool shown in Fig. 12.23, ease the rubber surround filler strip into position in its channel.
37. Finally using the Seelastick gun or suggested alternative method force the compound between the hardtop and outer lip of the glazing rubber. Any excess may be removed with a cloth moistened with paraffin.

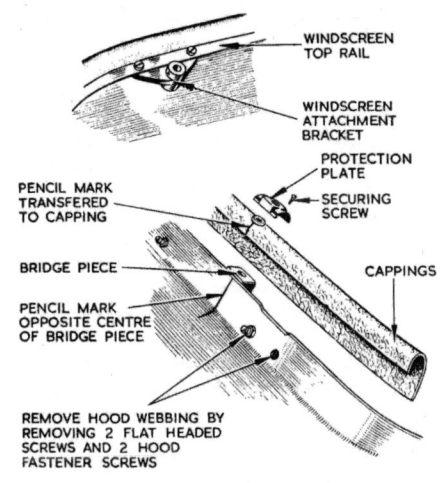

Fig. 12.17. Marking and fitting rear cappings

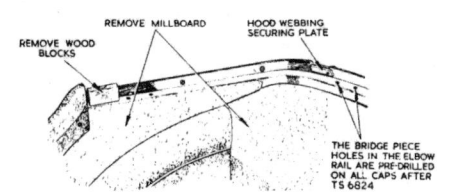

Fig. 12.18. Showing cappings removed

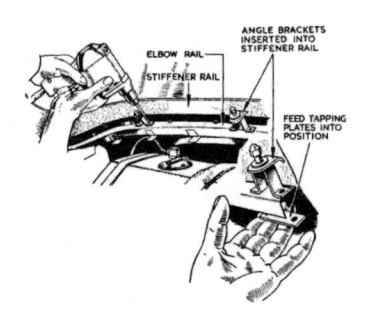

Fig. 12.19. Drilling the elbow rail and installing bridge pieces. Drilling necessary on cars prior to T.S. 6824 only

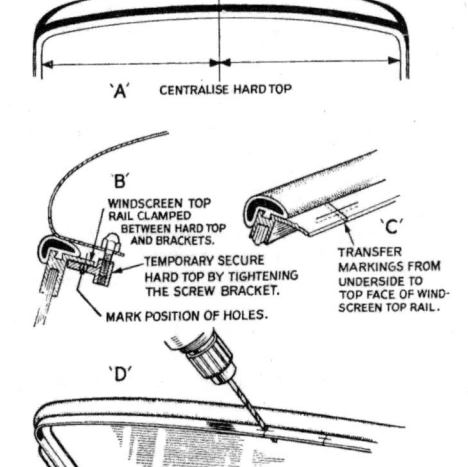

Fig. 12.20. a, b and c. Positioning 'Hard Top' and drilling screen rail.

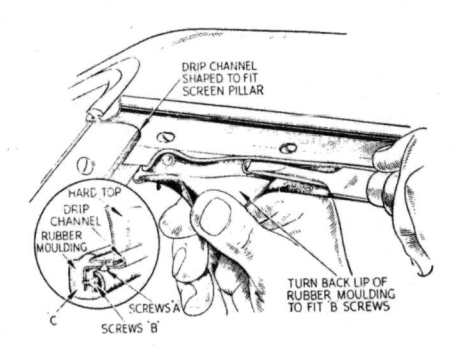

Fig. 12.21. Fitting drip channel and draught rubber

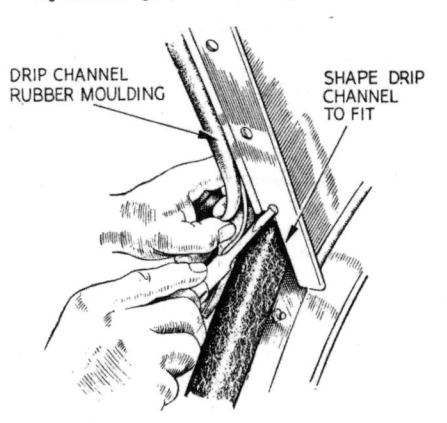

Fig. 12.22. Fitting lower part of drip channel

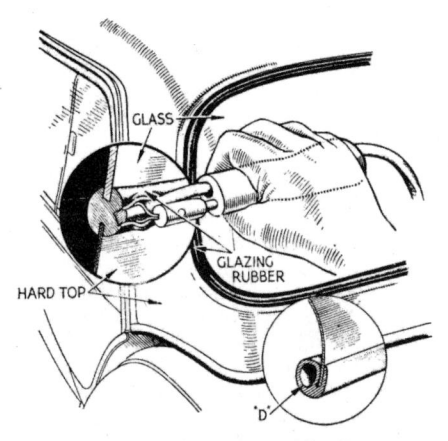

Fig. 12.23. Fitting rear window and waist rubber

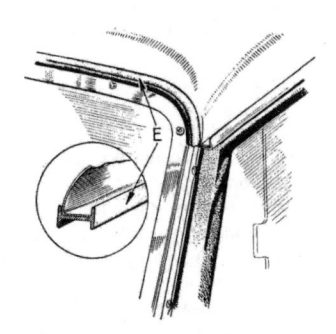

Fig. 12.24. Fitting screen rubber

289

Chapter 12/Bodywork & Underframe

41. Instrument - Removal and Refitting (All Models)

1. Each instrument is mounted to the back of the dashboard using a 'U' shaped bridge piece and knurled nuts screwed down onto threaded studs fixed to the rear of each instrument.
2. When an instrument is to be removed the battery earth terminal should be disconnected for safety reasons.
3. To give better access to the back of the dashboard undo and remove the four self tapping screws holding the lining casing of the glove compartment in place and lifting out the casing.
4. The tachometer (revolution counter) and speedometer have internal lights. These should be removed by pulling out the light sockets in each instrument before the instrument is removed.
5. To remove the oil pressure gauge first undo the union at the rear of the oil pressure gauge taking care to retain the leather washer which acts as a seal in the union. This can be easily misplaced.
6. The water temperature gauge is permanently connected to the bulb in the thermostat housing by a fine bore tube. The two parts must not be separated so before removing the water temperature gauge disconnect the bulb from the thermostat housing. Next remove the fine bore tube from its clips on the engine. Release the gauge from the rear of the dash panel and carefully feed the fine bore tube and bulb through the hole in the dashboard. Should the tube be damaged a complete new assembly must be fitted.

42. Heater and Demister Unit - Removal and Refitting (All Models)

The removal of the heater unit is the reverse sequence to fitting as covered in Sections 43 and 44 of this Chapter. The method of refitting is identical to that of installing the heater kit. The following additional points should be of assistance:-
1. When lifting away the heater unit keep upright or alternatively hold the two hoses up so that any water remaining in the heater does not drain out onto the carpets.
2. It is recommended that the heater is reverse flushed by connecting it to a garden hose and allowing a gentle stream of water to pass through the heater radiator matrix.
3. Inspect the rubber hoses for signs of perishing, cracking or hardening and fit new hoses if suspect.
4. The heater motor is a sealed unit so if its operation is proved faulty by connecting it directly to a charged battery a new motor must be fitted.
5. The heater motor control switch is also a sealed unit so if its operation is faulty it must be renewed.
6. It will probably be necessary to bleed the heater water system once the heater has been refitted.

43. Heater and Demister Unit Kit - Fitting (TR2, 3, 3A)

The earlier production cars were fitted with a heater and demister as an optional extra and not as standard production equipment. If a car does not have a heater fitted it is obtainable as a fitting kit being based on the Smiths C.H.S. 920/4 system using a circular type heater. The components of the kit are shown in Fig. 12.25.

When fitting the heater kit, follow the instructions below to ensure success first time. Numbers in brackets refer to Fig. 12.25 unless stated otherwise.
1. Disconnect the battery earth terminal for safety reasons.
2. Place a container having a capacity of 13 pints under the radiator drain tap and undo the tap. Drain the complete cooling system.
3. There are two square headed plugs which must be removed next. One is positioned on the rear top face of the cylinder head next to the rear inlet manifold branch and the second on the water pump housing. These may be a little tight due to corrosion so make sure that the square key used is a good fit.
4. Refer to Fig. 12.26 and fit the taper threaded tap (28) into the tapped hole at the rear of the cylinder head. Turn the tap until the tapped hole is facing the starter solenoid switch.
5. With the tap in position next screw the metal extension (27) rod into the hole in the side of the tap so that it fits between the rear of the cylinder head and the starter solenoid.
6. Screw the threaded end of the female adaptor (32) into the rear of the water pump housing and when secure attach the metal return pipe (29) to this adaptor using the olive and union nut.
7. Secure the end of the pipe steady bracket to the rearmost bolt fixing the ignition coil in position.
8. Undo and remove the two chamfer headed screws securing the two plates and rubber washers to the bulkhead. The plates are fitted one either side of the bulkhead.
9. Fit the metal water pipe connectors (22) and rubber washers (21) into these two apertures retaining each in place with the two chamfer headed screws.
10 Fit the two short lengths of rubber water hose (26) to the forward ends of the metal connectors positioned in the previous operation. The other ends of the rubber water hose should be fitted to the tap extension tube (27) and the metal return pipe on the rear of the water pump housing.
11 Undo and remove the four self tapping screws securing the trimmed glove casing in position. Lift away the casing.
12 Move the two front seats back as far as possible and working underneath the dashboard undo and remove four nuts, spring washers and plain washers, two on one side of the steering column 'U' shaped support bracket and the two securing the bracket to the body panel.
13 To enable this bracket to be disconnected from its two studs undo the two upper nuts, one on each arm of the rods of the 'U' shaped bracket so allowing the bracket to be moved out of contact with the studs.
14 Position the demister nozzles on the two pairs of studs checking that they are above and clear of the windscreen wiper drive cable. Refit the 'U' shaped bracket and refit the securing nuts, spring washers and plain washers. Tighten securely.
15 The heater control switch should next be fitted. There is a hole already in the dashboard but it has been covered with P.V.C. trim. Locate the hole between the overdrive switch and the tachometer and using a sharp knife cut away the trim over the hole.
16 Connect one side of the control switch (13) to the line side (left hand side) of the windscreen wiper switch with the cable supplied with the kit. Attach the other length of cable with a snap connector nipple to the other side of the switch.
17 Fit the mounting bracket (15) to the heater unit securing it with the three nuts and spring washers.
18 Fit the two longer lengths of rubber water hose (20) to the adaptors on the heater and secure with the two clips (19).
19 Fit the alloy elbow piece (5) to the heater unit.
20 Working again under the bonnet, remove the rubber grommet positioned centrally above the battery.
21 Assemble the two P.K. spire nuts onto either side of the heater and demister unit mounting bracket and fit the heater so that the stud on the forward stay of the bracket protrudes

Fig. 12.25. HEATER KIT PARTS TR2, 3, 3A

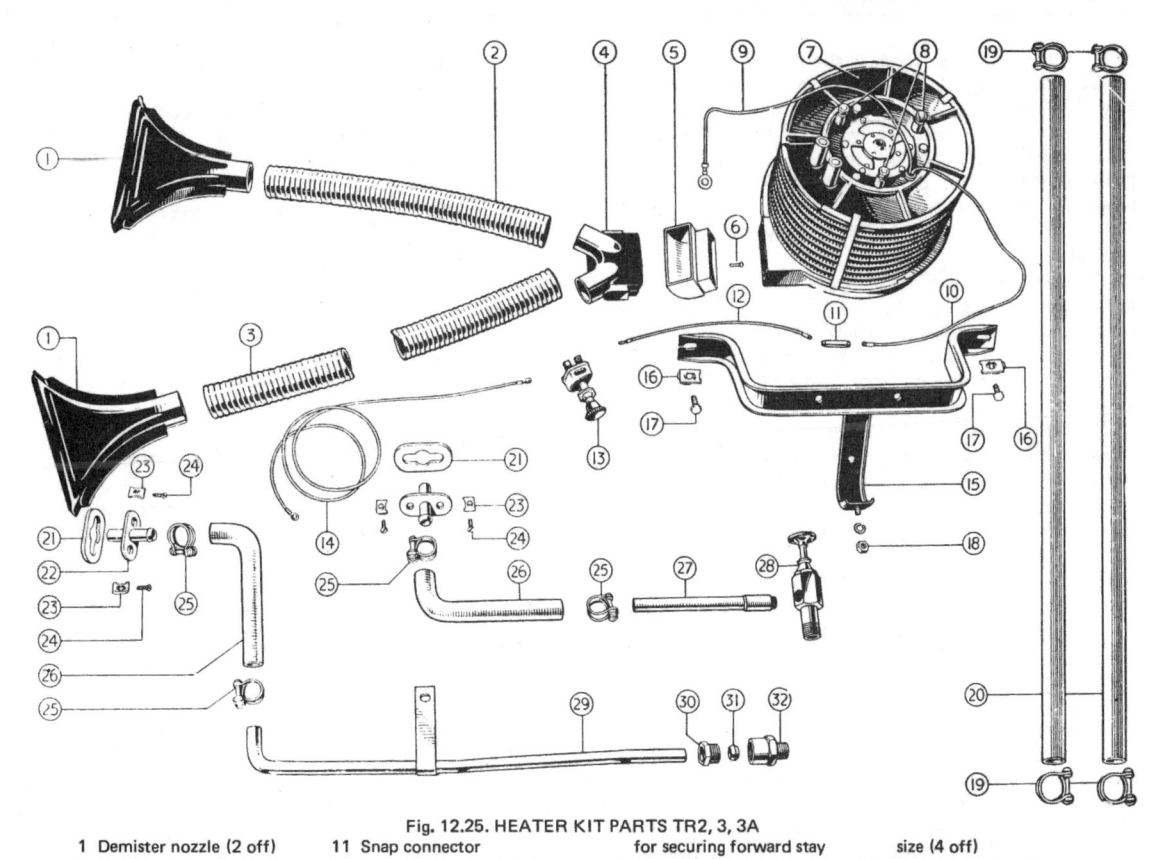

1. Demister nozzle (2 off)
2. Demister hose, R.H.
3. Demister hose, L.H.
4. Demister pipe 'Y' shaped air duct
5. Alloy elbow piece
6. Elbow piece securing screw
7. Heater unit
8. Securing nuts for attachment bracket (3 off), spring washers (3 off)
9. Earth wire
10. Feed wire to heater unit
11. Snap connector
12. Feed wire from control switch
13. Control switch
14. Feed wire from live side of windscreen wiper switch
15. Heater unit mounting bracket
16. P.K. spire nuts, large (2 off)
17. P.K. spire bolts (2 off)
18. Nut with spring washer for securing forward stay of attachment bracket
19. Large diameter pipe clip (4 off)
20. Long lengths of heater hose (2 off)
21. Rubber washer (2 off)
22. Metal water pipe connector (2 off)
23. P.K. spire nuts, small (4 off)
24. P.K. spire screws (4 off)
25. Heater pipe clip, small size (4 off)
26. Short length of rubber water hose (2 off)
27. Special tap extension
28. Taper threaded tap
29. Metal water return pipe
30. Union nut
31. Olive
32. Taper threaded female adaptor

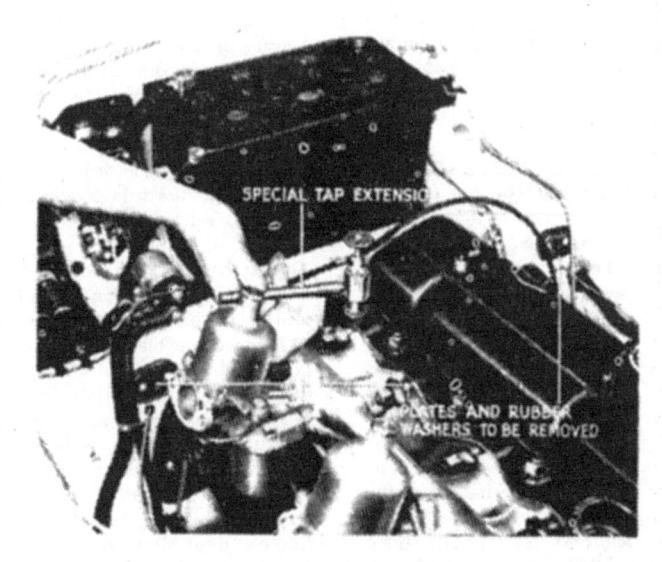

Fig. 12.26. Fitting the heater tap extension

291

Chapter 12/Bodywork & Underframe

through the hole from which the rubber grommet was removed. Secure this stud with a nut and spring washer (19).
22 Next attach the longitudinal section of the heater attachment bracket with the two bolts to the forward of the two central slots in each of the two panel stays.
23 Check the position of the overdrive unit relay. If it is being fouled by the heater unit there could be a short circuit so reposition the relay accordingly. Do not fit it in the inverted position.
24 The two free ends of the longer hoses already assembled to the heater unit should next be fitted to their respective connectors. The hose on the left hand side goes to the water pipe return connector and the hose on the right hand side goes to the connector from the feed hose. Tighten the securing hose clips.
25 Assemble the two lengths of demister hose (2, 3) to the demister 'Y' shaped air duct (4) and the union in the alloy elbow piece (5) previously fitted to the heater unit. The longer of the two hoses should be attached to the left hand side demister nozzle and the shorter piece to the right hand side demister nozzle.
26 Fit the nipple on the free end of the electric cable attached to the control switch into a snap connector (11) on the feed wire (10) which has already been attached to the heater unit.
27 Connect the earth cable (9) from the heater unit to the left hand dash bracket by undoing one of its forward screws, threading the screw through the terminal connector and refitting.
28 Replace the trimmed glove compartment casing and secure with the four self tapping screws.
29 Open the heater tap (28) and close the radiator drain tap. Refill the cooling system noting that the capacity of the cooling system will be increased by 1 pint.
30 Reconnect the battery earth terminal, start the engine, and allow to run until it reaches normal operating temperature.
31 Operate the heater boost motor checking that the heater and demister nozzles blow warm and cold air. If hot air is not blown when the heater tap is opened there is an air lock in the heater circuit.
32 To remove the air lock, first remove the radiator cap carefully with a rag over the top to prevent scalding. Working in the direction of water circulation through the heater and with the engine running at idling speed slacken each hose clip in turn and pull back the hose until water seeps out of the joint. Reconnect the hose and tighten the clip at each point. Do not forget to top up the radiator with hot water.
33 Finally check for water leaks at any of the joints.

44. Heater and Demister Unit - Fitting (TR4, 4A)

The earlier production cars were fitted with heater and demister as an optional extra and not as standard production equipment. If a car does not have a heater and demister one may be obtained as a fitting kit. The parts are shown in Fig. 12.27.

To fit the heater and demister kit follow the instructions below to ensure success first time. Numbers in brackets refer to Fig. 12.27 unless otherwise stated.
1. Disconnect the battery earth terminal for safety reasons.
2. Place a container having a capacity of at least 13 pints under the radiator drain tap and undo the tap. Drain the complete cooling system.
3. Undo and remove the bolt (34) (Fig. 12.28) spring washer (35) and plain washer (36) securing the forward end of the reinforcement bracket (33). Also undo and remove the two bolts (30), spring washers (31) and plain washers (32) securing the rear end of the reinforcement bracket (33) and then lift away the bracket.
4. Using a sharp knife carefully cut the forward edge of the P.V.C. trim concealing the outlets of the demister aperture. Apply a little adhesive to the end of the trim and turn it back under the fascia.
5. Position the two finishers (7) to the top of the fascia but do not secure yet.
6. Undo and remove the screws that secure the glove compartment lid hinges (50) to the fascia panel (49) and lift away the lid (40).
7. Undo and remove the six self tapping screws (57) (Fig. 12.28) that secure the glove compartment (55) to the fascia panel (49) and withdraw the compartment from the fascia panel.
8. Working behind the fascia panel fit the nozzle assembly (31) (Fig. 12.27) to the underside of the fascia with the deflector panel (32) between the nozzle (31) and the fascia. The wide section of the slot in the deflector should be positioned nearer to the centre of the fascia panel as shown in Fig. 12.27.
9. Undo the two drive cables from the rear of the speedometer and tachometer instrument heads and disconnect the cables. Bend the cables out of the way, if necessary tying with string.
10 Fit the second demister nozzle (31) and deflector panel (32) with the wide section of the lot in the deflector positioned nearer to the centre of the fascia panel as shown in Fig. 12.27.
11 Secure both nozzle assemblies with two nuts to each finisher (7) which has studs already attached.
12 Fit the hose (30) and clip (13) to the left hand nozzle (31) and tighten the clip. This hose should be the longer of the two.
13 Fit the hose (15) to the elbow (14) (if this is supplied in the kit) and secure it with the clip (13). Attach the elbow (14) to the right hand nozzle and secure with a clip (13). If the elbow (14) has been omitted secure the hose (15) directly onto the demister nozzle (12).
14 Disconnect the choke control inner and outer cables from the carburettor installation and carefully draw the cable back into the car.
15 Undo and remove the two screws (13) and pull the instrument panel (11) forwards. Note the cable colour coding and location of the cables to the rear of the instruments and disconnect the electric cables. Disconnect the oil pressure pipe from the rear of the gauge.
16 Remove the complete instrument panel.
17 Undo and remove the three blanking plate retaining bolts located on the underside of the fascia panel. Lift away and discard the plate as it is no longer required.
18 Fit the heater and demister unit to the underside of the fascia and secure it in position commencing by fitting the four bolts with plain washers and steel spacers on the right hand side of the unit.
19 Next fit the three bolts with plain washers and steel spacers to the underside of the heater and finally the bolt securing the bracket to the heater.
20 Remove the blanking plate and rubber grommet positioned below the bonnet locking mechanism and secured by two screws. In their place fit the bulkhead adaptor (17) suitably coated with a non setting sealing compound.
21 Note the positioning of the spark plug high tension leads and remove from the spark plugs.
22 Remove the square plug located at the rear of the water pump. Apply some Wellseal to the adaptor threads (6) and fit the adaptor (6) but do not tighten fully at this stage.
23 Place the nut (4) and olive (5) onto the pipe (2) and fit the pipe to the adaptor (6) again using Wellseal on the threads.

Fig. 12.27. HEATER UNIT KIT PARTS TR4, 4A

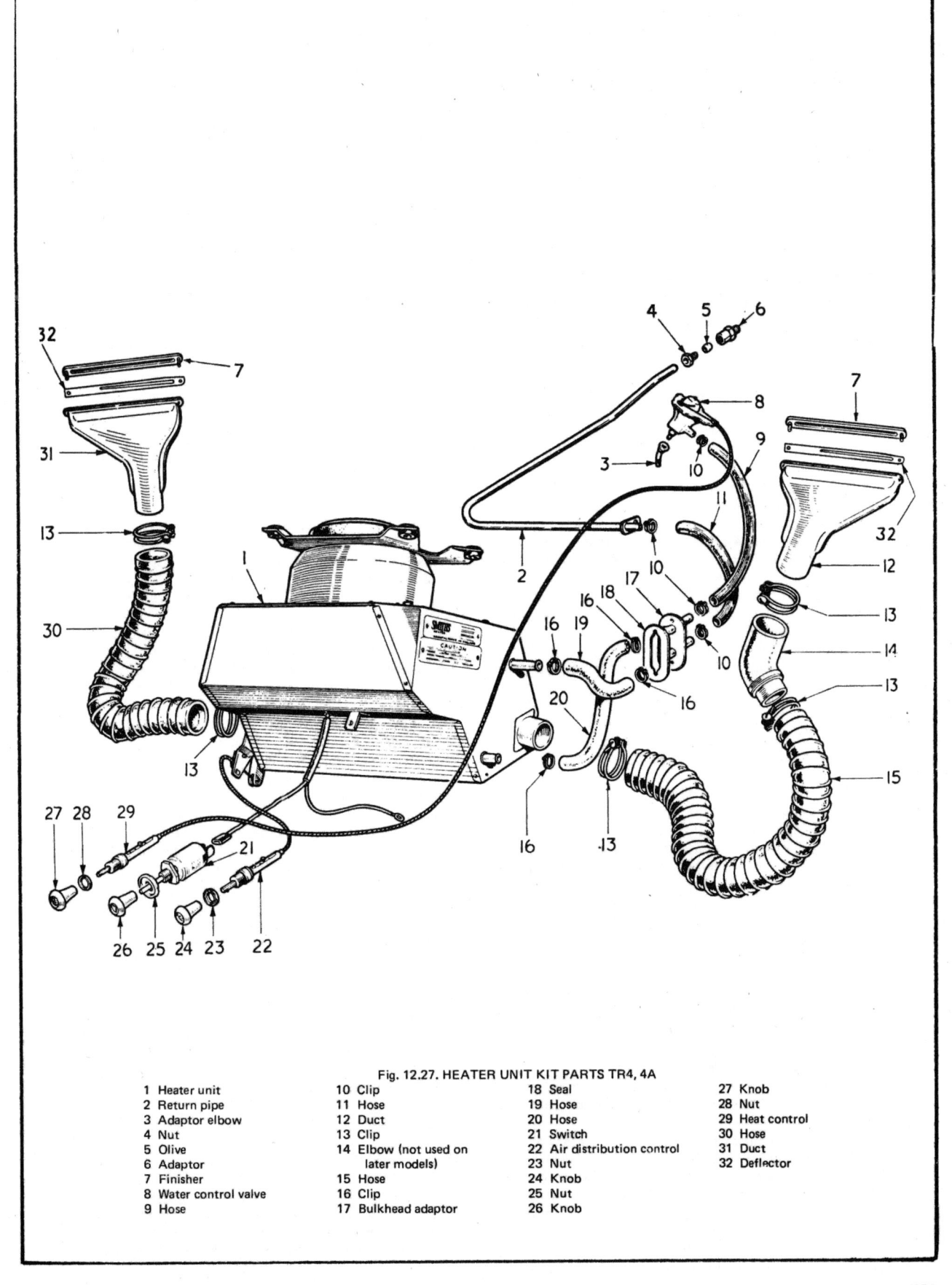

1 Heater unit	10 Clip	18 Seal	27 Knob
2 Return pipe	11 Hose	19 Hose	28 Nut
3 Adaptor elbow	12 Duct	20 Hose	29 Heat control
4 Nut	13 Clip	21 Switch	30 Hose
5 Olive	14 Elbow (not used on later models)	22 Air distribution control	31 Duct
6 Adaptor		23 Nut	32 Deflector
7 Finisher	15 Hose	24 Knob	
8 Water control valve	16 Clip	25 Nut	
9 Hose	17 Bulkhead adaptor	26 Knob	

293

Chapter 12/Bodywork & Underframe

24 Undo and remove the nut from the rearmost exhaust manifold retaining stud and attach the bracket on the pipe (2) to the stud. Refit and tighten the nut. It will probably be necessary to spring the bracket into position.
25 Using an open ended spanner securely tighten the adaptor (6) to the rear of the water pump and then the pipe (2) into the adaptor.
26 Reconnect the spark plug high tension leads to the correct spark plugs.
27 Undo and remove the plug from the elbow (3) located on the rear left hand side of the cylinder head and fit the water control valve (8) in place of the plug. Apply Wellseal to the threads.
28 Connect the hose (11) to the bulkhead adaptor (17) and the water pipe (2) as shown in Fig. 12.27 and tighten the two clips (10).
29 Connect the hose (9) to the bulkhead adaptor (17) and the control valve (8) and tighten the two clips (10).
30 Fit the two short hoses (19, 20) to the bulkhead adaptor (17) and heater unit (1) as shown in Fig. 12.27. It will be seen that the return pipe (19) is connected to the lower position of the adaptor and the upper position on the heater.
31 Fit the free ends of the demister hoses (15, 30) between the demister nozzle and heater at the heater unit and secure with clips (13).
32 The instrument panel and control panel should next be refitted. The sequence for refitting is a reversal of the removal instructions.
33 Using a sharp knife cut the trim covering the three holes for the heater controls in the fascia support bracket and fit the heater controls in the positions shown in Fig. 12.27. It will be seen that the heater control is in the left hand position, the blower switch is in the centre and the distribution air control in the right hand position.
34 Remove the blanking plug and fit the grommet to the hole in the dash panel above the bulkhead adaptor. Push the cable from the heat control (29) through the grommet and connect it to the water control valve. Adjust it by pushing in the heat control knob until it is within 1/8 inch of the fully closed position. Next turn the water control clockwise to the closed position and secure the trunnion screw.
35 Connect the air distribution control and adjust it by pushing in the air distribution control knob until it is within 1/8 inch of the full 'in' position. Close the flap valve and secure the trunnion on the heater.
36 The glove compartment and lid should next be refitted in the reverse sequence to removal.
37 Replace the fascia support bracket and secure with the bolts previously removed.
38 Reconnect the speedometer and tachometer drive cables to the instruments.
39 The earth cable from the booster motor should be connected to one of the securing bolts of the steering column to fascia support bracket.
40 Connect the white cable with the Lucar connector from the booster motor to the control switch.
41 The green coloured cable in the wiring harness, previously unused should be connected to the second terminal of the control switch. This cable should already have a Lucar connection on it.
42 The green coloured cable in the wiring harness should next be connected to the voltage stabilizer. It will be found that this cable has an unprotected Lucar connector fitted to the end. Should difficulty be found in locating the voltage stabilizer it will be found under the right hand side of the fascia next to the bonnet release cable.
43 Reconnect the battery earth terminal.
44 Close the radiator drain tap and refill the cooling system noting that the capacity of the cooling system has been increased by 1 pint.
45 Start the engine and allow to run until it reaches normal operating temperature.
46 Operate the heater boost motor and check that the heater and demister nozzles blow warm and cold air. If it blows cold air when the controls are set to blow hot air there is an air lock in the heater circuit.
47 To remove the air lock, remove the radiator cap carefully with a rag over the top to prevent scalding. Working in the direction of water circulation through the heater and with the engine running at idling speed, slacken each hose clip in turn and pull back the hose until water seeps out of the joint. Reconnect the hose and tighten the clip at each point. Do not forget to top up the radiator with hot water.
48 Finally check for water leaks at all of the joints.

45. Fascia Panel - Removal and Refitting (TR4, 4A)

1. Disconnect the battery earth terminal for safety reasons.
2. Undo and disconnect the drive cables at the rear of the speedometer and tachometer heads.
3. Disconnect the choke inner and outer control cable from the carburettor installation.
4. Refer to Chapter 11, Section 34 and remove the steering column complete with its cowling.
5. Refer to Fig. 12.28, undo the two screws (30) and remove them with the plain washers (32) and spring washers (33) positioned in line with the centre of the glove box casing (55).
6. Carefully move the reinforcement stay (33) outwards.
7. Undo and remove the six self tapping screws (57) securing the glove box casing (55) to the fascia panel (49).
8. With the glove box compartment removed it is easier to remove the speedometer and tachometer heads. Release the instrument illumination bulb sockets and undo the 'U' shaped bracket retaining knurled nuts. Lift away the nuts, spring washers and 'U' shaped brackets and withdraw the two instrument heads from the fascia panel.
9. Undo and remove the four nuts (42), bolts (23) and spring washers (41) that secure the fascia board (24). Lift away the fascia board.
10 The next part to be removed is the control panel. First undo and remove the screw (14), washer (15) and nut (21) that secures the choke control side of the control panel to the fascia panel.
11 Remove the two screws (17) and remove the panel complete with switch plate (18), switch plinth (19) and switch reinforcement (20) from the fascia panel until it is possible to gain access to the rear of the switches.
12 Make a note of the colour coding of the cables to the rear of the switches and then disconnect the cables. Lift away the complete control panel easing the choke control cable through its grommet in the bulkhead.
13 Undo the trunnion screw (63) that secures the scuttle ventilator rod to the control lever (62).
14 Undo and remove the instrument panel retaining screws (13) and ease the panel forwards. Note the electric cable colour coding to the rear of the instruments and disconnect the cables and oil pressure gauge pipe. Lift away the instrument panel.
15 Undo and remove the five bolts (68) and spring washer (69) that secure the upper edge of the fascia panel to the top of the scuttle. If difficulty is experienced in locating the bolts it will be found that one is in each upper corner of the glove compartment aperture, one is in the centre of the fascia panel, and one in each of the apertures for the speedometer and tachometer heads.

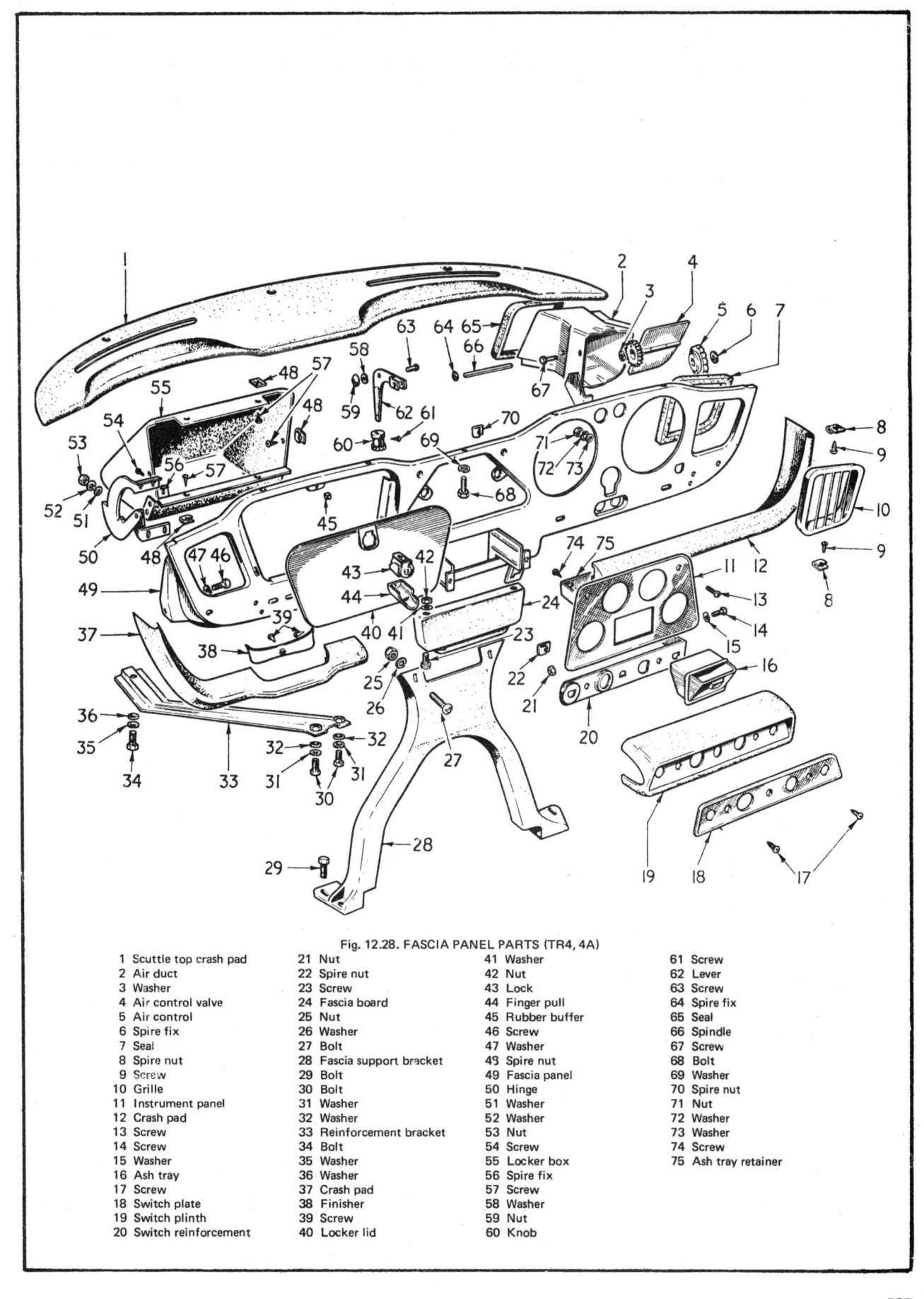

Fig. 12.28. FASCIA PANEL PARTS (TR4, 4A)

#	Part	#	Part	#	Part	#	Part
1	Scuttle top crash pad	21	Nut	41	Washer	61	Screw
2	Air duct	22	Spire nut	42	Nut	62	Lever
3	Washer	23	Screw	43	Lock	63	Screw
4	Air control valve	24	Fascia board	44	Finger pull	64	Spire fix
5	Air control	25	Nut	45	Rubber buffer	65	Seal
6	Spire fix	26	Washer	46	Screw	66	Spindle
7	Seal	27	Bolt	47	Washer	67	Screw
8	Spire nut	28	Fascia support bracket	48	Spire nut	68	Bolt
9	Screw	29	Bolt	49	Fascia panel	69	Washer
10	Grille	30	Bolt	50	Hinge	70	Spire nut
11	Instrument panel	31	Washer	51	Washer	71	Nut
12	Crash pad	32	Washer	52	Washer	72	Washer
13	Screw	33	Reinforcement bracket	53	Nut	73	Washer
14	Screw	34	Bolt	54	Screw	74	Screw
15	Washer	35	Washer	55	Locker box	75	Ash tray retainer
16	Ash tray	36	Washer	56	Spire fix		
17	Screw	37	Crash pad	57	Screw		
18	Switch plate	38	Finisher	58	Washer		
19	Switch plinth	39	Screw	59	Nut		
20	Switch reinforcement	40	Locker lid	60	Knob		

295

Chapter 12/Bodywork & Underframe

16 Remove the two bolts (46) and spring washers (47) on each end of the fascia panel.

17 The fascia panel may now be carefully withdrawn from its location in the car.

18 Refitting the fascia panel is the reverse sequence to removal. Take care that all electrical connections are made correctly bearing in mind the colour coding of the cables previously noted.

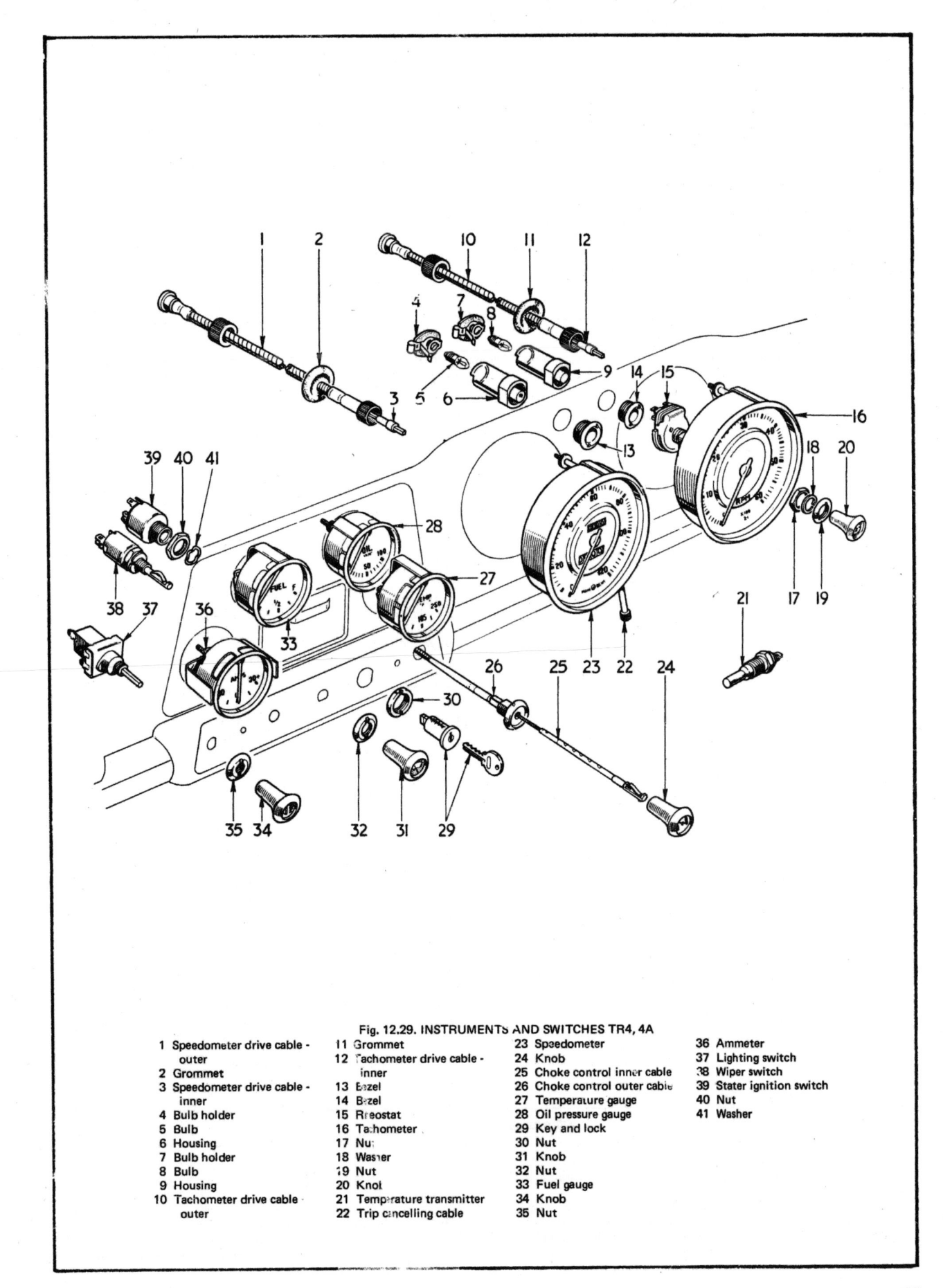

Fig. 12.29. INSTRUMENTS AND SWITCHES TR4, 4A

1 Speedometer drive cable - outer
2 Grommet
3 Speedometer drive cable - inner
4 Bulb holder
5 Bulb
6 Housing
7 Bulb holder
8 Bulb
9 Housing
10 Tachometer drive cable - outer
11 Grommet
12 Tachometer drive cable - inner
13 Bezel
14 Bezel
15 Rheostat
16 Tachometer
17 Nut
18 Washer
19 Nut
20 Knob
21 Temperature transmitter
22 Trip cancelling cable
23 Speedometer
24 Knob
25 Choke control inner cable
26 Choke control outer cable
27 Temperature gauge
28 Oil pressure gauge
29 Key and lock
30 Nut
31 Knob
32 Nut
33 Fuel gauge
34 Knob
35 Nut
36 Ammeter
37 Lighting switch
38 Wiper switch
39 Stater ignition switch
40 Nut
41 Washer

Use of English

As this book has been written in England, it uses the appropriate English component names, phrases, and spelling. Some of these differ from those used in America. Normally, these cause no difficulty, but to make sure, a glossary is printed below. In ordering spare parts remember the parts list will probably use these words:

English	American	English	American
Aerial	Antenna	Layshaft (of gearbox)	Countershaft
Accelerator	Gas pedal	Leading shoe (of brake)	Primary shoe
Alternator	Generator (AC)	Locks	Latches
Anti-roll bar	Stabiliser or sway bar	Motorway	Freeway, turnpike etc
Battery	Energizer	Number plate	License plate
Bodywork	Sheet metal	Paraffin	Kerosene
Bonnet (engine cover)	Hood	Petrol	Gasoline
Boot lid	Trunk lid	Petrol tank	Gas tank
Boot (luggage compartment)	Trunk	'Pinking'	'Pinging'
Bottom gear	1st gear	Propeller shaft	Driveshaft
Bulkhead	Firewall	Quarter light	Quarter window
Cam follower or tappet	Valve lifter or tappet	Retread	Recap
Carburettor	Carburetor	Reverse	Back-up
Catch	Latch	Rocker cover	Valve cover
Choke/venturi	Barrel	Roof rack	Car-top carrier
Circlip	Snap-ring	Saloon	Sedan
Clearance	Lash	Seized	Frozen
Crownwheel	Ring gear (of differential)	Side indicator lights	Side marker lights
Disc (brake)	Rotor/disk	Side light	Parking light
Drop arm	Pitman arm	Silencer	Muffler
Drop head coupe	Convertible	Spanner	Wrench
Dynamo	Generator (DC)	Sill panel (beneath doors)	Rocker panel
Earth (electrical)	Ground	Split cotter (for valve spring cap)	Lock (for valve spring retainer)
Engineer's blue	Prussian blue	Split pin	Cotter pin
Estate car	Station wagon	Steering arm	Spindle arm
Exhaust manifold	Header	Sump	Oil pan
Fast back (Coupe)	Hard top	Tab washer	Tang; lock
Fault finding/diagnosis	Trouble shooting	Tailgate	Liftgate
Float chamber	Float bowl	Tappet	Valve lifter
Free-play	Lash	Thrust bearing	Throw-out bearing
Freewheel	Coast	Top gear	High
Gudgeon pin	Piston pin or wrist pin	Trackrod (of steering)	Tie-rod (or connecting rod)
Gearchange	Shift	Trailing shoe (of brake)	Secondary shoe
Gearbox	Transmission	Transmission	Whole drive line
Halfshaft	Axleshaft	Tyre	Tire
Handbrake	Parking brake	Van	Panel wagon/van
Hood	Soft top	Vice	Vise
Hot spot	Heat riser	Wheel nut	Lug nut
Indicator	Turn signal	Windscreen	Windshield
Interior light	Dome lamp	Wing/mudguard	Fender

Miscellaneous points

An 'oil seal' is fitted to components lubricated by grease!

A 'damper' is a 'shock absorber', it damps out bouncing, and absorbs shocks of bump impact. Both names are correct, and both are used haphazardly.

Note that British drum brakes are different from the Bendix type that is common in America, so different descriptive names result. The shoe end furthest from the hydraulic wheel cylinder is on a pivot; interconnection between the shoes as on Bendix brakes is most uncommon. Therefore the phrase 'Primary' or 'Secondary' shoe does not apply. A shoe is said to be 'Leading' or 'Trailing'. A 'Leading' shoe is one on which a point on the drum, as it rotates forward, reaches the shoe at the end worked by the hydraulic cylinder before the anchor end. The opposite is a 'Trailing' shoe, and this one has no self servo from the wrapping effect of the rotating drum.

Conversion factors

Length (distance)
Inches (in)	X	25.4	= Millimetres (mm)	X 0.0394	= Inches (in)
Feet (ft)	X	0.305	= Metres (m)	X 3.281	= Feet (ft)
Miles	X	1.609	= Kilometres (km)	X 0.621	= Miles

Volume (capacity)
Cubic inches (cu in; in^3)	X	16.387	= Cubic centimetres (cc; cm^3)	X 0.061	= Cubic inches (cu in; in^3)
Imperial pints (Imp pt)	X	0.568	= Litres (l)	X 1.76	= Imperial pints (Imp pt)
Imperial quarts (Imp qt)	X	1.137	= Litres (l)	X 0.88	= Imperial quarts (Imp qt)
Imperial quarts (Imp qt)	X	1.201	= US quarts (US qt)	X 0.833	= Imperial quarts (Imp qt)
US quarts (US qt)	X	0.946	= Litres (l)	X 1.057	= US quarts (US qt)
Imperial gallons (Imp gal)	X	4.546	= Litres (l)	X 0.22	= Imperial gallons (Imp gal)
Imperial gallons (Imp gal)	X	1.201	= US gallons (US gal)	X 0.833	= Imperial gallons (Imp gal)
US gallons (US gal)	X	3.785	= Litres (l)	X 0.264	= US gallons (US gal)

Mass (weight)
Ounces (oz)	X	28.35	= Grams (g)	X 0.035	= Ounces (oz)
Pounds (lb)	X	0.454	= Kilograms (kg)	X 2.205	= Pounds (lb)

Force
Ounces-force (ozf; oz)	X	0.278	= Newtons (N)	X 3.6	= Ounces-force (ozf; oz)
Pounds-force (lbf; lb)	X	4.448	= Newtons (N)	X 0.225	= Pounds-force (lbf; lb)
Newtons (N)	X	0.1	= Kilograms-force (kgf; kg)	X 9.81	= Newtons (N)

Pressure
Pounds-force per square inch (psi; lbf/in^2; lb/in^2)	X	0.070	= Kilograms-force per square centimetre (kgf/cm^2; kg/cm^2)	X 14.223	= Pounds-force per square inch (psi; lbf/in^2; lb/in^2)
Pounds-force per square inch (psi; lbf/in^2; lb/in^2)	X	0.068	= Atmospheres (atm)	X 14.696	= Pounds-force per square inch (psi; lbf/in^2; lb/in^2)
Pounds-force per square inch (psi; lbf/in^2; lb/in^2)	X	0.069	= Bars	X 14.5	= Pounds-force per square inch (psi; lbf/in^2; lb/in^2)
Pounds-force per square inch (psi; lbf/in^2; lb/in^2)	X	6.895	= Kilopascals (kPa)	X 0.145	= Pounds-force per square inch (psi; lbf/in^2; lb/in^2)
Kilopascals (kPa)	X	0.01	= Kilograms-force per square centimetre (kgf/cm^2; kg/cm^2)	X 98.1	= Kilopascals (kPa)

Torque (moment of force)
Pounds-force inches (lbf in; lb in)	X	1.152	= Kilograms-force centimetre (kgf cm; kg cm)	X 0.868	= Pounds-force inches (lbf in; lb in)
Pounds-force inches (lbf in; lb in)	X	0.113	= Newton metres (Nm)	X 8.85	= Pounds-force inches (lbf in; lb in)
Pounds-force inches (lbf in; lb in)	X	0.083	= Pounds-force feet (lbf ft; lb ft)	X 12	= Pounds-force inches (lbf in; lb in)
Pounds-force feet (lbf ft; lb ft)	X	0.138	= Kilograms-force metres (kgf m; kg m)	X 7.233	= Pounds-force feet (lbf ft; lb ft)
Pounds-force feet (lbf ft; lb ft)	X	1.356	= Newton metres (Nm)	X 0.738	= Pounds-force feet (lbf ft; lb ft)
Newton metres (Nm)	X	0.102	= Kilograms-force metres (kgf m; kg m)	X 9.804	= Newton metres (Nm)

Power
Horsepower (hp)	X	745.7	= Watts (W)	X 0.0013	= Horsepower (hp)

Velocity (speed)
Miles per hour (miles/hr; mph)	X	1.609	= Kilometres per hour (km/hr; kph)	X 0.621	= Miles per hour (miles/hr; mph)

*Fuel consumption**
Miles per gallon, Imperial (mpg)	X	0.354	= Kilometres per litre (km/l)	X 2.825	= Miles per gallon, Imperial (mpg)
Miles per gallon, US (mpg)	X	0.425	= Kilometres per litre (km/l)	X 2.352	= Miles per gallon, US (mpg)

Temperature
Degrees Fahrenheit = (°C x 1.8) + 32   Degrees Celsius (Degrees Centigrade; °C) = (°F − 32) x 0.56

*It is common practice to convert from miles per gallon (mpg) to litres/100 kilometres (l/100km), where mpg (Imperial) x l/100 km = 282 and mpg (US) x l/100 km = 235

Safety first!

Professional motor mechanics are trained in safe working procedures. However enthusiastic you may be about getting on with the job in hand, do take the time to ensure that your safety is not put at risk. A moment's lack of attention can result in an accident, as can failure to observe certain elementary precautions.

There will always be new ways of having accidents, and the following points do not pretend to be a comprehensive list of all dangers; they are intended rather to make you aware of the risks and to encourage a safety-conscious approach to all work you carry out on your vehicle.

Essential DOs and DON'Ts

DON'T rely on a single jack when working underneath the vehicle. Always use reliable additional means of support, such as axle stands, securely placed under a part of the vehicle that you know will not give way.
DON'T attempt to loosen or tighten high-torque nuts (e.g. wheel hub nuts) while the vehicle is on a jack; it may be pulled off.
DON'T start the engine without first ascertaining that the transmission is in neutral (or 'Park' where applicable) and the parking brake applied.
DON'T suddenly remove the filler cap from a hot cooling system – cover it with a cloth and release the pressure gradually first, or you may get scalded by escaping coolant.
DON'T attempt to drain oil until you are sure it has cooled sufficiently to avoid scalding you.
DON'T grasp any part of the engine, exhaust or catalytic converter without first ascertaining that it is sufficiently cool to avoid burning you.
DON'T allow brake fluid or antifreeze to contact vehicle paintwork.
DON'T syphon toxic liquids such as fuel, brake fluid or antifreeze by mouth, or allow them to remain on your skin.
DON'T inhale dust – it may be injurious to health (see *Asbestos* below).
DON'T allow any spilt oil or grease to remain on the floor – wipe it up straight away, before someone slips on it.
DON'T use ill-fitting spanners or other tools which may slip and cause injury.
DON'T attempt to lift a heavy component which may be beyond your capability – get assistance.
DON'T rush to finish a job, or take unverified short cuts.
DON'T allow children or animals in or around an unattended vehicle.
DO wear eye protection when using power tools such as drill, sander, bench grinder etc, and when working under the vehicle.
DO use a barrier cream on your hands prior to undertaking dirty jobs – it will protect your skin from infection as well as making the dirt easier to remove afterwards; but make sure your hands aren't left slippery. Note that long-term contact with used engine oil can be a health hazard.
DO keep loose clothing (cuffs, tie etc) and long hair well out of the way of moving mechanical parts.
DO remove rings, wristwatch etc, before working on the vehicle – especially the electrical system.
DO ensure that any lifting tackle used has a safe working load rating adequate for the job.
DO keep your work area tidy – it is only too easy to fall over articles left lying around.
DO get someone to check periodically that all is well, when working alone on the vehicle.
DO carry out work in a logical sequence and check that everything is correctly assembled and tightened afterwards.
DO remember that your vehicle's safety affects that of yourself and others. If in doubt on any point, get specialist advice.
IF, in spite of following these precautions, you are unfortunate enough to injure yourself, seek medical attention as soon as possible.

Asbestos

Certain friction, insulating, sealing, and other products – such as brake linings, brake bands, clutch linings, torque converters, gaskets, etc – contain asbestos. *Extreme care must be taken to avoid inhalation of dust from such products since it is hazardous to health.* If in doubt, assume that they *do* contain asbestos.

Fire

Remember at all times that petrol (gasoline) is highly flammable. Never smoke, or have any kind of naked flame around, when working on the vehicle. But the risk does not end there – a spark caused by an electrical short-circuit, by two metal surfaces contacting each other, by careless use of tools, or even by static electricity built up in your body under certain conditions, can ignite petrol vapour, which in a confined space is highly explosive.

Always disconnect the battery earth (ground) terminal before working on any part of the fuel or electrical system, and never risk spilling fuel on to a hot engine or exhaust.

It is recommended that a fire extinguisher of a type suitable for fuel and electrical fires is kept handy in the garage or workplace at all times. Never try to extinguish a fuel or electrical fire with water.

Note: *Any reference to a 'torch' appearing in this manual should always be taken to mean a hand-held battery-operated electric lamp or flashlight. It does NOT mean a welding/gas torch or blowlamp.*

Fumes

Certain fumes are highly toxic and can quickly cause unconsciousness and even death if inhaled to any extent. Petrol (gasoline) vapour comes into this category, as do the vapours from certain solvents such as trichloroethylene. Any draining or pouring of such volatile fluids should be done in a well ventilated area.

When using cleaning fluids and solvents, read the instructions carefully. Never use materials from unmarked containers – they may give off poisonous vapours.

Never run the engine of a motor vehicle in an enclosed space such as a garage. Exhaust fumes contain carbon monoxide which is extremely poisonous; if you need to run the engine, always do so in the open air or at least have the rear of the vehicle outside the workplace.

If you are fortunate enough to have the use of an inspection pit, never drain or pour petrol, and never run the engine, while the vehicle is standing over it; the fumes, being heavier than air, will concentrate in the pit with possibly lethal results.

The battery

Never cause a spark, or allow a naked light, near the vehicle's battery. It will normally be giving off a certain amount of hydrogen gas, which is highly explosive.

Always disconnect the battery earth (ground) terminal before working on the fuel or electrical systems.

If possible, loosen the filler plugs or cover when charging the battery from an external source. Do not charge at an excessive rate or the battery may burst.

Take care when topping up and when carrying the battery. The acid electrolyte, even when diluted, is very corrosive and should not be allowed to contact the eyes or skin.

If you ever need to prepare electrolyte yourself, always add the acid slowly to the water, and never the other way round. Protect against splashes by wearing rubber gloves and goggles.

When jump starting a car using a booster battery, for negative earth (ground) vehicles, connect the jump leads in the following sequence: First connect one jump lead between the positive (+) terminals of the two batteries. Then connect the other jump lead first to the negative (–) terminal of the booster battery, and then to a good earthing (ground) point on the vehicle to be started, at least 18 in (45 cm) from the battery if possible. Ensure that hands and jump leads are clear of any moving parts, and that the two vehicles do not touch. Disconnect the leads in the reverse order.

Mains electricity

When using an electric power tool, inspection light etc, which works from the mains, always ensure that the appliance is correctly connected to its plug and that, where necessary, it is properly earthed (grounded). Do not use such appliances in damp conditions and, again, beware of creating a spark or applying excessive heat in the vicinity of fuel or fuel vapour.

Ignition HT voltage

A severe electric shock can result from touching certain parts of the ignition system, such as the HT leads, when the engine is running or being cranked, particularly if components are damp or the insulation is defective. Where an electronic ignition system is fitted, the HT voltage is much higher and could prove fatal.

Index

A

Air Filter
    Removal & Replacement - 76
Anti-Freeze Mixture - 11, 13, 66

B

Battery
    Charging - 210.
    Electrolyte Replenishment - 210
    Maintenance & Inspection - 210
    Removal & Replacement - 208
Big End Bearings
    Examination & Renovation - 34
    Reassembly - 42
    Removal - 28
Bodywork & Underframe
    General Description - 268
    Maintenance - Body Exterior - 272
                   - Body Interior - 272
                   - Hinges, Locks, etc. - 273
    Major Repairs - 273
    Minor Repairs - 270
Body Repair Sequence (colour) - 270, 271
Bonnet
    Adjustment - 278
    Removal & Replacement - 276
Boot Lid
    Adjustment - 278
    Removal & Replacement - 278
Braking System
    Bleeding the Hydraulic System - 186
    Disc Callipers - 196
    Disc Pads - 196
    Discs - 196
    Drums & Shoes - 182, 184, 186
    Dual Hydraulic System - 188
    Fault Finding Chart - 202
    General Description - 178
    Handbrake - 194
    Hydraulic Fluid Pipes - 184
    Master Cylinder - 190
    Pedal - 192
    Routine Maintenance - 180
    Servo Unit - 200
    Specifications - 178

    Tandem Master Cylinder - 190
    Wheel Cylinders - 188
Bumpers - Front & Rear
    Removal & Replacement - 273, 274

C

Camshaft & Camshaft Bearings
    Examination & Renovation - 36
    Removal - 28
Carburettors
    Fault Finding - 92
    General Description
    Stromberg - 86
    S.U. - 80
Clutch & Actuating Mechanism
    Bleeding - 108
    Faults - 118
    General Description - 108
    Inspection & Renovation - 110, 112
    Master Cylinder - 116
    Operating Cylinder - 114
    Pedal - 118
    Removal - 110
    Replacement - 110
    Routine Maintenance - 108

Condenser
    Testing & Removal - 96
Contact Breaker Points
    Adjustment - 96
Control Box
    Current Regulator Adjustment - 218
    Cut-Out Adjustment - 218
    Cut-Out & Regulator Contacts - 218
    General Description - 218
    Voltage Regulator Adjustment - 218
Cooling System
    Draining - 62
    Filling - 62
    Flushing - 62
    Routine Maintenance - 62
    Specifications - 60
Crankcase Ventilation System
    Description - 32
Crankshaft
    Examination & Renovation - 34
    Reassembly - 40
    Removal - 30
Cut-Out - 218
Cylinder Bores
    Examination & Renovation - 34
Cylinder Heads
    Decarbonisation - 40
    Dismantling of Rocker Gear, Valves & Springs - 28
    Reassembly - 48
    Removal with Engine in Car - 26
    Removal with Engine Out - 26

D

Dampers
    General Description - 236, 242
    Inspection - 242, 248, 252
Decarbonisation - 40
Differential Unit
    Overhaul - 166
    Removal & Replacement - 166, 170
Direction Indicator Flasher Circuit
    Fault Tracing & Rectification - 220
Disc Brakes - 196
Distributor
    Contact Breaker Points - 96
    Dismantling, Overhaul & Reassembly - 98
    Removal, Replacement & Ignition Timing - 98, 100
    Vacuum & Mechanical Advance - 94
Doors
    Alignment - 280
    Latch Striker Adjustment - 282
    Locks & Controls - 280, 282
    Windows - 282, 284
Drum Brakes - 182, 184, 186
Dynamo
    Dismantling & Repair - 212
    Removal & Replacement - 212
    Repair & Reassembly - 214
    Routine Maintenance - 212
    Testing in Position - 212

E

Electrical System
    Fault Finding Chart - 228
    General Description - 208
    Specifications - 206
    Wiring Diagrams - 207 209
Engine
    Ancillaries - Removal - 24
    Camshaft - Removal - 28

Index

Crankshaft Pulley Wheel - Removal - 28
Crankshaft Rear Seal - Removal - 30
Crankshaft - Removal - 30
Cylinder Heads - Removal - 26
Decarbonisation - 40
Dismantling - General - 24
Fault Finding Chart - 56
Flywheel - Removal - 30
General Description - 18
Gudgeon Pins - Removal - 30
Main Bearings - Removal - 30
Major Operations with Engine in Place - 18
Major Operations with Engine Removed - 20
Method of Engine Removal - 20
Oil Pump - Overhaul - 38
Oil Pump - Removal - 32
Oil Filter - Removal & Replacement - 32
Piston Rings - Removal - 30
Pistons, Connecting Rods & Big End Bearings - Removal - 28
Reassembly - Final - 52
Reassembly - General - 40
Removal with Gearbox - 22
Removal without Gearbox - 20
Replacement with Gearbox - 52
Replacement without Gearbox - 52
Rocker Gear - Examination & Renovation - 28, 38
Specifications - 14
Sump - Removal - 28
Tappets - Examination & Renovation - 38

Timing Chain Tensioner - Removal & Replacement - 34
Timing Gear & Cover - Removal - 28
Torque Wrench Settings - 17
Valve to Rocker Clearance - 48
Valve Guides - 40

F

Fan
    Removal, Overhaul & Replacement - 68
Fan Belt
    Adjustment - 68
Fault Finding
    Gearbox - 152
    Horn - 224
    Ignition System - 102
    Windscreen Wiper - 220, 222
Fault Finding Charts
    Braking System - 202
    Cooling System - 70
    Electrical System - 228
    Engine - 56
    Fuel System - 92
    Gearbox - 152
    Suspension - Dampers - Steering - 297
Faults
    Clutch - 118
    Direction Indicator Flasher Circuit - 220
    Ignition System - 102
Flywheel Starter Ring
    Examination & Renovation - 38
Front Wheel Alignment - 238
Front Wheel Bearings
    Adjustment - 238, 240
    Removal & Replacement - 238, 240,
Fuel Gauge Fault Finding - 226
Fuel Gauge Sender Unit
    Checking, Removal & Replacement - 226
Fuel Pump
    Dismantling, Examination & Reassembly - 78
    General Description - 76

    Removal & Replacement - 78
    Testing, Cleaning - 78
Fuel System & Carburation
    General Description - 76
    Specifications - 74
Fuses - 218

G

Gearbox
    Dismantling - 128
    Examination of Main Assemblies - 134
    Fault Finding - 152
    General Description - 124
    Input Shaft - Dismantling & Reassembly - 134
    Mainshaft - Dismantling & Reassembly - 134
    Reassembly - 136
    Remote Floor Gearchange - 142
    Removal & Replacement - 128
    Routine Maintenance - 124
    Specifications - 122
    Torque Wrench Settings - 124
Gudgeon Pins
    Removal - 30

H

Handbrake - 194
Headlamps
    Adjustment, Removal & Replacement - 224, 226
Heater
    Assembly - 290, 292
Hardtop - 288
Horn
    Fault Finding & Repair - 224

I

Ignition System
    Fault Finding - 102
    Firing Order - 94
    General Description - 94
    Specifications - 94
Ignition Timing - 100
Instrument Panel & Instruments
    Checking - 226
    Removal & Replacement - 226, 294

L

Lubricants - Recommended - 11, 13
Lubrication Chart - 10, 12
Lubrication - Distributor - 98

M

Main Bearings & Crankshaft
    Examination & Renovation - 34
    Removal - 30

O

Oil Filter
    Removal & Replacement - 32
Oil Pump
    Overhaul - 38
    Reassembly - 44
    Removal - 32
Overdrive - 144

P

Piston Rings
    Examination & Renovation - 36
    Reassembly - 45
    Removal - 30

Index

Pistons
    Examination & Renovation - 36
    Reassembly - 42
    Removal - 28
Points - Contact Breaker
    Adjustment - 96
    Removal & Replacement - 96
Propeller Shaft
    General Description - 154
    Removal & Replacement - 154
    Specifications - 154

R

Radiator
    Cleaning & Replacement - 62
    Grille - 284
    Removal & Inspection - 64
Rear Axle
    Bearings & Oil Seals - 164
    Differential Unit - 166, 170
    General Description - 160
    Half Shafts - 166
    Overhaul - 166
    Removal & Replacement - 160
    Routine Maintenance - 160
    Specifications - 158
Routine Maintenance
    Bodywork & Underframe - 272
    Braking System - 180
    Cooling System - 62
    Dynamo - 212
    Engine - 18
    Gearbox - 124
    Rear Axle - 160
    Summary - 7
    Suspension - Dampers - Steering - 238

S

Servo Unit - 200
Spare Parts - Ordering - 6
Sparking Plugs
    Examination - 100
    Chart (colour) - 105
Springs
    Front Suspension Unit - 240
    Inspection - 240, 248
    Rear - 248, 250
Starter Motor
    Dismantling & Repair - 218
    General Description - 214
    Reassembly - 216
    Removal & Replacement - 216
    Testing in Engine - 214
Steering
    Cam & Peg Steering - 256
    Rack & Pinion Steering - 260

Steering Wheel - 254
Suspension - Dampers - Steering
    Fault Finding Chart - 267
    Front Suspension Units - 238, 242, 244, 246
    Front Wheel Alignment - 238
    Front Wheel Bearings - 240
    General Description - 236
    Rear Springs & Dampers - 248, 250
    Routine Maintenance - 238
    Specifications - 232
Switches - 294

T

Temperature Gauge - 226
Thermostat - 64
Torque Wrench Settings

    Engine - 17
    Gearbox - 124
    Propeller Shaft & Universal Joints - 158
    Rear Axle - 158
    Suspension - Dampers - Steering - 236

U

Universal Joints
    Dismantling - 156
    General Description - 154
    Inspection & Repair - 154
    Reassembly - 156
    Specifications - 154

V

Vacuum Servo Unit - 200
Valves
    Clearances - Adjustment - 48
    Examination & Renovation - 36
    Reassembly - 48
Voltage Regulator - 218

W

Water Pump
    Dismantling & Reassembly - 66
    Removal & Replacement - 66
Water Temperature Gauge - 66, 226
Windows
    Aero Screen - 286
    Door - 282
    Regulators - 282
    Sidescreen - 284
Windscreen
    Removal & Replacement - 286
Windscreen Wiper Motor & Mechanism
    Dismantling & Reassembly - 224
    Fault Diagnosis - 220, 222
    Removal & Replacement - 222